Contemporary Archaeology in Theory

Social Archaeology

General Editor: Ian Hodder, University of Cambridge

Advisory Editors

Margaret Conkey, University of California at Berkeley
Mark Leone, University of Maryland
Alain Schnapp, U.E.R. d'Art et d'Archéologie, Paris
Stephen Shennan, University of Southampton
Bruce Trigger, McGill University, Montreal

Contemporary Archaeology in Theory

edited by

Robert Preucel and Ian Hodder

Blackwell
Publishing

© 1996 by Blackwell Publishing Ltd

350 Main Street, Malden, MA 02148-5018, USA
108 Cowley Road, Oxford OX4 1JF, UK
550 Swanston Street, Carlton South, Melbourne, Victoria 3053, Australia
Kurfürstendamm 57, 10707 Berlin, Germany

First published 1996 by Blackwell Publishing Ltd
Reprinted 1999, 2001, 2002

Library of Congress Cataloging-in-Publication Data

Contemporary archaeology in theory : a reader / edited by Robert W. Preucel and
Ian Hodder.
    p.   cm. — (Social archaeology)
  Includes bibliographical references.
  ISBN 0–631–19559–9 — ISBN 0–631–19561–0 (pbk.)
  1. Archaeology. I. Preucel, Robert W. II. Hodder, Ian.
III. Series.
CC173.C66   1996
930.1—dc20   96–2055
                                                      CIP

A catalogue record for this title is available from the British Library.

Printed and bound in the United Kingdom
by T. J. International Ltd, Padstow, Cornwall

For further information on
Blackwell Publishing, visit our website:
http://www.blackwellpublishing.com

Contents

Contents   vii

Contributors

Jack Anawak, Kivallia Consulting, Northwest Territories, Canada.

Bettina Arnold, Assistant Professor, Department of Anthropology, University of Wisconsin-Milwaukee, Milwaukee, Wisconsin.

John C. Barrett, Reader, Department of Archaeology and Prehistory, University of Sheffield, Sheffield, UK.

Lewis R. Binford, Professor, Department of Anthropology, Southern Methodist University, Dallas, Texas.

Michael Blake, Associate Professor, Department of Anthropology, University of British Columbia, Vancouver, British Columbia, Canada.

John E. Clark, Associate Professor, Department of Anthropology and Director, New World Archaeological Foundation, Brigham Young University, Salt Lake City, Utah.

Phillip Duke, Associate Professor, Department of Anthropology, Fort Lewis College, Durango, Colorado.

Timothy K. Earle, Professor, Department of Anthropology, Northwestern University, Evanston, Illinois.

Kent V. Flannery, Curator, Environmental Archaeology, Museum of Anthropology and Professor, Department of Anthropology, University of Michigan, Ann Arbor, Michigan.

Joan Gero, Associate Professor, Department of Anthropology, American University, Washington DC.

Antonio Gilman, Professor, Department of Anthropology, Northridge University, Northridge, California.

Christine A. Hastorf, Associate Professor, Department of Anthropology, University of California, Berkeley, California.

Contributors

Sissel Johannessen, Archaeologist, US Army Corps of Engineers, St. Paul, Minnesota.

Rosemary A. Joyce, Director, Phoebe Hearst Museum, and Associate Professor, Department of Anthropology, University of California, Berkeley, California.

Phillip Kohl, Professor, Department of Anthropology, Wellesley College, Wellesley, Massachusetts.

Mark P. Leone, Professor, Department of Anthropology, University of Maryland, College Park, Maryland.

Carlos Mamani Condori, Institute of Historical Research, La Paz and Universidad Mayor de San Andres, Bolivia.

Joyce Marcus, Curator, Latin America Museum of Anthropology, and Professor, Department of Anthropology, University of Michigan, Ann Arbor, Michigan.

Steven Mithen, Lecturer, Department of Archaeology, University of Reading, Reading, UK.

Charles E. Orser Jr., Director, Midwestern Archaeological Research Center, and Associate Professor, Department of Anthropology, Illinois State University, Normal, Illinois.

Parker B. Potter, Jr., Lecturer, Plymouth State College, Plymouth, New Hampshire.

Colin Renfrew, Professor, Department of Archaeology, Cambridge University, Cambridge, UK.

Dolores Root, Director, Exhibits and Programs, New England Science Centre, Worcester, Massachusetts..

Michael Shanks, Associate Professor, Department of Classics, Stanford University, Palo Alto, California.

Steven Shennan, Professor, Institute of Archaeology, University College, London, UK.

Janet D. Spector, Assistant Provost for Academic Affairs, University of Minnesota, Minneapolis, Minnesota.

Bruce Trigger, Professor, Department of Anthropology, McGill University, Montreal, Canada.

Gerald Vizenor, Professor of Native American Literature, University of California, Berkeley, California.

Alison Wylie, Associate Professor, Department of Philosophy, Washington University in St. Louis, Missouri.

Anne Yentsch, Associate Professor, Department of History, Armstrong Atlantic State College, Savannah, Georgia.

Preface

The idea for this book developed out of discussions between Ian Hodder, John Davey and Bob Preucel at Cambridge University in 1994. At that time we were intrigued by the challenge of trying to come to grips with the diversity of theoretical approaches in archaeology. In the last fifteen years there has been a proliferation of approaches often subsumed correctly or incorrectly under the heading of postprocessual archaeology. We felt that a Reader would be welcomed by teachers seeking to provide their students with a pathway through this diversity. We also wanted to show that there are strong historical and intellectual ties between specific versions of cultural historical, processual, and postprocessual archaeologies, and that we cannot talk of one framework replacing the other in any evolutionary or progressive sense. As we began working on the project we began to realize just how difficult it is to constrain different approaches to knowledge and why traditional disciplinary boundaries are breaking down. The present Reader is therefore not quite what we had envisioned, not a tidy summation of this diversity, but it is at least a start, a point of entry into the debates.

We would like to acknowledge the many individuals who have helped us in this project. We are especially grateful to those individuals who evaluated our proposal and assisted us in making selections of articles for inclusion. These include Barbara Bender, John Bintliff, Richard Bradley, Liz Brumfiel, Warren DeBoer, Tim Earle, Clive Gamble, Jean-Claude Gardin, Joan Gero, Antonio Gilman, Jim Hill, Matthew Johnson, Rosemary Joyce, Phil Kohl, Kristian Kristiansen, Vincente Lull Santiago, Randy McGuire, Bill Marquart, Richard Meadow, Isabel Martínez Navarette, Bjørnar Olsen, Bob Paynter, Chuck Redman, Jeff Reid, Colin Renfrew, Jerry Sabloff, Merrilee Salmon, Dean Saitta, Mike Schiffer, Steve Shennan, Andrew Sherratt, and Alison Wylie. The opinions expressed ranged from "very good attempt at a more or less impossible task," and "looking forward to using this collection" to "dearth of contributions from behavioral archaeology," "missing the non-Anglo-Saxon world," and "serious reservations about the tendency to create a new canon." We took each of these comments very seriously and have tried to make appropriate accommodations.

We also thank the individual authors who have agreed to allow their articles to be reprinted in this book. They have been extremely supportive and encouraging without knowing exactly how we would represent their work. We have chosen to use their writings to provide a context to explore the articulation of different theories and their applications. We have tried to be critical of processual and postprocessual approaches in what we hope is a constructive manner. But in the end these articles stand on their own. They were not produced for this Reader, but rather for different contexts – a book, a journal article, a pamphlet. We have extracted them for our purposes and used them to make specific points. Because of their pre-existence, they retain the ability to "talk back" and actively resist the interpretations we offer. This quality can be understood as their partial objectivity.

We would like to thank our respective colleagues and departments for providing intellectual and material support. Ian thanks Chris Hastorf, Meg Conkey, Ruth Tringham at Berkeley and Sarah Tarlow at Cambridge. Bob thanks Rosemary Joyce, Carl Lamberg-Karlovsky, Ofer Bar-Yosef, Richard Meadow, Michael Henzfield, Gordon Willey, K. C. Chang, David Rudner at Harvard and Greg Possehl, Wendy Ashmore, Clark Erickson, and Harold Dibble at Penn. He also wishes to acknowledge Churchill College, Cambridge where he spent his sabbatical in 1994.

We are most appreciative of Anna Harrison of Blackwell Publishers who secured the copyright permissions; Tony Grahame of Nineteen Daffodils who managed the project; Fred Schoch of the University Museum, University of Pennsylvania, who handled the photographic reproductions; Praveena Gullapali, Department of Anthropology, University of Pennsylvania, who assisted in the copying of the line drawings and in preparing bibliographies; and Anna Agbe-Davies, Department of Anthropology, University of Pennsylvania, who assisted with the copy-editing. We reserve our final thanks for John Davey whose vision, we hope, has been partially realized.

Acknowledgments

The editors wish to thank the following for permission to use copyright material:

Antiquity Publications Ltd and the author for Bettina Arnold (1990) 'The Past as Propaganda: Totalitarian Archaeology in Nazi Germany', *Antiquity*, 64, pp. 464–78.

Ashgate Publishing Ltd for M. Shanks (1993) 'Style and the Design of a Perfume Jar from an Archaic Greek City State', *Journal of European Archaeology*, 1, pp. 77–106.

Blackwell Publishers for J. Spector (1991) 'What This Awl Means' in *Engendering Archaeology*, ed. J. Gero and M. Conkey, pp. 388–406; C. A. Hastorf (1991) 'Gender, Space, and Food in Prehistory' in *Engendering Archaeology*, ed. J. Gero and M. Conkey, pp. 132–62; and A. Yentsch (1991) 'The Symbolic Divisions of Pottery: Sex-related Attributes of English and Anglo-American Household Pots' in *The Archaeology of Inequality*, ed. R. H. McGuire and R. Paynter, pp. 192–230.

Cambridge University Press for K. V. Flannery and J. Marcus (1993) 'Cognitive Archaeology', *Cambridge Archaeology Journal*, 3, pp. 260–70; P. L. Kohl (1987) 'The Ancient Economy, Transferable Technologies and the Bronze Age World-system: A View from the Northeastern Frontier of the Ancient Near East' in *Centre and Periphery in the Ancient World*, ed. M. Rowlands, M. Larsen and K. Kristiansen, pp. 13–24; J. E. Clarke and M. Blake (1993) 'The Power of Prestige: Competitive Generosity and the Emergence of Rank Societies in Lowland Mesoamerica' in *Factional Competition and Political Development in the New World*, ed. E. M. Brumfiel and J. W. Fox, pp. 17–30; T. K. Earle (1987) 'Specialization and the Production of Wealth: Hawaiian Chiefdoms and the Inka Empire' in *Specialization, Exchange and Complex Societies*, ed. E. M. Brumfiel and T. K. Earle, pp. 64–75; A. Gilman (1984) 'Explaining the Upper Palaeolithic Revolution' in *Marxist Perspectives in Archaeology*, ed. M. Spriggs, pp. 115–26; C. Renfrew (1986) 'Introduction: Peer Polity Interaction and Socio-political Change' in *Peer Polity Interaction and Socio-political Change*, ed. C. Renfrew and J. F. Cherry, pp. 1–18; and P. Duke (1992) 'Braudel and North American Archaeology' in *Archaeology, Annales and Ethnohistory*, ed. A. B. Knapp, pp. 99–111.

Center for Archaeological Investigations, Southern Illinois University, Carbondale, for C. A. Hastorf and S. Johannessen (1991) 'Understanding Changing

People/Plant Relationships in the Prehispanic Andes' from *Processual and Post-processual Archaeologies: Multiple Ways of Knowing the Past*, ed. R. W. Preucel, Occasional Paper No. 10, pp. 140–55. Copyright © 1991 by the Board of Trustees, Southern Illinois University.

Mark P. Leone and Parker B. Potter, Jr. (1984) for *Archaeological Annapolis: A Guide to Seeing and Understanding Three Centuries of Change*, Historic Annapolis Foundation, supported by the National Endowment for the Humanities and the Maryland Humanities Council.

The Prehistoric Society for S. J. Mithin (1989) 'Ecological Interpretations of Palaeolithic Art', *Proceedings of the Prehistoric Society*, 57, pp. 103–14.

Royal Anthropological Institute for B. Trigger (1984) 'Alternative Archaeologies: Nationalist, Colonialist, Imperialist', *Man*, 19, pp. 355–70.

Routledge for S. Shennan (1989) 'Cultural Transmission and Cultural Change' in *What's New? A Closer Look at the Process of Innovation*, ed. S. E. van der Leeuw and R. Torrance, pp. 330–46, Unwin Hyman; Carlos Mamani Condori (1989) 'History and Pre-history in Bolivia: What About the Indians?' in *Conflicts in the Archaeology of Living Traditions*, ed. R. Layton, pp. 46–59, Unwin Hyman; J. Gero and D. Root (1990) 'Public Presentations and Private Concerns: Archaeology in the Pages of *National Geographic*' in *The Politics of the Past*, ed. P. Gathercole and D. Lowenthal, pp. 19–37, Unwin Hyman; and J. Anawak (1989) 'Inuit Perceptions of the Past' in *Who Needs the Past? Indigenous Values and Archaeology*, ed. R. Layton, pp. 45–50, Unwin Hyman.

Society for American Archaeology for L. R. Binford (1980) 'Willow Smoke and Dogs' Tails: Hunter-Gatherer Settlement Systems and Archaeological Site Formation', *American Antiquity*, 45, pp. 4–20; and A. Wylie (1992) 'The Interplay of Evidential Constraints and Political Interests: Recent Archaeological Research on Gender', *American Antiquity*, 57, pp. 15–35.

Society for Historical Archaeology for C. E. Orser, Jr. (1992) 'Beneath the Material Surface of Things: Commodities, Artifacts, and Slave Plantations', *Historical Archaeology*, 26(3), pp. 95–104.

Sheffield Academic Press for John C. Barrett (1988) 'The Living, the Dead and the Ancestors: Neolithic and Early Bronze Age Mortuary Practices' in *The Archaeology of Context in the Neolithic and Bronze Age Recent Trends*, ed. J. C. Barrett and I. A. Kinnes, pp. 30–41.

University of Nebraska Press for Gerald Vizenor (1986) 'Bone Courts: the Rights and Narrative Representations of Tribal Bones', *American Indian Quarterly*, 10, 4 (Fall), pp. 319–31. Copyright © 1986 by The Regents of the University of California, Copyright © 1994 University of Nebraska Press.

University of Pennsylvania Press for R. A. Joyce (1994) 'Dorothy Hughes Popenoe: Eve in an Archaeological Garden' in *Women in Archaeology*, ed. C. Claassen, pp. 51–66.

Part I

Prologue

Communicating Present Pasts

We are all familiar with "Readers" as an established genre of writing. They typically consist of collections of previously published articles which are presented as illustrative of the range of views within an academic discipline. The pieces derive their authority from their position within established scholarly traditions. Introductory and bridging statements are written which contextualize the selections within the broader intellectual trends and perspectives and join them together in a disciplinary narrative. There is a sense of completeness, of totality. The final product is often regarded as a statement of 'the state of the art', a body of knowledge codified at a particular point in time in a way designed to be accessible to students or neophytes. This is why Readers can be so exciting when they first come out, and also why they become dated so quickly.

But the very term "Reader" draws attention to the process of interpretation as a creative act of engagement. Different people, with different perspectives, will read different things into what is written. This is true of all texts, and, of course, this Reader. Some will look for answers to practical questions. What organizational scheme is used to describe archaeological theory? How were the specific selections made? Why was my work left out? and so on. Others will look for answers to substantive questions. How is analogical reasoning used in archaeology? How does archaeological theory relate to theoretical developments in other fields? Still others will be interested in political questions. How has archaeological knowledge been used in the past? What is the proper role of archaeology in society today? How many women authors are represented? The act of reading thus permits multiple interpretations and the reader is free to identify themes and connections that enhance or contradict those of the author and/or editors.

This inherent multiplicity ensures that readings are always partial, incomplete, and ambiguous. As poststructuralists say, meaning resides not in the text itself, but rather in the chain of signifiers that connect the text to all other texts. Interpretation necessarily involves reconstructing webs of signification. This observation demonstrates why our text and the articles we have chosen cannot stand alone, complete in and of themselves. Readings also depend upon affective associations between the text and the reader. People bring to their reading a set of predispositions and beliefs that contour their engagement with the text. Sometimes we read what we want to see, and discover what we expect to find. But it is also the case that we are sometimes caught up short, challenged by a specific turn of phrase or an expression of ideas. This may stimulate the production of new ideas, or new ways of thinking. The act of reading is thus a thoroughly cultural process and one of the ways in which meaning is produced and reproduced.

Because of the power of the Reader to establish a canon, we feel it necessary to state our own interests at the outset. We regard archaeology as an increasingly diverse and changing discipline, with a growing multitude of perspectives espoused. Any attempt to congeal this proliferation, to categorize the moving diversity must ultimately be an attempt to impose a particular perspective from within a particular set of interests. Our aim, therefore, is to acknowledge this condition in constructing this Reader. We seek not to close down debate by asserting a stability, or declaring a new dogma. Rather we want to use this Reader as an opportunity to foreground some of the tensions which exist both within the discipline and across its boundaries. We view this Reader as a context for exploring these tensions as potential sites for future theoretical differentiation and development.

Categorization and Knowledge Production

One area we wish to problematize is the categorization of archaeological thought and its self-assumed developmental character. We could have carved up archaeological theory by identifying periods of research and organizing these so as to demonstrate a progressive movement. This is the approach Willey and Sabloff (1993) adopt in their review of the history of American archaeology. The assumption is that our field represents an orderly and progressive accumulation of knowledge from its speculative beginnings to its adolescent classificatory historical period to the more mature modern period. While we certainly agree that our understanding of the archaeological past has dramatically increased after over a century of research, we are concerned that this approach seems to imply that all of our theories have been equally progressive and that culture history has somehow been superseded or that processual is being replaced by postprocessual archaeology.

We could have divided up archaeological theory by focusing on different kinds of societies and subsystems. We could have identified family level, local group, Big Man collectivity, the Chiefdom, the archaic state, and the nation state or focused on variability in subsistence and settlement, technology and craft production, trade and exchange, and ideology and power. Johnson and Earle (1987) attempt the former and Renfrew and Bahn (1991) the latter. But this too is problematic since although these authors explicitly reject the notion of progress, these categorizations still preserve aspects of an unilinear evolutionary framework. And the subsystems approach assumes the validity of a functionalist systems theory which has come under increasing criticism because of its inability to account for change.

Or, we could have examined the subject and national character of archaeological theory as Trigger (1989) does. It is undoubtedly the case that Roman or Classical archaeology is different from Palaeolithic archaeology in many aspects, including the theoretical. Indian or Japanese archaeology tends to approach the past differently from French or Spanish archaeology. In other words, theories vary according to the material being studied (Palaeolithic Europe or Latin American cultures) and the historical traditions of each branch of the discipline. The limitations of this kind of approach are that it neglects the social context of theory production. None of these traditions developed in a vacuum and, in fact, Western culture has strongly influenced the rise of archaeology in many non-Western cultures. In any case, it would be invidious to "speak for" these other traditions, and we fully expect that they will, at some point, speak for themselves, perhaps in reaction to our and other attempts to describe the field of archaeological theory.

None of these approaches is wholly satisfactory. The historical approach tends to emphasize unilinear development and the accumulation of knowledge and it does not deal well with the diversity of approaches. The type-society or subsystem approach is problematic because its essentialist or typological character misrepresents variability by assuming that social systems possess certain structural or organizational principles that are good for all times and places: there is little concern for how these principles articulate with one another in specific historical contexts. The subject or nationalist approach tends to ignore the social and political context of global archaeology. This context cannot be understood without a consideration of the emergence of capitalism in the West and its impact on other nations throughout the world (Harvey 1985; Marcus and Fischer 1986).

This critique raises the question of whether it is possible to employ any organizational scheme that does not suffer from an evolutionary or imperialist bias. One answer, favored by cultural relativists perhaps, is that it is impossible for us to step outside our own culture and render an objective account of archaeological theory. There can be no definitive account of the various forms of theory in our discipline, much less of the forms of interpretation that characterize the world views of indigenous societies. In our view this response is too strong. It ignores the fact that we can communicate with one another and achieve partial understandings across theories, interests, and worldviews, even if these must, by definition, be provisional and temporary. These kinds of understandings need to be forged through a process of dialogue and discourse and not by fiat. For us, this is the justification for doing anthropology as well as for a socially committed archaeology.

So how have we organized this reader? We have constructed it using a scheme that respects historical stages, subsystems, kinds of societies, and nationalities, but focuses not on their essentialist character but rather upon their placement and interrelations within different holistic approaches to culture. Thus we have separated out approaches dealing with ecology, from those of political economy, symbolic meaning, gender, power, and so on. But within these broad areas of topical and theoretical interest in archaeology, we also consider approaches that cut across the categories we have constructed, thus demonstrating the arbitrariness of our classification. Gender is thus not restricted to Part VI nor is power limited to Part VII. Despite its many problems, this option seems best suited to challenge the rigid dichotomies of theoretical perspectives (e.g. positivist versus hermeneutic, or functionalism versus structuralism) often used in the literature, and it allows us to see how the different theories may interact in the examination of specific problems (e.g. exchange, symbolism, division of labor).

Theory in Archaeology

The theoretical landscape of archaeology consists of a kaleidoscope of approaches – often varying down to individual researchers – they can be visualized in terms of the extreme oppositions – materialist versus idealist, structure versus agency, objectivist versus subjectivist. Where any individual archaeologist would place any particular theory in this multidimensional space varies with that individual's interpretation of the theory. And where each individual would place herself or himself in that space will also vary and be unstable. For this reason, we choose to identify general contemporary research programs and then turn to a consideration of the level of theory and epistemology.

Archaeological theory is commonly described in terms of a set of historical oppositions. Processual archaeology is seen as a reaction to culture-historical archaeology while postprocessual archaeology is regarded as a response to processual archaeology (see, for example, Renfrew and Bahn 1991; Sharer and Ashmore 1993; Willey and Sabloff 1993). The often explicit assumption is that these oppositions represent distinct developmental stages in the maturation of archaeology as a scientific discipline. But is this accurate? Has processual really transcended culture-historical? Has postprocessual somehow moved beyond processual? We regard this developmental thesis as compromised by its dependence upon the widely discredited view of knowledge acquisition as progressive and evolutionary. As sociologists of science have shown, knowledge is produced within specific social contexts where different interests shape and guide the forms that knowledge takes (Barnes 1977; Harding 1986; Latour 1987). So rather than treating these oppositions as progressive stages, we wish to emphasize their contemporaneity and highlight some of their connections and interactions.

Culture history is presented as the dominant twentieth-century perspective prior to the New Archaeology of the 1960s, but much archaeology today is conducted within this framework. This research is often descriptive and uninterested in anthropological explanation or in the search for causes. It is sometimes seen as historical in approach although, as Trigger (1989) has long pointed out, history is not of itself descriptive and uninterested in generalization. Of course, some practitioners in the field prior to the 1960s did use well-developed theoretical perspectives such as Grahame Clark's ecological approach and Gordon Childe's Marxism. Thus although it is often associated with an empiricist view that inference must remain close to the data, culture history can also be seen as describing a facet of any archaeological research in a region, as sites and artifacts are categorized into cultural units which can be compared and dated. The description of the development, diffusion and movement of cultural traits establishes a space–time systematics which forms an essential building block for research in a new region.

Processual archaeology is the outcome of the New Archaeology of the United States in the 1960s and to a lesser extent British and North European archaeology in the 1970s. The New Archaeology critiqued culture history as normative and instead stressed the centrality of process – the relationships between variables in adaptive systems. The initial search for laws, prediction and the use of a rigid hypothetico-deductive reasoning was soon tempered by a looser concern with probabilistic generalization, the search for causal relationships, and a broad commitment to anthropology. The need to identify middle-range theory was embedded by Binford (1977) within a strong account of independence between theories and within a search for universal relationships between statics and dynamics. The processual emphasis on the functional relationships between systems was early linked to a concern with primary material and ecological factors. In later developments the concern shifted to social relations (e.g. burial ranking and settlement territories) as in the work of Flannery (1976) and Renfrew (1973), and then to mind and cognition as in Renfrew's (1982, 1994) "cognitive processual" archaeology (see Part V).

Postprocessual archaeology represents an incorporation of archaeological theory into a wider range of theoretical concerns within the social sciences – especially the various derivatives of structuralism (e.g. poststructuralism) and Marxism (e.g. critical theory, neo-Marxism, and agency theory), and the critique of positivism leading to the discussion of relativism, hermeneutics and realism. While postprocessual archaeology was based on a critique of processual archaeology, the development of a distinctive program of its own has often come to be termed interpretive archaeology (Tilley 1993; Shanks and Hodder 1995). The main tenets of the interpretive position are that the past is meaningfully constituted from different perspectives, that the role of agents actively using material culture needs to be considered, that there is a relationship between structure and practice, and that social change is historical and contingent. In some ways interpretive archaeology can be seen as a fulfillment of processual archaeology. The processual emphasis on theory building laid the foundation for a theoretical critique and development, and the processual discussion of variability rather than norms prefigured the postprocessual commitment to agency and diversity of interpretation. Indeed, rather than being "post" processual, interpretive archaeology has been described as the first truly processual archaeology (Hodder 1991a).

There has been and continues to be much movement within processual and interpretive archaeologies. For example, Renfrew (1989; Renfrew and Bahn 1991) has accepted many of the critiques of postprocessual archaeology (such as the importance of meaning, the active individual, structure and theory-laden data). Equally there have been moves away from a strong subjectivist position among some postprocessual archaeologists (e.g. Hodder 1991b). Overall there is enormous diversity within both positions and much blurring between them. The term "inter-

pretive" archaeology may, in fact, not be sufficient to encompass the postprocessual range from feminists to critical theorists to poststructuralists. Our response is
that while we will use the categories "processual" (and New Archaeology) and
"interpretive" (and postprocessual) where the occasion demands (particularly in
the context of the opposition between positivist and postpositivist approaches), it
is more helpful to focus on the specific theories within these two ranges. Thus we
will describe, for example, culture ecology or poststructuralism.

Another set of theoretical questions deals with issues of scale. One influential
approach has been to break down theory into low, middle, and high levels (Raab
and Goodyear 1984; Trigger 1989; Willey and Sabloff 1980). These levels are logically dependent upon one another, such that the process of interpretation
involves moving sequentially from one level to the next. Cultural historical
archaeology generally stresses interpretation from the bottom up (induction),
while processual archaeology favors top-down (deduction) approaches. In both
cases, low and high level theories are mediated by middle level theories.
Significantly, the use of these theories involves making relational analogies
(defined by Wylie 1985) which are concerned with placing inferences within a full
understanding of causal mechanisms.

Low level theories are empirical generalizations about the archaeological record.
These theories are routinely used in archaeology and include such things as artifact typologies and classifications, chronologies and seriations, and spatial
distributions. One of the most important developments in low level theory is the
study of site-formation processes stimulated by the recognition that the archaeological record rarely reflects past behavior in any direct fashion. Sites are subject to
a series of transformational processes which can often introduce patterns of their
own obscuring the behavioral context of interest. Schiffer (1976, 1987) has distinguished two kinds of transformational processes and these broadly correspond to
postdepositional theory in Clarke's (1973) framework. These processes are cultural
modifications (c-transforms) of an archaeological site after its abandonment and
the natural processes (n-transforms) that are related to geophysical and biochemical activity. This latter focus has stimulated research in geoarchaeology and
taphonomy.

Middle level theories link the archaeological record to behavioral dynamics –
this is depositional theory in Clarke's (1973) framework and behavior chains in
Schiffer's (1976) model of behavioral archaeology. Perhaps the most influential of
these theories is Binford's (1977, 1978) program of actualistic studies (termed
middle-range theory) which is designed to secure inferences about the archaeological record through direct observation of modern ethnographic peoples. This
approach is closely related to ethnoarchaeology or living archaeology (Gould 1980;
Hodder 1982; Kramer 1979). A second kind of middle level theory is experimental
archaeology. This approach often involves recreating particular technologies
under controlled conditions in order to understand tool use and manufacture (e.g.
Keeley 1980; Skibo, Schiffer, and Reid 1989). Yet a third kind is the use of written
records in conjunction with the archaeological context. In this case, documents are
not privileged over the archaeological record, but rather are used in the con-

struction of "descriptive grids" for the identification of ambiguity which can be explored through a consideration of organizational behavior (Leone and Potter 1988; Little 1992).

Finally, high level theories can be defined as general theories which integrate behavioral dynamics into broad, coherent explanatory frameworks (Trigger 1989). Clarke (1973) calls these "controlling models" and suggests four different kinds as being relevant for archaeology – ecological, anthropological, geographical, and morphological. Similarly, we can consider adaptationalism, evolutionary ecology, and structural Marxism as different kinds of high level theories which overlap to varying degrees. All of these theories deal with human behavior and their study crosscuts the social sciences. As Trigger (1989, p. 22) observes, there are no high level theories which are specific to archaeology and not shared by the other social sciences. Likewise, he notes that there is at present no commonly accepted unifying theory, like the New Synthesis in biology, for the human sciences.

While accepting the validity of some of the insights allowed by this approach, we take the view that the exclusive focus on scale issues obscures how theories mutually support and constrain one another. For example, c-transforms are conceptualized very differently from within an agency theory position than they are from a functionalist perspective. The successive occupation of a site may reflect social practices that play a central role in the constitution of society as may be seen, for example, with the burial of Bronze Age individuals in Neolithic mounds. This kind of intrusion would be regarded as noise to be factored out in a behavioral analysis. In our view, practitioners of high, middle, and low level theory have not sufficiently explored the interconnections between these levels; indeed, we suspect that these levels cannot be maintained in actual interpretation. This critique applies equally to postprocessualists who favor *Annaliste* perspectives that identify event, conjuncture, and the *longue durée* as well as to those who are exploring issues of agency and structure (see Part IV).

Yet another set of oppositions relates to differing epistemological frameworks. We can identify contemporary theory as consisting of analytic, hermeneutic and critical epistemologies (Preucel 1991, 1995). By analytic we refer to approaches which seek to explain systemic relationships in terms of cause and effect. There is a focus on sampling data in ways which enhance an objective evaluation of causal relationships. There is, above all, a belief that data can be isolated and used to test theories about causal relationships. In general terms, an analytic epistemology is associated with positivism or realism. It is positivism that has had the greatest impact in archaeology through the Vienna school and its deductive version cham-pioned by Carl Hempel in the United States. This influenced archaeology through Fritz and Plog (1970) and Watson, Redman, and LeBlanc (1971). The deductivism was later dropped (Salmon and Salmon 1979), but a separate and more general view was that archaeology should be like a natural science – on the questionable assumption that natural scientists worked through positivist hypothesis-testing procedures, even though this view of the natural sciences had been long contested, and even though physicists themselves have raised fundamental questions about the problem of the observer in measuring changes in subatomic physics.

Wylie (1989a) has pointed out that positivism, which assumes that theories can only be developed about observable phenomena against which they can be tested, was never an appropriate approach for archaeology, which tries to go beyond the material world in order to explain it. Nevertheless the general view that archaeology is a science and science is positivist was retained and this for a long time restricted the sorts of questions that could be asked. Following Hawkes's (1954) "ladder of inference" model it was and is felt by some archaeologists that a scientific archaeology should be restricted to environments, technologies and economies. Social and cognitive approaches to archaeology were later developments within the processual tradition (Renfrew 1973, 1982). But in order to extend a positivist view to such areas, the notion has to be retained that the social and symbolic meanings are objectively (universally, deterministically) linked to other observable variables in the system. This is logically contradicted by the arbitrary nature of the sign and the creativity of intentionality.

A hermeneutic epistemology focuses on eliciting meaning through interpretation. It attempts to provide an understanding of an event from the actor's point of view or from "inside" a particular society (Gadamer 1976). The emphasis on interpretation foregrounds the interpreting subject as playing a role in the construction of "facts," and it assumes that different people at different times in different social contexts will produce different interpretations. It seeks to be sensitive to particular contexts. As such, it tends to be suspicious of causal relationships. The whole notion of cause assumes that integrated events can somehow be divided up and interactions observed; whereas in historical events themselves, there are only purposeful human agents acting within conditions. Interpretive approaches thus tend to be less wary of description. While they accept that generalizations are brought to all archaeological enquiry, they believe that a full, "deep" or "thick" description of a series of events integrates the general and the particular and achieves a more complete understanding. Hermeneutic writers reject the possibility of testing theory against data, since the data are always theory laden. Rather than testing theory against data, we can talk of "fitting" theory and data to each other. The process is one of working between part and whole, until as much of the data as possible has been fitted together.

The third epistemological position in archaeology can be called critical. It is concerned with the evaluation of knowledge claims. One version seeks to assess theoretical adequacy and logical inconsistencies. The underlying premise is that science progresses through the dual processes of theory refinement and replacement. This position is favored by many processual archaeologists advocating positivism. Another version takes an explicitly political position, seeking to expose past and present ideological structures for the purposes of emancipation. The presumption here is that structures of power create ideologies to legitimize existing power relations as natural, universal, and inevitable, and that emancipation can be achieved by showing that they are actually artificial, particular, and constructed. This position is inspired in part by critical theory. Yet a third version represents a turn away from knowing the past on its own terms toward a focus on the way the past is constructed in the present. The argument is that we cannot know the past as it was, but we can examine the uses of the past in the present. This position draws liberally from deconstruction and literary theory.

But how different are these three epistemologies? Are they as incompatible as they seem or are there, in fact, areas of correspondence between them? The first point to make is that the critical position stands in a rather special position with regard to the other epistemologies discussed. It is not self-sufficient in the sense that it cannot be used to produce truth claims. This is because it does not contain a theory of data, or more specifically, a theory of subject–object relations. The analytic approach presumes a relationship between a real subject (the scientist) and a second real subject (the object) with the former acting on the latter. The hermeneutic approach, in contrast, acknowledges the interaction between a real subject (the scientist) and a second real subject (the co-subject). A critical approach is metadiscourse, theory about theory, and thus is detached from the subject–object relation. For this reason, we must speak of critical analytics or a critical hermeneutics to achieve explanation or understanding. In this sense the context of discovery cannot be divorced from the context of justification. So not only is a critical approach compatible with these other epistemologies but, in fact, it must be combined with them.

It can also be argued that the distinction between analytic and hermeneutic is false and all archaeology is interpretation. As we have seen, a hermeneutic understanding is based on constructing part–whole relationships. Parts can only be understood in relation to the whole, and the whole can only be understood in relation to the parts. We believe that regardless of the interest in recovering symbolism, ritual, meaning or intentionality in the past, all archaeology tends to use hermeneutic procedures, whether it is talking about past economies, technologies or symbolism. We have already noted that Wylie (1989a) argues that positivism is not an adequate description of what archaeologists actually do. In another paper (1989b), she argues that archaeologists tend to tack back and forth between theory and data. In our view this tacking, this dialectic, is best described in hermeneutic terms. The evaluation procedure is part of the whole that is taken into account by the archaeologist in making a particular interpretation. In practice, archaeologists always discover data which leads them to change theories, and they find theories which lead to a new view of the data. The whole process is one of linking together as much data and as much specific and general knowledge as possible in order to make a coherent and plausible argument. How that argument is evaluated (in terms of elegance, parsimony, amount of data explained, etc.) is itself part of the whole – in other words, how an interpretation is evaluated varies at different times and in different places. Thus what archaeologists and indeed all scientists actually do is a form of hermeneutics.

Towards Grand Theory?

Grand Theory is one of the centerpieces of Enlightenment thought. It is the view that all phenomena can potentially be subsumed under a single coherent model.

The model most commonly identified was physics. Accordingly, the laws of biology and culture were held to be reducible to the laws of physics. The philosophical position that introduced the modern version of this view was the logical positivism of the 1940s which held that all sciences could be integrated under a natural-science model, the famous "unity-of-science" thesis. Associated with this thesis was a formal method of scientific explanation. A causal explanation of an event involved deducing a connection with certain unique statements about initial conditions. This kind of explanation obtained its scientific status from being subject to empirical testing. As Popper (1959) argued, a belief is rationally grounded if and only if it has resisted the attempts to falsify it. In this context, the social sciences emerged as the sciences of the study of human behavior.

During the second half of the twentieth century, this unity-of-science model quickly extended from the natural sciences to those fields of study dealing with human relations and interactions. It resonated with certain Enlightenment concerns about rationalism, progress, and perfectibility. But at the same time, the seeds of criticism began to emerge. From within the positivist camp, Willard V.O. Quine (1951) called into question whether there can be a categorical distinction between concepts and facts; Thomas Kuhn (1970) questioned the nature of scientific rationality; and Paul Feyerabend (1975) drew attention to the tyranny of method. From without, Foucault (1972) explored the linkages between claims to knowledge and the exercise of power; Habermas (1975) stressed the relation of knowledge and human interests; and Derrida (1978) sought to demonstrate that modes of rhetorical analysis are central to understanding any discourse. More recently, feminist scholars and scholars from the sociology-of-knowledge school have elaborated and extended these arguments (e.g. Harding 1986; Latour and Woolgar 1979; Longino 1990). This "double critique" has effectively eroded the stature of positivism in the social sciences and has even had a considerable effect within the natural sciences.

Quentin Skinner (1985) has recently articulated a case for the return of Grand Theory in the social sciences. He makes the interesting, if rather controversial, claim that such leading social theorists as Jacques Derrida, Jürgen Habermas, Hans-Georg Gadamer, and Anthony Giddens can all be seen as Grand Theorists. His rationale is that these writers share a focus on the local and contingent, an interest in the social construction of knowledge, and a skepticism for metanarratives. He acknowledges that this core of beliefs might at first seem to be the very opposite of Grand Theory, but his point is that in the process of critiquing Grand Theory, each of these scholars has been committed to constructing a new Grand Theory. He gives an example from law where he claims that radical skepticism has cleared the way for a return to a consideration of the good life and the boundaries of a free and just society as seen in the work of John Rawls (Rawls 1971). The implication seems to be that theory develops through oscillations between periods of coherence and fragmentation and that ultimately Grand Theory can only be replaced by the next incarnation of Grand Theory.

From our perspective, Skinner glosses over some important differences between positivist and postpositivist theory. While it is true that many social theorists share an interest in the social construction of knowledge, it is decidedly not the case that a coherent consensus is emerging. For example, Gadamer has resurrected the German distinction between *Naturewissenschaften* and *Geisteswissenschaften*; Rorty has argued that all is interpretation; and Habermas has argued for the need for both instrumental and interpretivist approaches. In fact, some important debates have developed between Habermas and Gadamer (Gadamer 1976; Habermas 1977) and Foucault and Derrida (Derrida 1978). So while each of these social philosophers may legitimately be called a Grand Theorist, they are not constructing a grand unified theory in the same sense of positivism which dominated the scene in the 1950s and 1960s. The theories of these current social philosophers are contingent and provisional and cannot be subsumed one by the other. It is in this sense that we can perhaps speak of the "end of" Grand Theory and the "birth of" Local Narrative. What Skinner ultimately fails to appreciate is how theory is socially produced.

Archaeology permits a number of insights into these debates because of the way it has historically bridged the natural and social sciences. Given the prestige and success of the natural sciences, it is not surprising that attempts have been made to import the "unity-of-science" model and the scientific method. It is perhaps helpful to think of the natural sciences working within a "single hermeneutic" – there is only one frame of meaning, which is that imposed by the scientist. The natural scientist evaluates theories against data which do not themselves construct meanings of what they are doing. In the social sciences and humanities, on the other .hand, a "double hermeneutic" is used. Archaeologists have to translate between their frame of meaning and that of the people being studied. The argument is that the double hermeneutic raises fundamentally different problems for theory and method. According to this view there can be no over-arching archaeological theory since, for example, poststructuralist approaches may be appropriate for the interpretation of cultural meanings, but a positivist, natural-science approach seems more relevant for the analysis of sediments and chemical traces in residues.

The exploration of the single and double hermeneutic in archaeology has exposed a number of classic ontic and epistemic contradictions. Theories which emphasize structure and system (structuralism, poststructuralism, Marxism, social evolution, functionalism and systems theory) generally deny a role to the active agent, the ability of individuals to transform structures, in contrast to agency theories. Another fundamental difference concerns materialism versus idealism. Some theories (functionalism, structural Marxism) regard the ultimate causes of change as coming from the material, while others (neo-Marxism, agency theory) identify its roots in the ideological or social realm. And even more radically still, there are some theories (poststructuralism) which deny the possibility of comparison between cultures, while others (functionalism, systems theory, Marxism) base their argument on cross-cultural regularities. Some (poststructuralism) would even deny the possibility of causal explanation altogether, arguing that all we can do is examine the different representations of the past in the present.

There are three broad responses to this theoretical diversity. The first is alarm at the proliferation of theoretical perspectives in use today, on the grounds that many are incommensurable at best and nonscientific at worst (Binford 1987; Watson 1990, 1991). If different theories radically oppose each other, they cannot be used together to deal with different dimensions of the same problem. This argument is the polemical opposition of different worldviews, requiring the usurping of one position by another. The theoretical perspectives are totalizing, and are therefore either right or wrong. The second response is accommodation, an attempt to subsume aspects of this diversity and to construct from it a new Grand Theory. This is the direction taken, for example, by cognitive processual archaeology (Renfrew and Zubrow 1994). Thus from this second perspective, different theoretical perspectives are not so much wrong as different; they deal with different questions and scales. The third response is the denial of the possibility of Grand Theory in any form and the celebration of the local and contingent. Theories are held to be strategically developed in particular times and places, and to serve specific political interests. This view has elements of pragmatism or utilitarianism and underlies a variety of poststructural, feminist and neo-Marxist explorations (Bapty and Yates 1990; Conkey and Gero 1991; Shanks and Tilley 1987). In some cases, relativist rhetoric has been used to generate response and to stimulate reaction.

How is it possible to evaluate these theories and responses when there is even disagreement as to whether general explanations can be found? Our initial impression is that from within any one theoretical position, that position seems totalizing. The temptation is to argue that the theory accounts for everything, that it is a total worldview. This implies that all theories, however materialist, have an idealistic character. Local narratives always seem like grand theories from inside. Thus in our introductions to the different sections in this volume we will show how each article fits into and contributes to particular theoretical questions. But we will also challenge this internal view and refer across to other theoretical positions to explore the limitations and contributions of different theories in their larger context. In this way we can hope to learn whether the different perspectives have something to contribute to each other, and to explore the degrees to which they are complimentary or contradictory. We wish to see whether the polemical writings which have characterized archaeological theory over recent years are based on contradictions which are more apparent than real. We will thus, in effect, be exploring the limits of theory and the shape of archaeological knowledge.

Writing as a Social Practice

Another theme we wish to address is "writing" the past. Recent social theorists have shown why how we write is as important as what we write (e.g. Barnes and Duncan 1992; Clifford and Marcus 1986; White 1987). How we write tends to produce a certain kind of truth; writing is a technology of truth. Writing, as any other form of practice, involves meanings and resources. Who can write things, how and where things are written, what can be said: all these things depend on how writing is situated within a cross-cutting network of rules and resources, intentions and strategies. Reading too, as a practice, involves not only the active interpretation of words and texts but also the resources of knowledge and skill, the access to texts, the time resources and so on. The style and content of writing can act to transform these wider frameworks, the discourse within which texts are produced. Writing and reading can together form a set of transformative practices. On the one hand, writing can close off, and limit participation and reinterpretation. It can do this by emphasizing the authority and unquestionable scholarship of the individual writer, or by emphasizing the authority and scrutiny of objective science. These two strategies are often linked in the production of texts which expect the reader to be a passive consumer. On the other hand, writing can invite the reader to participate and take an active part in the construction of meaning. Within this approach there is more uncertainty and reading becomes a multiple and contingent process.

The first widely-read "Reader" in archaeology was edited over twenty years ago by Mark Leone (1970). This volume served to establish and legitimize the New Archaeology. The contributions all tended to be written in abstract scientific prose, reflecting archaeology's new self-conscious engagement with the natural sciences. The "reader" we have orchestrated here is equally a product of its time. It attempts to illustrate some of the diversity of positions that has emerged within Anglo-American archaeology since the 1980s. In this book, we have sought to construct an accommodation between content (theoretical contributions and worked examples), authors (men and women, Western and indigenous), and kinds of societies (hunter-gatherer, horticultural, and agricultural). Thus diversity and dialogue could be seen as the new canon. We favor this not as an end in and of itself, but as a necessary step toward creating the conditions for the possibility of a socially responsible archaeology.

Anglo-American archaeology has developed and is practised within a state-sponsored capitalist system (Gero 1985; Patterson 1995). As critical theorists have shown us, we cannot step outside our society and comment from a God's eye view. We can, however, choose to problematize this fact and to show some of the ways capitalism has marginalized certain voices. To make this point, we have included several views of Western archaeology from the perspectives of indigenous people, some of whom are archaeologists while others are not (Part VIII). These views have always been present within indigenous communities. What is new is that they are playing a more visible role in archaeological discourse (see, for example, Layton 1989a, b). Indigenous perspectives provide a poignant reminder of how contradictions between traditional and Western values are managed through lived experience. Some might object to our placing indigenous voices in a separate section rather than incorporating them throughout the volume, claiming that we are still marginalizing them. We acknowledge this criticism, but in our opinion an assimilationist approach would do the greater violence since it destroys the sense of difference or "Otherness" that we value. Many indigenous people do possess radically different worldviews and these need to be respected.

The selections we have chosen employ a wide range of writing styles which make various claims to being authoritative. Processual studies tend to be relatively conservative, written in a way deemed appropriate for the natural sciences while postprocessual and indigenous contributions demonstrate a wider range of styles, drawing from literary theory and experience. Thus Binford (**chapter 1**), a processualist, stresses classification and definitions to highlight his systemic approach. He talks about the "law of requisite variety" and about organizational principles such as logistic and residential mobility. He also makes use of rhetoric, challenging alternative views of mobility by calling them "opinions" which rely upon the "Garden of Eden" hypothesis. Shanks (**chapter 14**), a postprocessualist, begins with an artifact not a hypothesis, and moves outwards through a net of contextual associations. He writes in a rather fragmented style which seems to say "make of this what you can", inviting us to participate in the interpretation. He uses puns to link the past to the present. At the end of his article the object being interpreted remains a "riddle" – its meanings complex, ambiguous and multivalent. Anawak (**chapter 25**), a native American, makes use of a dialogic style whereby his written voice is virtually identical with his spoken voice. All of these examples have an effect and this is achieved in part through rhetoric and style.

As editors, we are also aware of the differences in our own backgrounds which predispose us to prefer certain interpretations over others. The collaborative nature of our project has required us to confront our own writing styles and explore their compatibility. We have edited and rewritten the texts for each of the introductory sections, a process that has been aided by electronic mail and our ability to send documents back and forth across the Atlantic almost instantaneously. We have chosen to write with a more or less consistent voice, to subsume our own personalities. This has both strengths and weaknesses. But we choose not to provide a totalizing narrative for the volume or for archaeological theory in general. So we have attempted to summarize the debates within the book in dialogic terms using the device of multiple voices and interests (Part IX). This strategy is designed to create an effect, to open the debate to a broader audience, to gain, we hope, your attention, and so to carry the dialogue forward.

By focusing on writing and reading, we are at the same time identifying and undermining our "Reader" as an authoritative work. Our section introductions represent our views of how the archaeological domain is structured in relation to theoretical perspectives. They bound and define the discipline, and say "read me, this is the way it is." And yet the very idea of coherent theoretical perspectives seems to be undermined by the fact that there is a tendency for theories to be grounded in practices in particular times and places. "The way it is" varies according to context. The articles we have chosen have been removed from their original contexts in books and journals but they can to some degree "respond back" to our categorizations and interpretations. Each reader of this "Reader" will, from within a particular tradition of practices, "write" a different book by evaluating these different discourses and adding in his or her own experience. We hope in our introductions, as far as we can, to open up the articles selected to different readings and different categorizations of the field, and to indicate the fluid and contingent nature of a developing archaeological theory.

Concluding Comments

We have produced this "Reader" because we think that theory is important. Theoretical discussion focuses attention on the assumptions we all use as archaeologists even in the most taken-for-granted moments – as when we say "this is a bevel rimmed bowl," "this is a flanged axe." Theory is also important because of the social context within which we live and work. Archaeology produces knowledge in the service of special interests. A "critically self-conscious archaeology," to use Clarke's (1973) term, depends on theoretical questioning. But it is all too easy for theory to become abstract and apparently irrelevant in the course of esoteric debate, divorced from practice. This is certainly the position taken by many involved in cultural-resource management, rescue archaeology, and the heritage industry. In this "Reader" we hope to have made theory more accessible – by providing our own assessments of contemporary archaeological theory, by including articles which demonstrate a variety of theoretical positions, and by emphasizing actual case studies. In this way, we hope to enable readers to form their own opinions and to develop their own critical perspectives.

We wish to draw attention to three trends we see emerging within archaeology. The first is the view of archaeology as a holistic discipline bridging the natural and social sciences. There is an increasing acceptance of the commensurability position, at least in terms of certain aspects of processual and postprocessual archaeologies (e.g. Brumfiel 1992; Cowgill 1993; Redman 1991). Attempts are now being made to show that each theoretical perspective has something to offer and that they all contribute to the "whole". The growing acceptance of history, of the fact that not only the universal is of interest, of the relevance of ideology and meaning, of our own ideological impact – all this makes for a broader discipline. We can look at things in multivariate ways, each of which can be seen as contributing to different aspects of scientific understanding.

The second is the attempt by some to shake off the dependence on other disciplines as the source of theory in archaeology: archaeology is a unique science, so the argument goes, and it should develop its own unique theory. Sherratt and Yoffee (1993), for example, suggest that the proper role of theory in archaeology is to build linkages between data and inference in which patterns of data are said to reflect social phenomena. They argue that, because archaeologists deal with certain kinds of problems that are not routinely dealt with by sociocultural anthropologists, archaeological theory cannot be regarded as a subset of anthropological theory. In some ways, this position is a return to the earlier views of Clarke (1968), who stated that "archaeology is archaeology is archaeology." It also recalls Schiffer's (1976) view of archaeology as the science of the archaeological record.

The third is the view of archaeology as a collection of incompatible theories tied to conflicting interests in the sciences, social sciences, and humanities (Bapty and Yates 1990; Shanks and Tilley 1987). This position derives from the postmodern condition of fragmentation and pluralism. Some argue that any attempt to define an integrated and unitary archaeological discipline implies that one theory must prevail. According to this view, the different theories are not just relevant at different scales and for different questions. They are intrinsically different, related to specific interests and aspirations in the present. This fragmentary perspective generates less interest in grand questions, such as the rise of the state or the origins of inequality, and encourages a concern with regional analysis and "thick descriptions" of specific events, sequences and meanings. This view accommodates a broad range of positions, from many indigenous perspectives to some forms of feminism to poststructural relativism.

We feel that each of these three trends – holism, exceptionalism, and pluralism – is limiting by itself, but anticipate the continuing development of archaeological theory as a result of interactions between them.

References

Bapty, I. and Yates, T. (eds) 1990. *Archaeology After Structuralism: Post-Structuralism and the Practice of Archaeology*, London.

Barnes, B. 1977. *Interests and the Growth of Knowledge*. London.

Barnes, T. J. and Duncan, J. S. (eds) 1992. *Writing Worlds: Discourse, Text and Metaphor in the Representation of Landscape*. London.

Binford, L.R. (ed.) 1977. *For Theory Building in Archaeology*. New York.

Binford, L.R. 1978. *Nunamiut Ethnoarchaeology*. New York.

Binford, L.R. 1987. Data, relativism and archaeological science. *Man* 22, 391–404.

Brumfiel, E. 1992. Breaking and entering the ecosystem – gender, class and faction steal the show. *American Anthropologist* 94, 551–67.

Clarke, D.L. 1968. *Analytical Archaeology*. London.

Clarke, D.L. 1973. Archaeology: the loss of innocence. *Antiquity* 47, 6–18.

Clifford, J. and Marcus, G.E. (eds) 1986. *Writing Culture: The Poetics and Politics of Ethnography*. Berkeley.

Conkey, M.W. and Gero, J.M. 1991. Tensions, Pluralities, and Engendering Archaeology: An Introduction to Women and Prehistory. In Gero, J.M. and Conkey, M.W. (eds) *Engendering Archaeology; Women and Prehistory*. Oxford, pp. 3–30.

Cowgill, G. 1993. Beyond criticizing new archaeology. *American Anthropologist* 95, 551–73.

Derrida, J. 1978. *Writing and Difference*. Chicago.

Feyerabend, P. 1975. *Against Method*. Thetford.

Flannery, K. (ed.) 1976. *The Early Mesoamerican Village*. New York.

Foucault, M. 1972. *The Archaeology of Knowledge*. London.

Fritz, J. and Plog, F. 1970. The nature of archaeological explanation. *American Antiquity*. 35, 405–12.

Gadamer, H-G. 1976. On the scope and function of hermeneutic reflection. In Linge, D. (ed.) *Philosophical Hermeneutics*, Berkeley.

Gero, J. 1985. Socio-politics of archaeology and the woman-at-home ideology. *American Antiquity* 50, 342–50.

Gould, R.A. 1980. *Living Archaeology*. Cambridge.

Habermas, J. 1975. *Knowledge and Human Interests*. London.

Habermas, J. 1977. A review of Gadamer's *Truth and Method*. In Dallmayer, F. and McCarthy, T. (eds) *Understanding Social Inquiry*, Notre Dame, p. 337.

Harding, S. 1986. *The Science Question in Feminism*. New York.

Harvey, D. 1985. The geopolitics of capitalism. In Gregory, D. and Urry, J. (eds) *Social Relations and Spatial Structures*. London.

Hawkes, C. 1954. Archaeological theory and method: some suggestions from the Old World. *American Anthropologist* 56, 155–68.

Hodder, I. 1982. *Symbols in Action: Ethnoarchaeological Studies of Material Culture*. Cambridge.

Hodder, I. 1991a. Postprocessual archaeology and the current debate. In Preucel, R.W. (ed.) *Processual and Postprocessual Archaeologies: Multiple Ways of Knowing the Past*. Center for Archaeological Investigations, Southern Illinois University, Occasional Paper 10, 30–41.

Hodder, I. 1991b. Interpretive archaeology and its role. *American Antiquity* 56, 7–18.

Johnson, A. and Earle, T.K. 1987. *The Evolution of Human Societies: From Foraging Group to the Agrarian State*. Stanford.

Keeley, L. 1980 *Experimental Determination of Stone Tool Uses: A Microwear Analysis*. Chicago.

Kramer, C. (ed.) 1979. *Ethnoarchaeology: Implications of Ethnography for Archaeology*. New York.

Kuhn, T. 1970. *The Structure of Scientific Revolutions*. Chicago.

Latour, B. 1987. *Science in Action*. Cambridge.

Latour, B. and Woolgar, S. 1979. *Laboratory Life: The Construction of Scientific Facts*. Beverly Hills.

Layton, R. (ed.) 1989a. *Conflict in the Archaeology of Living Traditions*. London.

Layton, R. (ed.) 1989b. *Who Needs the Past? Indigenous Values and Archaeology*. London.

Leone, M. (ed.) 1970. *Contemporary Archaeology*. Carbondale.

Leone, M.P. and Potter, P.B., Jr. 1988. Introduction: Issues in historical archaeology. In Leone M.P., and Potter, P.B., Jr. *The Recovery of Meaning: Historical Archaeology in the Eastern United States*. Washington D.C., pp. 1–22.

Little, B.J. 1992. *Text Aided Archaeology*. Boca Raton.

Longino, H. 1990. *Science as Social Knowledge*. Princeton.

Marcus, G.E. and Fischer, M.M.J. 1986. *Anthropology as Cultural Critique: An Experimental Moment in the Human Sciences*. Chicago.

Patterson, T. 1995. *Toward a Social History of Archaeology in the United States*. New York.

Popper, K. 1959. *The Logic of Scientific Discovery*. New York.

Preucel, R.W. 1991. The philosophy of archaeology. In *Processual and Postprocessual Archaeologies: Multiple Ways of Knowing the Past*. Center for Archaeological Investigations, Southern Illinois University, Occasional Paper 10, pp. 17–29.

Preucel, R.W. 1995. The postprocessual condition. *Journal of Archaeological Research* 3, 147–75.

Quine, W.V.O. 1951. The two dogmas of empiricism. In Quine, W.V.O. (ed.) *From a Logical Point of View*. New York, pp. 20–46.

Raab, L.M. and Goodyear, A.C. 1984. Middle range theory in archaeology. *American Antiquity* 49, 255–68.

Rawls, J. 1971. *A Theory of Justice*. Cambridge.

Redman, C. 1991. In defense of the seventies – the adolescence of new archaeology. *American Anthropologist* 93, 295–307.

Renfrew, A.C. 1973. *Social Archaeology*. Southampton.

Renfrew, A.C. 1982 *Towards an Archaeology of Mind*. Cambridge.

Renfrew, A.C. 1989. Comment on archaeology into the 1990s. *Norwegian Archaeological Review* 22, 33–41.

Renfrew, A.C. 1994. Toward a cognitive archaeology. In Renfrew, A.C. and Zubrow, E. (eds) *The Ancient Mind: Elements of Cognitive Archaeology*. Cambridge, pp. 3–12.

Renfrew, A.C. and Bahn, P. 1991. *Archaeology Theories, Methods and Practice*. London.

Renfrew, A.C. and Zubrow, E. (eds) 1994. *The Ancient Mind: Elements of a Cognitive Archaeology*. Cambridge.

Salmon, M.H. and Salmon, W.C. 1979. Alternative models of scientific explanation. *American Anthropologist* 81, 61–74.

Schiffer, M. 1976. *Behavioral Archaeology*. New York.

Schiffer, M. 1987. *Formation Processes of the Archaeological Record*. Albuquerque.

Shanks, M. and Hodder, I. 1995. Processual, postprocessual, and interpretive archaeologies. In Hodder, I., Shanks, M., Alexandri, H., Buchli, V., Carman, J., Last, J. and Lucas, G. (eds) *Interpreting Archaeology: Finding Meaning in the Past*. London, pp. 3–29.

Shanks, M. and Tilley, C. 1987. *Reconstructing Archaeology*. Cambridge.

Sharer, R.J. and Ashmore, W. 1993. *Archaeology: Discovering our Past*. Mountain View.

Sherratt, A.G. and Yoffee, N. (eds) 1993. *Archaeological Theory: Who Sets the Agenda?* Cambridge.

Skibo, J. M., Schiffer, M. B. and Reid, K. C. 1989, Organic-tempered pottery: an experimental study. *American Antiquity* 54, 122–46.

Skinner, Q. (ed.) 1985. *The Return of Grand Theory in the Human Sciences*. Cambridge.

Tilley, C. (ed.) 1993. *Interpretative Archaeology*. Oxford.

Trigger, B. 1989. *A History of Archaeological Thought*. Cambridge.

Watson, P.J., Redman, C. and Leblanc, S. 1971. *Explanation in Archaeology: An Explicitly Scientific Approach*. New York.

Watson, R. 1990. Ozymandias, king of kings: postprocessual radical archaeology as critique. *American Antiquity* 55, 673–89.

Watson, R. 1991. What the new archaeology has accomplished. *Current Anthropology* 32, 275–91.

White, H. 1987. *The Content of the Form: Narrative Discourse and Historical Representation*. Baltimore.

Willey, G.R. and Sabloff, J.A. 1983. *A History of American Archaeology*. Second edition. New York.

Willey, G.R. and Sabloff, J.A. 1993. *A History of American Archaeology*. San Francisco.

Wylie, A. 1985. The reaction against analogy. *Advances in Archaeological Method and Theory* 8, 63–111.

Wylie, A. 1989a. The interpretive dilemma. In Pinsky, V. and Wylie, A. (eds) *Critical Traditions in Contemporary Archaeology*. Cambridge, pp. 18–27.

Wylie, A. 1989b. Archaeological cables and tacking: the implications of practice for Bernstein's "options beyond objectivism and relativism." *Philosophy of Social Science* 19, 1–18.

Part II

Ecological Relations

Nature and Culture

Are humans "a part of" nature or are they "apart from" nature? This question lies at the very heart of the "Great Divide" between the natural and social sciences. Natural scientists have tended to emphasize the continuities between humans and other animals in areas such as physiology and behavior. Perhaps the most extreme example of this is sociobiology, the view that behavioral predispositions are genetically encoded (Wilson 1975). Social scientists generally stress culture as a uniquely human characteristic, drawing attention to the transformative potential of social structures. Some structural Marxists seem to view these structures as imbued with a life of their own, separate from the practices which reproduce them. In many ways this nature–culture dichotomy contours how we think about ourselves and our world.

Within these two broad approaches we can identify several subapproaches and varieties. For example, natural scientists, and here we include biologists, human ecologists, and evolutionary anthropologists, have explored ecosystems theory and evolutionary ecology. The former is the view that cultural variability and change are evidence for the different ways in which humans adapt to their environment (Hardesty 1971; Moran 1982; Netting 1968). The latter is the view that the differential persistence of cultural practices is due to the fact that they confer a selective advantage upon the group (Smith 1985; Smith and Winterhalder 1992). The main difference between the two turns on the role of selection in evolutionary theory. Social scientists, including sociologists, human geographers, and economic anthropologists, have explored various forms of economic theory. Some of these view human–environment relations in terms of transactions between individuals and resources (Halperin 1988; Plattner 1989) while others address social reproduction (Ingold 1986a; Lee 1992). Here the differences have to do with control over the means of production.

To varying degrees, archaeologists have made use of each of these different theories. Probably the most popular of the natural-science approaches has been some form of ecosystems modeling. This is the direction pioneered by Lewis Binford, Kent Flannery, and David Clarke. A small but significant approach is evolutionary biology, especially as it has been developed by scholars interested in

foraging theory. Steven Mithen (1994) for example is expanding this in the direction of cognitive processual archaeology. Against these natural-science approaches
are social approaches, including especially those stressing economic relations. The
work of the Cambridge school of paleoeconomy associated with Eric Higgs has
been especially influential as well as that of more recent cultural economists.
Another group of scholars, led by Michael Rowlands, Barbara Bender, and
Kristian Kristiansen, have emphasized social structures and transformations, in an
approach we term cultural materialism. In this section, we discuss each of these
approaches and then explore their uses in the interpretation of Paleolithic art and
landscape archaeology.

Ecosystems Approach

Although the ecosystems approach has important antecedents in the work of Julian
Steward (1955) and Leslie White (1949, 1959), its current prominence is due to the
rise of processual archaeology. In the 1960s processual archaeology consciously
sought to emulate the natural sciences by reformulating its theoretical and methodological base (Part VII). Accordingly, historical explanations such as diffusion and
migration were rejected in favour of those which implicated cultural dynamics
over time, that is, process. Following White, Binford (1962) proposed that culture
could be regarded as "man's extrasomatic means of adaptation" and that
cultural systems could be broken down into the economic, social and ideological
subsystems. Adopting a view firmly grounded in ecology, Flannery (1968, 1972)
stressed the importance of negative feedback in regulating cultural systems. Clarke
(1968) offered perhaps the broadest, and most complex, view, stressing the interconnectedness between different system components combining ecological,
anthropological, geographical, and morphological paradigms.
    The term "ecosystem" was originally proposed by A. G. Tansley (1935) to
describe both the biome (the total of interacting organisms), and the habitat. More
recent approaches in ecology emphasize the ecosystem as a self-regulated system
with an internal coherence, expressed in terms of energy flow, nutrient cycling, and
information feedback (e.g. Odum 1959). Changes in one part of the system automatically trigger changes in other parts as the system attempts to return to
steady-state by accessing a series of negative feedback loops. In human systems,
cultural practices serve first and foremost to maintain homeostasis in a process
termed adaptation (see Part V). Social systems, for example, are regarded as
functional components of the larger ecosystem. The unit of adaptation is usually
assumed to be the largest and most inclusive group that makes decisions. This may
seem superficially similar to group-selection arguments in evolutionary ecology
(Wynne-Edwards 1986), but there is an important difference. This is that there is
no consideration of natural selection, and change is instead seen as the result of
deviation-amplifying effects within the system. This distinction thus sets off
ecosystems from evolutionary ecology (see below).
    A pioneering example of the ecosystems approach is Kent Flannery's (1968)

study of the evolution of food production in formative Mesoamerica. He begins by defining the different components of the procurement system of the preagricultural inhabitants. These include the gathering of maguey, cactus fruit, tree legumes, and wild grasses, and the hunting of deer and other mammals. He suggests that the scheduling of hunting and gathering activities and the seasonal availability of plants and animals were part of the normal self-regulating mechanism that prevented the intensification of any one part of the procurement system. He then suggests that the emergence of agriculture can be understood as a process by which system equilibrium was disrupted due to scheduling conflicts. These developed as hunter-gatherers increasingly relied on maize, which in turn caused genetic changes which increased its yield. Maize agriculture thus grew preferentially at the expense of wild plant gathering and hunting and this eventually resulted in the spread of maize cultivation throughout all of Mesoamerica. This brought with it corresponding changes in group size and mobility. For Flannery, domestication did not arise *sui generis*, but rather came about as the result of human agency as certain plants and animals subject to human selection underwent genetic change.

A key concept in understanding ecological relations is mobility, how populations position themselves in the landscape in order to obtain natural resources, energy, and information. It is of theoretical interest because of the assumption that complexity is associated with sedentism and reduced mobility. Methodologically it has close connections to settlement archaeology and activity-area analysis. Mobility is often contrasted with sedentism as though they represent two poles along a continuum. This is problematic since sedentary people do not lack mobility strategies, although their movements may be channeled in certain ways by the presence of permanent villages. More recent studies have demonstrated that mobility is better regarded as an attribute of all populations, sedentary or not, and that different expressions cannot be uniquely linked to particular subsistence strategies (Kent 1989). In addition, some studies are exploring its political dimensions, particularly in the context of forced sedentarization and relocations (Lee 1979).

Binford (**chapter 1**) has offered an influential analysis of mobility from an ecosystems perspective. His main thesis is that variability in hunter-gatherer settlement systems can be explained in terms of the seasonal availability of resources. In a cross-cultural survey, he demonstrates that in environmental contexts characterized by high productivity and year-round resource availability, hunter-gatherers tend to adopt a seasonal round, moving to resources and leaving once the resources are consumed. In those contexts where productivity is low and resources are only seasonally available, hunter-gatherers make use of central places where they store food and from which they plan task-oriented forays into the landscape. Binford terms the former strategy "foraging" and the latter "collecting". He then goes on to explore some of the specific conditions under which these different strategies might be favored and then relates his typology to archaeological correlates (Kelley 1983). As with all ecosystemic studies, this model is more descriptive than explanatory, and fails to consider adequately how and why change takes place.

Most ecosystems modeling either explicitly or implicitly invokes the notion of carrying capacity. This refers to the maximum number of people that can be supported by a specific environment for a given mode of production. Systemic stress occurs when a population increases, either through immigration or biological reproduction (or both), beyond the limits imposed by the environment's carrying capacity (Zubrow 1975). Under these conditions, some form of adaptive response is required such as group fissioning or changes in the mode of production. Despite the fact that carrying capacity has proved extremely difficult to quantify, population pressure is commonly regarded as the "prime mover" in most adaptive models of culture change (Cohen 1977). More recent outgrowths of ecosystems modeling have sought to specify more accurately systemic variables, the conditions under which they interact, and the nature of non-linear and stochastic processes. Some of these directions being pursued include simulation modeling (Hodder 1978; Sabloff 1981), catastrophe theory (Renfrew and Cooke 1979), and information theory (Moore 1981, 1983).

The ecosystems approach has been criticized on several grounds. One problem is that its functionalism is incapable of explaining change. Presumably cultural behaviors emerge in response to changing environmental conditions. But there is little consideration of how these short-term behaviors may interact with longer-term "ecosystem imperatives" (Rappaport 1977). Another problem is the unit of adaptation. Ecosystem approaches focus on the largest inclusive decision-making unit. There is no recognition of the fluid and flexible nature of decision-making in human societies. At some times, individual families may make decisions while at other times, decisions may be made at a community level. The question then becomes one of who is adapting? Still another problem is that there is no general theory to account for why the systems take the form that they do. The presumption seems to be that variability is stochastic, but this denies that history channels this variability in specific ways.

Evolutionary Ecology

As noted above, evolutionary ecology differs from an ecosystems approach due to its explicitly Darwinian heritage. At present, it consists of a group of related theories covering foraging strategies, spatial organization, group size and formation, sex allocation, mating systems, life-history patterns, interspecific coevolution, the evolution of niches, and the equilibrium structure and dynamic behaviors of ecological communities (Krebs and Davies 1991). Many of these theories are subdivided into more specialized topics. For example, foraging theory is usually broken down according to decision stage into topics such as diet breadth, movement rules, time allocation, and group formation. The assumption underlying each of these different models is that individual organisms seek to maximize the net rate of energy capture so as to enhance their reproductive fitness. The decision rules used by organisms are thus continually being shaped by the forces of natural selection. But because fitness is extremely difficult to measure, proxy variables are typically used, such as protein and calories. Ecological relations are thus defined as all those interactions between the organism and its environment that affect its probability of survival and reproduction.

Foraging theory, also called optimal foraging theory, is among the best known of these theories in anthropology. Studies have now been conducted among the Aché (Hawkes, Hill, and O'Connell 1982), Alyawara (O'Connell and Hawkes 1981), Inuit (Smith 1985, 1991), and Cree (Winterhalder 1981) among others. The contributions are quite varied, ranging from the discovery that the uncertainties the Aché face in hunting are greatly outweighed by the net caloric return per foraging hour, to the finding that the use of Western hunting equipment greatly reduced handling time and allowed Cree hunters to target as prey fish and animals previously considered too small or too difficult to capture. This latter example points up one of the problems with foraging theory, namely that it ignores the importance of social and ideological factors in constraining choice – in this case it assumes that a superior technology is automatically adopted. This kind of critique is usually countered by arguing that the purpose of optimality studies is not to model reality, but rather to provide a set of guidelines against which to measure reality (Foley 1985).

In archaeology, evolutionary ecological theory has been touted as a source of middle-range theory linking general theory with predicted behavior (Winterhalder and Smith 1981). Yesner (1981) has introduced the notion of "coharvesting" to explain the taking of additional species as part of a specific hunting strategy. A hunter may kill an animal not originally targeted but randomly encountered so as not to return home empty-handed. Keegan (1986) has extended the optimal-foraging model to encompass diet breadth among horticulturalists. He suggests that gardens can be seen as "managed patches" and that the time required to prepare a patch can be considered as search time, a cost shared by all cultigens. Torrence (1983) has used optimization models to show that hunter-gatherers invest in technology that maximizes returns relative to time and not energy costs. Mithen (1989) has proposed replacing optimization with "meliorization" to enhance model realism. This approach acknowledges informational constraints and includes multiple, conflicting goals.

A number of simplifying assumptions are made by evolutionary ecological models. Speth (1990) draws attention to one of these in his review of food sharing in so-called "egalitarian" foraging societies. He starts with the widely held belief that food sharing is a hallmark of foraging societies and an indicator of the emergence of "humanness." He then questions whether equal access to sharing necessarily translates as equivalent nutritional benefits for all. In a carefully built argument, he shows how skilled hunters may receive a greater percentage of nutritionally valuable food by eating meat at the kill site and by differential sharing. This inequality would have the greatest negative effect on the diets of children, women, and the elderly, with potentially serious health consequences during stress periods. He further suggests that these asymmetries are better understood within a network of social, political and economic rights and that some of these can be inherited. This argument directly challenges the validity of neoevolutionism in general and the category of egalitarianism in particular (see Part III).

In a review of optimal foraging models, Keene (1983) has identified three problems that are associated with borrowing models from other fields. The first is use
without modification. This refers to the tendency to import theory directly into
archaeology without due consideration of the context from which it is borrowed.
He illustrates this point by discussing the debates over units of analysis and
currency in evolutionary biology. The second problem is the reification of theory
to the point that it becomes a tautology. In archaeology this has taken the form that
all behavior is assumed to be optimal in some way and all we need to do is to determine what is being optimized. On this view, nonoptimal behavior is never really
explained except as noise or random deviation. The third problem is that the
lending field often has a hidden agenda, a series of unstated assumptions about
how the world is ordered. For example, in evolutionary biology the intellectual
linkage to neoclassical economics is not often acknowledged. He suggests caution
in modeling foragers as "consumers in the environmental market."

One theory which seeks to transcend the problems of an evolutionary ecology
approach and provide a more general model of life is the new theory of complex
adaptive systems (CAS) (Gell-Mann 1992). This theory, often called complexity
theory, focuses on systems that have the capacity to learn or evolve by acquiring
needed information from their surrounding environments. These systems employ
"schemata" to describe the world and to predict future fitness landscapes. Selection
favors the differential survival of specific schemata, which in biological evolution
are the genome and in cultural evolution are social institutions, traditions and
beliefs. The application of these ideas to archaeology is still in an early stage,
and the few attempts are incomplete and highly speculative (e.g. Gumerman and
Gell-Mann 1994). There is a danger here that archaeologists will jump on yet
another band-wagon, as was the case to some extent with simulation and chaos
theory, without fully considering the broader implications of modeling cultural
systems as complex systems. Fortunately, two cautionary evaluations have been
offered. McGuire (1994) has argued that complexity is "too simple" because it
neglects history and conjuncture and Yoffee (1994) has drawn attention to some of
the problems of extending the biological notion of complexity to cultural systems.
Indeed, it seems highly unlikely that complexity theory can do more than describe
the form of cultural systems.

Cultural Economics

In the last fifty years the most important development in economic anthropology
has been the debate between two approaches known as substantivism and
formalism. Essentially, the debate turned on the universality of the principles of
modern market economics. Formalists argued that the differences between
capitalist and precapitalist societies were more of degree than of kind. They
regarded microeconomic concepts such as scarcity, maximization, and surplus as
universal properties of all societies. Substantivists countered that because pre-
capitalist societies generally lacked a market economy and a universal medium of

exchange, new principles needed to be discovered through empirical research. They stressed the embeddedness of the economy in social relations and contextual analysis. This debate is now moribund, but its historical legacy still continues to play an important role in economic theory.

In archaeology, an economic focus was introduced by Grahame Clark. Although he was not directly influenced by the formalist/substantivist debate, his view of economics as an aspect of culture suggests that he would have sided with the substantivists. His studies have addressed a wide variety of topics including diet and subsistence, agricultural land use, and trade and exchange (Clark 1952, 1953, 1954). Clark emphasized the economy not so much because of its significance in determining social organizations but because economics and technologies are shaped by forces that can be readily studied using the natural sciences. This is also the view expressed by Hawkes (1954) in his famous "ladder of inference" model. Clark appears to have regarded the economy as a means of adjusting to physical and biological conditions that generated specific needs, aspirations and values. The economy was thus a self-regulating subsystem that maintained the system at equilibrium. This approach has strong connections to ecosystems theory and indeed Clark represents the first use of the ecosystem concept in archaeology.

A formalist outgrowth of Clark's approach was the Cambridge school of paleo-economy, characterized by the work of Eric Higgs and Michael Jarman (Higgs 1972, 1975; Higgs and Jarman 1975). Paleoeconomy is the behavioral study of past subsistence systems, stressing cross-cultural regularities and general principles. It is closely related to the ecosystems approach, the primary difference being that economic approaches attempt to account for how subsistence strategies are chosen and why they change in terms of costs and benefits. The individual decision-maker is modeled as a rational economic person with perfect information. Like the eco-systems approach, it presumes that success depends upon the effectiveness and stability of the economic system, and sees culture as being largely determined by its economic adaptations. The method of paleoeconomy was site catchment analysis (Vita-Finzi and Higgs 1970). This technique involved determining the available resources in the immediate vicinity of an archaeological site and then comparing this with data gathered from excavation. Catchment size depended upon mode of subsistence and different catchment areas were drawn for hunter-gatherers and agriculturalists using ethnographic analogy.

The main limitation of the paleoeconomic approach is its view of the economy as divorced from social relations. A number of studies have sought to socialize economics by exploring such concepts as risk, uncertainty, surplus, exchange, and value (Earle and Ericson 1977; Ericson and Earle 1982; Halstead and O'Shea 1989; Sabloff and Lamberg-Karlovsky 1975; Sheridan and Bailey 1981). But many of these models can be criticized for their simplifying assumptions, particularly the neglect of symbolic behavior and agency. Few studies have systematically explored the strengths and weaknesses of economic and symbolic approaches. An exception is Hastorf and Johannessen's (**chapter 2**) study of prehispanic Andean fuel use. Beginning from a strict economic approach, they predicted that lower-quality fuel materials should be used as population increased, due to anthropogenic effects.

Their results, however, showed just the opposite: that there was a shift toward high-quality fuels, implying increasing fuel management over time. Their modern and ethnohistoric studies suggested that fuel and wood were conceptualized as something more than economic resources and had social, symbolic and political dimensions. They then concluded that the cultivation of trees, which could be interpreted in economic terms as a response to fuel shortages, was actually initiated because of the symbolic importance of trees as metaphors of life and lineage. Here a contextual analysis provides insights into the deeper workings of the pre-Inka economic system.

Cultural Materialism

We use the term cultural materialism to cover those approaches which emphasize the mode of production as structuring ecological relations. We refer explicitly to the studies influenced by the structural Marxism of Louis Althusser. These studies view social formations in terms of a hierarchy of levels (economic, political, and ideological), each of which is characterized by its own mode of production (the relations of producers, non-producers, and means of production). Although the economic level determines the shape of the social formation, the dominant mode varies according to each particular case. Cultural materialism shares some similarities with substantivist economics, the most obvious being that economic institutions are regarded as embedded within social relations. It is also closely associated with political economy (see Part III), although cultural materialism doesn't pay sufficient attention to history and social agency in the accumulation of power. And it also has linkages to the ecosystems approach, especially in the use of systems theory. Finally, we should note that we do not deal with Marvin Harris's (1979) version of cultural materialism because we regard it to be closer to the ecosystems approach.

There has now been considerable anthropological research addressing the mode of production (see Part III). Much of this has occurred in the debates between Claude Meillassoux, Emmanuel Terray and Pierre-Phillipe Rey. In his analysis of the Gouro, Meillassoux (1964) suggests that an original lineage mode of production was displaced by trade and then colonialism. Terray (1972) has criticized Meillassoux's reliance on a single mode, and interpreted the Gouro case as reflecting a tribal-village mode and a lineage mode with the latter dominant. Terray has himself been criticized by Rey (1975) for his static characterization and re-emphasized contradiction between modes. Another development only loosely connected to this debate is Sahlins's (1972) domestic mode of production. This concept refers to economies where the household is the primary unit of production and the key social dynamic is the relation between domestic groups and kinship affiliations. Wolf (1982) has explored the intersections of kin, tributary, and capitalist modes of production, showing how the Dutch capitalism and Bantu migrations pushed the !Kung into the Kalahari.

In archaeology, there has been a concern to explore the applicability of different modes of production to prehistoric societies. An example is Saitta and Keene's (1990) study of prehistoric village formation in the Zuni district. They define the communal mode as "organizational arrangements in which the social surplus labor performed by direct producers is appropriated by a collective body which includes those producers" (p. 213). Here Marx's notion of alienation is modified since producers retain partial access to the products of their labor. Significantly, they stress that this communal mode does not necessarily indicate egalitarianism, and indeed, under certain circumstances, it can actually lead to unequal access to various factors of production. They then proceed to look at the use of space at the Pettit site, which they interpret to reveal the existence of political agents who may have received shares of surplus in return for their role in managing the tensions between lineage and nonlineage interests. Here there is political complexity in a traditionally defined egalitarian society.

There has also been an interest in exploring the emergence of new relations of production. Patterson's (1991) study of state formation in the prehispanic Andes provides an example. He shows how the communal mode of production which developed during Conchas society broke down at the end of La Florida society. At that time, there is widespread evidence of fortified settlements, the taking of trophy heads, and elaborate weapons. This warfare and raiding favored the rise of temporary war leaders, some of whom seem to have been able to retain their power and authority. This is in part indicated by an increase in craft specialization, the use of prestige items, and the development of art styles to mark community boundaries. Approximately a century later, there is evidence for elaborate tombs with large quantities of grave goods. Patterson interprets all this as evidence for the emergence of a class-based society and a tributary mode of production. The reproduction of the state depends not so much on the exploitation of local kin communities, but rather on the goods and services appropriated from conquered states. But this mode of production set the stage for resistance and class struggle as subordinate states sought to regain control over the products of their labor.

Explaining Paleolithic Art

The variety of approaches to ecological relations can be demonstrated using Paleolithic art as a case study. Jochim (1983) has argued that Paleolithic art developed as a response to increasing population density during a period of environmental stress. He notes that by 25,000 years ago climatic conditions in northern Europe had become progressively harsh and this situation stimulated population movements south into the more favorable areas of southern France and northern Spain. He suggests that this region, already rich in anadramous fish resources, became a refugium for plants, animals, and humans. In this context, these groups of people intensified salmon fishing and this had social consequences, specifically the development of territorial fishing rights and sedentism. Jochim then argues that ritual mechanisms were needed to facilitate social interaction and cooperation.

Caves would have been the sites of these ritual activities and variability is reflected in localized styles of cave painting. A related interpretation dealing with a wider range of evidence is made by Gamble (1982).

Mithen (**chapter 3**) has offered a recent reinterpretation of Jochim's study. He points out some empirical problems with the refugium thesis and then offers his own approach which emphasizes cognition and decision-making (see Part V). According to Mithen, the refugium thesis does not adequately explain why certain images were chosen for illustration and, in fact, there are very few representations of fish in the cave art. In addition, he notes that fish remains are virtually absent in the archaeological record and that isotopic studies have shown that fish did not become important foods until the Magdalenian. Mithen then interprets cave art as linked to changes in hunting strategies. During the early Upper Paleolithic, individuals participated in the cooperative hunting of herd animals such as red deer and reindeer, but by the later Upper Paleolithic the populations of these herd animals fell dramatically causing individuals to hunt alone or in small groups. He suggests that during this changeover new hunting information was required and this was reinforced by close association with painted images of animals which cued the recall of specific animal habits and behaviors. In this way, art facilitated the retrieval of information stored in memory relating to the tracking of large animals.

Despite their different starting points, there are some important similarities between the two studies. Both adopt the art-as-function thesis. Jochim takes a classic cultural-ecological approach whereby the development of art is related to an external stress in the cultural system. Art emerges to solve a social problem. Mithen, on the other hand, adopts an evolutionary ecological approach by treating art as a "memory retrieval guide" which enhances the reproductive success of the society in question. Those groups that develop this particular form of communication are favored. But neither approach really addresses the issue of the individual as knowledgeable actor, as both the creator of human practices and created by past human practices (see Part V). In addition, there is no consideration of the transformative potential of art. Conkey's (1989) recent study comes closer because she explores the art in the context of the social processes of boundary formation, mediation, and maintenance.

Landscape and Culture

This variety of approaches can also be seen in the many different uses of the term "landscape" in archaeology. Here we wish to distinguish between four different approaches. The first is "landscape as environment." These studies involve the reconstruction of specific environments. They deal with what was out there that past people had to live in and adapt to. This approach underlies the paleoeconomic approach (see Part III) and especially the method of site catchment analysis. It is also widely associated with paleoenvironmental and climatic modeling. Thornes (1987), for example, has examined the paleoecology of erosion. A common assumption is that most environments have changed relatively little during the Holocene (with some obvious exceptions) and that present landscapes can be used as analogies to reconstruct past landscapes.

A second approach might be termed "landscape as system." These studies refer to the need to place sites within an overall pattern of site and off-site activities (Foley 1981). They refer to the integration of sites within settlement-subsistence systems. This is the approach pioneered by Willey (1953) and discussed here by Binford. These approaches are well suited to studies of economics and social structure since there is generally some relationship between the ways in which sites are distributed and the economic and political systems within which they exist. This is the focus of much locational archaeology, particularly central-place theory, network theory, and exchange theory (Hodder and Orton 1976).

A third approach is "landscape as power." This approach regards the landscape as ideologically manipulated in relations of domination and resistance. There is an emphasis on contradictions and conflict that emerge in the cognized environment and are embedded in power relations. An example at the local scale is Leone's (1984) study of a colonial house in Annapolis, in which the landscaped garden "naturalises" arbitrary relations of power. At a more regional scale a number of examples are provided by Bender (1992). Significantly, there is often a political awareness attached to this approach that requires activism in the face of contemporary environmental degradation, and in the face of the appropriation of monuments in the landscape by central planning agencies (ibid.).

A fourth approach is "landscape as experience". The term landscape can be taken to refer to how the environment was perceived and imbued with meaning (Part V), and this emphasis on the different cultural meanings given to the natural environment has been discussed by Flannery and Marcus (see **chapter 13**). But the concern of an experiential approach is more with the "phenomenology" of landscape (Tilley 1995) and with how bodies experience the world around them, how they move between monuments and settlements, along processional ways organised according to social and cosmological schemes, and so on (Bender 1992; Edmonds 1993). This is a move similar to the interest in lived experience currently being explored by some feminists (Part VI). The approach deals less with the landscape as perceived (as in studies of landscape painting and iconography) and more with the landscape as lived in, its features connected by routes, pathways and perspectives.

There is thus a gradation of views here, from the landscape as natural to the landscape as cultural. To some degree, these differences stem from issues of scale. The settlement approach is regional while the phenomenological approach is grounded in the individual. But it is also the case that some of the theories used are incomensurable. For example, there are ontological differences underlying whether landscape is considered independently of humans or as constructed by human agency. This raises serious questions about the calls for landscape as a unifying theoretical concept for archaeology. Ironically, there may be more chance for convergence at the methodological level. New developments in computer technology and software, particularly in Geographical Information Systems (GIS) and virtual reality, are enabling more sophisticated computer modeling applicable to each of these approaches (Allen et al. 1990; Reilly and Rahtz 1992).

Conclusion

To return to the nature–nurture question with which we started, it is clear that humans are both a part of nature and apart from it. As Ellen (1982, p. 277) puts it, this seeming paradox means that "every social action and idea, every rule, every category, is mediated by several million years of human and proto-human history and evolution" in a continuous process of reinterpretation and transformation. Seen this way the opposition, the either-or-ness of the nature and nurture debate is counterproductive and rather meaningless. But what does this insight really mean for an understanding of ecological relations? The answer may be that the very terms of the debate need to be rethought.

A key point which has been neglected by most studies of ecological relations is that material conditions are not simply determined by the environment or technology, but are predicated on notions of meaning and value. These are historically constituted and reproduced through cultural learning. Of the theories discussed here only the social-science approaches consider value. Cultural-economic approaches stress how value is created through the exchange of goods and services. Cultural-materialist approaches extend this to consider the construction of value through the exchange of symbols such as prestige goods. A complete analysis of value must then examine how symbols establish social obligations and act back to legitimize that which they create (see Part V). As Sahlins (1976, p. 211) writes, "culture is not merely nature expressed in another form. Rather the reverse: the action of nature unfolds in terms of culture, that is in a form no longer its own but embodied as meaning."

But what about evolutionary ecology? Are humans somehow immune from natural selection? Clearly this is not the case. Humans are, in fact, subject to natural selection in precisely the same ways that other animals are and this is best evidenced in marginal environments, such as islands or Arctic regions where they are particularly susceptible to extinction. But in culture humans possess something that assists in their survival that other animals do not have (see Part IV). It also follows that the variability we see in the archaeological record is due to the operation of cultural as well as natural selection. The problem is that the different approaches tend to divide up ecological relations into two camps and this only serves to perpetuate the traditional natural and social divisions. We need to recall how humans are both knowledgeable agents as well as actors in a pre-existing, historically constituted play.

But there may be a way in which these theories might be joined if the ontological grounds are shifted, if there is a move from conceptualizing systems in terms of unchanging essences to regarding them in terms of embedded relations. According to Ingold (1989) this would involve developing a theory of persons within a more general theory of organisms. This would link together the fields of psychology, anthropology, history, and biology in a common project. The challenge we would face if we were to follow this line would be to construct such a general theory without doing violence to human agency and creativity. In our view the result would be not a more general theory of complex adaptive systems, but rather a different kind of theory, a theory of life and consciousness.

References

Allen, K. S., Green, S. W. and Zubrow, E. B. W. 1990. *Interpreting Space: GIS and Archaeology.* Basingstoke, Hants.

Bender, B. 1992. Theorizing landscapes and the prehistoric landscapes of Stonehenge. *Man* 27, 735–55.

Binford, L.R. 1962. Archaeology as anthropology. *American Antiquity* 28, 217–25.

Clark, J.G.D. 1952. *Prehistoric Europe: The Economic Base.* London.

Clark, J.G.D. 1953. The economic approach to prehistory. *Proceedings of the British Academy* 39, 215–38.

Clark, J.G.D. 1954. *Excavations at Star Carr.* Cambridge.

Clarke, D.L. 1968. *Analytical Archaeology.* London.

Cohen, M.N. 1977. *The Food Crisis in Prehistory.* NewHaven.

Conkey, M. 1989. The structural analysis of Paleolithic art. In Lamberg-Karlovsky, C.C. (ed.) *Archaeological Thought in America.* Cambridge, pp. 135–54.

Earle, T.K. and Ericson, J. (eds) 1977. *Exchange Systems in Prehistory.* New York.

Edmonds, M. 1993. Interpreting causway enclosures in the past and in the present. In Tilley, C. (ed.) *Interpretive Archaeology.* Oxford, pp. 99–142.

Ellen, R. 1982. *Environment, Subsistence, and System: The Ecology of Small-scale Social Formations.* Cambridge.

Ericson, J. and Earle, T.K. (eds) 1982. *Contexts for Prehistoric Exchange.* New York.

Flannery, K.V. 1968. Archaeological systems theory and early Mesoamerica. In Meggers, B.J. (ed.) *Anthropological Archaeology in the Americas.* Washington D.C., pp. 67–87.

Flannery, K.V. 1972. The cultural evolution of civilizations. *Annual Review of Ecology and Systematics* 3, 399–42.

Foley, R. 1981. Off-site archaeology. In Hodder, I., Isaac, G. and Hammond, N. (eds) *Patterns of the Past.* Cambridge.

Foley, R. 1985. Optimality theory in anthropology. *Man* 20, 222–42.

Gamble, C. 1982. Interaction and alliance in Paleolithic society. *Man* 17, 92–107.

Gell-Mann, M. 1992. Complexity and complex adaptive systems. In Hawkins, J.A. and Gell-Mann, M. (eds) *The Evolution of Human Languages,* Santa Fe Institute Studies in the Sciences of Complexity, Proc. Vol. X, Reading, pp. 3–13

Gumerman, G.J. and Gell-Mann, M. (eds) 1994. *Understanding Complexity in the Prehistoric Southwest.* Santa Fe Institute Studies in the Sciences of Complexity, Proc. Vol. XVI, Reading.

Halperin, R. 1988 *Economies Across Cultures.* London.

Halstead, P. and O'Shea, J. (eds) 1989. *Bad Year Economics: Cultural Responses to Risk and Uncertainty.* Cambridge.

Hardesty, D. 1971. The ecosystem model, human energetics and the analysis of environmental relations. *The Western Canadian Journal of Archaeology* 2, 1–17.

Harris, M. 1979. *Cultural Materialism: The Struggle for a Science of Culture.* New York.

Hawkes, C. 1954. Archaeological theory and method: some suggestions from the Old World. *American Anthropologist* 56, 155–68.

Hawkes, K., Hill, K. and O'Connell, J.F. 1982. Why hunters gather: optimal foraging and the Ache of eastern Paraguay. *American Ethnologist* 9, 379–98.

Higgs, E.S. (ed.) 1972. *Papers in Economic Prehistory*. Cambridge.

Higgs, E.S. (ed.) 1975. *Paleoeconomy*. Cambridge.

Higgs, E.S. and Jarman, M.R. 1975. Paleoeconomy. In Higgs, E.S. (ed.) *Paleoeconomy*. Cambridge, pp. 1–8.

Hodder, I. (ed.) 1978. *Simulation Studies in Archaeology*. Cambridge.

Hodder, I. and Orton, C. 1976. *Spatial Analysis in Archaeology*. Cambridge.

Ingold, T. 1986. *Evolution and Social Life*. Cambridge.

Ingold, T. 1989. An anthropologist looks at biology. *Man* 25, 208–29.

Jochim, M. 1983. Paleolithic cave art in ecological perspective. In Bailey, G. (ed.) *Hunter-Gatherer Economy in Prehistory: A European Perspective*. Cambridge, pp. 212–19.

Keegan, W. 1986. The optimal foraging analysis of horticultural production. *American Anthropologist* 88, 92–107.

Keene, A. 1983. Biology, behavior, and borrowing: a critical examination of optimal foraging theory in archaeology. In Moore, J.A. and Keene, A.S. (eds) *Archaeological Hammers and Theories*. New York, pp. 137–55.

Kelley, R.L. 1983. Hunter-gatherer mobility strategies. *Journal of Anthropological Research* 39, 277–306.

Kent, S. (ed.) 1989. *Farmers as Hunters: The Implications of Sedentism*. Cambridge.

Krebs, J.R. and Davies, N.B. (eds) 1991. *Behavioral Ecology: An Evolutionary Approach*. Oxford.

Lee, R. 1992. Primitive communism and the origin of social inequality. In Upham, S. (ed.) *The Evolution of Political Systems: Sociopolitics in Small-scale Sedentary Societies*. Cambridge, pp. 225–46.

Leone, M. 1984. Interpreting ideology in historical archaeology: the William Paca garden in Annapolis, Maryland. In Miller, D. and Tilley, C. (eds) *Ideology, Power and Prehistory*. Cambridge, pp. 25–36.

McGuire, R. 1994. Why complexity is too simple. Paper presented at the Chacmool Conference, Calgary.

Meillassoux, C. 1964. *Anthropologie économique des Gouro de Côte d'Ivoire*. Paris.

Mithen, S. 1989. Modeling hunter-gatherer decision making: complementing optimal foraging theory. *Human Ecology* 17, 59–83.

Mithen, S. 1994. From the domain of specific to generalized intelligence: a cognitive interpretation of the Middle/Upper Paleolithic transition. In Renfrew, C. and Zubrow, E. (eds) *The Ancient Mind: Elements of Cognitive Archaeology*. Cambridge, pp. 29–39.

Moore, J.A. 1981. The effects of information networks in hunter-gatherer societies. In Winterhalder, B. and Smith E.A. (eds) *Hunter-Gatherer Foraging Strategies*. Chicago, pp. 194–217.

Moore, J.A. 1983. The trouble with know-it-alls: information as a social and ecological resource. In Moore, J.A. and Keene, A.S. (eds) *Archaeological Hammers and Theories*. New York, pp. 173–91.

Moran, E. 1982. *Human Adaptability: An Introduction to Ecological Anthropology*. Boulder.

Netting, R. McC. 1968. *Hill Farmers of Nigeria: Cultural Ecology of the Kofyar of the Jos Plateau*. Seattle.

O'Connell, J.F. and Hawkes, K. 1981. Alyawara plant use and optimal foraging theory. In Winterhalder, B. and Smith, E.A. (eds) *Hunter-Gatherer Foraging Strategies: Ethnographic and Archaeological Analyses*. Chicago, pp. 99–125.

Odum, E.P. 1959. *Fundamentals of Ecology*. Philadelphia.

Patterson, T.C. 1991. *The Inca Empire: The Formation and Disintegration of a Pre-Capitalist State*. Oxford.

Plattner, S. (ed.) 1989. *Economic Anthropology*. Palo Alto.

Rappaport, A. 1977. Ecology, adaptation, and ills of functionalism. *Michigan Discussions in Anthropology* 2, 138–90.

Reilly, P. and Rahtz, S. (eds) 1992. *Archaeology and the Information Age: A Global Perspective*. London.

Renfrew, C. and Cooke, K.L. (eds) 1979. *Transformations: Mathematical Approaches to Culture Change*. New York.

Rey, P.P. 1975. The lineage mode of production. *Critique of Anthropology* 3, 27–79.

Sabloff, J.A. (ed.) 1981. *Simulations in Archaeology*. School of American Research, University of New Mexico Press, Albuquerque.

Sabloff, J.A. and Lamberg-Karlovsky, C.C. (eds) 1975. *Ancient Civilizations and Trade*. School of American Research, University of New Mexico Press, Albuquerque.

Sahlins, M. 1972. *Stone Age Economics*. Chicago.

Sahlins, M. 1976. *Culture and Practical Reason*. Chicago.

Saitta, D. and Keene, A. 1990. Politics and surplus flow in prehistoric communal societies. In Upham, S. (ed.) *The Evolution of Political Systems: Sociopolitics in Small-Scale Sedentary Societies*. School of American Research, Cambridge University Press, Cambridge. pp. 203–24.

Sheridan, A. and Bailey, G. (eds) 1981. *Economic Archaeology: Toward an Integration of Ecological and Social Approaches*. BAR International Series 96. Oxford.

Smith, E.A. 1985. Inuit foraging groups: some simple models incorporating conflicts of interest, relatedness, and central-place sharing. *Ethnology and Sociobiology* 6, 27–47.

Smith, E.A. 1991. *Inujjuamiut Foraging Strategies: Evolutionary Ecology of an Arctic Hunting Economy*. New York.

Smith, E.A. and Winterhalder, B. 1992. *Evolutionary Ecology and Human Behavior*. New York.

Speth, J.D. 1990. Seasonality, resource stress and food sharing in so called 'egalitarian' foraging societies. *Journal of Anthropological Archaeology* 9, 148–88.

Steward, J. 1955. *Theory of Culture Change*. Urbana.

Tansley, A.G. 1935. The use and abuse of vegetational concepts and terms. *Ecology* 16, 284–307.

Terray, E. 1972. *Marxism and "Primitive" Society*. Monthly Review Press, New York.

Thornes, J.B. 1987. The Paleo-ecology of erosion. In Wagstaff, J.M. (ed.) *Landscape and Culture: Geographical and Archaeological Perspectives*. Oxford, pp. 37–55.

Tilley, C. 1995. *The Phenomenology of Landscape*. London.

Torrence, R. 1983. Time budgeting and hunter-gatherer technology. In Bailey, G. (ed.) *Hunter-Gatherer Economy in Prehistory*. Cambridge.

Vita-Finzi, C. and Higgs, E.S. 1970. Prehistoric economy in the Mount Carmel area of Palestine: site catchment analysis. *Proceedings of the Prehistoric Society* 36, 1–37.

White, L. 1949. *The Science of Culture*. New York.

White, L. 1959. *The Evolution of Culture*. New York.

Willey, G.R. 1953. Prehistoric settlement patterns in the Virú Valley, Perú. *Bureau of American Ethnology Bulletin* 153.

Wilson, E.O. 1975. *Sociobiology: The New Synthesis*. Cambridge.

Winterhalder, B. 1981. Foraging strategies in the Boreal Forest: an analysis of Cree hunting and gathering. In Winterhalder, B. and Smith, E.A. (eds) *Hunter-Gatherer Foraging Strategies: Ethnographic and Archaeological Analyses*. Chicago, pp. 66–98.

Winterhalder, B. and Smith, E.A. (ed.) 1981. *Hunter-Gatherer Foraging Strategies: Ethnographic and Archaeological Analyses*. Chicago.

Wolf, E. 1982. *Europe and the People without History*. Berkeley.

Wynne-Edwards, V.C. 1986. *Evolution Through Group Selection*. Oxford.

Yesner, D.R. 1981. Archaeological applications of optimal foraging theory: harvest strategies of Aleut hunter-gatherers. In Winterhalder, B. and Smith, E.A. (eds) *Hunter-Gatherer Foraging Strategies: Ethnographic and Archaeological Analyses*. Chicago, pp. 148–70.

Yoffee, N. 1994. Memorandum to Murray Gell-Man concerning: the complications of complexity in the prehistoric southwest. In Gumerman, G.J. and Gell-Mann, M. (eds) *Understanding Complexity in the Prehistoric Southwest*. Santa Fe Institute Studies in the Sciences of Complexity, Proc. Vol. XVI, Reading, pp. 341–58.

Zubrow, E. 1975. *Prehistoric Carrying Capacity: A Model*. Menlo Park.

1

Willow Smoke and Dogs' Tails: Hunter-Gatherer Settlement Systems and Archaeological Site Formation

Lewis R. Binford

An old Eskimo man was asked how he would summarize his life: he thought for a moment and said, "Willow smoke and dogs' tails: when we camp it's all willow smoke, and when we move all you see is dogs' tails wagging in front of you. Eskimo life is half of each."

This man was capturing in a few words a way of life now largely vanished from man's experience: mobile man pursuing food, shelter, and satisfaction in different places in his environment. This paper is a discussion of patterns that I have recognized through direct field study as well as long-term research in the historical and ethnographic literature dealing with hunting and gathering adaptations. I am interested in what, if anything, renders differences in man's mobility patterning, and in turn the archaeological "traces" of this behavior in the form of spatial patterning in archaeological sites, both "understandable" and "predictable".

The posture adopted accepts the responsibility for a systemic approach. That is, human systems of adaptation are assumed to be internally differentiated and organized arrangements of formally differentiated elements. Such internal differentiation is expected to characterize the actions performed and the locations of different behaviors. This means that sites are not equal and can be expected to vary in relation to their organizational roles within a system. What kind of variability can we expect to have characterized hunting and gathering adaptations in the past? What types of organizational variability can we expect to be manifest among different archaeological sites? Are there any types of regular or determined variability that can be anticipated among different archaeological sites? Are there any types of regular or determined variability that can be anticipated among the archaeological remains of people whose lives might be characterized as "willow smoke and dogs' tails"?

The archaeological record is at best a static pattern of associations and covariations among things distributed in space. Giving meaning to these contemporary patterns is dependent upon an understanding of the processes which operated to bring such patterning into existence. Thus, in order to carry out the task of the archaeologist, we must have a sophisticated knowledge and understanding of the dynamics of cultural adaptations, for it is from such dynamics that the statics which we observe arise. One cannot easily obtain such knowledge and understanding from the study of the archaeological remains themselves. The situation is similar to conditions during the early years of the development of medical science. We wish to be able to cure and prevent disease. Do we obtain such knowledge through the comparative study of the symptoms of disease? The symptoms are the products of disease. Can they tell us about the causes of disease? In a like manner the archaeological record is the *product* or derivative of a cultural system such that it is symptomatic of the past. We cannot hope to understand the causes of these remains through a formal comparative study of the remains themselves. We must seek a deeper understanding. We must seek to understand the relationships between the dynamics of a living system in the past and the material by-products that contribute to the formation of the archaeological record remaining today. In still more important ways we seek to understand how cultural systems differ and what conditions such differences as a first step toward meaningful explanation for patterns that may be chronologically preserved for us in the archaeological record. As in the earlier analogy with medical science, once we know something of the disease and its causes, we may codify the symptoms to permit accurate diagnosis. Similarly, in the archaeological world when we understand something of the relationship between the character of cultural systems and the character of their by-products, we may codify these derivatives to permit the accurate diagnosis from archaeological traces of the kind of cultural system that stood behind them in the past. These are not easy tasks to accomplish.

It has been my conviction that only through direct exposure to dynamics – the ethnoarchaeological study of living systems – does the archaeologist stand the best chance of gaining sufficient understanding to begin the task of giving meaning to the archaeological record, in short, of developing tools or methods for accurately diagnosing patterned variability.

My most extensive experience with living systems has been among the Nunamiut Eskimo (Inuit) of north-central Alaska. For this reason I will base my discussion of a "diagnostic approach" to settlement pattern on some of my Eskimo experiences. I will compare that understanding with a number of different settlement systems as documented ethnographically by others. I will then proceed to discuss how settlement systems may vary among hunters and gatherers living in different environments. In the course of these discussions. I will consider the types of archaeological sites generated in different environments as well as some of the probable spatial arrangements among such sites. Good diagnosis is "theory dependent." I will therefore be concerned with the factors that condition or "cause" different patterns of intersite variability in the archaeological record.

Collectors and Foragers

In several previous discussions of the Nunamiut I have described them as being "logistically organized." I have frequently contrasted their subsistence-settlement system with that of the San or "Bushman" peoples, whom, I have designated foragers.

Foragers

Figure 1.1 illustrates some of the characteristics of a foraging system (this figure is largely based on the /Gwi San as reported by Silberbauer [1972]). Several points should be made here regarding the characteristics of foragers. My model system as shown in Figure 1.1 illustrates seasonal residential moves among a series of resource "patches." In the example these include the "pans" or standing water sources, melon patches, etc. Foraging strategies may also be applied to largely undifferentiated areas, as is frequently the case in tropical rain forests or in other equatorial settings. One distinctive characteristic of a foraging strategy is that foragers typically do not store foods but gather foods daily. They range out gathering food on an "encounter" basis and return to their residential bases each afternoon or evening. In figure 1.1 residential bases are represented by solid black dots along tracks indicated by double dashed lines. The circles around each residential base indicate the foraging radius or the distance food procurement parties normally travel out into the bush before turning around and beginning their return trip. Another distinctive characteristic is that there may be considerable variability among foragers in the size of the mobile group as well as in the number of residential moves that are made during an annual cycle. In relatively large or "homogeneous" resource patches, as indicated by cross-hatching on the right of figure 1.1, the number of residential moves may be increased but the distances between them reduced, resulting in an intensive coverage of the resource "patch." On the other hand, if resources are scarce and dispersed, the size of the mobile group may be reduced and these small units scattered over a large area, each exploiting an extended foraging radius. This situation is indicated by the multiple residential bases on the lower left side of the "seasonal round" shown in figure 1.1. I might point out that when minimal forager groups (that is 5–10 persons) are dispersed, there is frequently a collapse of the division of labor, and foraging parties will be made up of both male and female members involved in procuring largely identical resources.

Perhaps the use of the desert San as a model for foraging strategies is somewhat misleading, since the most exclusive foragers are best known from equatorial forests. Table 1.1 summarizes some of the information from equatorial groups on numbers of residential moves, average distances between moves, and total distances covered during an annual cycle. What can be seen from table 1.1 is that there is considerable variability among foragers in the duration of stay at different sites. For some extremely mobile foragers such as the Punam, as reported by Harrison (1949), residential sites would be extremely ephemeral; one could expect little accumulation of debris and very low archaeological "visibility." There is another characteristic which may vary among foragers to further condition the "visibility" of the archaeological record: that is the relative redundancy of land use from year to year. One gains the impression from descriptions of such groups as

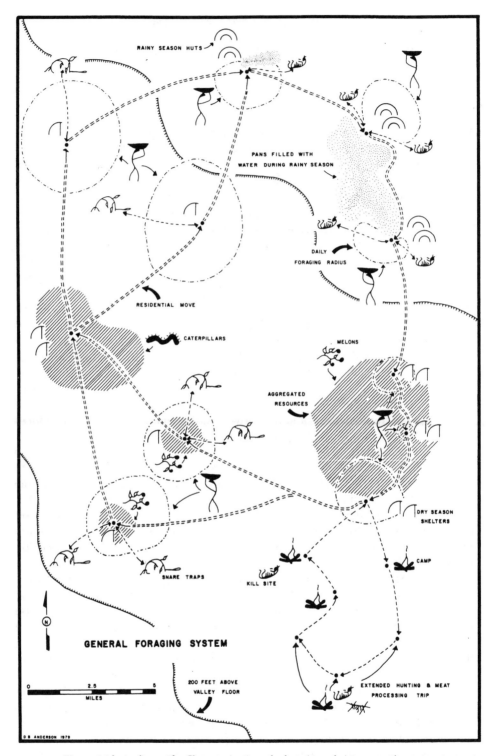

Figure 1.1 [orig. figure 1]   Characterization of a foraging subsistence-settlement system.

the Punam (Harrison 1949), the Guayaki (Clastres 1972), and other highly mobile foragers, that camps are not relocated relative to locations of previous use. The resources exploited are scattered but ubiquitous in their distribution and are not clumped or specifically localized as might be the case in deserts where waterholes

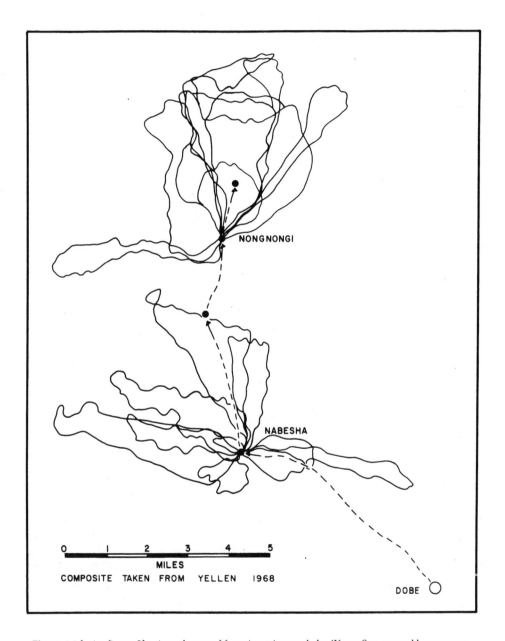

Figure 1.2 [orig. figure 2]   Actual map of foraging trips made by !Kung San around base camps.

Table 1.1 [orig. table 1]
Summary of group sizes and annual mobility for a number of equatorial and subequatorial groups of hunter-gatherers.

Group Name	Modal Group Size	Number of Annual Residential Moves	Mean Distance between Sites (miles)	Total Circuit Distance Covered Annually	References
Penum	65	45	4.2	195	Harrison 1949:135
Semang	18	21	7.1	150	Schebesta 1929:150
Mbuti	120	12	8.3	100	Bicchieri 1969:149
Siriono	75	26	14.2	370	Holmberg 1950
Guayaki	50–20	50	3.7	220	Clastres 1972:150
Aeta	45	22	8.0	178	Vanoverbergh 1925:432
Hadza	-	31	8.2	256	Woodburn 1972:194
Dobe !Kung	25	5	14.8	75	Lee 1968:35
G/wi	55–18	11–12	16.8	193	Silberbauer 1972:297

Note. These values are estimates from either the observers and interviewers or calculations made by me from indirect information provided by such authors.

are limited in number and discretely placed. Under the latter conditions we might expect more year to year redundancy in the occupation of particular places. Extreme examples of limited locations for critical resources may result in what Taylor (1964) has called *tethered nomadism,* indicating extreme redundancy in the reuse of identical places (water sources) over long periods of time. Such spatial discreteness tends to "tie down" the settlement system to specific geographical areas while other areas would be occupied little and rarely used because of their distance from such limited and crucial resources. We might think of a typical forager pattern of land use as looking like a daisy – the center is the residential base, and foraging parties move out, traversing search loops which resemble the petals of the daisy. Figure 1.2 illustrates this actual pattern as recorded by John Yellen (1972) for a mobile group of Dobe !Kung.

In recognition that there is an alternative strategy which may be executed occasionally by peoples who are basically foragers, I have indicated a different pattern in the lower right-hand corner of figure 1.1. We might think of this as a hunting trip where several men leave a residential base, establishing overnight camps from which they move out in search of game, frequently using what I (Binford 1978b) have termed an encounter of strategy. If they succeed in their hunting endeavors, and if the body size of the animal is large or the distance to camp is great and the temperature is warm, they may elect to dry the meat in the field and transport processed meat back to camp. This possibility is indicated by the little drying rack in the lower right-hand corner. They may then elect to return to the base by the original route or, if more meat is needed, they are more likely to return by a new route where they may even have further success in hunting. This little hunting trip represents a different type of strategy. It is a specialized work party, in this case made up of men, who establish camps for their own maintenance away from the residential base camp where they live. They may conduct special activities which may be only very rarely conducted in the residential base camp. This type of strategy may leave a very different kind of archaeological record and one we will explore in more detail in the next model.

Before going on, however, it may be useful to summarize something of our expectations regarding the archaeological remains of foraging strategies. The first point to be made regarding the archaeological remains of foraging strategies is simply that there are apt to be basically two types of spatial context for the discard or abandonment of artifactual remains. One is in the *residential base*, which is, as we have seen, the hub of subsistence activities, the locus out of which foraging parties originate and where most processing, manufacturing, and maintenance activities take place. I have indicated that among foragers residential mobility may vary considerably in both duration and the spacing between sites; in addition the size of the group may also vary. These factors would condition the character of the archaeological record generated during a single occupation. I have suggested that foragers may be found in environmental settings with very different incidences and distributions of critical resources. In settings with limited loci of availability for critical resources, patterns of residential mobility may be *tethered* around a series of very restricted locations such as water holes, increasing the year to year *redundancy* in the use of particular locations as residential camps. The greater the redundancy, the greater the potential buildup of archaeological remains, and hence the greater the archaeological visibility. Thus far, I have basically reiterated some of the generalizations Yellen (1977:36–136) formulated from his experiences with the Kalahari Bushman, as well as some of the arguments I (Binford 1978b:451–497) derived from my observations of Nunamiut Eskimo residential camps.

The further characteristics of the *residential base* will become clearer in contrast with the other type of archaeological occurrence that foragers are apt to produce: the *location*. A *location* is a place where extractive tasks are exclusively carried out. Since foragers generally do not stockpile foods or other raw materials. Such locations are generally "low bulk" procurement sites. That is to say, only limited quantities are procured there during any one episode, and therefore the site is occupied for only a very short period of time. In addition, since bulk procurement is rare, the use, exhaustion, and abandonment of tools is at a very low rate. In fact, few if any tools may be expected to remain at such places. A good example of a *location* generated by foragers, a wood-procurement site, is described by Hayden (1978:190–191).

As a rule, they are spatially segregated from base camps and are occupied for short durations (usually only a matter of hours at the most) by task-specific groups; ... the lithic tools employed are generally very distinctive and the assemblages highly differentiated in terms of proportional frequencies compared to base camp assemblages . . . the tools used are often obtained locally near the procurement site, and are generally left at the site after the activity is accomplished . . . if one walked extensively among the mulga grove, one could see an occasional chopping implement, usually left at the base of a decaying mulga trunk. Rarely were there more than two chopping implements, and the overall density must have been about one chopping implement per 2500 m² or less.

Under low-bulk extraction or low redundancy in localization, the archaeological remains of *locations* may be scattered over the landscape rather than concentrated in recognizable "sites." Understanding such remains would require data-collecting techniques different from those archaeologists normally employ. So-called "off-site" archaeological strategies are appropriate to such situations. Given that long periods of time are involved and certain resources are redundantly positioned in the environment, we might anticipate considerable palimpsest accumulations that may "look" like sites in that they are aggregates of artifacts; however, such aggregates would commonly lack internal structure and would be characterized by accretional formation histories. Very important research into this type of archaeological distribution was initiated in this country by Thomas (1975). Further provocative investigations of so-called "off-site archaeology" are currently being pursued by Robert Foley (personal communication) of the University of Durham in the Amboseli area of Kenya.

What can be summarized is that foragers generally have high residential mobility, low-bulk inputs, and regular daily food-procurement strategies. The result is that variability in the contents of residential sites will generally reflect the different seasonal scheduling of activities (if any) and the different duration of occupation. The so-called "functionally specific" sites will be relatively few; given low-bulk inputs and short or limited field processing of raw materials such locations will have low visability though they may well produce considerable "off-site" archaeological remains if long periods of land use are involved. Basically this type of system has received the greatest amount of ethnoarchaeological attention (e.g., Bushmen and central desert Australian Aborigines).

Collectors

In marked contrast to the forager strategy where a group "maps onto" resources through residential moves and adjustments in group size, logistically organized collectors supply themselves with specific resources through specially organized task groups.

Figure 1.3 illustrates some of the distinctive characteristics of a collector strategy. The model is generalized from my experiences with the Nunamiut Eskimo. In contrast to foragers, collectors are characterized by (1) the storage of food for at least part of the year and (2) logistically organized food-procurement parties. The latter situation has direct "site" implications in that special task groups may leave a residential location and establish a field camp or a station from which food-procurement operations may be planned and executed. If such procurement activities are successful, the obtained food may be field processed to facilitate transport and then moved to the consumers in the residential camp.

Logistical strategies are labor accommodations to incongruent distributions of critical resources or conditions which otherwise restrict mobility. Put another way, they are accommodations to the situation where consumers are near to one critical resource but far from another equally critical resource. Specially constituted labor units – task groups – therefore leave a residential location, generally moving some distance away to specifically selected locations judged most likely to result in the procurement of specific resources. Logistically organized task groups are generally small and composed of skilled and knowledgeable individuals. They are not groups out "searching" for any resource encountered; they are task groups seeking to procure *specific resources* in specific contexts. Thus we may identify specific procurement goals for most logistically organized groups. They go out to hunt sheep at the salt lick, or pursue big caribou bulls along the upland margins of the glaciers in July. They are fishing for grayling or white fish. They are not just out looking for food on an encounter basis.

This specificity and "specialization" in procurement strategy results in two types of functional specificity for sites produced under logistically organized procurement strategies. Sites are generated relative to the properties of logistical organization itself, but they are also generated with respect to specific types of target resources.

For foragers, I recognized two types of site, the *residential base* and the *location*. Collectors generate at least three additional types of sites by virtue of the logistical character of their procurement strategies. These I have designated the *field camp*, *the station*, and the *cache*. A field camp is a temporary operational center for a task group. It is where a task group sleeps, eats, and otherwise maintains itself while away from the residential base. Field camps may be expected to be further differentiated according to the nature of the target resources, so we may expect sheep-hunting field camps, caribou-hunting field camps, fishing field camps, etc.

Collectors, like foragers, actually procure and/or process raw materials at locations. However, since logistically organized producer parties are generally seeking products for social groups far larger than themselves, the debris generated at different locations may frequently vary considerably, as in the case of group bison kills on the Plains (see Frison [1970] or Wheat [1967]) or spring intercept caribou kill-butchering locations among the Nunamiut such as the site at Anavik (Binford 1978b: 171–178). Sites of major fish weirs or camas procurement locations on the Columbia plateau might be examples of locations with high archaeological visibility as opposed to the low-visibility locations commonly generated by foragers. Such large and highly visible sites are also the result of logistically organized groups, who frequently seek goods in very large quantities to serve as stores for consumption over considerable periods of time.

Stations and *caches* are rarely produced by foragers. *Stations* are sites where special-purpose task groups are localized when engaged in information gathering, for instance the observation of game movement (see Binford 1978b) or the observation of other humans. Stations may be ambush locations or hunting stands from

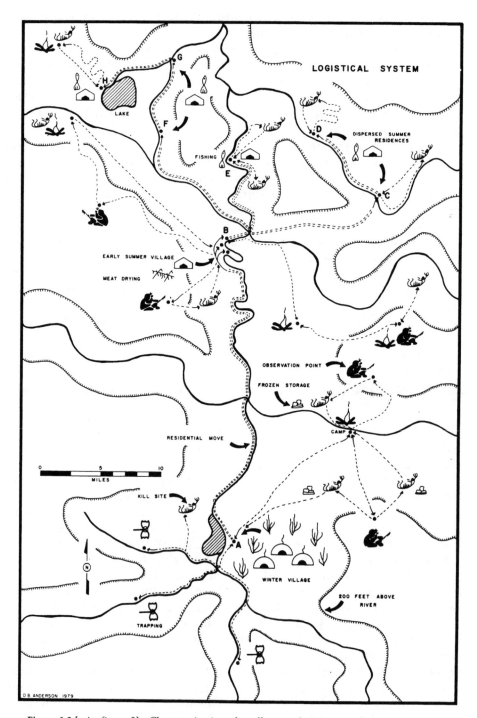

Figure 1.3 [orig. figure 3]   Characterization of a collector subsistence-settlement system.

which hunting strategy may be planned but not necessarily executed. These are particularly characteristic of logistically organized systems, since specific resource targets are generally identified and since for each target there is a specific strategy which must generally be "informed" as to the behavior of game before it can be executed.

Caches are common components of a logistical strategy in that successful procurement of resources by relatively small groups for relatively large groups generally means large bulk. This bulk must be transported to consumers, although it may on occasion serve as the stimulus for repositioning the consumers. In either case there is commonly a temporary storage phase. Such "field" storage is frequently done in regular facilities, but special facilities may be constructed to deal specifically with the bulk obtained (see Binford 1978a: 223–235). From the perspective of the archaeological record, we can expect *residential bases, locations, field camps, stations*, and *caches* as likely types of sites generated by a logistically organized system. Within each class we can expect further variability to relate to season and to the character of the resource targets of logistically organized task groups.

There is still an additional source of variability, since all the logistical functions may not necessarily be independently located. In some situations one might be able to use the field camp as an observation point, in others it may equally serve as a hunting stand. On occasion kills (*locations*) may be made directly from a hunting stand, and the meat may be processed and temporarily cached there. Many other combinations can be imagined. *The point is simple, the greater the number of generic types of functions a site may serve, the greater the number of possible combinations, and hence the greater the range of intersite variability which we may expect.*

Against this background it is perhaps instructive to follow out some of the conditions modeled in figure 1.3. Beginning with the winter village (site) at the lower center of the map, several conditions are indicated. The winter village is a cluster of relatively substantial houses located in a stand of willows (winter fuel). To the left of the village a series of expeditions are indicated; these are carried out by special trapping parties for the purpose of obtaining fur for winter clothing. To the right of the village are a series of site types: a *field camp*, where a hunting party is maintained while away from the residential camp; a station, or *observation site*, which is occupied and used basically for collecting information on game presence or movement; and several *locations*, kill sites and cache locations, which might also represent archaeological accumulations. With early summer a residential move is indicated (site B): this move results in a change in housing and a dependence upon dry rather than frozen meat as was the case in the winter village. From such a site, logistically organized parties may range out considerable distances to hunt such game as caribou or mountain sheep. *Field camps* and *stations*, like observation points and a variety of kill *locations*, might be generated. We see additional complexity caused by the differential combination of functions at different locations. For instance, to the far right of the map is a combined field camp and observation point; in other situations these functions might be spatially separated. In the upper part of the map an additional residential move is suggested. This move is accompanied by a reduction in group size as the local group breaks down into family units, each establishing independent residential camps having slightly different logistical patterning.

It should be clear by now that we are not talking about two polar types of subsistence-settlement systems, instead we are discussing a graded series from simple to complex. Logistically organized systems have all the properties of a forager system and then some. Being a system, when new organizational properties are added, adjustments are made in the components already present such that residential mobility no longer plays the same roles it did when the system had no logistical component, although important residential moves may still be made. Given basically two strategies, "mapping on" and "logistics," systems that employ both are more complex than those employing only one and accordingly have more implications for variability in the archaeological record. It should be clear that, *other things being equal, we can expect greater ranges of intersite variability as a function of increases in the logistical components of the subsistence-settlement system.*

Discussion

Thus far I have been talking about the patterning that I have perceived in the way hunters and gatherers are organized for subsistence purposes. I have been offering certain analytical and descriptive suggestions as to things one might look for in characterizing hunter-gatherer adaptations. I have been attempting to justify a particular way of looking at hunter-gatherers and suggesting that there are some interesting empirical patterns manifested by hunter-gatherers when they are looked at from the perspectives advocated.

Can we now begin the important task of building an explanation for the variability presented? Can we begin to understand the particular adaptive conditions which human groups differentially face by virtue of coping with different environments? Can we understand which conditions would favor "mapping on" versus "logistically organized" strategies? Beginning with a more specific question, are there any clues to the factors that favor or select for a foraging or logistical strategy? If we assume that technological and social characteristics contribute to making up the means and organization of production, we wish to know if there are not some basic "determinants" conditioning the distribution of differing "modes of production" (that is, the characteristic mixes of technology and social organization organized for subsistence purposes). Put another way, since systems of adaptation are energy-capturing systems, the strategies that they employ *must* bear some relationship to the energy or, more important, the entropy structure of the environments in which they seek energy. We may expect some redundancy in the technology or means, as well as the organization (labor organization), of production to arise as a result of "natural selection." That is the historical movement toward an "optima" for the setting. Put another way, technology, in both its "tools" sense as well as the "labor" sense, is invented and reorganized by men to solve certain problems presented by the energy-entropy structure of the environment in which they seek to gain a livelihood.

Given this viewpoint we would expect that a foraging mode of production would serve men well in certain environmental conditions, but not necessarily in all. What might some of these conditions be? Are there any environmental settings where we might expect foraging strategies to offer "optimal" security for groups of hunter-gatherers? I think it is fair to suggest that although most people view seasonal mobility of residential locations as being responsive to differences in food abundance, most have little appreciation for the environmental conditions which structure food abundance from the perspective of the human consumer. Perhaps Hollywood can be blamed for the widespread idea that "jungles" are food rich while deserts and arctic settings are food poor. In turn most laymen and beginning ecology students alike expect the greatest residential mobility in arctic and desert settings and most "sedentism" among non-food-producers in equatorial settings. Simply as a means of provocative demonstration I have adopted as a basis for further discussion data from Murdock (1967) regarding settlement patterns. Murdock rated 168 cases of hunters and gatherers as to their degree of residential mobility. Each group was scaled from one to four as follows (see Murdock 1967:159): (1) fully migratory or nomadic bands; (2) seminomadic communities whose members wander in bands for at least half of the year but occupy a fixed settlement at some season or seasons; (3) semisedentary communities whose members shift from one to another fixed settlement at different seasons or who occupy more or less permanently a single settlement from which a substantial proportion of the population departs seasonally to occupy shifting camps; and (4) compact and relatively permanent settings.

These 168 cases are summarized in table 1.2 which cross tabulates Murdock's estimates of residential mobility against a measure of environmental variability developed by Bailey (1960), called "effective temperature" (ET). This measure simultaneously describes both the total amount and yearly distribution of solar radiation characteristic of a given place. Stated another way, ET is a measure of both the length of the growing season and the intensity of solar energy available during the growing season. Since biotic production is primarily a result of solar radiation coupled with sufficient water to sustain photosynthesis, we can expect a general relationship to obtain between ET value and global patterns of biotic activity and hence production. Other things being equal, the higher the ET value, the greater the production of new cells within the plant or producer component of the habitat. This means that in a very simplistic sense we might expect "food rich" environments when ET is high and "food poor" environments when ET is low.

Table 1.2 illustrates some provocative facts. We note that "fully nomadic" strategies characterize 75% of the hunter-gatherer cases located in a fully equatorial environment (ET 25–21): high mobility is also found in 64.2% of the cases in semi-tropical settings. In warm temperate settings we note a drastic reduction of hunter-gatherers who are "fully nomadic" (only 9.3%), and in cool temperate settings the number is still further reduced (7.5%). Then as we move into boreal environments the number of fully nomadic groups increases slightly (11.1%), and in full arctic settings it increases drastically (reaching 41.6%). Thus we see that mobility, as measured by Murdock's categories, is greatest in equatorial settings,

Table 1.2 [orig. table 2]
Cross tabulation of settlement pattern as evaluated by Murdock (1967) and ET (Effective Temperature) values as calculated from world weather records.

Effective temperature	Fully Nomadic (1)	Semi-Nomadic (2)	Semi-Sedentary (3)	Sedentary (4)	Total	Index Value
25	2	0	0	0	2	
24	1	0	1	0	2	
23	3	1	0	0	4	
22	2	0	0	0	2	
21	1	1	0	0	2	
Sub-total	9 (75.0%)	2 (16.7%)	1 (8.3%)	0	12	1.33
20	1	1	1	0	3	
19	3	1	0	0	4	
18	2	1	0	0	3	
17	1	0	0	0	1	
16	2	1	0	0	3	
Sub-total	9 (64.2%)	4 (28.5%)	1 (7.1%)	0	14	1.42
15	2	11	2	0	15	
14	1	10	1	5	17	
Sub-total	3 (9.3%)	21 (65.6%)	3 (9.3%)	5 (15.6%)	32	2.31
13	3	17	4	4	28	
12	1	15	8	1	25	
Sub-total	4 (7.5%)	32 (60.3%)	12 (22.6%)	5 (9.4%)	53	2.33
11	2	15	9	3	29	
10	3	6	3	4	16	
Sub-total	5 (11.1%)	21 (46.6%)	12 (26.6%)	7 (15.4%)	45	2.46
9	5	3	1	1	10	
8	0	1	1	0	2	
Sub-total	5 (41.6%)	4 (33.3%)	2 (16.6%)	1 (8.3%)	12	1.91
Grand total	35 (20.8%)	84 (50.0%)	31 (18.4%)	18 (10.7%)	168	

where we have the highest production in the world, and in arctic settings, where we have the most consistently low production. Summarizing the data from table 1.2 another way, we observe the greatest concentration of sedentary and semi-sedentary hunters and gatherers in the temperate and boreal environmental zones and the least in equatorial and semiequatorial settings. This empirical pattern shows that mobility among hunter-gatherers is responsive to conditions other than gross patterns of "food abundance." This is indicated by the disproportionate occurrence of reduced mobility in the cooler, less productive environments.

I suggest that since mobility is a "positioning" strategy, it may well be most responsive to structural properties of the environment, that is to say the particulars of food distribution that are not directly correlated with the more intuitively appreciated conditions of food abundance.

A clue to the types of problems that different strategies solve is perhaps best sought in the contrasts between the two basic strategies themselves. *Foragers move consumers to goods with frequent residential moves, while collectors move goods to consumers with generally fewer residential moves.* The first strategy, that of "mapping on," would work only if all the critical resources were within foraging range of a residential base. Logistical strategies (by collectors) solve the problem of an incongruous distribution among critical resources (i.e., the lack of a reliable supply of a critical resource within the foraging radius of a residential base camp presumably located with regard to an equally critical resource). *Under conditions of spatial incongruity it must be appreciated that a residential move will not solve the problem.* A move toward one location reduces the access to the other. *It is under this condition that a logistical strategy is favored.* Hunter-gatherers move near one resource (generally the one with the greatest bulk demand) and procure the other resource(s) by means of special work groups who move the resource to consumers.

In the case of *temporal incongruity*, a storage strategy is the most likely means of solving the problem. One seeks to extend the time utility for one of the resources beyond its period of availability in the habitat. This is accomplished generally by either drying or freezing. *Storage reduces incongruous temporal phasing of resources, but it may increase the problem of spatial incongruity.* Spatial incongruity may be exacerbated in that storage accumulates considerable bulk in one place, which increases the transport costs of a residential move in favor of other resources that might be "coming in" or located some distance away. With increases in storage dependence there will be an expected increase in the logistical component of a settlement system. Finally, if the argument is made that incongruity among critical resources, whether temporal or spatial, is a condition favoring logistical strategies and a reduction and change in the role of residential mobility, it must also be realized that any condition which either (1) increases the numbers of critical resources and/or (2) increases the climatic variance over an annual cycle will also increase the probability of greater incongruities among critical resources.

Let us consider two logical expectations arising from this postulate. The law of requisite variety states that for maximum stability, the variety of homeostatic responses required in any system is equal to the variety of environmental challenges offered to it. We can expect, therefore, that the more unstable the thermal environment, the greater the number of operative homeostatic mechanisms, and hence the greater the number of critical resources, other things being equal. As the number of critical resources increases, there is a related increase in the probability that a lack of congruence will occur in their distributions. *Therefore, the greater the seasonal variability in temperature, the greater the expected role of logistical mobility in the settlement or "positioning" strategy.*

Given an equatorial environment in which species may exhibit patterns of differential production over an annual cycle, but the interdigitation of differing schedules among species ensures that there will be continuously available foods, a foraging strategy works very well. In temperate and still colder settings, such continuously available food is reduced as a function of decreases in the length of the growing season. Human groups attempting to "make a living" must therefore solve the "over-wintering" problem. Basically three methods are available: (1) exploiting species who have themselves solved the over-wintering problem (that is hunting other animals); (2) storing edible products accumulated largely during the growing season; or (3) storing animal resources accumulated during periods of high density and hence availability. *Although we must recognize that storage may not always be feasible, the degree to which it will be practiced can be expected to vary with decreases in the length of the growing season.* The degree to which storage is practiced will, in turn, increase the likelihood of distributional incongruities and hence condition further increases in logistically organized settlement systems with attendant reductions in residential mobility, at least seasonally. Both of these conditions are related to environmental reductions in the length of the growing season and to the implications of this for man, both in terms of foods and of other temperature-regulated resources. *This means that there is an environmental convergence of conditions acting simultaneously to increase the number of critical resources and to increase the conditions favoring storage.* Given the arguments presented here, we should therefore see a reduction in residential mobility and an increase in storage dependence as the length of the growing season decreases.

It should be pointed out that both of these expectations are supported empirically. As was previously indicated in table 1.2, there is a marked increase of cases classified as semisedentary and seminomadic in environments with ET less than 16°C. Stated another way, we see increases in seasonal sedentism, with attendant increases in logistically organized food procurement inferred, in such environments.

Figure 1.4 illustrates the relationship between ET and storage dependence as estimated by Murdock and Morrow (1970) for a sample of 31 ethnographically documented hunters and gatherers. Storage dependence is indicated by an ordinal scale distributed from one to six, where six indicates the greatest dependence upon storage. What is interesting in this small sample is that there is a clear curvilinear relationship between increased dependence upon storage and decreasing ET values, measuring decreases in lengths of growing season. It is notable that storage is practiced only among hunters and gatherers in environments with ET values less than 15 (i.e., in environments with growing seasons less than about 200 days). Exceptions to the general trend are interesting and perhaps instructive. In warm

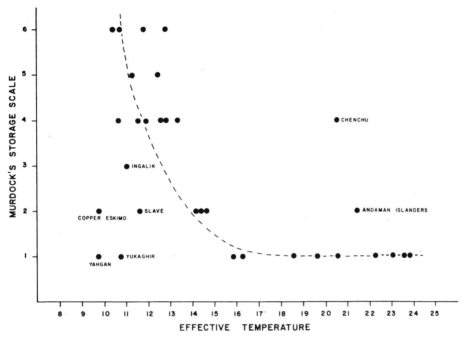

Figure 4. Graph of the relationship between storage dependence and effective temperature.

environments there are only two exceptions, the Andamanese and the Chenchu. It is my impression that the Andamanese are miscoded while the Chenchu are demonstrably in the process of adopting agriculture. Exceptions on the "cold" end of the distribution are the Yukaghir, Yahgan, Slave, Copper Eskimo, and Ingalik. I believe the Yukaghir to be miscoded, as well as the Ingalik, while the other cases are probably truly exceptional in being more mobile and not putting up stores for winter in appreciable amounts. Additional cases of cold-climate groups who do not put up appreciable stores might be the Micmac. Mistassini Cree, Igloolik and Polar Eskimo, and some groups of Copper and Netsilikmiut Eskimo, as well as some temperate cases like the Tasmanians. Many of these groups might be technically foragers with relatively high residential mobility, nevertheless they are foragers of a different type than most equatorial foragers.

As has been pointed out, equatorial foragers move their residences so as to position labor forces and consumers with respect to food-yielding habitats considered in spatial terms. The cold-environment foragers are what I tend to think of as serial specialists: they execute residential mobility so as to position the group with respect to particular food species that are temporally phased in their availability through a seasonal cycle. Leaving such interesting issues aside for the moment, it should be clear that there are definite geographical patterns to the distribution of environmental conditions that pose particular problems for hunter-gatherers. Some of these specifiable problems may be well solved or at least effectively dealt with through *logistically organized production strategies*. Such strategies answer the problem of incongruous distributions of critical resources. Incongruous distributions may occur spatially and may be further exacerbated by storage strategies. Storage always produces a high bulk accumulation in some place, which then has an increased likelihood of being incongruously distributed with respect to other critical resources such as fuel, water, shelter, etc. High bulk stores necessitate the determination of the relative cost of transporting consumers and stored goods to the loci of other critical resources versus that of introducing these other resources to the storage location through a logistically organized productive labor force.

   I should point out that if there are other factors that restrain mobility, such as increased numbers of social units in the area, competition among multiple social units for access to similar resources, etc., then we can expect an accompanying increase in logistically organized production. This is not the place to take up such important issues as the origins of agriculture and other density dependent shifts in both mobility and productive strategy, but I simply wish to point out that *with any condition that restrains residential mobility of either foragers or collectors, we can expect (among other things) a responsive increase in the degree of logistically organized production.*

Conclusions: Settlement Systems and Interassemblage Variability

The above discussion obviously has significant implications for our understanding of archaeological assemblages, their variability, and their patterning. I have argued elsewhere that we may think of an assemblage as a derivative of "some organized series of events characteristic of a system" (Binford 1978a:483). An assemblage that is the accumulated product of events spanning an entire year is rather gross and may be referred to as *coarse-grained* in that the resolution between archaeological remains and specific events is poor. On the other hand an assemblage accumulated over a short period of time, for instance a two-day camp, represents a *fine-grained* resolution between debris or by-products and events. Having made the above distinctions I previously argued:

> 1. Insofar as events are serially differentiated, and the composition of assemblages are responsive to event differences, the more fine-grained the assemblage, the greater the probable content variability among assemblages.
> 2. The factor which regulates the grain of an assemblage is mobility, such that high mobility results in fine-grained assemblages, whereas low mobility results in coarse-grained assemblages. (For further discussion see Binford 1978b:483–495.)

   In reference to the initial condition, "the degree to which events are serially differentiated," it was argued that from a subsistence perspective the major conditioner of event differentiation is seasonal variance in the basic climatic variables: rainfall and solar radiation. It was therefore suggested that interassemblage variability *"can be expected to increase with decreases in the length of the growing season"* and/or *"decreases in the equability of rainfall distribution throughout a seasonal cycle, given moderate to fine-grained assemblages"* (Binford 1978b:484).

The earlier arguments had reference primarily to *residential* mobility. In this paper I have explored something of the interaction and the determinants for differential degrees of residential versus logistical mobility. I have suggested here that there are two basic principles of organization employed by hunters and gatherers in carrying out their subsistence strategies. They may "map on" by moving consumers to resources, or they may move resources to consumers "logistically." I have suggested that the relative roles played by these two organizational principles in any given subsistence system will also condition the nature and character of archaeological intersite variability generated by the system. Foragers who practice primarily a "mapping on" strategy will generate basically two types of sites: the *residential base* and the *location*. Variability among forager systems will derive primarily from differences in the magnitude of residential mobility and environmental differences conditioning different subsistence activities through a seasonal cycle.

Collectors who tend toward a greater reliance on the logistical strategies can be expected to generate additional types of archaeological sites. That is, in addition to the *residential base* and the *location* we can expect *field camps, stations,* and *caches* to be generated. It was also argued that the character of residential bases, as well as that of locations, may well be expected to change in accordance with the relative degree of logistically organized activity characteristic of a system.

I then turned to the interesting question of what *conditions* the relative roles of "mapping on" versus "logistical" strategies in a subsistence-settlement system? It was argued that logistically based strategies are a direct response to the degree of locational incongruity among critical resources. It was further argued that the number of critical resources increases as climatic severity increases, and that the relative dependence upon stored foods increases as the length of the growing season decreases. It was pointed out that these characteristics are linked, and both tend to vary with geographical variability in the length of the growing season. *Therefore, as the length of the growing season decreases, other things being equal, we can expect increases in the role of logistical strategies within the subsistence-settlement system. It was also pointed out the any other conditions that restrict "normal" residential mobility among either foragers or collectors also tend to favor increases in logistically organized procurement strategies.* We would therefore tend to expect some increase associated with shifts toward agricultural production.

I can now integrate my earlier arguments regarding the factors conditioning interassemblage variability at residential bases with the arguments made in this paper regarding variability in the archaeological record stemming from organizational differences in the roles of mapping on and logistical strategies in the subsistence-settlement behavior of groups living in different environments. It was argued earlier that as seasonal variability in solar radiation or rainfall increased, given assemblage responsiveness to event differentiations, there would be an increase in residential interassamblage variability. This is assuming a roughly constant assemblage grain. In this paper it has been argued that under the same conditions increased logistical dependence with an accompanying reduction in residential mobility would be favored. This situation would have the effect of increasing the coarseness of the assemblage grain from such locations. *Increased coarseness, in turn, should have the effect of reducing interassemblage variability among residential sites of a single or closely related system occupied during comparable seasons. It would of course also have the effect of increasing the complexity and "scale" of assemblage content referable to any given uninterrupted occupation, assuming, that is, a responsiveness of assemblage content to event differentiations.*

The overall effect of what appears to be opposing consequences is normally some seasonal differentiation in the relative roles of residential versus logistical mobility. For instance, in some environments we might see high residential mobility in the summer or during the growing season and reduced mobility during the winter, with accompanying increases in logistical mobility. The overall effect from a regional perspective would be extensive interassemblage variability deriving from both conditions. We may also expect minor qualitative difference among assemblages from the winter villages (in the above examples). These are likely to be categorically different from mobile summer residences which would be highly variable and constitute a "noisy" category. Comparisons among winter residences would clearly warrant a categorical distinction of these from summer residences and they would be a "cleaner", less noisy category of greater within-assemblage diversity. Summer sites would be more variable among themselves but also less internally complex.

The point here is that logistical and residential variability are not to be viewed as opposing principles (although trends may be recognized) *but as organizational alternatives which may be employed in varying mixes in different settings.* These organizational mixes provide the basis for extensive variability which may yield very confusing archaeological patterning.

The next step in the arguments presented in this paper treats the production of special-purpose sites. It was suggested that with logistical strategies new types of sites may be expected: *field camps, stations,* and *caches.* It was further argued that the character and visibility at *locations* also changes in the context of increased use of logistical strategies. *We may therefore argue that, other things being equal, we may anticipate regular environmentally correlated patterns of inter-site variability deriving from increases in the number and functional character of special-purpose sites with decreases in the length of the growing season.* In addition to such quantitative changes, given the more specialized character of resource "targets" sought under logistical strategies, we can expect an increase in the redundancy of the geographic placement of special-purpose sites and a greater buildup of archaeological debris in restricted sections of the habitat as a function of increasing logistical dependence (for a more extended discussion of this point see Binford 1978b:488–495).

This last point addresses a subject not discussed in depth in this paper, namely, the long-term land-use strategies of hunter-gatherers in differing environmental contexts. This paper has primarily dealt with short-term organizational and strategy differences. "Short-term" here essentially means the dynamic of yearly cycle. I have argued that there are environmental factors conditioning variability in short-term mobility and land-use strategies among hunters and gatherers. I have not seriously considered the possibility that hunters and gatherers would ever remain *sedentary* as a security-seeking strategy unless forced to do so. I am aware of many arguments that essentially appeal to what I term the "Garden of Eden" principle, namely, that things were so "wonderful" at certain places in the environment that there was no need to move. I find that a totally untenable *opinion*, and one which can be countered easily by scholars who understand ecological relationships. This does, however, imply that an understanding of short-term strategies as discussed here is insufficient for treating patterning which derives from variable redundancy in geographical positioning of the total settlement-subsistence systems. A detailed consideration of the factors that differentially condition *long-term* range occupancy or positioning in macro-geographical terms is needed before we can realistically begin to develop a comprehensive theory of hunter-gatherer subsistence-settlement behavior. The latter is of course necessary to an understanding of archaeological site patterning.

Acknowledgments

This paper was originally prepared at the request of Peter Bleed, who graciously invited me to participate in the 1979 Montgomery Lecture Series at the University of Nebraska-Lincoln. For both the opportunity and the encouragement to prepare this paper I am most grateful.

My colleague Jeremy Sabloff read and made constructive comments on earlier drafts as did William Morgan and Robert Vierra; for this assistance I am most grateful. Ms. Dana Anderson developed and prepared the illustrations: certainly the quality of her work adds appreciably to this paper.

The field work opportunities which have provided the stimulus for much of the discussion and my appreciation of hunter-gatherer mobility were supported by the National Science Foundation, the Wenner-Gren Foundation, and the Australian institute of Aboriginal Studies. A grant from the Faculty Research Committee of the University of New Mexico aided in the preparation of the manuscript, particularly the drafting of the illustrations. For this I am most grateful. Colleagues who shared my interest in hunter-gatherer adaptations have provided me with stimulating intellectual environments; I would particularly like to mention Henry Harpending, James O'Connell, Nick Peterson and John Pfeiffer.

References Cited

Bailey, Harry P. 1960 A method of determining the warmth and temperateness of climate. *Geografiska Annaler* 43(1): 1–16.

Bicchieri, M.G. 1969 The differential use of identical features of physical habitat in connection with exploitative, settlement, and community patterns: the BaMbuti case study.

In *Contributions to anthropology: ecological essays*, edited by David Damas, pp. 65–72. *National Museums of Canada, Bulletin* 230, *Anthropological Series* No. 86.

Binford, Lewis R. 1978a   Dimensional analysis of behavior and site structure: learning from an Eskimo hunting stand. *American Antiquity* 43:330–361.

—— 1978b   *Nunamiut ethnoarchaeology*. Academic Press, New York.

Clastres, Pierre 1972   The Guayaki. In *Hunters and gatherers today*, edited by M. G. Bicchieri, pp. 138–174. Holt, Rinehart, and Winston, New York.

Frison, George 1970   The Glenrock buffalo jump, 48C0304. *Plains Anthropologist, Memoir* 7.

Harrison, Tom 1949   Notes on some nomadic Punans. *The Sarawak Museum Journal* V(1):130–146.

Hayden, Brian 1978   Snarks in archaeology: or, inter-assemblage variability in lithics (a view from the Antipodes). In *Lithics and subsistence: the analysis of stone tool use in prehistoric economics*, edited by Dave L. Davis, pp. 179–198. *Vanderbilt University Publications in Anthropology* 20.

Holmberg, Allan R. 1950   Nomads of the long bow; the Siriono of eastern Bolivia. *Institution Institute of Social Anthropology Publication* 10.

Lee, Richard B. 1968   What hunters do for a living, or how to make out on scarce resources. In *Man the Hunter*, edited by Richard B. Lee and Irven DeVore, pp. 30–48. Aldine, Chicago.

Murdock, G.P. 1967   Ethnographic atlas; a summary. *Ethnology* 6:109–236.

Murdock, G.P., and Diana O. Morrow 1970   Subsistence economy and supportive practices: cross-cultural codes 1. *Ethnology* 9:302–330.

Schebesta, Paul 1929   *Among the forest dwarfs of Malaya*, translated by A. Chambers, Hutchinson Press, London.

Silberbauer, George B. 1972   The G/wi Bushmen. In *Hunters and Gatherers today*, edited by M.G. Bicchieri, pp. 271–326. Holt, Rinehart, and Winston, New York.

Taylor, Walter W. 1964   Tethered nomadism and water territoriality: an hypothesis. *Acts of the 35th International Congress of Americanists*, pp. 197–203. Mexico City.

Thomas, David H. 1975   Nonsite sampling in archeology: up the creek without a site? In *Sampling in archaeology*, edited by James W. Mueller, pp. 61–81. University of Arizona Press, Tucson.

Vanoverbergh, Morice 1925   Negritos of northern Luxon. *Anthropos* 20:148–199, 399–443.

Wheat, Joe Ben 1967   A Paleo-Indian bison kill, *Scientific American* 216(1):44–53.

Woodburn, James 1972   Ecology, nomadic movement and the composition of the local group among hunters and gatherers: an East African example and its implications. In *Man, settlement and urbanism*, edited by P.J. Ucko, R. Tringham, and G.W. Dimbleby, pp. 193–206. Duckworth, London.

Yellen, John E. 1972   Trip V. itinerary May 24–June 9, 1968. In pilot edition of *Exploring human nature*. Educational Development Center, Inc., Cambridge, MA.

—— 1977   *Archaeological approaches to the present*. Academic Press, New York.

2

Understanding Changing People/Plant Relationships in the Prehispanic Andes

Christine A. Hastorf and Sissel Johannessen

The use of "natural" resources is the most conspicuous of human adaptations that can be studied by archaeologists, and the ecological and environmental issues implicit in resource use have been the heart and soul of processual archaeology. Changing resource use through time, seen exclusively in terms of a society's adjustment to its environment, has been a prominent research focus for the past 20 or more years (e.g., Binford and Binford 1968). Recently, postprocessual archaeology has turned from an interest in the purely physical adaptation of human beings to their environment toward a concern with human agency and the social construction of the world in which people live (Shanks and Tilley 1988).

Our contribution to the debate between processual and postprocessual archaeology centers on a data set that, dealing as it does with changing resource use over time, would be a likely subject of a processual interpretation. However, by illustrating the social, symbolic, and political dimensions to the change in resource use, we contextualize the data and enrich the interpretation, showing that even what might be considered the strictly economic aspect of the change is in fact uniquely shaped by the culture in which it takes place. In this chapter, we study how a culture interacted with its environment over time by focusing on the use of fuel in an Andean valley over a thousand years of prehistory. In doing so, we hope to illustrate how a group's interaction with, management, and use of its environment was socially constructed and culturally mediated.

There are many ways a human group can react to a fuel-scarce environment such as existed in the Andes of Peru. Highland people had more than one "optimal" solution to remedy their fuel problem. The ancestors of the Sausa chose a certain path based on their social and cultural views, thus constructing and changing their "natural" world as their society changed. We suggest that our results indicate that the prehistoric people were not just implementing a more productive fuel management system because of increased fuel needs but that fuel use was altered through social and political structures and actions. It is our task as archaeologists to try to learn about the cultural world of the people we are studying. We hope to show that an approach that sees cultural change as a result of constant interaction and negotiation channeled through the cultural principles of that world (Giddens 1979) can increase our understanding of past events.

Studying Resource Use in the Andes

We began this fuel project from an essentially economic, processual perspective. First, we believed that the study of long-term patterns of fuel remains could reveal shifts in human use and effect on the landscape (e.g., Lopinot and Woods 1988; Miller 1985; Minnis 1978). Given the relatively treeless conditions in the intermontane Andean study area, we thought that there would have been an increasing problem with fuel scarcity as the farming populations grew in the area. We expected that with increasing population the people would exhaust the local woody resources and resort to an increasing variety of lower quality fuel materials.

The project consisted of two parts: the laboratory analysis of woody plant remains from a number of archaeological sites in a Peruvian valley and a literature survey of Andean fuel resources and use. To date we have analyzed the woody remains from more than 300 flotation and screen samples covering a thousand years of occupation in the Jauja area in the central Andes, from approximately A.D. 500 to 1500 – a time span well within the period of settled farming life. The members of the Upper Mantaro Archaeological Research Project have excavated the remains of house compounds at a number of Late Intermediate and Inka period sites as well as earlier deposits at the stratified site of Pancán (Earle et al. 1987; Hastorf et al. 1989). From those household contexts we have direct evidence of fuel use in the form of charred woody material, such as grass stems, twigs, and wood fragments.

In addition, we researched the modern and ethnohistoric relations between Andean people, trees, and fuel (the major sources are Ansión 1986; Cobo 1890–1895 [1653]; Espinoza Soriano 1971; Gade 1975; Garcilaso de la Vega 1985 [1609–1617]; Guaman Poma de Ayala 1987 [1615]; Pachacuti Yamqui 1950 [1613]; and Sherbondy 1986 – for further detail see Johannessen and Hastorf 1990). From those sources we learned that the picture is more complex than we thought at first: wood and trees in the Andes are much more than fuel; they also have social, symbolic, and political dimensions.

As we studied the botanical remains and read the literature, we were forced to abandon two expectations that might typically be held by processual archaeologists. The first is that increasing population and more intensive agriculture in a fuel-scarce region should correlate with decreasing use over time of high-quality fuels such as wood. We found in fact that wood use, relative to less desirable fuels, increased and that the types of wood used changed in conjunction with political changes that occurred in the Late Intermediate period and with Inka hegemony. The second common viewpoint we have abandoned is that "natural" resources, especially fuel, are passive entities to be exploited, extracted, and utilized by human societies. We have found rather that fuel use involves a dynamic interaction between human groups and their perception of resources. We believe that our data show prehispanic tree management and perhaps tree cultivation in the central Andes. To begin our reading of fuel in the Andes, we first introduce the area and present the botanical data. We then discuss the cultural factors that add to their interpretation.

Methods and Data

The study area is the northern tip of the Upper Mantaro River valley near the modern town of Jauja in the Junín province of Peru (figure 2.1). The valley floor is

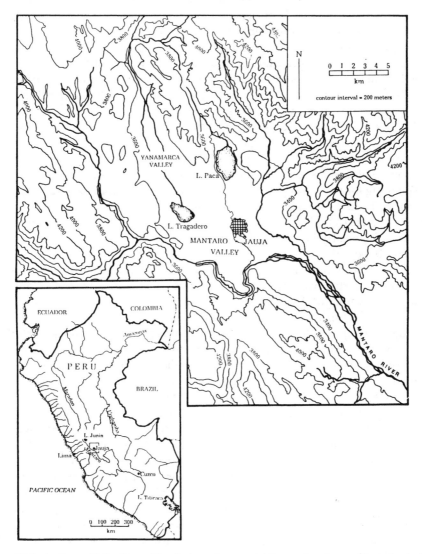

Figure 2.1 [orig. figure 12.1]   Map of the study region around the modern town of Jauja, Junín, Peru.

3200–3400 m above sea level and flanked by two high mountain ranges, the Cordillera Occidental on the west and the Cordillera Central on the east. The valley is about 60 km long, and the archaeological sites referred to in this chapter are in the upper (northwestern) end, including a series of small tributary valleys.

The sharp relief of the area creates a gradient of biological communities. The valley floors, with a mild, semiarid climate, are intensively settled and cultivated. They are surrounded by hillslopes with scattered rocky fields and grassy vegetation with a few shrubs and small trees. The high, cold puna plateau above 4000 m supports mostly grasses and grazing, rising beyond to the steep cordillera. Some 30–40 km away from Jauja on the eastern slopes of the Andes lies the *ceja de la montaña* where warm humid conditions allow the growth of dense forests (Pulgar Vidal 1972; Tosi 1960; Weberbauer 1945).

The landscape of the region has undoubtedly been greatly affected by thousands of years of occupation by herders and farmers. The extent of the effect has been debated. Some researchers argue that the Andes were originally forested and subsequently denuded by human activity (Budowski 1968; Cook 1916; Guillet 1985); others, that forests have been scarce since the retreat of the glaciers some 12,000 years ago. Pollen analysis completed in the central Andes suggests that the area has been relatively treeless since humans moved in, thus supporting the second hypothesis (Hansen et al. 1984; Wright 1983).

We have analyzed the remains of woody plant materials from six archaeological sites spanning four cultural phases in the Upper Mantaro region. The four phases are: Pancán 3 and 4 – the later part of the Early Intermediate period and the early Middle Horizon (A.D. 500–900); Pancán 1 and 2 – the later part of the Middle Horizon and the early Late Intermediate (A.D. 900–1300); Wanka II, the later Late Intermediate period (A.D. 1300–1460); and Wanka III, the Late Horizon or Inka period (A.D. 1460–1532). The first two phases are represented at the stratified site of Pancán, and the two later phases at five sites: Tunanmarca (Wanka II), Umpamalca (Wanka II), Hatunmarca (Wanka II and III), Marca (Wanka III), and Chucchus (Wanka III).

During excavation of house compounds at these sites, soil samples (6 liters) for flotation were collected and processed from every excavation unit. Proveniences for the study were systematically chosen to include a representative sample of all uncontaminated contexts in each of the four phases. At least one sample was then selected for analysis from each provenience. The contexts include floors, middens, pits, and hearths; most of the samples come from middens and floors. The charred woody material is similar in composition in all contexts, probably indicating that the material is the mixed refuse from fires accumulated over a number of months or years rather than from episodes of primary deposition. Charred woody plant remains can result from intentional, accidental, or catastrophic burning (Smart and Hoffman 1988). Samples from clear cases of catastrophic burning (e.g., a house that burned down, so that the woody material is thatch and roof beams rather than fuel) were not included in the analysis. We assume that the great majority of the charred woody remains from the floors, middens, and hearths sampled are the result of intentional burning (i.e., fuel use). Even if the primary use of the material was in manufacture, (e.g., discarded tool handles, posts, bedding, mats), their charred condition indicates a secondary use as fuel.

In all, we analyzed 47 samples from the earliest level, 89 samples from Pancán 1 and 2, 117 from Wanka II contexts, and 74 from Wanka III (Greenlee 1988; Johannessen and Hastorf 1990). The woody material from each sample was removed and weighed, and the fragments were counted. A total of 7,996 woody fragments were recovered from the 327 samples, and 3,670 of them were examined. The internal anatomy of the fragments was examined under 10X–70X magnification and was compared to specimens in a reference collection of woody parts of 60 Andean plant taxa. The material was first classified into three categories: the culm fragments of monocots such as grasses and rushes ("grass"), small diameter immature dicot stems or twigs ("stem"), and pieces of mature wood ("wood"). The first two categories could not be identified further, but the mature wood was classified by types, some of which have been identified to the genus level.

For the purposes of the present chapter, we look at the change in resource use over the 1,000-year period represented by this data set from two perspectives. First, we track the relative changes in the three fuel categories (wood, grass, and stems) by plotting their relative contribution to the assemblage of each phase. The rationale behind this analysis is that ethnohistoric and ethnographic studies indicate that the three types of material have long been perceived as separate fuel categories by the people of the area, with mature wood as the preferred fuel (Johannessen and Hastorf 1990); it is plausible that the ancestral people also categorized fuel in this way. The second perspective looks within the wood category itself and follows the frequencies of the most common wood taxa, allowing us to see the range of wood taxa used and how the range changed through time.

Fuel Composition Change

In the first analysis, we looked at the change in woody plant composition through time (figure 2.2). The bar charts in figure 2.2 compare the overall composition of the samples for each phase (each level of Pancán has been calculated separately) in terms of percentage of the total fragments recovered that are wood, stem, or grass. Plant remains are of course subject to differential preservation; therefore, the percentages are by no means assumed to reflect the actual proportions of aboriginal *use* of these categories. Since the form of the house compounds, the general subsistence remains, and the depositional contexts are similar throughout this 1,000-year record (Earle et al. 1987; Hastorf et al. 1989; Lennstrom 1988), there is no reason to suspect that the rates of preservation vary greatly from site to site. Therefore, major shifts in relative proportions of plant categories in a comparison *between or among* archaeobotanical assemblages are plausibly a result of differences in use rates (see discussion in Miller 1988).

Wood is always the dominant category throughout the sequence, making up from 60% to 90% of the total fragments at various times. However, wood drops in relative percentage throughout the four levels of Pancán so that in the later levels of that site close to 40% of the woody remains are stem, twig, and grass fragments.

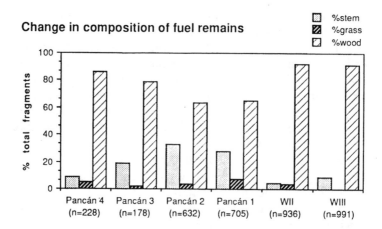

Figure 2.2 [orig. figure 12.2]   Barchart showing the change in the composition of fuel remains through time.

In the Wanka II and Wanka III phases the trend reverses, as wood increases in relative percentage, and stem and grass fragments drop to less than 10% of the fragments. The reversal of the trend in Wanka II times can be seen more clearly in figure 2.3, which plots the ratios of wood to stems and of wood to stem and grass fragments combined.

The trend seen throughout the Pancán sequence – an increasing proportion of twigs and grasses – is what we might expect if the landscape was being gradually filled in over time with an increasing population, denuding the land of its few trees and requiring the use of fuel sources less desirable and more costly to collect, such as small shrubby plants, twigs, and grasses. But the fuel composition changed in Wanka II and Wanka III times, with a marked proportional increase in wood

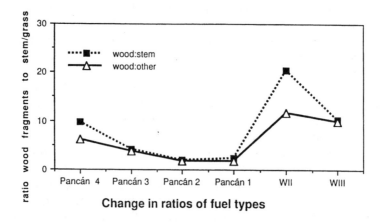

Figure 2.3 [orig. figure 12.3]   Graph of the changing ratios of wood to other fuel types through time.

remains. The change reversed earlier trends and challenged our initial expectation that increased population will increase pressure on the resources, resulting in the use of less desirable fuels. The change begins at a time (Wanka II) when people moved from dispersed clusters of small settlements into larger aggregations on high knolls. Political and social change is materially evident in many domains at this time, with differential production and access to an array of goods. Settlement pattern and artifactual analysis indicate a degree of political consolidation by an elite class in Wanka II times (Costin and Earle 1989; Earle et al. 1980; Hastorf 1990; LeBlanc 1981).

The reversal of the trend in fuel composition in Wanka II times may reflect some kind of fuel management, apparently occurring at a time of social and political consolidation by several groups in the valley. The new pattern is characterized by a higher proportion of mature wood, and we turn to the examination of this category for further information on the nature of the change in fuel use.

Change in Wood Taxa

Within the wood category, we see two patterns: overall high diversity and a change in the spectrum of wood types through time. The wood assemblages from the various time periods are all very diverse, containing as many as 40 different wood taxa; there is no marked change in diversity through time. No taxa are strikingly dominant; even the most commonly occurring taxa are present only in about 10–20% of the samples.

The wood taxa recovered most commonly do change through time. Figure 2.4 compares the ubiquities (percentage of the total samples from that phase in which the taxon was present) of the 13 overall most common wood taxa, that is, those present in the highest percentage of samples. The figure illustrates that rarely is a taxon present in more than 20% of the samples from any one phase. The top graph shows that five of the most common taxa in the earlier phases drop out completely by Wanka II times. We have as yet been unable to securely identify those early types. Other wood taxa are common throughout the sequence, as seen in the center graph. Two of them have been identified as *Polylepis* sp. (*quinhual*) and *Cassia* sp. (*mutuy*), both high-altitude shrubs or small trees that are favorite firewoods even today. The lowest graph of figure 2.4 demonstrates that some taxa appear for the first time in Wanka II contexts and then increase in ubiquity in Wanka III (Inka) times. Those taxa include *Buddleia* sp. (*quishuar*), a high-elevation tree, which in the Inka period becomes the most common taxon ever represented (present in 27% of the Inka period samples). Other common taxa identified only from the later time periods are *Colletia* sp. (*rokke*), a spiny bush nowadays favored as a fuel for bread ovens (Gade 1975), and *Cedrela* sp. (*cedro*), a tall tree. Interestingly, *Cedrela* is a tree of the *ceja de la montaña* forest to the east and was probably brought into the region from some 40 km away. Another taxon from the *ceja* region, *Chusquea* sp. (*carrizo*), a bamboo-like plant, is also present only in the Wanka II and Wanka III phases.

These particular late-occurring taxa are especially important because their

increase is part of the resurgence of wood to over 90% of the woody plant remains
in the Wanka II and Wanka III times. In the later periods, then, we have evidence
of local wood taxa (*Buddleia* and *Colletia*) being used in an increasingly intensive
way, as well as certain types (*Cedrela* and *Chusquea*) being brought into the region
from the outside.

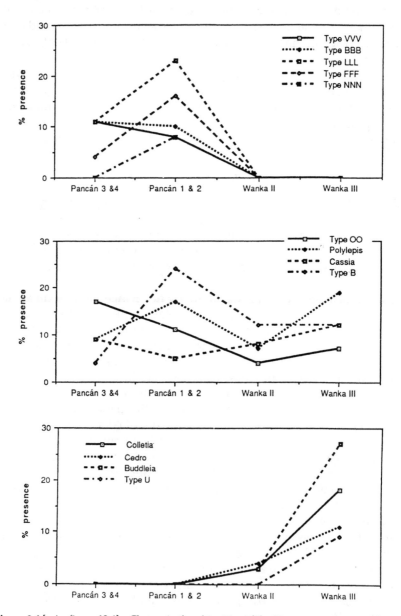

Figure 2.4 [orig. figure 12.4]   Change in the ubiquities of the 13 most common wood taxa
through time.

Discussion

Through the earlier phases, the woody remains were composed of increasing proportions of small stems, twigs, and grasses, as one might expect with a growing population in a fuel-scarce environment. That suggests a continuity of local fuel collection in the environmental zones surrounding the sites, which are mainly located in the valleys at this time. The later increase in the proportion of mature wood, together with the appearance and increase in certain wood taxa, suggests a fairly marked change in human interaction with the local resources beginning in Wanka II times.

We suggest that the botanical data may reflect some kind of fuel management, perhaps in the form of tree cultivation, beginning in Wanka II times. We know that tree cultivation is an ancient Andean custom and was practiced in Inka times (see below) and may well have been a pre-Inkaic practice. The new system of fuel management may have been a reaction to scarce resources and a growing population, but that does not seem to be a satisfactory explanation for several aspects of the phenomenon. For example, why do we see the change in Wanka II times and not, say, with the large settled farming population of Wanka I times, or later when the Inka entered and restructured the local production system? Why did the reaction to scarce fuel take this particular form (i.e., cultivation), instead, as has been shown in other cases, of going farther afield (e.g., Miller 1985; Minnis 1978), or moving to less favored fuel (e.g., Lopinot and Woods 1988; Pearsall 1983)? Why do particular taxa, such as *Buddleia*, dominate in the later time periods when they hadn't appeared before?

The Cultural Context

If the data presented above reflect increased fuel management and perhaps tree cultivation beginning in Wanka II times, how can the changes be interpreted? We could interpret these developments as an economic response to pressure on fuel resources, initiated by political leadership having the capacity to organize tree cultivation policy. But trees in the Andes are more than fuel. Perhaps some of the questions posed above about the specific time and form of the change can be addressed by looking at other dimensions of meaning that wood and trees have in Andean culture. Fuel and wood are linked to all aspect of Andean life. Change in fuel use has social and symbolic as well as economic implications. If we stopped our fuel use study with a strictly economic interpretation, we would not be able to address the aforementioned questions about why, when, and how fuel use changed.

Of course, fuel use has important economic aspects – fuel is a basic requirement in daily life. The gathering of fuel was a major life task, as it still is today, taking up to four hours a day to collect fuel to cook two meals (Skar 1982). Guaman Poma (1987 [1615]) illustrates major age class tasks from Inka times and lists collecting firewood as a major activity for several age classes. Figure 2.5 shows one example of an elderly man with a bundle of firewood (*leña*) on his back. We also know that,

SE GVNDA CALLE

PVRECMA HO

Figure 2.5 [orig. figure 12.5]   An old man collecting firewood
(Guaman Poma 1987 [1615]:191).

at least in Inka times, fuel was an important tribute item; huge quantities of fuel, including logs, kindling, and straw, were stored in the community and state store-houses in the Jauja area at the time of Spanish conquest (Espinoza Soriano 1971; Murra 1975).

Fuel has further dimensions of meaning. It was an important social resource, exchanged along with food to cement social relations. In figure 2.6, a drawing by Guaman Poma (1987 [1615]) shows the concrete symbols of reciprocity as a brother-in-law gives wood and straw fuel to relatives at a wake. In a recent study, Skar (1982) demonstrates by a series of household interviews how different social and political situations in the same region have created very different patterns of fuel access and use, thus illustrating the complex implications of these patterns.

Jeannette Sherbondy (1986) and Juan Ansión (1986) discuss the symbolic dimensions of Andean wood and trees, spanning cosmology, social relations, and access to land. In the Andes, certain trees have had symbolic connotations in the past. For example, Lumbreras (1974), González Carré and Rivera Pineda (1983), and Anders (1986) mention that the sacred *pati* tree was planted at Wari state sites. For the Inka,

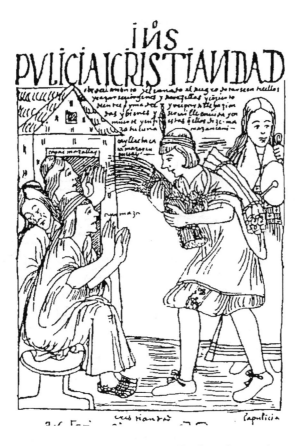

Figure 2.6 [orig. figure 12.6]   A man linking himself to his in-laws with a presentation of wood
and straw fuel at a wake
(Guaman Poma 1987 [1615]:919).

Buddleia (quishuar) appears to have been a tree with special symbolic value.
Quishuarkancha (quishuar enclosure) was the name of the sacred compound of the
creator deity Viracocha in the Inka capital of Cuzco. Wood in general, and especially *quishuar*, had an important role in ceremony as large quantities were used
in festival and sacrifice (Ansión 1986:39). Human figures carved from *quishuar*
wood were richly dressed and burned as sacrifice at Inti Raymi, festival of the Sun,
divine ancestor of the Inka dynasty (Cobo 1890–1895 [1653]). (Recall that it was
Buddleia that increased in ubiquity to dominate the Inka period wood remains).
These associations indicate that *quishuar* may have had a symbolic association with
the strength and legitimacy of the ancestral line; it is suggestive that the name
Collao, the area around Lake Titicaca that was the birthplace of the Sun, probably
refers to *Buddleia* (Soukup [1986:92–93] lists *colla* as another name for *Buddleia*).

Trees had an important place in Andean cosmology. Figure 2.7 is a picture of the
Inkaic cosmos drawn by Pachacuti Yamqui (1950 [1613]:226). On the right side is a

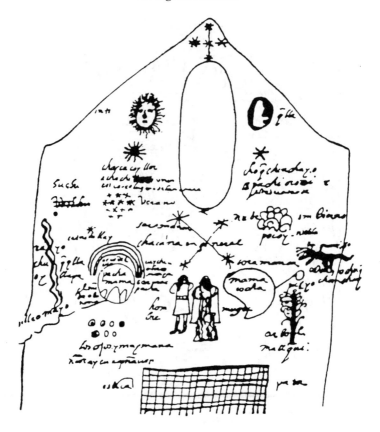

Figure 2.7 [orig. figure 12.7]   Pachacuti Yamqui's drawing of the Inkaic cosmos
(1950 [1613]:226).

tree labeled *árbol mallqui*, drawn beneath a spring (*pukyu*) flowing to the sea (*mama-cocha*). Trees are thus associated with water, the source of life, as well as with women, clouds, winter, and the moon, balanced against their complements on the left: men, summer, and the sun.

The Quechua word *mallqui*, used here with the Spanish *árbol* (tree), means the young tree ready for planting (Holguin 1952 [1608]:224–225). Sherbondy (1986) points out that the rich terminology in Quechua for various aspects of tree planting and tending indicates a considerable antiquity of the practice of tree cultivation in the Andes. Ethnohistoric sources indicate that the Inka controlled what forests there were (Polo de Ondegardo 1917 [1567]:80), appointed officials (*mallqui camayoc*) to direct the planting of trees (Murúa 1964 [ca. 1600]:87), and made ordinances concerning the cutting of planted trees (Murúa 1964 [ca. 1600]:89). Soldiers were forbidden to cut down the fruiting trees around an enemy's fortification because "if they had language they would complain of the offense done to them" (Murúa 1964 [ca. 1600]:90). One of the cultivated tree types often mentioned in ethnohistoric sources is *quishuar*, both in legend (Pachacuti Yamqui lists it as one of the tree types planted by the seventh Inka Viracocha [Pachacuti Yamqui 1950 [1613]:236) and in documents concerning the first years after the conquest (*Quishuar* was planted in the Jauja area in the 1580s [Henestrosa 1965 [1582]:171] and near Cuzco in 1590 [Sherbondy 1986:17]).

One of the central dynamics of Andean culture is interaction and reciprocity between land and people (Bastien 1978). The cultivation of plants and animals is thus essential to their notion of themselves. In Guaman Poma's story of the four ages of the world, the process of civilization in the Andean world is linked with the learning of agricultural skills (1987 [1516]:46–72). But even the first generation is portrayed as digging in the ground and contrasted with the savages, or *sacha runa* (people of the forest; Guaman Poma 1987 [1615]:47–48). Murúa (1964 [ca. 1600]:105) mentions that only domesticated animals (and cultivated plants?), as opposed to wild, were used in sacrifice, since the people offered nothing except that which had been raised (created? "*ubiesen criado*") and increased with their solicitude and care in order to show their esteem for the *huacas* (sacred person, place, or thing). It is logical that the process of cultivation, which was of central cultural importance, included trees as well as food plants.

The word *mallqui* means not only cultivated tree but also refers to the mummies of the ancestors (Sherbondy 1986). Even a century after the Spanish conquest, Joseph de Arriaga wrote that "after the sacred stones, their greatest veneration is for their *mallquis* . . . which are the bones or mummies of their pagan progenitors" (Arriaga 1968 [1621]:27). The ancestors and their mummified remains were important to the strength and prosperity of the *ayllu*, the Andean kin/political group, which were the principal landholders. The association between the ancestors and cultivated trees is clear in another drawing by Pachacuti Yamqui (1950 [1613]:217) that shows the three windows that are the place of origin of the Inkas, flanked by two trees with roots (figure 2.8). The two trees signify the mother and father from

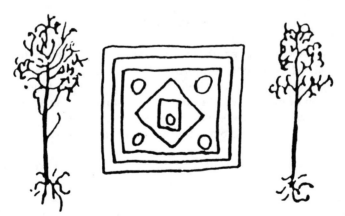

Figure 2.8 [orig. figure 12.8]   Pachacuti Yamqui's drawing of the place of origin of the Inka, with the mother and father on each side represented as trees
(1950 [1613]:217).

whom the Inka sprang "and that they were like fruits, and that the two trees were the trunk and the roots of the Inkas" (Pachacuti Yamqui 1950 [1613]:218). For Andean people in general, the ancestors legitimize the group's access to land and water. Ancestors dwell in the land in which the people of a community live. It is they who give the harvest, the water, and the life to the community (Bastien 1978). It was through tree roots, as well as caves and springs, that the lineage ancestors emerged into the lands assigned to them by the Creator, after an underground journey from their place of creation at Lake Titicaca (Molina 1947 [1572]:21). Trees grow in the ground with the ancestors, but also above it with the living, and thus are a link between the dead and the living, the past and the present. Trees seem to have been an important material link tying the people to their land and allowing them to remain on it.

The prosperity of the *ayllu* depends on its land and as Ansión (1986) and Sherbondy (1986) discuss, *mallqui* in its dual role as cultivated tree and ancestor legitimize an *ayllu*'s rights to use the land where the trees grow and are tended. Trees symbolize the ancestors of a group (certain trees are still addressed as "grandmother" and "grandfather" [Ansión 1986:78]), giving land-use rights to their living descendents. A *mallqui* is therefore the family continuing on that land: the roots are the ancestors; the fruits are the children. A ritual step in modern-day marriage ceremony called "to bring the branch," or *mallqui*, involves the bringing-forth of ritual offspring (Isbell 1978:124–125). In this way *mallqui* represents reproduction and the continuation of life through the generations.

From the ethnohistoric and ethnographic examples we can see several dimensions of meaning given to planted trees, linking the people to their land and to their ancestors, providing a reason to nurture and plant trees. This provides a fuller understanding of why an Andean people might plant trees, not just as a fuel source, but as a symbol of the linking reciprocal relationship of a kin group with their land.

Conclusions

With the understanding gained from the examples we can return to the questions posed earlier about the timing and form of the change in fuel use that we saw in the archaeological record. We have seen, beginning in Wanka II times, an upswing in the proportion of mature wood in the fuel remains and the appearance of new local and exotic wood taxa. We have suggested that it reflects a change in relationship to woody resources, plausibly including the cultivation of certain tree taxa.

In answer to our question about why the shift occurred in Wanka II times, the concept of *mallqui* reveals how planting trees could be part of the process of local political consolidation that took place at that time. That time saw the emergence of ridgetop fortified towns of up to 10,000 people, presumably as various kin groups formed closer alliances for the purposes of defense against other valley polities. Tree cropping may have been encouraged to fulfill increased fuel and building needs, but also for negotiating and legitimating access to land in the process of building a larger political group. Planting trees may have been a concrete expression with the purpose of strengthening ancestral rights to parcels of land. We know that the Inka ordered expanded agricultural activity as part of their civilizing and "beneficial" influence over conquered groups (Rowe 1946:265–267). The concept of increased cultivation could also have been used by earlier Andean leaders to promote their landholdings while linking the populace to a new social order.

The reason for the particular form of the change in people/plant interaction, that is, the cultivation of trees, becomes clearer with the understanding that reciprocity in human relationships to nature with emphasis on the nurture and care of land, animals, and plants is central to the Andean worldview. In other words, an action, which could be interpreted as a purely economic reaction to a fuel shortage, was chosen from a number of alternatives because of cultural values concerning the important roles of the process of cultivation and of trees as symbols of life and lineage.

The question of the significance of particular wood taxa that gained prominence in the archaeological record is clarified by a realization of their symbolic role in Andean thought. We noted that *Buddleia* first appeared in the Late Intermediate and became the most prominent wood in the remains from Inka times. It appears from the ethnohistoric sources that while *Buddleia* was not necessarily the best fuel, it was the best *mallqui*. It appears to have had an association with the principal deities of the Inka world, especially with the ancestral Sun. In the Jauja area, *Buddleia* had apparently already gained in importance some centuries before the Inka conquest, suggesting perhaps a similar pre-Inkaic role as *mallqui*.

We have proposed that the change in fuel use seen in the archaeological record is not purely an economic reaction to a fuel shortage but ties into the logic of the later prehispanic world view. We are not implying that economic factors are unimportant when trying to understand a cultural sequence but that a purely economic explanation is not sufficient. By examining the role of fuel and trees in Andean culture as a whole, we have been able to address aspects of the change in resource use not explainable in strictly economic terms. Are we able to enrich our interpretation of the archaeological sequence only because we have good ethnohistoric information and cultural continuity in the area? Perhaps in part that is true, yet even without any direct ethnographic analogy we should still be able to propose a set of hypotheses, not strictly economic, incorporating more complete dimensions of culture and leading to a fuller understanding of the past.

References

Anders, Martha Biggar,1986. *Dual Organization and Calendars Inferred from the Planned Site of Azangaro-Wari Administrative Strategies*. Ph.D. dissertation, Cornell University. University Microfilms, Ann Arbor.

Ansión, Juan, 1986. El arbol y el bosque en la sociedad Andina. Proyecto FAO-Holanda/ INFOR. Lima.

Arriaga, Pablo Joseph de,. 1968 [1621]. *The Extirpation of Idolatry in Perú*. Translated and edited by L. Clark Keating. University of Kentucky Press, Lexington.

Bastien, Joseph, 1978. *Mountain of the condor: Metaphor and Ritual in an Andean Ayullu*. Waveland Press, Prospect Heights, Ill.

Binford, Sally and Lewis R. Binford, 1968. *Postpleistocene Adaptations*. Aldine, Chicago.

Budowski, G., 1968. La influencia humana en la vegetación natural de montanas tropicales americanas. In *Geo-ecología de las regiones montanosas de las Américas tropicales*, edited by C. Troll, pp. 157–162. Ferd. Dummlers Verlag, Bonn.

Cobo, Bernabé de, 1890–95. [1653] *Historia del nuevo mundo*. Edited by Marcos Jiménez de la Espada. 4 vols. Sociedad de Bibiófilos Andaluces, Seville.

Cook, O. F., 1916 . Agriculture and Native Vegetation In Peru. *Journal of the Washington Academy of Sciences* 6: 284–93.

Costin, Cathy L. and Timothy K. Earle, 1989. Status Distinction and Legitimation of Power as Reflected in Changing Patterns of Consumption in Late Prehispanic Peru. *American Antiquity* 54(4): 691–714.

Earle, Timothy K., Terence D'Altroy, Cathy LeBlanc, Christine Hastorf, and Terry Levine 1980. Changing settlement patterns in the Yanamarca Valley, Peru. *Journal of New World Archaeology* 4(1). Institute of Archaeology, University of California, Los Angeles.

Earle, T. K., Terence D'Altroy, Christine Hastorf, Catherine Scott, Cathy Costin, Glenn Russell, and Elsie Sandefur, 1987. *Archaeological Field Research in the Upper Mantaro, Peru, 1982-83: Investigations of Inka Expansion and Exchange*. Monograph XXVII, Institute of Archaeology, University of California, Los Angeles.

Espinoza Soriano, W., 1971. *Los Huancas, aliados de la conquista. Tres informaciones inéditas sobre la participación indigena en la conquista del Peru, 1558, 1560 y 1561*. Anales Científicos de la Universidad de Centro del Perú 1:9–407. Huancayo, Perú.

Gade, Daniel W., 1975. *Plants, Man and the Land in the Vilcanota Valley*. Dr. W. Junk, The Hague.

Garcilaso de la Vega, 'El Inca', 1985 [1609–17]. *Comentarios reales de los Incas*. Biblioteca clasicos del Perú, No. 1. Editorial Andina.

Giddens, Anthony, 1979. *Central Problems in Social Theory. Action, Structure and Contradiction in Social Analysis*. London and Basingstoke: Macmillan Press.

González Carré, Enrique and Fermín Rivera Pineda, 1983. Pati, el árbol sagrado de los Waris. *Boletín de Lima* 27: 43–49.

Greenlee, Diana, 1988. The Woody Plant Remains from Pancán, Junín, Perú. University of Minnesota, Department of Anthropology, Archaeobotanical Report No. 16.

Guaman Poma de Ayala, F., 1987 [1615]. Nueva cronica y buen gobierno. Edited by J. V. Murra, R. Adorna, and J. L. Urioste. Cronicas de America, *Historia* 16, Madrid.

Guillet, D., 1985. Hacia una historia socio-económica de los bosques en los Andes Centrales del Perú. *Boletín de Lima*, Ano 7, No. 38.

Hansen, B., H.E. Wright, Jr., and J. P. Bradbury, 1984. Pollen studies in the Junín area, Central Peruvian Andes. *Geographical Society of America Bulletin* 95: 1454–65.

Hastorf, Christine A., 1990. One Path to the Heights: Negotiating Political Inequality in the Sausa of Peru. In *The Evolution of Political Systems*, edited by Stedman Upham, pp. 146–176. Cambridge University Press, Cambridge.

Hastorf, Christine A., Timothy Earle, Henry E. Wright, Jr., Lisa LeCount, Glenn Russell, and Elsie Sandefur, 1989. Settlement Archaeology in the Jauja Region of Peru: Evidence from the Early Intermediate Period through the Late Intermediate Period: A Report on the 1986 Field Season. *Andean Past* 2: 81–129.

Henestrosa, Juan de., 1965 [1582]. La descripcion que se hizo en la provincia de Xauxa por la instrucion de S. M. que a la dicha provincia se invio de molde. In *Relaciones geograficas de Indias – Peru* vol. 1, edited by m. Jiménez de la Espada, pp. 166–175. Biblioteca de Autores Españoles, Ediciones Atlas , Madrid.

Holguin, D. G., 1952 [1608]. *Vocabulario de la lengua general de todo el Peru llamada Quichua o del Inca.* Imprenta Santa Maria, Lima.

Isbell, Billie Jean, 1978. To Defend Ourselves: Ecology and Ritual in an Andean Village. Institute of Latin American Studies, University of Texas, Austin. *Latin American Monographs* 47.

Johannessen, Sissel, and Christine A. Hastorf, 1990. A History of Fuel Management (A.D. 500 to the Present) in the Mantaro Valley, Peru. *Journal of Ethnobiology* 10(1): 61–90.

LeBlanc, Catherine, 1981. *Late Prehispanic Huanca Settlement Patterns in the Yanamarca Valley, Peru.* Ph.D. dissertation, Department of Anthropology, University of California, Los Angeles. Ann Arbor: University Microfilms.

Lennstrom, H., 1988. Botanical Remains from Pancán. Paper presented at the 54th Annual Meeting of the Society for American Archaeology, Phoenix, Arizona.

Lopinot, Neal and William I. Woods, 1988. Archaeobotany, Environmental Degradation, and Collapse of Cahokia. Paper presented at the 54th Annual Meeting of the Society for American Archaeology, Phoenix, Arizona.

Lumbreras, L. G., 1974. *Las Fundaciones de Huamanga.* Editorial Nueva Edición, Lima.

Miller, Naomi F., 1985. Paleoethnobotanical Evidence for Deforestation in Ancient Iran: A Case Study of Urban Malyan. *Journal of Ethnobiology* 5(1): 1–19.

1988. Ratios in Paleoethnobotanical Analysis. In *Current Paleoethnobotany: Analytical Methods and Cultural Interpretations of Archaeological Plant Remains*, edited by Christine A. Hastorf and Virginia S. Popper, pp. 72–85. University of Chicago Press, Chicago and London.

Minnis, Paul E., 1978. Paleoethnobotanical Indicators of Prehistoric Environmental Disturbance: A Case Study. In *The Nature and Status of Ethnobotany*, edited by Richard I. Ford, M. F. Brown, M. Hodge, and Willian Merrill, pp. 347–366. Museum of Anthropology, University of Michigan, Anthropological Papers No. 67.

Molina, Cristóbal de., 1947 [1572]. *Ritos y Fábulas de los Incas.* Editorial Futuro, Buenos Aires.

Murra, John V., 1975. Formaciones económicas y políticas del mundo andino. Instituto de Estudios Peruanos, Lima.

Murúa, Fray Martín de., 1964 [ca. 1600]. *Historia general del Peru, II.* Coleccion Joyes Bibliograficas, Biblioteca American Vetus, Madrid.

Pachacuti Yamqui, J. de S., 1950 [1613]. *Relacion de antiguedades deste reyno del Perú.* In *Tres relaciones de antiguedades Peruanos.* Reproduction of 1897 edition, Ministerio Fomento de España: Editorial Garania.

Pearsall, Deborah M., 1983. Evaluation of the Stability of Subsistence Strategies by Use of Paleoethnobotanical Data. *Journal of Ethnobiology* 3(2): 121–37.

Polo de Ondegardo, Juan, 1917 [1567]. Del Linaje de los Incas y como Conquistaron. In *Colección de Libros y Documentos Referentes al la Historia del Perú*, edited by Horacio H. Urteaga and Carlos A. romero, vol. 4, pp. 45–95. Sanmartí, Lima.

Pulgar Vidal, Javier, 1972. *Geografía del Perú: Las ocho regiones naturales del Perú.* 7th edition. Editorial Universo, Lima.

Rowe, John H., 1946. Inca Culture at the Time of the Spanish Conquest. In *Handbook of South American Indians* vol. 2, edited by Julian H. Steward, pp. 183–330. Smithsonian Institution Press, Washington, D.C.

Shanks, Michael and Christopher Tilley, 1988. *Social Theory and Archaeology.* New Mexico University Press, Albuquerque.

Sherbondy, Jeanette E., 1986. Mallki: ancestros y cultivo de árboles en los Andes. Documento de Trabajo No. 5, Proyecto FAO-Holanda/INFOR GCP/PER/027/NET. Lima.

Skar, Sarah Lund, 1982. Fuel Availability, Nutrition, and Women's Work in Highland Peru. World Employment Programme Research Paper No. WEP 10/WP23, International Labour Office, Geneva.

Smart, Tristine L. and Ellen S. Hoffman, 1988. Enivronmental Interpretation of Archaeological Charcoal. In *Current Paleoethnobotany: Analytical Methods and Cultural Interpretations of Archaeological Plant Remains*, edited by Christine A. Hastorf and Virgina S. Popper, pp. 167–205. University of Chicago Press, Chicago and London.

Soukup Sdb., Jaroslav, 1986. *Vocabulario de los nombres vulgares de la flora Peruana y catalogo de los generos*. Editorial Salesiana, Lima.

Tosi, Joseph A., Jr., 1960. *Zonas de vida natural en el Perú*. Boletín Técnico, No. 5. Instituto Interamericano de Ciencias Agrícolas de la Organización de Estados Americanos, Zonal Andina, Lima.

Weberbauer, A., 1945. *El mundo vegetal de los Andes Peruanos*. Estacion Experimental Agrícola de la Molina, Ministerio de Agricultura, Lima.

Wright, H. E., Jr., 1983. Late Pleistocene Glaciation and Climate Around the Junín Plain, Central Peruvian Highlands. *Geofrafiska Annaler* 65(1–2): 35–43.

3

Ecological Interpretations of Palaeolithic Art

Steven J. Mithen

To describe, let alone explain, the paintings, engravings and sculpture of the Upper Palaeolithic as 'adaptations' may sound absurd. These are products of the human mind – a world of symbols and dreams, myths and fantasies. So to suggest that this art can be understood in an ecological framework may strike one as facile. Upper Palaeolithic art is one of the great cultural achievements of human kind. It testifies not only to an immense technical skill but to the human capacity for expressing emotion through the use of line, form and colour. Although we cannot know the meaning of the art, through it we can begin to share the sensitivies of the Palaeolithic hunters to their natural world and the animals of the chase. Like all great art, it transcends the boundaries of time and space to say something fundamental about the human condition – though that 'something' is forever elusive. The paintings, engravings and sculpture of the Upper Palaeolithic are indeed the epitome of human creativity. So when faced with either the great bulls of Lascaux or just a scratch upon a broken pebble, surely it must be trivial to invoke notions of adaptation and ecology. After all, is not adaptation solely about the more basic features of human life – the selfish struggle to survive and reproduce – hardly the basis for the fine arts.

But it is not trivial. It is the supposed contradiction between human creativity and human adaptation that is in error, not the idea that Palaeolithic art and ecology are fundamentally related. This error arises from a mistaken notion of what human adaptation entails. My argument will be that by invoking the term adaptation and operating within an ecological framework we can indeed move towards an understanding of the art without denying the human emotion and creativity by which it was produced. Indeed, that creativity will be seen as the core of an ecological interpretation of Upper Palaeolithic art. I must start with some definitions.

What is an 'Ecological Interpretation'?

The term ecology refers to the notions of wholeness and environment. Consequently an ecological approach is one that believes the art must be viewed as part of the whole set of thoughts and actions undertaken by the Palaeolithic hunters. It is simply one that seeks to place the art and its production into context. It is a misconception that this context is only the physical environment. An ecological approach can be concerned with making connections between the social life of the Palaeolithic hunters and patterning within their art. Indeed, human adaptation is quintessentially about social interaction. An ideal and complete ecological interpretation would show how all the many facets of the life of a Palaeolithic hunter were interwoven into a complex web and our divisions into 'art', 'society' and 'economy' are artificial – though of course necessary to provide routes into unravelling this complexity. Actual ecological interpretations quest towards this goal by making as many connections between patterning in art and that in other areas of existence as possible. As the number and diversity of connections increase so accordingly does the strength of the interpretation. Similarly, as they decrease the interpretation is weaker until it can no longer be properly called ecological. These connections between otherwise disparate elements of the archaeological record are made by invoking some unifying theme or concept. In an ecological interpretation this theme is adaptation.

What can it mean however to make an interpretation of *Palaeolithic art*? Does this mean that the interpretation must encompass and explain every single image in the art ranging from meagre scratches on broken pebbles to the Altamira ceiling? Clearly this is absurd. We recognize that no single interpretation can be so encompassing. But if this is not the case how can we evaluate the significance of the interpretation that has been made? We may be able to link one specific image to inferred economic or social activity but clearly this cannot be accepted as a significant interpretation for the entity we refer to as *Palaeolithic art*.

To solve this dilemma we need to view the art as we do the whole archaeological record. For pragmatic purposes, it is useful to divide Palaeolithic art into a series of overlapping problems that require explanation and that initially have no apparent relationship to each other. A proposed interpretation can then be judged by its effectiveness at drawing connections between patterns in these separate problem areas as well with the other elements of the archaeological record. The greater the number and the diversity of links that are made, the more significant the interpretation.

What sort of problem areas do I mean? The questions posed by Palaeolithic art can be divided into two domains, imagery and distribution. A significant ecological interpretation must be able to make connections between these two domains, i.e. to show how the imagery and the distribution of the art are dependent upon each other. The questions which concern the specific imagery in the art have of course been asked for many years. For instance why is the art dominated by adult, large mammals drawn in profile? Why are the majority of these bison and horse? Why are many animals only partly complete or deformed in shape? Why do different media contain different frequencies of animal species? Why are particular stylistic traits such as black outline method and twisted perspective used? Of course these questions are infinite in number. Some are controversial in themselves since they rest upon an interpretation of what has been represented prior to the asking of why it was engraved or painted. Indeed we have a hierarchy of ecological interpretations to make.

The second domain of problems does not make reference to specific imagery but to the spatial and temporal distribution of the art. For instance – why is it concentrated in south-west Europe during the later Upper Palaeolithic? Why do we find certain motifs (whatever their specific form) restricted to particular regions and localized areas? Why does the art first appear with the start of the Upper Palaeolithic and end with the end of the last glacial? As with the questions concerning imagery, we find here issues concerning both general features of the art as well as those concerning the details. A good interpretation will be one that can address issues at both of these large and small scales.

A question that cannot be easily fitted into either of the image and distributional domains is that concerning the origin of the art. This overlaps with the origin of symbolic behaviour in general at the start of the Upper Palaeolithic while also referring to the particular tradition established in late Pleistocene Europe. It is a question, however, that I am not addressing in this paper. The ecological interpretations I deal with below are principally concerned with the proliferation and florescence of Palaeolithic art in south-west Europe during the later Upper Palaeolithic. The scenarios they present for such developments have the existence of a Palaeolithic art tradition as a starting condition.

To summarize, we can characterize an 'ecological interpretation of Palaeolithic art' as one that seeks to take a holistic view of Palaeolithic society. It seeks to place the art into context by drawing links between as many patterns in the archaeological record as possible. These links are drawn within certain gross areas, such as art or economy, and between these areas so that art, economy, technology and society are shown to be interrelated. The strength of the interpretation can be measured by the number and diversity of links that are drawn. In addition, however, attention must be paid to the unifying principle or theme that allows such connections to be made. This is an issue that has not yet been addressed. I now want to look at one particular manner by which this can be done – that by invoking the concept of adaptation.

Adaptation and Palaeolithic Art

Adaptation is a very powerful concept. Archaeologists have used it in a variety of ways. Approaches ranging from palaeoeconomy to optimal foraging theory are all encompassed under the broad ecological umbrella. Frequently adaptation is used as a loose descriptive term. For instance Clark and Straus define adaptation, 'as the repertoire of collective social responses related to the procurement and processing of the plant and animal resources necessary for group maintenance and survival' (1983, 136). This ecological approach is focused on the group and appears to view the group as an independent organism with a life of its own. Clive Gamble is concerned with 'the problems which adaptive systems have to solve' and 'the adaptive repertoire of palaeolithic groups' (1986, 342). It is this use of the term

'adaptation' which is usually referred to when ecological interpretations of Palaeolithic art are invoked.

I prefer an alternative use of the term adaptation. I find this loose, all encompassing, descriptive usage inappropriate for archaeology and lacking adherence
to the biological meaning of the term. A more appropriate use makes reference to
individuals taking decisions about how to increase their chances of survival and
reproduction and the attainment of intermediate goals towards that end (Mithen
1989b). Such individuals must be characterized as having imperfect information.
They engage in both competition and co-operation with other individuals and
actively make behavioural choices on the basis of accumulated knowledge. Their
decision-making processes are seen to derive from an interaction between the
common biological endowment of the human species, providing them with
propensities to think and act in one way rather than another, and their environment, defined as their own unique historical, social and physical context. This
environment is viewed as constantly changing. Adaptation is recognized here as a
process of becoming, rather than a static state of being. Elsewhere I have used the
term 'thoughtful foragers' to capture the essence of this evolutionary ecological
approach to hunter-gatherer behaviour – individuals actively making decisions as
to how to act as they engage in the process of adaptation to a constantly changing
world (Mithen 1990).

This view of adaptation is related to the development of ecological interpretations by specifying that it is by reference to individuals making decisions by which
connections between the otherwise disparate elements of the archaeological record
are made. This recognizes that it is the short-term behaviour of individuals that
underlies all culture change, whether during the Pleistocene or in post-industrial
society. Individual decision-making is at the centre of the complex web of Palaeolithic culture to which I referred above. From this evolutionary ecological
perspective the appearance, nature and development of Palaeolithic art is under-
written by the activities of individuals while they go about their daily business.
That is, Palaeolithic art is an emergent property of the interactions between individuals as they pursue their own social and economic strategies.

Other concepts might be able to fulfil this connecting role but there are powerful
philosophical reasons to choose adaptation and hence an evolutionary ecological
perspective. By adopting this stance we are simply recognizing that the human
species, like all animals, is a product of biological evolution in which we assume
that natural selection has played a predominant role. We are explicitly recognizing
a continuum between human species and other animals. So by addressing human
behaviour and Palaeolithic art in an evolutionary ecological framework we are
addressing a fundamental question – how is it that the human species is so similar
and on a continuum with other species and yet at the same time so different? How
can there be such a tiny genetic difference between modern man and the chim-
panzee but such a gulf between their cultural capacities – illustrated so perfectly
in their artistic talents (Morris 1962)? This is, of course, one of the great questions
of philosophy. But it also has a pertinent political significance today as 'green'
politics begins to dominate our thoughts and we find ourselves needing to reassess

our relationship with the natural world. Palaeolithic art confronts us most forcefully with the paradox of similarity yet difference between humankind and other animals. For as I described in my introduction we might refer to that art when trying to define what is quintessentially human. Yet it was produced while humans were living in a manner so similar to other animals and which reminds us of our continuity with them, i.e. by hunting and gathering for their food.

Hunting Magic as an Ecological Interpretation

It is important to recognize that attempts to make an ecological interpretation of Palaeolithic art are not a recent trend. One of the earliest interpretations, hunting magic, meets certain of the 'ecological criteria'. At the centre of a hunting magic scenario is the drawing of a connection between the artistic/ritual life of the Palaeolithic hunters and their subsistence activities. Hunters were anxious about the availability of game, their chances of successfully killing animals, the danger from competing carnivores and from wounded prey. They turned to magic, involving the production and use of art, to alleviate this anxiety and to ensure hunting success.

I do not want to repeat all the criticisms against this interpretation that have been made elsewhere (e.g. Bahn and Vertut 1988, 150–58). Suffice to say that although this is an ecological interpretation we can recognize that it is not a very strong one by using the evaluation criteria I have described above.

The connections between the art and subsistence are few and fragile. Certainly the subject of both was large game but in general it differed markedly in the frequencies with which different species were represented and hunted. This is not in itself fatal however since there may be a correlation between the meat weights of species (and hence their attractiveness to hunters) and the frequency with which they were depicted (Rice and Patterson 1986). The connections between certain abstract images and hunting weapons/methods (e.g. that penniforms are arrows) are also weak (Bahn and Vertut 1988, 152) although certain cases may be convincing. While such criticisms can be easily made, I find the most significant weakness in being that no connections are made across the two domains of imagery and distribution. If hunting magic is a viable interpretation then an argument is required either for why it is only in the south-west region of Palaeolithic Europe that hunting magic was used or why it was only in this area that it became manifest in the production of art.

Jochim's Ecological Interpretation

The most notable ecological interpretation of Palaeolithic art in recent years is that by Michael Jochim (1983; 1987). Let me summarize his arguments and then discuss them critically in light of the evaluation criteria I have proposed above.

The crux of Jochim's (1983) interpretation is the regional perspective that he adopts to discuss Palaeolithic art. As he argues, by 25,000 bp climatic deterioration had begun as the last glacial approached its climax. Northern areas of Europe became progressively harsh as they turned into arctic desert. Jochim proposes that there were substantial population movements into the south-west region. This area acted as a refugium for plant, animal and human populations unable to survive in the northern regions. The south-west maintained a diverse and abundant set of resources, most notably large herbivores and, according to Jochim, rich salmon breeding grounds off the Atlantic coast.

Consequently, as from *c.* 25,000 bp population densities in the south-west region began to increase, causing an imbalance in population/resource levels. Jochim proposed that three types of response to the resulting economic stress were made. There was an intensification of the hunting of large game, particularly reindeer. Such intensification would put a premium on information sharing across regions and the maintenance of mobility and flexibility in settlement behaviour. Jochim links the proliferation of portable art to such developments seeing this as playing an essential role in maintaining communication and affiliation between groups. A second response was the diversification of the economic base. Greater numbers and varieties of small game, birds and fish were exploited.

The third response is of most significance for Jochim's arguments. He suggests that there was a substantial increase in the exploitation of salmon in the rivers running to the Atlantic coast. According to Jochim, intensifying on salmon would have very different implications for settlement than the intensification on reindeer. The supposed reliability and predictability of salmon would encourage sedentism and territorial claims to fishing grounds. As a consequence closed mating networks developed. Although it is not made explicit, the assumption appears to be that salmon were exploited in a similar manner as in historic times on the north-west coast of America.

Jochim suggests that to facilitate social interaction and co-operation within the resulting dense population an increase in the use of ritual would have been required. Such ritual would function to reinforce group solidarity and act to resolve conflict – traditional means of conflict resolution (e.g. mobility) would have been under severe stress due to the increase in sedentism. One should also expect to see territorial based ritual sites acting as land claims. It is precisely this role as territorial markers and locations for ritual that Jochim attributes to the decorated caves. Jochim makes an elaborate interpretation for the development of cave art styles (using Leroi-Gourhan's style phases) around this scenario of economic stress, salmon exploitation, increased sedentism and territoriality and the need for ritual to facilitate social integration.

If we examine Jochim's ecological interpretation for Palaeolithic art with the evaluation criteria I suggested above then we can recognize that it has some very powerful arguments. Of most significance is that Jochim does indeed draw a considerable number of links between otherwise disparate elements of the archaeological record. Settlement data from across Europe is linked to environmental change and the concentration of Palaeolithic art in the later Upper Palaeolithic of the south-west region. Evidence for exchange in the form of exotic items such as shells in assemblages from the south-west is linked to the distribution of portable art as complementary manifestations of information flow across regions. The appearance of localized styles in stone tools is linked to that of localized distributions of particular motifs, both suggesting increased territoriality. The faunal data, suggesting intensification on large game and a diversification of the resource base, are linked to all of these as evidence for the economic responses to cope with population pressure. Certainly, therefore, Jochim's ecological interpretation makes numerous and diverse links between otherwise disparate elements of the archaeological record.

There are however two major deficiencies with Jochim's ecological interpretation. The first is that, as with hunting magic, no contact is made between the domains of imagery and distribution. While hunting magic addressed imagery but not distribution, Jochim's interpretation addressed distribution but not imagery. According to the role that Jochim attributes to the art, it may have 'worked' with any type of images. Indeed, if it was principally produced to solve social problems we should perhaps expect a greater amount of human imagery in the art rather than the overwhelming dominance of animals. Similarly, if the decorated caves function as territorial markers for fishing grounds we should perhaps expect a higher frequency of fish imagery than the rather sparse representations we have in Palaeolithic art. In essence Jochim's arguments offer no interpretations for the imagery of the art. This is a fundamental weakness in his work if it is to be seen as an ecological interpretation for Palaeolithic art, rather than simply for the distribution of Palaeolithic ritual activity.

The second weakness in Jochim's ecological interpretation concerns the means by which he draws the connections between the patterns in the archaeological record. His unifying theme is not the concept of adaptation but the exploitation of salmon. It is this resource that enabled the south-west to act as a refugium. Salmon fishing encouraged sedentism, territoriality and, via the path of high population densities and the potential for social conflict, the ritual activity manifested in the cave art. But as Mellars (1985) argued, to claim that there was intensive salmon exploitation simply contradicts the archaeological evidence. In a second paper Jochim (1987) acknowledged this by agreeing that there is no predominance of fish remains, no evidence for intensive fishing technology and no evidence for bulk storage in the archaeological record. Carbon isotope techniques have demonstrated a low proportion of fish in the Palaeolithic diet prior to the later Magdalenion (Hayden *et al.* 1987). Nevertheless, Jochim continued to attribute an important economic role to salmon, now in the form of a back-up resource to exploit when the hunting of large game failed. As such, salmon may still be a critical resource but this risk-buffering role appears to undermine Jochim's original arguments. The role of decorated caves as ritual centres for conflict resolution, territorial claims and the enforcement of group solidarity depends upon the notion of sedentism and the need for territoriality to protect fishing grounds. This in turn rested on the idea that there was intensive salmon exploitation. If salmon in fact acted as a back up resource and the economy remained centred on reindeer exploitation then according to his own views concerning big game hunting (1983,

216), there would be a premium on maintaining mobility and flexibility in settlement behaviour.

Without the notion of intensive salmon exploitation Jochim's arguments are essentially the same as Mellars' (1985) who emphasized the economic security of the south-west region due to the abundance and diversity of large game. This must be criticized for being a 'Garden of Eden' scenario for the development of cultural complexity (Gamble 1986, 340: Binford 1983, 200). That is, the resources were so rich and abundant that populations simply settled down, became complex hunters and in the course of that produced their art.

Thoughtful Foragers and Palaeolithic Art

I now want to describe a third ecological interpretation for Palaeolithic art, although it is one that has significant links to both of those discussed above. This is an interpretation that has been developed from the 'thoughtful forager' perspective on hunter-gatherer behaviour (Mithen 1990), i.e. one that seeks to make explicit reference to individual decision making. It is an ecological interpretation that has a specific goal of drawing connections between patterns within the art and those within faunal assemblages.

As I discussed above, this interpretation attempts to use the concept of adaptation in a biologically sound manner but also one that is appropriate for archaeology. Consequently it focuses on individuals engaging in the process of adaptation to their environments. It recognizes that the art may play different functional roles for different types of individuals in Palaeolithic society, and may well change its role through time. Elsewhere (Mithen 1988) I have related certain aspects of the following ideas to the possible role of the art in education as discussed by Pfeiffer (1982), considering it to be concerned with the development of selective attention in young children. Here my concern is with the mature hunters within Palaeolithic society.

Let me begin by simply stating the 'thoughtful forager' model for the relationship between these hunters and Palaeolithic art. At times of hunting failure during the later Upper Palaeolithic hunters turned from participating in group co-operative killing of large game, particularly red deer and reindeer, to the stalking of individual animals either by themselves or in small groups. At this juncture between two different types of hunting methods the art facilitated the retrieval of information stored in the mind relating to the tracking of large mammals. It also facilitated the manipulation of that information so that multiple mental scenarios for the forthcoming hunting activity could be made. The art played this role by presenting visual images to the hunters that cued the recall of relevant information stored within encyclopaedic memory.

Note that this contrasts with other discussions concerning the relationship between Palaeolithic art and human memory. In the work of Pfeiffer (1982) the art has been associated with the imprinting of information on the human mind by drawing some rather dubious analogies with the art of Australian Aborigines. In

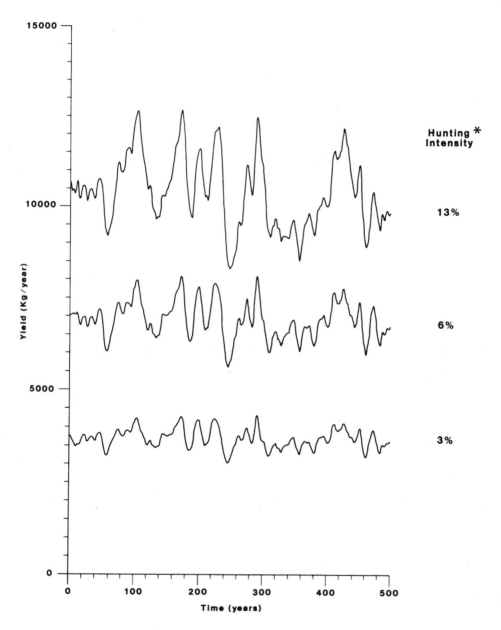

Figure 3.1 [orig. figure 1]   Fluctuations in red deer population/yields with time under increasing hunting intensity; * = percentage of population killed annually.

Table 3.1 [orig. table 1] Information gathering imagery in Upper Palaeolithic art.

Observation	Information	Manner in which referred to in Palaeolithic art	Examples
Hoof-prints	Presence, age/sex, activity patterns	Depiction of hoofs in ventral view ('twisted perspective')	Bovids and horses in Lascaux and Altamira
		Depiction of hoof-prints ('abstract signs') juxtaposed with same species	Bison in Font de Gaume; Horse in La Pieta; Reindeer in Les Trois Frères (Mithen 1990, fig. 8.1)
		Depiction of hoof-prints not juxtaposed with any animal	Indented circles from Pech Merle and Castillo; signs from Comarque (Mithen 1990, fig. 8.2)
Faeces	Presence, age/sex, feeding locations, state of health	Depiction of defecating animals with faeces	Ibex from Arudy, Bédeilhac and Mas D'Azil
		Depiction of defecating animals without faeces ('raised tail posture')	Reindeer from Les Combarelles; bison from Lascaux, Le Portel (Mithen 1990, fig. 8.3)
Marks on the ground (other than hoof-prints)	Locations where animals have been lying, rolling and sleeping	Depiction of animals lying, rolling and wallowing	Bison from Altamira; cow from lascaux; red deer from Gourdan (Mithen 1990, fig. 8.4)
Marks on vegetation	Locations where animals have been feeding, current feeding habits and movement of animals	Depiction of animals feeding	Reindeer from Limeuil; bovid from La Vache (Mithen 1990, fig. 8.5)

		Depiction of animals moving through vegetation	Horse and bovid from Laxcaux (Mithen 1990, fig. 8.5)
Sound	Location and activity of an animal	Depiction of animals calling and bellowing	Red deer from el Buxú Horteaux; bison from Altamira (Mithen 1990, fig. 8.6)
Antlers and horns	Age/sex and state of health of an animal	Frontal view ('twisted perspective')	Red deer and ibex from Lascaux
		Exaggerated size and omission of the rest of the body	Red deer from Lascaux and Le Portel; Reindeer from Teyjat (Mithen 1990, fig. 8.8)
Body size	Quantity of meat and fat on an animal	Exaggeration/distortion and omission of particular body parts	Bison from Font de Gaume; horse from Bédeilhac (Mithen 1990, fig. 8.9)
Animal species	The sight of an animal can provide information about species with which it is associated, either directly (e.g. predator-prey relationship) or indirectly due to shared behavioural characteristics	Juxtaposition of predators and prey	Wolf and deer from Lourdes; reindeer and fox from Altxerri
		Juxtaposition of birds and large animals	Bird and bison from Puy de Lacan; bird and horse from Lourdes
		Seasonal imagery	Batons from Lortet and Montgaudier
		Migratory waterfowl	Ducks and Geese from Escabasses, Lourdes, Gourdan (Mithen 1990, figs 8.10–13)

(See Mithen 1988; 1990, chap. 7)

the thoughtful forager model the emphasis is placed on the art as a means by which information is recalled. It is indeed the retrieval of information rather than its initial storage that is the principal problem facing human memory (Tulving 1983).

Now let me expand on the central features of this interpretation. First it recognizes that there was significant intensification on the exploitation of large game at the start of the later Upper Palaeolithic (Mellars 1985; Straus and Clark 1986). In particular, mass killing of reindeer in France and red deer in northern Spain, resulting in catastrophic mortality profiles, formed the central facet of the Palaeolithic economy. Following Jochim (1983), this intensification may indeed be due to the immigration of population from northern regions. One consequence of it is that the fluctuations in the size of the red deer and reindeer herds and the hunters' yields significantly increased (Mithen 1989a). This can be recognized by using simulation models for population dynamics of reindeer and red deer herds and exposing them to a range of predation intensities (figure 3.1). As a result the hunters experienced occasional, but severe, shortfalls in their yields as the reindeer/red deer populations entered a trough. It is probable that the Palaeolithic hunters recognized that this was going to occur but were unable to specify precisely when.

At the times when yields were particularly low hunters turned from mass co-operative hunting to working by themselves or in small groups to stalk and try to kill individual animals. This is a response to low yields/sparse populations that we find in the ethnographic record (e.g. Meldgaard 1983) and which accords with our understanding of cost-benefit-risk models of hunting strategies. The information requirements for hunting and stalking individual animals are very different from those necessary to participate in co-operative mass killing and it is to the satisfaction of these that the art played a functional role. The hunters will have had vast quantities of stored information within their minds about the tracks and trails of animals that they had observed in the course of their activities, i.e. by indirect information gathering (see Mithen 1990, chap. 3). At this switch to stalking strategies this stored information required rapid accessing and the art facilitated this process. In proposing this, a direct analogy is being made with scapulimancy among the Cree for whom ritual activity is believed to occur principally at the juncture between different economic activities and to facilitate thought about the future (Tanner 1979).

It would be unlikely that the stalking of individual animals by a lone hunter or a small group of hunters only occurred when an attempted mass kill failed. Modern hunter-gatherers are infinitely flexible in their hunting strategies and those with high degrees of logistic organization may at times turn to encounter foraging methods (e.g. Binford 1978). A change in hunting strategies may have been a regular part of the season to season or even day to day activity of a Palaeolithic hunter. However, at the sudden and perhaps unexpected juncture of hunting strategies following the failure of a mass kill, the art would have been essential in facilitating this switch. For on such occasions there would have been a rapid alteration in information requirements and the need to ensure that future hunting was successful.

This proposal that the art acted as a 'retrieval cue' (Tulving 1983) can be made since it contains a significant amount of imagery that is related to the stalking and killing of individual animals. This constitutes an information gathering theme which pervades the art and connects many otherwise disparate features of style and content.

The ethnographic record provides us with some knowledge of how hunters acquire information from their physical environment (Mithen 1990, chap. 3). They inspect tracks, hoofprints, scats and marks left on the ground and in vegetation. Through these, vast quantities of information can be acquired about animals in the vicinity. They also make careful observations on animals themselves, focusing particularly on the amount of fat they possess and the nature of their antlers/horns. Certain animals that are seen or inferred from tracks and trails act as clues to others. The sight of a predator may suggest that its prey is in the vicinity. Similarly some species may give general clues as to environmental conditions such as the sight of the first salmon swimming upstream. As I have described elsewhere (Mithen 1988; 1990, chap. 7) and summarize in table 3.1, I believe that Upper Palaeolithic art contains many references to this information gathering behaviour.

Now some, perhaps many, of the interpretations I have placed on particular images (table 3.1) are of course debatable. Whenever one says 'I think that this is a picture of . . .', someone else is sure to pounce with criticism. Let me anticipate certain criticisms with a few criteria that can help evaluate the interpretation put on any image. First I do not think that what the artist had intended to depict is of any great relevance. My interest is with the interpretations placed on the image by other individuals, either contemporary with the artist or many years later. These may no more coincide with the intention of the artist than my own. The artist may have intended to draw an arrow, a contemporary hunter may see it as a blade of grass, while another may have seen a phallus. Similarly the artist may not have intended to associate two images he/she painted side by side or when he placed his image next to one previously painted. But this does not prevent someone else viewing the art, in the Palaeolithic as much as the present, from making an association.

The interpretation placed on any single image may be strengthened over rival interpretations if it is compatible with interpretations for other images and hence relate to a common theme. For instance some of the raised tail imagery may be depicting animals inviting others to copulate. But this does not fit the information gathering theme (some of the animals with raised tails are also clearly males). The curled up bison from Altamira may be dead or giving birth but the idea that they are simply rolling on the ground and leaving signs of their presence is compatible with the way that their hoofs and horns are painted and hence receives support. Similarly the Kesslerloch reindeer has been interpreted as a male in rut rather than a grazing animal, but grazing fits the information gathering theme and is therefore preferred. This simply suggests that one means by which competing interpretations for particular images (e.g. whether a dented circle is a vulva, hoofprint or something else) can be evaluated is by their respective abilities to draw together otherwise disparate elements of the archaeological record into one coherent framework.

I am ready to recognize that there are few images in the art that can be directly and uncontroversially related to an information gathering theme. However further support for the art functioning at this switch from group mass hunting to that of individual stalking is found in a second complementary theme, 'information required' (Mithen 1989a). Rice and Patterson (1986, 665) have shown that the frequencies by which different animals are represented correlates with their meat weights. From a cost-benefit perspective this is likely to reflect the interest of the animal to a hunter who is using stalk methods. Bison and horse will be the prime targets. Consequently the art is making reference to the stalking of animals by the frequencies as well as the manner in which species are represented. By recognizing both the information gathering and required themes, the 'thoughtful forager' model is making reference to a large proportion of the imagery of Palaeolithic art.

So far I have shown how this interpretation has drawn numerous and diverse links between patterns within the art which had previously stood isolated from each other. Numerous features of the art are now related: the frequency of species representation, the depiction of animals in profile, the use of distortion, omission and exaggeration, twisted perspective, seasonal imagery, the association of carnivores and herbivores, the predominance of migratory wildfowl in the bird imagery and certain 'abstract' signs. All of these have previously been recognized as significant features of the art but have remained isolated from each other. The themes of information gathering and information required draw them together into one coherent framework. We can go further however and connect these themes to patterning in the faunal assemblages.

It has long been recognized that while the art is dominated by bison and horse, it is reindeer and red deer that proliferate in the faunal assemblages. Recent quantitative studies dealing with both individual sites and regions have emphasized this discrepancy (e.g. Altuna 1983; Delporte 1984; Rice and Patterson 1985, 1986; Sieveking 1984). There are some cases however when there is a general agreement between species frequencies in the art and the fauna, such as Covalanus and La Pasiega where both are dominated by red deer (Sieveking 1984; Bahn and Vertut 1988, 156). While this issue has now been well described, there has been little discussion of it other than simply to state that as a consequence the art can have little relationship with subsistence behaviour and hunting magic (e.g. Bahn and Vertut 1988; Straus 1987).

This pattern of frequent, but not total, art/fauna animal frequency discrepancy can be understood from the 'thoughtful forager' interpretation. Sites are dominated by red deer, reindeer or ibex since these were the mainstay of the economy and were hunted by group action resulting in mass kills, as suggested by the catastrophic mortality profiles (Klein *et al.* 1981; Straus and Clark 1986; Mithen 1989a). But within these assemblages there is a small frequency of other large game species such as bovids, horse and cervids. For instance within the classic mass kill assemblages of La Riera and Gare de Couze one finds occurrences of horse and bovids (figures 3.2, 3.3). These and perhaps some of the dominant species probably

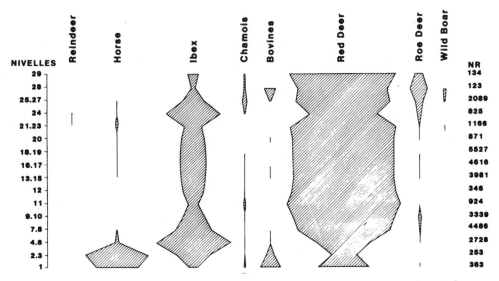

Figure 3.2 [orig. figure 2]   Percentage variations in ungulate remains throughout the Gare de Couze
sequence
(from Delpech 1983).

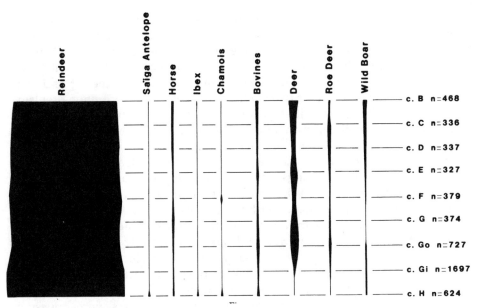

Figure 3.3 [orig. figure 3]   Percentage variations in ungulate remains throughout the La Riera
sequence
(from Straus and Clark 1986).

derived from the stalking and killing of individual animals. Consequently at such sites two types of hunting methods were taking place. The results of the mass hunting came to dominate the assemblages while the art related to the stalking of individual animals which only made a small though vital contribution to the Palaeolithic economy. We find therefore an overall discrepancy between species frequencies in the art and fauna.

However mass co-operative killing of red deer, reindeer and ibex could only have taken place from certain locations. It was dependent upon features of local topography and the mobility patterns of the herd animals. The stalking of individual animals would not have been so constrained. Consequently faunal assemblages at certain sites are likely to result from this hunting method alone and at these the species frequencies may show a much greater agreement with those within the art. One example may be Fontanet. Although there is little information on the fauna, that available (Bahn 1984, table 30) suggests a fairly even balance between bison, horse and ibex, in broad agreement with the frequencies of species in the parietal art of the Ariège. In contrast the assemblage from the nearby cave of Les Eglises is dominated by ibex (Delpech 1983) and probably results from co-operative mass killing of ibex herds. If these suggestions are correct then age/sex profiles and body part representation from these assemblages should differ indicating the contrasts in hunting strategies and associated butchery practices. Whether or not these suggestions are correct, the important point is that some concrete test implications concerning patterning in faunal assemblages are being proposed by which the 'thoughtful forager' interpretation for the art can be evaluated.

To conclude, let me return to the notion of an ecological interpretation of Palaeolithic art. The 'thoughtful forager' model does indeed meet the criteria for an ecological interpretation. There are numerous and diverse links made between otherwise disparate elements of the archaeological record. In particular patterns in the art are related to patterns in faunal assemblages. Within the art itself connections are made between the two realms of imagery and distribution problems. In turn, within the imagery itself many links are made between the style and content of depiction. Similarly, within the faunal assemblages connections have been made between the patterns of intensification and diversification and assemblages which are dominated by single species and those with a more even balance of different species. The unifying theme which enables all of these links to be made is the individual engaging in the process of adaptation during the late Upper Palaeolithic. An important point I wish to emphasize is that this interpretation is not addressing the origins of the artistic tradition but its proliferation towards and following the height of the last glacial. It takes as given that when individuals sought to cope with the problems that hunting intensification presented an artistic/ritual tradition existed which was co-opted to function in the manner I have described. Whether it had previously played a similar or indeed any role in the process by which individuals adapt to their environments is another question.

Finally I want to return to my opening remarks concerning human creativity, human adaptation and Palaeolithic art. In the interpretation I have proposed the imagery in the art is not simply aiding a mechanical like retrieval of information. It is acting as the stimulus for creative thought about the future. Hunters are creating multiple scenarios of future worlds within their minds and will attempt to achieve one of them through action. Such scenario building is the essence of the human mind and essential to learning and decision making. As the fore-runner of action it constitutes an individual's engagement in the process of adaptation. Consequently, in discussing the art it is simply impossible to separate the notions of human adaptation and creativity since they are dependent upon each other. I am left wondering about a possible connection between the creative act of producing images and the creative thoughts about hunting behaviour that such images helped generate. I feel that these must have fed off each other in a spiral of creativity leaving us today with the splendours of Palaeolithic art and enabling the Palaeolithic hunters to adapt to their uncertain world.

References

Altuna, J. 1983. On the relationship between archaeo-faunas and parietal art in the caves of the Cantabrian region. In J. Clutton-Brock and C. Grigson (eds), *Animals and Archaeology I: Hunters and their Prey*. Oxford: British Archaeological Reports.

Bahn, P. 1984. *Pyrenean Prehistory*. Warminster: Aris & Phillips.

Bahn, P. and Vertut, J. 1988. *Images of the Ice Age*. Leicester: Windward.

Binford, L. 1978. *Nunumiut Ethnoarchaeology*. New York: Academic Press.

Binford, L. 1983. *In Pursuit of the Past*. London: Thames & Hudson.

Clark, G. and Straus, L.G. 1983. Late Pleistocene hunter-gatherer adaptations in Cantabrian Spain. In G. Bailey (ed.), *Hunter-Gatherer Economy in Prehistory*. Cambridge: Cambridge University Press.

Delpech, F. 1983. *Les Faunas du Paléolithique Supérieur dans le Sud-Ouest de la France*. Paris: CNRS.

Delporte, H. 1984. L'art mobilier et ses rapports avec le faune Paléolithique. In H. Bandi *et al.* (eds), *La Contribution de la Zoologie et de l'Ethologie à l'Interpretation de l'Art des Peuples Chasseurs Préhistoriques*. Friborg: Editions Universitaires.

Gamble, C. 1986. *The Palaeolithic Settlement of Europe*. Cambridge: Cambridge University Press.

Hayden, B., Chisolm, B. and Schwarcz, H.P. 1987. Fishing and foraging: marine resources in the Upper Palaeolithic of France. In O. Soffer (ed.), *The Pleistocene Old World*, 279–91. New York: Plenum Press.

Jochim, M. 1983. Palaeolithic cave art in ecological perspective. In G. Bailey (ed.), *Hunter-Gatherer Economy in Prehistory*, 212–19. Cambridge: Cambridge University Press.

Jochim, M. 1987. Late Pleistocene refugia in Europe. In O. Soffer (ed.), *The Pleistocene Old World*, 365–75. New York: Plenum Press.

Meldgaard, M. 1983. Resource fluctuations and human subsistence: a zoo-archaeological and ethnographic investigation of a west Greenland caribou hunting camp. In J. Clutton-Brook & C. Grigson (eds), *Animals and Archaeology I: Hunters and their Prey*, 259–72. Oxford: British Archaeological Reports.

Mellars, P. 1985. The ecological basis of social complexity in the Upper Palaeolithic of south-west France. In T.D. Price and J. Brown (eds), *Prehistoric Hunter-Gatherers: The Emergence of Social Complexity*, 271–97. New York: Academic Press.

Mithen, S.J. 1988. Looking and learning: Upper Palaeolithic art and information gathering. *World Archaeology* 19, 297–327.

Mithen, S.J. 1989a. To hunt or to paint: animals and art in the Upper Palaeolithic. *Man (N.S.)* 23, 671–95.

Mithen, S.J. 1989b. Evolutionary theory and post-processual archaeology. *Antiquity* 63, 483–94.

Mithen, S.J. 1990. *Thoughtful Foragers: A Study of Prehistoric Decision Making*. Cambridge: Cambridge University Press.

Morris, D. 1962. *The Biology of Art*. London: Methuen & Co. Ltd.

Pfeiffer, J. 1982. *The Creative Explosion: An Inquiry into the Origins of Art and Religion*. New York: Harper and Row.

Rice, P.C. and Paterson, A.L. 1985. Cave art and bones: exploring the inter-relationships. *American Anthropologist* 87, 94–100.

Rice, P.C. and Paterson, A.L. 1986. Validating the cave art-archaeofauna relationship in Cantabrian Spain. *American Anthropologist* 88, 658–67.

Sieveking, A. 1984. Palaeolithic art and animal behaviour. In H. Bandi *et al.* (eds), *La Contribution de la Zoologie et de l'Ethologie à l'Interpretation de l'Art des Peuples Chasseurs Préhistoriques*, 91–109. Friborg: Editions Universitaires.

Straus, L. 1987. The Palaeolithic art of Vasco-Cantabria. *Oxford Journal of Archaeology* 6, 149–63.

Straus, L. and Clark, G.A. 1986. *La Riera: Stone Age Hunter-Gatherer Adaptations in Northern Spain*, Tucson: University of Arizona Press.

Tanner, A. 1979. *Bringing Home Animals: Religious Ideology and Mode of Production of the Mistassini Cree Hunters*. London: C. Hurst.

Tulving, E. 1983. *Elements of Episodic Memory*. Oxford: Clarendon Press.

Part III

Political Economy

The Production of Value

The term "political economy" has undergone many transformations since its origins in the seventeenth century and today has a wide range of meanings, some of which are sharply divergent. Generally speaking, it encompasses studies of production, circulation, accumulation and consumption of goods, services, and value. For many people, political economy is seen as synonymous with some variety of Marxism. This is somewhat ironic since Marx used the term to refer to the neoclassicism of Adam Smith and Ricardo and indeed the subtitle of *Capital* was *A Critique of Political Economy* (Marx 1967). More recently, the term has been used to refer to the analysis of political forces in the state and civil economy. Some of these studies have focused on the contradictions between the forces and relations of production, while others have emphasized the constitutive roles of power and ideology. Both of these approaches are in contrast to a third group which traces its lineage to the neoclassicists and stresses the workings of the market and the law of supply and demand.

In a recent review, Roseberry (1988) has identified two main strands in political economy. The first of these is world-systems theory and theories of underdevelopment which emerged in political sociology (Frank 1967; Wallerstein 1974, 1980). Both of these are dependency theories with practical applications for understanding the spread of capitalism. Those in the second strand are mainly concerned with the specification and articulation of different modes of production and have their origins in the writings of French anthropologists, which are highly theoretical and tend to be more difficult to apply in the real world (Godelier 1978; Rey 1975; Terray 1975). Roseberry's review, however, ignores those political-economy approaches with ties to the neoclassicism critiqued by Marx. These approaches seek to identify the regularities or universals that underlie economic interactions and to explore their specific expressions in non-Western contexts. And he also neglects the growing body of research on the politics of value (e.g. Appadurai 1986). These relatively new approaches explore authenticity and authentication, diversion and display, expertise and sumptuary control, connoisseurship and mobilized demand.

In archaeology, the term political economy has a similar range of meanings. We will restrict it here, however, to describing those approaches that focus on political control and legitimization, and this partially justifies separating it out from the cultural economics and cultural materialism discussed previously (Part II). Within this framework we identify three research directions. The first is concerned with exploring the political dimensions of precapitalist modes of production and their historical interconnections. Some of these address gender relations, ideology, the legitimization of power, and world economies. The second approach focuses on how past economies were financed and how political power was maintained. These approaches, with roots in neoclassical economics, have tended to treat economics and politics separately. The third approach deals with issues of commodity production and value. But before addressing these approaches we need to say a few words about the attempts to associate forms of sociopolitical organization with different types of economies, an approach commonly known as neoevolutionism.

Neoevolutionism

Neoevolutionism is popularly associated with the revival of evolutionary theory in anthropology in the 1950s and 1960s. Evolutionary theory was originally introduced by E.B. Tylor and Lewis Henry Morgan in the mid-nineteenth century to account for broad similarities in cultures worldwide. Morgan's typology of savages, barbarians, and civilization was the framework by which Victorians viewed themselves and "Others" (Part VIII) (Stocking 1987). At the turn of the century this theory fell into disfavor due to Franz Boas who with his students developed a comprehensive critique of the concept of evolutionary stages, the idea of progress, and the possibility of objectively evaluating cultures. Boas (1896) maintained that before seeking what is common to all cultures, each culture needed to be analyzed separately. Many anthropologists took this as a license to conduct particularist studies of different societies with no concern for process. As a result, the cultural-historical tradition in both anthropology and archaeology was dominated by descriptions and had little to say to the other social sciences.

Leslie White and Julian Steward reintroduced evolutionary theory in two rather different forms. White's universalism is the perspective that cultures can be studied in terms of universal characteristics. Culture could be measured objectively, ranking cultures by using the idea of "energy capture," thus cultures advance as the amount of energy captured per capita increases (White 1947). This view had a major impact in archaeology through the work of Binford (1962). Steward's multilinealism is the view that cultures develop along specific pathways and that these are particular to their local contexts. Steward (1955) regarded cultural variability as a response to local ecological adaptations and, like his teacher Boas, favored the detailed examination of specific cases in order to build up cultural regularities or general laws. This perspective was adopted by Willey and Phillips (1958). Steward and White did not regard their theories as compatible and a sharp debate emerged between them. Some of the confusion surrounding this debate was clarified by Marshall Sahlins and Elman Service (1960). In their model of general and specific evolution, they separated out general processes from their specific historical expressions. For them, general evolution could be equated with unilinear development since cross-culturally societies can be seen to evolve through a set number of stages. Specific evolution, however, is the realization of this process in particular contexts. It is not invariate since the trajectories different societies take may be quite different. This insight is a clear statement of the interdependence of history and process.

Service and Morton Fried modeled the processes of general evolution by means of more or less parallel stage typologies. Service (1962) subsumed social variability into four categories consisting of bands, tribes, chiefdoms, and states, while Fried (1967) used a tripartite approach identifying egalitarian, ranked and stratified societies. The main difference between the two typologies is Service's stress on forms of exchange and Fried's emphasis on political control. For example, Service identified chiefdoms on the basis of redistribution while Fried identified ranked societies by means of differentials in social status. Both positions share an implicit cultural-evolutionary assumption, namely that progress is a general feature of human society and that technological advancement ensures greater selective fitness. This thesis owes much to White's earlier formulations. These typologies have been extremely popular in archaeology and there has been considerable work correlating different stages with specific material culture manifestations. Much research focused on "middle-range" societies because of their transitional character, lying between bands and states. Renfrew (1973), for example, defined the European megalith societies as chiefdoms on the basis of twenty different characteristics and Peebles and Kus (1977) provided a similar inventory for Mississippian chiefdoms. But certain problems began to emerge with this typological approach. Earle (1978) showed that redistribution, previously regarded as a key attribute, was absent in the paradigm case of Hawaii. Similarly, in their cross-cultural ethnographic survey, Feinman and Neitzel (1984) demonstrated that so much variability existed among so-called chiefdoms that it was almost impossible to construct meaningful categories.

Currently, there is a general dissatisfaction with neoevolutionism in all its guises. This has led some away from typological approaches and toward those emphasizing social relations. Yoffee (1993), for example, sees social relations as fluid and regards social evolution as both gradualistic and transformational. For him, the entities that we call bands, tribes, chiefdoms and states might be better understood as different historical trajectories growing out of "bandishness", that depend upon different forms of power (economic, social, and political). Unfortunately, Yoffee's tripartite typology of power ignores the social relations between these domains and thus is subject to the same kind of criticism he makes of the Service and Fried typologies. Others have emphasized social relations of production, focusing on ethno-politics of acquisition, control and inheritance. Lourandos (1988), for example, regards the intensification of production as being closely connected to the demands of social relations. He argues that arenas of intergroup relations such as feasting, ritual and exchange provides the context for change. Shanks and Tilley (1987) have rejected neoevolutionism entirely, preferring to focus on social strategies, social transformation, power, ideology, altereity, plurality, relationality, displacement, substitution, and difference. For them, all social life is contingent and all social change is conjunctural.

Polity Formation and Interaction

A central problem in political economics is understanding how specific precapitalist sociopolitical formations emerge, interact with one another, and are transformed over time. A range of different theoretical approaches have been used (see Parts II and IV) and here we wish to emphasize three influential models, all of which focus on the regional scale, but employ rather different underlying assumptions. "Peer polity interaction" is a collection of empirical observations about the rise of cultural complexity and the growth of sociopolitical systems. "Prestige goods exchange" is a model of the emergence of dependency relations between core and peripheries created by the exchange of wealth items. World systems theory describes the origins of capitalism and has been applied in archaeology to deal with imperialism and empire in the ancient world.

Peer polity interaction was developed by Colin Renfrew (**chapter** 4) to understand the social dynamics underlying the emergence of state political economies (see Price 1977 for her similar cluster-interaction model). It identifies social structures (political institutions, ritual systems, and non-verbal language) as the product of interactions between adjacent early states over a long period of time. Three processes are implicated – competition, "symbolic entrainment," and increased trade. For Renfrew, both warfare and competitive emulation can favor the intensification of production and the emergence of leaders who establish their authority through gifts and feasting. "Symbolic entrainment," which involves the adoption of more complex symbolic and non-symbolic innovations, can lead to the adoption of writing systems and kingship. Increased trade can give rise to new facilities and institutions to manage goods, as well as craft specialization and mass production.

Renfrew has illustrated his model with a consideration of the emergence of Greek city states during the first millennium BC. He begins by criticizing the standard view of cultural evolution which regards the rise of Mediterranean civilizations as a secondary phenomenon dependent upon Egyptian developments. He then suggests that despite strong evidence for trade between the two areas, the Mediterranean case is better understood as a fundamentally Aegean event with its own historical processes. For Renfrew, the Greek city-states emerged together, each pulling the other up by their bootstraps. He identifies two new institutions which guided the trajectory of the political economy. These were the temple as a focus of religious expression, and a monetary system evincing pride in civic autonomy. He then argues that the simultaneous development of cultural innovations can be understood in terms of symbolic entrainment. This approach has seen wide use in both old world and new world contexts (Champion and Champion 1986; Cherry 1986; Freidel 1986; Sabloff 1986).

Prestige goods exchange was originally developed by Friedman and Rowlands (1977) as one of the pathways of their epigenetic model of social evolution (see Part IV). A prestige system is one where social status is based on access to prestige goods necessary for social reproduction. A dependency relation emerges between core and peripheral elites. In this case, core elites maintain centralized control over luxury goods and peripheral elites can only access these goods through the establishment of alliances with the core. This results in an increase in the intensity of exchange and in the quantity of goods produced. An increase in production specialization occurs as the core elites demand particular kinds of goods, and this can often lead to the standardization of form. They suggest that the prestige system is unstable, however, because of the difficulty of maintaining a clear monopoly over long-distance exchange contacts.

A sophisticated application is Parker Pearson's (1984) study of the political economy of the pre-state Iron Age societies of Jutland. He suggests that the Danish sequence can be understood as a series of three consumptive cycles which supported progressively unequal social relations with a widening gap between the rich and the poor. The ideological basis for this consumption rested on ritual gift giving by the living to the ancestors. Wealth items were interred in graves and buried in votive deposits. Prestige was thus accumulated by acquiring symbolic capital either by giving away prestige items or by taking them out of circulation. But gift giving was a potential source of transformation; it could be escalated until the point at which one of the participants was ruined and indebted to the other. This appears to have created the context for the Anglo-Saxon migrations. This model has been widely, and somewhat uncritically, applied in European and North American prehistory (Bender 1978; Cobb 1991; Kristiansen 1982).

World systems theory, developed by the political economist Immanual Wallerstein (1974, 1980), explores the structural linkages between the First and Third worlds such that development in one area creates underdevelopment in another. The central process is one of exploitation as nation-state cores abstract goods from peripheries and redistribute them according to specific rules of allocation. This process is dynamic and complex since the status of cores may fluctuate over time, resulting in unstable and changing boundaries. World systems theory has been particularly attractive to archaeologists because of the scale at which it operates. It places cultural entities within their larger historical, political, and economic contexts and is sensitive to the spatial dynamics of control. Most archaeological applications, however, have been generally uncritical and have imposed the theory directly upon archaeological data (Blanton and Feinman 1984; Champion 1989; Rowlands et al. 1987). Few studies have attempted to explore the limitations of the model for addressing precapitalist forms (see, however, Kohl 1989; Edens 1992; Sherratt 1994).

One of the best examples of the use of world systems theory is Phil Kohl's analysis of the Bronze Age of the Greater Middle East (**chapter 5**). Not only does he use the theory to lend insight into his case study but he also identifies several areas where Wallerstein's formation is inadequate and in need of additional theorizing. Kohl argues that the late third and early second millennium BC consisted of a series of multiple cores, each of which exploited its own hinterland. But the hegemony of cores was only partial and often short-lived. Peripheries could choose to establish or cease relations with cores according to their own interests. Kohl identifies two reasons for this. Precapitalist technologies were neither as specialized nor as controlled as they are in modern societies so that it was impossible for cores to maintain monopolies. In addition, precapitalist transportation systems were quite limited. This meant that it was difficult for the core to continually monitor the periphery. These observations represent an important start toward the reformulation of world systems theory as a theory of the history of precapitalist political economies.

These three models clearly stress different aspects of the regional political economy. Peer polity interaction identifies synergistic economic growth as a key factor in political development. Prestige goods exchange and world systems theory explore the dynamics of control as embedded in relations of dependency between core and periphery. It could be argued that a more comprehensive theory would result by combining these models into a single monolithic formulation of social change. But even if such linking could be achieved (and we are not convinced that synergy and the dialectics of dominance and dependence can be adequately accommodated), the resulting theory would be incomplete. This is because all of these theories tend to privilege core developments at the expense of the periphery. Local transformations of the items which had "prestige" need to be considered (Sørensen 1987), and it cannot be assumed that status was based on the control of exchange rather than, for example, land (Gosden 1989). This center bias means that reconstructions of the political economy using these models will always be incomplete and misleading.

Staple and Wealth Finance

Another research focus is on how political economic systems finance themselves. This is bound up in the processes of economic specialization and exchange. The most important evaluation of this issue is a result of the work of Timothy Earle, Terrance D'Altroy and Elizabeth Brumfiel. Their research has demonstrated the limitations of the standard adaptationalist account, which proposed that political economies specialize to solve specific environmental and economic problems (see Part II). They regard specialization not as the result of the political economy adapting to a new problem, but rather as the outcome of elites seeking to solidify and strengthen their political and economic control. This reversal of the standard adaptationalist argument has strong connections to structural-Marxist approaches, but retains an implicit notion of agency.

In order to understand the different contexts of exchange, D'Altroy and Earle (1985) make a distinction between staple finance and wealth finance. Staple finance refers to subsistence goods collected by the state as part of its juridical rights and redistributed to state subjects. These systems tend to be constrained by the perishability, bulk and weight of the subsistence goods that they circulate. In addition, as territorial size increases, storehouses must be decentralized and this makes the goods susceptible to being seized during rebellion. Wealth finance, by contrast, is a system where the state uses some form of wealth as currency to pay out to its subjects – currency which can then be exchanged for subsistence goods in the marketplace. Goods that circulate in these systems have a high value-to-weight ratio and high durability and thus permit a higher degree of centralization in the state economy with a lower risk of loss through forcible seizure. A dialectical relationship exists between the two kinds of finance since wealth is convertible into food and back again. Both staple and wealth finance are characteristic of many early complex societies. But Brumfiel and Earle (1987) emphasize the wealth-finance system as the primary force generating political development. It allows rulers to create alliances, to establish retinues and to legitimize power. It thus permits polity expansion while maintaining centralized control.

Earle (**chapter 6**) provides a useful example of the operation of these kinds of finance in his comparative study of Hawaiian and Inka political economies. Both the Hawaiian and Inka economies were characterized by staple finance. In the Hawaiian and Inka case wealth was not easily converted into subsistence goods because it circulated in a separate sphere of exchange. Linked not to goods but to access to goods, wealth acted as a visible symbol of status in both the Hawaiian and Inka contexts. Specialization developed as elites manipulated image and symbol to confront problems of control in the circulation of subsistence goods. The elaborately feathered cloaks worn by Hawaiian chiefs were physical markers of their elite status and symbolic manifestations of a system of rights to position and title to land. For the Inka different grades of clothing and metal adornments served much the same purpose. But unlike the Hawaiian case where wealth production was always organized at the community level, it became carefully managed by Inka state institutions. This approach has been applied in European and Mediterranean contexts (Gilman 1991; Kristiansen 1991).

But this focus on the context of exchange does not go far enough. It does not explore questions regarding the system of meaning within which certain items came to have elite-marking status, or how those meanings were maintained and reproduced. For example, it may be that specialization emerged in the Hawaiian case in the context of providing food and material goods to the deities and that chiefs (*tapu*) coopted this labor in order to establish linkages between themselves and the supernatural. In this way, they could control and distribute supernatural efficacy (*mana*) to others. They thus made themselves divine by association, by their claims to the same ritual practices and material-culture items previously the domain of the deities. Another issue is the division of staple and wealth items in the first place. Earle clearly uses this as a heuristic device, but in many societies, certain so-called staples can be wealth items. What may ultimately be more interesting is how the value of material culture changes as it moves in and out of different spheres of exchange.

Commodities and Value

A third area of research is the nature of commodities themselves. There are three main approaches. The economic view regards commodities as goods produced for exchange, their value being determined by their exchange value and the laws of supply and demand. Two kinds of commodity exchange are usually distinguished. Tribute presumes the existence of administrative organizations and is founded in the formalized political relations between sovereign entities. Market exchange refers to transactions between individuals that are regulated by the supply–demand mechanism. The social-reproduction view regards commodities as material manifestations of social relations. The exchange of prestige goods, for example, ties together two parties in a relationship of obligation. The cultural-commodity view treats commodities as having "a life of their own". It regards all objects as being potential commodities that acquire and lose value as they move in and out of different spheres of exchange.

According to the economic view, commodities are things which circulate throughout an economic system and can be exchanged for other things, usually money. Halstead and O'Shea's (1982) study of commodity production and the emergence of social ranking in the Aegean is a good example. For them, commodities are created through social storage as food surpluses are converted into material tokens of value. They suggest that this process of social storage was an important buffer against periodic food shortages and that the convertibility of tokens allowed for greater social differentiation than is permitted by direct reciprocity. This is because differentiated systems are predisposed to simplification as managerial elites take control and because the durability of tokens allows for the unequal accumulation of wealth and its transmission across generations. These factors also favor the symbolic and real manipulation of wealth and the emergence of social institutions.

The social-reproduction view borrows from Marx's notion of the commodity as a product of labor associated with a particular mode of production which is transferred to another by means of exchange. An example is Kristiansen's (1991) study of trends in wealth consumption, monument building, and symbolic behavior and the emergence of elites in northern Europe during the Bronze and Iron Ages. He shows that in both cases the adoption of international value systems was crucial. During the Bronze Age the transmission took place through a regional network of exchange systems linking Denmark to the military complexes of Mycenae and Asia Minor. Elite exchange goods included war chariots, stools, swords, razors, and tweezers. In the Iron Age it resulted through a center/periphery relation with the Roman Empire and the Celtic world. Social differentiation was based upon institutionalized access to land and the hoarding of exchange valuables was linked to taxation. There is thus a general trajectory from wealth finance to staple finance which transformed the social relations of production from kin-based to village-based modes.

A relatively new approach is the politics of value: how material goods move in and out of spheres of circulation and in the process reproduce and transform society (Appadurai 1986; Munn 1986; Weiner 1992). It has its origins in Mauss's (1950) notion of the "spirit of the gift" and Bourdieu's (1977) concern for practice. A provocative example is Orser's (**chapter 7**) study of material culture in plantation contexts. He suggests that in addition to use value and exchange value a third kind of value can be identified; this is the esteem or aesthetic value that an object instills in an individual. This move gives agency to the object, its presence in specific contexts can help perpetuate ideas and beliefs. Orser then gives an interesting example of how iron pots were often used in the household for cooking, but in the context of secret meetings they were turned over "to catch the sound" in a West African manner. He suggests that their esteem value transcended their use value in religious contexts. This implies that things are often not just what they appear, and that a full understanding of the political economy requires the compilation of a "cultural biography of things" (Kopytoff 1986).

The Archaeology of Capitalism

Finally, we wish to discuss a newly emerging focus within political economy. This is the archaeology of capitalism broadly construed. Capitalism can be simply defined as an economic system concerned with the production and sale of commodities in markets. But of course it is more than this. It embodies certain relations between people and institutional structures which have a particular history. And it enjoys a scale never before seen. Giddens (1984) calls it the first genuinely global type of social organization in history. Anthropologists have been particularly interested in the effects of this globalization upon indigenous peoples. Indeed, this is part of what Marcus and Fischer (1986) describe as world historical political economy, the positioning of subjects within history and the long-term operation of economic and political systems. In an influential book, Wolf (1982) has shown how the historical processes that led to capitalism both impacted on and were appropriated by the cultures that anthropologists study. This dual notion of active agency and world political economy has direct relevance for contextualizing the responses of "the Other" (Part VIII).

The archaeology of capitalism as a research project largely derives from over a decade of work by Mark Leone and his associates at Historic Annapolis, Maryland (see Leone and Potter, **chapter 22**). Their aim has been to do archaeology literally under the eyes of the public and in the process raise questions about how archaeology and archaeological knowledge is related to everyday life (Leone et al. 1987; Potter 1994). In the course of conducting the public tours, the directors realized that most tourists had only a fragmented picture of the history of Annapolis and this consisted of a series of disconnected oppositions – eighteenth versus nineteenth century, white versus black, historic district versus naval academy, residents versus tourists. This observation led them to explore how these histories were connected through the class structure of Annapolis society. One recent development has been the creation of a collaborative project with the local African-American community to explore African-American history (Leone 1995).

A number of related projects have been completed including studies of historical consciousness (Potter 1992), craft (Little 1988), and consumerism (Shackel 1993).

The archaeology of capitalism has now differentiated into several subfields and research topics, and some practitioners adopt a critical-theory perspective like that espoused by Leone, while others do not. One subfield is the study of plantation economic systems and the archaeology of slavery (Ferguson 1992; Orser 1988; Singleton 1985, 1988). Another area of interest has been how the built environment is used to support an ideology of class relations. The best known of these is Leone's (1984) study of William Paca's garden in Annapolis as an example of the Georgian ideology, although Johnson (1991, 1992, 1993) has completed a set of studies on how "polite" architecture was used within an emergent capitalism in post-medieval England in order to legitimize new forms of social power. Yet another area is the study of contemporary mortuary practices. McGuire (1988) has explored some of the complexity of the relations between ideology, death and capitalism in the Memorial Park cemetery in Broome County, New York, while Parker Pearson (1982) has shown how class and ethnicity are expressed in spatial differences in cemeteries in Cambridge, England. Related to Wolf's (1982) capitalist-expansion thesis are studies of domination and resistance collected in Leone and Potter (1988), Miller et al. (1989), and McGuire and Paynter (1991).

One might well ask why we need an archaeology of capitalism, given the wealth of historical research on capitalism. The answer is that although we live in capitalist societies, we really don't understand how capitalism conceals forms of exploitation, how it naturalizes its practices, and how in the process it reproduces itself. Historical studies of capitalism have made some important strides, but these typically focus on core political-economic developments and ignore how capitalism impacts on indigenous or marginalized peoples. In addition, historical studies ignore the constitutive role material culture plays in perpetuating this social form. An archaeology of capitalism is thus necessary to understand more fully the many different ways in which capitalism works. It has the potential to show us how we construct ourselves.

Conclusion

One problem we see with most of the work devoted to political economy is the extent to which it is adequate to explore the economy, however politically and socially embedded, separately from the systems of meaning which give value to things. In fact there has been little discussion in archaeology of the social construction of value, the third approach to the study of commodities discussed above. The archaeological focus on economy at the expense of value, or alternatively the reduction of value to labour or economic value, can be seen to mar many of the approaches discussed here. We are back with the problem of whether theory can be partitioned or whether a holistic, integrated approach is needed.

For example, a criticism of both the prestige goods exchange and world-systems models is that local meanings on the peripheries may have transformed the value of goods available in the centre. We cannot assume, because goods are found in the peripheries, that some form of dependency took place – the values of goods may have been constructed differently in core and periphery. Similarly, Renfrew's "symbolic entrainment" appears to assume that local polities did not transform the meanings of the symbols and rituals they copied from each other. Even the formalist–substantivist debate is ultimately about the local meanings of things – whether they had market value or were embedded in social relations. Similar issues beset the identification of gift versus commodity; and whether surplus is produced to reduce risk or for political purposes is a question of detailed contextual understanding. All this suggests that the study of the political economy is difficult to divorce from a broader understanding of social meanings and practices (Part V).

Similar critiques are relevant to an archaeology of power. It is difficult to see how the power to act or rule over people can be separated from the prestige of objects, goods, places, knowledge. Artifacts have to be given value within a system of meaning as well as within a system of power. It is not adequate to reduce everything to power. Issues such as the use of material culture in the formation of identities and in the construction of self take us beyond an account of power relations to broader questions of the construction of meaning. For example, we can ask why dominant ideologies become accepted or shared. How is the normativity which makes the wielding of power possible constructed and maintained? In answering such questions we need to move beyond power to a consideration of the cognitive schemes and bodily experiences through which ideologies are made persuasive and normativity is constructed.

It is clear that in the approaches discussed above there are fundamental differences in the way in which change is conceived. For some, political economies change in contingent fashion. This is true of writers influenced by Foucault and Giddens and in some neo-Marxist discussions (e.g. McGuire 1992). For others, change takes place within an evolutionary perspective linked, as in peer polity interaction, to the emergence of complex societies or to the rise of capitalism. The prestige-goods model, as we have seen, derives from an epigenetic evolutionary model and many of the classifications such as gift versus commodity, or part-time versus full-time specialists, are linked to developing forms of social complexity. Each of these approaches to change provides rich theoretical developments and useful insights but there has as yet been little consideration of the limits of these explanations.

References

Appadurai, A. 1986. (ed.) *The Social Life of Things*. Cambridge.

Bender, B. 1978. Gatherer-hunter to farmer: a social perspective. *World Archaeology* 10, 204–22.

Binford, L.R. 1962. Archaeology as anthropology. *American Antiquity* 28, 217–25.

Blanton, R. and Feinman, G. 1984. The Mesoamerican world system: a comparative perspective. *American Anthropologist* 86, 673–82.

Boas, F. 1896. The limitations of the comparative method of anthropology. *Science* 4, 901–08.

Bourdieu, P. 1977. *Outline of a Theory of Practice*. Cambridge.

Brumfiel, E. and Earle, T.K. 1987. Specialization, exchange, and complex societies: an introduction. In Brumfiel, E.M. and Earle, T.K. (eds) *Specialization, Exchange, and Complex Societies*. Cambridge, pp. 1–9.

Champion, T. (ed.) 1989. *Centre and Periphery: Comparative Studies in Archaeology*. London.

Champion, T. and Champion, S. 1986. Peer polity interaction in the European Iron Age. In Renfrew, C. and Cherry, J. (eds) *Peer Polity Interaction and Socio-Political Change*. Cambridge, pp. 59–68.

Cherry, J. 1986. Polities and palaces: some problems in Minoan state formation. In Renfrew, C. and Cherry, J. (eds) *Peer Polity Interaction and Socio-Political Change*. Cambridge, pp. 19–45.

Cobb, C. 1991. Social reproduction and the Longue Durée in the prehistory of the Midcontinental United States. In Preucel, R.W. (ed.) *Processual and Postprocessual Archaeologies: Multiple Ways of Knowing the Past*. Southern Illinois University, Center for Archaeological Investigations, Occasional Paper No. 10. Carbondale, pp. 168–82.

D'Altroy, T.N. and Earle, T.K. 1985. Staple finance, wealth finance, and storage in the Inka political economy. *Current Anthropology* 26, 187–206.

Earle, T.K. 1978. *Economic and Social Organization of a Complex Chiefdom: The Halelea District, Kaua'i, Hawaii*. Anthropological Papers, Museum of Anthropology, University of Michigan, No. 63. Ann Arbor.

Edens, C. 1992. Dynamics of trade in the ancient Mesopotamian "world system." *American Anthropologist* 94, 118–39.

Feinman, G. and Neitzel, J. 1984. Too many types: an overview of prestate sedentary societies in the Americas. *Advances in Archaeological Method and Theory* 7, 39–102.

Ferguson, L. 1992. Uncommon Ground: Archaeology and Early African America, 1650–1800. Washington D.C.

Frank, A.G. 1967. *Capitalism and Underdevelopment in Latin America: Historical Studies of Chile and Brazil*. New York.

Freidel, D. 1986. Maya warfare: an example of peer polity interaction. In Renfrew, C. and Cherry, J. (eds) *Peer Polity Interaction and Socio-Political Change*. Cambridge, pp. 93–108.

Fried, M.H. 1967. The Evolution of Political Society. New York.

Friedman, J. and Rowlands, M.J. 1977. Notes toward an epigenetic model of the evolution of civilisation. In Friedman, J. and Rowlands, M.J. (eds) *The Evolution of Social Systems*. London, pp. 201–76.

Giddens, A. 1984. *The Constitution of Society: An Outline of the Theory of Structuration*. Berkeley.

Gilman, A. 1991. Trajectories towards social complexity in the later prehistory of the Mediterranean. In Earle, T.K. (ed.) *Chiefdoms: Power, Economy and Ideology*. School of American Research, Cambridge University Press, Cambridge, pp. 146–68.

Godelier, M. 1978. The concept of the 'Asiatic mode of production' and Marxist models of social evolution. In Seddon, D. *Relations of Production*. London, pp. 209–88.

Gosden, C. 1989. Production, power, and prehistory. *Journal of Anthropological Archaeology* 8, 355–87.

Halstead, P. and O'Shea, J. 1982. A friend in need is a friend indeed: social storage and the origins of social ranking. In Renfrew, C. and Shennan, S. (eds) *Ranking, Resource and Exchange: Aspects of the Archaeology of Early European Society*. Cambridge, pp. 92–9.

Johnson, M. 1991. Enclosure and capitalism: history of a process. In Preucel, R.W. (ed.) *Processual and Postprocessual Archaeologies: Multiple Ways of Knowing the Past*. Southern

Illinois University, Center for Archaeological Investigations, Occasional Paper No. 10. Carbondale, pp. 159–67.

Johnson, M. 1992. Meanings of polite architecture in sixteenth century England. *Historical Archaeology* 26, 45–56.

Johnson, M. 1993. Notes toward an archaeology of capitalism. In Tilley, C. (ed.) *Interpretative Archaeology*. Oxford, pp. 327–56.

Kohl, P. 1989. The use and abuse of world systems theory: the case of the "pristine" West Asian state. In Lamberg-Karlovsky, C.C. (ed.) *Archaeological Thought in America*. Cambridge, pp. 241–67.

Kopytoff, I. 1986. The cultural biography of things: commoditization as process. In Appadurai, A. (ed.) *the Social Life of Things*. Cambridge, pp. 64–91.

Kristiansen, K. 1982. The formation of tribal systems in later European prehistory: Northern Europe, 4000–500 BC. In Renfrew, C., Rowlands, M.J. and Seagraves, B.A. (eds) *Theory and Explanation in Archaeology*. New York, pp. 241–80.

Kristiansen, K. 1991. Chiefdoms, states, and systems of social evolution. In Earle, T.K. (ed.) *Chiefdoms: Power, Economy and Ideology*. School of American Research, Cambridge University Press, Cambridge, pp. 16–43.

Leone, M.P. 1984. Interpreting ideology in historical archaeology: the William Paca Garden in Annapolis, Maryland. In Miller, D. and Tilley, C. (eds) *Ideology, Power, and Prehistory*. Cambridge, pp. 25–36.

Leone, M.P. 1995. A historical archaeology of capitalism. *American Anthropologist* 97, 251–68.

Leone, M.P. and Potter, P.B. Jr. (eds) 1988. *The Recovery of Meaning: Historical Archaeology in the Eastern United States*. Washington D.C.

Leone, M.P., Potter, P.B. Jr. and Shackel, P. 1987. Toward a critical archaeology. *Current Anthropology* 28, 238–302.

Little, B. 1988. Craft and culture change in the 18th-Century Chesapeake. In Leone, M.P. and Potter, P.B. Jr. (eds) *The Recovery of Meaning: Historical Archaeology in the Eastern United States*. Washington D.C., pp. 263–92.

Lourandos, H. 1988. Paleopolitics: resource intensification in Aboriginal Australia and Papua New Guinea. In Ingold, T., Riches, D. and Woodburn, J. (eds) *Hunters and Gatherers 1: History, Evolution and Social Change*. Oxford, pp. 148–60.

McGuire, R.H. 1988. Dialogues with the dead. In Leone, M.P. and Potter, P. (eds) *The Recovery of Meaning: Historical Archaeology in the Eastern United States*. Washington D.C., pp. 435–80.

McGuire, R.H. 1992 *A Marxist Archaeology*. New York.

McGuire, R.H. and Paynter, R. (eds) 1991. *The Archaeology of Inequality*. Oxford.

Marcus, G.E. and Fischer, M. 1986. *Anthropology as Cultural Critique: An Experimental Moment in the Human Sciences*. Chicago.

Marx, K. 1967. *Capital*. New York.

Mauss, M. 1950. *Essai sur le Don*. Paris.

Miller, D., Rowlands, M. and Tilley, C. (eds) 1989. *Domination and Resistence*. London.

Munn, N. 1986. *The Fame of Gawa: A Symbolic Study of Value Transformation in a Massim (Papua New Guinea) Society*. Cambridge.

Orser, C.E. Jr. 1988. Toward a theory of power for historical archaeology: plantations and space. In Leone, M.P. and Potter, P. (eds) *The Recovery of Meaning: Historical Archaeology in the Eastern United States*. Washington D.C., pp. 313–43.

Parker Pearson, M. 1982. Mortuary practices, society and ideology: an aspect of the relationship between social hierarchy and culture change. In Hodder, I. (ed.) *Symbolic and Structural Archaeology. Cambridge*, pp. 99–113.

Parker Pearson, M. 1984. Economic and ideological change: cyclical growth in the pre-state societies of Jutland. In Miller, D. and Tilley, C. (eds) *Ideology, Power and Prehistory.* Cambridge, pp. 69–92.

Peebles, C. and Kus, S. 1977. Some archaeological correlates of ranked societies. *American Antiquity.* 42, 421–8.

Potter, P.B. Jr. 1992. Establishing the roots of historical consciousness in modern Annapolis, Maryland. In Karp, I., Kreamer, C.M. and Lavine, S.D. (eds) *Museums and Communities: The Politics of Public Culture.* Washington D.C., pp. 476–505.

Potter, P.B. Jr. 1994. *Public Archaeology in Annapolis: A Critical Approach to History in Maryland's "Ancient" City.* Washington D.C.

Price, B. 1977. Shifts in production and organization: a cluster-interaction model. *Current Anthropology* 18, 209–33.

Renfrew, C. 1973. Monuments, mobilization, and social organization in neolithic Wessex. In Renfrew, C. (ed.) *The Explanation of Culture Changes: Models in Prehistory.* London, pp. 539–58.

Rey, P-P. 1975. The lineage mode of production. *Critique of Anthropology* 3, 27–79.

Roseberry, W. 1988. Political economy. *Annual Review of Anthropology* 17, 161–85.

Rowlands, M., Larsen, M. and Kristiansen, K. (eds) 1987. *Centre and Periphery in the Ancient World.* Cambridge.

Sabloff, J. 1986. Interaction among Classic Maya polities: a preliminary examination. In Renfrew, C. and Cherry, J. (eds) *Peer Polity Interaction and Socio-Political Change.* Cambridge, pp. 109–16.

Sahlins, M. and Service, E.R. 1960. *Evolution and Culture.* Ann Arbor.

Service, E.R. 1962. *Primitive Social Organization.* New York.

Shackel, P. 1993 *Personal Discipline and Material Culture: An Archaeology of Annapolis, Maryland, 1695–1870.* Knoxville.

Shanks, M. and Tilley, C. 1987. *Social Theory and Archaeology.* Albuquerque.

Sherratt, A. 1994. What would a Bronze Age world system look like? Relations between temperate Europe and the Mediterranean in later prehistory. *Journal of European Archaeology* 1:1–57.

Singleton, T.A. (ed.) 1985. *The Archaeology of Slavery and Plantation Life.* New York.

Singleton, T.A. 1988. An archaeological framework for slavery and emancipation, 1740–1880. In Leone, M.P. and Potter, P. (eds) *The Recovery of Meaning: Historical Archaeology in the Eastern United States.* Washington D.C., pp. 345–70.

Sørenson, M-L 1987. Material order and cultural classification: the role of bronze objects in the transition from Bronze Age to Iron Age in Scandinavia. In Hodder, I. (ed.) *The Archaeology of Contextual Meanings.* Cambridge, pp. 90–101.

Steward, J. 1955. *Theory of Culture Change.* Urbana.

Stocking, G.W. Jr. 1987. *Victorian Anthropolgy.* New York.

Terray, E. 1975. Classes and class consciousness in the Abron Kingdom of Gyaman. In Bloch, M. (ed.) *Marxist Analyses and Social Anthropology.* London, pp. 85–135.

Wallerstein, I. 1974. *The Modern World-System I: Capitalist Agriculture and the Origins of the European World Economy in the Sixteenth Century.* New York.

Wallerstein, I. 1980. *The Modern World-System II: Mercantilism and the Consolidation of the European World Economy.* New York.

Weiner, A.B. 1986. *Inalienable Possessions: The Paradox of Keeping-While-Giving.* Berkeley.

White, L.A. 1947. Evolutionary stages, progress, and the evaluation of cultures. *Southwestern Journal of Anthropology* 3, 165–92.

Willey, G.R. and Phillips, P. 1958. *Method and Theory in Archaeology*. Chicago.

Wolf, E. 1982. *Europe and the People without History*. Berkeley.

Yoffee, N. 1993. Too many chiefs? (or, safe texts for the '90s). In Yoffee, N. and Sherratt, A. (eds) *Archaeological Theory: Who Sets the Agenda?* Cambridge, pp. 60–78.

4

Peer Polity Interaction and Socio-political Change

Colin Renfrew

Introduction

The concept central to this paper – peer polity interaction – is a process in terms of which the familiar problem of the growth of socio-political systems and of the emergence of cultural complexity can be examined in a fresh and original way. Simply to name a process in itself, of course, establishes nothing. If, however, it brings new problems into clearer focus and offers an avenue towards their investigation, it can prove its usefulness. My claim is that the concept of peer polity interaction does that by bringing to the fore the question of the development of *structures* in society – political institutions, systems of specialised communication in ritual, conventionalised patterns of non-verbal language – and even of the development of ethnic groups and of languages themselves.

Peer polity interaction designates the full range of interchanges taking place (including imitation and emulation, competition, warfare, and the exchange of material goods and of information) between autonomous (i.e. self-governing and in that sense politically independent) socio-political units which are situated beside or close to each other within a single geographical region, or in some cases more widely.

The framework of analysis has two obvious properties. It avoids laying stress upon relations of dominance and subordination between societies, although such relations are indeed common enough and their discussion is, in the archaeological literature, the most frequent approach to questions of culture change. This is seen from the early days of the analysis of the 'diffusion' of culture, through the later treatment of 'primary' and 'secondary' states, to more recent investigations in terms of 'core' and 'periphery'. These are of course all terms which are valid in specific situations, but they have been applied very much more generally than the evidence sometimes warrants.

Secondly, the discussion here, by definition, does not simply consider the socio-political unit in isolation. *Die isolierte Stadt* is a concept whose examination has indeed yielded useful insights, and within which questions of the intensification of production and of the emergence of decision-making hierarchies in the face of increasing population density and other factors, can profitably be discussed. But the *form* of these control hierarchies and of the institutions by which intensification is achieved cannot so effectively be considered in isolation.

Spatial Relations and Power Relations

The underlying principle is conceived here primarily with reference to fairly complex societies (developed chiefdoms or early states), although it no doubt applies in many other instances of both lesser and greater scale and complexity. When we consider most early states, for instance, we find that they do not exist in

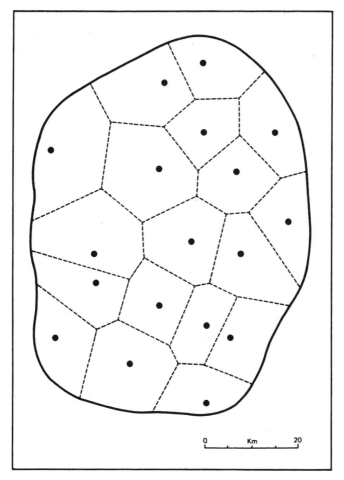

Figure 4.1 [orig. figure 1.1]   The early state module: idealised territorial structure of early civilisations showing the territories and centres of the ESMs within the civilisation (i.e. the area of cultural homogeneity).

isolation. On the contrary, it is possible to identify in a given region several autonomous political centres which, initially at least, are not brought within a single, unified jurisdiction. It is such autonomous territorial units, with their administrative centres which together constitute what is often termed a civilisation. They may be recognised as iterations of what I have called the *early state module* (ESM). Often the ESMs – which in any given case tend to be of approximately the same size – conform to a modular area of approximately 1,500 sq.km. In many early civilisations their number is of the order of ten, within a factor of two or so (Renfrew 1975: 12–21; figure 5.1).

To say this is to draw attention to the distinction, in spatial terms, between an *early state*, and a *civilisation*, seen here as a group or cluster of states sharing a number of common features. These usually include closely similar political institutions, a common system of weights and measures, the same system of writing (if any), essentially the same structure of religious beliefs (albeit with local variations, such as a special patron deity), the same spoken language, and indeed generally what the archaeologist would call the same 'culture', in whatever sense he might choose to use that term. The individual political unit – the states – are often fiercely independent and competitive (figure 4.2). Indeed, not uncommonly, one of them

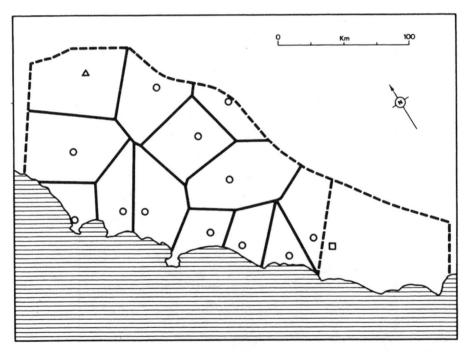

Figure 4.2. [orig. figure 1.2]   The early state module in Etruria: the twelve cities of ancient Etruria (circles) with hypothetical territorial boundaries. Rome is indicated by a square and Fiesole by a triangle. The Etruscan cities competed and were not united under a single rule till Roman times.

may come to achieve political dominance over the others, ultimately uniting the cluster into a single larger unit frequently coterminous in its extent with that of the entire 'civilisation'. This is a *nation state*, sometimes even an *empire*. The individual political units at the time of their independence are the peer polities of our title, whose interactions are the subject of our study.

The same general phenomenon may be seen at other scales, or to put it another way, at other levels of socio-cultural complexity. Precisely the same configuration may be recognised in almost any case where the archaeologist or the anthropologist speaks of chiefdom societies. The separate chiefdoms are effectively autonomous in terms of their power relations (figure 4.3), yet they do not exist in isolation for they have a large number of neighbours, among which each has much

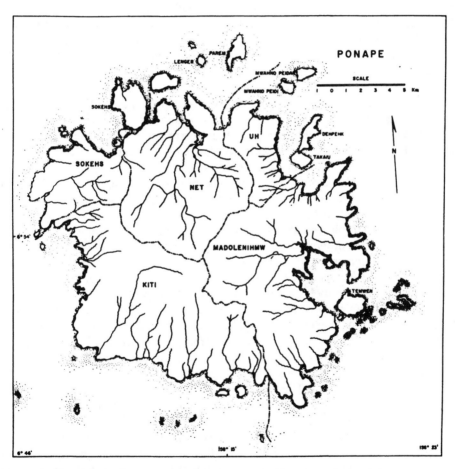

Figure 4.3 [orig. figure 1.3]   Peer polity interactions at chiefdom level: territorial divisions between the five independent tribes of the Pacific island of Ponape in the Caroline Islands
(after Riesenberg 1968:9).

in common with the others. That is not to say that such societies cannot exist in isolation. The case of Easter Island shows that sophisticated chiefdom society is not incompatible with remoteness (although even here the local region was usually divided territorially into a number of peer polities). It demonstrates only that such societies would be different if they did.

Nor is this configuration restricted to stratified or ranked societies. Among supposedly 'egalitarian' agricultural societies individual, politically autonomous units can usually be distinguished, whether as villages or tribal units. And at a greater territorial scale than these are those larger entities identified by many archaeologists and ethnographers where specific features or groups of features have a distribution sometimes taken to define a 'cultural' or ethnic unit. The problem of identifying such units (Clarke 1968: 367) is so acute that the utility of the archaeological concept of the 'culture' has been questioned (Renfrew 1978a:94; Shennan 1978). Nonetheless, the adjacent small polities do share a number of features: often a common language, and generally other symbolic systems, including belief systems. Their recovery from the archaeological record undoubtedly presents many problems. The difficulties are more acute in the case of less complex societies, which generally possess a more narrow range of symbolic expression and less formalised institutions. But ethnographic experience suggests that in nearly all cases of such societies, the extent of these structured symbolic systems is greater than the power span of the individual polities.

It should be clearly understood that the term 'polity' is not in this context intended to suggest any specific scale of organisation or degree of complexity, but simply to designate an autonomous socio-political unit. One of the first questions to face the archaeologist in any context, whether he is dealing with band societies or empires, is the scale of the autonomous unit. The polity is here conceived of as the highest order socio-political unit in the region in question. In many farming societies it will simply be the village or (with a dispersed settlement pattern) the neighbourhood. In others, the various villages or neighbourhoods may be aggregated into a larger unit with some socio-political coherence; such units are often termed 'tribes'. But it is now very clear that not all relatively egalitarian farming societies can realistically be termed 'tribal', nor do some of the loose aggregations or associations which have at times been referred to as tribes have any effective political institutions (Helm 1968). Chiefdoms, on the other hand, certainly do.

In hierarchically structured societies the term 'polity' is likewise reserved for the highest politically autonomous unit. The subordinate units, which may themselves have been independent polities at an earlier time, are often simply administrative or territorial subdivisions. Thus a nation state will normally contain several local areas or 'counties' which, at an earlier stage, may themselves have enjoyed independent status as early states, at that time ranking as polities.

It does not follow that a polity has to be territorially based or defined: many band societies and other egalitarian groups are formally defined in kinship terms. But the polity and its constituent members will nonetheless occupy a preferred area of land and will often enjoy privileged access to resources within it. Nearly all human groups, and hence nearly all polities, thus show territorial behaviour even when they are not formally defined in territorial terms. Nor need a polity display any notably developed or differentiated system of government or of administration; it is sufficient that there should exist procedures for decision-making which habitually work, and which in practice do modify or otherwise affect the behaviour of most of the members. Such a definition applies as much to a hunter-gatherer band as to an early state. It follows that a polity is not subject to the jurisdiction of a higher power.

Structural Homologies

So far the general observation has been made that autonomous political units do not generally exist in isolation, but have neighbours which are analogous in scale to them. But that assertion does not in itself make the simple and evident point that these neighbouring polities display a remarkable range of structural homologies in any specific case. Although this idea may be obvious it has not often been stressed, and it may prove to be remarkably important.

To take a familiar example, a typical Maya ceremonial centre consists of a central complex which is organised around a group of plazas, courtyards and platforms, surrounded by stepped pyramids (figure 4.4). The pyramids are generally approximately square in plan, and each was surmounted by a platform. At the more

Figure 4.4 [orig. figure 1.4]   The Maya ceremonial centre: a reconstruction of the site of Copan, Honduras, in the Late Classic period (drawn by Tatiana Proskouriakoff).

important centres carved stone stelae are found, bearing recognisably similar glyphs, which show the same system of numeration and other similarities.

Now *why* should this be? Why should we find these same *structures* (in the architectural sense) repeated throughout the region of this civilisation? Why are the architectural features of the sites in some respects homologous? Why do the numeration systems display a complete structural homology? Why do the writing systems show similar homologies? These are, we may be sure, simply the material manifestation of further homologies in social organisation, and in the belief system.

There is nothing in biological evolutionary theory that says we should expect such pronounced structural homologies in behaviour among members of a species within a given region, when at the same time finding a very different set of behaviour patterns among members of the same species in a different region. Of course, it could be argued that the various communities where these homologies of behaviour are observed are all the direct lineal descendants of a common ancestor community, whose behaviour patterns they have to some extent conserved. But such a simple explanation, except in a straightforward colonial situation, is rarely valid. Often the different communities developed simultaneously and their structural homologies developed with them. No individual centre can claim primacy for them all.

It would theoretically be perfectly possible for neighbouring early state modules (ESMs) to differ greatly in all these respects. Or at least they could differ as much between themselves within the ambit of a single civilisation as do ESMs when chosen for comparison from different civilisations. In the biological case that would often be so. Communities of a given species of social insect, for instance, show much the same structural homologies when compared with near neighbours as with other communities spatially remote from them. But this is not the experience with human societies.

Evidently the structural homologies which we see among the ESMs of a civilisation are the product of the interactions which have taken place between them, in many cases over a long time period.

In a strictly ecological sense we might regard some of the features which these societies share as necessary adaptations. These would be features which might have evolved quite independently in response to the similar environment in the different communities, each faced with analogous practical problems. Thus we might expect analogies in house structure among communities in arid lands, where mud is the only obvious building material. The *pisé* structures of the early Near East show many similarities with the adobe constructions of the American South-west, and a broadly 'functional' explanation along those lines could easily be constructed. If we are not surprised by similarities between Near Eastern and South-western structures, we have no cause to be any more so by comparable similarities between structures at different sites within the South-west.

Some social forms may be discussed and perhaps 'explained' in the same way. In a general sense, the recognition of the emergence of 'state' societies in different parts of the world implies the assertion of some measure of structural homology.

And since the different areas were (in some cases) not in significant contact with the others, the homologies in these instances cannot be ascribed to interaction.

The homologies upon which we are here commenting are, however, very much more specific than these in terms of structure. We are talking in terms of *specific* architectural forms, *specific* numerical systems, *specific* symbolic systems, and indeed, a very wide range of homologous structures which are seen within the social and projective systems of a given area.

The important question which we are asking is this: To what extent was the very emergence of such systems significantly determined by the interactions whose operation we may infer from the specific structural homologies observed? The distinction here is not a trivial one. We are concerned to explain certain important developments, such as the emergence of a particular governmental form, or the inception of specialised places of worship of monumental scale. In the cases which we have under consideration, these structures took on a specific form – specific, that is, to the civilisation in question, but shared among the constituent ESMs. The explanation for the shared elements within the civilisation, that is to say for the structural homologies, comes from the interactions between the polities – the peer polity interactions. To what extent were these peer polity interactions an indispensable and necessary element in the emergence of such systems, whatever their specific form?

The Analysis of Change

The approach advocated here differs from many earlier ones, where the dynamic for change is often viewed as operating outside the area and thus outside the societies which are the subject of study; this is exogenous change. Alternatively, several scholars have studied a single polity, effectively in isolation, and sought there the dynamic of change within the subsystems operating inside that polity or between those subsystems; this is endogenous change. It is relevant to note some of the properties of these two perspectives. Both offer useful approaches to the study of change, but they omit precisely that factor which is singled out for consideration here, namely the interactions of neighbouring polities of equivalent scale and status.

Exogenous change

Many analyses of societal change have utilised what may be termed 'models of dominance', where the changes within the area in question are explained largely in terms of the influence of, or of contact with, an adjacent area where the socio-political organisation is seen to be in some sense more 'advanced'. It is hardly necessary to recall the many early analyses of state formation and other processes of organisational growth conducted in terms of the 'diffusion' of culture. Morton Fried's use of the terms 'pristine' and 'secondary' to classify state societies into two categories, namely independent (parthenogenetic) and derivative, depending on the degree of purity and autonomy in their antecedents (Fried 1967: 231), is a popular and widely followed example of recent diffusionist thought. Another is the closely related idea of areas which are designated as 'core' and 'periphery' within a broader economic entity or 'world system', to use the terminology of Wallerstein (1974). Such concepts have been found useful in discussing the impact of the Western colonial powers in recent centuries upon what today is sometimes termed the 'Third World'. In my view, however, there are risks in projecting too vigorously onto the prehistoric past the particular circumstances of society, economy and transport which may make these terms appropriate, for instance, to the West Indies in the eighteenth century AD.

It should be noted that an emphasis upon exogenous change is not restricted to the 'cultural historical' school, which traditionally has favoured explanations based upon diffusion, nor to their neo-Marxist successors, in whose works a number of the same ideas are curiously reflected. Some of those advocating a systems approach likewise insist on looking outside the system for their explanatory thrust. Thus Hill (1977: 76) has written: 'no system can change itself; change can only be instigated by outside sources. If a system is in equilibrium, it will remain so unless inputs (or lack of inputs) from outside the system disturb the equilibrium.' Likewise, Saxe (1977: 116) writes: 'the processes that result in systematic change for all systems are and must be initiated by extra-systemic variables'.

It is not, of course, part of the case of Hill or Saxe that the outside sources instigating change need themselves be more complex societies than those under study, whereas that is precisely what the diffusionists and some of the neo-Marxists do argue. But either way, the exogenous approach, while entirely appropriate in those cases where the dominance relationship can clearly be demonstrated, is not an appropriate general model for all early socio-political change. In the words of Gordon Childe (1956: 154) it 'has the effect of relegating to the wings all the action of the prehistoric drama'.

There is a further class of models which may be considered here with the straightforward exogenous ones. These are the ones where there is a major regional diversity which the society manages to exploit. In such cases, the diversity may well be outside the territory of the society, but the organisational response is an internal one. Flannery's explanation for the rise of the Olmec (Flannery 1968), and those of Rathje (1973) and Tourtellot and Sabloff (1972) for the rise of the Classic Maya, fall within this category.

Endogenous change

At first sight the alternative to an emphasis on external forces or influences acting upon the area in question, and leading to transformations within the society which is under study, is to look at the territory and at the polity which it contains, considered in isolation. This has, in effect, been the approach adopted by many workers attempting 'processual' explanations, whether or not the idea of isolation is deliberately introduced as a positive feature of the model.

Many, although not all, of the 'prime mover' approaches hitherto proposed operate in this way. For instance, irrigation and the accompanying intensification of agriculture are often seen to relate functionally with certain organisational changes within the society, and a growth process is sustained by this interaction. In other models population increase is a 'prime mover', and accompanying it there is the ever greater efficiency of economies of scale and of administrative hier-archies, which favour more effective information flow as the number of units to be co-ordinated increases. Many of the most interesting growth models recently proposed, such as those of Wright (1977b), of Johnson (1978), and indeed the processes indicated by Flannery (1972), are essentially of this kind.

A systems approach can harmonise admirably with this view; there is absolutely no need for it to lay stress only upon homeostatis, as the authors cited in the previous section do. Maruyama (1963) long ago emphasised the importance of positive feedback leading to morphogenesis, and I have myself (Renfrew 1972; Cooke and Renfrew 1979) used this notion as the major explanatory mechanism for the emergence of complexity in the Aegean. The treatment has often been essentially an endogenous one.

Peer polity interaction

The peer polity approach is intermediate, from the spatial perspective, between the two preceding ones (figure 4.5). Change is not exogenous to the system as a whole in the region under study, as it generally is when agencies of 'diffusion' are invoked. Nor is it necessary to define the system so widely as to include whole continents, as is so soften the case when 'world systems' are brought into the

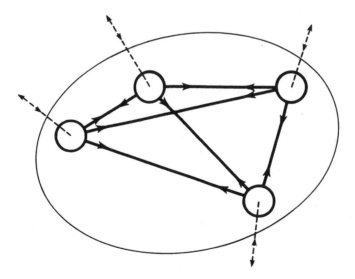

Figure 4.5 [orig. figure 1.5]   Peer polity interaction. Strong interactions between the autonomous socio-political units within the region are of greater significance than external links with other areas.

discussion. But, on the other hand, the locus of change is not situated uniquely within the polity under study, as sometimes seems the case with the endogenous approach.

Instead, change is seen to emerge from the assemblage of interacting polities, that is to say it operates in most cases at the regional level. Interactions at this scale have been largely ignored in many discussions of state formation, where, as noted above, the consideration has often been in terms of 'secondary' states (i.e. exogenous change) or 'pristine' states (where the change is often regarded as endogenous).

Interestingly, it is in the discussion of non-state societies that more careful consideration of significant contacts at the intermediate scale has taken place, notably with Caldwell's useful notion of the 'interaction sphere', initially applied to the North American Hopewell finds (Caldwell 1964).

While analysis at the local level, in terms, for instance, of the intensification of production, is always necessary, and an assessment of the significance of long-distance contacts equally desirable, it is suggested here that in many cases it is the intermediate-scale interactions between local but independent communities which are perhaps the most informative and certainly the most neglected. For it is at this level that those uniformities emerge which sometimes seem to have a significant role in determining the future pattern of development. The significant unit is thus seen, in this perspective, to be the larger community beyond the polity level, comprised of loosely related, yet politically independent, interacting groups. It is here, for instance, that the processes of ethnic formation must in many cases operate, and here too that the foundations for the later emergence of the nation state are laid.

Using the Concept

The real interest of this analytical perspective will emerge below. But it is first necessary to examine the risks of circular reasoning which a careless or loosely defined application of the notion of peer polity interaction can readily carry with it. The risk of circularity is most acute when the aim is not primarily to examine change, but simply to explain the existence in the archaeological record of the rather widespread distribution of a particular feature or trait.

In such a case the first stage might be the recognition and definition of the wide spatial distribution of the feature in question. This distribution, particularly if it is greater in areal extent than other comparable distributions at that time or earlier, clearly stands in need of explanation. It might be thought tempting, then, to assert the operation of some principle of peer polity interaction to explain the distribution – perhaps countering other diffusionist suggestions that the distribution is the result of contacts with some other area. Evidence for the operation of this process of peer polity interaction is then sought, and prominent among the supporting arguments is obviously the widespread uniformity in question.

This, however, is a purely circular argument. In effect, it has been possible to equate the *explanandum* and the *explanans* by separating them by means of a single hypothetical construct, namely peer polity interaction. The distribution is at once seen as explained by peer polity interaction and constitutes the evidence leading us to propose peer polity interaction as an explanation. Such an explanation is empty of meaning.

On the contrary, it is essential to bear in mind that our aim is the explanation of a temporal pattern, namely the changes which have taken place in the degree of complexity in the organisational aspects of a given society; simple trait distributions are not the appropriate subject of the explanatory exercise. And change in complexity must evidently be documented by some measure of complexity.

The causal role of the process of peer polity interaction can more legitimately be asserted when we have evidence of contact prior to the change in question in terms of information flow or the movement of goods, as well as at least the outline of some mechanisms whereby the interaction can be seen to have some role in facilitating the observed change. These circumstances may not be sufficient to document the explanation or even to make it entirely plausible, but they will at least save it from circularity.

Such then are the necessary conditions for the concept of peer polity interaction to be used as an explanatory or interpretive framework. Accompanying this general framework come some empirical observations, which it is worth setting out. For in this volume there is the opportunity to consider several interesting cases where the notion of peer polity interaction may be used. It is desirable therefore to make some positive statements which can be tested.

1   Within a given region with a human population, we shall term the highest order social units (in terms of scale and organisational complexity) 'polities'. It is predicted that, when one polity is recognised, other neighbouring polities of comparable scale and organisation will be found in the same region. (This is simply a statement of the early state module observation, which applies to other and simpler organisational forms, too.)
2   When a significant organisational change, and in particular an increase in complexity, is recognised within one polity, it is generally the case that some of the other polities within the region will undergo the same transformation at about the same time.
3   Leaving out of account the specific criterion which may be used in statement 2 above to recognise organisational change, we can predict that several further new institutional features will appear at about the same time. These may include architectural features, such as monumental buildings of closely similar form; conceptual systems for communicating information, such as writing or other sign systems (including systems of mensuration of number, length, weight and time); assemblages of specific and special artefacts which may be associated with high status in the society in question; and customs (including burial customs) indicative of ritual practices reflecting and perhaps reinforcing the social organisation.
4   The observed features will not be attributable to a single locus of innovation (at least not in the early phases of development), but, so far as the chronological means allow, will be seen to develop within several different polities in the region at about the same time.
5   It is proposed that the process of transformation is frequently brought about not simply as a result of internal processes tending towards intensification, nor in repeated and

analogous responses to a single outside stimulous, but as a result of interaction between the peer polities, which we can examine under the headings of:

(a)   competition (including warfare), and competitive emulation
(b)   symbolic entrainment, and the transmission of innovation
(c)   increased flow in the exchange of goods

6   Moreover, this general assertion – that many organisational transformations may be explained in terms of peer polity interaction – may be elaborated to make a further prediction. In a region with peer polities which are not highly organised internally, but which show strong interactions both symbolically and materially, we predict transformations in these polities associated with the intensification of production and the further development of hierarchical structures for the exercise of power.

The Nature of the Interactions

The nub of the matter, and the real focus of interest, lies in the *nature* of the interactions between these peer polities and *between whom*, precisely, they operate.

The emphasis here is not primarily upon interaction in terms of the exchange of material commodities, but rather in the flow of information of various kinds between the polities. The importance of information exchange as a fundamental component of exchange systems has been made elsewhere (Renfrew 1975: 22–3), but here we can go further and consider the importance of such symbolic exchange even in the absence of trade in material goods.

It may be suggested that the emergence of new institutions in society can often profitably be considered in terms both of intensification of production, and of peer polity interaction. Many significant social transformations are accompanied by increased production (of foodstuffs and other materials), which permits not only increased population density but also the accumulation of production beyond subsistence (PBS), which in turn allows the employment of craft specialists and other personnel at the behest of the élite, which in some cases controls that PBS. Within that framework, any interactions which serve to promote intensification of production are relevant to the discussion.

Warfare, to the extent that it uses up resources (whether as a result of destruction and looting, or in supporting an army), will promote intensification if it takes place on a sufficiently prolonged basis. (On the other hand, if it results in a great many deaths, so that food production can in consequence be substantially reduced, the converse is the case). Warfare (figure 4.6) is clearly one form of interaction between peer polities which may favour both intensification and the emergence of hierarchical institutions (initially for military purposes) within the various polities (Carneiro 1970; Webster 1975).

Competitive emulation is another form of interaction where neighbouring polities may be spurred to ever greater displays of wealth or power in an effort to achieve higher inter-polity status. There is a clear analogy here with individual behaviour, for instance in the well-known case of gift exchange, where positive reciprocity can be used to enhance status. The same process operates at group level in the

Figure 4.6 [orig. figure 1.6]   Warfare: a *condottiere* of Renaissance Italy, depicted outside a well-fortified hill town (Guidoriccio da Fogliano, in the painting attributed to Simone Martini in the Palazzo Pubblico, Siena).

familiar example of the potlatch, where the chief of a group engages the status of the whole group in the munificence of his feast-giving and gift-giving. This is a process favouring intensification, in that the resources utilised fall within the category of production beyond subsistence. But in an interesting way the emulation consists not only in the making of expensive gestures. The magnitude of these gestures has to be measured along some scale, and the gestures are thus similar in kind. If status is achieved, for instance, by erecting a particular kind of monument, the neighbouring polity will most readily acquire greater status by doing bigger and better.

There is reason to think that this is a significant factor in peer polity interaction. In several cases where there are concentrations of surprisingly large monuments – for instance the image *ahu* of Easter Island (figure 4.7) or the stone 'temples' of Malta – competitive emulation may help account for their otherwise rather puzzling scale. Within the present context of discussion it may in part also help explain the structural homologies of their form.

It would be wrong, however, to think of all the relevant interactions as essentially competitive. There is another process, perhaps of greater relevance, which I should like to term *symbolic entrainment*. This process entails the tendency for a developed symbolic system to be adopted when it comes into contact with a less developed one with which it does not strikingly conflict. For one thing, a well-developed symbolic system carries with it an assurance and prestige which a less developed and less elaborate system may not share. These remarks apply, for instance, to the adoption of writing systems (figure 4.8) as much as to the adop-

Figure 4.7 [orig. figure 1.7]   Competitive emulation: an image *ahu* of Easter Island, with colossal statue. The *ahu* were focal points within tribal territories.

tion of systems of social organisation (such as some of the institutions of kingship). We may imagine, for instance, in the Mesopotamia of the Protoliterate period, that several cities had centralised economies where an adequate system of recording would be a bureaucratic advantage, and indeed where some steps towards such a system had independently been taken. A really effective system developed in one would find ready adoption in many of the others.

A similar view may be developed for the adoption, or at least the parallel growth, of a political or administrative system, including that of kingship itself. The very existence of such a social order in one polity could tend to further the stability of a similar order in a neighbouring one. For it is the very nature of power that it is held by a few and accepted by many. The act of acceptance implies a sort of willing suspension of disbelief, an acquiescence in a belief structure or political philosophy, which neighbouring belief systems can do much to influence.

The *transmission of innovation* in a sense embraces symbolic entrainment within its scope, but refers also to innovations which are not, or do not at first seem to be, of a symbolic nature. Such innovations are perhaps 'transmitted' within the peer polities of the interacting group, and at first sight this would seem to be an example of the familiar process of 'diffusion'. Yet it differs from the standard view of that

Figure 4.8 [orig. figure 1.8]   Symbolic entrainment: writing in early Mesopotamia emerged in a number of cities, probably simultaneously – protoliterate tablets of limestone found at Kish, *c*.3500 BC, length *c*.6.4.cm.

process, not only in that the peer polities have the status of more-or-less equal partners (which is not the case in most studies of diffusion), but, as I have argued elsewhere (Renfrew 1978c) the crux of the matter, the true innovation, is not the original invention of the new feature or process but rather its widespread acceptance by the society or societies in question. Acceptance of an invention in one society may facilitate or even sanction it within another in which the invention itself may have occurred at an earlier time.

Although the emphasis here is primarily upon the exchange of information, there is no doubt that an *increased flow in the exchange of goods* can itself further structural transformations. For, clearly, if a society acquires an increasing proportion of its gross annual turnover from outside its own territory, those engaged in exchange are likely to become more numerous and new institutions may develop to cope with the reception, allocation and distribution of goods. The same applies to exports as to imports, and here the significant feature may be the increased level of production required to produce the materials to be exported. This may favour craft specialisation, perhaps mass production, and certainly other organisational features not hitherto required. All this is, of course, simply the familiar process of economic growth based partly on a developing import and export trade, and there is nothing very specific to peer polity interaction about it. Indeed, it applies to, and has been used with equal validity on, dominance models, where a more developed socio-political organisation enters into economic relations with, and perhaps 'exploits', a less developed one. Here we return to the neo-Marxist 'world system' approach. But economic growth is not an exclusive property of unequal partnerships. Moreover, with that growth and with the development of new organisational institutions, there is plenty of scope for the processes of emulation and symbolic entrainment to operate and hence to influence the specific forms and structures of these emergent organisations.

These observations only begin the task of considering the range of significant interactions operating between polities. And while the discussion has, for the sake of example, dealt primarily with early state societies, many of these points apply also to less highly structured social formations.

They also hint at problems as yet hardly broached by archaeologists, and rarely by anthropologists. One of these relates to the formation of ethnic groups. How do such groups form, sometimes over a long time period, and what governs their scale and extent? The same questions are pertinent to the understanding of the behaviour of specific languages. What determines the area over which a particular language is spoken and the number of people who speak it, and the expansion or contraction in its linguistic boundaries? There are few ready answers to such questions at present. Yet we are approaching them when we consider and seek to explain the widespread distribution in space of certain archaeological phenomena, such as Beaker burials, or Hopewell ceremonial behaviour. Our approach, however, specifically does not make assumptions about the equivalence of linguistic or ethnic or 'cultural' groups. It seeks instead a fresh grasp of the interaction processes underlying them.

An Example

The trajectories of development in the Greek islands at different times offer an appropriate example of the relevance of this approach. During the first millennium BC many individual and rather small islands achieved the explicit organisational structure which since the time of Plato and Aristotle has been the paradigm instance of the state – in this case the Greek city state. These islands, despite their small size, were self-governing, had a well-defined constitution, were subject to explicit law, issued coinage in the case of Naxos and Paros, and were famed for their accomplishments in sculpture (figures 4.9, 4.10). Yet it should be noted that the population of each was generally not more than 5,000 persons, and there was often little hierarchy of settlement since the population was generally concentrated in a single urban centre. Analogous developments can be seen in the third and second millennia BC, culminating in the second millennium in the emergence of small urban centres which lasted until the general organisational collapses in the Aegean before 1000 BC.

In the past, attempts have been made to represent both the Greek city states, and their Bronze Age predecessors in the Minoan and Mycenaean periods, as representing a 'secondary' civilisation, with states of earlier origin in the Near East or Egypt seen as 'primary'. But this view has increasingly been called into question (despite undisputed evidence for trading contacts with the Near East). Instead, it is possible to see the course of development in this area as fundamentally an Aegean one, a response to a number of processes which can be analysed primarily in Aegean terms, without denying a real role to external trade.

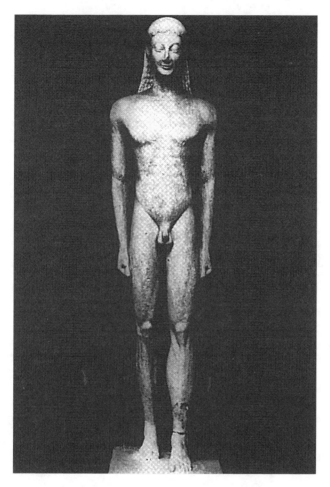

Figure 4.9 [orig. figure 1.9]   The *kouros*: life-sized male statue of marble seen widely in the city states of Greece in the sixth-century BC. The form is highly standardised, which illustrates a high degree of interaction between the independent cities.
(From Melos).

In this early period – certainly in the first millennium, and perhaps earlier – the communities in question were politically independent, although they were later incorporated into a larger political unit, dominated by Athens.

Attempts to explain the emergence of the state for any individual polity, considered in isolation, soon run into difficulties, however. In the case of Melos (Renfrew and Wagstuff 1982), for instance, it is possible to identify some of the processes of agricultural and industrial intensification which accompanied and underlay state formation, and to identify some of the political and cultural institutions involved. But while the intensification may in a sense be endogenous to Melos, the social, cultural and religious framework in which it took place is to a large extent shared with other islands (the peer polities) and other city states in the Greek world.

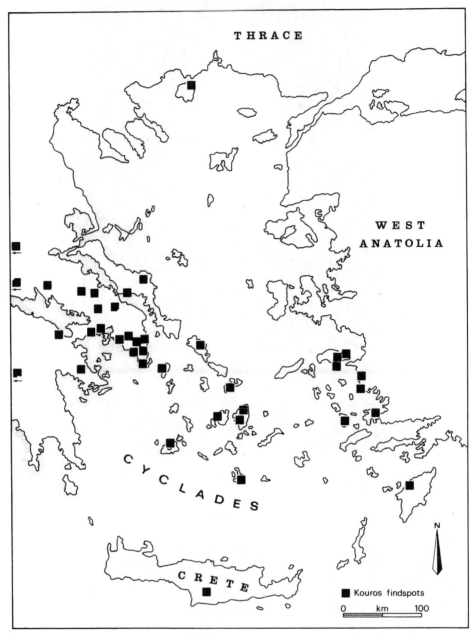

Figure 4.10 [orig. figure 1.10]   The distribution of *kouroi* in the Aegean: one indication of the extent of symbolic interaction in the sixth-century BC. (Nine finds outside the Aegean, notably from Italy and Sicily, are not shown.)

An entirely autonomous, endogenous explanation falls down: it is difficult to think of Melos, for instance, had it existed in magnificent solitude (the Easter Island scenario), beginning the move towards statehood. But at the same time Melos is not secondary to any identifiable primary centre. (The dominance of Athens then lay in the future.) The small states of Greece emerged *together*, pulling each other up by the bootstraps, as it were. What they shared were the common elements of Greek civilisation: language, religion, shared history, similar (but not identical) institutions, equivalent agricultural and commercial practices. If the exogenous and the isolated – endogenous explanations fall down, the focus must be upon the interactions among these peer polities which made possible what in some ways was a shared trajectory of development (notwithstanding their jealously guarded political independence). And while there were local variations in resources – marble in Paros, gold in Siphnos, particularly good grapes in Naxos – the model for growth cannot be based upon intra-regional diversity, any more than it can rest primarily upon inter-regional trade with areas outside the Aegean.

The interactions which merit study in this case are largely of a symbolic nature. For in the first millennium BC the new and emergent features, which ultimately came to characterise Greek civilisation as a whole, were not primarily technological. The solid agricultural base had been established centuries earlier (Renfrew 1982a). Instead, it is the new institutions that gave the civilisation its character and shaped its eventual trajectory. The importance of the Greek temple (figure 4.11), as the focus of religious expression is one such element. Pride in civic autonomy is

Figure 4.11 [orig. figure 1.11]   The Doric temple, the most striking civic manifestation of Greekness: The "Temple of Concord" at Akragas (Agrigento) in Sicily.

another, and this found significant commercial expression in the development of silver coinage throughout much of the region.

The interactions operating here undoubtedly included warfare, of which the earliest records certainly speak, and there are plenty of examples of competitive emulation – for instance in the magnificent treasuries and monuments which the richer islands (including Naxos and Siphnos) erected at pan-Hellenic sanctuaries such as Delphi and Delos, in an expression of civic pride (figure 4.12). But most of the simultaneous developments throughout this region can conveniently be subsumed under the term 'symbolic entrainment', as a first step in the discussion. To do so, however, simply underlines the need to understand the cultural dynamics by which important innovations, such as coinage, or large sculpture, or the adoption of the alphabet, came to be taken up so vigorously in so many different small and autonomous centres. There was a ferment of activity in the seventh, sixth and fifth centuries BC, which only at the end of that period resulted in the dominance of the Athenian or the Spartan state. Similarly, in the third

Figure 4.12 [orig. figure 1.12]   The Treasury of the Athenians at the sanctuary at Delphi: an outstanding example of civic pride and display, and dedicated to the god Apollo.

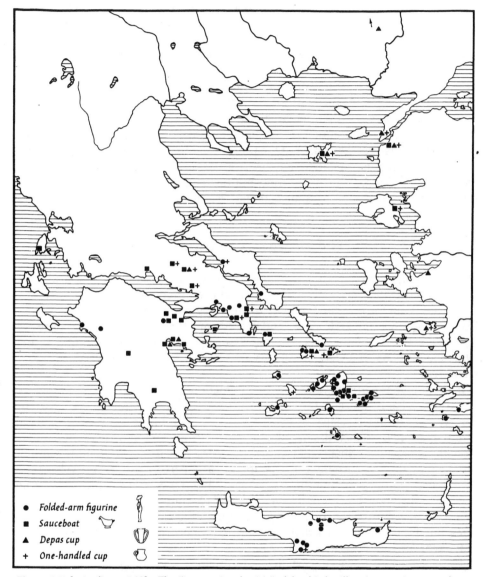

Folded-arm figurine

Sauceboat

Depas cup

One-handled cup

Figure 4.13 [orig. figure 1.13] The "international spirit" of the third millennium BC Aegean, whose small-scale interactions anticipated those of the early Greek cities by two thousand years. The most characteristic products of the Cycladic Islands were symbolic: the marble folded-arm female figurine whose distribution is shown. But no region of Greece was dominant at this time.

millennium BC it is possible to speak of an 'international spirit' (figure 4.13) operating *within* the Aegean, which culminated five hundred years later in the
emergence of the various centres of the Minoan and subsequently the Mycenaean
civilisation.

In the first millennium, and perhaps earlier, there are underlying ethnic patterns,
whose role in channelling these developments has not yet been analysed in a
processual framework. It is, of course, common enough to stress the significance
of the Greek language and to assert the 'Greekness' of Hellenic civilisation. But
hitherto these have been particularistic statements, claims – perfectly warranted
claims, in a sense – of uniqueness. At the same time, one can now see them more
clearly as a rather good example of the processes which are here under consideration. Their further investigation may prove rewarding on both the general and the
specific level. Snodgrass, in his contribution to this volume, has developed a
number of the relevant ideas, some of them already introduced in his earlier works.

The Emergence of Structure

The foregoing example perhaps illustrates the need for an analysis of this kind, at
a level intermediate between that of a close examination of processes within a
single polity on the one hand, and gross inter-regional, 'core–periphery' comparisons on the other. But in doing so, and in focusing attention on the importance, for
an understanding of the processes of change, of the specific institutions and
symbolic systems involved, it still leaves several questions unasked, let alone
answered.

In particular, the precise nature of the interactions, in personal terms, remains to
be explored. For instance, in the case of acts of competitive emulation – such as the
construction of the Treasury of the Siphnians at Delphi – exactly who, or what
group of people, reached the decision to construct it? And in precisely what way
were these persons influenced by earlier comparable acts of conspicuous community display (for instance the construction of earlier treasuries there)? Whom did
they hope to impress, both inside their own polity (i.e. Siphnos, which is far from
Delphi) and amongst the various peer polities? Of course the data of archaeology,
or indeed of early history, are not able to supply precise answers to all these questions. But it is pertinent to ask them if we are to frame an adequately detailed model
of the working of the system.

These very questions suggest that one obvious and important nexus is the
limited group of persons who are influential in making decisions, and who, in a
decision-making hierarchy, are located at a high level. Within the agonistic framework set out by Marx, these individuals are conceived of as manipulating
resources, symbols and people in such a way as to strengthen their own position
within their society with respect to other classes or social groups. This is clearly a
legitimate framework of analysis: to examine their control of communications, and
hence of interactions, in essentially self-interested terms. But it does not complete
the analysis; even if they were acting purely altruistically, they would remain the

Figure 4.14 [orig. figure 1.14]   The investment of resources in the media of internal communication: the great Ziggurat of Ur in southern Mesopotamia, photographed during excavation.

decision-making group. It is relevant to explore how the actions, including the symbolic actions of other peer polities, impinge upon them and how their own actions come to be known and perceived by the members of other polities. The distinct and related question as to how the interactions between the polities are seen and interpreted by others within them who are less centrally placed in the decision-making process, and how their reactions nonetheless affect that process, is also an interesting one. Nor is this as abstract as it at first sounds: most early state societies invested substantial resources in the media of internal communication (figure 4.14), and all the great buildings and large-scale monuments erected within them can be interpreted in this way.

If we are studying peer polity interaction, it is thus of particular importance to consider the circumstances in which individual members of different polities are likely to have met, circumstances where competition and emulation could operate (figure 4.15), and where symbolic utterances or displays could have their effect. Obviously this could happen on neutral ground, and one may suggest that the whole phenomenon of pan-polity gatherings is one of special interest (figure 4.16). The pan-Hellenic games and festivals at centres such as Olympia, Isthmia, Nemea, Delphi and Delos (figure 4.17) are an excellent example, and no doubt many other early state societies had some kind of framework where members of different

Figure 4.15 [orig. figure 1.15]   Investment in communication through games: the Late Classic Maya ball court at Copan, Honduras.

polities came into contact. Even warfare can operate in this manner: the way in which war in some New Guinea societies often takes place without serious consequences of territorial loss or gain, and sometimes without great loss of life, emphasises that war can be a channel for communication as much as for destruction. The role of the warrior as a communicator, for instance in heroic societies like those of the Celts, would prove an interesting field of study.

Such questions as these need to be asked. Until we have some clearer idea of the way communications within and between non-literate (and early literate) societies are structured, we shall not properly understand the change and development of their institutions. Yet happily, since those communications were to a large extent effected by means of material symbols, the archaeological record has much to offer about them.

In discussing these differential patterns of communication within and between social groupings, we are, of course impinging upon a field which has been considered by sociologists. Barnes (1969), for instance, has considered decision-making in terms of a social network approach, utilising graph theory. Network analysis studies (Boissevain and Mitchell 1973) have the merit of applying formal and quantitative techniques to the examination of specific aspects of social groups. Braun (this volume: Ch.9) and others have advocated a network approach of rather a

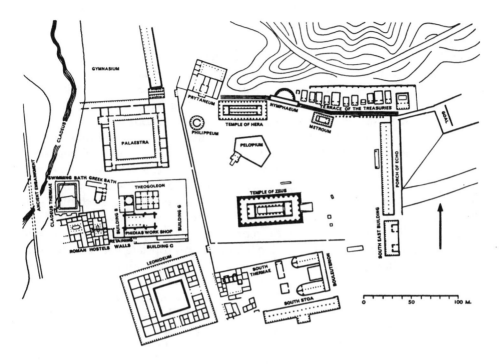

Figure 4.16 [orig. figure 1.16]   Plan of the great pan-Hellenic sanctuary, dedicated to Zeus, at Olympia, indicating (at the top) the treasuries dedicated by the individual city states whose athletes regularly competed and won there
(after Mallwitz).

Figure 4.17 [orig. figure 1.17]   Reconstructed elevations of three of the treasuries at the pan-Hellenic sanctuary of Apollo at Delphi, dedicated by the citizens of Cnidus, Massalia and Siphnos. Siphnos was an independent island state with a population of less than 4,000 people
(after Dinsmoor 1950: Fig. 50).

different sort, which perhaps stands closer to that used by contemporary geographers (e.g. Haggett and Chorley 1969). Simulations of a related kind have indeed been conducted in considering examples of morphogenesis in self-organising systems, such as the development of urban structure (Allen 1982).

In a sense, of course, any pattern of interactions can be regarded or defined as a network, and, as Braun indicates, to do this establishes a useful relationship with work undertaken in other fields. Such an approach is perhaps most effective when the network is a relatively undifferentiated one – when the nodes, for instance, may be visualised as single individuals, or perhaps as small village communities, which stand in a symmetrical relationship one to another. With very simple polities of this kind the network need not be too overpoweringly complicated. But when the polities themselves are more complex, as Braun indicates, with pronounced hierarchical structures within them, the degree of differentiation of activities – or of subsystems of the culture system – is such that the linkages between individuals within the polities can no longer be represented as single edges in a simple network. They become multidimensional, and an appropriate network diagram would need to show several different channels linking each pair of interested individuals. It is precisely with this differentiation in channels of communication, with the different *kinds* of interactions, between individuals and between polities, that we are concerned here. And in my own view the problem for research, to which the peer polity interaction approach is designed to respond, is not so much the examination of the spatial configuration of the interactions, which the network approach is well equipped to undertake, but rather their very nature. Who impresses whom, and how, and what effect does that have upon the future actions of both? That question has already been posed by some workers within the framework of the endogenous approach, and indeed answered in a rather simplistic way by others within the framework of the exogenous approach, where, for instance it has been hypothesised that petty chieftains have used imported manufactured goods to amaze the rural populace and thereby enhance their own status. It becomes a more interesting and complex problem when considered within the context of the emerging symbolic and communication systems which are shared by a number of peer polities.

In each of the papers which follow there is a concern with what I have termed the structural homologies visible between neighbouring and autonomous polities, and in the interactions responsible for them. This emphasis on forms, and on symbolic interactions, distinguishes our approach to some extent from that of Barbara Price (1977), with whose cluster interaction model the present approach has otherwise much in common.

It could be argued that our emphasis on specific structures makes our approach a 'structuralist' one, and in a sense this is so. We are concerned with social and symbolic forms which are specific to human society, and are the product of the specifically human ability to conceptualise. Our very emphasis on structural homologies may to some evoke comparisons with French *structuralisme*. But our work differs fundamentally from that approach in its concern with diachronic processes, with specific development through time. Our observations, like those of all archaeology, are rooted in the material world and this, for all its obvious limitations, gives to them a certain concreteness not always obvious in the discussion of myth and oral tradition.

Our aim, however, is not to ascribe labels, or to define new 'isms', but to ask fruitful questions. These do indeed pertain to human beliefs and human symbolic systems, and to the way human societies have sought to conceive their world in order to shape it more effectively. The framework which we have chosen to adopt allows the same questions to be posed in relation to societies in different parts of the world, and of very differing degrees of complexity. The intention is to develop a cross-cultural approach, with the hope of obtaining general insights.

Acknowledgements

The following are gratefully acknowledged as sources or as copyright holders for the illustrations to this chapter: figure 4.3 [orig. figure 1.3], Copyright, Smithsonian Institution, Washington D.C.; figures 4.4 and 4.15 [orig. figures 1.4 and 1.15], Peabody Museum, Harvard; figure 4.8 [orig. figure 1.8], Ashmolean Museum, Oxford; figure 4.9 [orig. figure 1.9], National Museum, Athens; figures 4.11, 4.12, 4.16, and 4.17 [orig. figures 1.11, 1.12, 1.16 and 1.17], Thames and Hudson, London, and Hirmer Verlag, Munich (from Berve and Gruben 1963); figure 4.14 [orig. figure 1.14], British Museum.

References

Allen, P. M. 1982. The genesis of structure in social systems: the paradigm of self-organisation. In C. Renfrew, M. J. Rowlands and B. A. Segraves (eds.) *Theory and Explanation in Archaeology: The Southampton Conference*, pp. 347–76. New York, Academic Press.

Barnes, J. A. 1969. Graph theory and social networks: a technical comment on connectedness and connectivity. *Sociology* 3: 215–32.

Boissevain, J. and Mitchell, J. C. (eds.) 1973. *Network Analysis Studies in Human Interaction*. The Hague, Mouton.

Caldwell, J. A. 1964. Interaction spheres in prehistory. In J. R. Caldwell and R. L. Hall (eds.) *Hopewellian Studies* (Illinois State Museum Papers 12, No, 6), 133–43.

Carneiro, R. L. 1970. A theory of the origin of the state. *Science* 169: 733–8.

Childe, V. G. 1956. *Piecing Together the Past*. London, Routledge and Kegan Paul.

Clarke, D. L. 1968. *Analytical Archaeology*. London, Methuen.

Cooke, K. L. and Renfrew, C. 1979. An experiment in the simulation of culture changes. In C. Renfrew and K. L. Cooke (eds.) *Transformations: Mathematical Approaches to Culture Change*, pp. 327–48. New York: Academic Press.

Dinsmoor, W. B. 1950. *The Architecture of Ancient Greece*. London, Batsford.

Flannery, K. V. 1968. The Olmec and the Valley of Oaxaca: a model for inter-regional interaction in Formative times. In E. P. Benson (ed.) *Dumbarton Oaks Conference on the Olmec*, pp. 79–110. Washington D.C., Dumbarton Oaks.
    1972. The cultural evolution of civilizations. *Annual Review of Ecology and Systematics* 3: 399–426.

Fried, M. H. 1967. *The Evolution of Political Society*. New York, Random House.

Haggett, R. and Chorley, R. J. 1969. *Network Analysis in Geography*. London, Edward Arnold.

Helm, J. (ed.) 1968. *Essays on the Problem of the Tribe*. New York, American Ethnological Society.

Hill, J. N. 1977. Systems theory and the explanation of change. In J. N. Hill (ed.) *Explanation of Prehistoric Change*, pp. 59–104. Albuquerque, University of New Mexico Press.

Johnson, G. A. 1978. Information sources and the develpment of decision-making organisations. In C. L. Redman et al. (eds.) *Social Archaeology: Beyond Subsistence and Dating*, pp. 87–112. New York, Academic Press.

Maruyama, M. 1963. The second cybernetics: deviation amplifying mutual causal processes. *American Scientist* 51: 164–79.

Price, B. J. 1977. Shifts in production and organisation: a cluster interaction model. *Current Anthropology* 18: 209–34.

Rathje, W. L. 1973. Models for mobile Maya: a variety of constraints. In C. Renfrew (ed.) *The Explanation of Culture Change: Models in Prehistory*, pp. 731–60. London, Duckworth.

Renfrew, C. 1972. *The Emergence of Civilisation: The Cyclades and the Aegean in the Third Millennium BC*. London, Methuen.

1975. Trade as action at a distance: questions of integration and communication, In J. A. Sabloff and C. C. Lamberg-Karlovsky (eds.) *Ancient Civilisation and Trade*, pp. 3–59. Albuquerque: University of New Mexico Press.

1978a. Space, time and polity. In J. Friedman and M. J. Rowlands (eds.) *The Evolution of Social Systems*, pp. 89–112. London, Duckworth.

1978b. The anatomy of innovation. In D. Green, C. Haselgrove and M. Spriggs (eds.) *Social Organisation and Settlement* (BAR S47), pp. 89–117. Oxford, British Archaeological Reports.

1982. Polity and power: interaction, intensification and exploitation. In C. Renfrew and J. M. Wagstaff (eds.) *An Island Polity: The Archaeology of Exploitation in Melos*, pp. 264–90. Cambridge, University Press.

Renfrew, C. and Wagstaff, J. M. (eds.) 1982. *An Island Polity: The Archaeology of Exploitation in Melos*. Cambridge, University Press.

Riesenberg, S. H. 1968. *The Native Polity of Ponape* (Smithsonian Contributions to Archaeology 10). Washington D.C., Smithsonian Institution Press.

Saxe, A. 1977. On the origin of evolutionary processes: state formation in the Sandwich Islands. In J. N. Hill (ed.) *Explanation of Prehistoric Change*, pp. 105–52. Albuquerque, University of New Mexico Press.

Shennan, S. J. 1978. Archaeological 'cultures': an empirical investigation. In I. Hodder (ed.) *The Spatial Organisation of Culture*, pp. 113–39. London, Duckworth.

Tourtellot, G. and Sabloff, J. A. 1972. Exchange systems among the Maya. American Antiquity 37: 126–35.

Wallerstein, I. 1974. *The Modern World System*. London, Academic Press.

Webster, D.L. 1975. Warfare and evolution of the state: a reconsideration. *American Antiquity* 40: 464–70.

Wright, H. T. 1977. Toward an explanation of the origin of the state. In J. N. Hill (ed.) *Explanation of Prehistoric Change*, pp. 215–30. Albuquerque, University of New Mexico Press.

5

The Ancient Economy, Transferable Technologies and the Bronze Age World-system: A View from the Northeastern Frontier of the Ancient Near East

Phil L. Kohl

Scholarly reaction to the publication of I. Wallerstein's initial volume (1974) on the modern world system was surprisingly strong. Initial enthusiastic responses were elicited from historians of the *Annales* school and from historians and anthropologists working within a more critical or Marxist tradition. Opponents represented an equally broad spectrum of political and academic traditions with criticisms extending from empirical inaccuracies to theoretical objections over Wallerstein's view of history or, more specifically, over the teleological determinism implicit in his reified concept of a supra-historical world system (e.g. Brenner 1977; Hunt 1978; for a balanced but critical assessment Wolf 1982: 21–3). The work clearly was related to the writings of dependency theorists, such as Amin (1974) and Frank (1976), but was distinguished by its longer and more detailed historical perspective.

Ancient and medieval historians were less drawn into the creative furor stimulated by the study for the simple reason that Wallerstein was interested in the formation of the modern world system, which he viewed as a process that began in the sixteenth century and which he considered qualitatively distinct from earlier large-scale developments. Ancient empires, which encompassed 'worlds' of their day, functioned and were structured differently from the unique system that ushered in the modern era:

> Empires were a constant feature of the world scene for 5,000 years. There were continuously several such empires in various parts of the world at any given point of time. The political centralization of an empire was at one and the same time its strength and weakness. . . . Political empires are a primitive means of economic domination. It is the social achievement of the modern world, if you will, to have invented the technology that makes it possible *to increase the flow of the surplus from the lower strata to the upper strata, from the periphery to the center, from the majority to the minority by eliminating the 'waste' of too cumbersome a political structure.* (1974, 15–16, emphasis added)

The modern world system is distinguished by primarily economic as opposed to political, cultural, or presumably even ideological linkages among its constituent parts. Political diversity, primacy of the economic sphere, and control and development of a technology capable of supporting and expanding such a system are the critical variables, according to Wallerstein, that distinguish the modern era from ancient and medieval times. The modern world system also is characterized by a highly complex global division of labor which results in major regional differences: some areas become exporters of primary resources, while others produce and successfully market industrial products. The exchange uniting different regions is not symmetrical but structurally weighted or tipped in favor of the politically more powerful and technologically advanced core states of the West. The exchange relations which develop are thus beneficial to the core areas and detrimental to the peripheries which essentially are exploited or 'underdeveloped' by these relations. Wallerstein's model becomes even more complex when he shows how specific nation-states' core status shifts over time and how certain countries, termed semi-peripheries, provide a built-in flexibility to the world system.

The question naturally arises as to whether or not Wallerstein is correct in his insistence that such a system only emerged during the beginnings of the modern era in the sixteenth century AD. One intelligent and generally laudatory review of Wallerstein's original study criticizes the book precisely for its perpetuation of this great divide between modern and ancient/medieval times:

> From the point of view of social science, Wallerstein's most significant contribution is the suggestion that processes of interaction and unequal exchange might explain events not only in Third World areas transformed by European hegemony in the nineteenth and twentieth centuries, but in earlier periods within Europe itself. This establishes a unity of theory between Western and non-Western peoples, the absence of which has long been problematic in unilineal models of change whose ethnocentrisms are consistent with their inability to account for the disparity between Europe's precocious advances and other people's 'lag'. . . . The Modern World-System suffers from too narrow an application of its own theory. For, although Wallerstein admires Owen Lattimore's description of the differentiation process according to which ancient Chinese civilization 'gave birth to barbarism', . . . he does not view the pre-capitalist world as systematically integrated through the operations of world economic forces. (Schneider 1977:20)

According to the reviewer, Wallerstein too easily dismisses the external economic linkages forged by non-Western political empires, denigrates the effects and importance of earlier long-distance trade in luxury goods, and, consequently, fails to adequately explain or understand the motivations and stimuli which led to the Great Discoveries and the beginnings of the modern era. The book suffers, in short, from an unnecessary, self-limiting ethnocentrism which bestows special status upon modern European development.

Thus, through their insistence upon the unique features of the modern capitalist world system, Wallerstein and his disciples join the ranks of the 'substantivists' in economic anthropology and the 'primitivists' in ancient history who qualitatively distinguish ancient from modern economies and who argue against the applicability of contemporary economic theory to primitive and ancient social formations. Perhaps the most celebrated theorist of this school, Karl Polanyi, set his Great

Transformation in the nineteenth, not the sixteenth, century and emphasized different factors, such as the relative lack of alienation, commercial exchange, and formal marketplaces in precapitalist societies. Wallerstein's view of earlier times is less developed but also far less utopian: a politically non-unified world-economy never emerged in ancient times for the technology necessary 'to increase the flow of surplus' sufficient to maintain it was never developed.

This chapter cannot review, much less settle, this hallowed, perhaps irresoluble debate (cf. Pearson 1957 for a now dated over view but cf. now Hall 1985) over qualitative or only quantitative differences between modern and precapitalist societies. Application of Wallerstein's model of a world system to earlier periods does not imply a rejection of the substantivist argument for essential differences or incomparabilities, a position which grapples with other issues besides the articulation of separate societies in external networks of exchange. The important problem is to determine the degree to which the world system's model can be employed to elucidate the development of precapitalist societies. Points of non-correspondence may be as instructive as similarities, or, in other words, the utility of the model can only be assessed by attempting to apply it to earlier social formations. This chapter will selectively review archaeological materials from early class societies in the ancient Near East that illustrate external exchange relations over widely separate areas.

Political Empires and Intercultural Exchange in the Ancient Near East

Wallerstein's characterization and dismissal of earlier world-empires must be examined in greater detail. According to Wallerstein, empires are political units; they expand by incorporating new territories and obtain necessary resources and materials through the coercive imposition of tributes and taxes. Goods flow to the political center and – in classic Polanyi-like fashion – are redistributed by the State according to its own specific rules of allocation. Earlier 'world-economies' may have existed, but they always were transformed into political empires. The argument for the unique character of modern times again seems to emphasize differences in the forces of production or have a technological base:

> *The modern world-economy might have gone in that same direction [towards empire] – indeed it has sporadically seemed as though it would – except that the techniques of modern capitalism and the technology of modern science, the two being somewhat linked as we know, enabled this world-economy to thrive, produce, and expand without the emergence of a unified political structure. (1974:16)*

Certainly, ancient political empires levied tributes on conquered areas and imposed taxes, either of labor services of goods, on its subjected citizenry. Some early civilizations may have expanded politically, as Wallerstein suggests, to incorporate areas from which they obtained essential resources. Although known almost exclusively from archaeological data, the Harappan or Indus Valley civilization may have expanded in precisely this fashion. Unlike the Old Assyrian settlement at Kanesh (cf. below) where traders adopted the local material culture, entire Harappan colonies, containing exclusively Harappan materials, have been discovered well beyond the confines of the Indus Valley. The Harappan settlements at Shortughai on the Ai Khanoum plain of northeastern Afghanistan provide the most striking illustration of this difference (cf. Francfort and Pottier 1978). J. Shaffer (1982:44–5) has suggested that the distributional evidence from Harappan sites indicates that foreign trade was unimportant to this early civilization for Harappans built their complex social order through elaborate *internal* exchange networks that redistributed local resources throughout their vast domains; even more intriguingly, Lamberg–Karlovsky (n.d.) recently has proposed that the striking uniformity of Harappan remains and other evidence peculiar to this early civilization may indicate that their society was structured by some incipient *caste* principles which require separate tasks to be performed by specific endogamous groups.

Regardless of whether or not these interpretations are correct, Harappan materials always have been considered enigmatic, if not unique, and its pattern of expansion is not shared by the best-documented early civilization: Mesopotamia. Indeed, consideration of the development of early Mesopotamian civilization reveals that, at least, two features of Wallerstein's analysis are incorrect: (a) 'world-economies' and political empires were not always commensurate with one another, and (b) there existed no irreversible trend for the former to transform itself into the latter. Mesopotamian civilization developed over the course of roughly three millennia: political empires and periods of expansion alternated with periods of breakdown, nomadic or semi-nomadic incursions, and times of intense competition and struggle between local, culturally related, but politically autonomous city-states. Individual cities remained the basic building blocks of state formation in Mesopotamia at least through the third and into the second millennia BC. The well-documented example of the old Assyrian trading network in the early second millennium BC (cf. Larsen, this volume) clearly demonstrates how the economic life and prosperity of a city, Assur, depended upon its middleman role in the long distance exchange primarily of silver and gold from Anatolia for tin and textiles from regions to the east and south. This profit-motivated trade extended far beyond the political borders of any state and linked into a single world system areas stretching from the Anatolian plateau to southern Mesopotamia east across the Iranian plateau possibly to western Afghanistan (Cleuziou and Berthoud 1982). Similarly, the earlier royal archives from Ebla in northern Syria unequivocally demonstrate that even when cities expanded into kingdoms of considerable size they still engaged in essential 'international' exchange, transporting raw materials, luxury goods, textiles, and even livestock and agricultural products, such as olive oil, across recognized political boundaries (Pettinato 1981:chapter VII).

An even earlier reliance on intercultural exchange can be reconstructed from archaeological materials dated to Early Dynastic times. Sumerian civilization, of course, developed on an alluvial plain that was noteworthy for lacking most essential natural resources besides clay and possibly salt (Potts n.d.). The trade that developed partly as a result of this deficiency cannot be dismissed as the relatively unimportant luxury exchange of status markers among participating elites. As Schneider (1977:23) correctly has emphasized. Wallerstein's distinction between luxury and staple exchanges is misleading and discredits the political importance of the former.

> *The relationship of trade to social stratification was not just a matter of an elevated group distinguishing itself through the careful application of sumptuary laws and a monopoly on symbols of status; it further involved the direct and self-conscious manipulation of various semiperipheral and middle level groups through patronage, bestowals, and the calculated distribution of exotic and valued goods.*

Moreover, since trade was one means by which the competing city-states of Early Dynastic Sumer obtained non-indigenous resources, it was essential for them to produce commodities that could be exchanged. Textual and archaeological evidence (cf. Adams 1981:147–51) together confirm that they succeeded primarily by engaging in the surplus production of woollen textiles or a production for exchange that was intimately related to the internal structure of Sumerian society. Analyses of the distribution of archaeological materials in the mid-third millennium have demonstrated that finished commodities, as well as raw materials, were imported into Sumer (Kohl 1978; 1979). In other words, the intercultural trade which developed between resource-poor Mesopotamia and the resource-rich highland areas of Anatolia and Iran necessarily transformed the productive activities of all the societies participating in the exchange network without the development of an overarching polity or empire. For example, a specialized center for the production of elaborately carved soft stone vessels has been excavated at the small, non-urban settlement of Tepe Yahya in southeastern Iran. There is no evidence to suggest that this centre was incorporated into a larger political unit encompassing the urban centers that imported its vessels.

It also has been proposed that Sumerian and other lowland cities held a competitive advantage in this exchange at least insofar as that they could obtain commodities and natural resources from multiple, isolated, and autonomous communities, such as Tepe Yahya, while the highland communities came to rely exclusively upon the goods – textiles and possible foodstuffs – that they received from Mesopotamia and Khuzestan (Kohl 1978:471–2); the highland settlements became locked into unequal exchange relationships for both internal and external reasons. Needs and demands, of course, were artificially created, but, more importantly, the small communities that engaged in the production of highly crafted commodities were themselves internally transformed. Emergent elites who directed these productive activities came to depend upon the continuance of the trade to maintain their newly acquired privileged positions within society. If correct, this pattern seems to resemble Wallerstein's model of the modern world system and leads us to question his reasons for rejecting comparisons between ancient and modern times.

Multiple Cores, Unequal Exchange, and Underdevelopment in the Bronze Age

However, the nature of this unequal exchange and the problem of detecting structurally induced underdevelopment and dependency demand closer scrutiny. Cultural evolution throughout the greater Middle East during the third and second millennia BC was not exclusively nor even dominantly related to developments within Mesopotamia. Reference already has been made to the geographically more extensive and culturally more uniform Harappan civilization, and any complete discussion must consider Egypt and, as shall be examined below, southern Central Asia. There were multiple core areas which co-existed and intermittently came into direct or indirect contact with one another. Each 'core' manipulated an adjacent hinterland which at times it may have attempted to control. Egypt's relations with Nubia, the Levantine coast, and the Sinai peninsula provide a striking illustration of such a regionalized 'world system'. Meluhhan or Indus villagers may have resided in Mesopotamia (Parpola, Parpola, and Brunswig 1977), and now direct archaeological evidence suggests that the Harappans, like the Sumerians, were interested in the copper resources of Oman (Weisgerber n.d.; 1981). Southern Central Asia or what has been termed the Namazga civilization (cf. Kohl 1981) exchanged some materials with Harappan centers as is evident from the discoveries of Indus seals, ivory sticks, and etched carnelian beads at Altyn-Depe in southern Turkmenistan (Masson 1981). Sites along the piedmont strip of southern Turkmenistan and in the lowland plains of Bactria and Margiana contain numerous objects made from materials, such as lapis lazuli, turquoise, and various metals, which were not available locally but which existed in adjacent regions and which must have been procured through some regularized intercultural exchange network. In short, the Bronze Age world system of the late third and early second millennia BC was characterized not by a single dominant core region economically linked to less developed peripheral zones, but by a patchwork of overlapping, geographically disparate core regions or foci of cultural development, each of which primarily exploited its own immediate hinterland.

The existence of such multiple cores in sporadic contact with one another is not a peculiar anomaly of the Bronze Age world system but points to a basic disconformity between this system and that postulated by Wallerstein for the modern era. Specifically, peripheries situated between cores were far from helpless in dictating the terms of exchange; they could develop or terminate relations depending upon whether or not these relations were perceived to be in their best interest. For example, recent archaeological excavations in the United Arab Emirates and Oman at sites such as Hili (Cleuziou n.d.; 1980), Bat (Frifelt 1976), and Maysar (Weisgerber 1981) have revealed the existence of a fairly uniform late third–early second millennia culture characterized by distinctive architecture, ceramics, and mortuary practices which, at least at Maysar, was engaged in the large-scale production of copper for exchange. Evidence also suggests that many more mining and copper refining sites of this period once existed throughout the mountainous interior of Oman but subsequently were destroyed by later Islamic sites exploiting the same deposits. The archaeological data are consistent with cuneiform documents recording extensive trade with Makkan, a region which exported copper and diorite to Mesopotamia, but ceramics, ingot forms, and an excavated triangular-shaped seal from Maysar also indicate metallurgical relations with South Asia (Weisgerber 1980: 106, fig. 77; n.d.). Although it is still too early to determine whether or not this prehistoric Omani culture maintained exchange relations simultaneously or successively with Sumer and Harappa, it seems impossible to refer to the systematic under-development of this autonomous culture. If anything, prehistoric Oman appears to have prospered or been sustained at a more complex level of cultural development than would have been possible in the absence of these exchange relations. While circumstantial, this evidence seems to contradict a model of exchange so unequal as to foster 'the development of underdevelopment'.

There is little reason to doubt that patterns of dependency or, perhaps better, interdependency were established as a result of intercultural exchange in the Bronze Age world system. Less developed peripheral societies probably were more strongly affected by participation in this exchange than were the more densely populated, internally differentiated civilizations which emerged on lowland alluvial plains. Dependency could lead to exploitation, and, if later myths, such as Enmerkar and the Lord of Aratta, are a guide (cf. Kohl 1978:472 and criticisms pp. 476–84), it is possible that in exceptional circumstances – during a drought or famine – the more powerful urban societies could dictate the terms of the exchange. But the relations between ancient cores and peripheries were not structurally analogous to those which underdevelopment theorists postulate are characteristic of First–Third World relations today. Unless conquered (i.e., incorporated into a larger polity), ancient peripheries could have followed one of several options ranging from withdrawal from the exchange network to substitution of one core partner for another. Archaeological and historical evidence converge to suggest that most intercultural exchange systems in antiquity were fragile, lasting at most a few generations before collapsing. This inherent instability is related to the relative weakness of the bonds of dependency that existed between core and peripheral partners.

Transferable Technologies: the Case of Central Asia

Peripheral societies of the Bronze Age not only had more options available to them, but they also did not necessarily suffer from a technological gap which doomed them to politically and militarily inferior positions *vis-à-vis* civilized cores. That is, consideration of the technological base of these early Bronze Age civilizations also reveals a fundamental structural discrepancy between ancient and modern world systems. It is not that the scale of intercultural trade in the late third–early second millennia BC was a fraction of that which united the world in the sixteenth century AD, nor that the speed, reliability, and capability of transportation and communication systems in the Bronze Age were greatly circumscribed relative to the systems which developed at the beginning of the modern era. These are relative phenomena. Rather, a qualitative difference exists because critical technologies, such as metal working and later horse breeding, were not controlled by core areas alone. Bronze Age technologies could not be monopolized but quickly diffused from one area to another or, in this sense, were transferable. Moreover, important technologies often initially developed or were further refined in peripheral areas close to the natural sources of the necessary resources.

The uses to which transferable technologies could be put varied from society to society depending upon their needs and internal structure. In his final summary of the Bronze Age Childe contrasted progressive barbarian Europe with the stultified, despotic societies of the ancient Near East:

> *Yet the relations of production that thus made possible the establishment of a metallurgical industry, fettered its development. So the types of tools and weapons and the technical methods for their production, established by 3000 bc, persisted in Egypt and Hither Asia with hardly any progressive change for the next two millennia. The reasons for such stagnation are not far to seek. The urban revolution in the Orient liberated craftsmen and specialists from the necessity of procuring their own food, but only at the cost of complete dependence on a court or a temple. It gave them leisure to perfect their skills but no encouragement to do so along progressive lines; for the last thing to interest a divine king or high priest would be labour-saving devices. . . . The more progressive character of Aegean industry and craftsmenship is legitimately explicable by reference to the social and economic structures within which they functioned. Craftsmen had not been reduced, as in the Orient, to an exploited lower class because no class division had as yet cleft Aegean societies. Their patrons were themselves practical men who would appreciate the efficiency of tools and weapons. (Childe 1957: 8–9)*

Childe's analysis, of course, is dated, and his insistence on Europe's progressive and the Orient's despotic character – questionable and embarrassingly ethnocentric. Childe consistently underestimated the potential surpluses that could have been generated by Neolithic economies (Kohl and Wright 1977) and thus incorrectly asserted that the first 'regular use of metal' had to have occurred within the highly productive river valleys which spawned the earliest civilizations of the Old World. Though based on the evidence available at the time, Childe's model neglected to consider the potential of peripheral areas for internal technological innovation or for their adoption of easily transferable technologies due to their own internally generated needs; smiths or 'immigrant specialists' simply ventured forth from cores to ply their skills and wares under less repressive social conditions. The model was mechanical and highly diffusionary or core-focused. However, it nicely linked technological development to social structure and, if properly modified, can be used to illustrate another fundamental discrepancy between ancient and modern core-peripheral relations; viz., major technological innovations which made possible new forms of social organization and which could alter existing balances of power often appeared in peripheries or along the frontiers of civilized society. Peripheral societies not only exercised a considerable range of options in dealing with more powerful trade partners but, in certain times and places, also developed new techniques or applied nearly universal skills in a broadly 'progressive' fashion that ultimately had far-reaching social and political consequences.

The remainder of this chapter will illustrate the potential for innovation characteristic of ancient peripheries through consideration of Late Bronze developments in Central Asia.

Western Turkestan, an area that has been referred to as the northeastern frontier of the ancient Near East (Tosi 1973–4) stretches from the Caspian Sea in the west to the Fergana valley in the east and from the Aral Sea in the north to the Hindu Kush and Atrek valley of northeastern Iran in the south. It can be defined as the vast area of interior drainage formed by the streams draining the Kopet Dagh and northern Hindu Kush mountains and by the Atrek, Tedjen, Murghab, Amu Darya, Zeravshan, and Syr Darya rivers and their tributaries (figure 5.1). Today, it is divided among three nation-states: Iran; Afghanistan; and the republics of Turkmenistan, Uzbekistan, Tadjikistan, and part of Kirghizia in the Soviet Union. The boundaries of prehistoric culture areas and modern political borders rarely coincide, but the existence of the latter usually implies a different history of archaeological investigation for regions separated by the borders, and this fact strongly affects current understanding. Specifically, most of the data presented below has been gathered by Soviet archaeologists working along the fertile *atak* or piedmont strip of southern Turkmenistan and on the lowland plains of Margiana (lower Murghab) and Bactria (southern Uzbekistan-northwestern Afghanistan).

Western Turkestan consists of largely uninhabited deserts (Kara Kum and Kyzyl Kum, in particular), rugged mountain ranges, lowland alluvial plains, watered piedmont zones, and intermontane valleys. Important rivers, such as the Amu Darya and Zeravashan, that rise in the high eastern mountain ranges are fed largely

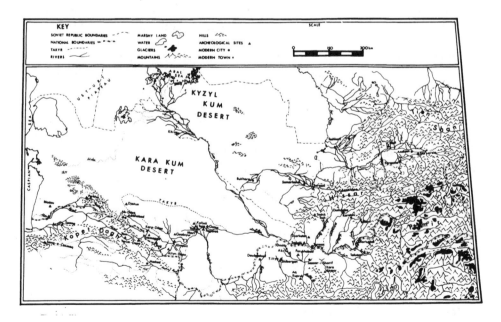

Figure 5.1 [orig. figure 2.1]   Western Turkestan: major prehistoric archaeological sites.

by melting snows, while those in the west, such as the Murghab, Tedjen, or numerous streams of the Kopet Dagh, rely more on rainfall or, in some cases, tap groundwater sources (Dolukhanov 1981). Southern Central Asia is a landlocked basin with a sharply continental climate and is very arid, particularly throughout its low-lying plains. While Soviet specialists disagree on the extent of environmental change during the Holocene (contrast Lisitsina 1978: 189–93 with Vinogradov and Mamedov 1975: 234–55), a longer term pattern of general desiccation is clear. Neolithic archaeological remains deep in the Kyzyl Kum and Bronze Age settlements far to the north of the area currently watered by the lower Murghab suggest, at least, that waters flowed much farther into the deserts as recently as the early second millennium BC.

Systematic prehistoric investigations in Central Asia began with the work of R. Pumpelly at Anau in 1904, but this initial work only was refined and extended on a large scale by Soviet archaeologists after World War II. Soviet scholars, such as B.A. Kuftin (1956) and V.M. Masson (1956), documented a rich prehistoric sequence along the northern foothills of the Kopet Dagh in southern Turkmenistan which extended from Neolithic through Iron Age times and which related to developments on the Iranian plateau. Soundings at the major urban site of Namazga-Depe (50 ha.) yielded a basic six-period sequence (NMGI–VI) which has been confirmed and further refined by subsequent work, particularly at Altyn-Depe (c. 26 ha.; cf. Masson 1981). While regional differences were detected in specific periods, most scholars were impressed with the uniformity of the Namazga or southern Turkmenistan culture which stretched nearly the entire 600 km. length of the piedmont strip and emphasized that developments in this area led to the appearance of socially differentiated urban societies (Masson 1968). Moreover, ties between southern Turkmenistan and southern areas, like Pakistani Baluchistan, particularly the Quetta valley, and Iranian Seistan, were recognized and even led to speculations of colonization or movements from southern Turkmenistan south as early as the Late Aeneolithic of NMG III period (late fourth millennium) that may have been partly responsible for the emergence of such large centers of Shahr-i Sokhta in eastern Iran (Tosi 1973). In other words, in our terms, southern Turkmenistan was recognized early as its own core area, not perhaps as spectacular or as densely populated as the better known cores of the Tigris–Euphrates, Nile, and Indus valleys, but on which developed a distinctive, internally complex culture that occasionally seemed to have significantly influenced developments in adjacent peripheral areas.

According to Soviet investigators, the NMG-related settlements in southern Turkmenistan continued to expand through the Middle Bronze NMG V (end of third millennium BC) or so-called urban period, but during the subsequent Late Bronze NMG VI period large settlements along the piedmont strip, like Namazga and Altyn, either were abandoned or only continued to be occupied on a sharply reduced scale. Several interpretations – none of which is mutually exclusive – have been advanced to explain this decline, including: (a) environmental degradation due both to natural causes and to human overexploitation of the environment (Dolukhanov 1981); (b) 'barbarian' invasions from the northern steppes, possibly representing the arrival of Indo-Aryan groups (a theory first proposed by E.F. Schmidt at Anau but later accepted by many Soviet investigators, such as A.A. Marushchenko and A.M. Mandel'shtam); (c) a shift from primarily overland to maritime long-distance trade in the late third millennium BC leading to the decline of settlements not only in southern Turkmenistan but in the Gorgan plain (Tureng Tepe, Shah Tepe), the Iranian plateau (Hissar), and Seistan (Shahi-i Sokhta); this shift may have been associated with the consolidation and southern expansion of the Harappan civilization (Dales 1977); (d) an ingenious thesis of overurbanization (Biscoine 1977), which is based upon an analysis of known settlement size, postulates that too great a percentage of the total population lived in the cities and towns of southern Turkmenistan creating an artificial situation that could not sustain itself; and (e) a theory of colonization or emigration from southern Turkmenistan to the recently discovered and clearly related Bronze Age settlements in Margiana and Bactria (cf. Sarianidi 1981). Reasons for such a colonization need to be established; and determination of when such a movement actually began, how suddenly it occurred, and whether or not it proceeded only from west to east constitute some of the unresolved difficulties with this last explanation.

We cannot review the merits and demerits of each theory; some, like Dales' provocative hypothesis of a shift from overland to maritime trade, are extremely difficult, if not impossible, to establish conclusively on the basis of archaeological evidence. In a very real sense, however, the discoveries of numerous Bronze Age settlements in Margiana and Bactria suggest that a false problem has been posed; a crisis in urbanization or social devolution in southern Central Asia (and by extension throughout areas farther to the south) never occurred. Urban life did not collapse, but settlements shifted in Central Asia to the lowland plain formed by the lower Murghab and to the southern and northern Bactrian plains. These settlements were clearly related in terms of their material features to the earlier ssettlements in southern Turkmenistan, but they also were different. Sites were obviously planned and fortified; burial practices changed; and more numerous and advanced metal tools and weapons were produced on the Margiana and Bactrian sites. Known area of occupation in Margiana alone during its so-called Gonur or second stage of development (cf. Sarianidi 1981) is roughly double that documented in southern Turkmenistan or the core area during its period of urban florescence (NMG V). If southern and northern Bactria also are considered, the estimated area of *expansion*, not contraction or collapse, doubles once more. That is, present evidence suggests that settled life minimally was four times as extensive in Bactria and Margiana during the Bronze Age than in southern Turkmenistan (cf. Kohl 1983: chaps. 11, 13, 14, 15 for these estimates). While chronological correlations between the different regions need further clarification, it is obvious that the development of settled life in Bactria and Margiana cannot be accounted for solely or even primarily on the basis of emigration from southern Turkmenistan. In addition, hundreds of archaeological sites or stations, comprised chiefly of lithic remains, have been documented north of Margiana in the Kyzyl Kum desert (Vinogradov and Mamedov 1975) and immediately north of the

Bronze Age sites in southern Bactria (Vinogradov 1979). It is likely that the relatively sudden appearance of planned Bronze Age sites on these lowland plains also involved the incorporation of these less technologically advanced peoples (cf. Kohl 1983: chap. 5 for a discussion of the Kyzyl Kum sequence and its apparent shift in orientation roughly at this time). The known core area of southern Turkmenistan was replaced by new centers in Bactria and Margiana at the end of the third and beginning of the second millennium. The cultures which developed in these newly settled areas clearly were related to the earlier cultures that evolved over several millennia in southern Turkmenistan but also exhibited new features, perhaps reflecting their mixed origins. We will briefly review materials from two Bactrian sites: Sapalli and Dashly 3.

The most informative and supposedly earliest North Bactrian site is Sapalli-Tepe in southwestern Surkhandarya province (Uzbekistan), *a.c.* 4 ha. settlement with a central fortified area (82 × 82m.) which was totally excavated by A. Askarov from 1969 to 1973 (figure 5.2; Askarov 1973; 1977). The excavated structures at this obviously planned site were fortified from the outset and consisted of eight separate multi-roomed complexes, termed 'patriarchal households' by the excavator (cf. Askarov 1973: 136–9 for an interesting, if speculative, comparison and contrast of

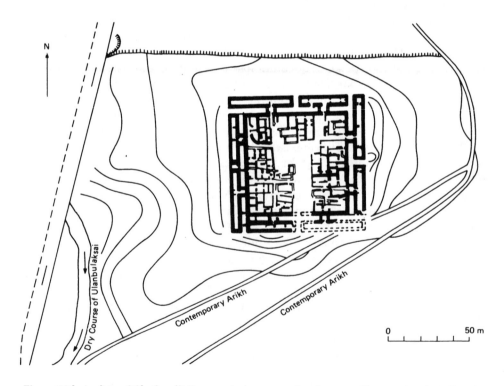

Figure 5.2 [orig. figure 2.2]   Sapalli-Tepe: central compound and surrounding area, northern Bactria (southern Uzbekistan).

Sapalli's social organization, as reconstructed from its architecture, with that recorded in the *Avesta*), grouped around a central open area and separated from one another by streets and alleys. These quarters seem to be generally self-sufficient, each containing several domestic hearths and evidence for pottery production. Thirty such hearths, possibly representing as many individual families, were found in the earliest period. While pottery-making was attested for each quarter through the discovery of two-tiered, two-chambered, and one chambered-combined kilns, conditions for production must have been terribly cramped with some kilns having only a *c*. one sq. m. section. Despite the general picture of independence and self-sufficiency for each quarter, there is some evidence for specialization: bread ovens occur only in certain quarters; quarter 1 has a craft shop for the production of bone and antler tools; quarter 6 has a particularly elaborate potters' workshop; and quarter 3 has a shop for preparing bronzes.

138 graves were excavated under the houses and in the walls at Sapalli, and the preservation was excellent with remains including figured metal pins, shaft-hole axe-adzes (which also can be paralleled on southern Bactrian tombs, at Hissar IIIC, and in the Mehrgarh VIII cemetery and site of Sibri in Pakistani Baluchistan), drilled bead seal-amulets, and food offerings and textiles, including the remains of silk clothing in four cases and caches of wheat and millet seeds. The graves included 125 individual and 13 collective burials or a contrast with the slightly earlier graves from Altyn where roughly 2/3 of the adult burials occurred in collective graves. The richest tombs contain only *c*. 50 objects, primarily pottery vessels, and female burials in general were richer than those of males. The number of goods in the graves seemed to depend upon the age of the deceased with infant and children's graves containing fewer gifts, possibly suggesting that status was achieved, not ascribed nor inherited. In general, little social differentiation beyond that of sex and age was evident in the Sapalli graves despite the high craftmanship and sophistication of the grave goods, particularly the metals.

Sites from southern Bactria or northwestern Afghanistan were discovered and excavated by the Soviet–Afghan archaeological expedition from 1969–1979. At least sixty-four Bronze Age sites were recorded in four separate oases along the dried-up extensions of streams, such as the Balkh-ab, flowing down from the western Hindu Kush. Dating of the sites is problematic: a sequence of some duration, probably extending back towards the middle of the third millennium is suggested, though it is also clear that most of the materials should be contemporaneous with the North Bactrian and Margiana settlements which can be dated to the end of the third through the first half of the second millennium BC. Sites include small planned fortified settlements, such as Dashly 1 (110 × 90m.), reminiscent of Sapalli; industrial or craft production sites of uncertain dimensions marked by extensive scatters of debitage, including slag and wasters of lapis lazuli and turquoise; and very large settlements, like the *c*. 90 ha. site of Farukhabad 1.

The site of Dashly 3 contained two interesting groups of structures: a complex centered around a circular building or 'temple' (figure 5.3; Sarianidi 1977:34–40); and a fortified compound or 'palace' similar to those excavated at Sapalli and

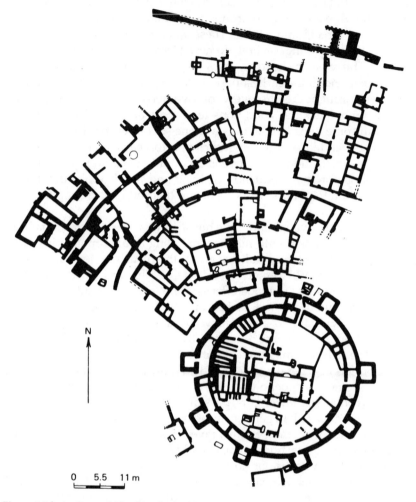

Figure 5.3 [orig. figure 2.3]   Circular building at Dashly 3: southern Bactria (northwestern Afghanistan).

Dashly 1 (figure 5.4; Sarianidi 1977:41–50). The circular building, which was enclosed within a rectangular wall 130–150 m. to a side, was formed by a double row of walls encircling an area *c.* 40 m. in diameter. While the interpretation of the site as a temple is speculative, the central building complex contained several enigmatic features, such as hearths built on brick platforms, which were filled with white ash, and pits, which contained lightly burned animal bones, suggesting some possibly non-utilitarian activity associated with the use of fire. Three rings of domestic structures outside the building but within the wall were thought to represent the residences of the separate temple community, though no direct evidence supports this problematic interpretation.

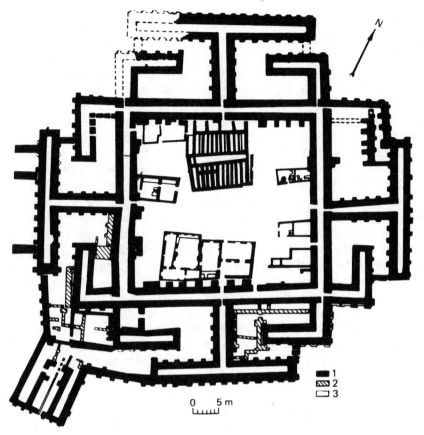

Figure 5.4 [orig. figure 2.4]   Dashly 3 'palace' or planned compound: southern Bactria (northwestern Afghanistan).

As at Sapalli, the Dashly 3 'palace' appeared to have been built largely at one time. It consisted of a symmetrical, rectangular walled area (84 × 88 m.) with an inner central court (38 × 40 m.) and had several false entrances and narrow T-shaped corridors. Access to the compound was deliberately restricted. After the original buildings were abandoned, new structures were built within the former central court and older rooms were reused, one of which functioned as a place for casting metal. In this room (no. 51) a two-part kiln was situated together with a clay mold for casting an axe-adze and copper ingots. More evidence for metallurgical production was discovered during the final or fourth period of occupation when the original planned architecture had further decayed and poorly built rooms were constructed.

The mortuary evidence from southern Bactria consists of roughly 100 properly excavated burials from Dashly 1 and Dashly 3 and thousands of illegally plundered tombs. In several highly specific respects the former excavated burials closely resemble those from Sapalli and other sites in northern Bactria and suggest relatively little social differentiation. It is more difficult to interpret the plundered tombs since their context has been destroyed. Some of the objects, particularly the metals, from these tombs are truly spectacular (cf. Sarianidi 1977; Amiet 1977, 1978; and the systematic catalogue of objects from the Kabul bazaar by Pottier (1981) offers striking parallels to excavated materials from sites farther south in Baluchistan and southeastern Iran. Some Bactrian seals, for example, appear to have been cast from the same mold as those found in the rich cemetery at Shahdad on the western edge of the Dasht-i Lut in southern Iran (compare Sarianidi 1977:94, Fig. 48, no. 12 with Hakemi 1972: pl. XXIB.). In fact, the plundered Bactrian materials necessitate a re-evaluation of assemblages earlier collected by Stein and other scholars throughout Baluchistan (Jarrige 1982); seemingly incongruous and unexpected discoveries, such as a limestone column and shaft-hole axe from Shahi Tump (Stein 1931:90–4), can be related to the Bactrian materials, suggesting some intensive trade or, more likely, north to south movements of peoples among the regions. Unfortunately, it is impossible to assess properly the significance of the plundered materials, and, until an undisturbed cemetery is scientifically excavated, one can only assume that the same relative similarity of grave lots recorded at Sapalli, other North Bactrian sites, Dashly 1, and Dashly 3 characterized all tombs – even those containing highly crafted objects. That is, despite the beauty and obvious craftsmanship of the Bactrian materials, there are no known royal or disproportionally wealthy tombs; present mortuary evidence suggests relatively little stratification within the society that produced them, an interpretation consistent with the relatively sudden appearance and mixed character of these settlements.

Analysis of these Central Asian materials is not illuminated by a simple reference to Wallerstein's world system's model. Rather, significant discrepancies emerge: an older core (southern Turkmenistan) appears to have been quickly superseded immediately subsequent to its florescence through a large-scale expansion onto formerly uncultivated, natural fertile plains; the new settlements appear to have been remarkably self-sufficient and well-organized, though less internally differentiated than the earlier urban centers of southern Turkmenistan; at the same time, metallurgical technology, in particular, and the scale of subsistence and craft-related productive activities seem to have increased substantially. Peripheral frontier areas were transformed into cores which were both more and less developed than the societies that they replaced. In addition, the recorded shifts in settlements appear to have been accompanied by significant changes in methods of transportation related to the introduction of the horse and utilization of the spoked wheel.

Horse bones are found at Kelleli 1 and/or Taip (Kuzmina 1980:27, 33) and at the later Takhirbai 3 site in Margiana and at Tekkem-Depe and Namazga-Depe in the piedmont strip. The horse initially was domesticated on the south Russian steppe from the Don to the Volga in the fourth millennium and was introduced into Central Asia on a significant scale during the Late Bronze period (ibid.). Such an introduction or contact might be suggested by the presence of diagnostic incised 'steppe' ceramics on many of the sites in the lower Murghab and at Tekkem-Depe;

in addition, a clay model head of a horse was found at Namazga-Depe. Although one cannot confidently speak of the advent of mounted pastoral nomadism or the extent of true horsemanship at this time, it seems likely from what is known of immediately succeeding periods (e.g. at Pirak to the south, Jarrige and Santoni 1979) that riding skills were developing at the end of the third and the beginning of the second millennia and that these must have profoundly affected the entire area of southern Central Asia. The evidence for spoked, as opposed to solid, wheels consists of a model wheel with four brown painted spokes and an emphasized hub from Namazga, a wheel with six red painted spokes from Tekkem, and another spoked wheel from El'ken-Depe (Kuzmina 1980: 27). The significance of this development is unclear, though it presumably led to increased mobility and ease of wheeled transport for hauling goods and/or also for military purposes.

The new settled societies in Bactria and Margiana, some of whom may have moved farther south into Baluchistan and eastern Iran, adopted pre-existing, easily transferable technologies in strikingly innovative and politically significant ways. This adoption, possibly analogous to that postulated by Childe for his 'progressive' European barbarians, resulted in the abandonment of an older core area and indeed may have been partly responsible for the collapse of early urban civilization in south Asia (cf. Allchin and Allchin 1982: 298–308). Core areas, in short, were not terribly stable, and critically important technologies, capable of transforming or being transformed by political relations among interacting areas, were readily transferable to less developed regions, some of which were situated closer to natural source deposits or breeding plains for live resources, such as horses. Technologies, of course, did not diffuse automatically, and their importance, even use, differed from one social context to the next. But the model of a world system, which Wallerstein defined for the modern era, only imperfectly describes structured interactions in antiquity. *Economic* development and dependency were not linked phenomena during the Bronze Age in the manner postulated by contemporary critical theory for – to paraphrase their terminology – the development of underdevelopment in the Bronze Age was sharply constrained or itself under–developed. Critical technologies, such as metal working, could diffuse relatively easily and new means of transportation and sources of power, such as horses, could be raised in peripheral zones and radically restructure this ancient world system. Technological gaps, which dependency theorists argue pervade First–Third World relations today, simply did not exist in the Bronze Age in a manner that signified permanent political dominance or subjugation. Gatherer-hunter and nomadic stockbreeding populations on the Central Asian steppes or on the previously uncultivated plains of Margiana and Bactria rapidly adopted and transformed technologies that developed elsewhere, and these innovations made it possible – not inevitable – for them to alter established methods of interaction and political relations throughout many disparate regions of the greater Middle East.

Central Asia clearly interacted with South Asia and Iran in the late third millennium, but it was neither a core, periphery, or semi-periphery in terms of economic exchange with any of these areas. Contact was at best indirect and sporadic with

Mesopotamia and non-existent with the eastern Mediterranean. A stray chlorite weight carved in an immediately recognizable 'Intercultural Style' (cf. Brentjes 1971) or the discovery of etched carnelian beads in Thailand and Southeast Asian spices in second millennium Mesopotamian contexts do not demonstrate the existence of a unified world system in any meaningful economic sense; materials and ideas simply could have diffused throughout Eurasia in a variety of ways. For Wallerstein's model to apply one must demonstrate economic dependency, and this one can do for only separate, relatively restricted areas of Eurasia during the third and early second millennia BC.

The neo-evolutionary models of regional autonomous development, which can be legitimately criticized for ignoring history or, in Braudelian terms, the conjuncture(s) of different structures, remain popular precisely for this reason. Prehistoric materials from the Balkans may bear some resemblance to those from western Turkey but to link them in turn to the Caucasus or, worse yet, Iran and points farther east is to invite ridicule. There was not a single Bronze Age world system but, if you will, over-lapping world systems which constantly shifted and modified their boundaries due to unpredictable historical events, technological changes, or the formation and dissolution of larger political units and alliances. Thus, in the early to mid-third millennium southern Iran, extending the length of the Zagros, was united into a world system dominated by Khuzestan and possibly south-central Iran at the site of Anshan. The Namazga civilization of southern Central Asia formed part of another world system, perhaps spatially resembling that defined by Biscoine and Tosi as prehistoric Turan (1979). Relations with South Asia and its Harappan-dominated world system changed during the latter part of the third millennium, possibly related to the previously mentioned hypothesis of a shift from overland to maritime long-distance exchange and to the development of metallurgy, particularly the production of weapons, and the introduction of horses.

The Bronze Age world systems lacked an equivalent – if we follow Wallerstein – to western Europe in the late fifteenth and sixteenth centuries. There was no direct contact from one end of these Bronze Age world systems to the other. There was no single core, but a patchwork of core areas which succeeded only fleetingly in dominating their peripheral neighbors. The relative impermanence of core and peripheral areas was one of the major distinguishing features of Bronze Age world systems; means of communication and transportation simply were not sufficiently advanced to allow core areas to control and dominate their peripheries for long periods of time. Successful, long-lived political empires only emerged later, and they were explicitly distinguished by their politically imposed unity from the world system of modern times. Moreover, developments that occurred in peripheral zones soon transformed these backward societies, as on the plains of Bactria and Margiana and, perhaps, at Shah-dad in southeastern Iran, into core areas of their own. Expansion and colonization during the Bronze Age into largely unsettled areas continuously stimulated development and were structurally similar to the Greek overseas ventures of the seventh and sixth centuries BC, if not to the much later discovery and conquest of the New World and Australia. However, the

Bronze Age colonies, as in Bactria, soon became more advanced than their home-lands for they quickly achieved, if they did not originally possess, political autonomy and could develop relatively freely of limiting historical and social constraints.

The currently fashionable regional ecosystemic perspectives on the development of Bronze Age societies represent an advance over earlier diffusionary theories for they compel us to consider long-term structural phenomena, but they are still inad-equate because they refuse to acknowledge the importance of historical events and the coming together of different cultural systems. Although it is notoriously diffi-cult to assess the scale of the exchange of materials and ideas between prehistoric societies, archaeological data unequivocally demonstrate that contact occurred, and it is reasonable to assume that in many cases its effects were substantial. Utilization of Wallerstein's concept of a world system has the singular advantage of emphasizing that such contacts were based on fundamental economic consid-erations that were not necessarily to every society's adaptive advantage but were the products of stronger societies or elites within those societies attempting to impose their will and desire for material gain upon less developed areas.

However, the correspondence between a Bronze Age (or ancient) and modern world system is far from exact for precisely the reason that the control exercised by core areas was circumscribed and dependent upon relatively egalitarian or transferable technologies and primitive means of transportation and communica-tion. Thus, for example, the advent of mounted warriors and effective chariots transformed interregional relations throughout the ancient Near East during the second millennium BC, ushering in various Dark Ages in older core areas and the emergence of new power centers, as in central Anatolia. For reasons of control and the complexity of the technology upon which this control is based, it is difficult to believe that a structurally similar rapid shift in the balance of power will occur to alter relations between underdeveloped and advanced countries today – at least without the prior internal transformation of the latter.

Cynics might argue that the Wallerstein model, questionable at best for the modern era, is so inapplicable to earlier periods as to make reference to it misleading or meaningless. Models that fail, however, also instruct, and consider-ation of the economic and political linkages among disparate societies is essential to advance beyond the theoretically simple-minded and empirically inaccurate alternative provided by neo-evolutionism. For both modern *and* ancient times Wallerstein's model of an interacting world system raises the essential, though often over-looked, problem of determining the most appropriate spatial and temporal unit of analysis. One cannot deny the open-ended nature of social systems in the past any more than one can ignore the interconnections among soci-eties in the modern era (Wolf 1982). Moreover, because such interconnections have intensified during modern times, it is obvious that cultural evolution primarily must be reconstructed from archaeological, not ethnological, evidence. That Wallerstein's model cannot be applied literally to the Bronze Age does not mean that the search for interconnections and structured interaction is unproductive. Rather, the task now is to determine how and why interactions at different, archaeologically attested stages of cultural development both resembled and differed from those of today. The model cannot be applied literally to earlier social formation, but its necessary alteration may help us better understand the development and character of pre- and early State societies and, perhaps more hopefully, gain insights into the nature of the contemporary world.

References

Adams, R. McC. 1981 *Heartland of Cities,* Chicago: University of Chicago Press

Allchin, B. and Allchin, R. 1982 *The Rise of Civilization in India and Pakistan* Cambridge University Press

Amiet, P. 1977 'La Bactriane proto-historique', *Syria* LIV (1-2): 89–121,
    1978 'Antiquites de Bactriane', *La Revu du Louvre et des Musées de France* XXXVIII 30: 153–64

Amin, S. 1974 *Accumulation on a World Scale* New York: Monthly Review Press

Alkarov, A. 1973 *Sapallitepa* Tashkent: FAN
    1977 *Drevnezemledel'cheskaya Kultura epokhi bronzi iuga Uzbekistana* Tashkent:FAN

Biscoine, R. 1977 'The Crisis of Central Asian Urbanism in 2nd Millennium B.C. and Villages as an Alternative System' in J. Deshayes (ed.) *Le Plâteau Iranien et L'Asie Centrale dès Origines à la Conquête Islamique* Paris: CNRS, oo. 113–27

Biscoine, R. and Tosi, M. 1979 *Protostoria degli Stati Turanici.* Supplemento n. 20 ogli Annali Dell'Istituto Universitario Orientale, XXXIX, 3 Naples

Brenner, R. 1977 'The origins of capitalist development: a critique of neo-Smithian Marxism', *New Left Review* 104: 25–93

Brentjes, B. 1971 'Ein Elamitischer Streufund aus Soch, Fergana (Usbekistan)', *Iran* IX: 155

Childe, V. G. 1957 'The Bronze Age', *Past and Present* 12: 2–15

Cleuziou, S. 1980 'Three seasons at Hili: toward a chronology and cultural history of the Oman Peninsula in the 3rd Millennium B.C.', *Proceedings of the Seminar for Arabian Studies* 10: 19–32 n.d. 'Oman Peninsula and Western Pakistan during the 3rd millennium, B.C.' Cleuziou, S. and Berthoud, T. 1982 'Early tin in the Near East: a reassessment in the light of new evidence from Western Afghanistan', *Expedition* 25(1): 14–25

Dales, G. F. 1977 'Shifting trade patterns between the Iranian Plateau and the Indus Valley in the third millennium B.C.'. . . in J. Deshayes (ed.) *Le Plâteau Iranien et L'Asie Cetnrale dès Origines à la Conquête Islamique* Paris: CNRS

Dolukhanov, P. M. 1981 'The Ecological Prerequisites for Early Farming in Southern Turkmenia' in *the Bronze Age Civilization of Central Asia: Recent Soviet Discoveries,* Armonk, NY: M. E. Sharpe, pp. 359–85.

Francfort, H. -P. and Potter, M. -H. 1978 'Sondage préliminaire sur l'établissement protohistorique Harapéen et post-Harapéen de Shortugai (Afghanistan du N. -E.)', *Arts Antiques* XXXIV: 29–79

Frifelt, K. 1976 'Evidence of a third millennium B.C. town in Oman', *Journal of Oman Studies* 2: 57–73

Hakemi, A. 1972 *Catalogue de l'exposition Lut-Xabis* (Shahdad) Teheran

Hall, J. A. 1985 *Powers and Liberties: the causes and consequences of the rise of the West.* Oxford: Blackwell

Hunt, V. 1978 'The rise of feudalism in Eastern Europe: a critical appraisal of the Wallerstein World System thesis', *Science and Society* XLII 1: 43–61

Jarrige, J. -F. 1982 'Syvazi Beludzhistana v Stendnei Azii vo vtoroi polovine III tis, do n.e. v svete novikh rabot raione Mergara (Les rapports du Baluchistan avec L'Asie Centrale meridionale dans la deuxième moitié du 3 eme millenaire à la lumière de travaux recents (dans la region de Mehrgarh)', in R. M. Munchaev, V. M. Masson, N. N. Negmatov, and V. A. Ranov (eds.) *Drevneishie' Kul'turi Baktrii: Sreda, Razvitie, Svyazi*

Jarrige, J. -F. and Santoni, M. 1979 *Fouilles de Pirak*, vols I and II. Paris: Diffusion de Boccard

Kohl, P. L. 1978 'The balance of trade in southwestern Asia in the mid-third millennium B.C.', *Current Anthropology* 19: 463–92

1981 'The Namazga Civilization : An Overview' in P. L. Kohl (ed.) *The Bronze Age Civilization of Central Asia: Recent Soviet Discoveries*, Armonk, NY: M. E. Sharpe, pp. vii–xxxviii

1983 *L'Asie Central: dès origines a l'âge du Fer (Central Asia: Palaeolithic Beginnings to the Iron Age). Synthese 8, Editions Recherche sur les Civlizations.* Paris

Kohl, P. L. and Wright, R. 1977 'Stateless cities: the differentiation of Societies in the Neolithic in the Near East', *Dialectical Anthropology* 2: 271–83

Kuftin, B. A. 1956 'Polevoi otchet: o rabote XIV otrade IuTAKE po izucheniiu kul'turi pervobitno-oshchinikh osedlozemledel'cheskikh poselenii epokhu medui bronzi v 1952 g.', *Trudi Iu.T.A.K.E.* VII: 260–90

Kuzmina, E. E. 1980 'Etapi razvitiya kolesnogo transporta Sredne Asii v epokhu eneolita I bronzi', *Vestnik Drevnei Istorii* (4): 11–35

Lamberg-Karlovsky, C. C. n.d. "Caste or Class Formation within the Indus Civilization' to appear in E. C. L. During-Caspers (ed.) *A Felicitation Volume for Beatrice de Cardi on the Occasion of Her 70th Birthday* Academic Publishers Association

Larsen, M. T. 1987 'Commerical networks in the Ancient Near East,' in M. Rowlands, M. Larsen and K. Kristiansen (eds.) *Centre and Periphery in the Ancient World* Cambridge: Cambridge University Press, pp. 47–56

Lisitsina, G. N. 1978 *Stanovlenie I razvitie oroshaemogo zemledeliya v iuzhnoi Turkmenii* Moscow: Nauka

Masson, V. M. 1956 'Raspisnaya keramika iuzhnoi Turkmenii po raskopkam B. A. Kuftina', *Trudi Iu.T.A.K.E.* VII: 291–373

1968 'Urban revolution in southern Turkmenia', *Antiquity* XLII: 178–87

1981 Altyn-depe. *Trudi Iu.T.A.K.E.* vol. XVIII. Leningrad: Nauka

Parpola, S., Parpola ,A. and Brunswig, R. H. 1977 'The Meluhha village: evidence of acculturation of Harappan traders in late third millennium Mesopotamia?' *Journal of the Economic and Social History of the Orient* XX(2): 129–65

Pearson, H. W. 1957 'The secular debate on economic primitivism' in K. Polanyi, C. M. Arensberg, and H. W. Pearson (eds) *Trade and Market in the Early Empires* Chicago: Free Press, oo. 3–11

Pettinato, G. 1981 *The Archives of Ebla: An Empire Inscribed in Clay* New York: Doubleday

Pottier, M. -H. 1981 *Materiel Funeraire de la Bactriane meridionale de l'Age de Bronze*, vols. I and II, Thèse pour le Doctorat de IIIe Cycle. Universite de Lille III. Unpublished

Potts, D. n.d. 'On Salt and Salt Gathering in Ancient Mesopotamia' to appear in *Journal of the Economic and Social History of the Orient*

Sarianidi, V. I. 1977 *Drevnie Zemledeltsi Afganistana* Moscow: Nauka

1981 'Margiana in the Bronze Age', in P. L. Kohl (ed.) *The Bronze Age Civilization of Central Asia* pp. 165–93

Schneider, J. 1977 'Was there a pre-capitalist world system?' *Peasant Studies*, vol. VI, no. 1: 20–9

Shaffer, J. 1982 'Harappan culture: a reconsideration', in G. L. Possehl (ed.) *The Harappan Civilization: A Contemporary Perspective*, New Delhi: Oxford and ISB Publishers, American Institute of Indian Studies, pp. 41–50

Stein, A. 1931 *An Archaeological Tour in Gedrosia* (Memoires of the Archaeological Survey of India no. 43)

Tosi, M. 1973 'Early urban evolution and settlement patterns in the Indo-Iranian Borderlands', in C. Renfrew (ed.) *The Explanation of Culture Change: Models in Prehistory*, London: Duckworth

1973–4 'The northeastern frontier of the Ancient Near East', *Mesopotamia* VII-IX: 21–76

Vinogradov, A. V. 1979 'Issledovaniya pamyatnikov kammenogo veka v severnom Afganistane', *Drevanaya Baktriya* 2: 7–62

Vinogradov, A. V. and Mamedov, E. D. 1975 *Pervobitnii Lyavlyakan* (materiali Khorezmskoi Ekspeditsii, no. 10). Moscow: Nauka

Wallerstein, I. 1974 *The Modern World-System: Capitalist Agriculture and the Origins of the European World-Economy in the Sixteenth Century* vol. 1, New York: Academic Press

Weisgerber, G. 1980 '. . . und Kupfer in Oman', Der Anschnitt-Zeitschrift fur Kunst und Kultur im Berghou 32(2–3): 62–110

1981 'Mehr als Kupfer in Oman – Ergebnisse der Expedition 1981', *Der Anschnitt-Zeitschrift fur Kunst und Kultur im Bergbau* 33(5–6): 174–263

n.d. 'Makan and Meluhha – 3rd millennium B.C. copper production in Oman and the evidence of contact with the Indus Valley'

Wolf, E. R. 1982 *Europe and the People Without History* Berkeley: Univ. of California Press

6

Specialization and the Production of Wealth: Hawaiian Chiefdoms and the Inka Empire

Timothy K. Earle

Introduction

Specialization is the economic essence of complex society. Economic efficiency, interdependence, and control are various outcomes of specialization that have been linked to the evolution of chiefdoms and states (Brumfiel and Earle, Chapter 1). Economic efficiency permits both higher population densities and the production of a surplus to support a non-subsistence sector of the population. Economic interdependence resulting from specialized production and distribution of food and crafts is both the cause and the effect of larger societies, which become economically intertwined by food exchange as real energetic systems. Economic control derived from proprietorship and management is the necessary element of finance, the channeling of resources differentially to support the elaboration of institutions of government, stratification and legitimization.

Specialization is undeniably important in any explanation of complex societies, but its highly variable role in evolutionary processes needs to be specified and investigated. In our introduction we lay out the different kinds of specialization, independent and attached, and the economic conditions under which they have become important. The two general perspectives on the role of specialization have been discussed – the adaptationist explanations involving independent specialists for markets and the political explanations involving attached specialists for elite/institutional patrons. We do not claim that one perspective is right and the other necessarily wrong, but they both play a role that varies according to specific environmental, social, and economic conditions. We need to specify those conditions under which different kinds of specialization arise and how they are linked to evolutionary processes.

To do this, I will evaluate the role of specialization in two critical cases of complex society – the Hawaiian chiefdoms and the Inka empire. Explicitly I disclaim any general application to the evolution of *all* complex societies. Quite to the contrary, the Hawaiian and Inka cases together represent variants of one type of society, similar in their control of surplus staple production, but different in their scale and complexity. Staple finance underlies many, but not all, early complex societies. The main point of the Hawaiian and Inka cases is that specialization in complex societies may be quite limited and related closely to political finance and control.

The Cases

The Hawaiian islands at the time of first western contact (1778) were occupied by Polynesians organized as complex chiefdoms (Malo 1951 [1898]; Sahlins 1958, 13–22; Earle 1978). Characteristically, following violent wars of succession and conquest, a paramount chief ruled a major island (Hawai'i, Maui, O'ahu, or Kaua'i) and nearby smaller islands (such as Moloka'i or Ni'ihau). Repeatedly the paramounts attempted to extend political control through marriage and conquest, but limits imposed by sea transport caused these attempts to fail or to be quite fragile. Within any Hawaiian chiefdom, there was a hierarchy of chiefs tracing their relationships to the senior ruling line. These chiefs received community land grants, *ahupua'a*, according to their status and their support for the paramount in his wars of succession and conquest. A hierarchy of priests, chiefs in their own right, was also involved in elaborate rituals of legitimization, demonstrating the sanctity of the ruling chiefs and their significance for the fertility, stability and livelihood of the commoner population.

The economic basis of the Hawaiian chiefdoms was control of subsistence production. Primary subsistence came from irrigated agriculture and intensive shifting cultivation. All land was owned by the paramount chief who granted community land to loyal, ranking chiefs. These community chiefs, through their appointed land manager *konohiki*, allocated subsistence land parcels to commoners in return for their labor on the chief's land. Produce from the chief's land went to the community chief who retained part for his own support and the support of his retainers such as the land manager. A portion then was given over to the ruling paramount, as rent for the initial land grant. Rights to use land were thus distributed down the social hierarchy and produce from the land was mobilized up through the hierarchy.

As discussed in a moment, the *ahupua'a* community was largely the social segment within which production was managed and controlled. Importantly this community was economically self-sufficient and more generally isolated by endogamy from other local communities (Earle 1978).

The Andes at time of first western contact (1532) was dominated by the mighty Inka empire (Cobo 1956 [1653]; Rowe 1946; Moore 1958; Murra 1980 [1956]; Schaedel 1978). The empire began as a chiefdom in Peru's southern highlands and expanded rapidly during the 1400s to control at contact perhaps 980,000 km 2 and 8 to 14 million people. The empire was structured as an administrative hierarchy with vertically arranged offices. The empire was partitioned into four quarters, each subdivided into provinces and districts (*saya*) based on existing ethnic distinctions. Administration at these highest levels was handled by ethnic Inka. The *saya* were then divided into local land holding units (*ayllu*). Administration of the *ayllu* was handled indirectly through its own ethnic leaders. The overriding principle of administration was to emphasize vertical ties of dependence through the state hierarchy (Schaedel 1978, 308). This control depended on the independence of units such as the *ayllu* community from other similar units, and their ultimate dependence on the state for basic rights to land (Earle 1985a).

Very similar to the Hawaiian island chiefdoms, the Inka empire was based on the control of subsistence production. Primary subsistence depended on massive irrigation complexes in the coastal and some intermontane valleys and on intensive shifting cultivation cycles throughout the rolling highlands. All land was owned by the state based on rights of conquest and allocated to commoner communities in return for their *mit'a* labor on state lands and in other productive activities. A local chief *kuraka* served the double function of local leader and state representative. He was responsible for managing local production to support the community and to generate a surplus to finance the state.

Throughout the empire were administrative centers spaced along the major road network. At these centers were large warehouse complexes (Morris 1967; D'Altroy 1981; Earle and D'Altroy 1982) where the staples collected from the local communities were stored to support state administrative and religious personnel and the mobile army.

In the next two sections, I examine the role of specialization and exchange in subsistence goods and wealth. In both Hawai'i and the Andes, specialist production and exchange in subsistence objects were remarkably limited. This point demonstrates the inapplicability of the adaptational model of specialization in these early complex societies based on staple finance. Rather, economic specialists developed in these and similar cases to produce a highly stable and exchangeable wealth used to strengthen and centralize political control.

The Adaptationist Approach to Specialization

The adaptationist approach characterizes the work by cultural ecologists (Steward 1955; Service 1962; Harris 1979) and by the 'New Archaeologists' (Binford 1964; Sanders and Price 1968; Hill 1977). In general terms, cultural evolution is seen as adaptation. New cultural forms, such as the complex governing institutions of the state, are seen as developments to solve specific environmental and economic problems. As population grows in a region, problems are created that require management to guarantee that the needs of the population are adequately met. The specific requirements for management vary according to particular environmental conditions – management of irrigation in dry environments, management of warfare in circumscribed regions, the management of exchange in regions of resource diversity. It is of course the causal linkage between environmental diversity, specialization, exchange, and complex social forms that concerns us here.

The adaptations position with regard to specialization has been articulated clearly by Sanders (1956) and Service (1962, 1975). In areas of high environmental diversity (i.e., where different locales are optimally suited to produce different things), local communities become specialized in their optimal production strategies, and then the communities become economically interdependent as they exchange specialized products. Local community specialization can involve food production (for example, one locale specializing in grain agriculture and exchanging for meat produced by pastoralists or fishermen) or craft production (one locale, impoverished agriculturally, may specialize in crafts that are traded for food [Arnold 1975]). What actually causes the increased specialization is population growth. As production increases to support a growing population, declining yields (increasing costs) will not be uniform in a diverse environment but will be highly localized according to particular conditions of elevation, rainfall, soils, and the like. To compensate for these differences, local populations should emphasize production in their best local strategy.

The resulting community specialization then leads to a regional exchange in subsistence products (food and procurement tools). Communities that had formerly been at war find themselves dependent on each other for their very livelihood. A new level of regional integration is necessary to mediate the conflicting interests over resources access which if unchecked break out in conflict. The chief and eventually the state government evolve to regulate these regional relationships and keep the peace of the market.

This scenario is certainly appealing; it combines a formalist economic theory of decision making to the biological motor of population growth in environmentally constrained circumstances. In the past two decades, anthropologists have come almost to assume that it must be true. But is it? Perhaps in some circumstances, but in both Hawai'i and the Andes where all conditions seem to be met, actual outcomes of development were very different.

In the Hawaiian islands, environmental diversity is very high. Resource availability and productivity change radically as one moves inland from the coastal fisheries and lowland irrigation complexes to the upland forests and as one moves from the rainy windward side of the islands to the near desert leeward side. Major environmental contrasts, as between leeward and windward, certainly determined major differences in subsistence production. Leeward communities emphasized sweet-potato cultivation, and windward areas emphasized taro.

Population density at contact was moderate (39/mi), but locally much higher where productive lowland alluvium was concentrated. Recent research (see Kirch 1982) has documented a leveling off of population growth after AD 1600, a pattern suggesting a density-dependent mechanism.

Despite both environmental diversity and comparatively high population density, regional exchange in subsistence products was remarkably limited in prehistoric Hawaiian chiefdoms (Earle 1977, 1978). Because of the high environmental diversity, community territories could be laid out as a strip from the coast to the mountains that contained within their boundaries a range of necessary resources. In many communities, individual households were within several hours walk of all elevations. What specialization existed, as between fisherman and farmer, was contained within the social bounds of the community. Where community resources differed, the result was not large-scale exchange; rather productivities in crops simply resulted in different local diets and community sizes.

Exchange in Hawaii consisted of two forms. First and most important was 'redistribution' used to mobilize subsistence products and certain raw materials as a means to finance the chiefly institutions (Earle 1977). Quite explicitly this exchange did not distribute goods among specialized commoner communities; rather it provided for the elites and their retainers. Second was reciprocal exchange apparently on a small-scale, unregulated by the chiefs. Some stone materials with unusual properties, fine grain basalt for polished axes and basaltic glass for cutting flakes, were limited in their availability to specific geological sources. Production, possibly involving independent specialists, concentrated at quarries such as the basalt source at Mauna Kea where a considerable volume of adze blanks were manufactured presumably for exchange (McCoy 1977).

In the Andes, environmental diversity is also very high. In the central highlands of Peru, for example, a number of distinct ecological zones are found at different elevations: on the intermontaine valley floors below 3400 m were the maize-producing lands which were often irrigated; between 3400 and 3900 m were the rolling uplands and hill slopes farmed in rotation to produce potatoes and other indigenous tuber and grain crops; above 3900 m were the grasslands where herds of llama and alpaca grazed.

Recent archaeological surveys (Parsons 1976a; Parsons and Hastings 1977; LeBlanc 1981) have documented a long-term and consistent growth in settlements and human population in the central highlands of Peru. Prior to the rapid expansion of the Inka empire, population density reached high levels and intensive systems of production included drained fields, elaborate terracing, and irrigation (Earle et al. 1980).

With high environmental diversity and high population densities, the adaptationist theories would argue for the evolution of community specialization and a regional market system. One would expect either major exchange developing prior to state formation or at least expanding after state formation as regional peace was established.

Ethnohistorical work, however, has claimed that the Central Andes under the Inka empire was a marketless society (Murra 1980 [1956]; La Lone 1982). The Inka empire itself was financed by the mobilization, local storage, and disbursement of staple goods (D'Altroy and Earle 1985). This aspect of the economy was centrally managed by the state. It did not involve movement of goods between specialized producers, but involved the local mobilization of subsistence goods used to support state personnel. Movement of goods was thus limited to state finance.

Instead of developing markets, local communities extended their territories across the landscape to incorporate within their boundaries colonies isolated several days walk from the main settlement in remote areas where special products, such as coca, were procured (Murra 1972). Was this possible and, if so, why?

Recent archaeological work in the Mantaro valley (Earle *et al.* 1980; Earle and D'Altroy 1982; Hastorf 1983; Earle 1985a) unambiguously supports the limited nature of exchange. We have been conducting extensive excavation to contrast economic production and exchange in the periods immediately before Inka conquest (Wanka II; AD 1300–1460) and during Inka domination (Wanka III; AD 1460–1532). Evidence from basic commodities, namely food and household utensils and tools, shows considerable localism with limited specialized production and intercommunity exchange.

Foods are being studied from systematic flotation sampling of all proveniences and from ¼" screening of excavated soils. Plant remains are unexpectedly well preserved with consistent recovery of seeds and plant parts from domesticated and wild species. Virtually all domesticated plant remains derive from species such as maize, quinoa and various tubers, that are produced in the area immediately (<10 km) surrounding the sites. Out of 611 flotation samples already analyzed for the Mantaro region, only three (0.5%) contained traded plant products (Hastorf 1983). Settlements located at different elevations practiced different agricultural strategies, as seen in the stone tools (Russell and Hastorf 1984), but this resulted simply in different diets without exchange (Hastorf 1983). Although analysis of faunal remains is at present more limited, all species identified were clearly from local highland species, such as the camelids, guinea pig, dog, and deer (Earle *et al.* 1985). A handfull of mussels (*Aulacomya alter* and *Choromytilus chorus*) indicates possible trade in food with the coast, but mussel occurrence is very low (1.4% of proveniences) and would not have been significant. No other tropical or coastal species have been identified.

Household utensils and tools included an extensive inventory of domestic ceramics and lithics. For ceramics, sherds have been identified as local (probably manufactured within 10 km of the target site), regional (within 10–15 km), and interregional (beyond 50 km). The majority (82%) of ceramics were locally produced (Earle 1985a). This percentage dropped from 89% in Wanka II to 75% in Wanka III because of the introduction of Inka ceramics (18%) that were apparently state produced and regionally distributed. Definite regional ceramics were not common (decreasing from 6% in Wanka II to 5% in Wanka III). Ceramic types from outside the region were rare (0.4% of the ceramics); they decreased slightly in abundance (0.5–0.3%) following Inka conquest.

For lithics, the majority (83%) were locally (10 km) procured (Earle 1985a). The percentage of local materials actually increased from pre-Inka (79%) to Inka times (86%). The regionally traded materials (a chert and phyllite) were not traded broadly (less than 20 km), but there is good evidence for their specialized production similar to the Hawaiian case. The one traded chert was procured from a large quarry to the west of our main research area; it was then removed as prepared cores to settlements where blades were produced for exchange. At the Wanka II site at Umpamalca, large quantities of manufacturing debris (exhausted cores, substandard blades, and shatter) were recovered in all households excavated; this contrasted with other sites, such as the nearby Wanka II site of Tunanmarca, where used blades were recovered but without manufacturing debris. Evidence for limited village-level specialization in lithic manufacture is clear, but this never represented a large-scale or long-distance operation. Long-distance exchange was very limited. Such a desirable material as obsidian, which is available from the productive Quispisisa source in Huancavelica only 130 km to the south, is represented by only a handful of scattered flakes (0.2% of the lithic assemblage).

To summarize, despite the prerequisite conditions (environmental diversity and high population density) and despite the evolution of social complexity, specialization in subsistence products was of limited importance. Rather the opposite was true. Levels of community self-sufficiency were high in both Hawai'i and the Andes, and if anything increased with the establishment of regional peace. Food commodities were apparently not exchanged between communities except as a system of political finance. Local environmental differences resulted in differences in production but not exchange and symbiosis; the simple outcome was differences in diet. Exchange in household goods was more common (perhaps 20% of the inventory) but it was limited to certain unusual goods with properties not locally replaceable – such as the fine-grain basalt and basaltic glass for Hawai'i, and the chert for the Andes. Long-distance exchange was negligible. Although some exchange undoubtedly existed for both Hawai'i and the Inka empire, it was remarkably restricted in range of goods and considerably less than some egalitarian societies, such as California hunter-gatherers (Ericson 1977) and Italian horticulturalists (Ammerman 1979). Evidently the adaptationist hypothesis linking environmental diversity and population growth to community specialization and regional symbiosis to the evolution of complex societies does not apply well to the Hawaiian and Inka cases.

The Political Approach to Specialization and Exchange in Complex Societies

If the adaptationist approach to cultural evolution is inadequate, can the evolution of complex society still be linked to specialization by drawing on the alternative political approach? Obviously, I think it can.

In essence the political approach reverses the primary direction of causality in the model. Specialization, induced by environmental and demographic conditions, is not seen as causing political complexity; quite the opposite, political complexity causes the elaboration of specialization as a means to strengthen political and economic control. Some might say that this is simply a 'chicken and the egg' dilemma common in the feedback relationships of cultural evolution. In part this may be true, but the *kind* of specialization and the way it articulates to the broader social and economic system is quite different in the two models. In the adaptationist model, specialists produce for a general market of commoners; specialist producers exist because of gains in *efficiency* resulting from underlying economic conditions. In the political model, specialists are attached to elite patrons or governing institutions for whom they produce special products or provide special services; attached specialists exist because of gains in *control* that they provide to the ruling segments of society.

For the political approach, primary is the evolution of social stratification. As argued elsewhere (Johnson and Earle n.d.), the evolution of social stratification is based on economic control arising characteristically from dominion over resources (land). Status rivalry then involves intense competition among elites for dominion and results in a distinctive growth-oriented political economy (Earle 1978). Elites are under constant competitive pressure and must search out opportunities to maximize economic control through prudent investment and management. (The parallels to the capitalist entrepreneur are obvious). Institutional elaboration as related to attempts to maintain and extend economic and political control underlies the increasing scale of complex societies (cf. Johnson 1978). It is in this context that we must understand specialization as linked to explicit strategies to extend control.

In the Hawaiian and Inka cases, I will examine how specialization is linked to the financial base of expanding governing institutions. Two major alternative forms of finance can be recognized – staple finance and wealth finance (D'Altroy and Earle 1985). It is in the operation of these systems of finance that specialists played such an important role in early complex societies (Brumfiel and Earle, Chapter 1).

Staple finance is the simpler tribute system whereby subsistence goods, needed by all, are mobilized from the commoner producers and distributed to support the ruling elite, their retainers, and other institutional personnel. The basic logic is that resources are held by the ruling elites and access to these is granted in return for labor or goods. Considerable variation existed in the centralization of the staple finance system from feudal systems to fully fledged state bureaucracies. Taking an explicitly sociopolitical view of these societies, specialists (retainers of the ruling elites) work to maintain, extend, and legitimize elite economic control.

In the Hawaiian chiefdoms, a proliferation of specialists provided at least five basic roles in the operation of the system of social stratification. First and perhaps most prominently the ruling paramount chief and other chiefs were surrounded by retainers who provided special goods and services to support a sumptuous lifestyle. The paramount moved, surrounded by retainers entrusted with particular jobs such as carrying his feather flyswatter or his elaborate spit bowl. Second were those specialists involved in information processing and administration. Particularly important were the district administrators who established specific personnel and product quotas in order to meet general chiefdom requirements for upcoming wars or ceremonies. Genealogists retained through memory the very lengthy and often complicated pedigrees of chiefs necessary to establish their rank and potential rights. Third were the land managers, who were responsible for guaranteeing the smooth operation of the subsistence economy so as to generate the necessary staple surplus used in finance. They allocated lands to the commoners and supervised work on chiefly lands and on special projects, such as the construction of irrigation systems. Fourth were the military specialists, chiefs trained in the art of war and responsible for combat in battles. Directly associated with the paramount chief and military men were specialists who manufactured the equipment of war, that included special clothing such as wicker helmets, wooden spears, and the large double hulled sailing canoes used for seabased invasions. Fifth were the religious specialists who conducted annual and special ceremonies related to warfare and legitimization. Most important were the annual Makahiki ceremonies in which the paramount chief representing the god Lono proceeded around the island accompanied by his priests. As Lono he received annual gifts, as part of his staple finance, and performed ceremonies to ensure the fertility of the communities' land and people. The list of specialists in the Hawaiian chiefdom was long indeed and most were involved directly in the ruling operation of the chiefs.

In the Inka empire, the general list of specialists included the same five basic functions described above. With the much greater scale of the empire, the number and specific jobs of the specialists were expanded. This can be illustrated in two areas of particular importance for state integration – information handling and military support. Information handling in the Inka empire involved several kinds of specialists including administrators at the different levels of the hierarchy, inspectors sent out from the capital at Cuzco, record keepers, and message carriers. The record keepers, using a mnemonic device of knotted strings (*khipu*), monitored the payment and disbursement of staple goods through the warehousing system. The message carriers (*chaski*) were runners stationed along the roads who would carry messages rapidly in relay throughout the vast empire. Military support was greatly expanded because of the size of the army involved in external conquest and in suppression of internal rebellion. The amount of equipment, such as clothing, sandals, shields and maces, must have been staggering. Semi-industrial production of clothing for the army may have become quite common (see later discussion of weavers on Lake Titicaca).

The new institutions of chiefdom and state were always associated with such diverse specialists as we have described for the Hawaiian and Inka cases. A few general points should be emphasized about these specialists. Their involvement with a general population was limited to situations where the chiefdom or state was directly involved. The specialists rather served the social elite and newly developed institutions involved in finance and control. The number and specificity of specialists proliferated with increasing scale of the chiefdom and state institutions.

As I have indicated, staple finance was the simplest, and I believe most common, basis for early complex society. It, however, has a major liability, namely decentralization. Because of the bulkiness and weight of staple products, transportation of the goods is prohibitively expensive over long distances (D'Altroy and Earle 1985). Staple finance is therefore suitable only for regionally compact societies, such as Hawaiian island chiefdom, or a decentralized state, such as the Inka. In the Inka case, for example, each region had its own administrative center and maintained its own, separate storage system for support. Local staples were collected to pay for local state activities and, because of the cost of moving staples long distances (cf. Drennan 1984), little was moved through the empire.

This decentralization created severe problems of control for the developing state. The locally produced and stored staples, in addition to creating local finance, created opportunities for local revolt. Rebels could seize the stores and use them to fund their revolt against the central government. In order to solve this problem, most developing complex societies used some elements of wealth finance in which attached specialists played a central role.

Wealth finance consists of the procurement and use of exchange valuables to pay personnel (D'Altroy and Earle 1985). The use of exchange valuables (wealth) as payment exists in all societies (Earle 1982); however, the elaboration of its use, eventually with true currency, plays a critical role in the development of finance in states. The main advantage of wealth as a basis for finance is its high value to weight ratio; this of course minimizes the cost of transportation and permits movement across great distances. In the evolution of the state, a shift to wealth finance permits an expansion in the regional scale of the polity while retaining centralized control. Wealth collected from incorporated populations can be moved into the state's center, where it is held until used as payment. The central storage of the wealth gives central control over finance which deprives peripheral areas of financial independence and a base to fund rebellion. The central control of wealth strengthens vertical ties of dependence and inhibits the growth of opposition coalitions (cf. Brumfiel, Chapter 9). Storable wealth used as a fund for payment and as a display of eliteness becomes monopolized.

Now it is essential to consider the significance of wealth in the societies under consideration. Personnel working for the chiefdom or state must have a means to obtain necessary subsistence goods. In the elemental staple finance system, the needed subsistence goods are collected by the ruling government and distributed directly to its support personnel. But what role does wealth play in the operation of a staple finance system? No matter how valued are metals and cloth they cannot be eaten. In a system of wealth finance, the solution is to have the wealth convertible to subsistence goods in a market exchange; this is the apparent solution for the Aztec state (Brumfiel 1980). In the Hawaiian and Inka cases, and I suspect in most early stratified societies, wealth was *not* easily convertible into subsistence goods because it circulated in a separate sphere of exchange (cf. Earle 1982). Although not directly convertible into subsistence goods, wealth was inextricably linked to access to subsistence goods. To be specific, as I will try to show, wealth acted as a highly visible symbol of status, meant not as abstract prestige but as a status position the holder of which had explicit rights to income in the staple finance system. Without written contracts, the physical demonstration of status is essential to define one's rights in the sociopolitical hierarchy, especially the rights of subsistence support (Earle 1985b).

At this point, specialization in craft manufacture as it relates to state development takes on a different significance. Wealth objects must be scarce; this limited availability can reflect the natural rarity of the raw material used, as in the case of the Hawaiian feather cloaks and the Inka metal, but it also reflects the amount of skilled labor required in manufacture. Wealth, made by specialists, can be controlled by controlling the production process.

The Hawaiian and Inka cases illustrate the control of wealth production in the development of complex societies with similar staple finance bases. Hawaiian and pre-Inka (Wanka) societies were similar chiefdoms organizing polities in the tens of thousands. The Inka were an imperial state organizing an overall population in the millions. Production of wealth in the chiefdoms was handled by specialists attached to elite patrons who distributed the wealth as symbols of authority along with direct right to land. In the imperial state, some production continued in this manner but much changed. The use of wealth in status display and legitimization remained unaltered, but the control over the production and distribution was centralized as a direct means for strengthening political control over the decentralized empire. Production shifted from the many attached specialists of local elites to semi-industrial workshops under direct state management.

In the Hawaiian chiefdoms, staples were not stored or moved over distances; staple finance was highly decentralized such that the paramount chief and his large retinue of advisors and functionaries moved through the chiefdom living in turn on the staple products of dependent communities. This 'moveable feast', as it was called in feudal Europe, was necessary as the large retinue quickly devoured locally available surpluses. Obviously this decentralized staple base was fraught with problems of control that resulted in a repeated pattern of local rebellion against the paramount chief. It is my argument that the wealth, as symbols of legitimacy and explicit rights of economic access, helped to overcome this weakness. Wealth objects, that included cloaks, helmets, standards (*kahili*), and necklaces, were crafted of rare raw materials, feathers and whale ivory, by skilled specialists. Wealth was scarce because of its natural rarity (especially of certain feathers) and the skill required in its manufacture. The Hawaiian case illustrates both the symbolic importance of wealth and the role of attached specialists in controlling its availability.

The most important objects of wealth and symbols of power were the feathered cloaks, *'ahu'ula* (Malo 1951 [1898], 76–7; Brigham 1899, 1903, 1918; Buck 1957, 215–31; Cummins 1984; Earle 1985b). The finest cloaks were full length and brilliant yellow with contrasting red designs. They were made with a fine fibre net base onto which were attached small bundles of feathers. On a single cloak, hundreds of thousands of these feathers created a shining, velvet finish of incomparable beauty.

Access to and control over such wealth items illustrates well the linkage between craft specialization, wealth, and symbolic representation in complex polities (see also Brumfiel, Chapter 9). In Hawai'i, feathered cloaks could only be worn by high ranking, male chiefs 'as an insignia in time of war and when they went into battle' (Malo 1951 [1898], 77). They were also worn on special ceremonial encounters between high chiefs to demonstrate potential power and thus intimidate a potential foe and/or attract a valuable ally. In full dress, Kalani'opu'u, ruling chief of Hawai'i, and his supporting chiefs came out to meet Captain Cook, the first westerner to contact the islands:

> *The next day, about noon, the king, in a large canoe, attended by two others, set out from the village, and paddled toward the ships in great state. Their appearance was grand and magnificent. In the first canoe was Terreeoboo [Kalani'opu'u] and his chiefs, dressed in feathered cloaks and helmets, and armed with spears and daggers; in the second, came the venerable Kaoo, the chief of the priests, and his brethren, with their idols displayed on red cloth. These idols*

*were busts of a gigantic size, made of wicker-work, and curiously covered with small feathers
of various colors, wrought in the same manner with their cloaks. (King 1784, 16–7)*

The accompanying illustration by Webber (figure 6.1) shows a large double-hulled
sailing canoe with about twenty paddlers and forty people standing on the platform between the hulls. At least seven of these, including Kalani'opu'u, were
wearing feathered cloaks. In a very similar meeting Kamehameha I, the new paramount of Hawai'i, dressed in a full length yellow cloak, came out in his large canoe
to greet Vancouver (1798, 126). Vancouver, as representative of the British crown,
was obviously an important potential ally for Kamehameha. Other occasions when
cloaks were worn included the confrontation when Captain Cook was killed by the
Hawaiians and later when his bones were returned to the British (King 1784, 137).

Cloaks varied considerably in size, shape, and color (type of feathers used)
which denoted the relative status of the high chiefs and distinguished warriors
who wore them. For example, the brilliant large circular cloaks of *Mamo* feathers
were battle regalia for an island's paramount (Malo 1951 [1898], 77). The smaller
rectangular cloaks with tropic bird and man-of-war feathers were worn by lower
ranked chiefs (King 1784, 136–37).

Cloaks were physical representatives of status with its system of rights to position and land title. "*Ahu'ula* means literally red ('*ula*) garment ('*ahu*), red being the
symbolic color of the gods and chiefs through Polynesia (Buck 1957, 216; Cummins
1984). In fact, the finest cloaks in the Hawaiian islands were not red but yellow,
because the yellow feathers from the *mamo* and '*o'o* were exceedingly scarce and

Figure 6.1 [orig. figure 6.1]   Kalani'opu'u, paramount of Hawai'i, coming out to greet Captain James
Cook
(Webber engraving in King 1784).

highly valued. Each bird had only a small tuft of yellow feathers (most of the bird being black) such that ten thousand birds might be caught to make a single magnificent cape. The natural rarity of the feathers created the limited availability necessary to establish and maintain value. This rarity was also coupled to a control over the production process that was necessary to the political manipulation of their distribution.

The control was manifest at all steps in the system – initial procurement of the feathers, their fabrication into cloaks, and presentation. The feathers themselves were procured by professional bird hunters (*po'e hahai manu*) who used sticky bird lines and nets (Buck 1957, 217). The bird skins or feather bunches were then valuables apparently used in exchange but especially used as tribute payments. When Captain Cook first landed on the island of Kaua'i, he was offered 'great numbers of skins of small red birds for sale, which were often tied up in bunches of twenty or more, or had a small wooden skewer run through their nostrils' (Cook 1784, 207). Later, on the island of Hawai'i, when Cook first visited the paramount chief Kalani'opu'u, Cook observed an abundance of tributary gifts to the chief that included 'a vast quantity of red and yellow feathers, tied to the fibres of cocoa-nut husks' (King 1784, 28).

Feathers were an important annual tributary payment made to the paramount chief by communities where birds were found. As described by Malo (1951 [1898], 77).

> *The lands that produced feathers were heavily taxed at the Makahiki time, feathers being the most acceptable offering to the Makahiki idol. If any land failed to furnish the full tale of feathers due for the tax, the landlord was turned off (hemo).*

The paramount chief, as the earthly manifestation of the Makahiki god Lono, received the feathers directly. The stable finance system was thus extended to require payment in a rare raw material from which his valuables (the cloaks and other feathered objects) were to be fabricated.

Little is known about the actual organization of production for the valuables, but it seems highly probable that this was done by specialists attached directly to the paramount and perhaps other high ranking chiefs. Kepelino (Beckwith 1932, 134) states that the cloaks were 'woven by persons skilled in the art into fine nets.' Kepelino's description is found in a general account of chiefs and attached specialists (military guards, genealogists, land experts, and personal attendants). The implication by context is that the feather weavers were also part of a high-ranking chiefly household.

The paramount chief by controlling the surplus flow of staple goods was in the best position to support attached specialists including feather weavers. In this situation, the craft specialist functioned as a converter. He was personally supported by staples mobilized by the chiefly hierarchy for which he manufactured a highly visible and storable wealth. The craft specialist in this role was the main link between the mobilization of food and raw material production and the creation of wealth for distribution (cf. D'Altroy and Earle 1985).

The distribution of the feather cloaks by the paramount chief is a clear indication of their use in the definition of political statuses. In his inventory of the feather cloaks, Brigham (1899, 1903, 1918) records the history of all capes known at that time. The history of transfer is recorded for fifteen capes: one by inheritance and fourteen by gift from a paramount chief. The majority of these were given by Kamehameha III to western dignitaries or others in his service. Recipients included William Lee (first Chief Justice of the Hawaiian Islands), William Miller (British representative), Fredrick Byny (who attended Liholiho on his visit to London), Samuel Whitney (first missionary to Kaua'i), J.H. Aulick (Commander, USN), and L. Kearny (Commander, USN on diplomatic errand). Two dramatic examples of cloak gifts were recorded in early explorer accounts. When Captain Cook was first visited by the Hawaiian paramount, he was given several cloaks:

> they [Kalani'opu'u and Captain Cook] had scarcely been seated, when the king [paramount chief] rose up, and in a very graceful manner threw over the Captain's shoulders, the cloak he himself wore, put a feathered helmet on his head, and a curious fan [feathered kahili] into his hand. He also spread at his feet five or six other cloaks, all exceedingly beautiful, and of the greatest value. (King 1784, 17)

Similarly, Vancouver received a fine cloak from the new paramount Kamehameha I:

> Kamehameha conceiving this might be his last visit, presented me with a handsome cloak formed of red and yellow feathers, with a small collection of other native curiosities; and at the same time delivered into my charge the superb cloak that he had worn on his formal visit on our arrival. This cloak was very neatly made of yellow feathers; after he had displayed its beauty and had shown me the two holes made in different parts of it by the enemy's spears the first day he wore it, in his last battle for the sovereignty of this island, he very carefully folded it up, and desired that on my arrival in England, I would present it in his name to H.M. King George; and as it had never been worn by any person but himself, he strictly enjoined me not to permit any person whatever to throw it over their shoulders, saying it was the most valuable in the island of Hawaii, and for that reason he had sent it to so great a monarch, and so good a friend, as he considered the King of England. (Vancouver 1789, 271)

These two formal presentations show clearly the importance of the cloaks as gift exchanges between highest ranking individuals. Almost surely the exchanges were meant as a ceremony of formal alliance. (See Brumfiel's Chapter 9 for additional discussion of wealth exchange as a means of validating political relationships).

The other main context for transfer involved warfare. Cloaks, worn in battle, were given to great warriors in recognition of their valor and were seized from those defeated in battle.

> The ahu-ula was also conferred upon warriors, but only upon those who had distinguished themselves and had merit, and it was an object of plunder in every battle.
> Unless one were a warrior in something more than name he would not succeed in capturing his prisoner nor in getting possession of his ahu-ula. (Malo 1951 [1898], 77)

Although it is implied that a successful warrior received a cloak directly in plunder, this appears not to be strictly the case. The only historically documented case of such seizure is one cape in the Bishop Museum (number 2 in Brigham's [1899] inventory); this cape was seized by Kamehameha I when he slew Kiwala'o, rightful heir to the paramountcy of Hawai'i. The large number of cloaks listed by Brigham as given by the Hawaiian rulers early in the historic period strongly suggests that the cloaks captured in the rapid expansion of the newly formed Hawaiian state went not to the victorious warriors but to the victorious paramount who then distributed the cloaks to his supporters and allies.

Ownership and distribution of the cloaks were thus very similar to the system of land tenure and in fact may have been linked to it. All lands were the property of the paramount chief, and, on his victories in wars of succession and conquest, the lands were then distributed by the paramount to his high ranking relatives and close military supporters. Access to land through conquest and central distribution was apparently identical to that for the cloaks. Based partly on this clear parallel it seems reasonable to suggest that the elite regalia including the cloak was a declaration of right to a landed estate on which the chiefs depended for their income.

What I am arguing is that the Hawaiian cloaks, a highly visible and limited wealth, were symbolic of a system of status and resource access on which the Hawaiian chiefdoms depended. Control over the raw material and fabrication of the cloaks translated into a control of the symbolism of power and its religious legitimization.

In the Inka empire, the role of specialist-manufactured wealth is similarly apparent, especially in cloth and metals. These wealth objects served primarily to define visually the status divisions within society, and the objects were important commodities of exchange. In clothing, status was marked not by tailoring but by different grades of cloth and kinds of ornamentation (especially of metal and shell) (Murra 1962, 711). Access to this visual wealth was thus essential to demonstrate one's position with its concomitant economic and political rights.

Cloth was of particular importance in the Andes because of its symbolism and exchange value (see especially Murra 1962 for a summary of the ethnohistoric evidence). Often a simple distinction is drawn between rough, domestic cloth used in everyday contexts and the fine *kumpi* cloth used for elite clothing, to wrap the idols, in sacrifice, and in similar special contexts. The *kumpi* was smooth and tightly woven, and it was often decorated with shells and feathers.

The major life crises and marriage ceremonies were marked in the Andes by exchanges that frequently involved cloth. At birth, puberty, marriage and death cloth was displayed, ceremonially worn, and exchanged. After death the Inka mummies were annually taken out and paraded around dressed in sumptuous cloth (Guaman Poma 1936 [1613], 256). In order to function in society – to define one's status, to obtain a wife, and to create and maintain social relations – access to cloth and other valuables was essential. This was not a creation of the state, as identical conditions characterized stateless societies generally (Earle 1982); however, it created an opportunity for control that was enhanced by the state through its central management of production, storage, and distribution of the wealth.

   Production of cloth was organized in at least three ways that illustrate the nature of state involvement in this critical process. First, thread was spun and cloth was woven at the household level. Presumably much of this was used for family consumption, but the household was also required to produce a certain quota of cloth, perhaps one blanket a year, for the state. As described by Murra (1962, 715), the household was obligated to produce cloth for the state in return for access to community herds residually owned by the state through rights of conquest. Cloth production at the household level therefore fitted into the broader pattern of mobilization in the staple finance system. The cloth derived would have been of common quality and would have served the daily uses of state personnel.
   Second, specialists involved in weaving of the fine cloth that represented wealth were attached to elite households for which they produced objects for elite use and exchange. Generally, the high quality of Andean textiles argues convincingly for specialized manufacture predating the Inka empire by at least a thousand years. Examples of such fine textiles include the technically elaborate Necropolis textiles decorated with embroidery that date to about 200 BC (Lumbreras 1974). In its simplest form, multiple wives of local leaders may have been specially involved in weaving. Cock (1977), in his analysis of Collagua *kuraka*, mentions that artisans, especially weavers and smiths, belonged to local elites for whom they produced goods for distribution. In the Mantaro Valley excavations, spindle whorls and needles were recovered characteristically from all households but were more abundant in elite households for both the Inka and pre-Inka period (Costin 1984). Following conquest, the products of these attached specialists became gifts to the Inka.
   Third, and as far as the argument goes most important, specialist weavers, who were attached formerly to elite households, became involved in semi-industrial large-scale production directly for the Inka state. Weavers, recruited from local communities, were brought together to form specialist villages like Millerea on the northern shore of Lake Titicaca. There, 'one thousand' Aymara weavers manufactured cloth for the heavy demands of the military which used cloth both to differentiate status and to reward participation (Murra and Morris 1976; Murra 1982). *Aqllacuna* were a singular group of 'chosen women' recruited from the local communities but removed to the regional administrative centers where they were involved in a number of functions but most importantly in the manufacture of the fine *kumpi* cloth. Cieza (1862 [1551], 432) mentioned the presence of *aqllacuna* at Hatun Xauca in the Mantaro valley. At the administrative center of Huánuco Pampa, Morris (1974) has identified a large, enclosed compound that he believed housed *aqllacuna*. The compound contained forty-five large, regular structures, spacious plazas and corridors, and a distinctive concentration of spindle whorls and weaving instruments. At present, we do not know the kind of cloth being manufactured, whether *kumpi* or domestic, but the semi-industrial scale of production is well documented. LeVine (1985) has identified a similarly organized compound at the nearby center of Pumpu where large-scale production may also have taken place.
   The state received cloth through all forms of production – as part of corvée labor

obligation, as gifts from regional chiefs, and as production from institutional specialists. The large amounts of cloth received filled many of the state warehouses through the empire. The extent of the cloth stores must have been impressive even to the conquistadors whose interests were more in the precious metals:

> *Among the eyewitnesses of the invasion, Xerez reports that in Caxamarca there were houses filled to the ceiling with clothes tied into bundles. Even after 'the Christians took all they wanted,' no dent was made in the pile. 'There was so much cloth of wool and cotton that it seemed to me that many ships could have been filled with them.' As Pizarro's army progressed across the Inka realm, similar stores were found at Xauxa and in Cuzco. In the capital, it was 'incredible' to see the number of separate warehouses filled with wool, rope, cloth both fine and rough, garments of many kinds, feathers, and sandals. Pedro Pizarro mused some 40 years later about what he had seen as a youth: 'I could not say about the warehouses I saw, of cloth and all kinds of garments which were made and used in this kingdom, as there was no time to it, nor sense to understand so many things.' (Murra 1962, 717)*

The state used these massive stores of cloth as a means of payment. Cloth was paid for state services such as carrying tribute or a regional idol to Cuzco. Particularly important were the payments from the ruling Inka to local chiefs in return for their special services. Cloth, with its symbolic definition of status and its exchange value, was given over to the local leaders who could use the cloth directly in ceremonial display of his status or exchange it for desired goods and services.

The Inka state centralized the distribution of cloth by establishing payment in cloth both from commoners and elites. More revolutionary, it established large-scale production of the cloth by specialists which provided a large volume of wealth for distribution similar to the feathered cloaks of the Hawaiians.

The manufacture and use of metal in the Inka state illustrates a pattern of production and distribution similar to the cloth. The Andes witnessed the independent development of complex metallurgical technology involving smelting and fabrication of gold, silver, copper, lead, and a number of alloys (Lechtman 1979, 1984). Metal working was quite sophisticated involving such techniques as smelting sulfide ores (Lechtman 1979), plating (Lechtman 1979, 1984), and lost-wax casting. Simpler procedures using native metals and oxide ores, and fabrication with sheet-metal hammering and cutting were common through the region. Uses for the metal were quite varied including institutional decoration (gold and silver sheet covered walls, of the Inka), personal ornamentation (pins, discs, head bands, ear spools, and the like) and simple technology (needles, axes, bola weights).

Metal was highly valued for its symbolic identification and exchange value. From at least Chavin times (800 BC), gold and silver were symbols of rank, power and religious force (Lechtman 1984). In Inka cosmology, gold was the sweat of the sun and silver, the tears of the moon, two central high gods. Helms (1981) has argued that Inka nobility used metals in their lives to identify themselves with the celestial realm, symbolized by the colors of metal. Lothrop's (1938) description of the sumptuous metal wealth of the Inka is remarkable. Included were elaborate symbols of the high gods (golden suns, silver moons), lifesize golden statues of ancestors, and great vessels of gold and silver. The use of metals in status and political display was central to the legitimization of relationships within the Andean world. Annual ceremonies featured public displays of metal wealth as with the parading of the ancestral idols; artificial golden gardens of maize and other plants were probably aspects of fertility rites (Lothrop 1938). Status and worldly or spiritual power were conveyed by restricting the wearing of certain metal objects, such as the beautiful ear spools, to the Inka rulers (Lechtman 1984). The wearing of the ear spools, along with special cloths, was a visual statement of status and associated position. Along with cloth, metal was also a standard gift at life-crisis ceremonies (Murra 1962). During the marriage ceremony, the woman gave the man metal and a wool tunic (Rowe 1946, 286). Morúa (1946 [1590], 64–65; referenced in Murra 1962, 719) described the gift by an Inka ruler to his bride of a fine cloth and a metal pin. Metal was also frequently included as part of the burial offering.

The conquering Spanish were of course first and foremost in search of precious metals, and it was in the Andes where their dreams were realized. The famous ransom of the Inka Atawalpa is said to have been 238,000 oz. of gold, filling the ruler's cell higher than a man could reach (Lothrop 1938). Certainly the Empire was manufacturing and stockpiling massive amounts of metal, but why? Partly the metals displayed at ceremonies of legitimization were the critical prop of defining the distinctiveness and sanctity of the ruling Inka. In addition, however, metal may have come to be an important means of payment.

Some of the best information on the uses of metal and how these uses changed with Inka conquest come from the recent excavation of twenty-nine domestic patio groups in the Mantaro Valley (Earle *et al.* 1985). Although it has long been recognized that metal was an important component of burial offerings, its uses in domestic context have not been systematically studied. Metal products, including pieces of silver, copper, and lead were recovered from 120 of 2,168 nonburial proveniences excavated (total ubiquity = 5.5%). Forms included ornaments (silver and copper pins, discs, and pendants), various copper and tin bronze tools (needles, axes, chisels, and weights), and lead tools (possible spindle whorls or weights) and ceramic mends or plugs. In all, metal increased somewhat in overall occurrence from pre-Inka (3.8% of proveniences) to Inka (7.0% of proveniences).

More dramatic were certain shifts in the types of metals recovered. During the pre-Inka period, the most common metal recovered was silver used in ornamentation. As seen in figure 6.2, silver was concentrated in elite households and probably denoted high status. During Inka domination, silver became significantly rarer. Although it is possible that silver production decreased, it seems more likely that the silver produced locally in Mantaro Valley was expropriated by the Inka and used as display and payment primarily among the highest levels. Silversmiths worked at the Mantaro administrative center of Hatun Xauxa (Cieza 1862 [1551], 432). The increase in frequency of lead (0.1% of proveniences in pre-Inka to 0.6% of provenience in Inka) probably indicates silver smelting from galena with lead as a byproduct. If the silver were won from galena, lead oxide would have been produced. Since the lead would have to have been smelted from the galena, a complex process, it would seem unjustified by the very simple and mundane uses

	Ubiquity of metal artifacts					Uniquity of production byproducts	Number of proveniences
	Ag	Cu	Pb	Other	Total		
Wanka II							
elite	3.0	2.2	0.2	0.2	5.2	0.5	594
commoner	0.8	0.5	0	0.3	1.5	0.3	389
Wanka III							
elite	1.6	8.1	0.7	0.3	10.3	2.2	669
commoner	0.2	2.3	0.4	0	2.7	0.6	516
Total	1.5	3.7	0.4	0.2	5.5	1.0	2168

Figure 6.2 [orig. figure 6.2]   Ubiquity of prehistoric metals: percentage of excavated proveniences containing metal for pre-Inka (Wanka II) and Inka (Wanka III) contexts.

of lead documented and more likely to have been derived from a silver smelting byproduct.

Copper increased dramatically in overall occurrence (1.5% of provenience in pre-Inka to 5.6% in Inka). In part, copper replaced some ornamental uses of silver. For the first time, copper discs were found, as silver discs became quite rare. Small pins of both silver and copper were made in identical forms during the Inka period.

Importantly, the Inka state may well have been directly involved in the manufacture and distribution of these copper objects. Prior to Inka conquest of the Mantaro, coppers were an arsenic bronze, most probably derived from smelting local sulphide ores (Howe 1983; Lechtman 1976). During the Inka period, the coppers contained significant amounts of tin that must have come through long-distance exchange with the southern highlands. As Lechtman (1976) has discussed, tin bronze became a uniform metal throughout the Inka empire. Although a major study of this point is wanting, I would argue that the manufacture of the coppers had become centralized and under direct state supervision.

Direct evidence for the organization of metal production under the Inka is quite limited. Mining is said to have been done as part of the annual labor tax (*mit'a*) (Rowe 1946). Moore (1958, 39) suggests, based on her analysis of the ethnohistoric documents, that mines were the property of the Inka state, similar to agricultural and pastoral resources, but that ore production and metal fabrication were under the control of local leaders who delivered the wealth objects as gifts to the Inka. Specialists, miners and craftsmen, were then exempted from regular labor tax. At least in part, therefore, the production of metals was closely tied to the more general system of mobilization through staple finance. Attached specialists working for local leaders were supported by local elites who then delivered up the finished goods as gifts to the state. This is *not* state controlled production; rather it was a continuation of the pre-Inka pattern redesigned by the Inka.

In the Mantaro Valley, ore, slag, casting spill and other manufacturing debris is quite rare in domestic contexts (ubiquity = 1.0%), suggesting that the level of production at the household was very low (figure 6.2). What evidence we did recover was concentrated in elite household contexts, especially during Wanka III. This pattern fits Moore's suggestion of local production by specialists, attached to local elites; however, the evidence for production is really very limited. In our survey of the settlements, no debris of metal production was noted. Smelting was probably not practiced locally and metal fabrication was probably on a limited scale. Metal production off the settlements investigated may have been handled at other local settlements, but it is plausible that metal production, like cloth, had come under direct state control.

Murra (1980 [1956]) has brought together ample evidence for full-time specialist smiths attached to the state. These individuals, such as the highly skilled smiths of the Chimor state, were moved to the capital at Cuzco and to other administrative centers where they produced goods for the state, its direct institutional use, and distribution to local leaders. Cieza (1862 [1551]) mentioned smiths located in all the Inka administrative settlements. These smiths were most probably *yanacona*, individuals removed from their community association and working full time for the state (Rowe 1946, 268).

To summarize briefly, prior to Inka expansion in the central Andes, the production, distribution and use of wealth was very similar to the pattern seen in the Hawaiian chiefdoms. Production appears to have been mainly by specialists attached to elite households and the metal goods were distributed over relatively short distance to be used as status markers. With the Inka expansion, the local production at elite households continued and became part of the more general mobilization of goods to support the state. Dramatically, the state appears to have taken charge of production in key wealth objects, especially the metal and cloth, and to have created large-scale systems of manufacture, warehousing, and long-distance movement. At this point, production had taken on a semi-industrial scale with direct state involvement.

Murra (1980 [1956]) develops a most interesting argument for a possible economic transformation under Inka domination. At first production of cloth and metals appears to have been handled indirectly; a requirement of each community was to provide goods (cloth and metal) as part of the broader labor assessment. The Inka shifted emphasis to production of key wealth items by specialists removed from their local community contexts. The implication is that wealth, used in ceremonies of legitimization, as status markers, and as exchange valuables, was being produced by full-time specialists working for Inka state institutions.

The reasons for this significant change in the nature of production appear to be two. First the larger volume of production surely had certain economies of scale. Second, and probably more important, the centralization of production brought it under direct state control. This would have strengthened the economic basis of the empire and helped counterbalance the centrifugal forces inherent in a staple finance system (D'Altroy and Earle 1985). The development of specialized production of course underlay this critical move.

Conclusion

To return to the initial question, what is the relationship between specialization and the evolution of complex societies? In complex societies such as the Hawaiian chiefdoms and the Inka empire, the economic basis of stratification was control over staple production. Ownership of productive resources, especially land, was most basic. In these situations regional exchange, linking local communities, was remarkably little developed except in certain raw materials and craft goods. In this context, where regional exchange was limited and on a small scale, the independent specialists working for a general market were comparatively unimportant. In at least these cases, local specialization and intercommunity interdependence were neither the preconditions for nor the outcome of complex society.

Rather, specialization appears to have developed as an outcome of the development of social stratification and large political and religious institutions. These attached specialists performed a variety of functions that included monopoly of force, economic management, and ceremonial legitimization. In terms of craft production, the manufacture of special wealth (feathered cloaks, cloth, and metal) served strategically to control the society economically and symbolically. The items of wealth served as means of payment, as symbols of legitimate power, and as evidence of sanctity. To understand the evolution of attached specialists from the retainers of complex chiefdoms to the semi-industrial workshop of states is to understand the role of their products, i.e., the society's wealth, in the developing system of stratification.

Acknowledgements

This paper was first presented at XIth International Congress of Anthropological and Ethnological Sciences, Vancouver (1982). I am grateful for discussions with the audience and symposium panel. Cathy Costin, Glenn Russell, and Bruce Owen have helped critically evaluate the paper's ideas, and have made available their own data on ceramic (Costin) and lithic (Russell) production and exchange. Elizabeth Brumfiel's work as seen in this volume and earlier papers has influenced my consideration of the linked economic and symbolic aspects of wealth. The Mantaro Valley research was supported by a grant from National Science Foundation (BNS82 03723).

References

Ammerman, A. 1979. A study of obsidian exchange in Calabria. *World Archaeology* 11: 95–110.

Arnold, D. E. 1975. Ceramic ecology of the Ayacucho Basin, Peru. *Current Anthropology* 16: 183–205.

Binford, L. 1964. A consideration of archaeological research design. *American Antiquity* 29: 425–41.

Beckwith, M. W. 1932. Kepelino's traditions of Hawaii. *Bernice P. Bishop Museum Bulletin* 95.

Brigham, W. T. 1899. Hawaiian feather work. *Bernice P. Bishop Museum Memoir* 1(4).

    1903. Additional notes on Hawaiian feather work. *Bernice P. Bishop Museum Memoir* 1(5): 437–53.

    1918. Additional notes on Hawaiian feather work. *Bernice P. Bishop Museum Memoir* 7(1): 1–64.

Brumfiel, E. M. 1980. Specialization, market exchange, and the Aztec state: A view from Huexotla. *Current Anthropology* 21: 459–78.

1987. Elite and utilitarian crafts in the Aztec state, in E. M. Brumfiel and T. K. Earle (eds.) *Specialization, Exchange, and Complex Societies.* Cambridge: Cambridge University Press, pp. 102–118.

Brumfiel, E. M. and Earle, T. K. 1987. Specialization, exchange, and complex societies: an introduction, in E. M. Brumfiel and T. K. Earle (eds.) *Specialization, Exchange, and Complex Societies.* Cambridge: Cambridge University Press, pp. 1–9.

Buck, P. H. (te Rangi Hiroa). 1957. Clothing, in P. Buck (ed.) *Arts and Crafts of Hawaii* (Section V). Honolulu, Bernice P. Bishop Museum Press.

Cieza de Leon, Pedro de. 1862. La cronica del Perú. *Biblioteca de Autores Españoles* 26: 349–458. Madrid, Ediciones Atlas [orig. 1551].

Cobo, B. 1956. Historia del nuevo mundo, II. *Biblioteca de Autores Españoles*, v. 92. Madrid, Ediciones Atlas [orig. 1653].

Cock, C. G. 1977. Los kurakas de los Collaguas: poder político y poder económico. *Historia y Cultura* 10: 95–118.

Cook, J. 1784. *A Voyage to the Pacific Ocean*, vol. II. Dublin: H. Chamberlaine.

Costin, C. 1984. The organization and intensity of spinning and cloth production among the late prehispanic Huanca. Paper presented at the Annual Meeting of the Institute of Andean Studies, Berkeley.

Cummins, T. 1984. Kinshape: design of Hawaiian feather capes. *Art History* 7: 1–20.

Drennan, R. D. 1984. Long-distance transport costs in prehispanic Mesoamerica. *American Anthropologist* 86: 105–12.

D'Altroy, T. 1981. *Empire growth and consolidation: the Xauxa region of Peru under the Inkas.* Doctoral dissertation, Department of Anthropology, University of California, Los Angeles.

D'Altroy, T. and Earle, T. K. 1985. State finance, wealth finance, and storage in the Inka political economy. *Current Anthropology* 26: 187–206.

Earle, T. K. 1977. A preappraisal of redistribution: Complex Hawaiian chiefdoms, in T. K. Earle and J. E. Ericson (eds.) *Exchange Systems in Prehistory* New York: Academic Press, pp. 213–29.

1978. *Economic and Social Organization of a Complex Chiefdom: The Halelea District, Kaua'i, Hawaii* (Anthropological Paper, No. 63). Ann Arbor: The University of Michigan Museum of Anthropology.

1982. The ecology and politics of primitive valuables, in J. G. Kennedy and R. B. Edgerton (eds.) *Culture and Ecology: Eclectic Perspectives* (Special Publication No. 15) Washington D.C.: American Anthropological Association, pp. 65–83.

1985a. Commodity exchange and markets in the Inca state: Recent archaeological evidence, in S. Plattner (ed.) *Markets and Marketing* (S.E.A. Monographs in Economic Anthropology, No. 4), pp. 369–77. Lanham, MD: University Press of America.

1985b. The uses of style in complex chiefdoms. Paper delivered in symposium *Anthropological Approaches to Style.* Minneapolis, Minn., January.

Earle, T. and D'Altroy, T. 1982. Storage facilities and state finance in the upper Mantaro Valley, Peru, in J. Ericson and T. Earle (eds.) *Contexts for Prehistoric Exchange* New York: Academic Press, pp. 265–90.

Earle, T.K., D'Altroy, T., Hastorf, C., Scott, C., Costin, C., Russell, G. and Sandefur, E. 1985. Preliminary report of the 1982 and 1983 field research of the Upper Mantaro Archaeological Research Project. Ms. under preparation for the Institute of Archaeology, University of California, Los Angeles.

Earle, T. K., D'Altroy, T., LeBlanc C., Hastorf, C. and LeVine, T. 1980. Changing settlement patterns in the Upper Mantaro Valley, Peru. *Journal of New World Archaeology* 4(1): 1–49.

Ericson, J. 1977. Egalitarian exchange systems in California: a preliminary view, in T. Earle and J. Ericson (eds.) *Exchange Systems in Prehistory* New York: Academic Press, pp. 109–26.

Guaman Poma de Ayala, F. 1936. *Nueva Cronica y Buen Gobierno.* Paris: Institut d'Ethnologie [orig. 1613].

Harris, M. 1979. *Cultural Materialism.* New York, Random House.

Hastorf, C. 1983. *Prehistoric Agricultural Intensification and Political Development in the Jauja Region of Central Peru.* Ph.D. dissertation, Department of Anthropology, University of California, Los Angeles.

Helms, M. 1981. Precious metals and politics: style and ideology in the Intermediate Area and Peru. *Journal of Latin American Lore* 7: 215–37.

Hill, J. (ed.). 1977. *Explanation of Prehistoric Change.* Albuquerque: University of New Mexico Press.

Howe, E. 1983. Metals provenientes del alto Mantar: un analisis preliminar. Report submitted to the Instituto Nacional de Cultura, Lima.

Johnson, A. and Earle, T. n.d. *The Evolution of the Human Society.* Palo Alto: Stanford University Press [in press].

Johnson, G. A. 1978. Information sources and the development of decision-making organizations, in C. Redman et al., *Social Archaeology.* New York: Academic Press.

King, J. 1784. *A Voyage to the Pacific Ocean*, Vol. III. Dublin, H. Chamberlaine.

Kirch, P. 1982. Advances in Polynesian prehistory: three decades in review, in F. Wendorf and A. E. Close (eds.) *Advances in World Archaeology*, vol. 1 New York: Academic Press, pp. 51–97.

LaLone, D. 1982. The Inka as a nonmarket economy: supply on command versus supply and demand, in J. Ericson and T. Earle (eds.) *Contexts for Prehistoric Exchange* New York: Academic Press, pp. 291–316.

LeBlanc, C. 1981. *Late prehistoric Huanca settlement patterns in the Yanamarca Valley, Peru.* Ph.D. dissertation, Department of Anthropology, University of California, Los Angeles.

Lechtman, H. 1976. A metallurgical survey in the Peruvian Andes. *Journal of Field Archaeology* 3: 1–42.

   1979. Issues in Andean metallurgy, in E. Benson (ed.) *Pre-Columbian Metallurgy of South America.* Washington: Dumbarton Oaks.

   1984. Andean value systems and the development of prehistoric metallurgy. *Technology and Culture* 25: 1–36.

LeVine, T. 1985. *Inka administration of the central Andes.* Ph.D. dissertation, Archaeology Program, University of California, Los Angeles.

Lothrop, S. K. 1938. Inka treasure as depicted by Spanish historians. *Frederick Webb Hodge Anniversary Publication Fund* 2. Los Angeles: Southwest Museum.

Lumbreras, L. 1974. *The Peoples and Cultures of Ancient Peru*, B. Meggers, trans. Washington, D.C., Smithsonian.

Malo, D. 1951. Hawaiian antiquities. *Bernice P. Bishop Museum Special Publication* 2 (2nd ed.). [orig. 1898].

McCoy, P. C. 1977. The Mauna Kea adz quarry project: a summary of the 1975 field investigations. *Journal of Polynesian Society* 86: 223–44.

Moore, S. F. 1958. *Power and Property in Inka Peru.* New York: Columbia University Press.

Morris, C. 1967. *Storage in Tawantisuyu.* Ph.D. dissertation, Department of Anthropology, University of Chicago.

   1974. Reconstructing patterns of non-agricultural production in the Inka economy, in C.

Moore (ed.) *The Reconstruction of Complex Societies*. Cambridge, MA. American School of Oriental Research, pp. 49–68.

Morua, M. 1946. *Historica y Genealogia Real de Los Reyes Inka*, C. Bayle (ed.). Madrid: Consejo Superior de Investigaciones Cientifices, Instituto Santo Toribio de Mongrovejo [orig. 1590].

Murra, J. V. 1962. Cloth and its functions in the Inka state. *American Anthropologist* 64: 710–28.
   1972. El control vertical de un maximo de pisas ecologicos en la economia de las sociedades andinas, in J. Murra (ed.) *Vista de la Provincia de Leon de Huanuco Tomo 2.* Huanuco, Peru: University of Hemilio Valdizan, pp. 427–76.
   1980. *The Economic Organization of the Inca State*. Greenwich, CT: JAI Press [orig. 1956].
   1982. Public talk to the Department of Anthropology, University of California, Los Angeles, January.

Murra, J. and Morris, C. 1976. Dynastic oral tradition, administrative records and archaeology in the Andes. *World Archaeology* 7: 270–78.

Parsons, J. 1976. *Prehispanic settlement patterns in the Upper Mantaro, Peru: a preliminary report of the 1975 field season*. Unpublished ms. submitted to the Instituto Nacional de Cultura, Lima and to the National Science Foundation, Washington, D.C.

Parsons, J. and Hastings, C. 1977. *Prehispanic settlement patterns in the Upper Mantaro, Peru: a progress report for the 1976 field season*. Unpublished ms. submitted to the Instituto Nacional de Cultura, Lima and to the national Science Foundation, Washington, D.C.

Rowe, J. 1946. Inka culture at the time of the Spanish conquest. *Bureau of American Ethnology Bulletin* 143(2): 183–330.

Russell, G. and Hastorf, C. 1984. Stone Tools as a Measure of Agricultural Change in the Andes. Paper delivered at the 49th Annual Meeting of the Society for American Archaeology, Portland.

Sahlins, M. D. 1958. *Social Stratification in Polynesia* (American Ethnological Society, Monograph 29). Seattle: University of Washington Press.

Sanders, W. T. 1956. The Central Mexican symbiotic region, in G. R. Willey (ed.) *Prehistoric Settlement Patterns in the New World* (Viking Fund Publications in Anthropology No. 23). New York: Wenner-Gren Foundation for Anthropological Research, pp. 115–27.

Sanders, W. T. and Price, B. J. 1968. *Mesoamerica: The evolution of a civilization*. New York: Random House.

Schaedel, R. 1978. Early state of the Inkas, in H. Claessen and P. Skalnik (eds.) *The Early State.* The Hague: Mouton, pp. 289–320.

Service, E. R. 1962. *Primitive Social Organization*. New York: Random House.
   1975. *Origins of the State and Civilization*. New York: Norton.

Steward, J. 1955. *Theory of Culture Change*. Urbana: University of Illinois Press.

Vancouver, G. 1798. *A Voyage of Discovery to the North Pacific and Round the World*, Vol I. London: G. G. and J. Robinson.

7

Beneath the Material Surface of Things: Commodities, Artifacts, and Slave Plantations

Charles E. Orser, Jr.

Introduction

Artifacts provide one of the most important sources of information in archaeology. The *Oxford English Dictionary* (*OED* 1971:108), an authoritative source on the English language if not exactly an archaeological source, defines "archaeology" in one sense as a word meaning "the scientific study of the remains and monuments of the prehistoric period." Although archaeology encompasses much more than the simple examination of artifacts, the study of objects made and used in the past and their contexts does comprise a large part of the archaeological endeavor. Even in historical archaeology, where access to sources of information other than artifacts and their site contexts are common, artifacts – their points of origin, associations, and styles – still provide a significant source of information.

Although artifacts are important in archaeology, the definition of the word "artifact" has not always been exactly the same. Artifacts have been variously defined as "anything that has been constructed or modified by man [sic]" (Joukowsky 1980:279), as "portable objects whose form has been modified wholly or partially from human activity" (Sharer and Ashmore 1987:65), as "objects found in archaeological sites that exhibit features which are the result of human activity" (Fagan 1983:33), and as "anything which exhibits any physical attributes that can be assumed to be the results of human activity" (Dunnell 1971:117). A respected social theorist has even stated that artifacts are "relics or remains, the bric-a-brac washed up on the shore of modern times and left there as the social currents within which [they were] created have drained away" (Giddens 1984:357).

Historical archaeologists also have had some problem agreeing on an exact definition of "artifact." In fact, the developmental history of historical archaeology has included a debate over an ontological question of whether artifacts are historical documents or whether historical documents are actually artifacts.

The view that artifacts constitute a special kind of historical document was perhaps the first position adopted by historical archaeologists. In an important article explaining the scope and direction of the developing field of historical archaeology, Harrington (1952:337) argues that the excavation of an archaeological site is similar to "the study of a new collection of documentary material." In this view, archaeological data are intended to supplement already extant written records and to function as documents. In agreement with this perspective, artifacts were subsequently defined as "three-dimensional" documents (Russell 1967:387), "three-dimensional additions to the pages of history" (Noël Hume 1972:5), and "sources of history" that can be "read" (Glassie 1975:12). The term "manufact" has even been used to indicate the close relationship between artifacts and manuscripts (Washburn 1964:247).

In contradistinction to this artifacts-as-documents view is the perspective that manuscripts are really nothing more than artifacts, objects produced by conscious human activity. Although rarely explicitly advocated, perhaps being axiomatic in anthropology, the clearest statement of this position was made by Fontana (1965:61) when he wrote about treating "documentary evidence as if it were another artifact" (cf. Fontana 1978:78).

In addition to debating the theoretical aspects of how to perceive artifacts, archaeologists also have long been interested in how the artifacts found at archaeological sites actually came to be there. In the absence of other sources of information, prehistorians have conducted sophisticated petrographic analyses to determine the source locations of artifact raw materials and have used this geologic information to extrapolate the distances various stone materials would have had to travel to reach archaeological sites (e.g., Cann et al. 1970; Weigand et al. 1977). Historical archaeologists, because of the greater availability of information, have used other means to examine artifact source-to-site distances. One popular approach has been to use geographic models to investigate historic-period trade networks and commodity flow to archaeological sites (Adams 1976; Miller and Hurry 1983; Riordan and Adams 1985). These kinds of studies, like those in prehistory, focus on macro-economic issues. For example, Riordan and Adams (1985), in their analysis of commodity flow to four archaeological sites – one on the East Coast, two in the South, and one near the West Coast – test a hypothesis about the relationship between the access of individuals in certain regions in the United States to the national market. Their postulate is that artifact collections from different sites within the same region will tend to be similar because of the likelihood that their inhabitants had roughly equal access to the market. Their analysis suggests that the four sites did indeed exhibit distinct artifact "profiles" that could be defined on the basis of market access.

These macro-level studies link individual sites to national and even international market economies and go far toward showing that historic-period sites in North America were indeed part of the world market economy explored by Wallerstein (1974), Wolf (1982), and Curtin (1984). Such studies demonstrate what kinds of goods were available in particular geographic regions at particular points in time, and they suggest what market forces may have affected archaeological site inhabitants. Such analyses generally concentrate on artifacts as economic entities; artifacts are primarily seen to move through the market as saleable objects. This perspective, while certainly not wrong, provides only a partial understanding of the place of artifacts in living societies. Another perspective also can be used in which the artifacts represent commodities that have both an economic and a social existence.

The purpose of this article is to explore the nature of commodities in historical archaeology. As an example, special reference is made to slave plantations found in the American South during the first half of the 19th century. Plantations, as archaeological sites containing commodities, are distinctive because of the power relations inherent in slavery and because of the social networks maintained by slaves. Plantations are not so unique, however, as to make the ideas of this essay inapplicable to other sociohistorical situations. This article does not seek to offer a final statement on artifacts as commodities or to establish a concrete methodological tool for devising such a statement. Instead, the goal here is to provide a framework within which to formulate ideas for future research.

Commodities and Exchange

All human societies fashion physical objects in order to mediate between themselves and nature. This act of manufacture, the self-consciousness it entails, and the fixing of both concrete and abstract meanings to physical objects helps to distinguish humans within the animal kingdom (Mumford 1967). In the course of human history individuals and social groups discovered that they wanted exotic material objects for which they themselves did not possess the knowledge, raw materials, or perhaps even skill to make themselves. In order to obtain these desired items, people learned that they would have to make contact with those who had the items and attempt to acquire them peacefully, through exchange, or violently, through conquest and theft. The act of peaceful acquisition entailed the production of goods that could be used in exchange for the desired nonlocal objects.

Many scholars have argued that exchange is a universal cultural element (Homans 1961; Ekeh 1974; Emerson 1976; Befu 1977) and that "without exchange, there is no society" (Braudel 1977:15). In such a perspective, one way in which individual societies differ is in how exchanges occur, the cultural and ideological meanings of the exchanges, and the place that exchange has within the social structure (Kopytoff 1986:68).

Commodities are items created specifically for exchange. Since commodities are generally not consumed by their producers, commodities embody social labor, or labor in service to society. Commodities represent the abstraction of social labor, or "the separation of generalizable qualities and inherent properties from the concrete persons whose activities make up the social whole" (Hart 1982:40). As a result, a commodity cannot be something that is not useful, something that is not in some way the product of human labor, or something that is not objectified as a produced thing capable of being exchanged for a good or service judged to have roughly equal value.

The simple exchange of one commodity for another represents "the circulation of materialised social labor" (Marx 1967:106), with the members of the exchanging societies appearing as atomistic individuals linked together only through exchange

(Cohen 1978:121–122). Without the exchange situation the various actors would not interact.

The true essence of commodities lies beneath their physical surface because commodities are more than the sum of their material attributes. As Lewis Mumford (1967:23) has noted, "material artifacts may stubbornly defy time, but what they tell about man's [sic] history is a good deal less than the truth, the whole truth, and nothing but the truth." Commodities have social lives and tend to rule their producers rather than being ruled by them (Marx 1967:75). Commodities, like all material things, carry social meaning and have socially relevant values (Douglas and Isherwood 1979:59). These social meanings indicate that commodities are more than simple economic entities. The unique character of commodities relates perhaps most strongly to the concept of value. The consideration of value extends to Aristotle and appears in many philosophical traditions, and extensive debate has occurred in the social sciences about the values that commodities embody. In general, however, commodities are minimally thought to exhibit use value and exchange value. Use value is generally defined as the ability of an object to satisfy a human want, while exchange value generally refers to the number of objects or services a single object can command in an exchange situation. Use value is often seen as a prerequisite for exchange, with price – exchange values expressed in a standard medium, like money – being the basic regulatory mechanism of a market economy (Lichtenstein 1983:27). Use values are overtly qualitative and covertly quantitative, whereas exchange values transform qualitative relationships into quantitative ones. In classical Marxian economics, where a great deal of thinking about commodities has occurred, an object's exchange value exists totally independent of its use value, and the common denominator is the value of the object in terms of the labor expended in its production (Marx 1967:35–41). This reasoning forms the basis of the controversial Labor Theory of Value (Lichtenstein 1983:153–163; Thompson 1983; Valtukh 1987:71–77; Roemer 1988:47–51).

In addition to use value and exchange value, however, a third kind of value also has been defined. Termed "esteem" (Walsh 1901:1) or "aesthetic" (Simmel 1978:73–74) value, this kind of value originates in an individual's perception of an object, from a personal feeling that an object evokes, or from the pleasure that an object brings to people.

These three kinds of value show that commodities are complex entities that have socially endowed characteristics conferred upon them that may have nothing to do with their physical appearances. These endowed properties are culturally defined, socially relevant, and historically situated. The endowment of these properties transfers power to objects. This power has been termed "fetishism" (Marx 1967:72; Cohen 1978:115–133; Geras 1983). In capitalist economies, commodities are fetishized because their value appears to derive from their material properties, not from the social relations that brought about these objects. At least some of the power, however, is attributed to the objects *after* they are produced, in a separate cognitive process that is far removed from production (Kopytoff 1986:73). In this perspective, "objects can help make autonomous forces out of ideas by remaining the physical environment long after their production" (Mukerji 1983:15).

Although in anthropology the concept of the commodity leads directly to such topics as the evolution of the division of labor and exchange (Bloch 1985:95) and the cultural valuation of material objects, Arjun Appadurai (1986) has argued that the commodity, as explained in economics and political economy and explored perhaps most thoroughly by Marx, is difficult for anthropologists to use cross-culturally because of Marx's focus on 19th-century industrial capitalism. For Appadurai, the key issue facing anthropologists is to discover the mechanisms and processes of commodity exchange rather than to determine precisely what commodities are. Such an approach allows anthropologists to study commodities in non-Western, non-capitalist, and pre-capitalist settings. Thus, Appadurai (1986:13) focuses on what he terms the "commodity situation," or the situation in which the exchangeability of one object for another is the socially relevant feature of that object. Because objects move in and out of a commodity state and have "social lives," commoditization is "best looked upon as a process of becoming rather than as an all-or-none state of being" (Kopytoff 1986:73). Objects enter and exit from a commodity state at various points in their social lives.

The distinction between the economic and the social aspects of a commodity is analogous to Braudel's (1977:17, 19) distinction between the "economic life," involving market forces and exchange values, and the "material life," involving the daily interaction between people and things. In this perspective, people – like material objects – can move back and forth between their material and economic lives with relative, albeit socially relevant, ease.

The significance of viewing material objects as having social lives can be further explained by Kopytoff's (1986) concept of the "cultural biography" of an object. In his view the "life history" of an object can be traced throughout its existence in order to determine the cultural changes that it has experienced. As an example he uses the huts of the Suku of Zaire, which commonly begin their lives as houses, but which with time become transformed into guest houses, widows' houses, meeting places for unmarried teenagers, kitchens, or goat or chicken houses before collapsing (Kopytoff 1986:67).

The writing of an object's cultural biography is different from the social history of things (Appadurai 1986:34). In a cultural biography, a particular object is followed through time, with its changing context noted at each stage of its life. The social history of things focuses on the large-scale dynamics of supply, demand, and meanings of whole classes of items and tracks their changes through time.

The Increasing Significance of Commodities through Time

While it cannot be doubted that commodities were used by many cultures at many times in the past, and perhaps even universally, it also cannot be doubted that commoditization has become increasingly important over time (Samhaber 1964; Casson 1984). This increase is particularly notable in those cultures typically studied by historical archaeologists.

Little doubt exists that the world was transformed after about A.D. 1500. Part of the reason for this change was the worldwide search for wealth begun by European national powers. Even though these changes have been variously described as "capitalist" (Wallerstein 1974; Frank 1978) and as "pre-capitalist" (Banaji 1977; Brenner 1977), this period of expansion might be characterized best as "mercantilist" (Brewer 1980:3), a period exemplified at least partly by the search for mercantile wealth (Wolf 1982:79), or a period of pre-capitalist colonial rule (Alavi 1983:81). Capitalism has been periodized in many hotly contested ways, but the important point here is that capitalism represents historically created and re-created social relations that include a large place for commodities. In fact, it has been argued that capitalism represents "the highest form of commodity production" (Valtukh 1987:71).

Most of the artifacts found on historic-period sites in the New World were once commodities produced as part of this developing capitalist framework. These artifacts were generally produced in settings far removed from the place of their consumption, and the vast percentage of producers and consumers never met. Even though a few cases of commodity manufacture might be found in the prehistoric period, only after about A.D. 1500 did large numbers of people have the opportunity to buy objects manufactured in various places around the world. Only in the historic period could common men and women become part of a global network of commerce that linked Europe, Asia, Africa, and the New World.

Still, the materialism that developed after A.D. 1500 was not entirely new, but was really a continuation of medieval patterns of thought (Lopez 1971; Postan 1973). For example, in the early part of the expansion period, the Portuguese, perhaps the first global colonialists of the modern age, continued to think as they had in medieval times, using the material innovations that made global expansion possible – new kinds of ships, sails, and maps – to engage in a Holy War with the Islamic empire. They treated explorers' maps and travel memoirs as craft secrets not intended for public use. As soon as these innovations were found to have economic benefit for Portugal, however, these items lost their medieval meanings and became part of the internationalist "material culture of the early modern period" (Mukerji 1983:255). With time, a consumer revolution occurred in the European world as goods that were once only available to the wealthy could be purchased by commoners. Men and women who once could only hope to acquire material things through inheritance could suddenly buy their own objects (McKendrick 1982:9–13). Items that were formerly out of reach became "objects of desire" for the masses (Forty 1986:6–10).

The increasing role of commodities in the economic and material lives of historic-period societies suggests that commodities and commoditization should be topics of growing interest to historical archaeologists. Certainly, both cultural biographies and social history of things are relevant to archaeological research, although the development of a cultural biography of a specific thing may have more applicability in cultural anthropology where the "life changes" of an object might be directly observed. Still, cultural biographies are not unknown in historical archaeology. South (1977:183–185) provides a partial example in his discussion of the changing use of a flax hackle, and Fontana (1965), in his "The Tale of the Nail," speaks of nails starting "out in life as square cut tacks." Thus, while cultural biographies are not impossible in archaeology, especially given the range of research materials available in historical archaeology, much of the research conducted in archaeology will probably fall into the realm of the social history of commodities.

Commodities, Artifacts, and Slave Plantations

The introduction of commodities to historic-period archaeological sites, the institution of such objects into the material life of the sites' inhabitants, and the giving of meaning to these items has relevance to historical archaeological research. Even though such topics can be pursued at many types of sites occupied during the historic period, slave plantations stand out as one kind of site wherein such an analysis might be particularly fruitful. It has been argued, in fact, that "an understanding of the material environment of slavery . . . would seem to be an indispensable prelude to comprehending other aspects of their [slaves'] culture" (Joyner 1984:90). Plantations provide a potentially important place in which to view the changing role of commodities because of the spatially bounded nature of plantations, the power relations inherent in plantation slavery, and the social networks maintained by slaves.

It has been argued elsewhere (Orser 1988:741–742) that a slave plantation can be conceptualized as the "power domain" of the plantation slave-holder. When power is defined as the ability of one person or group of people to control another person or group, the slave plantation is seen as a distinct physical place in which some people controlled the lives of others. This control extended to both the economic and material lives and was often so absolute that it has been argued that slaves should be viewed as members of their master's household rather than as members of distinct slave households (Fox-Genovese 1983:245). This determination rests on both economic and material grounds, because slaves "had no independent economic bases worthy of the name, and they could not withstand the exercise of the master's will or the fluctuations of the economic features of his household," and because "slaves rarely, if ever, determined their own relation to income" since the masters controlled the distribution of food, clothing, living space, and other elements of daily life (Fox-Genovese 1983:239, 242).

At the same time, plantation slaves are well known to have maintained their own social networks and lifeways (e.g., Rawick 1972; Blassingame 1979; Joyner 1984). These networks, like all networks composed of living individuals, consisted of a series of "weblike, netlike connections" (Lesser 1961:42). These connections changed and were altered as attitudes and circumstances changed and as individuals entered and left the network. Thus, the slave community was composed of a series of fluid social relations that tied the net together, yet allowed it to be flexible.

Even though it cannot be doubted that slaves controlled aspects of their lives, it also cannot be doubted that plantation owners controlled much of what occurred on their estates. This control can be assumed to have extended to the realm of material culture, so that archaeologists excavating plantation remains, particularly slave quarters, must be concerned with how slaves acquired the objects found in their building remains. The question of acquisition, no matter how hard to answer, lies at the heart of understanding the dynamics of material life. The uniqueness of the slave plantation stems partly from the ability of the slaveowner or his or her agent to act as an intermediary between the producers and suppliers of commodities and the plantation's slaves. This situation obtained for many commodities even though slaves are known to have fashioned items from locally available materials, such as gourds, and to have visited markets with their owner's permission (Blassingame 1977:402–403).

The perspective of viewing archaeologically recovered objects as commodities was tacitly suggested in a widely used study of plantation ceramics (Otto 1977). Although the subject of ceramic acquisition by slaves was approached from a perspective that emphasized status considerations – for comments see Orser (1988), the study does contain a distinctly social element. For example, in confirming the hypothesis that the planter issued ceramics to slaves at Cannon's Point Plantation, Otto (1977:97–101) is also implying that the ceramics began their social lives as commodities in distant factories, came of age in the hands of merchants who sold them to the planter, and then died as commodities when they were given to slaves as gifts. The slaves' association with these ceramics is entirely material; no economic relation occurs between slaves and masters where these particular items are concerned, and the slaves do not enter the marketplace. Conversely, by confirming the hypothesis that slaves may have purchased many of their own ceramics, Otto (1977:100) places the slaves directly in the marketplace as purchasers. Of course, it remains possible that these slaves obtained their ceramics in both ways, sometimes entering the marketplace and sometimes not.

While some archaeologists might argue that how slaves actually acquired their ceramics – and by extension all their artifacts – is not important, careful reflection shows that such a determination plays a large role in the conceptualization of slave–master relations. Clearly, a different relation obtained when slaves purchased their own ceramics and when they were given them as gifts. Such a difference might contain information about the social histories of artifacts after they had entered the plantation contexts. In the case of ceramics, for example, it might be obvious to assume that they were used in the preparation and serving of foodstuffs.

The problem with such a readily apparent, functional interpretation is that it does not take into account the cultural biography of the object. An historical illustration can serve as an example. One of the objects that is mentioned in many descriptions of the 19th-century slave cabins is the iron kettle that often appeared inside the cabin near the fireplace. Miss Towne, upon visiting St. Helena Island, South Carolina, in the early 1860s, noted, for instance, that the typical slave cabin she visited contained "household utensils" consisting of "one pot, in which they cooked their hominy or peas with salt pork" (Towne in Cooley 1926:121). Charles Ball (1837:143), an escaped slave who later wrote about his experiences in slavery, noted that in one cabin he visited he saw a "common iron pot, standing beside the chimney; and several wooden spoons and dishes hung against the wall." Such descriptions lead archaeologists to place the use context of the iron kettle within a foodways environment. As such, the kettles have use value within the context of slave cooking.

Different sources suggest, however, that iron pots could have had an equally important alternative use in the slave quarters. This alternative use involved the use of kettles in religious observances. According to one former slave, Wednesday night prayer meetings were usually held in the slave cabins at the discretion of the master. However, when permission to hold a meeting was denied, the slaves held them "by stealth" (Williams 1885:67). These secret meetings were facilitated by iron kettles because slaves used them to catch the sound of the meetings: "Cause some of the masters didn't like the way we slaves carried on [at prayer meetings] we would turn pots down, and tubs to keep the sound from going out" (Perdue et al. 1976:141). Thus, these pots were used in a West African manner (Rawick 1972:42–45) to defy the master and to continue the cultural practices of slaves. In this particular case, an apparent commodity was used in a manner that upheld cultural beliefs bearing no apparent relation to economics. The kettles lost their use value in favor of esteem value when they were used in religion.

A similar example derives from an archaeological source. In their careful research at the Jordan Plantation in Texas, Kenneth L. Brown and Doreen C. Cooper (1990:16–18) argue that a number of artifacts, including sections of cast-iron kettles, found in the deposits of one slave cabin may represent objects used in a traditional African healing ceremony. Their determination is made by understanding that the social life of the artifacts found in the slave cabins may have had values that were not simply use values in the general sense of the term.

Conclusion

These brief examples demonstrate that the social lives of historic-period artifacts at plantations are extremely complex and that no easy interpretations will be typically apparent. Certainly, no definitive statement can be offered here on the values that specific commodities may have had or the changes that they may have undergone in terms of value and meaning. The concept of the artifact as commodity illustrates, however, that the social histories of artifacts are multifaceted. The slave plantation poses specific problems because of the life that any single artifact could have "lived." The ceramic sherd found at a slave cabin site was commoditized in a factory setting and was later sold to a merchant, who in turn sold it to a planter or in some cases directly to a slave. If the planter bought the item, the continued life of the artifact might illustrate the power of the planter – if the item was given to a slave as part of an allotment, or even the power of the slave – if the item was stolen from the planter household and hidden in the quarters. Thus, the cultural biography of one such object would represent a transformation from exchange value (market item) to use value (food service item) to esteem value (stolen item). Within the plantation context, the exchange and use values would be fairly clear, but the esteem value would be more problematic.

This kind of complex life history could exist for any artifact found by any archaeologist. For example, a particular plate found in a mining town somewhere might
have esteem value for a miner's immigrant wife because she had obtained it from
her mother, who continued to live in Europe. Upon finding sherds at this woman's
former home, an archaeologist could never know, even in the presence of an
exceedingly abundant documentary record, whether any particular sherd was a
piece of the esteemed plate or whether the sherd was simply from a common
kitchen plate. This kind of determination can never be made by archaeologists. The
pertinent point here is that archaeologists, particularly historical archaeologists,
must come to recognize the true nature of commodities and the information that
they can carry. In terms of plantations, whether a master allowed his slaves to visit
local markets played a major part in shaping the composition of the archaeological
record. The power relations between masters and slaves, and all that this interaction entailed in historical, social, cultural, and economic terms, is at least partly told
by the commodities found at archaeological sites.

This consideration leads to the conclusion, in terms of artifacts at least, that plantation archaeology – and all archaeology of this sort – will progress slowly as
archaeologists at particular sites or groups of sites make efforts to discover the
social histories of the commodities they recover from the earth. Thus, the concept
of "reading" the past that is becoming popular in archaeology (after Hodder 1986)
might be partially accomplished by understanding the dual economic/material
aspects of historic-period artifacts. Obviously, this understanding will be neither
easy nor straightfoward.

In this particular article only a brief attempt is made to indicate some of the
concepts that might be useful in such a study and to illustrate some of the complexities that will be encountered. This kind of intellectual exploration most certainly
will not be easy, but the difficulty of a research problem should not determine
whether someone can profitably study it. Historical archaeology has only
advanced through the creative and thoughtful research efforts of its practitioners.

References

Adams, William H. 1976. Trade Networks and Interaction Spheres: A View from Silcott. *Historical Archaeology* 10:99–112.
Alavi, Hamaz. 1983. Colonial and Post-Colonial Societies. In *A Dictionary of Marxist Thought*, edited by Tom Bottomore, pp. 81–83. Harvard University Press, Cambridge.
Appadurai, Arjun. 1986. Commodities and the Politics of Value. In *The Social Life of Things: Commodities in Cultural Perspective*, edited by Arjun Appadurai, pp. 3–63. Cambridge University Press, Cambridge.
Ball, Charles. 1837. *Slavery in the United States: A Narrative of the Life and Adventures of Charles Ball, a Black Man*. John S. Taylor, New York.
Banaji, J. 1977. Modes of Production in a Materialist Conception of History. *Capital and Class* 1:1–44.
Befu, Harumi. 1977. Social Exchange. *Annual Review of Anthropology* 6:255–281.
Blassingame, John W. 1979. *The Slave Community: Plantation Life in the Antebellum South*. Revised and enlarged edition. Oxford University Press, New York.

Blassingame, John W. (Editor). 1977. *Slave Testimony: Two Centuries of Letters, Speeches, Interviews, and Autobiographies*. Louisiana State University Press, Baton Rouge.

Bloch, Maurice. 1985. *Marxism and Anthropology: The History of a Relationship*. Oxford University Press, Oxford.

Braudel, Fernand. 1977. *Afterthoughts on Material Civilization and Capitalism*, translated by Patricia M. Ranum. Johns Hopkins University Press, Baltimore.

Brenner, R. 1977. The Origins of Capitalist Development: A Critique of Neo-Smithian Marxism. *New Left Review* 104:25–92.

Brewer, Anthony. 1980. *Marxist Theories of Imperialism: A Critical Survey*. Routledge and Kegan Paul, London.

Brown, Kenneth L., and Doreen C. Cooper. 1990. Structural Continuity in an African-American Slave and Tenant Community. In Plantation and Farm: Archaeological Approaches to Southern Agriculture, edited by Charles E. Orser, Jr. *Historical Archaeology* 24(4):7–19. Society for Historical Archaeology, California, Pennsylvania.

Cann, J. R., J. E. Dixon, and Colin Renfrew. 1970. Obsidian Analysis and the Obsidian Trade. In *Science in Archaeology*, edited by Don Brothwell and Eric Higgs, pp. 578–591. Praeger, New York.

Casson, Lionel. 1984. *Ancient Trade and Society*. Wayne State University Press, Detroit, Michigan.

Cohen, G. A. 1978. *Karl Marx's Theory of History: A Defense*. Princeton University Press, Princeton, New Jersey.

Cooley, Roosa B. 1926. *Homes of the Freed*. New Republic, New York.

Curtin, Philip. 1984. *Cross-Cultural Trade in World History*. Cambridge University Press, Cambridge.

Douglas, Mary, and Baron Isherwood. 1979. *The World of Goods*. Basic Books, New York.

Dunnell, Robert C. 1971. *Systematics in Prehistory*. Free Press. New York.

Ekeh, Peter P. 1974. *Social Exchange Theory: The Two Traditions*. Harvard University Press, Cambridge.

Emerson, Richard M. 1976. Social Exchange Theory. *Annual Review of Sociology* 2:335–362.

Fagan, Brian M. 1983. *Archaeology: A Brief Introduction*. Second edition. Little, Brown, Boston.

Fontana, Bernard. 1965. The Tale of the Nail: On the Ethnological Interpretation of Historic Artifacts. *Florida Anthropologist* 18:85–90.

——1978. Artifacts of the Indians of the Southwest. In *Material Culture and the Study of American Life*, edited by Ian M. G. Quimby, pp. 75–108. W. W. Norton, New York.

Forty, Adrian. 1986. *Objects of Desire: Design and Society, 1750–1980*. Thames and Hudson, London.

Fox-Genovese, Elizabeth. 1983. Antebellum Southern Households: A New Perspective on a Familiar Question. *Review* 7:215–253.

Frank, Andre Gunder. 1978. *World Accumulation: 1492–1789*. Monthly Review Press, New York.

Geras, Norman. 1983. Fetishism. In *A Dictionary of Marxist Thought*, edited by Tom Bottomore, pp. 165–166. Harvard University Press, Cambridge.

Giddens, Anthony. 1984. *The Constitution of Society: Outline of the Theory of Structuration*. University of California Press, Berkeley.

Glassie, Henry. 1975. *Folk Housing in Middle Virginia: A Structural Analysis of Historic Artifacts*. University of Tennessee Press, Knoxville.

Harrington, J. C. 1952. Historic Site Archaeology in the United States. In *The Archaeology of the Eastern United States*, edited by James B. Griffin, pp. 335–344. University of Chicago Press, Chicago.

Hart, Keith. 1982. On Commoditization. In *From Craft to Industry: The Ethnography of Proto-Industrial Cloth Production*, edited by Esther N. Goody, pp. 38–49. Cambridge University Press, Cambridge.

Hodder, Ian. 1986. *Reading the Past: Current Approaches to Interpretation in Archaeology*. Cambridge University Press, Cambridge.

Homans, George C. 1961. *Social Behavior: Its Elementary Forms*. Harcourt, Brace, Jovanovich, New York.

Joukowsky, Martha. 1980. *A Complete Manual of Field Archaeology: Tools and Techniques of Field Work for Archaeologists*. Prentice-Hall, Englewood Cliffs, New Jersey.

Joyner, Charles. 1984. *Down by the Riverside: A South Carolina Slave Community*. University of Illinois Press, Urbana.

Kopytoff, Igor. 1986. The Cultural Biography of Things: Commoditization as Process. In *The Social Life of Things: Commodities in Cultural Perspective*, edited by Arjun Appadurai, pp. 64–91. Cambridge University Press, Cambridge.

Lesser, Alexander. 1961. Social Fields and the Evolution of Society. *Southwestern Journal of Anthropology* 17:40–48.

Lichtenstein, Peter M. 1983. *An Introduction to Post-Keynesian and Marxian Theories of Value and Price*. M. E. Sharpe, Armonk, New York.

Lopez, Robert S. 1971. *The Commercial Revolution of the Middle Ages, 950–1350*. Prentice-Hall, Englewood Cliffs, New Jersey.

Marx, Karl. 1967. *Capital: A Critique of Political Economy*, Vol. 1. International, New York.

McKendrick, Neil. 1982. Commercialization and the Economy. In *The Birth of a Consumer Society: The Commoditization of Eighteenth-Century England*, by Neil McKendrick, John Brewer, and J. H. Plumb, pp. 7–194. Indiana University Press, Bloomington.

Miller, George L., and Silas D. Hurry. 1983. Ceramic Supply in an Economically Isolated Frontier Community: Portage County of the Ohio Western Reserve, 1800–1825. *Historical Archaeology* 17(2): 80–92.

Mukerji, Chandra. 1983. *From Graven Images: Patterns of Modern Materialism*. Columbia University Press, New York.

Mumford, Lewis. 1967. *The Myth of the Machine: Technics and Human Development*. Harcourt, Brace, and World, New York.

Noël Hume, Ivor. 1972. *A Guide to Artifacts of Colonial America*. Alfred A. Knopf, New York.

Orser, Charles E., Jr. 1988. The Archaeological Analysis of Plantation Society: Replacing Status and Caste with Economics and Power. *American Antiquity* 53:735–751.

Otto, John Solomon. 1977. Artifacts and Status Differences: A Comparison of Ceramics from Planter, Overseer, and Slave Sites on an Antebellum Plantation. In *Research Strategies in Historical Archaeology*, edited by Stanley South, pp. 91–118. Academic Press, New York.

Oxford English Dictionary (OED). 1971. *Oxford English Dictionary*. Compact edition. University Press, Oxford.

Perdue, Charles L., Jr., Thomas E. Barden, and Robert K. Phillips (Editors). 1976. *Weevils in the Wheat: Interviews with Virginia Ex-Slaves*. University Press of Virginia, Charlottesville.

Postan, M. M. 1973. *Medieval Trade and Finance*. Cambridge University Press, Cambridge.

Rawick, George. 1972. *From Sundown to Sunup: The Making of the Black Community*. Greenwood, Westport, Connecticut.

Riordan, Timothy B., and William Hampton Adams. 1985. Commodity Flows and National Market Access. *Historical Archaeology* 19(2):5–18.

Roemer, John E. 1988. *Free to Lose: An Introduction to Marxist Economic Philosophy*. Harvard University Press, Cambridge.

Russell, Carl P. 1967. *Firearms, Traps, and Tools of the Mountain Men*. Alfred A. Knopf, New York.

Samhaber, Ernest. 1964. *Merchants Made History: How Trade Has Influenced the Course of History Throughout the World*, translated by E. Osers. John Day, New York.

Sharer, Robert J., and Wendy Ashmore. 1987. *Archaeology: Discovering Our Past*. Mayfield, Palo Alto, California.

Simmel, Georg. 1978. *The Philosophy of Money*, translated by Tom Bottomore and David Frisby. Routledge and Kegan Paul, London.

South, Stanley. 1977. *Method and Theory in Historical Archaeology*. Academic Press, New York.

Thompson, Richard H. 1983. The Ox, the Slave, and the Worker. A Pedagogic Exercise in Marx's Labor Theory of Value. *Dialectical Anthropology* 8:237–240.

Valtukh, K. K. 1987. *Marx's Theory of Commodity and Surplus-Value*, translated by Boris Kutyrev. Progress, Moscow.

Wallerstein, Immanuel. 1974. *The Modern World-System*. Vol. 1, *Capitalist Agriculture and the Origins of the European World-Economy in the Sixteenth Century*. Academic Press, New York.

Walsh, Correa Moylan. 1901. *The Measurement of General Exchange-Value*. Macmillan, New York.

Washburn, Wilcomb E. 1964. Manuscripts and Manufacts. *The American Archivist* 27:245–250.

Weigand, Phil C., Garman Harbottle, and Edward V. Sayre. 1977. Turquoise Sources and Source Analysis: Mesoamerican and the Southwestern U.S.A. In *Exchange Systems in Prehistory*, edited by Timothy K. Earle and Jonathon E. Ericson, pp. 15–34. Academic Press, New York.

Williams, Isaac D. 1885. *Sunshine and Shadow of Slave Life*. Evening News Printing and Binding House, East Saginaw, Michigan.

Wolf, Eric R. 1982. *Europe and the People without History*. University of California Press, Berkeley.

Part IV

Social and Cultural Evolution

Process, Structure and History

Archaeology obtains much of its disciplinary identity from the study of how and why cultures change. The theories of change used today are highly diverse and have been forged through a complex history of intellectual cross-fertilization between the social and natural sciences and represent different accommodations to issues such as scale, process, structure and agency. We can distinguish two distinct, but interconnected, traditions. The first is cultural evolution. This approach regards changes in culture as the product of adaptations to the natural environment. This area has been taken up mainly by human ecology, biological anthropology, and processual archaeology. The second might be called social evolution. This is the idea that change is best evaluated with regard to changes in social and political organization, changes which are in turn driven by modifications in the economic sphere. It has been the traditional domain of sociology, social anthropology, and postprocessual archaeology. Crudely put, the main differences have to do with whether primacy is given to environmental interactions or social relations, whether to system or to structure.

Cultural evolution is strongly Darwinian in character. However, there is broad disagreement as to how far Darwinian principles, such as natural selection, can go in explaining the differential persistence of cultural traits. There are three major approaches: one which favors an analogous relationship between biological and cultural evolution, another which postulates a homology between the two, and a third which regards cultural evolution as a result of interactions between the biological and the cultural. The analogy or adaptationalist view is currently the dominant view in archaeology and has the closest ties to social evolution. The homology view is a recent development with a growing following, but seems debilitated by its overly restrictive handling of cultural transmission. The co--evolutionary view, also a recent development, may offer more promise because of its recognition of mutualism between culture and nature.

Social evolution, by contrast, draws largely from the writings of Marx, Parsons, Durkheim, and Weber (Sanderson 1990). Several varieties can be distinguished within the broader social-evolutionary approach. Historical materialist approaches stress the importance of contradictions between the forces and relations of production in transforming society. Generally the economic base is regarded as primary. Structuralist approaches emphasize the evolution of social formations as dependent upon the properties of local systems, local constraints, and their place within the larger system. In this case, the economic cannot be separated out since it is inextricably bound up in the social structures which organize production and reproduction. There are, in addition, neo-Marxist approaches which identify ideology and politics as active factors in social change. Here the focus is on the negotiation of power relations between individual actors and interest groups.

At present there is a sharp debate both within and across these two general evolutionary frameworks, but both have made important contributions. Cultural evolutionary theories, for example, have identified some of the local factors involved in sociocultural change, such as population increase, climatic change, trade, and social competition. Social evolutionary theories have identified long-term evolutionary trajectories based on social conflict. But none of these theories provides a satisfactory explanation of why large-scale trends should emerge. None of them have identified causal processes which seem universally applicable to the local creativity variability of which humans are uniquely capable. One direction which does aim to accommodate the existence of evolutionary change with local variability returns to the biology of Darwin, but to a Darwin untrammeled by ideas of evolutionary progress. Another is the exploration of theories of agency and structure as embodied in the work of the sociologist Anthony Giddens and the Annaliste historians.

Cultural Evolution as Adaptation

As we have seen in the introduction to Part II, one of the main contributions of the processual archaeology of the 1960s was the application of ecosystems theory to cultural change, in an approach known as adaptationalism. Cultural systems and configurations were defined as being composed of three discrete but interrelated subsystems – the economic, the social, and the ideological (Binford 1962). The principal way these three subsystems articulated with the natural environment was through technology. It was assumed that a culture's natural state was equilibrium, and that this stability was achieved through the operation of social strategies as homeostatic mechanisms. Changes in the cultural system were thus regarded as adaptive responses to different environmental conditions (see Binford, **chapter 1**), the source of change being external to the system. Culture is thus the preeminent "adaptive system," or to use Clark's (1968) term, an "information system."

The adaptationalist approach borrows the concepts of variation, selection and transmission from biological evolution, but reinterprets them in rather different ways. Cultural variation is regarded as a product of innovation. Variation in evolutionary biology is the result of genetic recombination and mutation, genetic drift and the like. Cultural selection is seen as the primary selection mechanism. Cultural values, and not nature, largely determine the success or failure of a new adaptation. This is grounds for arguing that cultural change is, at least in some respects, Lamarkian. Cultural transmission is accomplished through social learning. This is a form of biased transmission. In biology, transmission is accomplished through sexual reproduction. The operating assumption is that cultural selection operates at the group level; that under changing environmental conditions certain behaviors confer greater adaptedness upon the population. In biology, the consensus is that natural selection takes place primarily at the level of the reproductive individual (Mayr 1988; although see Wynne-Edwards 1986).

One of the difficulties with adaptationalism is its inability to deal effectively with two areas – interactions between subsystems and sudden change. This led to more sophisticated systems-modeling and computer simulation whereby different components were given different explanatory weights. Hosler, Sabloff and Runge (1977), for example, have suggested that the collapse of the Maya state was due to a growing imbalance between subsistence and ideological systems. Food stress due to population growth was accompanied by increased monument construction to placate the gods, in a runaway feedback loop. Problems with adaptationalism have also led to the exploration of catastrophe theory. Renfrew (1979) has drawn attention to regularities in cultural collapses and state formation that follow specific system trajectories. And most recently, scholars inspired by the work of the complexity theorists at the Santa Fe Institute have begun to explore the implications of understanding culture as a complex adaptive system (Gumerman and Gell-Mann 1994, 1995) (see Part II).

All.adaptationalist studies share certain limitations. Many tend to be teleological in the sense that they often assume that if a particular strategy exists, it must be adaptive in some way. (For a similar critique in biology see Gould and Lewontin 1979). Yet very little work has been done on how to determine if behaviors are adaptive or not and how behaviors that are adaptive may become neutral or even maladaptive (but see Flannery 1972). In addition, adaptationalist studies generally adopt a passive view of human behavior. That is to say, they assume that societies react to external stimuli and do not initiate change for any reasons of their own. This grossly neglects social dynamics within society, which are the focus of social evolutionary approaches. Finally, adaptationalism provides no rationale for the persistence of specific cultural forms over time. It neglects the importance of local history in guiding variation.

Natural Selection and Cultural Evolution

Since the mid to late 1980s, Robert Dunnell and his associates have sought to develop a theory of cultural evolution that conforms to Darwinian principles. Their goal is to integrate archaeology and contemporary evolutionary biology so as to construct a more general scientific theory. This approach stresses the central role of natural selection in cultural change and for this reason is often called "selectionism" (Teltser 1995). Most of the efforts of this school have focused on theoretical developments at the expense of application.

Dunnell (1980, 1989) has offered a comprehensive critique of the dominant adaptationalist program. He regards adaptationalism as a series of empirical generalizations about the course of human history. For him, it is tautological in the sense that the rules that are used to explain the archaeological record are re-statements of intuitive observations on that same record. This circularity ensures that there can be no adequate testing. He sees the common attribution of causality in cultural change to human intentionality as vitalistic. Human history is not the way it is because people made it that way, but rather it is the result of unintended acts. Intentionality is at best a proximate cause, important in the generation of vari-ability but not in its transmission.

Dunnell (1989) asserts that biological evolution is directly applicable to cultural phenomena on the grounds that humans are not qualitatively different from other organisms. He acknowledges that cultural transmission is responsible for the large majority of human behavior. But, citing the work of Bonner (1980), he suggests that culture is not unique to humans and can be seen, albeit in a more rudimentary form, in animals. This leads him to consider artifacts as the "hard parts of the behavioral segment of phenotypes" in much the same way that nests are part of the phenotype of birds. He concludes that artifact frequencies are, therefore, explainable by the same processes as plant and animal species in biology. He suggests that the principal modification needed to convert biological theory into a more general theory is to increase the number of mechanisms of trait transmissions. To accomplish this program requires a new systematics where the archaeological record is divided into traits that are functional (those which enhance an organism's fitness) and those which are stylistic (those which are neutral).

An example of a selectionist approach is given by O'Brien and Holland (1992). They show a dramatic shift in the frequency of three different kinds of tempering materials in prehistoric ceramics from the Woodland to Mississippian periods in the American Midwest. During the early Woodland there was an increase in pottery production using grit temper. This stabilized by 200 BC and then fell off dramatically by AD 1000. Small quantities of limestone-tempered ceramics were made between 250 BC and AD 700. At approximately AD 700 shell temper replaced limestone temper and then by AD 1000 replaced grit temper. They interpret these data as evidence for the operation of both stabilizing (grit temper) and directional selection (grit and shell temper) in the performance characteristics of ceramic vessels. Shell-tempered pottery may have increased fertility as infants were shifted to starchy foods at earlier ages. In this case, changes in ceramic technology occurred in step with increased sedentariness, shifts in household composition and size, population growth, and increased dependence on starchy plants.

Several problems are associated with selectionist theory. Crucially, it has not demonstrated that it can distinguish between those traits which enhance the fitness of the population and those which have no selective value. And even if it could be shown that certain traits have a positive fitness value, selectionists offer no consid-eration of how functional and stylistic features articulate with one another in a coherent cultural system. Cultures are open systems, with information constantly flowing in and out. Interaction between cultures (e.g. Kohl's transferrable technologies, **chapter 5**), to a large degree, serves to insulate culture against environmental stresses of the kind faced by plants and animals, and thus greatly reduces, (but does not eliminate) the effects of natural selection upon humans. Therefore there seem to be no grounds for subsuming cultural selection under natural selection since cultural evolution has its own distinctive properties which are species specific (Shennan 1991).

Coevolution

Coevolution refers to those theories which examine the interactions between biology and culture (Boyd and Richerson 1985; Cavalli-Sforza and Feldman 1981; Duhem 1991). One of the most widely cited in archaeology is Boyd and Richerson's (1985) "dual-inheritance theory." This theory, actually a collection of related models, focuses on identifying the structures of cultural transmission, relating these to models of genetic evolution, and specifying the circumstances under which specific modes of cultural transmission might be favored. Contra Dunnell, they do not regard culture as a phenotypic response to environmental stress. This is because the cultural-inheritance system is based upon social learning by individuals and the culturally acquired variations transmitted across generations are evolving properties of the population.

Dual-inheritance theory identifies the forces of variation as random variation, an analog of genetic drift; guided variation; biased transmission; and natural selection. Of these, the latter three are the most important. Guided variation refers to trial-and-error learning and rational calculation combined with cultural transmission, which account for the so-called "Lamarkian effect" of culture. Biased transmission includes the acquisition of behaviors on the basis of judgments about the properties of the behaviors themselves (direct bias), decisions about the prevalence of specific behaviors within society (frequency-dependent bias), and imitation of role models exhibiting culturally valued behaviors (indirect bias). Natural selection acts on cultural variation but it does so in ways which are not predicted by standard Darwinian theory since it may favor behaviors associated with acquiring status and prestige at the expense of reproduction.

Of the different coevolutionary models, dual-inheritance theory has attracted the most attention in archaeology (Earle 1991; Spencer 1993; but see Rindos 1984, 1989 for a different coevolutionary approach tied to selectionism). At present, the only case study is Bettinger's (1991) somewhat sketchy analysis of the emergence of frequency-dependent and indirect bias during the European Upper Paleolithic. His thesis is that the evolution of style in lithic assemblages, the elaboration of non-utilitarian art forms, such as the famous cave paintings, and the emergence of ethnicity and group ritual behaviors are cases where proxy measures of adaptive success became increasingly exaggerated. This follows from his argument that late Pleistocene climatic change and population growth created the conditions for local technological and procurement specialization and that intergroup contact became more problematic as hunting behaviors appropriate in one region may not have been appropriate to others. Conformism and altruistic behavior would have been fostered by the rise of ethnicity, formal social groupings, and group ritual activities. In this way, cultural evolution is the unintended consequence of biased transmission in the cultural-inheritance system.

Several critiques of coevolutionary theory are now beginning to appear. Shennan (1991) has challenged Boyd and Richerson on their static view of cultural transmission. He suggests that social learning and the asymmetric nature of cultural transmission over time may lead to a culture's increasing disconnectedness from genetic fitness. This implies that cultural transmission is a distinctive process with its own properties. And Ingold (1989) has pointed out that the neo-Darwinians commit the fallacy of supposing that information can exist prior to the processes that give rise to it. The reduction of human choice to natural selection divorces it from the very social contexts that imbue it with meaning.

Social Transformation and Structural Contradiction

In the introduction to Part III we introduced Marxist approaches to the political economy. These theories are transformational and thus deal with social change at varying levels and scales. They regard social practices as existing within dialectical relationships, and the development of society is assumed to occur through the unity of opposites. Underlying the visible social system are relationships which embody incompatibilities, the resolution of which can potentially generate change.

The two main types of contradiction are those between the interests of social groups (as in the class struggle) and those between the forces and relations of production. In the first type of contradiction, the dominant class controls the means of production and appropriates surplus produced by the subordinate class. The interests of the two classes are contradictory because the expansion of one class is at the expense of the other. This general notion has been applied in precapitalist societies to social divisions based on age, sex, lineage and so on. Thus Faris (1983) suggests that in the Upper Paleolithic in Europe men appropriated the products of labor of women and maintained a position of dominance at the expense of women. The notion of "structure" in such studies, although weakly developed, concerns the relations of production and appropriation that lie behind the apparent social relations (between men and women, chief and commoner, etc).

The second type of contradiction, clearly linked to, and often underlying, the first type, is structural incompatibility. Here the forces of production are in conflict with the relations of production. One view of these terms and their relationships has been provided by Friedman (1974). The social formation is comprised of the base (infrastructure) and the superstructure. The base is further subdivided into the forces of production and the relations of production. The former refer to the means of production (technology, the ecosystem) and the organization of production (the organization of the labor force). The latter, by contrast, are the social relations which correspond with the forces of production. These social relations will vary from society to society; for example, in some societies kinship orders the forces of production while in the contemporary West it rarely does. The social relations of production organize the way in which the environment is to be used within the available technology; they also determine who works and how the product of labor is appropriated.

An example of a materialist approach is Gilman's (**chapter 8**) study of how the Upper Paleolithic Revolution was brought about by the development of the forces of production. He argues that the domestic mode of production (Sahlins 1972) characteristic of the period has internal contradictions. On the one hand local groups need external alliances in order to survive, but on the other they wish to maintain control over their own resources. As technology improves, the more self-sufficient groups want to move out of the alliance network. This leads to bounded alliances, which establish closed circles of mutual aid and limit obligations to assist others. Although Gilman claims that technology does not specifically determine the social changes, it does appear that it is primary. Technological changes are generated as the result of the selection of primary adaptive improvements in stone tools.

Epigenesis and Multiple Trajectories

The primacy given to technology in Gilman's model, and thus to the forces of production, can be contrasted with an emphasis on the social relations of production. As used in archaeology, the latter approach derives in large part from Jonathan Friedman and Michael Rowlands's (1978) influential epigenetic model of evolutionary trends. The term epigenesis refers to the principle that all social forms are dynamic processes and contain within themselves the seeds of their own transformation.

For Friedman and Rowlands, social evolution can be understood as a socially determined set of productive relations that distribute labor, work processes, and natural resources within constraints established by technology. These constraints determine the limits of functional compatibility between levels or subsystems. Relations of production dominate the superstructure as well as the productive forces and ecosystem, organizing and structuring the entire process of social reproduction. Friedman and Rowlands stress that a complete model must incorporate time/space so that temporal transformations are related to spatial variations. The evolution of specific social formations thus depends upon the internal processes of local systems, upon local constraints, and upon their place within the larger system. For example, the evolution of tribal systems into Asiatic states depends not only on the existence of the locally expressed structure of the tribal system, but also on the existence of a larger system within which tribal social systems can expand.

It is important to point out how this conception of society differs from the systemic view. The social subsystem, for example, is not equivalent to the social relations of production since the latter only includes those aspects of "the social" that are involved in production. In capitalist societies, for example, kinship is not always involved in productive relations – thus in these societies kinship (which is part of the social subsystem) is not part of the social relations of production. Another important difference is that the Marxist view of the dialectic differs from negative feedback. The latter occurs when subsystems or environments constrain interactions within the system. However, the idea of the dialectic is not constraint on growth, but rather it is that growth is an embedded part of the system. All relations of production involve opposing forces – the development of societies is a product of the continual tension between these opposites – change is endemic. Thus it may be in the interests of the slave to work for his master, but at the same time the interests of the master and slave are opposed.

A good example of work in this general structural-Marxist area is Bender's (1978) account of the origins of agriculture. Competitive feasting between local groups leads to demands for increased production and for increased control over the exchange of valuables. At some point the forces of production (based on wild resources) are no longer able to support the demands of the social relations of production (feasting and exchange). Some groups therefore maintain their dominance by intensifying production and adopting agriculture. In this case, clearly, the driving force is provided by the social relations of production rather than by the forces of production. This kind of approach has been widely applied, with particular reference to the "prestige-goods" models (see Part III) whereby increased social ranking is linked to the control of prestige goods (Bender 1978 Frankenstein and Rowlands 1978; Haselgrove 1982).

Shanks and Tilley (1987, pp. 171–2) have criticized materialist approaches on three grounds. First, the contradictions between different levels of social formation are assumed to be functional. Functionalist explanations, however, fail to account for change for exactly the same reasons that systems theory and adaptationalism are inadequate (see above). Secondly, the model artificially separates the base and superstructure. This gives rise to the false presupposition that the economy somehow precedes the political. Thirdly, the model is essentialist and reductionist. It assumes that relations of production have essences irrespective of their expression in a particular society. This denies the importance of conjuncture and contingency. They argue instead for a truly dialectical theorization where the political, economic, and cultural are seen as embedded in relations of mutual determination.

Power and Ideology

The materialist approaches described above differ with respect to the emphasis they place upon the forces and relations of production. However, both approaches neglect the superstructure (juridical–political and ideological) and indeed to a large extent they treat it as epiphenomenal. The centrality of ideology and power in social evolution has been championed by scholars critical of base determinism (e.g. Miller and Tilley 1984; Shanks and Tilley 1987). These new approaches reject naive positivism and are concerned with relating theory to material culture in nonessentialist ways.

At the core of these approaches is a reconception of the concepts of power and ideology that incorporates the work of Foucault (1977, 1980, 1981). There are two kinds of power to be distinguished, "power to" and "power over." "Power to" refers to the ability that all individuals possess to effect a desired outcome. This is similar to Giddens's (1984) conception of agency. "Power over" refers to coercive power, the ability of individuals, institutions, and organizations to ensure compliance. In contrast to classical materialist approaches where power is located in the economic, power is regarded as a component of all social action, embedded in all social relations. "Power over" involves the accomplishment of outcomes through the agency of others, but because others always possess the resources to resist, power is always contingent. One can argue that social evolution is an unceasing struggle in which power relations are transformed, strengthened, and sometimes reversed by the manipulation of symbolic and material capital, the two being fully interdependent and often difficult to distinguish.

In standard Marxist approaches ideology is regarded as false consciousness, the ideas and values of the ruling class which are taken as givens. Ideology works to legitimate the dominant order by hiding or mystifying the objective conditions of existence. This formulation is challenged through an ideology critique which questions the dominant ideology thesis and relates the concept to different interest groups and modes of representation in conflict. Following Giddens (1979, 1981), we can distinguish three ways in which ideologies function: (1) the representation of sectional interests as universal; (2) the denial or transmutation of contradictions; and (3) the naturalization of the present, or reification. These ideas have immediate implications for archaeologists. For example, if burial remains are seen as ideological naturalizations of the social order, then burial variability within cemeteries (how the bones are laid out, the contents of the graves, and so on) will be correlated directly with the structure of the society. But if burial remains in a particular society deny contradictions, then the archaeological burial data cannot be used to "read off" the social organization (see Barrett, **chapter 15**). Material culture, then, is a type of social reality, but its meaning is not fixed and varies across contexts.

Tilley (1984), for example, has interpreted the collapse of the Funnel Neck Beaker (TRB) tradition in southern Sweden in terms of a legitimization crisis (Habermas 1975). He shows that local groups were involved in competitive status displays which led to differential ranking. These differences were supported through feasting and funerary displays in which elders consumed wealth items and, in the process, converted them into individual power and prestige. During the late phase of the TRB, there is a breakdown of the lineage-based social system and tombs no longer appear to be the sites of such displays. He suggests that this transformation was engendered by increasing contradictions between the structuring principles defining the relationships of individuals and groups. The dominant lineages were no longer able to assert their claim to social control through traditional ritual practices. The ground had shifted out from under them.

The reactions to such work on power have been varied and from several different directions. Historical materialists, such as Trigger (1985), find it compromised by its radical interpretation of Marxist concepts and its rejection of positivism. Postprocessualists, such as Hodder (1986), accept much of its agenda, particularly its focus on structures of meaning, but question whether it is sufficiently committed to history and contingency. Feminists, such as Engelstad (1991), have pointed out that in its exploration of power it has neglected the relationship of gender to power.

Structure and Practice

Another group of critics have recast the evolutionary debate in terms of agency and structure, meaning and practice (see Part IV). Rather than focusing on regularities in the differential transmission of cultural forms, the emphasis is instead on contingency and conjunction (Shanks and Tilley 1987). The social world is seen as both a practical world of social action and a conceptualized world consisting of signs and symbols which are constantly in the process of production and reproduction. This means that evolution is simply the working out of day-to-day practices in the long run.

A clear attempt to identify types of structure working at different scales is provided by the historian Fernand Braudel (1972). In terms of the *"longue durée,"* environmental factors such as mountains or seas are linked to aspects of a recurring *"mentalité."* Thus mountains in the Mediterranean region are continually used through time as refuges. Against this backdrop of long-term continuities are the rise and fall of social and economic trends – population increases and decreases, aggregation and dispersal, monetary inflation and deflation. These medium-term trends or "conjunctures" mask individual decisions and vicissitudes. These small-scale events can be separated out but work within the larger-scale structures and trends.

The formalized structure of Braudel's account is unsatisfactory, as also is the lack of mechanism for the relationship between levels or scales. More recent work by the Annales school (e.g. Duby 1983; Le Goff 1985; Le Roy Ladurie 1980) emphasizes detailed ("thick") description of historical events, placed within broader trends. There is an emphasis on contingency and indeterminacy. In some cases, ideology can play a determining role in directing agency. In other cases, economic factors may be dominant. The aim is to explore the complex links between multiple factors at all levels. Here totalizing narratives seem to have given way to more complex and individuated processes.

An example of an Annaliste approach is Philip Duke's (**chapter 9**) study of different temporal scales of change in southern Alberta, Canada. Here he takes Braudel's view of time and adds to it a consideration of structure and event. He argues that procurement and processing tools can be understood as components of *mentalité*, and thus need to be considered not only in their economic capacities but also as symbols of negotiation. For example, he suggests that Avonlea phase projectile points were linked to long-term structures of power and prestige associated with hunting, perhaps going back as far as the Paleoindian period. He sees the adoption of pottery during the Avonlea phase as taking place precisely because it was not fundamental to processing and storage. This may mean that ceramic use was part of a sphere of social discourse only loosely linked to subsistence-related activities.

The Annales school has been widely discussed in archaeology (e.g. Bintliff 1991;

Hodder 1987; Knapp 1992). Its popularity may be due to its multiscale approach, which is attractive in a discipline which deals both with the long term and with individual events. In addition, the approach offers some resolution of the tension between theories based on structure (neo-Marxism, structuralism) and those based on process. However, there is a need for a fuller understanding of the relationship between scales, particularly with regard to how *mentalité,* is formed and transformed. Probably the most important failing is that the relationship between structure and event is insufficiently theorized. For this we need to turn to theories of agency or structuration.

The sociologist Anthony Giddens (1979, 1981, 1984) has developed an influential theory of social change known as structuration theory. Its central premise is that change is the historical product of situated social practices implemented by knowledgeable human agents. Social life consists of the conflicts and struggles between agents and social structures in the ongoing process of reinterpretation and transformation. Giddens developed his theory as a critique of adaptation and evolutionism. For him, human history does not have an evolutionary "shape" and positive harm can result from trying to compress it into one. This is because humans act in cognizance of their own history in what he calls the reflexive nature of social life. Thus state formation needs to be understood in the context of preexisting intersocial relations and in terms of the structural principles relevant to the generation of social forms.

Clarke and Blake (**chapter 10**) use aspects of structuration theory in their study of the emergence of ranked society during the Early Formative period of West Central Mexico. Their argument is that the development of permanent social inequality among the Mokaya was an unanticipated consequence of a political process of individual "aggrandizers" competing for prestige in public arenas. However, previous social structures as well as perceived environmental pressures strongly contoured the emerging system. They support this claim with archaeological evidence for the emergence of elites, the creation of factions, and competitive feasting. Significantly, they regard aggrandizers as acting within an emerging elite network reminiscent of Renfrew's peer-polity model (see **chapter 4**). There are now a number of other examples of agency, structurationist or practice theories in archaeology. Indeed, British and northwestern European prehistory is now routinely interpreted in these terms (e.g. Barrett 1994; Edmonds 1993; Thomas 1991). However, since these approaches usually include structures of meaning and symbolism we will deal with them in Part V.

Another approach also emphasizing the recursive relation between structure and action is Pierre Bourdieu's (1977) theory of practice. This theory identifies "*habitus*" as a collection of dispositions that enable agents to reproduce the conditions of their existence. They are strategy-generating principles enabling agents to cope with unforeseen situations. Rather than seeing *habitus* as abstract sets of mechanistic rules in a filing cabinet in the mind, Bourdieu emphasizes the importance of practical logic and knowledge. All the schemes of categorization and perception are included, but the *habitus* is unconscious, a linguistic and cultural competence. In day-to-day activities, there is a practical mastery involving tact, dexterity, and *savoir faire* which cannot be reduced to rules. It is transmitted from generation to generation without going through discourse or consciousness. And in this process it plays an active role in social action and is transformed in those actions.

Donley (1982) has implemented some of these ideas in her ethno-archaeological study of houses on the island of Lamu off the coast of Kenya. She shows how the symbolically organized space of the house defined the roles of different categories of people. Slaves, for example, were considered unclean and relegated to ground-floor rooms with no washing facilities and simple pit toilets. Women were to be kept pure and were thus strictly segregated in special quarters on the second floor. Muslim traders were only allowed to stay within the house if they had developed a longstanding relationship with the household, otherwise they had to remain on their ships or sleep on the floor of the mosque. The contradiction between purity and defilement was mediated by protective charms and carved inscriptions.

Shennan (**chapter 11**, 1991) has recently evaluated the potential of different theories of practice in understanding cultural change. He regards structuration theory as an important model, especially in its attempt to account for everyday behavior and the ways in which structures are reproduced within it. He notes that by breaking down the distinction between rules or norms on the one hand and behaviors on the other, structuration theory is similar to Bourdieu's theory of practice. But for Shennan, by themselves, theories of practice provide an inadequate account of cultural transmission. This is because they tend to be more preoccupied with practical consciousness and the instantiation of action than with the ways in which its principles are transmitted.

Conclusion

The history of the debates on evolutionary theory is one of continual tensions between biology and culture, individual and society, system and structure. The underlying problem is how to allow for particularism and local history, and how to accommodate intentionality and social strategies, within a wider model of the selective constraints which undoubtedly influence or even channel human social and cultural development. This problem is itself a product of the evolutionary pathway down which the human species has followed. Uniquely, human evolutionary success is linked to a dependence on culture (tools, language, and symbols). It is that cognitive development that led to selection and expansion of the modern human species. And yet, in the process, humans became dependent on the culture which they had created; they "made themselves" (Childe 1936) historically. They created an infinite variety of forms of society.

There is thus a "natural" tendency for us to take the line of a Boas and argue for historical uniqueness, creativity and contingency. And yet it is hard to deny that larger trends can be identified. In the postglacial period sedentary village societies and forms of agriculture emerged independently in widely different parts of the globe. In some areas more complex societies gradually emerged, again independently. An overall trend does seem to run through the local variability at least in some areas of the world. The evolutionary theories described above have identi-fied some of the local factors involved in sociocultural change, such as population increase, climatic change, trade, social competition. Marxist theories in particular have identified long-term evolutionary trajectories based on social conflict. But none of these theories provide an overall explanation of why large-scale trends should emerge. None of them have identified causal processes which seem universally applicable to the local creativity variability of which humans are uniquely capable.

What then are the prospects for a single general theory of cultural change? An optimistic answer is to argue that such a theory can be fashioned by combining aspects of current social and cultural evolutionary theory. In fact, these theories could be seen as complementary since social evolution addresses short-term social dynamics and cultural evolution, particularly with its focus on selection (either nat-ural or cultural), deals with the long-term persistence of cultural forms. On this account the difference is really one of scale and personal interest. But this solution is really no solution at all since it glosses over a crucial problem. Ingold (1986, p. 366) puts it like this, "only when culture is understood in the former sense (innate), as a passively learned tradition not open to discursive formation, can a strict analogue of the Darwinian processes be applied; yet only when it is understood in the latter sense (artificial), as a series of innovations based on explicit, taught rules, can we posit an adequate principle of selection." This paradox turns on the notion of social being as linked to consciousness and irreducible to the interactions of individuals. It seems then that these theories may not be so compatible after all.

Of course, to say that our current frameworks for understanding cultural change are incompatible is entirely different from saying that a unified theory is im-possible and should not be attempted. Indeed, there are good reasons to believe that genetic and cultural transmission are interrelated, if only because the capacity to acquire culture is genetically encoded. Some version of the coevolutionary thesis thus seems on the right track. It is the case, however, that no social or natural science has yet developed a satisfactory theory of cultural change that includes intentionality, symbolic communication, and the persistence of social structures. These are better dealt with by theories of agency and structure. But perhaps we are asking the wrong question; perhaps what we should be concerned with is the incredible diversity of ways in which humans perceive and organize their world, the ways in which they historically construct their own identities. The very intractableness of the evolutionary debate may reveal more about our own assumptions grounded in Platonic idealism, than it does about the development and evolution of culture.

References

Barrett, J.C. 1994. *Fragments from Antiquity: An Archaeology of Social Life in Britain, 2900 – 1200 BC*. Oxford.

Bender, B. 1978. Gatherer-hunter to farmer: a social perspective. *World Archaeology* 10, 204–22.

Bettinger, R.L. 1991. Hunter-Gatherers: Archaeological and Evolutionary Theories. New York.

Binford, L.R. 1962. Archaeology as anthropology. *American Antiquity* 28, 217–25.

Bintliff, J. (ed.) 1991. *The Annales School and Archaeology*. Leicester.

Bonner. J.T. 1980. *The Evolution of Culture in Animals*. Princeton.

Bourdieu, P. 1977. *Outline of a Theory of Practice*. Cambridge.

Boyd, R. and Richerson, P.J. 1985. *Culture and the Evolutionary Process*. Chicago.

Braudel, F. 1972. *The Mediterranean and the Mediterranean World in the Age of Phillip II*, vol. 1. New York.

Cavalli-Sforza, L.L. and Feldman, M.W. 1981. *Cultural Transmission and Evolution: A Quantitative Approach*. Princeton.

Childe, V.G. 1936. *Man Makes Himself*. London.

Clark, D.L. 1968. *Analytical Archaeology*. London.

Donley, L. 1982. House power: Swahili space and symbolic markers. In Hodder, I. (ed.) *Symbolic and Structural Archaeology*. Cambridge, pp. 63–73.

Duby, G. 1983. *The Three Orders: Feudal Society Imagined*. Chicago.

Duhem, W.H. 1991. *Coevolution: Genes, Culture and Human Diversity*. Stanford.

Dunnell, R.C. 1980. Evolutionary theory and archaeology. *Advances in Archaeological Method and Theory*, 35–99.

Dunnell, R.C. 1989. Aspects of the application of evolutionary theory in archaeology. In Lamberg-Karlovsky, C.C. (ed.) *Archaeological Thought in America*. Cambridge, pp. 35–49.

Earle, T.K. 1991. Toward a behavioral archaeology. In Preucel, R.W. (ed.) *Processual and Post-processual Archaeologies: Multiple Ways of Knowing the Past*. Southern Illinois University; Center for Archaeological Investigations, Occasional Paper No. 10. Carbondale, pp. 83–95.

Edmonds, M. 1993. Interpreting causewayed enclosures in the past and the present. In Tilley, C. (ed.) *Interpretative Archaeology*. Oxford, pp. 99–142.

Engelstad, E. 1991. Feminist theory and post-processual archaeology. In Walde, D. and Willows, N. (eds.) *The Archaeology of Gender*. University of Calgary Archaeological Association, Calgary, pp. 116–20.

Faris, J. 1983. From form to content in the structural study of aesthetic systems. In Washburn, D. (ed.) *Structure and Cognition in Art*, Cambridge.

Flannery, K.V. 1972. The cultural evolution of civilizations. *Annual Review of Ecology and Systematics* 3, 399–42.

Foucault, M. 1977. *Discipline and Punish*. New York.

Foucault, M. 1980. *Power/Knowledge*. New York.

Foucault, M. 1981. *The History of Sexuality*. Harmondsworth.

Frankenstein, S. and Rowlands, M.J. 1978. The internal structure and regional context of Early Iron Age society in southwestern Germany. *Bulletin of the Institute of Archaeology* 15, 73–112.

Friedman, J. 1974. Marxism, structuralism and vulgar materialism. *Man* 9, 444–69.

Friedman, J. and Rowlands, M.J. 1978. Notes towards an epigenetic model of the evolution of civilisation. In Friedman, J. and Rowlands, M.J. (eds.) *The Evolution of Social Systems*. London, pp. 201–76.

Giddens, A. 1979. *Central Problems in Social Theory*. London.

Giddens, A. 1981. *A Contemporary Critique of Historical Materialism*. London.

Giddens, A. 1984. *The Constitution of Society: An Outline of the Theory of Structuration*. Berkeley.

Gould, S.J. and Lewontin, R. 1979. The spandrels of San Marco and the Panglossian paradigm: a critique of the adaptationalist programme. *Proceedings of the Royal Society London* B205, 581–98.

Gumerman, G.J. and Gell-Mann, M. (eds) 1994. *Understanding Complexity in the Prehistoric Southwest*. Santa Fe Institute Studies in the Sciences of Complexity, Proc. Vol. XVI, Reading.

Habermas, J. 1975. *Legitimation Crisis*. Boston.

Haselgrove, C. 1982. Wealth, prestige and power: the dynamics of political centralisation in South-east England. In Renfrew, C. and Shennan, S. (eds) *Ranking. Resource and Exchange*. Cambridge, pp. 79–88.

Hodder, I. 1986. *Reading the Past: Current Approaches to Interpretation in Archaeology*. Cambridge, pp. 11–31.

Hodder, I. 1987. (ed.) *Archaeology as Long-term History*. Cambridge.

Hosler, D., Sabloff, J. and Runge, D. 1977. Simulation model development: a case study of the Classic Maya collapse. In Hammond, N. (ed.) *Social Processes in Maya Prehistory*. New York, pp. 553–90.

Ingold, T. 1986. *Evolution and Social Life*. Cambridge.

Ingold, T. 1989. An anthropologist looks at biology. *Man* 25, 208–29.

Knapp, A.B. 1992. (ed.) *Archaeology, Annales and Ethnohistory*. Cambridge.

Le Goff, J. 1985. *The Medieval Imagination*. Chicago.

Le Roy Ladurie, E. 1980. *Montaillou: Cathars and Catholics in a French Village 1294–1324*. Harmondsworth.

Mayr, E. 1988. *Toward a New Philosophy of Biology: Observations of an Evolutionist*. Cambridge.

Miller, D. and Tilley, C. 1984. *Ideology, Power, and Prehistory*. Cambridge.

O'Brien, M.J. and Holland, T.D. 1992. The role of adaptation in archaeological explanation. *American Antiquity* 57, 36–59.

Renfrew, C. (1979). Systems collapse as social transformation: catastrophe and anastrophe in early state societies. In Renfrew, C. and Cooke, K.L. (eds) *Transformations: Mathematical Approaches to Culture Change*. New York, pp. 481–506.

Rindos, D. 1984. *The Origins of Agriculture: An Evolutionary Perspective*. New York.

Rindos, D. 1989. Undirected variation and the Darwinian explanation of culture change. In Schiffer, M.B. (ed.) *Archaeological Method and Theory Vol. 1*. Tucson, pp. 1–45.

Sahlins, M. 1972. *Stone Age Economics*. Chicago.

Sanderson, S.K. 1990. *Social Evolutionism: A Critical History*. Oxford.

Shanks, M. and Tilley, C. 1987. *Social Theory and Archaeology*. Cambridge.

Shennan, S. 1991. Tradition, rationality, and cultural transmission. In Preucel, R.W. (ed.) *Processual and Postprocessual Archaeologies: Multiple Ways of Knowing the Past*. Southern Illinois University, Center of Archaeological Investigations, Occasional Paper No. 10. Carbondale, pp. 197–208.

Spencer, C. 1993. Human agency, biased transmission, and the cultural evolution of chiefly authority. *Journal of Anthropological Archaeological* 12, 41–74.

Teltser, P. (ed.) 1995. *Evolutionary Archaeology: Methodological Issues*. Tucson.

Thomas, J. 1991. *Rethinking the Neolithic*. Cambridge.

Tilley, C. 1984. Ideology and the legitimation of power in the middle Neolithic of southern Sweden. In Miller, D. and Tilley, C. (eds) *Ideology, Power, and Prehistory*. Cambridge, pp. 111–46.

Trigger, B. 1985. Marxism in archaeology: real or spurious? *Reviews in Anthropology* 12, 114–23.

Wynne-Edwards, V.C. 1986. *Evolution Through Group Selection*. Oxford.

8

Explaining the Upper Palaeolithic Revolution

Antonio Gilman

Any attempt to provide a Marxist account of the social processes of pre-class societies (including the extinct ones known to us through the archaeological record) faces the serious difficulty that the works of Marx and Engels provide little sure guidance for the enterprise. The founders of historical materialism were familiar with European pre-capitalist social formations, but with respect to pre- and early class societies they could only know what was just beginning to be discovered and synthesized. The views of Marx and Engels were, accordingly, subject to continual review through their lifetimes as new information became available. Thus, the 'Asiatic Mode of Production' of the *Grundrisse* (Marx 1965 [orig. 1857–8]), a construct developed on the basis of early nineteenth-century British accounts of India, was set aside in the *Origin of the Family* (Engels 1972 [orig. 1884]), which relied on the more up-to-date ethnology of Morgan. At the same time, Engels dropped the functionalist account of the origins of ruling classes which he had set forth in the *Anti-Dühring* (1935 [orig. 1877]: 181–3) in favour of a conflict model stressing the importance of commodity exchange in generating social divisions. We have every reason to suppose, therefore, that the masses of prehistoric and ethnographic information and analysis made available over the course of the past century would have led to even greater changes of position. Marxists today must make their own prehistory aided by only the most general guidelines provided by historical materialism (cf. Meillassoux 1972).

The difficulty of constructing a properly Marxist account of pre-class social systems is exacerbated by the fact that these are fundamentally different from the social formations with which historical materialism has typically concerned itself. 'The history of all hitherto existing society is the history of class struggles', says the *Communist Manifesto* (Marx and Engels 1968 [orig. 1848] : 35) and Engels's footnote to this slogan ('That is all *written* history') only serves to emphasize that the quintessence of Marxism is class analysis. To propose to conduct such an analysis on social systems in which social positions are determined by age, sex and achievement (that is to say, in which social classes as usually defined do not exist) is paradoxical, if not problematical. It is clear that an analysis of the end of pre-class societies (of their transformation into or inclusion within class societies) can be conducted along more or less orthodox Marxist lines. Marxism leads one to distinguish straightforwardly between 'tributary' and 'kin-ordered' modes of production (cf. Wolf 1981). It is not so clear, however, that the contrasts and changes between and within kin-ordered societies can be subjected to an analysis which remains Marxist as such. Leacock (1972: 246) has noted, for example, that Engels's (1972 [orig. 1876]: 251–4) treatment of the role of tools in early human evolution anticipates Washburn's ideas on the same subject 80 years later (e.g. Washburn 1960): this shows not that Washburn is a Marxist, but that Engels understood Darwinism and could apply it creatively. The question, then, is whether an analysis of pre-class societies can be developed which, apart from its jargon, is specifically Marxist, as opposed to being generically evolutionist, structuralist or functionalist.

In any attempt to construct a distinctively Marxist account of the social dynamics of pre-class societies, an essential first step must be to emphasize the archaeological record. Marxism seeks to explain/predict/direct social change, and the rate of such change in pre-class societies is not high. Almost inevitably, then, Marxist accounts of such societies based on ethnography have tended to emphasize the social statics of the systems they examine. It is not surprising, therefore, that ethnographically oriented Marxists have converged with cultural ecology (e.g. Lee 1979) – a tendency criticized as 'vulgar' Marxism – or with structuralism (e.g. Godelier 1975) – a tendency for which the appropriate critical designation might be 'effete' Marxism (T.K. Earle, personal communication). The time-span over which ethnographic evidence has been collected is hardly sufficient to provide evidence to test hypotheses concerning the dynamics of social change within a still egalitarian social system. The very forces which make ethnographic research possible bring to an abrupt end the 'kin-ordered' nature of the society under study. The only way out of this practical and theoretical impasse is to place at the centre of our attention the archaeological record. With all its defects this provides the only (and thus the best) evidence for the long-term trajectories of societies which remain kin-ordered.

Since Marxism is primarily a theory of social change, we must look at those segments of the archaeological record which give manifest evidence for universal and pervasive transformations in social arrangements. There are two such metamorphoses within the time-span in which kin-ordered modes of production were universal. One is the Neolithic Revolution, associated with the introduction of farming and initially defined within a Marxist framework (Childe 1951 [orig. 1936]). This has been one of the central objects of archaeological research in the past 35 years, and the many empirical studies devoted to its elucidation are complemented by a variety of theoretical positions, some idealist (e.g. Isaac 1962), many ecological materialist (e.g. Flannery 1968), and a few attempting to trace a Marxist path between these (e.g. Bender 1978; Kohl and Wright 1977). The other great social change before the emergence of class societies is the Upper Palaeolithic Revolution (Feustel 1968; cf. the 'Broad Spectrum Revolution' of Flannery 1969). Although the transformation in human political economies associated with this latter process is no less fundamental than the changes associated with the Neolithic Revolution, theoretical work on the nature of the dynamics involved remains scanty and rudimentary. As part of the task of seeing how far one can go in building a distinctively Marxist prehistory, it will be useful, then, to outline briefly the changes involved in the Upper Palaeolithic Revolution and to review the general explanatory accounts which are currently proposed in the literature.

Main Features of the Upper Palaeolithic Revolution

The transition from the Middle to the Upper Palaeolithic involves changes in all aspects of the archaeological record, in artifact technology and typology, in the evidence for subsistence patterns, in the nature and distribution of habitation sites, in burial patterns, in the regional configuration of artifact type distributions, and in the material expression of symbolic behaviour. Similar changes occur throughout the Old World, but are best documented in southwest France. Mellars's (1973) description of the transition in the classic area of Palaeolithic research and White's (1982) updating of Mellars's work provide the basis of the following summary.

Archaeologists have traditionally concentrated their attention on artifacts, so that changes in the stone and bone implements are the best documented features of the Upper Palaeolithic Revolution. As far as the stone tool industry is concerned, the Revolution is characterized by a complete shift in predominant artifact types. The tool categories which form the overwhelming bulk of Mousterian assemblages – sidescrapers, denticulates, etc. – are in the minority in all Upper Palaeolithic assemblage types except the Chatelperronian (Chung 1972); they are replaced by endscrapers, burins, etc., tool classes which in the Mousterian had been rare. This change in typology is facilitated by the greater use of the blade core to produce blanks for artifact manufacture. The bone industry changes even more dramatically. In contrast to the rudimentary bone implements found in Mousterian assemblages, the Upper Palaeolithic has a sophisticated range of production: the groove-and-splinter technique of splitting bone and antler into workable pieces is the first step in the all-over shaping of a variety of points, awls, harpoons, mobiliary art, etc. These general changes in the bone and stone industries are accompanied by the constant development of novel, specific artifact types (e.g. split-based bone points, Noailles burins, laurel leaf points) with restricted spatial and temporal distributions. The Middle Palaeolithic completely lacks such a rich variety of specialized types. In the Upper Palaeolithic bone and stone are combined into composite tools much more complex than the simple hafted instruments which may have been made in the Mousterian. In the later Upper Palaeolithic, furthermore, there appear the first mechanical devices to assist human muscle power: spearthrowers and bows. The stylistic and technical perfection of the best Upper Palaeolithic artifacts strongly suggests, as Binford (1973) has pointed out, that tools were 'curated' rather than expediently made and discarded. Upper Palaeolithic industries are more elaborate stylistically and functionally than their

Mousterian predecessors, and it is fair to conclude that they were more effective in handling nature.

Faunal remains from Middle and Upper Palaeolithic habitation sites have, until recently, been collected and studied for their environmental rather than economic significance, so that it is difficult to evaluate systematically the shifts in subsistence patterns associated with the Upper Palaeolithic Revolution. Reviewing the available evidence from the Périgord, Mellars (1973: 260–4) concludes that (a) in the Upper Palaeolithic there was greater concentration on single species (usually reindeer) as the main food resource, and (b) in later phases the hunting repertoire expanded to include fishing and fowling. Recent detailed studies of Middle and Upper Palaeolithic assemblages from Cantabria (Freeman 1973a; Straus 1977) reveal a somewhat different pattern. In the Upper Palaeolithic the range of fauna regularly exploited expands to include Alpine species, nocturnal animals (which must have been trapped), and molluscs (which in the final phases are even overexploited: Straus *et al.* 1980), but evidence of specialization on a particular species seems to be restricted to just one Magdalenian site (red deer at El Juyo). Throughout the Upper Palaeolithic, however, faunal collections reveal a 'catastrophic' mortality profile (dead animals are of all ages) (Klein *et al.* 1981); this suggests that hunters were not restricted in their kills to the weaker of their prey. The accomplished technique such a killing pattern implies would naturally translate itself both into exploitation of a wider range of species and into specialization on a single, wild-harvested species, as conditions rendered either strategy more cost-effective.[1] It would seem, then, that the greater techno-environmental control suggested by Upper Palaeolithic tool kits is also reflected in hunting patterns.

If indeed the Upper Palaeolithic exhibited broad advances in technique with respect to the Mousterian, the resultant increase in adaptive effectiveness should be reflected in increased population densities. This is confirmed in the Périgord where, as Mellars (1973) has indicated, the number of sites per unit time is some ten times larger for the Upper than for the Middle Palaeolithic. Similar results are reported from Cantabria, another well-canvassed region (Straus 1977). This increase in the number of sites cannot be wholly attributed to the loss of earlier sites over time and is not compensated by any decrease in site size. On the contrary, the much larger size of some Upper Palaeolithic occupation horizons suggests not only that population was higher, but also that it was grouped into larger aggregates.

The development of technique which characterizes the shift from Middle to Upper Palaeolithic is accompanied by extensive changes in the archaeological evidence for social organization. The comparison of Middle and Upper Palaeolithic burial practices by Binford (1968a), systematically reviewed and updated by Harrold (1980), shows that the latter exhibit a greater variety of ritual contrasts, possibly reflecting a greater complexity in the social arrangements requiring

---

[1] Bahn (1978) even defends the hypothesis that Upper Palaeolithic animal exploitation practices included incipient forms of husbandry.

certification when the participants died. Another facet of the social aspect of the Upper Palaeolithic Revolution is manifested archaeologically in the profound change in the way in which assemblage types are differentiated spatially and chronologically. The Middle Palaeolithic assemblage types distinguished by Bordes (1953) are characterized by variability in the proportion of major tool classes and by differences in the proportions of flakes manufactured by different techniques. The various Upper Palaeolithic assemblage types also differ in the proportions of major tool classes and in various technological respects, but in addition each assemblage type is characterized by differing proportions of the specialized artifact types discussed above. In spite of the abundance of stratified sequences of assemblages, the general absence of such type fossils has led directly to the failure to establish a clear, widely accepted cultural sequence within the time-span of 40,000 years or more covered by the Mousterian (cf. Binford 1973; Bordes and de Sonneville-Bordes 1970; Mellars 1969; Rolland 1981). By contrast, the general outlines of the Upper Palaeolithic succession have been accepted since the beginning of the century (Breuil 1912). Spatially, the contrast is equally striking: Upper Palaeolithic assemblage types form distinct regional groups, but experts who shun references to a 'Solutrean' or 'Gravettian' in, say, the Near East find no difficulty in identifying the Near Eastern Middle Palaeolithic as 'Mousterian' (e.g. Bordes 1968; cf. Rolland 1981). [2] The contrast in pattern has been concisely summarized in diagrammatic form by Isaac (1972: 401). The 'stylistic and artisan investment' (Binford 1973: 251) in artifact production (which permits the prehistorian to differentiate assemblages spatially and temporally) is also manifested in the personal ornaments and in the artistic representations which constitute the most striking novelties of the Upper Palaeolithic. These, together with the annotated bone pieces studied by Marshack (1972), are often interpreted vitalistically as expressions of emergent human cognitive capacities. More significantly, however, spatially clustered, stylistically distinctive material remains are, as Wobst (1977) points out, a by-product of (and useful contributor to) the maintenance of communication within the social groups that manufacture them. That 'cultures', in Childe's (1929: v–vi) classic definition of the term, do not appear until the Upper Palaeolithic can, then, be interpreted as indicating that, before then, 'ethnicity may not . . . have been a component of the cultural environment of man' (Binford 1973: 244; cf. Freeman 1973b: 131; Leroi-Gourhan 1964: 221). The appearance of art and ornament, the more elaborate burial patterns, the change in archaeological systematics, the production of highly stylized artifacts, all are manifestations of the appearance in the Upper Palaeolithic of a 'new form of social organization, one in which greater corporate awareness . . . played a role' (Binford 1968a: 148).

The Middle to Upper Palaeolithic transition is best documented in western Europe, but it is apparent that after about 40,000 years ago changes in the lithic and

---

[2] At the same time, raw materials at Upper Palaeolithic sites are sometimes procured from distant sources, which may indicate, as White (1982: 176) says, more 'structured relationships between the inhabitants of different geographic areas'.

bone industries similar to those just discussed occur in eastern Europe and Africa. In each of these, furthermore, some at least of the additional innovations associated with the Upper Palaeolithic are definitely present, e.g. ornaments and art in southern Russia (Klein 1973), intensification of faunal exploitation in southern Africa (Klein 1979), etc. Thus, in every area of the world where reliable assemblages are numerous enough to permit systematic comparisons, the occurrence of an Upper Palaeolithic Revolution is the salient feature of the Upper Pleistocene archaeological record. But while the Upper Palaeolithic Revolution is widespread, it is not abrupt. Conceptually, it may be a 'quantum advance' (Klein 1973: 122) and, cumulatively, it is certainly far-reaching, but the transition is nothing if not gradual. The slow nature of the change can be illustrated in two ways. First, most Upper Palaeolithic innovations in fact occur with lesser frequency or intensity in the Middle Palaeolithic. This is clear in the lithic industry, where the major Upper Palaeolithic tool categories, as well as the blade technology used to make them, all occur (in low frequencies) in Mousterian assemblages. Likewise, worked bone is not altogether lacking in the Mousterian. Hafted (composite) tools are probably present as well. Burials may be simpler, but they are, after all, a Mousterian innovation. Some regionalization of distinctive style zones is apparent in later phases of the Middle Palaeolithic (e.g. the Aterian). Even decorated and inscribed pieces are not unknown (e.g. Freeman 1978). Second, the characteristic features of the Upper Palaeolithic often only achieve full expression in its later phases. Expansion and/or intensification of faunal exploitation only becomes manifest in the Solutrean and Magdalenian, both in Cantabria and in the Périgord (Mellars 1973; Straus 1977); earlier Upper Palaeolithic faunal exploitation does not differ markedly from that of the Mousterian (cf. Gamble 1979). Regionalization of assemblage types is less pronounced in the earlier than in the later Upper Palaeolithic: Aurignacian assemblages cover a wider geographical area than Magdalenian ones. The climactic phase in the development of Palaeolithic art is, once again, the Magdalenian. As a result of these two tendencies, it is not surprising that at the chronological dividing point between Middle and Upper Palaeolithic there are often 'transitional' cultures: in France, the 'B' facies of the Mousterian of Acheulian tradition and the Chatelperronian; in east-central Europe, the Szeletian; in southern Africa, the Umguzan complex (Sampson 1974). All of these share Middle and Upper Palaeolithic features. The Upper Palaeolithic Revolution, like the Neolithic Revolution later on, encompasses the entire inhabited world in a gradual process of immense significance.

Current Explanatory Approaches

Apart from being consistent with the content and tempo of the changes involved, a successful account of the Upper Palaeolithic Revolution must meet two requirements. First, it must be comprehensive enough to link together all the various technical and social features of the transition into a single, causally plausible explanatory web. Second, the account must be structurally basic enough to be able to explain the occurrence of the Revolution in all the very diverse areas in which it took place. There are three major approaches to the problem of the Middle to Upper Palaeolithic transition and it will be instructive to examine them with these requirements in mind.

The biological approach

Mousterian artifact assemblages are mostly associated with skeletal remains of *Homo sapiens neanderthalensis*, Upper Palaeolithic assemblages mostly with *Homo sapiens sapiens*. In Europe transitional specimens are unknown. Before the Second World War, when the outlines of the Middle to Upper Palaeolithic transition were well known in Europe and when very little information was available from other regions, the generally accepted explanation of the cultural changes involved was to attribute them to the associated biological changes. As Sackett (1968: 66–7) has pointed out, artifact types were considered to be analogues to biological fossils and differences in artifact types were seen as indicative of biological differences. A wholesale change in typology, such as that associated with the Upper Palaeolithic Revolution, could only be brought about by a wholesale change in biology. The idealist inclinations of artifact connoisseurs converged with an abject biological reductionism in a nice example of the unity of opposites.

After the Second World War the biological approach to Palaeolithic culture change was fairly generally abandoned (see below), but recently it has been revived, notably by Richard Klein:

> [The] physical characters [of Neanderthals], in combination with such cultural facts as the absence of undoubted art objects in Mousterian sites, suggests that they may have been 'primitives' in the narrowest imaginable sense of that word. Thus, in addition to possessing simpler cultures than we do, they may have been bio-physically less complex. (Klein 1973: 123)

> The people who appeared 35,000 years ago knew how to do an awful lot of things their predecessors didn't. Something quite extraordinary must have happened in the organization of the brain . . . I'm quite convinced . . . that in Europe it was a physical replacement of one kind by another. And I'm prepared to bet that that's what happened in Africa too and at about the same time . . . I would think that the behavioral gulf between these two very different kinds of people would have been so great that there would have been no desire at all to mate. (Klein, quoted in Rensberger [1980: 7, 8])

A somewhat more subtle version of this approach explains the cultural changes of the Middle to Upper Palaeolithic transition in terms of biological changes permitting the development of full linguistic competence.

> Whether it was only with the appearance of *Homo sapiens* or before, that the lowered larynx and mobile tongue developed, . . . at whatever point in human evolution the symbolic mode of communication . . . became established as a regular component of human behavior, the adaptive advantage it conferred upon its users must have been significant . . . Not only is it a plausible hypothesis that a cultural informational transformation contributed to the 'replacement' of Neanderthals by fully sapiensized populations, but also it is easy to see how a

communication advantage could have enhanced the learning of new adaptive tasks. (Conkey 1978: 73–4; cf Isaac 1972: 403; 1976: 286)

In short, the Upper Palaeolithic Revolution is the technological and social manifestation of the biological achievement of a full capacity for culture.

Empirically, the biological approach to explaining the Middle to Upper Palaeolithic transition faces the difficulty that the skeletal differences between *Homo sapiens neanderthalensis* and *Homo sapiens sapiens* have no direct bearing on their respective intellectual/cultural capacities. The changes in facial and cranial morphology have no clear explanation (certainly not an intellectual one) and the decrease in robustness in the post-cranial remains can be plausibly interpreted as the *result* of more effective extrasomatic adaptations (Trinkaus and Howells 1979).[3] Even if, for the sake of argument, one were to allow that *Homo sapiens sapiens* was biologically more capable of cognitive representations such as language than his immediate predecessors, however, one would still not be able to use his increased abilities as a sufficient explanation for the new elements in his cultural repertoire. To say, for example, that Cro-Magnons were capable of painting caves (and that Neanderthals were not) does not explain why they painted them. Conversely, if painting caves is part of a more effective adaptive system, then one need not appeal to the capability of painting them in order to explain why the painting took place. Because biological changes underdetermine cultural ones, the biological approach fails to establish a plausible link between the assumed causes and the known manifestations of the Upper Palaeolithic Revolution.

The particularist approach

The overtones of *Rassengeschichte* inherent in the biological approach to Palaeolithic culture change led to a widespread revulsion among prehistorians. After the Second World War the focus of much of the research was to emphasize the continuities between the Middle Palaeolithic and its successors: the existence of intermediate cultures in a number of areas and the presence of Upper Palaeolithic elements in earlier contexts (Bordes 1971; Bricker 1976: 139–43) were deployed as evidence to debunk the catastrophism implicit in the classic biological model. Like other cultural particularist responses to racialist evolutionary theories, this approach has the great merit of encouraging the detailed documentation of variation in the anthropological record and the defect of blurring broad contrasts which still demand an explanation. Thus, although Bordes does not deny that differences exist in the nature and distribution of assemblage types between the Middle and the Upper Palaeolithic, he considers them to be the material expression of 'tribes' in both instances (e.g. Bordes 1968: 144–5, 157–8). In his last statement on the

---

[3] In fact, of course, the only evidence for *Homo sapiens sapiens'* biological superiority is his cultural production. The evidence for the assumed cause is its supposed effect. It is this circularity that makes the biological approach irrefutable.

subject, Bordes clearly reveals the thrust of his position: 'Il est d'ailleurs curieux que [certains] auteurs dénient aux Moustériens tout sentiment d'identité, ethnique au moment où les paléontologues rattachent l'homme du Néanderthal ... á l'espèce *Homo sapiens* comme une simple race . . . ou démontrent que certaines industries mousté,riennes ont été l'oeuvre d'*Homo sapiens sapiens*' (Bordes 1981: 87). This simply turns the biological argument on its head. The existence of detailed similarities and continuities between the Mousterian and its successors does not obliterate the major differences which exist and require explanation.

The cultural materialist approach

Sally Binford (1968b; 1970) has put forward the theory that the changes involved in the Upper Palaeolithic Revolution were brought about by the hunting of herds of migratory herbivores. First proposed tongue-in-cheek as the achievement of 'a level of primary predation efficiency' (Binford and Binford 1966), the central idea is expressed as follows:

> *The cooperative hunting of a few males to capture one or two animals characterized human subsistence from at least Mindel times . . ., but the large-scale systematic exploitation of migratory herd mammals is a qualitatively different kind of activity, one that makes totally different structural demands on the human groups involved. This kind of hunting is known to characterize Upper Palaeolithic adaptations, and it is proposed . . . that . . . not only did this hunting pattern appear before the Upper Palaeolithic, but that the formal changes documented from Neanderthal to modern man and from Mousterian to the Upper Palaeolithic occurred in response to this basic structural change in ecological relationships. (Binford 1968b: 714)*

The detailed steps in the model as applied to the Near East are summarized in flow-chart form in figure 8.1, but its essential features might be replicated in other areas with appropriate changes in empirical variables. The central thrust is to provide an ecological explanation for the development of the group co-operation which is the practical basis of the hunter-gatherer band in the classic model of Service (1962).

The co-operative hunting account of the 'origin of Band Society' has been amplified by Wobst's (1976) interpretation of the significance of the appearance of style zones in the light of his simulations of Palaeolithic demographic processes (Wobst 1975). The latter show that a local exogamous group (the 'minimal band' of c. 25 individuals) must be part of a mate exchange network (a connubium: Williams 1974) of some 500 individuals in order to survive. At population densities of Palaeolithic sparseness this means that travel time to maintain necessary social contacts would constitute a significant cost. The existence of style zones is interpreted as the material expression of the demarcation of its social identity by a closed connubium (cf. the 'dialectical tribe' of Birdsell 1953). Because peripheral groups within a closed connubium must forego mates obtainable from 'alien' neighbours, the travel cost of maintaining the exchange of mates is higher than in an open connubium. Therefore, the appearance of style zones is interpreted to mean (a) that population densities had become high enough to make the longer travel for mates feasible, and

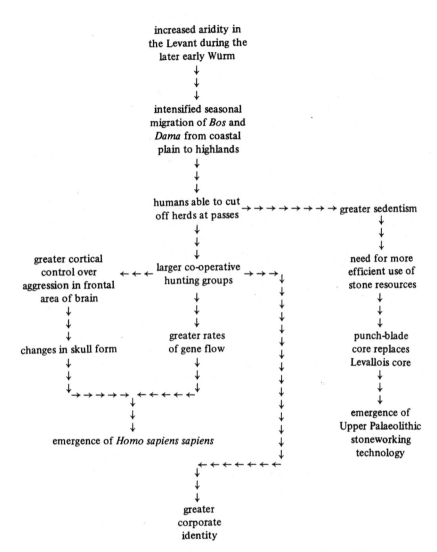

Figure 8.1 [orig. figure 1]   The Upper Palaeolithic Revolution according to Binford
(1968b; 1970).

(b) that the closed connubium conferred practical benefits which compensated for the higher cost of procuring mates.

It was at this time that work groups, requiring more personnel than a single local group could provide, had achieved a sufficient pay-off to have become a predictable part of the seasonal round of activities and . . . that additional pay-off could be gained by minimizing the turn-over in this personnel. Such pay-offs may well have derived from large scale game drives that effectively exploited the windfall of the spring and fall migrations of large herbivores. (Wobst 1976: 55)

The causal chain involved in Wobst's elaboration of the Binford model is summarized in flow-chart form in figure 8.2.

The cultural materialist accounts just outlined have the merit of focusing research on subsistence techniques, demography, and social organization, aspects of the archaeological record too often neglected in Palaeolithic studies, but the specificity which gives the approach its heuristic value is carried to the point of becoming a theoretical defect. On the one hand, the argument is tied to specific ecological settings, those where co-operative hunting of large, seasonally migratory herd animals would have been advantageous in mid-Würm times. Even assuming that such opportunities had the predicted consequences for *Bos* and *Dama* hunters in the Levant or for *Rangifer* hunters in the Périgord, how can the model help us understand the transition to the Upper Palaeolithic in Cantabria (where quite different faunal exploitation patterns are attested), let alone in the Maghreb or southern Africa? The Upper Palaeolithic Revolution is an Old-World-wide event and cannot be explained by local ecological gimmicks. On the other hand, even where the ecological conditions are arguably appropriate for the

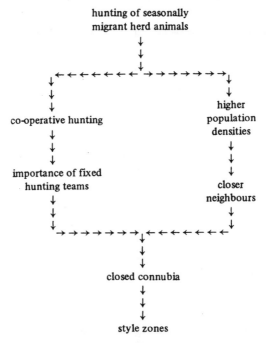

Figure 8.2 [orig. figure 2]   The development of Upper Palaeolithic style zones according to Wobst (1976).

co-operative hunting theory, the causal links between the change in hunting patterns and the remaining cultural changes have an implausible, Rube Goldberg-like quality. It is proposed, for example, that the increased sedentism required in order to cut off migrating herds at fixed localities would encourage the adoption of the more parsimonious punch-blade technique in order to husband the relatively scarcer flint resources locally available (Binford 1970: 282). Would this mean that Middle Palaeolithic techniques survived longer, *ceteris paribus*, in areas with abundant flint resources, like the Périgord? Similarly, the link between co-operative hunting and the closed connubium proposed by Wobst depends on an assessment of the relative effectiveness of set v. pick-up hunting teams which is hardly supported by the available ethnographic record on hunting practices.[4] Cultural materialism, here as elsewhere (cf. Friedman 1974), fails to link technical and social changes in a convincing causal sequence.

  The available literature on the Middle to Upper Palaeolithic transition, in so far as it transcends a purely descriptive level, does not contain a satisfactory account of the nature of the processes involved. We are left to choose between positions which reduce the cultural changes to epiphenomena of undocumented biological changes, positions which minimize the significance of the transformation (and thereby suggest that no explanation is nesessary), and positions which explain the transformation in terms of mechanically conceived ecological devices. It is clear that there is room for a more convincing approach, Marxist or otherwise.

Theory, Discussion, and Conclusions

Wobst (1976), Conkey (1978), and White (1982) are correct in emphasizing that the key feature which requires explanation in the Upper Palaeolithic Revolution is the appearance of style in its various manifestations. The changes in artifact and subsistence technology constitute straightforward adaptive improvements, but the development of art and tools worked with an elaboration far beyond functional requirements and the increased regional clustering of types of such objects reflect social changes whose causes are not so immediately explained in terms of Darwinian rationality.[5] The widespread interpretation of these changes as reflecting the appearance of increased corporate solidarity, the development of closed connubia, or more generally the introduction of ethnicity constitutes a major first step in understanding the processes involved, but this idea has not been articulated satisfactorily with the techno-environmental aspects of the Upper

---

[4] Among the !Kung San, for example, 'the composition of the hunting party is not a matter of strict convention or of anxious concern. Whoever the hunters are, the meat is shared and everyone profits. The men are free to organize their hunting parties as they like . . . Men from different bands may hunt together' (Marshall 1976: 357). In Australia, 'collective hunting can be carried out by men who are not clansmen, and knowledge of animal behaviour and personal skill are more important than detailed local knowledge in most conditions' (Peterson 1975: 63).

[5] The question of the nature and pace of Upper Pleistocene human biological evolution (which may include local population replacement events) is an interesting research area, but (for the reasons noted earlier) not one which can easily contribute to an understanding of the cultural changes of the period.

Palaeolithic Revolution. The proposed explanations to date – that these social changes are epiphenomena either of biological changes in the human species or of technical changes in ways of exploiting the environment – are demonstrably inadequate. As Bender (1981: 153) has suggested, in order to connect the social and technical changes of the Upper Palaeolithic Revolution in a plausible framework, it will be useful to review some of the principal conclusions of alliance theory in social anthropology, since this provides us with a basic understanding of the social relations of production in the primitive social formations which emerged in the Late Pleistocene.

The adaptive necessity for local groups to maintain alliances with their neighbours was expressed aphoristically by Tylor (1889: 267) as 'the simple, practical alternative between marrying out and being killed out'. Tylor's dictum emphasized a group's need for alliances in order to maintain access to its own territory, but subsequently the utility of alliance was recognized to include the assurance of access to the territory and resources of others in times of shortage. Alliances established by means of the exchange of spouses (by exogamy) promote security by preventing conflict and facilitating economic assistance between groups. Beyond a certain social distance, however, the costs of alliance outweigh its benefits. As Lévi-Strauss (1969 [orig. 1949]: 46) notes: 'A very great number of primitive tribes simply refer to themselves by the term for "men" in their language . . . In all these cases, it is merely a question of knowing how far to extend the logical connotation of the idea of a community, which in itself is dependent on the effective solidarity of the group.' The occasional and dispensable contacts with strangers can be governed by the norms of what Sahlins (1965) has termed 'negative reciprocity'.

Within the circle of the co-operative, maximally endogamous group (the connubium), mutual assistance is not absolute, however. Members of the same household and their close kinsmen may entertain relations governed by 'generalized' reciprocity, but, as Sahlins (1972: 123–30) has emphasized, the sphere of 'balanced' reciprocity is replete with variable and grudging co-operation, especially in moments of crisis. Within the 'Domestic Mode of Production' relations between households are governed by contradictory forces: on the one hand, the household desires to establish external ties in order to insure against inevitable failures in its own production; on the other hand, it desires to limit its external ties in order to husband its resources. Beyond the intimate domestic sphere of unquestioning mutual assistance, the household establishes ties whose scope and intensity are inversely proportional to the security of its autonomous production. To the extent that the household assures its production security by its own efforts, it both diminishes its need for the assistance of other households and increases the likelihood that it will be subject to the importunities of other households. Maintaining the necessary web of social relations requires the balancing of contradictory interests and it is this that makes ritual reinforcement of reciprocity necessary.

Archaeologists have tended to interpret the existence of style zones as the material expression of actual co-operation between local groups (see Brown and Plog 1982 for a well-developed expression of this view). Indeed, the diagram by which Wobst (1977: Fig. 1) expresses the functional sphere of artifact style in facilitating the transmission of information corresponds precisely to the sphere of balanced reciprocity as expressed diagrammatically by Sahlins (1965: Fig. 1). But the solidarity of households engaged in balanced reciprocity must be sanctified by ritual (or, in the material expression of ritual in artifacts, by style) not because co-operation between households exists, but because it is liable to break down.[6] The lesson of alliance theory is, therefore, that rituals expressing corporate solidarity came to have increasing salience in Upper Palaeolithic material culture, not because co-operation between local groups/households/minimal bands had increased, but because, although co-operation was necessary, the basis for it had become more problematical.

Alliance theory suggests how the technical and social aspects of the Upper Palaeolithic Revolution may be integrated into a single, coherent, plausible account. A local group in the Palaeolithic would have obtained the wherewithal with which to survive, on the one hand, from its own co-operative efforts assisted by whatever level of technique was known to it and, on the other hand, by pooling its resources (or risks, as Wiessner [1982: 173] puts it) with those of neighbouring groups. No group would have been able to dispense with outside assistance, but the frequency with which it would have to make appeal to other groups and the number of needed allies would be inversely proportional to the effectiveness of its own techniques. Thus, as technique improved, relations between groups would become more problematical: the need for positive co-operation would be balanced by the defensive needs indicated by Tylor. The Upper Palaeolithic Revolution involves, then, a critical change in the balance of social security, a change brought about by the development of the forces of production.

The low level of technology possessed by Lower and Middle Pleistocene human groups logically would have had two consequences. First, local groups would often require the help of their neighbours: the local production shortages which are not uncommon among ethnographically documented hunter-gatherers (Colson 1979) can only have been more frequent for foragers with more limited equipment. Second, population densities must have been very low, so that any particular local group would have had little choice in its allies. All help would be welcome and, conversely, help would be granted to all. The give-and-take of mutual aid would have been so essential that it would have known no social boundaries. In the Upper Pleistocene there was continual and accelerating improvement in the level of human technology. The innovations vary from region to region, but to the extent that the techno-environmental efficiency of the forces of production increased, there would logically be two outcomes. First, population densities would rise.

---

[6] The notion that ritual serves to alleviate uncertainty is , of course, a functionalist commonplace, but one contemporary example may be to the point: in American society the increasing prevalence of rituals (in which artifacts play no little part) asserting the sanctity and permanence of the nuclear family (Mother's and Father's Days, wedding anniversaries, renewed wedding vows, etc.) does not reflect any increasing unity of the family in fact. Rather, these practices are meant to ward off whatever disruptive forces have led to a rising divorce rate.

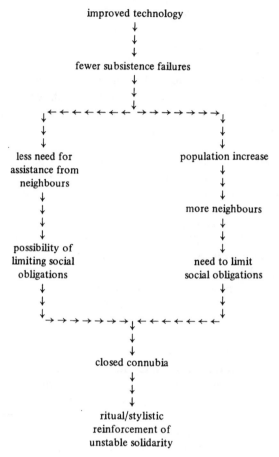

Figure 8.3 [orig. figure 3]   The relation between technological improvements and social change over the course of the Upper Palaeolithic Revolution.

Second, the frequency with which any local group would find itself unable to obtain the necessities of life on its own would decrease. Thus, as more neighbours became available (to whom help might have to be given), fewer occasions would arise on which help from one's neighbours would be required. The clear solution to this shift in the balance of a group's interests would be to restrict the scope of its alliances. The establishment of closed circles of mutual aid would fulfil the need of each group to obtain occasional assistance and to limit its obligations to assist others. Given the increase in population density, this shift could be performed at fairly low cost (cf. Wobst 1976). The closed connubium of friends-in-need would require ceremonies to symbolize and cement their alliance and style to represent it, not because innovations in technique had made mutual aid more necessary, but because higher production security (made possible by innovations in technique) had made social co-operation more unstable.[7] The overall process is summarized in flow-chart form in figure 8.3.

The approach just proposed to account for the salient features of the Upper Palaeolithic Revolution has several points to recommend it. First, it is consistent with the empirical record of change in the prehistoric remains. The pace of change assumed by the model is a gradual one and the correlative technological and social aspects predicted by it are confirmed archaeologically. Thus, many of the characteristic technical advances of the Upper Palaeolithic are present in a small way in the Mousterian, while the first foreshadowing of the elaborate collective representation of the Upper Palaeolithic are the formal burials of the preceding period. The model proposed here sees in the Upper Palaeolithic Revolution gradual cumulative processes which eventually culminate in critically significant qualitative changes.[8] Second, the model links the technical and social aspects of the Revolution in a manner structurally basic enough to accommodate the diversity of ecological circumstances in which it took place, and concrete trajectories by which it took place. The changes in social organization attendant on the cumulation of technical advances are not tied, as in the cultural materialist accounts of Binford or Wobst, to specific settings, but rather to an overall increase in production security.[9] The changes in technology are seen as primary adaptive improvements to be explained within a Darwinian framework of the kind elucidated by Hayden (1981). The changes in social organization arise from a shift in group interests ultimately caused, but not specifically determined, by more effective technologies. That is to say, the materialist determination of social structure is in the last, not the first, instance. Finally, unlike other accounts, this theory embodies specific suggestions concerning the nature of 'pre-Band Society' social structure. The idea that the social structure of human groups before the Upper Palaeolithic was based on unlimited co-operation is in accord with the emphasis on sharing which Isaac (1971) has made the basis of his social analysis of the earliest known human cultural remains.

---

[7] Wiessner's (1982) useful analysis of the social relations of hunter-gatherer production helps define the nature of the changes brought about by improvements in technique. Of the four approaches used to reduce the variance in mean subsistence income – prevention of loss, storage, negative transfer of risk (expropriation), and pooling (sharing) – the first two would be immediately and directly affected by increases in technological effectiveness. Improvement in these strategies, however, would tend to affect the social approaches to risk prevention by increasing the feasibility and profitability of expropriation and by reducing the incentive to share. In short, technological improvements in the security of production would lead to potential decreases in social security, a recurrent pattern in social evolution (cf. Gilman 1981). The emergent social tensions would be mediated by stylistic intensification. Pfeiffer (in White 1982: 184) points in the right direction when he sees 'the spectacular increase in . . . art and ceremony' as 'an effort to reduce conflict'.

[8] My model implies that technological and social changes unfold over the course of both the Middle and the Upper Palaeolithic. Evidence for such 'progress' is available for the latter period, but remains to be developed for the former.

[9] The idea of 'primary hunting efficiency' lampooned by Binford and Binford (1966) may not, after all, be such a bad one.

To date, explanations of the Upper Palaeolithic Revolution have been character-ized by a considerable theoretical poverty. We have been left to choose between an idealism that considers the cultural information of the Upper Palaeolithic so much more complex than that of preceding periods that it necessarily reflects genetic changes in the capacity for culture and a mechanical materialism that reduces the social and ideological developments of the Upper Palaeolithic to instruments necessary to make new technologies effective. By focusing on the social relations of production, I have tried to steer a course between these extremes. Such an approach is characteristically, but not exclusively Marxist. The central ideas of alliance theory go back, after all, to Durkheim and Tylor, who were not Marxists. What is muted in the work of Durkheim and of most of his successors, however, is any emphasis on the tensions and divisions underlying the corporate solidarity of the social group. Sahlins's essentially Marxist addition to alliance theory is to show how internal economic tensions served as a stimulus for the change from egalitarian to complex social systems (Sahlins 1972: 123–48). It is this same emphasis on conflict and contradiction, cast backwards so to speak, that permits one to arrive at a better account of the Upper Palaeolithic Revolution.

This essay is Marxist, not only in its analytical approach, but also in its conclu-sions. Marx and Engels took up the idea that primitive communism was the pristine form of human social organization in order to show, as Pershits (1981: 85) puts it, 'the historically conditioned and, therefore, transient character of [the] basic institutions of class society'. Morgan provided Marx and Engels with the oppor-tunity to convert a philosophical theory into a scientific one. In response, opponents of Marxism have tended to emphasize the great differences between pre-class societies. This criticism has been all the more effective in that Marxist syntheses of prehistory have tended to emphasize the stages, rather than the processes, of social evolution. To articulate the archaeological evidence for the earliest human social formations to a coherent account of the social dynamics of pre-class societies will contribute, I hope, to the revitalization of the basically correct notion of primitive communism.

Acknowledgements

Earlier drafts of this paper received useful criticisms from Harvey Bricker, Glynn Isaac, Susan Kus, Paul Mellars, Kathryn Maurer Trinkaus, Keith Morton, Erik Trinkaus, and Gregory Truex. All remaining errors are of course mine.

References

Bahn, P.G. 1978. The unacceptable face of the West European Upper Palaeolithic. *Antiquity* 52: 183–92.

Bender, B. 1978. Gatherer-hunter to farmer: a social perspective. *World Archaeology* 10: 205–22

    1981. Gatherer-hunter intensification. In A. Sheridan and G. Bailey (eds.), *Economic Archaeology: Towards an Integration of Ecological and Social Approaches*. B.A.R. International Series 96: 149–57. Oxford: British Archaeological Reports.

Binford, L.R. 1973. Interassemblage variability – the Mousterian and the 'functional' argument. In C. Renfrew (ed.), *The Explanation of Culture Change: Models in Prehistory*, pp. 227–54. London: Duckworth.

Binford, L.R. and S.R. Binford, 1966. The predatory revolution: a consideration of the evidence for a new subsistence level. *American Anthropologist* 68: 508–12.

Binford, S.R. 1968a. A structural comparison of the disposal of the dead in the Mousterian and the Upper Palaeolithic. *Southwestern Journal of Anthropology* 24: 139–54.

1968b. Early Upper Pleistocene adaptations in the Levant. *American Anthropologist* 70: 707–17.

1970. Late Middle Palaeolithic adaptations and their possible consequences. *Bioscience* 20: 280–83.

Birdsell, J.B. 1953. Some environmental and cultural factors influencing the structure of Australian aboriginal populations. *American Naturalist* 87: 171–207.

Bordes, F. 1953. Essai de classification des industries 'mousté,riennes'. *Bulletin de la Société Préhistorique Française* 50: 457–66.

1968. *The Old Stone Age*. London: Weidenfeld and Nicolson.

1971. Du Palolithique moyen au Paléolithique supérieur, continuité, ou discontinuité. In F. Bordes (ed.), *The Origin of Homo sapiens*, pp. 211–18. Paris: UNESCO.

1981. Vingt-cinq ans aprés: le compléxe moustérien revisité. *Bulletin de la Société Préhistorique Française* 78: 77–87.

Bordes, F. and D. Sonneville-Bordes, 1970. The significance of variability in Palaeolithic assemblages. *World Archaeology* 2: 61–73.

Breuil, H. 1912. Les subdivisions du Paléolithique supérieur et leur signification. *C.R. XIV Congrès International d'Anthropologie et d'Archéologie Préhistoriques, Genève*, pp. 165–238.

Bricker, H.M. 1976. Upper Palaeolithic archaeology. *Annual Review of Anthropology* 5: 133–48.

Brown, D.P. and S. Plog, 1982. Evolution of 'tribal' social networks: theory and prehistoric North American evidence. *American Antiquity* 47: 504–25.

Childe, V.G. 1929. *The Danube in Prehistory*. Oxford: Clarendon Press.

1951. *Man Makes Himself*. New York: Mentor Books.

Chung, Young-Wha, 1972. L'outillage de type archaïque dans le Paléolithique supérieur du sud-ouest de la France. Thèse Dr. de l'Université, Bordeaux 1.

Colson, E. 1979. In good years and bad: food strategies of self-reliant societies. *Journal of Anthropological Research* 35: 18–29.

Conkey, M.W. 1978. Style and information in cultural evolution: toward a predictive model for the Palaeolithic. In C. Redman *et al.* (eds.), *Social Archaeology: Beyond Subsistence and Dating*, pp. 61–85. New York: Academic Press.

Engels, F. 1935. *Herr Eugen Dühring's Revolution in Science*. Chicago: Charles H. Kerr.

1972. *The Origin of the Family, Private Property, and the State*. New York: International Publishers.

Feustel, R. 1968. Evolution und Revolution im Ablauf der Steinzeit. *Ethnographisch–Archälogische Zeitschrift* 9: 120-47.

Flannery, K. 1968. Archaeological systems theory and early Meso-america. In B. Meggers (ed.), *Anthropological Archaeology in the Americas*, pp. 67–87. Washington, DC: Anthropological Society of Washington.

1969. Origins and ecological effects of early domestication in Iran and the Near East. In P.J. Ucko and G.W. Dimbleby (eds.), *The Domestication and Exploitation of Plants and Animals*, pp. 73–100. London: Duckworth.

Freeman, L.G. 1973a. The significance of mammalian faunas from Palaeolithic occupations in Cantabrian Spain. *American Antiquity* 48: 3-44.

1973b. El Musteriense. In J. Gonzá lez Echegaray *et al* (eds.), *Cueva Morín: Excavaciones 1969*, pp. 15–140. Santander: Patronato de las Cuevas Prehistóricas.

1978. Mousterian worked bone from Cueva Morín (Santander, Spain): a preliminary description. In L.G. Freeman (ed.), *Views of the Past: Essays in Old World Prehistory and Palaeoanthropology*, pp. 29–51. The Hague: Mouton.

Friedman, J. 1974. Marxism, structuralism, and vulgar materialism. *Man* (n.s.) 9: 444–69.

Gamble, C. 1979. Hunting strategies in the central European Palaeolithic. *Proceedings of the Prehistoric Society* 45: 35–52.

Gilman, A. 1981. The development of social stratification in Bronze Age Europe. *Current Anthropology* 22: 1–23.

Godelier, M. 1975. Modes of production, kinship, and demographic structures. In M. Bloch (ed.), *Marxist Analyses in Social Anthropology*, pp. 3–27. New York: John Wiley.

Harrold, F.B. 1980. A comparative analysis of Eurasian Palaeolithic burials. *World Archaeology* 12: 195–210.

Hayden, B. 1981. Research and development in the Stone Age: technological transitions among hunter-gatherers. *Current Anthropology* 22: 519–48.

Isaac, E. 1962. On the domestication of cattle. *Science* 137: 195–204.

Isaac, G. 1971. The diet of early man. *World Archaeology* 2: 278–99.

1972. Chronology and the tempo of culture change during the Pleistocene. In W.W. Bishop and J.A. Miller (eds.), *Calibration of Hominoid Evolution*, pp. 381–400. Edinburgh: Scottish Academic Press.

1976. Stages of cultural elaboration in the Pleistocene: possible archaeological indicators of the development of language capabilities. *Annals of the New York Academy of Sciences* 280: 275–88.

Klein, R.G. 1973. *Ice Age Hunters of the Ukraine*. Chicago: University of Chicago Press.

1979. Stone Age exploitation of animals in southern Africa. *American Scientist* 67: 151–60.

Klein, R.G., C.Wolf, L.G. Freeman and K. Allwarden, 1981. The use of dental crown heights for constructing age profiles of red deer and similar species in archaeological samples. *Journal of Archaeological Science* 8: 1–31.

Kohl, P.L. and R.P. Wright, 1977. Stateless cities: the differentiation of societies in the Near Eastern Neolithic. *Dialectical Anthropology* 2: 271–83.

Leacock, E.B. 1971. Editor's introduction to 'The part played by labor in the transition from ape to man'. In Engels 1972: 254–9.

Lee, R.B. 1979. *The !Kung San: Men, Women, and Work in a Foraging Society*. Cambridge: Cambridge University Press.

Leroi-Gourhan, A. 1964. *Le Geste et la Parole*. vol. 1: *Technique et Langage*. Paris: Albin Michel.

Lévi-Strauss, C. 1969. *The Elementary Structures of Kinship*. Boston: Beacon Press.

Marshack, A. 1972. Cognitive aspects of Upper Palaeolithic engraving. *Current Anthropology* 13: 445–77.

Marshall, L. 1976. Sharing, talking, and giving: relief of social tensions among the !Kung. In R.B. Lee and I. DeVore (eds.), *Kalahari Hunter-Gatherers: Studies of the !Kung San and Their Neighbors*, pp. 349–71. Cambridge, Mass.: Harvard University Press.

Marx, K. 1965. *Pre-Capitalist Economic Formations*. New York: International Publishers.

Marx, K. and F. Engels, 1968. *Selected Works in One Volume*. New York: International Publishers.

Meillassoux, C. 1972. From production to reproduction. *Economy and Society* 1: 93–105.

Mellars, P.A. 1969. The chronology of Mousterian industries in the Périgord region of southwest France. *Proceedings of the Prehistoric Society* 35: 134–71.

1973. The character of the Middle-Upper Palaeolithic transition in southwest France. In C.

Renfrew (ed.), *The Explanation of Culture Change: Models in Prehistory*, pp. 255–76. London: Duckworth.

Pershits, A.I. 1981. Ethnographic reconstruction of the history of primitive society. In E. Gellner (ed.), *Soviet and Western Anthropology*, pp. 85–94. New York: Columbia University Press.

Peterson, N. 1975. Hunter-gatherer territoriality: the perspective from Australia. *American Anthropologist* 77: 53–68.

Rensberger, B. 1980. The emergence of *Homo sapiens. Mosaic* 11 (6): 2–12.

Rolland, N. 1981. The interpretation of Middle Palaeolithic variability. *Man* (n.s.) 16: 15–42.

Sackett, J.R. 1968. Method and theory of Upper Palaeolithic archaeology in southwestern France. In S.R. Binford and L.R. Binford (eds.), *New Perspectives in Archaeology*, pp. 61–83. Chicago: Aldine.

Sahlins, M.D. 1965. On the sociology of primitive exchange. In M. Banton (ed.), *The Relevance of Models for Social Anthropology*, pp. 139–236. London: Tavistock.

1972. *Stone Age Economics*. Chicago: Aldine-Atherton.

Sampson, C.G. 1974. *The Stone Age Archaeology of Southern Africa*. New York: Academic Press.

Service, E.R. 1962. *Primitive Social Organization*. New York: Random House.

Straus, L.G. 1977. Of deerslayers and mountain men: Palaeolithic faunal exploitation in Cantabrian Spain. In L.R. Binford (ed.), *For Theory Building in Archaeology: Essays on Faunal Remains, Aquatic Resources, and Systemic Modeling*, pp. 41–76. New York: Academic Press.

Straus, L.G., G.A. Clark, J. Altuna and J.A. Ortea, 1980. Ice Age subsistence in northern Spain. *Scientific American* 242 (6): 142–52.

Trinkaus ,E. and W.W. Howells, 1979. The Neanderthals. *Scientific American* 241 (6): 118–33.

Tylor,· E.B. 1989. On a method of investigating the development of institutions: applied to laws of marriage and descent. *Journal of the Royal Anthropological Institute* 18: 245-72.

Washburn, S.L. 1960. Tools and human evolution. *Scientific American* 203 (3): 3-15.

White, R. 1982. Rethinking the Middle/Upper Palaeolithic transition. *Current Anthropology* 23: 169–92.

Wiessner, P. 1882. Beyond willow smoke and dogs' tails: a comment on Binford's analysis of hunter-gatherer settlement systems. *American Antiquity* 47: 171–8.

Williams, B.J. 1974. A model of band society. *Memoirs of the Society for American Archaeology* 29.

Wobst, H.M. 1975. The demography of finite populations and the origins of the incest taboo. *Memoirs of the Society for American Archaeology* 30: 75–81.

1976. Locational relationships in Palaeolithic society. *Journal of Human Evolution* 5: 49–58.

1977. Stylistic behavior and information exchange. In C.E. Cleland (ed.), *For the Director: Research Essays in Honor of James B.* Griffin

9

Braudel and North American Archaeology: An Example from the Northern Plains

Philip Duke

Introduction

It has long been recognized that temporal change in the archaeological record of the Northern Plains of North America was, with few exceptions, predominantly slow and sporadic. This feature has set the tone for all archaeological research in the area but has, in the process, generated two research strategies which have hindered understanding of the past. The first strategy is based on the view that human cultures in the region are highly adapted to their local environments with little need for change. Although adaptation does explain certain features of cultural behavior, it leaves unanswered the specific question of why some artifacts in the region show more temporal change and/or greater embellishment than others (see Burnham [1973] and Sahlins [1976] for general critiques of adaptation).

The second research strategy, which has created a more insidious problem, arose from a comparison by archaeologists of the apparently slow tempo of change in prehistoric societies with the more rapid cultural changes of the historic period. Consequently, a classic Lévi-Straussian division was created in Northern Plains archaeology in which the prehistoric past was peopled by "cold" societies studied by archaeologists and the succeeding historic period was peopled by "hot" societies studied by ethnographers and historians. To all intents and purposes, the past has, therefore, been created as two separate worlds, prehistoric and historic/ ethnographic. The primary relationship between the two, as far as archaeologists are concerned, is analogical, and this has reinforced their separation. Differences between the historic and prehistoric pasts, however, should not be overstated. The prehistoric/historic interface gains any paramount epistemological significance it might have over other periods of cultural change only because of its concerns and contacts with our own society (Fabian 1983). Furthermore, stressing the paramount importance of the change from the prehistoric to the historic period may inadvertently keep alive the nineteenth-century conception of the division between primitive and advanced (Young 1988).

In adopting such a posture toward the past, archaeologists have allowed their discipline to remain subordinate to ethnography: any intellectual "traffic" between the two has been predominantly one-way. This has been reified institutionally by subsuming archaeology within the wider field of anthropology. One specific result of this is that North American archaeologists have overlooked the important contribution which their discipline's reliance on the long term can make to studies of the short term, the latter reliant on documentary- or informant-based sources. So far, the opportunity has been lost to create models of the past which, while acknowledging the different data of prehistory and history/ethnography, analyze these data sets within a framework complementary to both. If this situation is to be rectified, and archaeology is to make a more independent contribution to historical and ethnographic understanding, it must adopt models which are suited to its own data and apply these models to other types of data.

In this chapter, I propose an explanation of why certain artifacts in the Northern Plains show more temporal change and embellishment than others and, in so doing, I hope to break down the barrier between the prehistoric and historic pasts as epistemologically separate entities. My arguments will be based on an examination of the processes of long-term continuity and change in the Northern Plains from the viewpoint of certain *Annales* conceptions of time and change. They will recognize the long-term nature of archaeological data and, in emphasizing the continuity between prehistory and history, will move the study of the past toward a single ontology (see Duke 1991).

For the sake of argument, discussion is restricted to the cultures of southern Alberta, Canada, the extreme northwestern tip of the Northern Plains, during the past 2,000 years of prehistory and early history. This particular area creates problems of analysis not found in other case studies in this volume. Most significantly, it does not have a long documentary history. Thus, in using a model which attempts to reconcile both material culture and ethnohistoric evidence, these data sets are regarded as essentially sequential, rather than as contemporary and complementary to each other. This problem, however, should be recognized as a problem of data, not of epistemology. Because many of the explanations offered depart radically from those common in southern Alberta archaeology, they must be regarded as tentative. Nevertheless, they provide a potentially powerful way of explaining the data.

The Contribution of *Annales*

Despite the many contributions which *Annales* thinking can make to archaeological interpretation, two specific elements characterize the present analysis. The first is the notion of time itself. For a discipline so concerned with the past, archaeology has given surprisingly little serious attention to time as a theoretical and culturally specific concept: Bailey (1983) and Shanks and Tilley (1987: 118–36) are exceptions, and they approach the phenomenon, respectively, from methodological and ideological perspectives (see also Knapp and Smith, this volume). However, the notion of time was addressed consistently by Fernand Braudel in both his seminal discussion of Mediterranean society (1949, English translation 1972/1973) and in many later writings. Braudel argued that historical phenomena operate on different temporal scales and that, depending on the scale, their impact on societies and individuals differs. He categorized historical phenomena into three time scales of *courte, moyenne,* and *longue durée,* which are, to a large degree, situational and operate as scales along a continuum (Knapp, this volume). As Braudel himself emphasized, these temporal models "are valid for as long as the reality with which they are working" (Braudel 1980: 44–5). Braudel's emphasis on geographical structures has been replaced in later Annaliste writings by an emphasis on structures of *mentalité,* concerned with notions of ideology and symbolism within a specific cultural context. The implications of *mentalité,* for the analysis of structural change will be considered later.

An immediate benefit to archaeology of such a temporal model is, firstly, that it reasserts the value of the long term, a concept first stressed in archaeology by the palaeoeconomic school (Higgs and Jarman 1975) but one which never became popular in North America. Secondly, Braudelian concepts of time introduce the notion that certain phenomena have different rhythms of change, and that these rhythms have different effects on society and the individuals in it. In adapting Braudel's model for archaeological use (note that it is a model *for,* rather than a model *of*) in the present study, analysis is restricted to a consideration of structure and event, avoiding conjunctures (*moyenne durée*). This decision recognizes the practical problems of temporal resolution in the archaeological record, but keeps untouched the important relationship between short-term events and long-term structures.

The second element of *Annales* thinking incorporated into this study concerns the notion of structural change. This can occur in two ways, First, structures can "clash" with other structures so that some are overwhelmed and temporarily subdued (Braudel 1980). Secondly, the impact of individual human action can affect structural change. Both types of change may be recognized in events, which serve as etically defined "thresholds" of change that allow us to analyze the precise processes by which change occurred.

Although Braudel seemingly rejected short-term events as unimportant phenomena, there is some evidence that he was not completely hostile to them, as some critics would suggest (for example, Beales 1981). And whereas Braudel rejected history as merely a sequence of events peopled by famous individuals, he stated that "I am by no means the sworn enemy of the event" (Braudel 1973: 901), and referred on a number of occasions to the relationship between structure and event as analogous to an hourglass (Braudel 1973; 1980). Later *Annales* historians have regarded the event as an important explanatory concept with an equal relationship to structure (Stoianovich 1976; Le Roy Ladurie 1979; Clark 1985: 196), a shift which brings them much closer to earlier positions held by Febvre and Bloch (Clark 1985: 182).

This shift amongst later Annalistes is paralleled by recent developments in post-processual archaeology, which questions the notion of passivity and determinism in at least certain areas of human behavior (Hodder 1985). Rather than seeing basic organizational structures as inevitably deterministic, post-processual archaeology recognizes the recursive relationship between structure and human action, as individuals negotiate their everyday existence. This relationship, and the encapsulation of change within continuity that it implies, has recently been investigated from an explicitly archaeological viewpoint by Hodder (1987a; 1987b). He accurately describes artifact change, for instance, as "the stream of continual variability and change as one artifact type is transformed into another;" (1987b: 2). Thus, change is recognized as important to the continued existence of long-term structures and is seen, in the words of a commentator on *Annales* thinking, "as part of a process of structuring, destructuring, and restructuring" (Stoianovich 1976: 38).

In this study, the event is defined by its relationship to structure, not just by its length of time. It constitutes a marker of transition (Abrams 1982: 195), and serves as a point of analysis of changing social structural configurations. Clearly such events need not have been consciously recognized by their participants – and in this they differ fundamentally from the "events" of contemporary mass media. Rather they serve as etic reconstructions enabling us to understand social processes and individual action.

If these notions of time are combined with the structure-event model, we have a powerful tool for explaining processes of change. In the following pages I attempt to show how this tool contributes to an understanding of why only certain artifacts on the Northern Plains show much temporal variation. This discussion is then expanded to consider other aspects of human behavior in the study area, namely the ways in which long-term structural continuity contributed to processes through which gender relationships were transformed by the impact of European culture on aboriginal society, and the ways in which the long-term structure of specific economic subsistence practices of aboriginal society was affected not just by changes in the environment but also by human action.

Southern Alberta: a Case

The natural environment

Southern Alberta, apart from its mountainous western edge, occupies the extreme northwestern portion of the North American Plains grasslands and is characterized by a relatively flat topography and a generally treeless environment. It has low precipitation, low mean annual temperatures and short growing seasons (Sanderson 1948). The Saskatchewan river system is the area's major aquifer (figure 9.1).

Prior to European contact, the animal most numerous, and most important to aboriginal culture, was the American buffalo or bison (*Bison bison bison*), a herd animal which weighed up to 1,000kg. Other fauna included the wapiti (*Cervus elaphus*), deer (*Odocoileus* spp.), pronghorn antelope (*Antilocapra americana*), bear (*Ursus* sp), coyote (*Canis latrans*), swift fox (*Vulpes velox*), bobcat (*Lynx rufus*), beaver (*Castor canadensis*), and muskrat (*Ondatra zibethicus*). European immigration

Figure 9.1 [orig. figure 7.1]   Map of Alberta showing archaeological sites and natural features mentioned in the text.

caused the near extinction, or radically altered the distribution, of many of these animals. A variety of resident and migratory birds still inhabit the area.

Grasses are the most important floral component of southern Alberta. Their specific distributions depend on local climate and moisture: xeric grasses have an especially high frequency in the southeastern part of the province, with more mesic types found at higher elevations and along the western and northern edges of the Plains (Morgan 1980). The seasonally varying nutritional content of the grasses helped to determine the seasonal movements of the bison (Morgan 1980). Various shrubs and trees such as willow and cottonwood are found along water-courses.

Paleoclimatic research has identified short-term climatic changes in North America during the last two thousand years (Baerreis and Bryson 1965; Bryson and Wendland 1967). Pending specific studies in southern Alberta, however, descriptions of paleoclimate in the area must remain tentative, although there is a high probability that at least some of these episodes affected southern Alberta (figure 9.2). Such climatic changes as did occur would have been quantitative, involving the density and frequency of different grass types and thus the fitness of many of the animals inhabiting the area.

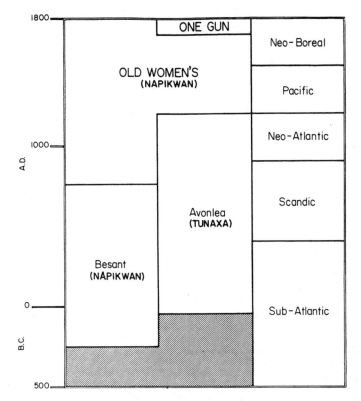

Figure 9.2 [orig. figure 7.2]   Cultural and paleoenvironmental sequence of southern Alberta. Dates are only approximate.

Cultural setting: the historic Blackfoot

The historic period begins in southern Alberta in the second half of the eighteenth century when Canadian trappers made contact with aboriginal groups (Ray 1974), although for some time prior to this European goods and horses had circulated through the area. During this time, southern Alberta was exploited by several different tribal groups: the Blackfoot, Cree, Assiniboine, Gros Ventres, Kutenai, Sarcee, Shoshone, and Crow, of which the Blackfoot were the area's primary occupants. Throughout the nineteenth century, both Canadian and American settlers moved west and increasingly threatened Blackfoot territory. The result was that by the final quarter of that century, the Blackfoot had lost their independence and had been relocated on reservations in southern Alberta and northern Montana (Ewers 1958).

The exact length of time the Blackfoot occupied southern Alberta is still undetermined (Byrne 1973; Brink 1986), although their occupation certainly extends some distance into prehistory. Furthermore, although they have existed as a separate linguistic group for a considerable time (Kroeber 1939), it is not at all clear that they existed during the prehistoric period as a separate political-ethnic group in a manner similar to that of the historic period. Indeed, their historical political separateness from other tribes may have been the result of European pressure, rather than a long-term condition.

The Blackfoot are well documented in rich ethnographies (e.g., Wissler 1911; Ewers 1958). The band was the primary social and subsistence unit and varied in size and membership (Dempsey 1982), although tribal solidarity beyond the band was encouraged by pan-tribal societies that fulfilled various policing and judicial roles. The Blackfoot are formally characterized as egalitarian, but the effects of the fur trade and the acquisition of the horse created social rankings, a shift to individualism from communalism, and changes in the status of females throughout the historic period (Lewis 1942; Ewers 1955; Klein 1983).

The Blackfoot relied on the bison for food, clothing, tipi (lodge) covers, utensils, and many other artifacts (McHugh 1974), and used techniques like driving the animals *en masse* over cliffs or into specially constructed timber pounds. The use of such communal techniques lessened, however, as the acquisition of the horse encouraged the killing of individual animals by mounted warriors. Other animals, such as deer and antelope, were taken in smaller numbers for specific purposes such as clothing (Wissler 1910; Ewers 1958). Vegetable foods were utilized to some degree, mainly for medicine and as dietary supplements. Native tobacco (*Nicotiana attenuata*) was grown until European-cured leaves became available through trading (Lowie 1954: 26).

The Blackfoot used the tipi for their domestic living structure. This was a portable, skin- (later canvas-) covered, circular, four-poled structure. The availability of European goods caused a rapid loss of traditional Blackfoot material culture, but the few studies available (e.g. Wissler 1910) suggest that their material culture was largely indistinguishable from that of other tribes of the Northern Plains region.

The prehistoric record

The recency of archaeological investigations in the province means that the vast majority of work is still culture-historical in nature. Because of its morphological changes through time and space, the most useful artifact for understanding the prehistoric culture-history of southern Alberta is the stone projectile point. Other stone tools include shaped and unworked awls, knives, scrapers, and chopping tools. Ceramics were introduced to southern Alberta about 1,500 years ago. Bone tools, both formed and unformed, are also found.

Because of their long stratigraphic sequences invaluable for culture-historical studies, the most important sites in southern Alberta are the large, communal kill-sites. The two most important of these are Head-Smashed-In, with a use sequence going from the historic period back to about 3500 BC (Reeves 1978), and Old Women's Jump, dating back about 2,000 years (Forbis 1962). Both are located in the southwestern part of the province (figure 9.1). Habitation sites comprise hearths, cooking pits, and lithic and bone debris indicative of a wide range of domestic activities. Stone circles are interpreted as the remains of a domestic structure essentially identical to the historic Plains tipi (Kehoe 1958). Some stone circles, particularly those lacking artifacts, may have been used for other specialized purposes. Rock art panels, in both pictographic and petroglyphic form, are occasionally found on suitable cliff faces. Isolated finds, usually of stone tools or debitage, are nearly ubiquitous, but their archaeological implications are limited.

The culture-history employed in this study relies heavily on that presented in Reeves' 1970 doctoral dissertation (1983). It is acknowledged that relying on only one authority simplifies the current debate on the area's culture-history. The last 2,000 years of prehistory in southern Alberta are characterized by two separate cultural traditions, each comprising sequential phases (figure 9.2). The *Tunaxa* Tradition is indigenous to southern Alberta and dates back to about 2000 BC. The terminal phase of this tradition is the Avonlea, which dates from approximately AD 200 to 1200; it marks the first use of the bow and arrow in southern Alberta. Overlapping the Avonlea Phase is the Besant Phase, the initial phase of the intrusive *Napikwan* Tradition, which is thought to represent an immigration from the northeastern edge of the Plains. The Besant Phase dates from approximately 200 BC to AD 750. Increasing contact between participants of the Avonlea and Besant Phases resulted in the appearance of the Old Women's Phase in the eighth century, although the Avonlea Phase continued as an independent entity for another 400 to 500 years. In the middle of the eighteenth century, the One Gun Phase is recognized. This has been widely interpreted as an immigration into the area, based on differences in pottery as well as on a unique fortified structure at the Cluny site (Byrne 1973; Forbis 1977). The One Gun Phase was rapidly assimilated into the Old Women's Phase.

The material cultures of these four phases have much in common. Major differences are found in projectile point types and in other items of material culture such as ceramics. Avonlea arrow points, distinguished by their thinness, symmetry, and meticulous body flaking, represent a climax in the quality of point manufacture on the Northern Plains (Kehoe and McCorquodale 1961: 184). The Besant atlatl dart point has a more varied shape. The quality of Besant flaking is far lower generally than that of Avonlea points, both in the techniques of flake removal and point symmetry. About AD 450 the Besant point was replaced by the Samantha Side-Notched, an arrow point which, while identical in shape to the Besant atlatl dart, is smaller. Besant sites prior to AD 450 are further characterized by a high frequency of Knife River Flint, a silicified wood imported from quarries in North Dakota. Points of the Old Women's Phase comprise a variety of temporally seriated arrow forms (Forbis 1962). These point types are not temporally exclusive. At Old Women's Jump, for example, different types are found in the same components. The early point types of the Old Women's Phase are very similar to Samantha Side-Notched points. Through time, however, the side-notching of Old Women's Phase points becomes more marked, and there is an increase in their symmetry and quality of flaking which approaches those on Avonlea points.

Pottery in all phases is unpainted, and decoration consists mainly of impressions from a variety of materials. The ceramic component of the Avonlea Phase in southern Alberta has been classified by Byrne (1973) as the early variant of the Saskatchewan Basin Complex (AD 150/250–1150). As yet Besant pottery in the province has not been formally classified. Ceramics of the Old Women's Phase belong to the late variant of the Saskatchewan Basin Complex (Byrne 1973: 354). The ceramics of the One Gun Phase belong to the Cluny Complex (Byrne 1973).

Other items of material culture show much less qualitative variation. Although Reeves (1983) used a wide variety of artifacts to define phases on the Northern Plains, it remains the case that sites cannot be phase-assigned without diagnostic points or ceramics: other items simply do not show the variation necessary for this type of segregation.

In summary, therefore, the archaeological record of southern Alberta shows little radical change. The major qualitative changes occur in projectile points and ceramics. One way of explaining this phenomenon requires the division of the material culture into two major categories: procurement, represented in the archaeological record by projectile points; and processing, represented by tools such as scrapers, awls, chopping tools, and ceramics. These categories are based on a generalized analogy from historic groups of the area, including the Blackfoot, where these two sets of tasks correspond to a sexual division of labor. Such a categorization also has validity in other areas: a similar contextual model is employed by Sinclair (1988), for example, in his analysis of Upper Palaeolithic tool assemblages in France.

Procurement and processing as long-term structures

In this section, tools of procurement and processing are examined as components of long-term structures of *mentalité*, and it is argued that they not only reflect economic behavior, but also operate as symbols in the field of human action and social negotiation. Change in these tools cannot be due solely to an assumed teleological need for greater efficiency; it must also be explained within its specific historical context. The structures of procurement and processing have a long-term "flow" to them, and cross-cut the temporal boundaries defined by traditional culture-history. Despite their long-term nature, these structures are not immune to the impact of other structures or individual action. All artifacts have many layers of symbolic meaning: the meanings adduced in this study are only one of many potential sets.

Procurement

Tools of procurement, specifically projectile points, constitute a long-term structure, manifested archaeologically by the intense investment of time and effort made in Avonlea points and in the later varieties of the Old Women's Phase, particularly those which appear after AD 1200, when the Avonlea Phase as an independent cultural system begins to break down. This structure, however, did not originate in the Avonlea Phase; indeed, the investment of effort and care in flaking can be traced back to the preceding Pelican Lake Phase, and perhaps all the way back to the finely worked points of the Paleoindian period, 8,000 years earlier (which would provide a striking example of *la longue durée*).

The care and detail invested on these points may be interpreted in the light of the symbolic role such objects played in a society with a long tradition of hunting large game (Duke 1991); these points were tied into notions of power and prestige associated with killing, a symbolic investment well documented elsewhere (Evans-Pritchard 1956: 236; Hodder 1979; Larick 1985). It is also worth considering that more rapid changes in point types characteristic of the Old Women's Phase might be tied into the same notions of power and prestige. Larick (1985), for instance, has suggested that amongst Maasai males, more rapid replacement of point types is tied into their perception of their own worldliness and status. Consequently, rapid style evolution takes place. Clearly this analogy will not suffice unmodified for a prehistoric situation taking place over a considerably longer time period, but it does demonstrate at least one process by which punctuated change can occur.

The adoption of the bow and arrow, associated with the Avonlea Phase, is also tied into this notion of hunting power and prestige. Not only is this "event" recognized archaeologically as a marker of transition, but it is also the product of structural change, intimately connected to individual negotiations of power within existing structures. An explanation of greater adaptive efficiency for point embellishment and the adoption of the bow and arrow has been rejected, since there is apparently no greater killing efficiency of Avonlea and later Old Women's Phase points compared to Besant points which lack such embellishment: all are found in the same area, all are of the same general time period, and all fulfilled eventually the same function in a communal kill situation where a long trajectory was not needed.

The same degree of symbolic importance does not seem to have been attached to Besant and Samantha points. While many are well made (although never equal to Avonlea points), most are much more asymmetrical than Avonlea and show much less control in body flaking. The heavier and slower atlatl continued in use. These differences perhaps result from the socio-structural character of the people of the Besant Phase. Were they an immigrant group from an area where there was less concentration on single animal species and, therefore, less of a tradition in hunting symbolism? Their movement into the Plains would have necessitated a rapid readjustment to bison-hunting practices and, through emulation, they would rapidly have become as efficient as indigenous groups. In such a scenario, the importance attached to hunting as a symbolic action was less quickly adopted, since it was a product of a historically specific long-term structure in indigenous cultures.

This structure of *mentalité* – hunting as symbolic action – may be traced through an approximately two thousand-year period, and probably originated well before that. Although it cross-cuts the temporal boundaries established by culture-historical studies, it is not consistently present in specific phases, as evidenced by its absence during the early part of the Old Women's Phase. The waxing and waning of the symbolic importance attached to hunting have implications for a greater understanding of the processes of cultural transmission during the period, and enhance notions based on traditional culture-history alone. The structure is transformed and amplified by the adoption of the bow and arrow, a product of individual action within an existing structural framework.

Processing

In contrast to the embellishment and more rapid stylistic change of Avonlea and Old Women's projectile points, artifacts concerned with processing seem more resistant to change. Certainly, there is no equivalent amongst processing tools of the Avonlea point, and it has proven extremely difficult to date sites by processing tools alone because of their more standardized shapes. This conservatism would have been encouraged actively by society and is reflective of different values attached to procurement and processing activities. Ethnoarchaeological studies in the material culture of females in Kenya's Baringo district, for example, show that conservatism is tied into notions of individualism within society; females are expected to conform to traditional notions of behavior, whereas men achieve status by being "worldly" and innovative (Hodder 1979; 1981).

There is evidence, however, for long-term change in the structural continuity of processing activity in one area: the adoption of pottery. A number of functional arguments can be given for the adoption of this technology, ranging from the appearance of new foodstuffs to the development of new cooking styles. Other complementary explanations, however, are also feasible for the adoption of an artifact not particularly well suited to this socio-technic environment (a friable and fragile object that had to be fired in an area devoid of surplus combustible material and then transported).

Avonlea groups may have adopted pottery within the context of its role in social negotiation, specifically between procurers and processors. An analogous situation has been explored by Braithwaite (1982) and Hodder (1982) in African agricultural societies, where pottery has a high utilitarian value, and where social power is negotiated through the decoration of pots, in such a way that the overall efficiency of the pot is not reduced. In southern Alberta, pots may have been used to achieve similar social goals, although in a slightly different way. Pottery was adopted precisely because it was not fundamentally necessary to processing and storage facilities. Brumley (1983: 185), for instance, noted that fire-broken rock, used to heat food or water in skin containers, is still found in ceramic-bearing sites in southern Alberta, the implication being that existing processing practices continued. Social discourse in material culture could then be carried out in a cultural sphere which would not interfere with existing practices. The long-term continuity of the processing structure is thus marked off and transformed by a recognizable event, the adoption of pottery. This event is best explained not by functional adaptation alone, but by its recursive relationship to other structures in society, within the context of individual action and social negotiation.

There is no reason to explain the adoption of ceramics by groups of the Besant Phase in the same way. Since the Besant Phase was intrusive, different contextual arguments are relevant. These relate, for instance, to Besant social organization prior to their movement into the Northern Plains, and to the economic and cultural ties of Besant Phase groups with groups located farther east. These topics deserve more detailed examination.

Historic period gender relations

The dialectical relationship between procurement and processing structures can be used as a means of assessing the specific dynamics of gender relationships of the area's aboriginal groups, specifically the Blackfoot, during the historic period. The traditional anthropological view of gender relations in historic Blackfoot society is that males were dominant, while females were essentially menial drudges: the mechanics of the fur trade made females into objects of capital needed by males to process furs and hide for profit (Klein 1983). Furthermore, different standards of morality applied to males and females (Ewers 1958). Some contradictory evidence, however, suggests that females may have had power in society. For example, females made, owned, and looked after the tipi (Wissler 1910; Lowie 1954), played significant roles in religious ceremonies (Weist 1980: 260), and in some Plains societies, including the Blackfoot, undertook men's roles in certain circumstances (Weist 1980). Alternative roles, of which the best known is the "manly-hearted women" (Lewis 1941), allowed some women access to the high levels of social status normally reserved for males (Medicine 1983).

The contradictory nature of this evidence has been reinterpreted by recent anthropologists as indicative of greater female equality, with the traditional interpretations of male dominance perceived as arising from the specific ideological positions of earlier observers, both specialist and non-specialist (Kehoe 1983; Weist 1983). At the risk of simplifying what was a very complex situation, it is suggested that the different interpretations are reflective not just of ambivalence on the part of anthropologists, but also of a real ambivalence in gender relations in the historic period: European contact rapidly altered gender relationships, and resulted in the confusing and sometimes contradictory appearances described above.

For example, European contact throughout the nineteenth century had a profound influence on the self-perception of the Indian male. From being an independent warrior, he became increasingly controlled by the European fur and hide trade. Territorial control was lost as settlers began to move west. Conversely, females became more important because of their ability to process hides and fur. One response was that males "over-reacted" in order to retain their sense of control and their position in society. Thus, males exerted greater dominance over females: there was a shift to polygyny as males became aware that more wives meant more wealth in trading (Lewis 1941). Male control of the mode of production was further stimulated by the particular form of European gender relations, itself a long-term structure of *mentalité*. European males imposed their own value system of gender inequality on the Indian, in trading only with Indian males; females in European society were generally prohibited from entering into such economic activity.

These gender relationships of the nineteenth century Blackfoot did not spring up spontaneously. Rather, they are the direct product of individuals in aboriginal society altering and intensifying – through the event of European contact – the intertwined, long-term structures manifested archaeologically in procurement and processing. A clash of external and internal long-term structures thus contrived to produce the particular short-term situation described ethnographically.

Environment and economy

Long-term structural continuity in subsistence strategies and responses to the natural environment can be traced from the prehistoric into the historic periods. The environment exerted fundamental influences on aboriginal cultures of southern Alberta. The unpredictability of cultivated plant yields made the area unsuitable for any subsistence economy other than hunting and gathering. Seasonal variation in climate resulted in certain areas being used consistently through time. This is most noticeable in the Foothills belt where warming westerly winds called Chinooks create a more amenable winter habitation zone. The demands of living in this environment created similar adaptations throughout much of the Northern Plains.

Such conservatism is evidenced in the circular habitation structure, capable of being transported and withstanding the wind and temperatures of the Plains. On the evidence of stone circles or configurations, this type of structure has a long antiquity. There is some evidence for buried stone structures as early as the late Paleoindian period, for example, with more secure evidence dated to the ensuing Archaic period (T. Kehoe 1983: 338). Stone circles are numerous in southern Alberta, as in the Northern Plains generally; Wormington and Forbis (1965: 143) conservatively estimate a total of 600,000 for the former area alone.

Kill sites, whose location was determined by the presence of appropriate topographical features like a natural gathering basin and a cliff of a particular height, provided a means of dispatching the animals which took advantage of their instincts to stampede. These sites also show long-term continuity of use, as evidenced at Head-Smashed-In, Old Women's, and many others; evidence for communal bison hunting may be found as early as the Paleoindian period (Wilson and Davis 1978). These patterns of human-environmental relationships showed a remarkable resilience through time; incoming groups apparently adopted existing subsistence techniques, whether they were those of the Besant Phase, the One Gun Phase, or the strategies of the aboriginal immigrants into the Northern Plains in the historic period (Wissler 1914). The subsistence economy constitutes one example of the structure of *la longue durée*.

Although this bison-hunting pattern remained essentially unchanged, fluctuations in the environment may well have had some effect on human occupation of the area. Periods of higher precipitation not only increased the numbers of bison and other animals but also favored an increase in woodland animals like deer (Reher 1977; Duke 1981). Such a change is hypothesized for at least three climatic episodes: the Sub-Atlantic (500 BC–AD 400), the Neo-Atlantic (AD 900–1200), and the Neo-Boreal (AD 1500–1800).

There is evidence in at least two of these episodes, the Sub-Atlantic and Neo-Boreal, for population movement into southern Alberta. During the Sub-Atlantic, peoples represented by the Besant Phase entered the area and, although evidence is scant, their initial movement may have been caused by an increased demand in Hopewellian trading networks for Rocky Mountain obsidian, and possibly for bison meat and hides (Reeves 1983). Another indigenous population movement occurred during the Neo-Boreal with the appearance of the intrusive One Gun Phase, representing immigrants from the Middle Missouri. Thus, it may be concluded that during periods of higher precipitation population levels in southern Alberta rose because of immigration. There is no evidence for increases in indigenous populations during these periods, although this is extremely difficult to recognize.

In periods of lower precipitation, bison populations fell. It is also plausible that the decrease during the Scandic Episode (AD 400–900) was responsible for the decline after AD 450 in Alberta Besant sites of Knife River Flint imported from South Dakota (Reeves 1983). If Besant populations were part of a Northern Plains exchange network, their connections to the east would have become more tenuous as bison became scarcer, and as meat and hides became less available. Also, the loss of social ties with the east would have reduced the need (or ability) for Besant populations to remain as independent entities. Thus, they initiated the slow merger with indigenous populations, a process manifested archaeologically in the emergence of the Old Women's Phase.

In any comprehensive assessment of the impact of the environment on human behavior, it is necessary to view the environment not just as an external, determining phenomenon, but also as a cultural construct of the societies inhabiting it (Collingwood 1946: 200). This view introduces the notion of human action into the interpretation of economic behavior, and moves away from a strict determinism.

In this instance, hunting techniques must be placed within the context of procurement and processing and the dialectical relationship between the two. Viewing the process of change as *structure-event-structure* (Le Roy Ladurie 1979: 113–31) (the event being the adoption of the bow and arrow) may help to explain the evidence for a possible intensification in hunting practices during the last 2,000 years of Northern Plains prehistory (Kehoe 1973; Frison 1978; cf. Reeves 1978). In southern Alberta, there is evidence for larger numbers of animals being killed at one time and for shorter periods between kills (Duke 1981). This intensification continues into the historic period where the relationship between humans and bison may have approached what Higgs and Jarman (1972) defined as animal husbandry (Kehoe 1973).

The role of hunting as a symbolic activity is further affected by another event: its clash with European gender structures. A shift to individualism from communalism is manifested in the popularity of individual mounted hunting and in the heavy toll taken on bison herds, and this is tied into the changes in male self-perceptions during the nineteenth century (already discussed). Since hunting intensification seems to have been a continuous process throughout the last 2,000 years, spanning climatic episodes with different environmental carrying capacities, its explanation should not rely solely on ecological factors.

Concluding Summary

The contributions which Braudel and *Annales* thinking generally can make to archaeological interpretation may be divided into two types: empirical and conceptual. This study has concentrated on empirical methods of analysis that allow explanations of specific data sets. Particular notions of time and structural continuity and change have been adduced to explain varying rates of artifactual and behavioral change in the later prehistory of southern Alberta. Different prehistoric phenomena, therefore, changed at differential rates that affected individuals in society in different ways. Structural change may be induced by a series of different events, ranging from structural clashes (as in the case of European worldviews and aboriginal structures) to the impact of internal human action on those structures, as evidenced by differential rates of change in procurement and processing artifacts. Inasmuch as these structures are transformed by events, new social conditions are created upon which human action operates in an endless *structure-event-structure* cycle.

The conceptual contribution of *Annales*, in terms of "Grand Theory" (Clark 1985), involves most importantly new notions about the flow and rhythms of history. These notions are particularly relevant for North American archaeology, which has been implicitly defined as a cultural anthropology of the past, with emphasis on short-term models of change. Braudel's concept particularly, with its sweep through time and space, offers to North American archaeologists a workable model which may transcend the restrictions of past analyses, and allow a reassessment of the traditional relationship between archaeology and ethnography; the outcome may allow archaeology to contribute independently to a better understanding of the human past. This has profound implications not just for archaeology but also for anthropology.

Acknowledgements

This chapter developed out of a wider research project on structure and event in the Northern Plains. I am most grateful to the following for their helpful comments and criticisms: Ian Hodder, Alice and Thomas Kehoe, Michael Wilson, Bernard Knapp, Tony Sinclair, Kathleen Fine, and Cynthia Duke.

References

Abrams, P. 1982 *Historical Sociology*. Shepton Mallet: Open Books.
Bailey, G. 1983 Concepts of time in Quaternary prehistory. *Annual Review of Anthropology* 12: 165–92.
Baerreis, D. and R. Bryson 1965 Climatic episodes and the dating of the Mississippian cultures. *Wisconsin Archaeologist* 46: 203–20.

Beales, D. 1981 *History and Biography*. Cambridge: Cambridge University Press.

Braithwaite, M. 1982 Decoration as ritual symbol: a theoretical proposal and an ethnographic study in southern Sudan, in I. Hodder, ed., *Symbolic and Structural Archaeology*, pp. 80–8. Cambridge: Cambridge University Press.

Braudel, F. 1972 *The Mediterranean and the Mediterranean World in the Age of Philip II*, vol. 1. London: Collins.

　1973 *The Mediterranean and the Mediterranean World in the Age of Philip II*, vol. 2. London: Collins.

　1980 *On History*, London: Weidenfeld and Nicolson.

Brink, J. 1986 *Dog Days in Southern Alberta*, Archaeological Survey of Alberta Occasional Paper 28. Edmonton.

Brumley, J. 1983 An interpretive model for stone circles and stone circle sites within southeastern Alberta, in L. Davis, ed., *From Microcosm to Macrocosm: Advances in Tipi Ring Investigation and Interpretation*, pp. 171–91. Plains Anthropologist Memoir 19. Lincoln: Augstums Printing Service.

Bryson, R. and W. Wendland 1967 Tentative climatic patterns for some late glacial and postglacial episodes in Central North America, in W.J. Mayer-Oakes, ed., *Life, Land and Water*, pp. 271–98. Winnipeg: University of Manitoba Press.

Burnham, P. 1973 The explanatory value of the concept of adaptation in studies of culture change, in C. Renfrew, ed., *The Explanation of Culture Change: Models in Prehistory*, pp. 93–102. London: Duckworth.

Byrne, W. 1973 *The Archaeology and Prehistory of Southern Alberta as Reflected by Ceramics*. Archaeological Survey of Canada, Mercury Series 14. Ottawa.

Clark, S. 1985 The "Annales" historians, in Q. Skinner, ed., *The Return of Grand Theory in the Social Sciences*, pp. 177–98. Cambridge: Cambridge University Press.

Collingwood, R. 1946 *The Idea of Prehistory*, Oxford: Oxford University Press.

Dempsey, H. 1982 History and identification of Blood bands, in D. Ubelaker and H. Viola, eds., *Plains Indian Studies: A Collection of Essays in Honor of John C. Ewers and Waldo R. Wedel*, pp. 94–104. Washington: Smithsonian Institution.

Duke, P. 1981 Systems dynamics in prehistoric southern Alberta: 2000 B.P. to the historic period. Unpublished Ph.D. dissertation. University of Calgary, Calgary.

　1991 *Points in Time: Structure and Event in a Late Period Northern Plains Hunting Society*. Boulder: University of Colorado Press.

Evans-Pritchard, E. 1956 *Nuer Religion*. Oxford: Oxford University Press.

Ewers, J. 1955 *The Horse in Blackfoot Indian Culture*, Bureau of American Ethnology, Bulletin 159. Washington: U.S. Government Printing Office.

　1958 *The Blackfoot. Raiders of the Northwestern Plains*, Norman: University of Oklahoma Press.

Fabian, J. 1983 *Time and the Other: How Anthropology Makes its Object*, New York: Columbia University Press.

Forbis, R. 1962 The Old Women's buffalo jump, Alberta. *National Museums of Canada, Bulletin* 180: 56–123. Ottawa.

　1977 *Cluny. An Ancient Fortified Village in Alberta*. Department of Archaeology, University of Calgary Occasional Paper 4, Calgary.

Frison, G. 1978 *Prehistoric Hunters of the High Plains*. New York: Academic Press.

Higgs, E. and M. Jarman 1972 The origins of plant and animal husbandry, in E. Higgs, ed., *Papers in Economic Prehistory*, pp. 3–13. Cambridge: Cambridge University Press.

　1975 Palaeoeconomy, in E. Higgs, ed., *Palaeoeconomy*, pp. 1–7. Cambridge: Cambridge University Press.

Hodder, I. 1979 Social and economic stress and material culture patterning. *American Antiquity*, 44: 446–54.

1981 Reply to Davis. *American Antiquity* 46: 668–70.

1982 *Symbols in Action*. Cambridge: Cambridge University Press.

1985 Postprocessual archaeology. *Advances in Archaeological Method and Theory* 8: 1–26.

1987a The contextual analysis of symbolic meanings, in I. Hodder, ed., *The Archaeology of Contextual Meanings*, pp. 1–10. Cambridge: Cambridge University Press.

1987b The contribution of the long-term, in I. Hodder, ed., *Archaeology as Long-Term History*, pp. 1–8. Cambridge: Cambridge University Press.

Kehoe, A. 1983 The shackles of tradition, in P. Albers and B. Medicine, eds., *The Hidden Half*, pp 53–73. Lanham: University Press of America.

Kehoe, T. 1958 The direct ethnological approach applied to an archaeological problem. *American Antiquity* 60: 861–74.

1973 *The Gull Lake Site: A Prehistoric Bison Drive Site in Southwest Saskatchewan* 1. Milwaukee Public Museums, Publications in Anthropology 1, Milwaukee.

1983 A retrospectus and commentary, in L. Davis, ed., *From Microcosm to Macrocosm: Advances in Tipi Ring Investigation and Interpretation*, pp. 327–42. Plains Anthropologist Memoir 19. Lincoln, NE: Augstums Printing Service.

Kehoe, T.F. and A. McCorquodale 1961 The Avonlea: horizon marker for the Northwestern Plains. *Plains Anthropologist* 6: 179–88.

Klein, A. 1983 The political economy of gender: a 19th century Plains Indian case study, in P. Albers and B. Medicine, eds., *The Hidden Half*, pp. 143–73. Lanham: University Press of America.

Kroeber, A. 1939 *Cultural and Natural Areas of North America*. University of California Publications in American Archaeology and Ethnology 8. Berkeley.

Larick, R. 1985 Spears, style and time among Maasai-speaking pastoralists. *Journal of Anthropological Archaeology* 4: 206–20.

Le Roy Ladurie, E. 1979 *The Territory of the Historian*. Chicago: University of Chicago Press.

Lewis, O. 1941 Manly-hearted women among the North Piegan. *American Anthropologist* 43:173–87.

1942 *The Effects of White Contact upon Blackfoot Culture, with Special Reference to the Role of the Fur Trade*. American Ethnological Society Monograph 6. Seattle: University of Washington Press.

Lowie, R. 1954 *Indians of the Plains*. New York: McGraw-Hill.

McHugh, T. 1974 *Time of the Buffalo*. Lincoln, NE: University of Nebraska Press.

Medicine, B. 1983 "Warrior women" – sex role alternatives for Plains Indian women, in P. Albers and B. Medicine, eds., *The Hidden Half*, pp. 267–80. Lanham: University Press of America.

Morgan, R. 1980 Bison movement patterns on the Canadian Plains: an ecological analysis. *Plains Anthropologist* 25: 143–60.

Ray, A. 1974 *Indians of the Fur Trade*. Toronto: University of Toronto Press.

Reeves, B. 1978 Head-Smashed-In: 5000 years of bison jumping in the Alberta Plains, in L. Davis and M. Wilson, eds., *Bison Procurement and Utilization: a Symposium*, pp. 151–74. Plains Anthropologist, Memoir 14. Lincoln, NE: Augstums Printing Service.

1983 *Culture Change in the Northern Plains 1000 B.C. to A.D. 1000*. Archaeological Survey of Alberta Occasional Paper 20. Edmonton.

Reher, C. 1977 Adaptive processes on the shortgrass plains, in L. Binford, ed., *For Theory Building in Archaeology*, pp. 13–40. New York: Academic Press.

Sahlins, M. 1976 *Culture and Practical Reason*. Chicago: University of Chicago Press.

Sanderson, M. 1948 The climates of Canada according to the new Thornwaite classification. *Scientific Agriculture* 28: 501–17.

Shanks, M. and C. Tilley 1987 *Social Theory and Archaeology*. Cambridge: Polity Press.

Sinclair, A. 1988 Foraging for meaning; seeking structure in Palaeolithic society. Unpublished ms on file with author.

Stoianovich, T. 1976 *French Historical Method: The* Annales *Paradigm*. Ithaca, NY: Cornell University Press.

Weist, K. 1980 Plains Indian women: an assessment, in W. Wood and M. Liberty, eds., *Anthropology on the Great Plains*, pp. 255–71. Lincoln, NE: University of Nebraska Press.

1983 Beasts of burden and menial slaves: nineteenth century observations of Northern Plains Indian women, in P. Albers and B. Medicine, eds, *The Hidden Half*, pp. 29–52. Lanham: University Press of America.

Wilson, M. and L. Davis 1978 Epilogue: retrospect and prospect in the man-bison paradigm, in L. Davis and M. Wilson, eds., *Bison Procurement and Utilization: A Symposium*, pp. 312–35. Plains Anthropologist, Memoir 14. Lincoln, NE: Augstums Printing Service.

Wissler, C. 1910 Material culture of the Blackfoot Indians. *Anthropological Papers of the Museum of Natural History* 5: 1–78.

1911 The social life of the Blackfoot Indians. *Anthropological Papers of the Museum of Natural History* 7: 1–64.

1914 Material Cultures of the North American Indians. *American Anthropologist* 16: 447–505.

Wormington, H. and R. Forbis 1965 *An Introduction to the Archaeology of Alberta, Canada*. Denver: Denver Museum of Natural History.

Young, T.C. Jr. 1988 Since Herodotus, has history been a valid concept? *American Antiquity* 53: 7–12.

10

The Power of Prestige: Competitive Generosity and the Emergence of Rank Societies in Lowland Mesoamerica

John E. Clark and Michael Blake

Introduction

Explanations of the origins of institutionalized social inequality and political privilege must resolve the central paradox of political life – why people cooperate with their own subordination and exploitation in non-coercive circumstances (Godelier 1986: 13). In the following pages we address this paradox for an archaeological case from Mesoamerica.

The first chiefdoms in lowland Mesoamerica, the focus of this discussion, appear to have developed some 3300 years ago among the Mokaya in the Mazatan region of Chiapas, Mexico, during the first part of the Early Formative, 1550–1150 BC (all dates are in radio-carbon years). This period also witnessed the adoption of maize agriculture in the coastal lowlands, the founding of sedentary villages, the adoption of ceramic technology, a rapid population increase, and the beginnings of patronized craft specialization.

To explain these developments, we first offer a general model for the development of hereditary rank distinctions as the outcome of competition among political actors vying for prestige and social esteem. We then apply this model to the issues of technological and demographic change in the development of social inequality in the Mazatan region.

Resources, Prestige and Privilege

It is difficult to imagine why people would voluntarily submit to non-egalitarian political systems. Despite this perception, the institutionalization of political privilege may have been quite simple; it may at first have been in people's best interest. Nowadays, in addressing this issue, we are hindered by hindsight and evolutionist and functionalist thinking that regards change as reaction to existing social problems. Binford (1983: 221), for example, states: "When I am faced with a question such as why complex systems come into being, my first reaction is to ask what problem people were attempting to solve by a new means." As will become clear, we disagree with this perspective. The development of social inequality was neither a problem nor a solution. Rather, it was a long-term, unexpected consequence of many individuals promoting their own aggrandizement.

Briefly, we argue that the transition from egalitarian to rank societies was a process that occurred on a regional scale under special historical and techno-environmental circumstances. The engine for change was self-interested competition among political actors vying for prestige or social esteem. We refer to such political entrepreneurs as "aggrandizers," paralleling Hayden and Gargett's (1990) term "accumulators." Over time, some aggrandizers became chiefs with institutionalized authority. Parlaying temporary prestige into legitimate authority was the key process.

Primary Assumptions

Our view of the origins of social inequality rests on several propositions concerning human action, the formation of factions, and the creation and deployment of physical and social resources. Our most critical assumptions concern culture, society, and individual behavior.

Social systems are regularized practices. They lack reason, purpose, or needs and are incapable of adaptation (Giddens 1979: 7). Only the actors within a system share these attributes and are capable of adaptive response. Purposive, motivated action becomes the point of articulation between structure and the human agent (Vincent 1978; Giddens 1979; Callinicos 1988). Importantly, such action often sparks unintended consequences for the system.

It is clear that actors are constrained by past practice (history of system and structure) and opportunities for future practice (e.g. available technology, physical and social environment, personal social networks, etc.). Each actor knows a great deal about his/her social system and its constraints and limits under varying circumstances – even to the extent that (s)he can manipulate aspects of the system for personal advantage. We presume a primary motivation of self-interested action based upon culturally bound rational choice (i.e. "minimal rationality," see Cherniak 1986). Obviously, individual motivations, desires, and reasons for action cannot be the same for everyone (Callinicos 1988). Where numerous people pursue self-interests, their interaction is characterized by frequent conflicts of interests, internal social tensions, and social constraints on behavior.

Specifically, in emergent chiefdoms or transegalitarian societies, we postulate the necessary presence of ambitious males (aggrandizers) competing for prestige within a regional setting.[1] Aggrandizers do not strive to become chiefs; the end

---

[1] Our use of masculine pronouns is intentional. Female aggrandizers remain a theoretical possibility, but their minor representation in the ethnographic record requires explanation. An aggrandizer's competitive ability derives in large part from his immediate access to the productive labor of his wife (or wives) and children, a form of familial exploitation socially justified by gender ideology. Schrijvers (1986: 25–6) observes that "women cannot achieve political power [since] women cannot marry wives to work for them and increase their wealth."

result of political competition cannot be foreseen by participants in the system. Aggrandizers simply strive to become more influential. It is the successful deployment of resources and labor that ultimately ensures the social and political longevity of an aggrandizer, and only certain environments can sustain such behavior on a regional scale and a chronic basis (Hayden and Gargett 1990).

Competition for "prestige" consists of rivalry for continual public recognition by supporters (with access to their resources). Prestige is maintained by establishing a coalition of loyal supporters, or a faction (Salisbury and Silverman 1977; Bailey 1977). In this view, vying for prestige is the equivalent of competing for people or their labor power and support (Binford 1983: 219; see also Sahlins 1968: 89–90; Gulliver 1977: 44; Silverman 1977: 72; Price 1984). It also involves competition over the "management of meaning" and "interpretation of behavior and relationships" (Cohen and Comaroff 1976: 102); this probably relates to the emphasis on oratory among tribal leaders (Clastres 1977).

Although our argument requires the presence of a particular personality type, we consider psychology a constant. Ambitious individuals are probably present in most societies. The presence of such individuals is a necessary but insufficient condition for the transition to non-egalitarian systems.

Structure and Social System

We assume that "all social systems, whatever their structure, contain the seeds of inequality" (Josephides 1985:1; see also Béteille 1977). We do not view social evolution as unfolding from inner forces, but we do maintain that all egalitarian systems mask fundamental structural contradictions which necessitate leveling mechanisms to assert egalitarianism (Woodburn 1982; Matson 1985; Lee 1990).

Cohen (1974: 78) argues that all social systems involve hierarchy, which suggests the presence of leadership with attendant prestige, no matter how ephemeral. In egalitarian groups, hierarchy is likely to be based on age, gender, and aptitude. Rivalries for temporary hierarchical positions develop among many of those with requisite ability to fill them. In addition to social differentiation, all societies require a system of social evaluation (Béteille 1977: 9). These two necessary conditions for any society lay the basis of social inequalities.

In our model we assume egalitarian groups or communities where great latitude exists in the degree to which individuals may maneuver for prestige, that is, societies in which prestige is possible, personal ambition is allowed, and agents have control over the fruits of some of their labor. The deployment of resources (or property) as actors see fit involves usufruct rights within a defined territory (Sack 1986; Hayden 1990).

Two more specific aspects of structure and social system inform our model. The first concerns biological reproduction. We concur with Friedman and Rowlands (1978: 204) that "reproduction is an areal phenomenon in which a number of separate social units are linked in a large system" (see Wobst 1974). Furthermore, we assume patrilocality, with patrilineal descent favored but not strictly necessary (cf. Allen 1984; Coontz and Henderson 1986).

Environment and Technology

Considerations of the environment should acknowledge actors with conventional perceptions and constructions of their "world" in symbolic interaction with other people and objects (Blumer 1969: 11). In short, "nature" (including resources, physical features, and concepts of space and distance) is subject to interpretive shifts and even manipulation by interested individuals within a given social system (Sack 1986; Helms 1988).

Using these resources, aggrandizers compete for "prestige"; *competition over physical resources is not an end in itself.* Nature is handed a passive role in this process. Resources and technology circumscribe individual choice but otherwise neither impede nor promote social competition or development.

Only certain kinds of environments and resources will sustain escalating exploitation by aggrandizers. Resources must be accessible, productive, and relatively immune to normal environmental perturbations (Coupland 1985: 219; Matson 1985) – characteristics of r-selected species, such as fish, rodents, and cereals (Hayden 1986, 1990). Resource availability and productivity determine potential levels of accumulation for social display and competition. In addition, the periodicity and extent of resource shortfalls is critical to the development of political inequality on a permanent basis.

The environment must be productive enough to support a rapidly growing labor force, the followers attached to an aggrandizer. In other words, aggrandizers fare best in "intensifiable habitats" (Price 1984: 225). Of course, the elasticity of a habitat to labor influx varies according to basic technology, social relations of production, and subsistence techniques.

Any transition to a non-egalitarian system requires the emergence of new practices as a necessary prelude to structural change. And these must be maintained and financed long enough to make the practices habitual (Berger and Luckmann 1966; Bourdieu 1977). Therefore, factional leaders must have access to important resources continuously over a period of years or even decades (Binford 1983: 219; Earle 1987: 294). One or two bad seasons can undo years of public posturing, faction building, and prestations, with loss-of-face and depletion of stored resources and social credits.

While resource productivity and reliability act as relaxed restraints on individual action, they alone cannot explain the specific location, timing, or extent of social development. An equally important consideration is the geographic configuration of resources and physical features which channel communication and social interaction.

Demography, Social Interaction and Rank

Demographic increase does not and cannot force people to invent and adopt non-egalitarian social formations (Netting 1990). Although there is a strong correlation between population size and level of sociopolitical complexity (Cohen 1985; Keely 1988), we view population as a necessary precondition or threshold phenomenon. Population must reach a certain size and density before the complex social interactions that lead to the emergence of rank can occur.

Both intra- and inter-community interactions are essential in faction building (see Spencer, Chapter 3). Interaction within (1) the community, (2) the region, and (3) various regions (the area) includes both positive and negative social discourse, from trade and marriage to warfare (Price 1977, 1984). Cooperation and competition are complementary principles. To compete effectively, aggrandizers require the cooperation and support of indebted clients, probably including many kin, and other patrons or trade partners. Competition is undertaken to maintain or enlarge this cooperative unit or interest group.

Effective competition at the community level requires aggrandizers to traffic outside their home communities and establish significant ties to individuals elsewhere, preferably other aggrandizers who also seek outside contacts. The physical and social resources and knowledge thus gained allow an aggrandizer to compete more effectively within his own community. The aggrandizer capitalizes upon innovation and risk taking (Schmookler 1984: 28). Enhancing prestige through innovation depends on an aggrandizer's ability to convince potential beneficiaries/clients of the value of his innovations.

The conversion of external resources into social leverage locally requires (near) exclusive access to outside goods, material, or information (Gosden 1989). This also allows the aggrandizer to operate partially outside the sanctioning norms of his local group, where local norms are more ambiguous and easier to manipulate. Our model presumes a plurality of structurally similar, autonomous social groups or communities within a region and a complex web of rivalry and cooperation among aggrandizers and their supporters, in what has been called "peer polity interaction" (Renfrew and Cherry 1986).

Even the first steps of an aggrandizer's career involve interaction both within and beyond his home community. Building renown commences in the nuclear unit of production. An aggrandizer first accumulates deployable resources by the sweat of his brow, and through the efforts of his wife (wives) and children. The more wives and children the better (Coontz and Henderson 1986). Since intensified resource procurement is a consequence of increased labor input, it follows that larger families may produce larger surpluses to invest in prestige competition. Multiple wives also provide the aggrandizer with a larger group of affines for exchange partnerships (Strathern 1966: 360). In addition, multiple wives engender more offspring who later become a source of additional alliances (Redmond, Chapter 4).

The potential for social development of a community is a function of its access to *social resources*, notably people in neighboring communities and kinship structures. Such access depends upon relative topographic position within the region (Johnson 1977: 492). Some basic features of the landscape (e.g. mountains, canyons, and rough ocean) will inhibit travel and communication to some areas; other features (e.g. mountain passes, fords, and navigable rivers) funnel social contact into specific areas. Inherent potential for travel, coupled with distribution of critical resources, delimits settlement locations, sizes, population densities, permanence, and future growth. Some communities will be central and others peripheral to

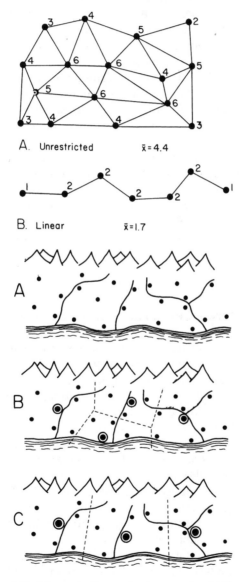

Figure 10.1 [orig. figure 2.1]   Measures of interaction in unrestricted (A) and linear (B) networks.

critical natural and social resources. So too, some people are more centrally placed than others vis-à-vis various social and physical resources and can avail themselves of this advantage. Thus, some aggrandizers will be better placed than others to mobilize resources. Those with the most numerous or strongest ties to different outside resources should be best off.

The settlement pattern may be linear or non-linear (or open). In linear settlement systems, each aggrandizer has unimpeded access to only one or two significant neighboring groups, as shown in figure 10.1. In open settlement systems, however, potential for interaction varies significantly from center to periphery; a community's territory can border the territories of two to six neighboring groups. Note the difference in mean interaction between linear and open systems shown in figure 10.1. Centrally placed aggrandizers within open settlement systems enjoy an advantage with more possibilities for inter-group alliances and for manipulating the ambiguities of several different systems for their own benefit.

We expect social change at focal points of regional social interaction, or in the central sectors of open settlement systems. Rank societies emerge within a network of interacting groups. One society does not hoist itself from one social level to another; the process involves the simultaneous emergence of a network of *chiefdoms* from a network of interacting *chiefs*. In this sense, all pristine developments are secondary developments dependent on outside resources, alliances, and events. However, the process is irreversible in most instances. Because social competition is elevated to a new level among a plurality of like units, there is no practical way to reverse the process – and little incentive for doing so. Structural and systemic changes shift the conditions for future development and possibilities for action.

Perks, Persuasion, and Clientage

Returning to the question of the emergence of institutionalized inequality, why would individuals in a subordinate position surrender their liberty, equality, and fraternity to a non-egalitarian system? Traditionally, two answers have been proposed, one emphasizing voluntary "social contracts" and the other stressing "coercion" (Service 1975). Both proposals have serious flaws.

Theories of coercion often stress the importance of warfare and conquest in the construction of social inequality. Raiding does play an important role in emerging systems of inequality as one way that leaders can gain reputation and undercut the prestige of rivals (Kirch 1984: 197), seize booty that can be shared with one's followers, or even obtain captives (Redmond, Chapter 4). Of equal importance is the hostile "meaning" attributed to the exterior social environment and the increased prestige accrued by successful negotiation in that domain. But theories based upon conquest and subjugation are inappropriate for egalitarian societies (see Fried 1967: 213–23; also Otterbein's 1985: Ch. 2 for a cross-cultural study of war). On the other hand, social contract theories are all teleological and/or functional and thus logically flawed (see Dahrendorf 1968: 165; Fischer 1970: 155). In contrast to either of these theories, we suggest that social inequality was an unanticipated consequence of aggrandizers vying for followers.

Aggrandizers cannot force anyone to join their group or faction. Followers must be persuaded, coaxed, cajoled, begged, bribed, and otherwise won over. Consequently, aggrandizer strategies and tactics for persuasion must appear to conform to the self-interests of their followers (Doob 1983: 41; Bailey 1988; Spencer, Chapter 3). Simply put, followers tag along because they benefit from doing so, retaining the option of shifting their loyalty to other aggrandizers should enough benefits not be forthcoming (Wolf 1966: 17). The most successful aggrandizers are those who provide the most physical, social, and/or spiritual benefits to the most people on the most reliable basis. Thus, aggrandizers are strongly motivated to increase rewards through increased production and innovation.

Aggrandizers and followers, as social creditors and debtors, construct complex webs of relationships as they interact on different levels (see Lederman 1986). These relationships are in constant flux and vary according to the particular dyadic relationships considered. An aggrandizer can be creditor to his group and at the same time be indebted to other powerful partners (Strathern 1966). All successful aggrandizers begin as followers of powerful patrons and acquire prestige from their prestigious mentors.

The self-aggrandizing process is fundamentally a political one based upon the simple principle of reciprocity. We view personal generosity as the key competitive process for forging a coalition of clients (Price 1984: 224–5). Aggrandizer gifts are eventually returned by their followers in reciprocal exchanges. When this is not possible, unreciprocated benefits create obligations of social indebtedness which become deployable social resources themselves (Blau 1964; Sahlins 1968: 88; Orenstein 1980; Gosden 1989). Periodically aggrandizers must "draw on the fund of good will" (Paynter and Cole 1980: 66) created by previous acts of generosity to mobilize labor and resources. The most successful aggrandizers are those who can maintain a positive balance of generosity and "gift-credits" (Lederman 1986); they give more than they receive. This puts them in a socially superior position which, if sustained long enough, can lead to the institutionalization of social inequalities (Friedman 1975; Hayden and Gargett 1990). Apical rank societies or chiefdoms are clearly prefigured in the organization of personal followings or factions.

Rank or chiefdom societies, however, can only be said to be truly in place when special privileges get passed on to the leader's heirs. "Attention to processes of consolidation of power shifts the focus from individual actors to families" (Vincent 1978: 187). The general process of establishing succession is clear. Men of wealth, renown, and influence can create opportunities for favored dependants, "to effect differential patterns of marriage choice" (Wolf 1966: 6). Strategies for passing benefits to heirs may also involve creation of heritable wealth through patronized craft production (Clark and Parry 1990) or monopolization of important outside resources (Gosden 1989). Orenstein (1980: 76) demonstrates that "rules of inheritance" are the key; we would also add marriage rules and arrangements (Friedman and Rowlands 1978; Collier 1988). To become habitual, at least two generations are probably needed to allow for the socialization of the majority of a society's members to the changed social reality.

Summary

Our model of structural transformation considers historical antecedents (system and structure *sensu* Giddens), environment and technology, scales of social interaction, and human agency, action, and personality. It focuses upon "action" rather than "reaction" (i.e., in response to ecological variables). In particular, the main motivation is the self-interested pursuit of prestige, or competition for followers, using a strategy of competitive generosity.

Forming a coalition is inherently competitive. Successful competition involves elements of luck, chance, personality, and mobilization of social and physical resources over a continuous period. As the process depends on an unpredictable concatenation of factors and contexts negotiated in social interaction, we cannot predict *specific* timing nor precise location of initial occurrence within a generally favorable environmental and demographic milieu.

The Mokaya and the Origins of Rank

Background

The Mazatan region lies in the highly productive section of the southern Chiapas coast known as the Soconusco – an area long famed for its productivity (Voorhies 1990). Mazatan consists of closely packed environmental zones, with a narrow, low-lying coastal plain sandwiched between a linear beach/estuary complex and the formidable piedmont/Sierra Madre mountain range 20–30 km inland (figure 11.2). Specialized hamlets were located within the estuary system, but the largest Early Formative communities occupied the central strip of the coastal plain, between 10–15 m above sea level. The plain is crossed by numerous abandoned river channels radiating in a semicircular fan; until twenty years ago these served as runoff channels during the rainy season and supported garden plots at the end of the dry season. These seasonal rivers and streams divided the tropical forest into a patchy mosaic of trees, shrubs, small lagoons, and swamps, ideal for a great variety and density of small fauna. The abundance of game is implicit in the Aztec name – Mazatan, "place of the deer."

Late Archaic (Chantuto phase) shell middens in the estuary zone probably represent seasonal accumulations from occupations by residentially mobile hunter/fisher/gatherers (Voorhies 1976, 1990). Towards the end of the Late Archaic the Chantuto people engaged in long-distance exchange for highland Guatemalan obsidian (Nelson and Voorhies 1980).

The Early Formative transition began about 1550 BC, or 200 years after the last reliable data on the Archaic. The Barra phase (1550–1400 BC) witnessed the

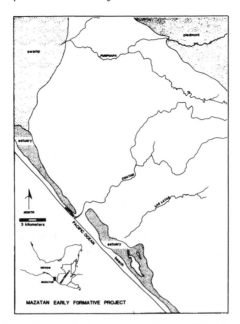

Figure 10.2 [orig. figure 2.2]   Environmental zones of the Mazatan region.

founding of sedentary villages, presumably with agriculture, and the introduction of ceramics. We refer to these Early Formative villagers as the "Mokaya," an indigenous term meaning "corn people." The estuary shell middens saw only minimal use after the Chantuto phase (Voorhies 1976), perhaps as a consequence of a shift in the settlement-subsistence system from residential mobility to sedentism.

Hints of rank distinctions first appear towards the end of the Barra phase, with more convincing evidence for the following Locona phase, beginning about 1400 BC. Briefly, the indicators of Locona rank systems are (1) a two-tiered settlement pattern comprising small villages and hamlets centered around large villages, (2) elite and non-elite domestic architecture (Blake, Clark, Feddema *et al.* 1993), (3) differential mortuary practices, (4) unequal access to sumptuary goods and long-distance imports, (5) attached craft specialization centered around elite housemounds, and (6) redistribution within each large community (Clark 1991). Artisans made ceramic vessels and figurines, elaborate carved stone bowls that imitated fancy ceramic forms, greenstone beads, and, perhaps, textiles and cordage.

The following events or processes are implicated in the emergence of rank in the Mazatan region: (1) a shift from residential mobility to sedentism; (2) increased emphasis on agriculture, including the adoption of highland cultigens such as corn and beans; (3) the beginnings of ceramic technology; (4) rapid population growth; and (5) the beginning of craft specialization. Rather than causal, these processes are probably all related as secondary indicators of a more fundamental process of prestige building and competitive generosity. In the remainder of this paper we assess the roles of (1) population pressure, (2) the adoption of ceramic technology, and (3) the beginnings of agriculture in this process as it evolved in the Mazatan area.

Population pressure

As presented by Carneiro (1970), population pressure on limited resources provokes agricultural intensification and, later, when this temporary measure proves inadequate, wars of conquest and subjugation. In this view, the transition to institutionalized inegalitarianism occurs within a circumscribed zone once the limits of its carrying capacity are exceeded.

Our hypothesis of competing aggrandizers turns Malthus on his head. The objective of competitive generosity is to *attract* more followers to one's locale and to foment rapid population growth, including local increases in family sizes and fertility rates. The emergence of rank is coupled with strategies that bring more people into a zone that is well below carrying capacity (see Kirch 1984). Rank emerges in regions able to absorb this increased population without deleterious effect. Increase in local population is achieved through mechanisms such as promoting immigration, younger marriage, a higher birth rate, or even the capture of slaves. In the Mazatan area, competition among aggrandizers for secondary wives could have effectively lowered the age of marriage for women, and consequently increased the fertility rate (see Hayden 1992). We expect the emergence of rank societies to occur well below carrying capacity. The process as we see it results from a long-term distribution of benefits rather than the exercise of naked force.

The uniformity in subsistence tools and remains during the Early Formative suggests that the carrying capacity of Mazatan was virtually constant throughout this period; it may even have increased slightly as the number of fallow fields increased (creating a greater "edge" effect), and with genetic improvements in cultigens such as corn (Kirkby 1973). Survey data for the zone provide the basis for the demographic estimates shown in figure 10.3. This population curve is based upon the estimated hectares of occupation per phase for a 50 km² survey block of 100 percent coverage. As figure 10.3 demonstrates, the first major shift in population corresponds to the emergence of rank societies, countering the predictions of population pressure advocates. Interestingly, the next major change anticipated another important political shift in the zone – from a network of simple chiefdoms to a single paramount chiefdom.

Had the transition to rank society been prompted by population pressure, one would expect it to have taken place at or shortly after the peak of demographic growth (i.e. near carrying capacity). Wars of conquest, as argued by Carneiro (1970), merely reshuffle usufruct rights of critical resources rather than provide a basis for additional growth. In contrast, population growth as part of the transformation process should evince rapid change to the degree that nascent leaders compete for followers. The Mazatan data support the notion of population growth as outcome of social complexity rather than cause.

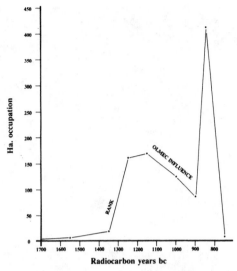

Figure 10.3 [orig. figure 2.3]   Population estimates for the Mazatan region during the Early Formative period. Estimates are based upon a 50 km² survey block.

Although settlement survey coverage of adjacent areas is not complete, available data suggest that during the Early Formative period the Mazatan area was ringed by uninhabited or sparsely occupied land, signaling the absence of any environmental or social circumscription and, of equal importance, some population movement from these areas into the Mazatan region.

Ceramic technology

Technological and ecological explanations of the origins of Mesoamerican ceramics cannot account for the technical and aesthetic sophistication of the early ceramics from coastal Chiapas and Guatemala. Barra-phase ceramics (figure 10.4) from the Mazatan area are currently the earliest securely dated examples (1550–1400 BC) in Mesoamerica, but these thin-walled, hard ceramics are finely finished and elaborately decorated (bichromes, trichromes, incised, grooved, carved, fluted, and gadrooned). This assemblage is clearly well developed, suggesting an origin and development elsewhere. Alternatively, some investigators conjecture that earlier, less complex ceramics will yet be found in the Soconusco region.

Were these early ceramics a local development, or were they brought in from elsewhere? Both Coe (1960) and Lowe (1975) speculate about Central or South American origins. But with the benefit of more complete assemblages from Mazatan and the areas to the south, we now recognize only vague similarities between the Mazatan pottery and pottery from Central and South America. Notable, however, are (1) the apparent temporal progression of the earliest ceramic assemblages as one moves northward from Ecuador to Mesoamerica (Hoopes 1987) and (2) the stylistic dissimilarities among adjacent early assemblages.

Figure 10.4 [orig. figure 2.4]   Reconstruction of Barra vessels from the Mazatan region.

The Central and South American data suggest that the earliest Mokaya did adopt the basic ceramic technology from people to the south. Central questions, then, are (1) why they chose to adopt pottery when they did, (2) what functions the pottery served, and (3) how the process of adoption occurred. We argue that the adoption of ceramics was a result of competition among aggrandizers who brought in foreign technology and products as part of their pursuit of prestige.

To place this hypothesis in perspective, we need to consider probable historical antecedents to the adoption of ceramics. First, we postulate the presence of numerous aggrandizers within the Mazatan region and a dynamic egalitarian network – a society of complex hunter-fisher-gatherers (see Price and Brown 1985). Second, these hunter-fisher-gatherers inhabited the zone for at least 2000 years prior to the adoption of ceramics (Blake, Clark, Voorhies *et al.* 1993). Undoubtedly, the adaptation of these archaic Chantuto foragers to their tropical coastal environment already included viable container technology and food preparation techniques. The adoption of ceramic technology, therefore, involved the *replacement* of some perishable containers with ceramic vessels. Attributes of the first ceramic vessels suggest they served a specialized function.

All Barra ceramics are finely made, flat-bottomed tecomates or deep incurved bowls (figures 10.4 and 10.5). To date, no plain, unslipped, undecorated vessels have been recovered. Ceramic vessels mimic gourd forms (Lowe 1975; Marcus 1983a). We suggest these first ceramic vessels copied then extant fancy gourd vessels. All the techniques used to embellish the surface of Barra pots are still used today to decorate gourds (see Lathrap 1977). Such techniques may have been used initially to decorate gourds and only later transferred to the new ceramic medium.

We postulate that aggrandizers borrowed foreign ceramic technology for personal advantage in displays of competitive feasting. The aggrandizers might have sent someone to the pottery-producing areas to learn the techniques (or gone themselves) or, alternatively, sponsored a potter to come to the Mazatan region.

But if ceramic technology was brought in fully developed, how do we explain the differences in pottery styles in the borrowing area (Mazatan) and the donor area (Central America)? If gourd vessels (which may have been elaborately decorated and expensive) were already functioning in a competitive sphere of public/ritual display, the containers most likely imitated by ceramic forms would have been stylistically elaborate and socially bounded already. That is, vessel style would already have been socially meaningful or semantically complex within special social contexts (cf. Steinberg 1977). Producing these vessels in a new and more expensive medium (fired clay) would have enhanced their value but not tampered with meaningful social conventions. In contrast, the direct transfer of

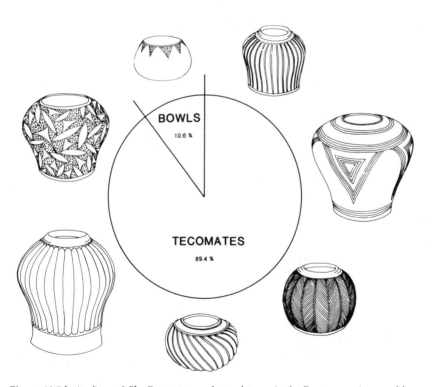

BOWLS

10.6 %

TECOMATES

89.4 %

Figure 10.5 [orig. figure 2.5]   Percentages of vessel types in the Barra ceramic assemblage.

foreign vessel forms and styles would not have been immediately meaningful, in traditional conventions, and may have been of less value to those seeking prestige through conspicuous consumption. McCracken (1987) demonstrates that material codes, unlike language codes, lack generative capacity or combinatorial freedom. To recombine the stylistic elements into a new form is to render them meaningless. The material code (or combination of elements) must be known in advance to be culturally meaningful in social interaction. Consequently, different social messages are conveyed by local and foreign styles.

Technological transfer in a milieu of competing aggrandizers can account for those aspects of ceramic technology that previous investigators found puzzling. It would explain (1) the timing of the adoption, (2) vessel style or exterior decoration, (3) vessel forms, (4) workmanship, (5) the general function of these first ceramic vessels, and (6) the development of ceramics during the following phases. Timing was dictated by the heightened level of social competition in Mazatan. Vessel style and forms were predicated upon the style and forms of the non-ceramic ritual/feasting vessels already functioning in competitive social displays; all that changed was the base material and *some* processes of surface manipulation and finish. The sociopolitical functions of pottery also account for the superior quality of the first vessels (they were preciosities) and the unexpected absence of plain, utilitarian vessels. Functions later relegated to plain pottery continued to be performed, in the Barra phase, by gourds or *jicaras*, net bags, and baskets. Unslipped pottery became more common during the following Locona phase, a time when techniques of ceramic manufacture were more widely known and consequently less "expensive," and probably when the use of ceramic vessels in competitive displays had lost its novelty.

Barra vessels do not appear to have been designed or used for cooking; instead, they are appropriate for preparing and serving liquids (figures 10.4 and 10.5).[2] Large quantities of fire-cracked rock, dating to the Barra and early Locona phase, may indicate non-ceramic-vessel cooking techniques such as roasting and/or stone boiling. But during the Locona phase (figure 10.6), cooking wares were introduced, and the frequency of fire-cracked rocks declined. In sum, we suspect that ceramics were initially adopted more for their power to impress others in competitive social displays than for their culinary potential in food preparation.

---

[2] Two objections to our interpretation of Barra tecomates as vessels used for brewing, storing, and/or serving liquids have been raised. First, tecomates are poorly designed to pour or dispense liquids – but pouring liquids is not implicated in our argument. Some of the smaller tecomates could have been passed among participants, or participants could drink from one large tecomate with straws (illustrated by Katz and Voigt 1986: 28, fig. 6a for the Tiriki of Kenya). Small gourd tecomates are still used by Maya groups in Chiapas for ritual drinking. The second objection, that large gourd tecomates are used today to store tortillas and so may have served this function in the past, stems from a naïve use of ethnographic analogy. The first clear evidence of tortillas in Chiapas dates only to the Early Postclassic period, c. AD 1000. If tortillas or tamales were involved with the function of these early ceramic vessels, we would expect to find evidence of a greater contribution of corn to the diet and evidence of using vessels in cooking.

Figure 10.6 [orig. figure 2.6]   Reconstruction of Locona vessels from Mazatan region.

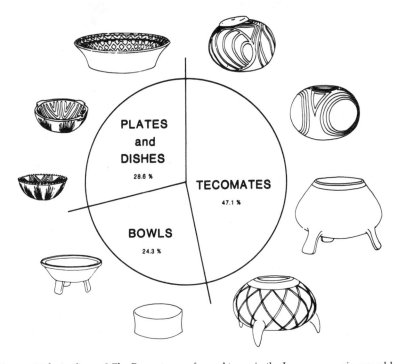

Figure 10.7 [orig. figure 2.7]   Percentages of vessel types in the Locona ceramic assemblage.

We argue that the first Barra ceramics mimicked functionally specialized gourd vessels and that the range of forms increased with time as ceramic technology was applied to other functions. We would expect to see an increasing diversity of functional types over time and a greater range of execution (fancy vs. plain pottery). In addition, the per capita consumption of functionally analogous vessels should remain constant between phases. All these trends are evident in Barra phase and Locona phase (figures 10.6 and 10.7) ceramics.

Ceramic diversity increased through time with a Locona-phase proliferation of fancy dishes and plates as well as relatively plain tripod tecomates, perhaps used for storage and/or boiling. Consumption rates between phases, as gauged by ceramic counts per volume of excavated fill, remained remarkably constant for highly polished, slipped, decorated tecomates (table 10.1). The smaller proportion of fancy tecomates in the Locona ceramic assemblage (figure 10.7) results from the addition of new forms, including utilitarian tecomates, rather than a decreased use of fancy tecomates during the Locona phase.

Table 10.1 [orig. table 2.1]   Consumption of tecomates during the Early Formative, based upon the minimum number of individual (MN1) pots. MN1 calculated by refitting and analyzing rim sherds.

Tecomates	Barra phase*		Locona phase**	
	MN1	MN1/m³	MN1	MN1/m³
Fancy, slipped	74	9.7	118	10.0
Grooved	6	0.8	44	3.7
Plain	0	0.0	44	3.7
Total	80	10.5	206	17.4

* based upon 7.5 m³ of deposit.
** based upon 11.8 m³ of deposit.

Beginning of agriculture

The first clear evidence of agriculture in the Mazatan region consists of domesticates brought in from the highlands. This may be another example of aggrandizers appropriating materials from outside areas in their never-ending quest for self-promotion (see Hayden 1990). Domesticated corn and beans were both clearly present in Mazatan by Locona times, and we suspect that these highland cultigens were first brought into the area during the Late Archaic. But several lines of evidence suggest that maize may not have been very important in the diet. We cannot evaluate the importance of beans at this time.

Corn cobs in Locona deposits are quite small (3–4 cm long) and not very productive. Our analysis of C13/C12 ratios from twenty-eight human bone collagen samples spanning the Late Archaic to Late Postclassic periods show that maize (or other C-4 plants) was not a significant part of the diet until the Middle Formative

Conchas phase (*c.* 850–650 BC). For all Early Formative samples, the stable carbon isotope ratios are as low as those for hunter/fisher/gatherers in many other regions of the world (Blake, Chisholm *et al.* 1992).

We suggest that the adoption of maize may have been linked to the adoption of ceramic technology. Clearly, maize was imported into a system already self-sufficient in basic foodstuffs. Even the highland peoples who domesticated maize were still not fully sedentary agriculturalists at this time (MacNeish 1964; Flannery and Marcus 1983c; Flannery 1986); Mesoamerican corn was not that productive 4000 years ago. In line with our model, we suggest that maize may have been adopted as a status food and not as some sort of far-sighted, prehistoric agricultural improvement project. We should not assume that plants were imported to Mazatan 4000 years ago for reasons having to do with their function today.

We have argued that Barra ceramics were designed for liquids, presumably liquids with ritual significance and prestige value for the giver. Maize may have been part of this complex, introduced to the coastal area prior to the adoption of ceramics primarily for making corn beer, or *chicha*. Alternatively, it may have been used with chocolate or as a drink in its own right such as *atole*; *atole* is still an important ritual drink in Chiapas. Hayden (1990) argues that the domestication of plants and animals resulted from their deployment as status foods. While this may not explain the development of agriculture, it may explain the spread of some cultigens. Use of corn as a ritual ingredient, or as an alcoholic beverage could explain (1) the initial importation and special cultivation of this unproductive highland cereal, (2) the rarity of seed-processing implements, and (3) the minor contribution of maize in the overall diet during the Early Formative period.

Summary and Conclusions

Our explanation of the emergence of permanent social inequality from egalitarian sociopolitical structures rests on six propositions:

1 Egalitarian social systems contain the seeds of permanent social inequality in their structure of age, kin, gender, and aptitude distinctions.
2 The development of permanent social inequality is an unanticipated consequence of individuals pursuing self-interests and personal aggrandizement.
3 Temporary positions of prestige become hereditary and legitimate positions of authority under limited social and natural environmental conditions.
4 These changes result from the purposive action of individuals pursuing individual strategies and agendas within the structural constraints of their cultural system.
5 The engine of change is competition for prestige – constituted as public recognition of status, rights, and responsibilities – among a network of aggrandizers.
6 Effective competition within one's community requires that aggrandizers traffic outside their respective communities and establish enduring ties with individuals elsewhere.

These propositions have archaeological implications that differ significantly from those generated by functionalist/ecological approaches. Ecological approaches see hierarchical, chiefly political organization as an adaptive, structural response to social/ecological needs. Therefore, to explain the change it is sufficient to document the conditions or needs stimulating the adaptive response. In contrast, we suggest that chiefdom emergence must be explained in terms of the political process.

Anterior social structure as well as perceived environmental constraints shape the emergent system. This means that a great deal of variability may be expected in the paths to permanent inequality taken by different societies. Aggrandizers in different cultural-environmental contexts may employ some but not all of the various options available. Although the broad outlines of structural change may be similar, specific conditions of inequality will vary considerably from case to case as each will have its own history.

But the focus on individual historical sequences need not degenerate into a particularistic view of social process that negates generalization and the search for patterns. Our model for the transition to institutionalized inequality has several implications which can be verified archaeologically for any test case. First, if the emergence of hereditary inequality is indeed an unanticipated consequence of competition among aggrandizers in transegalitarian systems, this transitional period from egalitarian societies to chiefdoms should appear, archaeologically, neither egalitarian nor ranked. Many of the standard trappings of chiefly societies will be absent during the transitional period because they are still unnecessary or, in some cases, not permitted. Once clear evidence of hereditary inequality appears, the transition is long past. On the other hand, if in emergent chiefdoms constraints to wealth accumulation and public display were undergoing modification, aggrandizers would be allowed to produce and distribute subsistence and craft items in excess of existing norms. Therefore, one might find archaeological evidence of elaboration and experimentation with status objects and social structures which might become embedded in subsequent chiefdoms.

Second, change would be rapid in transitional societies because innovation would be useful for competing aggrandizers. In contrast, material culture, symbols, and sociopolitical structure in both egalitarian societies and developed chiefdoms would be more stable with an emphasis on perpetuating the traditional bases of power. As sociopolitical structures develop so does the symbolism of chiefly power and inter-regional alliances. Their very existence leads to conservatism, thereby dampening their own rates of change. Elite competition within a chiefdom or among chiefdoms takes place within the newly established, legitimate symbol system based upon a limited range of recognized status markers (Anderson, Chapter 5). Radical and innovative change in symbol systems accompany major social structural changes.

Third, aggrandizers, like big-men and chiefs, must control or maintain access to a large labor pool in order to sustain the high levels of production that both demonstrate and further their influence. Thus, an aggrandizer will value all innovations that (1) attract more followers and (2) increase production to sustain those followers. Novelties, whether arising from emulation or invention, will be valued, especially those items that can be controlled, managed, or manipulated by aggrandizers.

In evaluating this model of chiefdom emergence we reviewed three lines of archaeological evidence as they relate to population dynamics, development of ceramic technology, and adoption of agriculture. As noted, we expect population growth and nucleation to occur during the transition to non-egalitarian society. At the very least, population should not remain stable or decline within the region of the aggrandizer interaction network as long as resources can be intensified and the system does not collapse. Survey data for the Mazatan region show significant population increase and nucleation during the early part of the Early Formative period. The first evidence of population growth is coeval with the first indications for competition among aggrandizers, during the Barra phase. This suggests that population growth and nucleation – and the increasing labor pool they imply – could have been consequences of social and political strategies.

New technology is another expectation for a competitive political environment favoring innovation. In the Mokaya case, the first use of ceramics began during the Barra phase. These highly decorated and well-made ceramic containers were probably first used in beverage preparation and consumption as an adjunct to public feasting rather than in utilitarian functions such as cooking. Such activities would have been crucial for an aggrandizer trying to attract, impress, and retain followers.

Finally, the adoption of agriculture in coastal Chiapas suggests a sociopolitical dynamic quite different from those postulated for other parts of Mesoamerica. Maize and bean cultivation in the highland valleys go back several millenia before the Chiapas Early Formative period. By the Locona phase (*c.* 1350–1250 BC) in Mazatan, maize and beans were used frequently enough to enter the archaeological record. However, it was not until the Middle Formative that maize became significant enough in the diet to influence the stable carbon isotope ratio in human bone collagen. One possibility is that aggrandizers adopted an agricultural complex as a means of growing new foods, one of which (maize) could be used in making alcoholic beverages useful in competitive feasting. They may also have cultivated a range of other plants of which we have no material evidence. However, the faunal evidence clearly indicates that the Early Formative Mokaya were fishers, hunters, and gatherers. Hunter-fisher-gatherers in other highly productive regions of the world developed simple chiefdoms. The Mokaya appear to have done so also. Maize cultivation may have initially been a dietary supplement of greater political than nutritional value.

Much more research remains to be done to understand the transition from egalitarian to permanently ranked social organizations. We are confident, however, that the avenues for inquiry suggested by a focus on transitional political processes differ substantially from traditional functionalist/ecological approaches – especially those that consider established, early chiefdoms. Once the transitional process began, the socio-political order became fundamentally different, both from what it had been and from what it was to become.

Acknowledgements

Our research was generously funded by the New World Archaeological Foundation of Brigham Young University, then directed by Gareth W. Lowe. We are grateful for the opportunity to undertake the Mazatan Project. Barbara Stark, Barbara Voorhies, Jim Brown, Brian Hayden, Peter Peregrine, Elizabeth Brumfiel, and John Fox offered many constructive suggestions on previous drafts of this paper, for which we extend our appreciation. The second half of this paper is a modification of our paper presented at the Circum-Pacific conference.

References

Allen, M. 1984. Elders, chiefs and big men: authority legitimation and political evolution in Melanesia. *American Ethnologist* 11: 20–41.

Bailey, Frederick G. 1977. The definition of factionalism. In M. Silverman and R.F. Salisbury, eds., *A House Divided? Anthropological Studies of Factionalism*, pp. 21–32. Toronto: University of Toronto Press.

1988. *Humbuggery and Manipulation: The Art of Leadership*. Ithaca: Cornell University Press.

Berger, Peter L. and Thomas Luckmann. 1966. *The Social Construction of Reality: A Treatise in the Sociology of Knowledge*. Garden City, NY: Doubleday.

Béteille, André. 1977. *Inequality Among Men*. Oxford: Basil Blackwell.

Binford, Lewis R. 1983. *In Pursuit of the Past: Decoding the Archaeological Record*, New York: Thames and Hudson.

Blake, M., B.S. Chisholm, J.E. Clark, B. Voorhies, and M. Love. 1992. Prehistoric subsistence in the Soconusco region. *Current Anthropology* 33: 83–94.

Blake, M., J.E. Clark, V. Feddema, M. Ryan, and R. Lesure. 1993. Early Formative architecture at Paso de la Amada, Chiapas, Mexico. *Latin American Antiquity* 4.

Blake, M., J.E. Clark, B. Voorhies, G. Michaels, M. Love, A.A. Demarest, M. Pye, and B. Arroyo. 1993. The Archaic and Early Formative chronology for the Soconusco region of Mexico and Guatemala. *Ancient Mesoamerica* 4.

Blau, Peter M. 1964. *Exchange and Power in Social Life*. New York: John Wiley and Sons.

Blumer, Herbert. 1969. *Symbolic Interactionism: Perspective and Method*. Berkeley: University of California Press.

Bourdieu, Pierre. 1977. *Outline of a Theory of Practice*. Cambridge: Cambridge University Press.

Callinicos, Alex. 1988. *Making History*. Ithaca: Cornell University Press.

Carneiro, Robert L. 1970. A theory of the origin of the state. *Science* 169: 733–8.

Cherniak, Christopher. 1986. *Minimal Rationality*. Cambridge MA: MIT Press.

Clark, John E. 1991. The beginnings of Mesoamerican: apologia for the Soconusco Early Formative. In W.R. Fowler, Jr., ed., *The Formation of Complex Society in Southeastern Mesoamerican*. pp. 13–16. Boca Raton: CRC Press.

Clark, John E. and William J. Parry. 1990. Craft specialization and cultural complexity. *Research in Economic Anthropology* 12: 289–346.

Clastres, Pierre. 1977. *Society Against the State: The Leader as Servant and the Humane Uses of Power among the Indians of America*. R. Hurley, trans. New York: Urizen Books.

Coe, Michael D. 1960. Archaeological linkages with North and South America at La Victoria, Guatemala. *American Anthropologist* 62: 363–93.

Cohen, Abner. 1974. *Two-Dimensional Man: An Essay on the Anthropology of Power and Symbolism in Complex Society*. Berkeley: University of California Press.

Cohen, A.P. and J.L. Comaroff. 1976. The management of meaning: on the phenomenology of political transactions. In B. Kapferer, ed., *Transaction and Meaning: Directions in the Anthropology of Exchange and Symbolic Behavior*, pp. 87–107. Philadelphia: Institute for the Study of Human Issues.

Cohen, Mark N. 1985. Prehistoric hunter-gatherers: the meaning of social complexity. In T.D. Price and J.A. Brown, eds., *Prehistoric Hunter-Gatherers: The Emergence of Cultural Complexity*, pp. 99–119. New York: Academic Press.

Collier, Jane. 1988. *Marriage and Inequality in Classless Societies*. Stanford: Stanford University Press.

Coontz, Stephanie and Peta Henderson. 1986. Introduction: 'explanations' of male dominance. In S. Coontz and P. Henderson, eds., *Women's Work, Men's Property: The Origins of Gender and Class*, pp. 1–42. London: Verso.

Coupland, Gary. 1985. Restricted access, resource control and the evolution of status inequality among hunter-gatherers. In M. Thompson, M.T. Garcia and F.J. Kense, eds., *Status, Structure and Stratification: Current Archaeological Reconstructions*, pp. 217–26. Calgary: Archaeological Association, Department of Archaeology, University of Calgary.

Dahrendorf, Ralf. 1968. *Essays in the Theory of Society*. Stanford: Stanford University Press.

Doob, Leonard W. 1983. *Personality, Power and Authority: A View from the Behavioral Sciences*. Westport, CT: Greenwood Press.

Earle, Timothy K. 1987. Chiefdoms in archaeological and ethnohistorical perspective. *Annual Review of Anthropology* 16: 279–308.

Fischer, David Hackett. 1970. *Historian's Fallacies: Toward a Logic of Historical Thought*. New York: Harper and Row.

Flannery, Kent V., ed. 1986. *Guilá Naquitz: Archaic Foraging and Early Agriculture in Oaxaca, Mexico*. New York: Academic Press.

Flannery, Kent V. and Joyce Marcus, eds., 1983c. *The Cloud People: Divergent Evolution of the Zapotec and Mixtec Civilizations*. New York: Academic Press.

Fried, Morton H. 1967. *The Evolution of Political Society: An Essay in Political Anthropology*. New York: Random House.

1975. *The Notion of Tribe*. Menlo Park, CA: Cummings.

Friedman, Jonathan. 1975. Tribes, states, and transformations. In M. Bloch, ed., *Marxist Analyses and Social Anthropology*, pp. 161–202. New York: John Wiley and Sons.

Freidman, Jonathan and Michael J. Rowlands. 1978. Notes toward an epigenetic model of the evolution of "civilisation." In J. Friedman and M.J. Rowlands, eds., *The Evolution of Social Systems*, pp. 201–76. Pittsburgh: University of Pittsburgh Press.

Giddens, Anthony. 1979. *Central Problems in Social Theory: Action, Structures and Contradiction in Social Analysis*. Cambridge: Cambridge University Press.

Godelier, Maurice. 1986. *The Menial and the Material*. M. Thom, trans. London: Verso.

Gosden, Chris. 1989. Debt, production, and prehistory. *Journal of Anthropological Archaeology* 8: 355–87.

Gulliver, P.H. 1977. Networks and factions: two Ndendeuli communities. In M. Silverman and R.F. Salisbury, eds., *A House Divided? Anthropological Studies of Factionalism*, pp. 37–65. Toronto: University of Toronto Press.

Hayden, Brian. 1986. Resources, rivalry, and reproduction: the influence of basic resource characteristics on reproductive behavior. W.P. Handwerker, ed., *Culture and Reproduction: An Anthropological Critique of Demographic Transition Theory*, pp. 176–95. Boulder, CO: Westview Press.

1990. Nimrods, piscators, pluckers, and planters: the emergence of food production. *Journal of Anthropological Archaeology* 9: 31–69.

1992. Conclusions: ecology and complex hunter-gatherers. In B. Hayden, ed., *Complex Culture of the British Columbia Plateau*, pp. 525–63. Vancouver: University of British Columbia Press.

Hayden, Brian and Rob Gargett. 1990. Big man, big heart? A Mesoamerican view of the emergence of complex society. *Ancient Mesoamerica* 1: 3–20.

Helms, Mary W. 1988. *Ulysses' Sail: An Ethnographic Odyssey of Power, Knowledge and Geographical Distance*. Princeton: Princeton University Press.

Hoopes, John W. 1987. Early ceramics and the origins of village life in lower Central America. Ph.D. dissertation, Harvard University, Ann Arbor: University Microfilms.

Johnson, Gregory A. 1977. Aspects of regional analysis in archaeology. *Annual Review of Anthropology* 6: 479–508.

Josephides, Lisette. 1985. *The Production of Inequality: Gender and Exchange among the Kewa*. London: Tavistock.

Katz, Solomon H. and Mary M. Voigt. 1986. Bread and beer: the early use of cereals in the human diet. *Expedition* 28: 23–34.

Keeley, Lawrence H. 1988. Hunter-gatherer economic complexity and "population pressure": a cross-cultural analysis. *Journal of Anthropological Archaeology* 7(4): 373–411.

Kirch, Patrick V. 1984. *The Evolution of the Polynesian Chiefdoms*. Cambridge: Cambridge University Press.

Kirkby, Anne V.T. 1973. *The Use of Land and Water Resources in the Past and Present Valley of Oaxaca, Mexico*. Ann Arbor: The University of Michigan Museum of Anthropology, Memoir 5.

Lathrap, Donald W. 1977. Our father the cayman, our mother the gourd: Spinden revisited, or a unitary model for the emergence of agriculture in the New World. In C.A. Reed, ed., *Origins of Agriculture*, pp. 713–51. The Hague: Mouton.

Lederman, Rena. 1986. *What Gifts Engender: Social Relations and Politics in Mendi, Highland Papua New Guinea*. Cambridge: Cambridge University Press.

Lee, Richard B. 1990. Primitive communism and the origin of social inequality. In S. Upham, ed., *The Evolution of Political Systems: Sociopolitics in Small-Scale Sedentary Societies*, pp. 225–46. Cambridge: Cambridge University Press.

Lowe, Gareth W. 1975. *The Early Preclassic Barra Phase of Altamira, Chiapas: A Review with New Data*. Provo, UT: New World Archaeological Foundation, Papers 38.

McCracken, Grant. 1987. Clothing as language: an object lesson study of the expressive properties of material culture. In B. Reynolds and M.A. Scott, eds., *Material Anthropology: Contemporary Approaches to Material Culture*, pp. 103-28. Lanham, MD: University Press of America.

MacNeish, Richard S. 1964. Ancient Mesoamerican civilization. *Science* 143: 531–7.

Marcus, Joyce. 1983a. The Espiridion complex and the origins of the Oaxacan Formative. In Flannery and Marcus 1983c: 42-3.

Matson, R.G. 1985. The relationship between sedentism and status inequalities among hunters and gatherers. In M. Thompson, M.T. Garcia, and F.J. Kense, eds., *Status, Structure and Stratification: Current Archaeological Reconstructions*, pp. 245–51. Calgary: Archaeological Association, Department of Archaeology, University of Calgary.

Nelson, Fred W. and Barbara Voorhies. 1980. Trace element analysis of obsidian artifacts from three shell midden sites in the littoral zone. Chiapas, Mexico. *American Antiquity*, 45(3): 540–50.

Netting, Robert McC. 1990. Population, permanent agriculture, and polities: unpacking the evolutionary portmanteau. In S. Upham, ed., *The Evolution of Political Systems: Sociopolitics in Small-Scale Sedentary Societies*, pp. 21–61. Cambridge: Cambridge University Press.

Orenstein, Henry. 1980. Asymmetrical reciprocity: a contribution to the theory of political legitimacy. *Current Anthropology* 21: 69–91.

Otterbein, Keith F. 1985. *The Evolution of War: A Cross-Cultural Study.* New Haven: Human Relations Area File Press.

Paynter, Robert and John W. Cole. 1980. Ethnographic overproduction, tribal political economy, and the Kapauku of Irian Jaya. In E.B. Ross, ed., *Beyond The Myths of Culture: Essays in Cultural Materialism*, pp. 61–99. New York: Academic Press.

Price, Barbara J. 1977. Shifts in production and organization: a cluster-interaction model. *Current Anthropology* 18: 209–33.

1984. Competition, productive intensification, and ranked society: speculations from evolutionary theory. In R.B. Ferguson, ed.,*Warfare, Culture and Environment*, pp. 209–40. Orlando: Academic Press.

Price, T. Douglas and James A. Brown, eds. 1985. *Prehistoric Hunter-Gatherers: The Emergence of Cultural Complexity.* Orlando, NJ: Academic Press.

Renfrew, Colin and John F. Cherry, eds. 1986. *Peer Polity Interaction and Socio-Political Change.* Cambridge: Cambridge University Press.

Sack, Robert David. 1986. *Human Territoriality: Its Theory and History.* Cambridge: Cambridge University Press.

Sahlins, Marshall D. 1968. *Tribesmen.* Englewood Cliffs, NJ: Prentice-Hall.

Salisbury, Richard F. and Marilyn Silverman. 1977. An introduction: factions and the dialectic. In Silverman and Salisbury 1977, pp. 1–20.

Schmookler, Andrew Bard. 1984. *The Parable of the Tribes: The Problem of Power in Social Evolution.* Boston: Houghton Mifflin Company.

Schrijvers, Joke. 1986. Make your son a king: political power through matronage and motherhood. In M.A. van Bakel, R.R. Hagesteijn, and P. van de Velde, eds., *Private Politics: A Multi-Disciplinary Approach to 'Big-Man' Systems*, pp. 13–32. Leiden: E.J. Brill.

Service, Elman R. 1975. *Origins of the State and Civilization.* New York: W.W. Norton.

Silverman, Marilyn. 1977. Village council and factionalism: definition and contextual issues. In Silverman and Salisbury 1977, pp. 66–98.

Steinberg, Arthur. 1977. Technology and culture: technological styles in the bronzes of Shang Chin, Phrygia and Urnfield Central Europe. In H. Lechtman and R. Merrill, eds., *Material Culture: Styles, Organization, and Dynamics of Technology*, pp. 53–86. New York: West.

Strathern, Andrew J. 1966. Despots and directors in the New Guinea highlands. *Man* 1: 356–67.

Vincent, Joan. 1978. Political anthropology: manipulative strategies. *Annual Review of Anthropology* 7: 175-94.

Voorhies, Barbara. 1976. *The Chantuto People: An Archaic Period Society of the Chiapas Littoral, Mexico.* Provo, UT: New World Archaeological Foundation, Papers 41.

1990. *Ancient Economies of the Soconusco: The Prehistory and History of the Economic Development in the Coastal Lowlands of Chiapas, Mexico.* Salt Lake City: University of Utah Press.

Wobst, H. Martin. 1974. Locational relationships in Paleolithic society. *Journal of Human Evolution* 5: 49–58.

Wolf, Eric R. 1966. Kinship, friendship and patron-client relationship in complex societies. In M. Banton, ed., *The Social Anthropology of Complex Societies*, pp. 1–22. London: Tavistock.

Woodburn, James. 1982. Egalitarian societies. *Man* 17: 431–51.

11

Cultural Transmission and Cultural Change

Stephen Shennan

Introduction

At the beginning of the 1960s a broadly cultural-historical or 'normative' view of the past prevailed in archaeology: prehistory was written in terms of a changing kaleidoscope of 'cultures' held to correspond in some sense to 'peoples' (Shennan 1989). Particular peoples had particular 'mental templates' or 'norms' for conducting their lives. The mechanisms of change which were held to operate were twofold: the replacement of one people by another and thus the replacement of their templates, or the modification of the templates by the diffusion of influences from outside; the latter mechanism was based on various assumptions about the processes of innovation, imitation and diffusion.

This 'normative view' was attacked in the early 1960s by Binford (e.g. 1962, 1964) and others, who showed that it was inadequate. It did not address the question of how people interacted with their environment and other people, nor with how material culture was used as a tool in such situations. The New Archaeologists went on to do this, from a functionalist perspective, without any reference to questions of cultural transmission and treating cultural content purely from an adaptive viewpoint.

Despite the clearly stated intention to study prehistoric change, a by-product of this approach at the level of empirical work has been a tendency to see synchronic reconstruction as a necessary prerequisite for such study. Thus, for example, patterns are constructed from cemeteries or settlements on the basis of the extent and form of covariation between different types of data, and inferences are made about the type of social-economic-ideological situation which they represent. More recent theoretical approaches have tended to follow a similar reconstructionist line and have also devoted little attention to questions of cultural transmission, despite seeing themselves in some respects as returning to the concerns and concepts of traditional archaeology. The need for analyses of this type cannot be denied but they have the dangerous tendency to lead to a stultifying view of prehistoric archaeology as synchronic reconstructionism – prehistorians as ethnographers *manqués* of the prehistoric present, struggling to achieve a goal which they know in advance is unattainable, and failing to get as far as the questions of long-term change which are supposed to be archaeology's privileged domain.

Arguments such as this, however, together with a new emphasis on the importance of individuals as agents, creators as well as products of their sociocultural environment (e.g. Hodder 1982, 1986, Miller & Tilley 1984; and see below), have recently led some archaeologists towards a renewed interest in dealing with change directly. By this is meant a renewed interest in diachronic trajectories in material culture, including the tracing and explaining of the frequency curves representing the rise and decline in the popularity of artefact types or cultural traits which were traditionally used for constructing chronologies and culture histories.

One of the most important theoretical sources for this renewed concern has been an interest in the concept of emulation, and what emulation patterns have to tell us about the nature of the societies in which they are at work. This has been examined by Miller (1982) and Cannon (1987), for example, although their perspectives are incompatible with one another. Both are preoccupied with the relationship between emulation and social hierarchy, and the way in which material items associated with élites are copied by lower levels within society, so prompting further symbolic elaboration by the élite in order to maintain their differentiation. However, they differ substantively in their theoretical assumptions, in that Miller appears to envisage emulation as a process which can occur in the absence of other kinds of social change – an ongoing static cyclical process – while Cannon sees emulation as associated with social mobility, so that faster rates of emulation correspond to faster rates of social change.

These particular studies do not give any great attention to the spatial aspects of emulation as a process, but this too has come back into focus, with the formulation of such ideas as peer polity interaction (see the papers in Renfrew & Cherry 1986), which attempts to explain the way in which similar patterns of social change often occur over wide areas and are associated with similarity in such aspects as symbolic and ideological systems, and in material culture.

In addition, there are signs of reviving interest in art historical approaches to archaeological data, subjecting the attributes of material culture items to detailed examination to establish their origin and inspiration.

What all this amounts to is a renewed concern with diffusion, albeit from a different perspective from that in which it had its importance in the earlier part of this century. In fact, if one wishes to link the concern with peer polity interaction and emulation to earlier trends within the social sciences, the connections are less with the cultural geographers who initially inspired an archaeological interest in diffusion and much more with the work of Veblen (1899) on the social and cultural characteristics of élites.

Nevertheless, what we may perhaps call the 'neo-diffusionist' perspective adopted by these recent studies is still relatively partial and narrow and it is argued in this chapter that the key to its integration with other areas of social and economic action within the context of specific cultural situations is its inclusion in a broader framework by means of a general model of cultural transmission, of which emulation is only one specific variety. This model also provides a basis for considering innovation – the generation of new cultural variety.

Cultural Continuity as a Problem

The framework to be adopted is fundamentally that of Boyd & Richerson (1985). However, the starting point for its adoption is recent work not just in evolutionary theory but also in social theory belonging to a very different tradition. Where they come together is in an emphasis on the relationship between individual and society as a recursive one, in which the continuity of society, or more accurately of social production and reproduction, is taken as problematical. The biologists and other evolutionary theoreticians have been concerned with the nature of cultural transmission – with how cultural traditions are handed on and modified through time; while the social theorists have emphasized social action and its causes and consequences – how individual social actors realize their goals from one day to the next with the resources at their disposal, and the causes and consequences of their actions. In this latter field the most important theorists have been Giddens (e.g. 1984) and Bourdieu (e.g. 1977), whose work has already played an important rôle in some recent archaeological discussions (e.g. Braithwaite 1982, Moore 1982, Shanks & Tilley 1982, 1987, Hodder 1986).

The essence of Giddens' theory is the construction of what he believes to be a satisfactory link between individual behaviour and larger scale structures, which gives appropriate weight to the knowledgeability of human agents. Some of this knowledge is discursive – individuals can and do articulate it – but much of it is at the level of practical consciousness: individuals know how to take part in their way of life without a great deal of conscious thought and simply get on with it. Thus, in their daily lives people produce and reproduce the institutionalized practices of their society. Of key importance here is the idea of routine, since this makes up the bulk of day-to-day activity.

It is in this day-to-day activity that what Giddens calls the 'duality of structure' is realized: social life as constituted in social practices is recursive, in that structure is both the medium and the outcome of the production of practices (Archer 1982). We can only realize this by doing away with the idea that structure is synchronic and constant while change is diachronic. All social activity takes place in a flow of time and its recursiveness arises as a result of repetition through time. However, we are not dealing with homeostatic causal loops but with what Giddens calls the reflexive self-regulation of human agents: the capacity for conscious evaluation which can be called up as and when required. This, of course, is not to imply that all individuals correspond to modern Western notions of such entities, since it arises quite clearly from Giddens's concept of the duality of structure that what individuals are like cannot be taken as obvious: specification of this cannot be done outside of their social context since this affects the way the individual is constituted (cf. Carrithers *et al.* 1985).

However, in understanding how structures are produced, reproduced and changed we have to take into account the limits which exist both on the knowledgeability of human actors and in their capacity to produce the outcomes which they desire. Social practice is also affected by unacknowledged conditions of action and produces unintended consequences which form part of the context of subsequent interaction. (Giddens 1979, Archer 1982). It is the unacknowledged conditions and unintended consequences which have been at the centre of functionalist sociology, but Giddens asserts that it is possible to study them without the use of functionalist concepts: even defining what is unintentional presupposes a knowledge of intentions.

> *All explanations will involve at least implicit reference both to the purposive reasoning behaviour of agents and to its intersection with constraining and enabling features of the social and material contexts of that behaviour. (Giddens 1984, p. 179)*

Giddens's theory has considerable attractions as an account of everyday social behaviour and the way the structuring principles of society are reproduced in it. Furthermore, by its move towards the dissolution of the distinction between 'rules' or 'norms' on the one hand and 'behaviour' on the other, it provides a framework within which change can be conceptualized. We don't have to postulate one realm of abstract 'rules' and another of 'behaviour' and construct convoluted models of the relation between the two: the principles and resources in terms of which social interactions take place may be modified by the interactions themselves, as people go about their daily business. In this sense then, like Bourdieu (1977), Giddens is offering a 'theory of practice'.

Giddens's views have been criticized for taking insufficient cognizance of the importance of structural constraint on social action (e.g. Archer 1982, Thompson 1984). For present purposes, however, this question is less important than the *completeness* of his theory with regard to questions of cultural transmission. His preoccupation with the short term means that he is more concerned with the instantiation of practical consciousness in day-to-day social action than with the way its principles are transmitted. Such is not the case with Bourdieu who devotes a considerable amount of attention to precisely this. The point is conveniently summarized by Hodder (1986, p. 72):

> *The child adjusts and accommodates subjective and objective patterns, patterns 'in here' and 'out there', giving rise to systematic dispositions. The habitus [Bourdieu's term for practical consciousness] which results is based on the child's own social position as he/she sees how others react to him/her. In particular, the house, and the use of space and objects in a house, lead a child to an understanding of the habitus . . . It is the practices, in the process of enculturation, that act back on the habitus.*

Nevertheless, while Bourdieu's ideas are undoubtedly stimulating, not least to the archaeologist, who sees sketched out ways in which the domestic routine and its material aspects relate to social structure, they still give us nothing like an analytical scheme to explain how and why the structuration processes take the form they do. It is at this point that the evolutionary theory perspective becomes relevant.

Culture and the Evolutionary Process

To explain this assertion, and provide a more adequate framework for archaeological accounts of change, it is necessary to turn to the now fairly extensive literature on the rôle of selection in cultural change. Here the emphasis will be on the work of Boyd & Richerson (1985) concerning *cultural transmission* (cf. especially Cavalli-Sforza & Feldman 1981, Cavalli-Sforza 1986), but an examination of the ideas of Harre (1979) will also play a rôle. Inevitably, the exegesis will be rather lengthy since the ideas are relatively complex and have not yet received wide currency within the archaeological literature.

Boyd & Richerson define culture as 'the information affecting [their] phenotype acquired by individuals by imitation or teaching' (1985, p. 283). They argue that there is sufficient evidence to suggest that culture can usefully be seen as a system of inheritance, and that large amounts of heritable cultural variation exist within and between populations. As is well known, cultural transmission differs from the genetic variety in that the transmission to the next 'generation' of traits acquired during the individual's lifetime can and does occur. Nevertheless, they suggest that:

> there is no necessary logical connection between Darwin's idea of evolution by natural selection and the particular features of genetic inheritance. There are two necessary conditions in order for natural selection to operate: (1) There must be heritable variation in phenotype. (2) Phenotypic variation must be associated with variation in individual survival and reproduction. (1985, p. 173)

Sources of cultural variation are several, including random errors, which can be regarded as corresponding to genetic mutations. In other words, in the same way as mutations arise from random copying errors in the process of gene replication, random errors can also arise in the process of imitating or repeating cultural practices as a result of failures of memory and unintentional mistakes in imitation. This source of cultural variation arising from the transmission process, however, is in many way less interesting than other factors which affect what is transmitted not in a random fashion but systematically. Boyd & Richerson outline several such factors, beginning with what they call 'guided variation'.

This arises from a model of the transmission process in which individuals acquire a pattern of behaviour from their (cultural) parents and then modify it in the light of their own experience – learning through interaction with the environment. It will be this modified form of behaviour which is then passed on to subsequent (cultural) offspring, who will no doubt modify it in their turn. The strength of this learning effect relative to cultural transmission is contingent; it will vary with particular circumstances. The basic rationale for cultural transmission is that it cuts the costs of learning, but this will only be true in certain situations and the models suggest that, as far as its origin is concerned, it will only be favoured over genetic transmission and individual learning where environmental fluctuations of large size and reasonable predictability occur, and where individual trial-and-error learning makes only relatively slight improvements to the phenotype of any single individual.

A second force is what Boyd & Richerson call *bias* (which corresponds to 'cultural selection' *sensu* Cavalli-Sforza & Feldman 1981). With regard to any given activity an individual will often have a number of different models from which to choose. Decisions may be made on the basis of the properties of the models themselves, or on their frequency in the population, and these represent possible forces of *direct* bias in transmission. A rather different phenomenon is *indirect* bias. This refers to a situation where individuals take some aspect of another individual as a model, not on the basis of an evaluation of the range of possibilities with regard to the aspect being imitated, but because the particular individual who possesses this trait is already being used as a model for other activities.

Boyd & Richerson conclude that guided variation and direct bias are often relatively weak, in that many traits are acquired by imitation rather than learning, and there appears to be a substantial heritability of cultural traits; furthermore, they suggest that human ability to make correct choices is relatively limited. This conclusion has important implications in that it indicates the possibility of substantial cultural variation unaffected by individual learning and decisions. They suggest that in these circumstances natural selection will be important:

> It seems likely that individuals characterized by some cultural variants will be more likely to survive or attain social positions that cause them to be imitated than individuals characterized by other variants. When this is true, natural selection will increase the frequency of those variants. (1985, p. 285)

Here, the success of individuals and the success of their associated cultural traits are directly linked, in a formulation apparently very similar to that of the human sociobiologists: certain cultural traits are more successful, in that the individuals possessing them are more successful; the traits will thus tend to spread through the population. However, the similarity to a hard-line genetic determinism is only apparent, in that the traits are cultural rather than genetic, and selection for fitness in cultural terms can override that for fitness in genetic terms.

This point had already been demonstrated by Cavalli-Sforza & Feldman (1981), who showed how cultural transmission could counteract negative natural selection and maintain traits with negative Darwinian fitness in a population; even traits with fitnesses as low as 50 per cent of a competing trait could remain with the population under certain circumstances.

Essentially the same argument is also made by Boyd & Richerson, and the situation arises because of the differing patterns of transmission. In cultural transmission, models for values and behaviour other than the genetic parents are likely to be relevant to a greater or lesser extent, while the rôles of the two parents may well also differ. Within the general sphere of cultural transmission there are likely to be different modes of transmission for different areas of the cultural repertoire; some patterns may be learned from parents and others from contemporaries.

> *If models occupying social roles other than that of genetic parent are important in cultural transmission, and if cultural variation affects which people attain these roles, then selection can increase the frequency of cultural variants that reduce ordinary genetic fitness. (Boyd & Richerson, 1985, p. 286)*

The reason for this is the separability of cultural traits as opposed to genetic traits from individuals:

> *The [cultural] variant that maximises the probability of attaining social roles other than that of parent may often be different from the variant that maximises the probability of becoming a genetic parent. If individuals occupying social roles other than parents are involved in cultural transmission, then many of the selection processes that act on cultural variation may increase the frequency of genetically maladaptive cultural variants.*
>
> *The competition for many social roles, especially those with high prestige, is likely to be much more intense than the competition to become a parent. If these roles are even moderately important in socialization, there will be very strong selection on asymmetrically transmitted cultural variation. (Boyd & Richerson 1985, p. 198)*

In addition, as Cavalli-Sforza & Feldman (1981, pp. 351–7) point out, the speed at which change occurs may also be affected by the mode of transmission. Patterns of behaviour and values transmitted from generation to generation by parents to children, for example, may change more slowly than patterns transmitted between peers.

Before turning to some of the implications of the model for the innovation process, it remains to explicate briefly two other aspects of the cultural transmission process already briefly referred to, which distinguish it from genetic transmission. 'Frequency-dependent bias' refers to the tendency, which may or may not exist in any particular case, for individuals to imitate the more common, or the less common, of two different versions of a behaviour pattern precisely because it is more common, or less common. As Boyd & Richerson point out, it may well be advantageous to a given individual on a given occasion to opt for the majority pattern, because it is likely to be a sensible one for the local circumstances and saves the cost of evaluating alternatives. It also has the interesting and important effect of decreasing variation within groups and preserving variation between groups. This is one of the major respects in which cultural and genetic variation differ from one another, since the latter tends to be characterized by great within-group variation and relatively little between groups (Cavalli-Sforza & Feldman 1981, pp. 355–6). In addition, the phenomenon has interesting implications for the origins and nature of archaeological 'cultures'.

Some of the implications of indirect bias are equally interesting. In this case, the fact that an individual is considered an appropriate model for some trait or traits has an effect on his/her attractiveness as a model with regard to other traits. Like frequency-dependent bias, this can be a sensible strategy for individuals to follow: imitating all the characteristics of individuals who appear to be locally successful can be a short-cut to a generally successful decision pattern. However, it is also a potential source of runaway effects not unlike those which seem to be relevant to sexual selection in animals:

> *If the average person prefers to accord high prestige to (and imitate the behaviour of) people with above average values of the indicator trait, the preferences can continue to evolve, dragging the indicator trait up another notch as well. In imitating the Joneses' new car purchase, we may also have acquired the Joneses' heightened sensitivity to cars as markers of status, doing our bit to feed the further evolution of the system. (Boyd & Richerson 1985, p. 287)*

Innovation and the Transmission Process

It is appropriate to consider innovation in the context of the transmission process because it never takes place in a vacuum, but in the context of a pre-existing culturally transmitted state of affairs, in which new cultural variety is created.

As we have seen, the logic of Boyd & Richerson's arguments is that it is continuity which is the norm, rather than radical change; this follows from the basic concept that culture can appropriately be seen as an inheritance system. Various factors act to change the pattern of what is transmitted over time, in terms of its relative frequency or prevalence, but the majority of these factors act on already existing variation; this is true of all the varieties of bias even though, as we have also seen, the force of indirect bias can potentially have runaway effects.

The two sources of new variation are random errors in transmission, analogous to genetic mutations, which it does not seem plausible to see as having a major influence on the innovation process in human societies, and what Boyd & Richerson call 'guided variation', which in effect means modification of what was transmitted as a result of direct interaction with the environment (meant in the widest possible sense), as opposed to following the existing cultural respertoire – trial-and-error learning in other words. Boyd & Richerson suggest that in most circumstances, at least once a system of cultural transmission has become established, this tends not to pay off, so the tendency will be in the first place not to innovate, and secondly for the innovation not to be adopted. The implication is that where innovation does occur it is at some level a conscious decision in response to a particular situation, in which the usual routine is suspended; its scale and significicance can, of course, vary from minor fashion change to major technological innovation. It also follows, since we are not dealing (for the most part) with random cultural mutations but with some level of conscious decision-making, that rates of both innovation and innovation adoption will be variable and respond to variation in social, economic, and environmental conditions.

This point leads on to the consideration of a more general theme, of interest to both the social and the evolutionary theorists: the relationship between small-scale and large-scale processes, and between individuals and populations:

Processes on an evolutionary time-scale affect contemporary behaviour because they determine the nature of the cultural traditions that characterise any society. On the other hand, to understand evolutionary processes we must understand the forces that act on an ecological time-scale to affect cultural variation as it is carried through time by a succession of individuals.

Boyd & Richerson illustrate their point by means of a very simple hypothetical example postulating two groups with independent histories, one with an agricultural subsistence base, the other a group of hunters and gatherers, moving into the same new ecological zone, which is well suited to pastoral nomadism. The possible reactions range from both groups immediately becoming nomadic pastoralists to them both retaining their earlier way of life, however adverse the circumstances. In fact, as they suggest, these two extreme options are both extremely unlikely; but even if they were likely it would be essential to explain whichever extreme occurred within a single framework, rather than adopting an 'ecological' framework to account for the first possibility and a 'historical' framework to account for the second. Within that single framework we would have to explain why an instant change in way of life occurred in the one case and why it did not in the other. Furthermore, the explanation would have to involve both the cultural inheritance and the decisions of individuals.

In reality, of course, there are likely to be different patterns of change with regard to different spheres of activity. Thus, subsistence techniques may change rapidly in the new context while social organization or basic cultural values may change much more slowly. In Giddens' terms 'cultural inheritance' corresponds closely to 'routinization', persisting in existing patterns and not exercising the available potential for choice. Indeed, the two terms rather complement one another, in the sense that Boyd & Richardson's 'cultural inheritance' has an explanatory background, outlined above, which is not present in Giddens, while the idea of routinization spells out clearly the implications of cultural inheritance in terms of everyday patterns of action. In general Boyd & Richerson, with their emphasis on transmission, have relatively little to say about action, which is presupposed rather than analysed. Giddens, on the other hand, as we have already noted, says very little about the transmission processes which are in fact vital to his framework, since without them he cannot achieve his aim of explaining how it is that societies persist across space and time. As we have suggested already, together the two processes provide a justification for the long-standing archaeological assumption that it is *change* and not stability which needs explaining, a justification more convincing than an appeal to what tend to be theoretically vacuous ideas of 'homeostasis'.

The rôle of individual choice, however, which may or may not be conscious, is clear in both perspectives. In Boyd & Richerson it corresponds to the so-called 'bias' factors and the process of 'guided variation' which affect the cultural inheritance of the next cultural generation, while in Giddens it is the exercise of agency and calculation in social transactions in specific contexts by individuals already formed in specific ways by their previous experience, along the kinds of lines described by Bourdieu.

Boyd & Richerson complete their hypothetical example as follows:

*both societies will acquire new traits by invention and diffusion over a period of several gener-
ations as new adaptations are developed. Some techniques and values will spread more rapidly
than others, and the rates will likely be different in the two societies . . . Historical differences
may lead the two societies to develop quite different adjustments to the new zone, particularly
if they compete . . . After many generations, each society will contain some traits that are recognisably related to those of its distant past, some that have developed and spread in the recent
past, some that are still developing and spreading, and some that have been borrowed from
other groups.*

*Cultural transmission leads to persistence of behavioural traits through time, but genera-
tion by generation, even day by day if our measurements were fine enough to detect it,
traditions are modified by accident, individual choices and natural selection. (Boyd & Richerson 1985, p. 291)*

With the exception of the reference to natural selection this is a formulation with
which Giddens would surely largely agree. In effect, it tells us that we cannot
prejudge the explanatory factors relevant to history, as such authors as Marvin
Harris would have us do: we will only arrive at them from a process of analysis of
the particular case. To some this may seem like commonsense, and indeed in the
very simple and summary form presented here it is little more, but it is not quite
that straightforward. The point is that it is grounded in a theoretical perspective
which explains why this approach is the valid one, and which provides a set of
mechanisms relevant to the understanding of particular situations. This does not
make history predictable in the way that the early New Archaeologists hoped
when they were attempting to develop general laws of culture process. An appropriate analogy is with the study of the history of biological evolution. Darwin
provided a mechanism explaining the processes operating in the production of the
sequence of forms recovered and studied by geologists and palaeontologists.
The knowledge of this mechanism does not permit the course of evolution to be
predicted because the number of possibilities present in what Dawkins (1986) calls
the 'genetic space' is simply colossal, but it does tell us about the way in which it
occurred.

However, it is necessary to note two points. From the archaeological point of
view the emphasis on seeing culture and behaviour in terms of traits and their
transmission has its dangers, in that it is precisely what Binford so cogently criticized in the early 1960s because it may, and in the past did, lead to a neglect of the
rôle of those traits in action. Secondly, the formulation as it stands does not recognize the significance of such phenomena as social institutions.

Failure to provide an adequate account of social institutions has already been
noted as a point of criticism against Giddens (Archer 1982, Thompson 1984) and is
clearly a danger in any individual-centred approach to social reality. Boyd &
Richerson respond to the problem in two ways. The first concerns the way in which
the individual and the group are linked together. Their definition of cultural evolution as referring to the changing content of knowledge, values and other factors
influencing behaviour which is transmitted from cultural generation to cultural

generation means that, like genetic evolution, it is a group phenomenon, in the sense that it is concerned with changing distributions of values of certain variables across a population, as a result of cultural transmission and factors affecting the decisions made by individuals in the light of their cultural inheritance (Boyd & Richerson's 'biasing factors' and Cavalli-Sforza & Feldman's 'cultural selection').

The question then arises of the level at which the factors operate which affect the distribution of values across the population; of course, in studies of the animal world the key concept recently has been that of individual-centred inclusive fitness (see e.g. Barash 1982). In the social sciences functionalists have argued for the level of group adaptation and methodological individualists for the individual level, on the basis of certain philosophical and methodological assumptions. What is required, however, and it presupposes a starting point at the individual level, is empirical and theoretical analysis to actually find out what is the case with regard to particular aspects of particular situations; once again, philosophy and assumptions cannot prejudge the outcome of actual work. Because cultural transmission creates heritable variation between individuals and between groups, different social processes can increase or decrease the frequency of some kinds (culturally defined) of individuals and groups through the force of selection. Boyd & Richerson demonstrate that the strength of selection at the group level as opposed to the individual level will depend on the relative amounts of culturally transmitted variation within and between groups, so that if, for example, a form of frequency-dependent bias is in operation which means that individuals tend to select the most common of the cultural variants available to them, then group-level selection may predominate. In this sense then, apart from the fact that the cultural evolution process operates at a population level anyway, as noted above, groups can have a reality and a significance distinct from the individual which is at the same time a product of individual decisions and behaviour; whether the outcome of the aggregated decisions corresponds to what the individuals want is, of course, another matter. (cf. Elster 1985).

This is only part of the answer, however, since it does not fully address the existence of so-called 'World 3' phenomena (Popper 1972), the products of human thought and action, including social institutions, which have a continuing existence beyond the lifespan of individuals and which are not entirely assimilable in a satisfactory fashion into concepts of structural principles and unacknowledged conditions of action, in Giddens' formulation, or into models of cultural transmission in the way outlined by Boyd & Richerson. The question is clearly more relevant in the case of societies with a greater degree of institutional differentiation.

Boyd & Richerson conceptualize the problem in a preliminary way as concerned with 'the transmissible environment':

> *Examples include the inheritance of money and artifacts of various kinds, especially the persistence of expensive capital facilities such as improved agricultural land, transportation infrastructure, and so forth . . . Information is not being directly transmitted to the next generation, but environmental modifications made by one generation do constrain [and, one might*

add, enable] the decisions, or condition the ordinary learning of the next. Thus, unlike ordinary environmental effects, they are endogenous to the evolving system of behaviour. (Boyd & Richerson 1985, pp. 295–6; item in parentheses my addition)

This, then, is an area which needs to be modelled in the future, and it is clearly of considerable relevance to archaeology, since material culture, and other products of human action, operate precisely as an endogenously generated transmissible environment in the way outlined above, channelling future decisions in particular directions and acting as a source of cultural transmission, in addition to, and conditioning, the imitation and teaching/learning processes which Boyd & Richerson largely discuss. Furthermore, from an historical perspective, the transmissible environment has clearly had a major effect on modes of transmission through time. This is most striking in the case of literacy (e.g. Goody 1977; cf. Harre 1979, p. 374).

Ideas based on a selectionist perspective have been current in certain areas of the social sciences for some time. Models of technical change within economics, for example, have used the idea of selection, taking Darwinian natural selection as an analogy and noting areas of positive and negative analogy (Elster 1983, Ch. 6). At the general level with which this paper is concerned, however, the most fully developed Darwinian view is Harre's (1979) mutation-selection theory, which in many ways runs parallel with what has been outlined here. Like Elster (1985), Boyd & Richerson, and Giddens, Harre is concerned to establish a satisfactory link between micro-scale action and macro-scale social properties. For social change to occur small-scale changes must spread through populations and a Darwinian perspective provides an appropriate way of viewing this:

Populational theories depend on the separation of the mutation-conditions . . . and selection conditions . . . Let us call the general conceptual system of which particular Darwinian theories of the change of particular species are instantiations, the M/S [mutation/selection] dynamics . . . Even in biological applications the M/S conceptual system is not an axiomatic super-theory from which, as intermediate-level deductive consequences, explanations of particular changes flow. Rather, the propositions and iconic models of the Darwinian 'theory' serve to define the system of concepts and acceptable modes of explanation that will be used in different particular forms and in different concrete applications in the construction of explanations of particular changes . . . In considering the legitimacy of borrowings from it, it will be necessary to discriminate amongst the various M/S conceptual systems to identify a model source precisely enough to examine its viability as a basis for the construction of concepts. (Harre 1979, pp. 352–3)

Harre sees two main reasons for adopting such an approach: first it provides a basis for explaining the way in which different aspects of social and economic activity are linked to one another, without invoking a teleology. In the absence of some kind of theory to explain these links, Harre suggests, 'it seems insuperably difficult to explain the tendency that many changes seem to have towards social practices that are more adaptive to the conditions in which they have come to flourish than those they have displaced' (1979, p. 353).

The second reason is that this view provides a basis for conceptualizing the rôle of the properties of large-scale collectives of people: they can be seen as a selection environment which 'can be taken to have differential effects on different innovatory social practices effective in a Darwinian fashion, augmenting or diminishing the population of such practices in the next time-phase of that society' (1979, p. 353).

Many of the issues he raised there are also covered in a rather different form by Boyd & Richerson and have therefore already been discussed. However, it is worth drawing attention to a number of points that he makes in the course of his outline which helpfully amplify the argument that this chapter is seeking to make, since they relate closely to the concerns of the other authors who have been discussed.

What Boyd & Richerson, Cavalli-Sforza & Feldman, and others are offering is not merely an analogy with Darwinian theory but a series of hypotheses about the actual nature of cultural transmission and the selective and biasing factors acting upon it. The insight that cultural transmission is, in certain respects, like genetic transmission is only a starting point. Furthermore, as emphasized already, their hypotheses do not involve biological reductionism but actually exhibit parallel features, and share a similar view of human capacities of agency, with positions such as those of Giddens or Bourdieu.

Harre shares the concern to specify the mechanisms relevant to social and cultural, as opposed to biological, change. In the biological case mutation and selection conditions are totally independent of one another, in a strict Darwinian fashion, but in the social case there can be some degree of linkage between the two, in other works a Lamarckian element. Furthermore, the strength of this link will be variable with regard to different aspects of social practice in different cases, and depending on the nature of the transmission process, for example whether written records are involved.

Harre, too, is aware of the importance of the transmission process for a mutation-selection model of the kind he is advocating, although on the basis of the discussion of 'theories of practice' above one might argue with his precise formulation:

> the social practices of one generation are conceived not to generate the social practices of the next directly. There must be a replicator node. In socio-evolution this would be the replication of the rules held to by one generation or by the same generation at different times. New practices would be produced by the following of a new rule. In effect this condition on socio-evolution is equivalent to the condition that social change must involve a social psychological theory, involving the changing competences of the individual members of the collective. (1979, p. 372)

As Harre says, this consequence is very welcome and again links up with points made earlier in this chapter, as well as with the general emphasis on the indispensability of the individual.

In summary, social action and cultural transmission do not belong in separate spheres, as Ingold (1986) would have us believe. Indeed, a linkage between them of the type sketched out on the basis of the authors examined here is essential for the development of an adequate social theory and for the explanation of cultural change, including the rôle of innovation within it.

Conclusion

The demise of the functionalist-adaptationist position does not leave prehistorians bereft of a convincing theoretical position, condemned to an unsatisfactory cultural relativism. The attacks which have led to its demise are in fact the key to further progress. From the side of the social sciences has come an emphasis on human agency and intentionality (which may be at the practical or the discursive level), on conflict and contradiction, on meaning in material culture, and on the importance of history. The Darwinian evolutionary perspective has produced a parallel emphasis on the importance of the individual, including a rôle for individual intentionality, a distinction between cultural and genetic transmission, and a detailed analysis of the properties of cultural transmission and of the various processes which act upon it. It has been suggested that a Darwinian approach to human societies and cultures need not, and indeed must not, be reductionist, and that history has a vital rôle in the understanding of particular situations.

As far as prehistory and archaeology are concerned, the synthesis of the two approaches has a number of specific implications, some of which have been outlined. Its potential fruitfulness at the level of generating hypotheses about the evolution of human culture should be obvious. However, it also provides a potentially powerful theoretical background for the dynamic studies of diffusion and emulation which are increasingly coming to complement the rather static processual analyses of social and economic relations which have dominated the prehistory of the past 20 years.

The key point of the Neo-Darwinian evolutionary approach to culture is not that it is biological, which, as we have seen, it is not. Rather, from a biological inspiration it postulates mechanisms and processes that are central to the generation of change and the maintenance of stability (cf. Harre 1979). In the synthesis with recent social science interests, which has been outlined here, there exists the potential for a productive complementary relationship between the two.

Acknowledgements

I would like to thank Clive Gamble, James Steele, Peter Ucko, Todd Whitelaw, and Alison Wylie for their comments on a previous version of this chapter. Needless to say, I am responsible for the inadequacies that remain.

References

Archer, M.S. 1982. Morphogenesis versus structuration: on combining structure and action. *British Journal of Sociology* 33, 455–83.
Barash, D. 1982. *Sociobiology and behaviour*, 2nd edn. London: Heinemann.

Binford, L. 1962. Archaeology as anthropology. *American Antiquity* 28, 217–25.

Binford, L. 1964. A consideration of archaeological research design. *American Antiquity* 29, 425–41.

Bourdieu, P. 1977. *Outline of a theory of practice*. Cambridge: Cambridge University Press.

Boyd, R. & P.J. Richerson. 1985. *Culture and the evolutionary process*. Chicago: University of Chicago Press.

Braithwaite, M. 1982. Decoration as ritual symbol: a theoretical proposal and an ethnographic study in southern Sudan. In *Symbolic and structural archaeology*, I. Hodder (ed.), 80–89. Cambridge: Cambridge University Press.

Cannon, A.D. 1987. Socioeconomic change and material culture diversity: nineteenth century grave monuments in rural Cambridgeshire. Unpublished PhD dissertation. University of Cambridge.

Carrithers, M., S. Collin & S. Lukes (eds) 1985. *The category of the person*. Cambridge: Cambridge University Press.

Cavalli-Sforza, L.L. 1986. Cultural evolution. *American Zoologist* 26, 845–55.

Cavalli-Sforza, L.L. & M.W. Feldman 1981. *Cultural transmission and evolution: a quantitative approach*. Princeton: Princeton University Press.

Dawkins, R. 1986. *The blind watchmaker*. London: Longman.

Elster, J. 1983. *Explaining technical change*. Cambridge: Cambridge University Press.

Elster, J. 1985. *Making sense of Marx*. Cambridge: Cambridge University Press.

Giddens, A. 1979. *Central problems in social theory*. London: Macmillan.

Giddens, A. 1984. *The constitution of society*. Cambridge: Polity Press.

Goody, J. 1977. *The domestication of the savage mind*. Cambridge: Cambridge University Press.

Goody, J. 1980. Thought and writing. In *Soviet and Western anthropology*, E. Gellner (ed.), 119–133. London: Duckworth.

Harre, R. 1979. *Social being*. Oxford: Basil Blackwell.

Hodder, I. 1982. Theoretical archaeology: a reactionary view. In *Symbolic and structural archaeology*, I. Hodder (ed.), 1-16. Cambridge: Cambridge University Press.

Hodder, I. 1986. *Reading the past*. Cambridge: Cambridge University Press.

Ingold, T. 1986. *Evolution and social life*. Cambridge: Cambridge University Press.

Miller, D. 1982. Structures and strategies: an aspect of the relationship between social hierarchy and cultural change. In *Symbolic and structural archaeology*, I. Hodder, (ed.), 89–98. Cambridge: Cambridge University Press.

Miller, D. & C. Tilley 1984. Ideology, power and prehistory: an introduction. In *Ideology, power and prehistory*, D. Miller & C. Tilley (eds.), 1–15. Cambridge: Cambridge University Press.

Moore, H.L. 1982. The interpretation of spatial patterning in settlement residues. In *Symbolic and structural archaeology*, I. Hodder (ed.), 4–79. Cambridge: Cambridge University Press.

Popper, K.R. 1972. *Objective knowledge*. Oxford: Clarendon Press.

Renfrew, A.C. & J.F. Cherry (eds) 1986. *Peer polity interaction and sociopolitical change*. Cambridge: Cambridge University Press.

Shanks, M. & C. Tilley 1982. Ideology, symbolic power, and ritual communication: a reinterpretation of Neolithic mortuary practices. In *Symbolic and structural archaeology*, I. Hodder (ed.), 129–54. Cambridge: Cambridge University Press.

Shanks, M. & C. Tilley 1987. *Re-constructing archaeology*. Cambridge: Cambridge University Press.

Shennan, S.J. (ed.) 1989. *Archaeological approaches to cultural identity*. London: Unwin Hyman.

Thompson, J.B. 1984. *Studies in the theory of ideology*. Cambridge: Polity Press.

Veblen, T. 1899. *The theory of the leisure class*. New York: Macmillan.

Part V

Meaning and Practice

Material Symbols

The so-called "linguistic turn" in the social sciences has thrown into sharp relief many of our modernist assumptions about how we give meaning to the world. This movement can be traced in part to the emergence of poststructuralism in the late 1960s, through the writings of the French scholars Michel Foucault, Roland Barthes, Jacques Derrida and Paul Ricoeur. Poststructuralism developed out of a critique of structuralism which was itself based upon Fernand Saussure's analysis of language. Many of the aspects of this critique concern the space between an abstract language and a particular concrete text written in that language.

Within structuralism a sign obtains its meaning by its position within an abstract and internally structured system of codes of presences and absences, similarities and differences. The sign itself is composed of two parts, a signifier (symbol) and a signified (concept). As Saussure (1960) put it, "a linguistic system is a series of different sounds combined with a series of differences of ideas." Poststructuralism has questioned the stability of the signification process. It shows that the sign is not a coherent entity, but rather a temporary association between two different sliding systems. The meaning of a signifier comes about as a result of that signifier's position within a structured set of similarities and differences. Thus culture might be opposed to nature (see Part II). But in order to understand what is meant by "nature" we might have to refer to other ideas and concepts, such as "wild", "outside," "untamed". Thus the meaning of a signifier begins to slip away, always depending on other terms, which have to be defined in relation to other terms in an endless sequence. Meaning is thus entirely relational. It depends, not on a stable structured set, but on some arbitrary closure of meaning within what is a highly unstable process. Meanings are thus always provisional and local, they can always be reread and reinterpreted.

Poststructuralism has also challenged the authority of the text. It argues that the search for ultimate meaning is futile because the author's intentions constitute only one among many different meanings. In archaeology, Hodder (1986) has proposed "reading" the archaeological record as text. This is not, however, a simple matter of transferring the familiar literary practice to archaeology since there are a number of important differences between material culture and linguistic meanings

(Hodder 1989). Material-culture meanings are often more practical and less imme-diately concerned with abstract meaning, and these meanings are often non-discursive and subconscious. Material-culture meanings are multiply coded and multidimensional while linguistic meanings are singly coded and linear, which implies that material culture is more ambiguous than language. Material symbols possess a durability unlike the spoken word, which means that control of symbols is an effective social strategy in the control of meaning. Thus material-culture meanings are less logical and more immediate, use-bound and contextual than linguistic meanings.

The very attempt to define "meaning" in archaeology might seem presumptuous and even misguided in the absence of informants. However, archaeology has always addressed meaning, if only in the attribution of function to material culture. Given the increasing interest in symbolism and style in archaeology, the issue of meaning cannot be avoided. It will become clear in this section that all aspects of material culture have their symbolic components. Thus the issue of symbolic meaning can no longer be ignored in the discipline. With regard to breaking out of a self-fulfilling and arbitrary definition of meaning, we will see that the conundrum of defining the "meaning of meaning" raises acutely the issue of the relationship between "our" and "their" meanings. Attempts to define the "meaning of meaning" lead some to argue that the construction of meaning is always a social practice. According to this view there can be no non-social, ahistorical definition of "meaning". This section addresses the issue of meaning and explains why mean-ings have increasingly come to be interpreted through practices.

Function as Meaning

It is commonplace in processual archaeology to oppose function and meaning (often in terms of function versus style, or function versus symbol). Thus certain attributes of artifacts are isolated as pertaining to practical, utilitarian activities. The paste and temper used in making a pot have an effect on the shape of the pot, how it can be used and so on. The retouch on the edge of a flint blade may be related to the blade's use as a scraper. These functional attributes are seen as distinct from the secondary meanings people might attribute to the pot or scraper – for example, whether the artifacts symbolize a particular social group. The separation of func-tion and meaning tends to support a wider set of dichotomies between materials, adaptation, and objective science on the one hand, and symbolism, history and interpretive approaches on the other.

In colloquial terms, that the edge of a stone tool is shaped in order to carry out some function is part of its meaning. It may be more helpful, therefore, to start by considering function as a type of meaning, and to distinguish between types of functional meaning. For example, we can identify the utilitarian and social func-tions of artifacts. This is equivalent to distinguishing the lower and upper rungs of Hawke's (1954) "ladder of inference." By utilitarian functions we refer to the use of an artifact in exchanges of matter and energy – the use of an axe in cutting down a tree, the use of a pen in writing. By social functions we mean the use of an arti-fact in exchanges of information – the use of an artifact to symbolize a social position or to legitimate positions of authority.

In fact, however, it has proved increasingly difficult to keep these functions, the different rungs of the ladder, separate. This merging of utilitarian and social func-tions is particularly clear in recent work on technology (e.g. Lemonnier 1986). Technological activities prove to be socially constituted in that all aspects of tech-nologies, from craft specialization to the details of the "chaines opératoires" used in flint knapping, are embedded in a seamless material and social web (Latour 1988). It might be argued that at the macroscale, prehistoric technologies are best studied in relation to long-term adaptive demands, the availability of raw mate-rials, and so on. But even over the long term, Lechtman (1984) has shown that technologies can only be fully understood as embedded in an ideological web. At the microscale, it is undoubtedly the case that technologies are enacted in specific times and places. They involve social interactions, gendered relations, and so on. Thus Dobres (1995) has argued that Upper Palaeolithic bone and antler technolo-gies vary considerably between sites, and that this variability must be partly understood in terms of the ways in which technical skills were negotiated as part of the jockeying for social position and recognition.

In processual archaeology the social functions of artifacts are understood largely in terms of information exchange and the symbolic expression of identities. Some examples of this approach are provided in the chapters by Earle (**chapter 6**) and Renfrew (**chapter 4**). An important early statement of this approach was provided by Wobst (1977). He argued that systematic relations could be identified between the amount of information exchange and the adaptive strategies of social groups. Thus, for example, larger groups needed more information exchange and would thus have more symbolic elaboration or style. Similar approaches were developed by Wiessner (1983, 1984) in terms of the emblems of social groups and the assertion of individual identities. But since these approaches allowed that artifacts would be used by ethnic groups to express social and cultural distinctiveness, they did not differ radically from culture-historical attempts to equate "cultures" with "peoples" (Childe 1951). While they provided a more systematic basis for such arguments within a cross-cultural and adaptive framework, they still remained normative. Thus they assumed that the symbols would have common and un-ambiguous meanings within social groups. Sackett (1986) has pointed out that not all group symbols are iconological, in the sense that they are not all used consciously to express group affiliation. Many are arbitrary historical choices, part of a local tradition – "just the way things are done." Here the normativity within a common way of doing things is yet more marked.

The Marxist view of the social function of artifacts is rather different. Rather than symbols being normative, they are seen as the site of conflict between social groups within society. In classical Marxist terms, the symbols function ideologically to represent or misrepresent the interests of dominant groups (e.g. Leone 1984). In these approaches symbols are used as part of repressive social strategies; they support "power over" (see Part IV). But following Foucault, many archaeologists now accept that even subordinate groups use symbols to represent or misrepresent their own interests – that ideologies are a pervasive aspect of social life and that the manipulation of symbolic knowledge is an integral part of the power to achieve all social ends (e.g. McGuire and Paynter 1991; Miller, Rowlands, and Tilley 1989; Miller and Tilley 1984). Such approaches, as seen in Western neo-Marxist writings such as that of McGuire (1992), move beyond a simple functional view. Meaning and symbol are not just passively assisting groups but are actively involved and creatively negotiated in the formation of social strategies. They have to be understood as involved in daily practices.

More generally, Marxist contributions to the debate about meaning emphasize that meaning is not "free" – things cannot just mean anything we might want them to. Meanings are embedded in relations of power and enacted in discourse. The notion of "discourse" draws attention to the situated character of communication (Shanks and Tilley 1987). Not all people can say things, or say things with the same force. It requires control of resources to gain a particular form of education, to read certain books, and to understand certain cultural messages. This point is even more forcefully made in relation to material-culture symbols. Use of a prestige object in order to symbolize or to constitute positions of authority depends on control of exchange routes, control of raw materials, and of labor in order to gain access to those prestige objects. This idea is the basis for the structural-Marxist "prestige-goods model" which has had such widespread impact in European prehistory and elsewhere (see Part III). The study of prestige-goods systems has concentrated on access to the exchange systems and has paid scant attention to the meanings of the prestige goods themselves (see Sørensen 1987). Indeed, approaches which focus on the conditions within which objects have meaning can be contrasted to structuralist, hermeneutic, and poststructuralist approaches, which focus on how things have meaning within the constraints set by material forces.

Meaning as Structure

The main limitation of the functional view of meaning is that it ignores the fact that signs and symbols themselves are patterned and that this patterning reflects a grammar or code or structure. We might assume that a symbol has the meaning "high prestige" because it is made of material that is scarce or because it occurs in rich burials. But knowing the utilitarian and social functions of an artifact does not ensure that we will understand its specific meanings. Why is the symbol of a particular shape? Why was this design chosen? Why was that rim form chosen? Specific questions of this type often demand a move beyond function to the rules which lie behind the choice of particular words or motifs. In language we are used to the idea of a grammatical code (Hodder 1989). It can be argued that material culture is "language-like" in that it too is organized by codes. For example, in choosing which tie or skirt to wear we consider color combinations with other items of clothing we are wearing – we choose that which "fits" according to some code.

Structuralist archaeology has come a long way since the pioneering attempts of Leroi-Gourhan (1965). Derived from the structural linguistics of Saussure, structuralism is most frequently associated with the work of the anthropologist Lévi-Strauss (1963). In its initial form it was associated with the search for universals in underlying binary opposites (such as culture/nature, male/female, public/private) and with analyses which lacked a historical or dynamic context. But in archaeology a historical dimension was soon added (e.g. Deetz 1977). Most structuralist analysis in archaeology nowadays tries to situate symbolic codes (including but not confined to binary opposites) within social and historical contexts. A clear example of this approach is provided in the chapter by Yentsch (**chapter 12**).

Yentsch argues that a culture/nature opposition underlying ceramic manufacture and use was part of the negotiation of social inequality in early-historic North America. Her interpretation of the meaning of white-toned and earth-toned vessels is built up from associations and contrasts in the placing of ceramics in male and female, public and private parts of houses. Parallels are also drawn between changes through time in ceramic assemblages and changes in the use of space. Links are also made to variation in the use of spices, in the complexity of recipes, and in the proliferation of knives, forks and spoons. These similarities and differences in apparently disconnected spheres are made sense of in terms of structures. For example, nothing obviously links the use of natural building materials to a lack of separation in the use of ceramics and in the use of space. But such a link is made possible by the abstraction of "organic solidarity". Yentsch uses the abstractions culture/nature and public/private to draw out the similarities in her covarying data. She goes on to argue that these abstractions were used as metaphors in the creation of inequality.

One criticism of structuralist analyses is that they too easily assume universal binary oppositions. Thus there has been much criticism of the idea that women are linked universally to nature and to the private (see Part VI). For this reason most analysts who use abstract binary oppositions as a provisional methodological tool in their work try to situate the general terms within the particular historical context being considered. Women often act in public and may act as "culturers" in many contexts, and the very terms culture, nature, public, private may be given different meanings or not even exist within different historical schemes. Certainly indigenous writers such as Mamani Condori (**chapter 24**) argue that meanings have to be understood as radically different, and that the internal view is relevant.

But the structuralist analysis of material-culture meanings has other limitations as well. These limitations include the separation of abstractions such as culture/nature from practical activities, social functions and social agency. Individuals seem caught in some abstract code which is little responsive to changing conditions of meaning. As a result of these failings, while structuralism is widely used as a stage in the analysis of symbolic meaning it is often allied with some form of social analysis of particular historical contexts, including the analysis of changing power relations through time as is the case with Yentsch's focus on gender ideologies (see the discussion of power and politics in Parts III and IV). We do not have to assume that the codes are "in the mind". Rather, they are "in society" and are subject to material and social constraint.

A more general problem with the idea of code, and material culture as language, is that much material-culture meaning does not work in a language-like way (Hodder 1989). In language the relation between the signifier and signified is nearly always arbitrary. There is nothing necessary about the relation between the signifier "tree" and the signified concept of tree. But if the tree itself is taken as a signifier of, for example, a "Nature Conservancy" group, or a "Save This Planet" movement, the relation between signifier and signified is no longer wholly arbitrary – it is iconically or materially motivated. Unlike language, nearly all material symbols have some non-arbitrary connection with that which they denote. As a result, it becomes increasingly difficult to separate structure from material and social relations, to separate structural from functional meaning. Material culture is thus coded in more complex ways than is language.

Whether one takes the view that structures are in the mind or in society, it is widely recognized, particularly in relation to material practices, that they are often not discursively conscious. If people are asked to explain why they are making a pot in a certain way, most people will often be unable to explain their actions and choices. This is because we are generally unaware of the unconscious reasons which contribute to our behavioural choices. We may know that something "works" for us, without knowing why it does. Thus the interpretation of symbolic meaning is not necessarily concerned with the discerning of conscious intentions; it is more concerned with non-discursive knowledge about "how to go on" in the world (Giddens 1979), and with the unconscious and social and material construction of that knowledge.

Meanings in Context

The structuralist method thus involves the search for patterned similarities and differences in the data. Associations and oppositions are explored in order to build up an account of the codes in use, and these codes are then understood as working, often non-discursively, within an active social context. But this procedure, by itself, is insufficient to complete our understanding of the various types of meaning. One of the problems which remains is that knowing the code does not ensure that we know what a sign or symbol means – there still seems to be a gap of understanding. As a linguistic example we can take the phrase "I love you". We could get the meaning of such a phrase by looking up the words in a dictionary and by learning English grammar. But this would not equip us to understand when it is used ironically – when it really means "I hate you". In fact such a phrase can be used in an endless variety of ways which no dictionary or grammar could hope to encompass. In order to understand these variations of meaning, including the use of irony, we need to understand what is going on locally. Thus we might understand the irony of "I love you" by knowing that in the particular case two people do not love each other, and that the phrase is said in order to show anger or to be dismissive.

The two main dimensions of symbolic meaning are thus (1) the structured sets of similarities and differences, and (2) context. While the first is normative, the second is situated and contingent. While there is continual interchange between the two, leading to dynamic processual change, there is a methodological need to separate them during analysis – and this separation is found even in the most radical postprocessual studies (e.g. contributors to Tilley 1993). But the consideration of context necessitates a shift from a structuralist to a hermeneutic understanding. This is because, as the "I love you" example shows, it is not enough simply to place the coded message within a social context. What is needed in order to understand the irony of the phrase is to interpret the intentions of the speaker within a specific social setting. The irony of "I love you" is only understandable in terms of the intention to anger or put down.

Hermeneutic interpretation incorporates the analysis of codes worked out in active social contexts, but it argues that codes and social action have to be understood within the whole of a local context. The meaning of a part can only be fully understood, not by separating it from its whole, but by integrating it with that whole. An essential part of the whole is what people intended, either discursively or non-discursively, when they did things. A hermeneutic approach argues not only that we should, but that we have to, get at what things meant to "them" in the past.

But if local meanings are to be derived from contextual analyses, how are the inferences to be made? A widespread assumption is that symbolic meanings are recoverable in so far as they have an impact on the material world. Thus, Renfrew (1994) argues that social and symbolic knowledge has an impact on material actions. Those actions are thus patterned in repeated ways by symbolic rules. The rules can therefore be inferred and "tested" against the repeated patterning in the artifact remains. The examples given by Flannery and Marcus (**chapter 14**) of the impact of cosmologies and religions on use of the landscape and trade patterns make this point well. A hermeneutic interpretation uses the same materialist starting point.

Hermeneutic interpretation also generally assumes, in common with structuralist analysis, that local meanings are built up from similarities (associations) and differences (oppositions) (Hodder 1992; Tilley 1991). It is a universal characteristic of all languages and material-symbol systems that meaning is closely related to similarity and difference in form, context, function etc. The point made in the preceding paragraph implies that the patterned similarities and differences in the material world are systematically related to meaning systems. The symbolic meanings are "objectified" or "materialized" in "real" similarities and differences in hard data. They are also "actualized" in social contexts. But the interpretive problem which remains is that of moving beyond the symbolic and social codes and norms. What contextual meanings were given?

The hermeneutic move involves scrutinizing the elements which are grouped by their material similarities (or differences) in order to identify general themes which tie them together at a more abstract level. The data are made to "cohere" by positing some idea or abstraction which "makes sense" of disparate findings. In other words a "whole" is hypothesized that includes the meanings which would have made sense to the actors involved. The hypothetical whole is "tested" or "fitted" by seeing whether it makes sense of the way in which people acted – their observable material behaviour. These abstractions or "wholes" are evaluated in order to see whether they "make sense" in terms of social function, ecological adaptation and so on. The more different types of data that can be made similar, or to cohere within an interpretation, the more plausible the interpretation becomes.

Hermeneutic strands can be found in many, if not most, interpretations of past symbolism. We can take the example of Linares's iconographic analysis of Panamanian art discussed by Flannery and Marcus (**chapter 13**). She recognized that the animals used in the art were similar in that aggressive species had been selected. The abstraction "aggression" or "predation" made sense of the animals grouped in the art and made them similar, and different from those not depicted, which were (another abstract grouping) prey species and animals with soft body parts. Barrett's (**chapter 15**) methodology appears to be similar. He observes a series of activities which occur in the British Neolithic around the tombs and which are organized by familiar oppositions such as front/back. The activities are similar to each other (and different from the Bronze Age examples) in that they are to do with more than burial. Barrett therefore suggests the abstraction "ancestors" as a theme which makes coherent the activities around the Neolithic tombs.

A more self-conscious use of hermeneutic principles is provided in **chapter 14** by Shanks. His text starts with an individual Greek *aryballos* pot and follows lines of reference and association in a cycle of interpretation. He shows that the scenes on the pots predominantly concern males, contests and hunting and he builds up steadily a set of statistical associations and oppositions. An abstraction is then identified which makes coherent the patterning observed. Shanks identifies the idea of risk as the common thread that links the parts together into a whole. This is not risk in the sense of optimal foraging behaviour (Part II), but rather a social risk to be enhanced and overcome as part of a particular competitive male elite. The ideology of risk links together not only the motifs used on the pots (males, the symposium, weapons, hunting, fighting, violent monsters) but also associated practices such as the making of pottery, using perfume oil, and drinking from the cup. Abstractions of this type allow a structuralist set of oppositions to be proposed, but this is only a stage in the analysis of social strategies. The idea of risk is an abstraction, but it aims to tell us about "their" meanings and intentions. These meanings are shown to make sense in terms of a highly competitive aristocratic life style. This is a life style and an ideology that not everyone would have shared. The "whole" is only a segment of society – in this case elite males. It is only such males who go through the bodily entraining and who participate in the practices of risk.

Both hermeneutic and poststructuralist approaches lead to a radical concern with the relationship between past and present. In hermeneutics, the dependence on the part–whole relationship implies that the whole needs to be known before the parts can be interpreted. But the whole can only be known from an understanding of the parts. This conundrum can be resolved, as noted above, by positing a "whole" that acts as a schema, which is fitted to or tested against the data. But the data themselves are always initially understood within a prior "whole", which is the set of assumptions that the analyst brings to the data. The task is the gradual fusion of past and present "wholes" or horizons (for applied examples, see Hodder 1990, 1992). But the reconstructed "whole" will always include the present – so different presents will always construct different pasts – indeed, the past is integrally part of the present, however much we might try to separate them.

An awareness of the situated and multiple character of meaning requires self-reflexivity. In our case this must imply a skepticism even to the idea of defining "meaning" in some general and overarching way. As noted at the outset, the very term "the meaning of meaning" draws attention to the arbitrary and self-referential nature of the task. The point has been well made by Bloch (1995). We take it for granted that we know what we mean by meaning and that any such discussion involves getting at essentials and universals. And yet, as Bloch shows, in French there is no equivalent to the English verb "to mean." As for the Zafimaniry being discussed by Bloch, one can ask a range of questions about meaning in Malagasy. These include questions rather like "what is the point of that?", or "what is the root cause of this?", or "what are those pictures of?", or "what are you doing?" None of these questions really conveys what either the French or English terms to do with meaning convey. Our own account of meaning has itself to be seen as situated.

Such discussion must lead to a skepticism about the hermeneutic idea of getting at "their" meaning – the meanings given by people to things in the past. Archaeologists often make a distinction between emic and etic; the former term describes the internal understanding of behaviour, the latter the external, objective account in the analyst's terms. The poststructuralist account not only undermines any notion that we can get at the original emic meanings. It also undermines any attempt to distinguish emic and etic. According to Derrida, there is "nothing outside the text." By this is meant that our very consciousness of ourselves derives from language, which is always already given. We come to our understanding of ourselves through a linguistic system of differences which is socially constructed. The self is defined through language – there is no originary, centered self. Thus, in a sense, there is no "emic," only various forms of "etic," linguistically constructed from a wide variety of different perspectives, both past and present. We can only ever understand the past in our own terms.

Recently two different approaches have emerged which claim to get at aspects of past meaning while avoiding attempts to reconstruct meanings in "their" heads. These are cognitive processual archaeology and the archaeology of the body and practice, one comes from developments in processual archaeology while the other comes from developments in postprocessual, interpretive archaeology.

Cognitive Processual Archaeology

Cognitive processual archaeology has been described as the next "new synthesis" for archaeology, which transcends the limitations of the standard processual approach (Renfrew and Bahn 1991; Renfrew and Zubrow 1994). It represents a considered response to the radical critique while claiming roots in the processual tradition. The main tenets of the approach include a desire to incorporate information about the cognitive and symbolic aspects of early societies, a recognition of the active role of ideology, an acknowledgment of the constitutive potential of material culture, and an interest in internal conflict as a significant force in cultural change. In terms of epistemology, cognitive processual archaeology seeks to revitalize historical explanation and adopt a modified form of positivism that acknowledges that theory and data mutually interact with one another.

The embrace of the term "cognitive" by cognitive processual archaeology is itself of importance. In other disciplines, such as cognitive anthropology and cognitive psychology, a cognitive approach is associated with the computational and mathematical analysis of decision-making, formal structures and generative schemes. In processual archaeology, cognition is associated with the study of ideology and belief systems, broadly defined. This focus emerged cautiously due to the empiricist base of processualism. We can trace an interest in symbolic meanings as expressed by systems of weights and notation (Renfrew 1982), to the study of religion (Renfrew 1985), to the analysis of the development of human cognitive abilities (Mithen 1994). The main problem faced by processual archaeology was how to deal with the contextuality of meaning. If meanings are local and historical and contingent, how can we understand them? Two solutions are suggested by cognitive processual archaeology. The first seeks to identify aspects of meaning and mind which are universal. The second links an understanding of symbolic meaning to historical contexts where ethnohistorical texts allow insight into people's thoughts.

Renfrew's (1985) study of cult is an example of this first approach. He attempts to apply a "scientific," hypothesis-testing approach to ritual and cult. His methodology involves compiling a series of cross-cultural indicators of shrines which include such things as attention-focusing devices, boundary markers between the sacred and profane, images of the divine, and evidence for offerings. But just how are we to recognize these indicators in the archaeological record? To assert that a bench focused the attention of those in a building assumes that "we" can experience a building as "they" did. We cannot "test" the cult hypothesis against objective data, because in order to do so we have to interpret what the bench, the image, the gestures and so on meant in each context. A bench may mean one thing in a kiva and quite another in a temple. This essentialist approach severely limits the variability within the archaeological record and illustrates one of the problems faced by cognitive archaeology in trying to retain positivism while exploring the meaning of symbols.

An example of the second approach is Flannery and Marcus's (**chapter 13**) study, which emphasizes the importance of ideational aspects of life and insists that a rigid materialism must be rejected. In their early work they saw societies adapting to their environments through ideational schemes. In their more recent work they acknowledge that cosmologies, religions etc. have an impact on the way the landscape is used (cf. Hastorf and Johannessen, **chapter 2**) and the way trade is organized. But, as already noted, recognition of the importance of symbolism and meaning creates a quandary for processual archaeologists. How can rigor and scientific analysis be protected from the danger of wandering off into fiction – Flannery and Marcus's "bungee jump into the Land of Fantasy"? How can one deal with the arbitrary nature of the sign or the contextuality of meaning? Flannery and Marcus respond by saying that the cognitive should be seen as only one of many subsystems, and that cosmologies and religions can only be constructed where there is historical data.

But this desire to return archaeology to its role as the "handmaiden of history" raises its own problems. For example, it unnecessarily restricts the possibilities of understanding the deep past in terms of symbolism and meaning. And is the retreat into historical particularism really what is intended? In the end, Flannery and Marcus describe what is very close to a hermeneutic position. They argue for a contextual analysis of ritual paraphernalia, but more generally they suggest that a specific understanding of specific contexts is required, and that the richer the data, including historical data, the more the analyst is able to get at "their" meanings. While they provide no theoretical basis for privileging texts (texts are, after all, just another form of material culture), they clearly feel that texts allow something of an insider's view. As historical archaeologists have demonstrated such a perspective is undermined by the fact that there are many viewpoints in society and historical texts typically give only a few of these views (McGuire and Paynter 1991).

An Archaeology of Practice and the Body

We have seen that cultural meanings are often understood in terms of practice at the level of non-discursive knowledge about "how to go on." We know a particular social act works even if we do not know why. Or we may not know much about art but we know what we like when we see it. Shanks (**chapter 14**) has suggested that an ideology of risk is part of the bodily experience of elite Archaic Greek males. It is in the body and through the regulated practices of the body taking risks that a whole social code of ethics and conduct is reproduced. Bourdieu (1977) has been widely used by archaeologists because he demonstrated that how we move around the space within houses can be the medium for inculcating a wide range of cultural knowledge about status, gender relations and the like. In other words, we learn cultural rules and norms in the movements of our body.

This emphasis on practice is an important development going beyond studies of cultural meaning found in culture historical and processual archaeology. In both the latter approaches, what cultural symbols meant to people in the past was assumed to be non-problematic. Indeed, in processual archaeology the purpose of material symbols was the communication of information amongst all members of a cultural group – the information was thus shared normatively. More recently, the various approaches termed postprocessual (Hodder 1985) have adopted a more fragmented and contextual view of cultural meanings – material culture is meaningfully constituted by individuals and groups in their relations with each other. Ironically this non-normative view of cultural meanings was explicitly noted by Binford (1965) when he observed that culture was participated in differentially. Indeed, the whole of processual archaeology was set up in contrast to the normative assumptions of the culture historical school. Unfortunately, the implications of this were never pursued and the differential participation in culture was reduced to functional variation. The radical view that culture is a process rather than a series of rules or norms was never explored. An emphasis on practice is in effect an emphasis on process – cultural meanings are seen as being worked out from day to day in the contingent interactions between agents.

An example of this commitment to practice is provided by Barrett (**chapter 15**). Here landscape and architecture are explored in terms of the activities and movements of people. From a description of these practices, a difference is suggested between ancestral and burial sites. The non-normative emphasis is clear in that cultural rules are continually being worked out in practice, in bodily movements. This insight has also been used to understand the social implications of sites and landscapes (see the contributors to Tilley 1993). The layout of stone circles, avenues, monuments is studied not in terms of a two-dimensional map or plan, but in terms of the ways in which bodies would have moved round them. This understanding of the choreography of place has brought the monuments alive again, and the differences between those taking part in processions and those looking on, between those inside the tombs and those excluded on the outside, give an indication of how the movements through space set up social differences – they had social meaning.

We should be cautious, however, in moving too far afield, focusing too much on the practices themselves as if they took place outside a conceptual framework. Barrett seems guilty of this in suggesting that "the evolution of each monument was not a matter of forward planning". But it seems highly unlikely that design or plan played no role in their layout and re-use. How would similarities in the final form of henges result if there was no concept beyond practices? It would seem difficult to argue that practices can be studied disembodied from the structures, rules, norms which they reproduce. If the study of practices aims to avoid making inferences about past frameworks of social meaning (what was "in their heads"), it is bound to be inadequate. It would be impossible to understand the social meaning of processions, for example, without having some idea about what the processions meant conceptually. The social relationships between those involved in and those watching a procession depend very much on whether those processing are "priests" or, for example, "war captives." It is not enough simply to describe a series of practices; the practices themselves have to be given a certain meaning content.

In fact, as already noted, Barrett's methodology comfortably fits within the hermeneutic tradition. Barrett uses concepts such as burial or ancestral site to make sense of the practices at a conceptual and social level. An archaeology of practice cannot, therefore, by-pass the methodological process of hermeneutic under- standing. There is a danger, particularly given the difficulty of making inferences about past minds from archaeological data, that a split is occasioned between mind and body within an archaeology of practice. But to rob practice of intentionality would be to deny agency and return archaeology to a narrow behaviorism. Certainly indigenous writers such as Mamani Condori (**chapter 24**) want us to try to understand what things mean and meant to "them"; simply to describe a set of practices is to deny a full cultural significance.

Some recent attempts to integrate practice within a total framework of being have turned to phenomenology (Gosden 1994; Shanks 1992). Tarlow (1992), for example, has criticized the postprocessual assumption that burial practices func- tion ideologically to support dominant groups. She argues that this restriction of burial and death to questions of power denies the full meaning of those who ex- perience death (see also Kus 1992). It is not enough simply to describe burial practices and relate them socially to power. A fuller understanding of the practices surrounding death must take into account the way people made sense of traumatic experiences, and must interpret the metaphors through which death was made sensible. This experiential approach integrates burial practices into a total bodily experience. It does not arbitrarily separate practice from mind within the body.

Conclusion

When it comes to the interpretation of meaning, positivist and hermeneutic approaches seem poles apart; their base theories seem radically incommensurable. Because the consideration of symbolic meaning invites discussion of intentionality and particular historical meaning, the limitations of materialist and positivist approaches in this area are readily brought out. Even technology, a central focus of processual archaeology, appears to be best understood using a hermeneutic approach for the interpretation of past symbolism and communication. The emphasis on meaning and agency adds to, or "socializes," technical studies. All is interpretation.

But perhaps the differences between these two viewpoints results from different accommodations to scale. For example, Yentsch (**chapter 12**) interprets pottery in terms of agency, power and ideology, while O'Brien and Holland (1992) consider pottery in terms of enhancing reproductive fitness. Agency theory and structuralism may be telling us about intent and the production of variability while cultural-evolutionary theory is telling us about the differential persistence of that variability. Perhaps selective pressures are unacknowledged conditions and selec- tive advantages are unintended consequences of human action. Both theories accept that human agents may be unaware of all the conditions and outcomes of their actions. The two perspectives may be simply asking different questions, interested in different scales of analysis, and they may not appear contradictory. Where the problem lies, however, is in how these different scales articulate with one another. How and why do local practices persist over the long term? In some ways, this problem is similar to the challenges the Annalistes face in bridging event, conjuncture and the *longue durée* (Part IV). The main error of some cultural-evolutionary approaches is to ignore the interaction effects between these scales and their transformative potential in generating change. Events, traits, or practices cannot be boxed up and studied in isolation.

What about the differences between functional and contextual interpretation of symbols? Wobst's (1977) account of symbolism and style as information exchange appears to contradict the hermeneutic and poststructuralist emphasis on multiple and contested meanings. For Wobst, the power of symbols is that they give clear unambiguous messages. For Shanks, however, the power of symbols is that they are ambiguous, complex and multivalent. But Shanks's *aryballoi* are used to form the identity of a particular group of elite men. Presumably they were recognized as identifying that group by others in Archaic Greek society, and by those on the peripheries of that society. For Shanks, such uses of the pots as identity markers may be unintended consequences of the construction of the self through the control of the body. But presumably the use of common pots and practices of the body did contribute to a certain social cohesion, even in the context of an internally competitive elite. So functional meanings cannot be ruled out, but they may be only one of many different kinds of meanings.

Perhaps, the main difference between these approaches turns on the acknowledgment of the provisional nature of interpretation and the instability of meaning. From an information-exchange point of view, the degree of local variability in meaning is partly a function of the degree to which local groups need to identify with larger social units. But from an interpretivist perspective, group identity is an integral part of the construction of self. Here the incompatibility between theories seems contrived since functional meanings can be subsumed by social practice. The same seems to be true of methods. We have noted in a number of cases the appearance of hermeneutic methods in explanatory, cross-cultural, and hypothesis-testing accounts. Flannery and Marcus, for example, define what is really a contextual, hermeneutic approach. On the other hand, most interpretive approaches use quantification and "objective" data, even if bracketed within a provisional, uncertain interpretation. Both Shanks and Barrett ally an interpretive position with the use of generalization and concern for theory–data coherence. Some sort of hermeneutic, inductive method is widely used in archaeology. But within this framework, there is often the provisional, guarded, and bracketed use of data as if they were objective.

References

Binford, L. 1965. Archaeological systematics and the study of culture process. *American Antiquity* 31, 203–10.

Bloch, M. 1995. Questions not to ask of Malagasy carvings. In Hodder, I. et al. (eds) *Interpreting Archaeology*. London, pp. 212–15.

Bourdieu, P. 1977. *Outline of a Theory of Practice*. Cambridge.

Childe, V. G. 1951. *Social Evolution*. New York.

Deetz, J. 1977. *In Small Things Forgotten*. New York.

Dobres, M-A. 1995. Gender and prehistoric technology: on the social agency of technical strategies. *World Archaeology* 27, 25–49.

Giddens, A. 1979. *Central Problems in Social Theory*. London

Gosden, P. 1994. *Social Being and Time*. Oxford.

Hawkes, C. 1954. Archaeological theory and method: some suggestions from the Old World. *American Anthropologist* 56, 155–68.

Hodder, I. 1985. Post-processual archaeology. *Advances in Archaeological Method and Theory* 8, 1–2.

Hodder, I. 1986. *Reading the Past: Current Approaches to Interpretation in Archaeology*. Cambridge.

Hodder, I. 1989. Post-modernism, post-structuralism and post-processual archaeology. In Hodder, I. (ed.) *The Meaning of Things: Material Culture and Symbolic Expression*. London, pp. 64–78.

Hodder, I. 1990. *The Domestication of Europe: Structure and Contingency in Neolithic Societies*. Oxford.

Hodder, I. 1992. *Theory and Practice in Archaeology*. London.

Kus, S. 1992. Toward an archaeology of body and soul. In Gardin, J-C. and Peebles, C. S. (eds) *Representations in Archaeology*. Bloomington, pp. 168–77.

Latour, B. 1988. The prince for machines as well as for machinations. In Elliott, B. (ed.) *Technology and Social Process*. Edinburgh.

Lechtman, H. 1984. Andean value systems and the development of prehistoric metallurgy. *Technology and Culture* 15, 1–36.

Lemonnier, P. 1986. The study of material culture today. *Journal of Anthropological Archaeology* 5, 147–86.

Leone, M. 1984. Interpreting ideology in historical archaeology. In Miller, D. and Tilley, C. (eds) *Ideology, Power and Prehistory*. Cambridge, pp. 25–35.

Leroi-Gourhan, A. 1965. *Préhistoire de l'art Occidental*. Paris.

Lévi-Strauss, C. 1963. *Structural Anthropology*. New York.

McGuire, R. 1992. *A Marxist Archaeology*. New York.

McGuire, R. and Paynter, R. (eds) 1991. *The Archaeology of Inequality*. Oxford.

Miller, D. and Tilley, C. 1984. *Ideology, Power and Prehistory*. Cambridge.

Miller, D., Rowlands, M. and Tilley, C. (eds) 1989. *Domination and Resistance*. London.

Mithen, S. J. 1994. From domain specific to generalized intelligence: a cognitive interpretation of the Middle / Upper Paleolithic transition. In Renfrew, A.C. and Zubrow, E. (eds) *The Ancient Mind: Elements of a Cognitive Archaeology*. Cambridge, pp. 29–39.

O'Brien, M. J. and Holland, T. D. 1992. The Role of Adaptation in Archaeological Explanation. *American Antiquity* 57, 36–59.

Renfrew, A. C. 1982. *Towards an Archaeology of Mind*. Cambridge.

Renfrew, A. C. 1985. *The Archaeology of Cult*. London.

Renfrew, A. C. 1994. Towards a cognitive archaeology. In Renfrew, A. C. and Zubrow, E. (eds) *The Ancient Mind: Elements of Cognitive Archaeology*. Cambridge, pp. 3–12.

Renfrew, A. C. and Bahn, P. 1991. *Archaeology*. London.

314   *Meaning and Practice*

Renfrew, A. C. and Zubrow, E. 1994. *The Ancient Mind: Elements of Cognitive Archaeology*. Cambridge.

Sackett, J. 1986. The meaning of style in archaeology: a general model. *American Antiquity* 42, 369–80.

Saussure, F. 1960. *Course in General Linguistics*. London.

Shanks, M. 1992. *Experiencing the Past: On the Character of Archaeology*. London.

Shanks, M. and Tilley, C. 1987. *Reconstructing Archaeology* Cambridge.

Sørensen, M-L. 1987. Material order and cultural classification. In Hodder, I. (ed.) *The Archaeology of Contextual Meanings*. Cambridge, pp. 90–101.

Tarlow, S. 1992. Each slow dusk a drawing down of blinds. *Archaeological Review from Cambridge* 11, 125–40.

Tilley, C. 1991. *Material Culture as Text: The Art of Ambiguity*. London.

Tilley, C. 1993 (ed.) *Interpretative Archaeology*. London.

Wiessner, P. 1983. Style and social information in Kalahari San projectile points. *American Antiquity* 49, 253–76.

Wiessner, P. 1984. Reconsidering the behavioural basis for style: a case study among the Kalahari San. *Journal of Anthropological Archaeology* 3, 190–234.

Wobst, M. 1977. Stylistic behaviour and information exchange. *University of Michigan Museum of Anthropology, Anthropological Paper* 61, pp. 317–42.

12

The Symbolic Divisions of Pottery: Sex-related Attributes of English and Anglo-American Household Pots

Anne Yentsch

Introduction

Objects and metaphors

People communicate with metaphors. English metaphors include those of pottery: a "drinking-pot" is a man who imbibes heavily (Beaudry 1980); a "honey-pot" is a woman who openly expresses a strong degree of sexuality to attract men (Fraser 1985). Not only the English, but also the New World Indians used the imagery of pots to describe people, speaking of pregnant women as becoming pot-shaped or as "big-pots" (Levi-Strauss 1988:181). By taking the neutral word *pot* and attaching to it adjectives with culturally attributed masculine and feminine connotations, people speak about behavior and relationships between men and women. Yet, people do not speak with words alone. Men and women also use the world of objects to convey information through the use of analogy. In metaphorical analogies, one or more attributes of a person, animal, plant, or object correspond to one or more attributes of something else; by speaking of one, men and women speak indirectly of the other. In nonverbal communication even something as common as a household pot can have a metaphorical or symbolic association existing side by side with its ostensible utilitarian function. This chapter uses household pots to illustrate the ways in which pottery could serve as metaphors through which people "spoke" about social relationships, the roles of men and women, the ways in which social class arbitrarily divided men from women, woman from woman, man from man, and the boundary between culture and nature.

The argument builds on ideas expressed by James Deetz (1972, 1977). In "Ceramics from Plymouth: The Archaeological Evidence" (1972), Deetz considered change in the ceramic assemblages from coastal New England sites between the seventeenth and the late eighteenth centuries. He associated the appearance of matched sets of ceramic vessels with the rise of individualism discussed by historians, and observed in architectural plans of Virginia folk houses (Glassie 1975). Despite Deetz's plea that ceramics be understood in terms of their utilitarian *and* symbolic functions, the possibility that household ceramics had symbolic values of equal importance with or parallel to their more pragmatic use as food and beverage containers has not been widely explored by historical archaeologists in the United States (Deetz 1977:50).

The symbolism of pottery and porcelain vessels is a consequence of (a) the social rank of the people who use the vessels, (b) the social space wherein the vessels are used and/or stored, and (c) access to them. The latter reflects the ease with which they may be acquired which is, in turn, a combination of availability, price, and a family's purchasing power. Critical to understanding the symbolism associated with different functional sets of household ceramics are the uses of domestic space. The appearance of specific ceramic forms and ware-types in different household areas is not accidental; rather, ware-type, decoration, and form signal who uses particular vessels and what their uses are. Both the who and the what are related to the cultural restrictions of household space.

In this chapter, the discussion of common and uncommon pots is cast in a structuralist framework because structuralist analyses highlight how people were able to use the symbolic language of objects to speak of other aspects of daily life, reinforcing social principles with physical analogies. The symbolic messages were not only conveyed by those ceramic vessels that were used for display, but were reiterated by the differential use of pots. The impact of those used in display was heightened as they were cast against the background of those in daily use. The result was a cultural division of pottery which can be seen as repeating a series of binary discriminations highly visible in food use (i.e., hot/cold, wet/dry), and in spatial designations (i.e. inner/outer, heaven/earth), and in social rank (higher/lower). The two basic divisions of concern are the culturally defined dichotomies of culture/nature and male/female: the ways in which foods and pottery relate to them are schematically outlined in figures 12.1A and 12.1B. Integral to the analysis is a concern with the symbolic expression of relationships of dominance and subordination. The analysis indicates that ceramic vessels were elements in boundary maintenance. Over time, as cultural boundaries in English and Anglo-American society were more sharply defined, earth-toned vessels became the primary vessels used in the foodways system in social spaces assigned to women, while white-toned vessels were increasingly used to denote status in social display, an element of the food domain that traditionally fell within the masculine sphere of activity.

As Macfarlane (1988:195) notes, concepts of power and property were merged in the medieval English world. Power was mysteriously and indirectly expressed in different forms of property of which the lowly household pot is one small example. The hierarchical relationships that constituted the social structure of the culture were repetitively illustrated within different cultural domains. In a manner akin to mythic thought, these illustrations constituted a number of statements set side by side. Levi-Strauss views myth as a series of texts and writes: "Imagine a text, difficult to understand in one language, translated into several languages; the combined meaning of all the different versions may prove richer and more profound than the partial, mutilated meaning drawn from each individual version" (1988:171). These domains included and used elements of material culture

Masculine	Feminine
Culture	Nature
Heaven	Earth
Ritual	Secular
Public	Private

Elite Englishman	Women, children, servants
(*Dominant social group*)	(*Subordinate social groups*)
Instrumental social action	Expressive social action

Figure 12.1A [orig. figure 10.1A]   Basic cultural categories used to classify social space, food, and pottery.

Divisions of space

Public space: market area	Private space: household area
Cultivated land: farm, field	Uncultivated land: forest, marsh
Built access: road, bridge, walk	Natural access: ocean, river, creek

Divisions of food[1]

Courtly cuisine (mysterious	Daily cooking (everyday)
transformations of nature)	transformations of nature)
Cooked foods	Raw foods
Exotic foods	Common foods
Swans and blackbirds	Geese, hens, partridges
Wild boar or deer	Beef and pork
Whales, porpoises, sturgeon	Herring or mackerel
Rice-based potage	Cereal-based potage
Peaches and oranges	Apples and pears
Almonds	Walnuts
Oriental spices	Potherbs
Cinnamon, nutmeg, etc.	Parsley, rosemary, thyme
Exotic beverages	Common beverages
Wine, tea, coffee, chocolate	Beer, ale and cider

Divisions of pottery

Display pottery	Utilitarian pots
Plates, chargers, harvest jugs	Butter pots, crocks, storage jars
Experimental use (ca. 1680)	Customary use (ca. 1680)
Tea and coffee pots, punch bowls	Dish, mug, jug
Exotic ware: porcelain, delft	Basic ware: earthen and stone
Finely hand-painted decoration	Trailed or combed decoration
Visual appearance: white-toned	Visual appearance: earth-toned

[1] See the work of Levi-Strauss (1958, 1965), Douglas (1972), and Goody (1982) for detailed discussions of the categories and transformations of food. See Wilson (1974), Henisch (1976), and Mennell (1985) for information on specific food items.

Figure 12.1B [orig. figure 10.1B]   Analytic classifications of space, food, and pottery that align with the basic dichotomies shown in figure 12.1A.

to reinforce the principles whereby they were organized; these principles included beliefs about the proper roles of men and women. In studying the masculine and feminine symbolism of a common class of artifacts found in the archaeological record, and thinking of them as metaphorical statements about the society at large, an archaeologist begins to see the wide range of ethnographic information conveyed by objects. Such research expands the discussion of archaeologically recovered ceramic vessels beyond the readily observable attributes of form, material, temper, glaze, decoration, distribution, and economic value by placing artifacts within their social context.

If an archaeologist can and does separate masculine and feminine domains of culture within the archaeological record, what does she learn? Does it shed a new light on a culture or open up different avenues for study? As I thought of artifacts as being either masculine or feminine, it became clear that as Schuyler (1980) and Handsman (1984) noted earlier, there is very little discussion of women's lives in the archaeological literature. A number of imaginative, sensitive, and informative books and articles have been written about women in English and Anglo-American society using historical resources (Amussen 1985, 1987; Cahn 1987; Cott 1977; Hanawalt 1986; Mertes 1988; Nicholson 1986; Norton 1980; Stansell 1987; Ulrich 1982, to name but some). There are very few (Deagan's (1973, 1983) work on Spanish sites, and Wall (1987) are exceptions) that have dealt with women's lives as seen through the archaeological record. Yet the bulk of any domestic assemblage is food-related refuse, and the foodways system *was* an institution in which women were deeply involved (see table 12.3); and although men controlled ceremonial food consumption, within household space women were primarily responsible for its production. When historical archaeologists ignore the data available from artifact analysis that contains information about gender, about the relations between men and women, and about the activities characteristic of each, they dispossess women from their past. Society is depersonalized; the fact that all cultures have male and female members can be ignored. Inevitably the analysis is biased towards one segment – the politically dominant segment – of the society.

It is not simply that women are overlooked. Archaeologists are also beguiled into ignoring many provocative aspects of men's lives. Men in the past, as men do today, spoke to each other about themselves, their power, their prestige, and rank in the same terms, using the same metaphors of pottery and of space, as they did about the relationships between men and women. This was surprising to learn, but perhaps it should not have been, for Marc Bloch concluded after a study of ritual that there were many examples where *gender symbolism was used as the basis for all types of ideological schemes* (1985:46). Starting with a consideration of relations between men and women, the symbolism in pottery inevitably leads one to look at how space is used and then to consider different facets of men's lives and their relationships with each other. This occurs because the axes in the prestige structure that patterned male–female relationships in terms of deference, respect, and obedience on the one hand and condescension, disregard, and authority on the other guided relationships between individuals of the same sex belonging to different status groups as well (Ortner and Whitehead 1982).

Gender and space

The relation between gender and space helps explain differences in vessel form, decoration, and function in earth-toned and white-toned medieval and post-medieval pottery. As space was reorganized making new areas in houses and yards more isolated and private (i.e., feminized), the symbolic attributes of artifacts normally used within these areas went from either gender-neutral or masculine to feminine. Household pots, predominantly earth-toned, became associated with women's tasks and with subordinate activities in the hierarchical food system. In this, their earth-toned colors aided, for natural lands were traditionally viewed as feminine. There was a cultural repertoire of symbols that described male and female qualities and activities as derivative aspects of either culture or nature. By extension, other earth-toned vessels also came to be associated with subordinate positions.

In feudal English society, a major social bond was the relation between surbordinate men and those above them, including that of "lord and man, a relation implying on the lord's part protection and defense; on the man's part protection, service, and reverence, the service including service in arms" (Maitland 1919:143–4, quoted in Macfarlane 1988:196). This might be viewed as the primary hierarchical public relationship. A primary private relationship was the social bond between a man and his wife, implying on the man's part protection and defense, on the woman's part, service and reverence, the service including a wide range of domestic chores. Although elements of these relationships changed over time, women still held subordinate roles in Anglo-American families (Norton 1980:3). While there were gradations of rank among women, and some women possessed extraordinary economic, social, or political power, female hierarchy is collapsed here to facilitate discussion of male/female relationships. Women are treated as one set of individuals – a social group subordinate, for the most part, to adult Englishmen.

Similarly, the gradations that existed in rank among servants and slaves are not germane. Of course they used their material culture to express nuances of rank among themselves. But the basic argument still holds – that women, indentured servants, and slaves as social groups held lower positions in the hierarchically organized New World communities than did male free-holders, and that their respective positions were denoted by the objects they used.

Once one understands the masculine and feminine attributes of household space and customary male and female roles within the household, the dual role of ceramic objects (i.e., utilitarian and symbolic) is easier to perceive. For example, domestic or inner space (i.e., feminine space) parallels and mirrors community or exterior space (i.e., masculine space) while men's and women's roles within the home reiterate other positional relationships among men of differing social status in the wider community (cf. those between English nobility and ordinary men described by Maitland). Within the home domestic space can be thought of as public or private, ceremonial, commercial, domestic, or even defensive. Often it is classified by its use (i.e., as an activity area), and by the access people have to it.

Use can be inferred from the artifact assemblages associated with specific areas as illustrated in table 12.1, which clearly shows (1) variations in the ceramic assemblage from different rooms at Corotoman that relate to (2) public and private uses of household space. Similar information drawn from probate inventory data is presented in table 12.2 for the Thomas Bordley residence in Annapolis, Maryland. Archaeologists are perhaps less aware of the way social relationships are organized by space within the home than of the role of space in organizing the activities of a community.

Table 12.1 [orig. table 10.1]   Location of ceramic vessels found at Corotoman.[a]

Room	White-toned vessels	Earth-toned vessels
Parlor		Pudding pans Serving jugs Drinking jugs
	Plates (delft, porcelain) Bowls (delft, porcelain) Tea bowls (porcelain) Chocolate cups (white salt-glaze)	
Central Hall or passage		Basins Chamber pots Milk pans Pudding pans Storage pots Serving jugs Drinking jugs Mugs and drinking pots
	Porringers (delft)	
Chamber		Basins Chamber pot Mugs
Chamber closet		Basin Bottles Serving jug
	Plate (delft)	

[a] Corotoman was Robert "King" Carter's home on the Rappahannock River in Tidewater Virginia. The house burned down in 1729 providing an excellent sealed context for the finds (unpublished data provided by Alice Guerrant, personal communication 1980, and Conrad M. Goodwin, personal communication July 1988).

Table 12.2 [orig. table 10.2] Placement of ceramic vessels in the Thomas Bordley House, Annapolis, Maryland, based on a room-by-room probate inventory of 1727.

	White-toned vessels [a]		Earth-toned vessels	
Room	Form	Use	Form	Use
Inner room	Custard cups	Tea consumption		
	Sugar dish	Tea consumption		
	Punch bowl	Wine consumption		
Parlor	Tea cups and saucers	Tea consumption		
	Dishes	Social dining		
	Plates	Social dining		
	Bowls	Social dining		
	Plates (delft)	Social dining		
	Saucers (delft)	Social dining		
Passage	Custard cups	Tea consumption		
Parlor Chamber	Custard cups	Tea consumption		
	Punch bowl	Wine consumption		
Kitchen			Stone pots	Storage
			Earthen pots	Storage
			Stone jugs	Ale/beer
			Earthen pans	Baking
			Chamber pots	Hygiene

[a] All the vessels are Chinese porcelain unless noted otherwise.

An Overview of Gender-related Use of Space

Certainly there was a sexual division of labor in medieval and post-medieval cultures, but the primary association of women with unpaid domestic labor and men with monetarily supported labor is a product of capitalism. The medieval woman's economic sphere was limited when compared with her father's, husband's, brother's, and son's. She rarely took part in activities that extended beyond the spatial boundaries defined by the location of her home and immediate neighborhood. While the eighteenth century saw the extension of cash labor to women, paid tasks were done as piecemeal labor within the home. In this they supplemented the small monies a woman might earn by selling her butter, eggs, or cheese at market.

Additionally, a man's professional life and his private life were merged because household buildings and family lands formed the major work areas for both sexes. Thus both men's and women's work was closely tied to household space. It is these qualities of family life that Deetz (1977) had in mind when he described seventeenth-century New England families as possessing organic solidarity; divisions between production and consumption, income-producing labor and reciprocal or domestic labor, work and home, public and private life differed radically from modern divisions which emphasize the separation of these domains. Neither regional lifestyles nor rural–urban variations created sufficient difference to alter the dominant, underlying form of medieval and post-medieval culture. There was an inescapable aura of organic unity between a household's living space and the physical terrain, emphasized by the natural building materials drawn from the regional environment. The bounds between activity areas were blurred; segmentation of activities was minimal. Workshops, ware-houses, and offices might be parts of domestic establishments; animals might be kept within a household's building walls, and grain crops were frequently stored in house lofts.

Craftsmen and artisans residing in towns blended income-producing and domestic activity inside their houses and in their yards with minimal spatial distinctions (Yentsch and McKee 1987). There was social heterogeneity. Rich and poor households mingled together within town and city neighborhoods. Residen-tial location, in contrast to size and style of house, was not a meaningful status indicator either in England (Reed 1983:146) or in America. Because there were few clearly defined, mutually exclusive social spaces, the emblems of rank were indi-vidually specific (i.e., clothing and personal utensils identified an individual's rank).

Elite households in the Old and New Worlds differed from average households because they were larger and contained individuals with more extensive kinship ties as well as a range of servants and, in the New World, slaves. An elite house-hold entertained a constant flow of people whose visits were simultaneously friendly, social, and professional. It also provided social services to the community. In other words, wealthy families lived in larger, more complex households whose functions were multi-faceted, often including commercial or administrative governmental elements not found in the average household. Within such households, the economic and political domains were fused.

Until the mid-eighteenth century, few households had rooms set aside as public rooms where visitors were separated from the household. As Hamilton writes, "People ate, met, talked, slept, made love and made deals all in the same rooms" (1978:34). The endless succession of guests made demands on the household for provisions far above those of other households. The merging of social space reiterated the merging of power, property, economic, and social relationships. Although possessing greater complexity, undifferentiated space and a co-mingling of people and activities was as characteristic of wealthy households as it was of poorer ones throughout the seventeenth century and into the early years of the eighteenth century.

In English medieval culture, the marked spatial boundary was between the sacred and the profane, not between public and private. Women's work spilled over into public space when women sold butter, cheese, milk, eggs, and poultry at local markets. Feminine domains included the dairy, springhouse, hen house, and kitchen garden; and farmers' wives occasionally brought grain to the mill. As shown in table 12.3, women were in charge of many of the processes which transformed raw plant materials and the by-products of domesticated animals into usable goods: milk to butter and cheese, flax and wool to yarn, malt and other grains to ale, plants (pot vegetables and herbs) to soup and medicine. Still, their use of public space was episodic. Men, however, routinely used community or public space and were the individuals who traversed less settled reaches of the countryside. Men controlled the transformation of wild and domestic animals into edible meats through their mastery of the butchery process. As artisans and craftsmen, they were also in charge of the more mysterious transformation of metal ores into usable objects.

The allocation of space into masculine and feminine domains described above continued in Anglo-America. Domestic space was not highly differentiated, nor were activity areas restricted to a single activity. St George (1982) suggests that the parlor inside the house was masculine space while the hall comprised feminine space; to my mind, the hall might better be described as "unmarked" space because it was used by people of both sexes and all ages for a broad range of activities and daily tasks. It was also the center of household sociability. As the seventeenth century progressed domestic space was reclassified; the space represented by a hall was increasingly referred to as the kitchen. Presumably this change in nomenclature was accompanied by a separation of hall and kitchen activities. By the early eighteenth century most cooking areas were removed to a back room, often in a lean-to addition to the central house.

Table 12.3 [orig. table 10.3]   Major phases in the cycle of food use among English communities

Food or beverage	Activity area	Characteristic activities	Workers	Domain
Phase 1: Food procurement				
Fish	Oceans, rivers, etc.	Seining, fishing	Men	Male
Crabs and shellfish	Creeks and bays	Gathering, trapping	Men	Male
Wild meats	Forests or marshes	Hunting, trapping	Men	Male
Wild birds	Fields and marshes	Hunting, trapping	Men	Male
Marketable grains	Farm fields	Tillage	Men	Male
Marketable fruits	Orchards	Harvest	Men	Male
Domestic meats	Farm pastures	Animal husbandry	Men	Male
Domestic poultry	Barnyard	Animal husbandry	Women	Female
Dairy products	Barn or barnyard	Milking/egg collection	Women	Female
Kitchen vegetables	House garden	Kitchen gardening	Women	Female
Cultivated herbs	House garden	Kitchen gardening	Women	Female
Spices (exotic)	Outside community	Sale/trade	Men	Male
Wines, hard liquors	Outside community	Sale/trade	Men	Male
Phase 2: Food preparation and storage				
Step 1. Initial processing				
Meat	Farm yard	Butchery	Men	Male
Grains	Barn, barnyard, mill	Winnowing, milling	Men	Male
Kitchen vegetables	Kitchen	Washing/drying	Women	Female
Herbs	Kitchen	Washing/drying	Women	Female
Dairy products	Kitchen or dairy	Curd separation, etc.	Women	Female
Step 2. Initial storage				
Meat	Smokehouse, cellar	Curation	Men?	Male?
Grains	Barns, house lofts	Curation	Men?	Male?
Dried herbs	Kitchen	Curation	Women	Female
Root crops	Kitchen cellars	Curation	Women	Female

Butter, cheese	Dairy, springhouses	Curation	Women	Female
Step 3. Meal preparation and brewing				
All foodstuffs	Kitchen	Roasting, baking, etc.	Women	Female
Ale, beer, cider	Kitchen	Brewing	Women	Male
Tea, coffee, cocoa	Dining areas	Brewing	Women	Male
Step 4. Storage of prepared foods and beverages				
Meats	Springhouse?	Curation	Women	Female
Vegetables	Kitchen	Curation	Women	Female
Fruits	Kitchen	Curation	Women	Female
Baked goods	Kitchen	Curation	Women	Female
Phase 3: Household food distribution				
Food and beverages	Kitchen and work area	Serving	Women	Female
Food and beverages	Formal dining areas	Serving	Women or young men	Male
Meat	Formal dining areas	Carving	Adult men	Male
Phase 4: Food consumption				
Daily meals	Kitchen or work area	Food consumption	Household	Female
Feasts	Formal dining area	Social display	Family and guests	Male
	Exterior public spaces			
Phase 5: Refuse disposal				
All garbage	Interior house	Cleaning	Women	Female

Aries (1962) contends that the concept of private, familial space did not develop until the 1500s and then spread slowly. Sixteenth- and seventeenth-century paintings show a blending of domestic and social activities within houses and within the same room. Late seventeenth-century room-by-room inventories, whether from England, New England, or the Chesapeake, provide additional evidence of the way activities merged within single rooms. There are also, however, a series of townscapes by Dutch genre painters, including Tenniers, that show men engaged in games or other social activities outside the house while women remain in doorways or near the doorsteps. The association of women with interior, or private space, and men with exterior, or public space, is given symbolic meaning in these and other contemporary paintings. It was repeated in Jacob Cats' 1628 admonition "The husband must be on the street to practice his trade, The wife must stay at home to be in the kitchen" (quoted in Schama 1987:400). The idea is perhaps most vividly expressed in New Jersey Governor William Livingstone's essays of 1790 which praised as a cultural ideal the American women who "enjoyed happiness in their chimney corners" (quoted in Norton 1980:5).

The way in which English and European culture was reorganized from the time of the Renaissance has been described by a number of historians. Different lines were drawn between culture and nature (Thomas 1983); boundaries between time, space, activities, and events became more finely drawn, readily distinguishable, and less easily crossed. The symbolic content of space was critical because it was a major axis organizing, separating, or conjoining activities. Since the reorganization emphasized the asymmetry that characterized relationships between men and women as well as other perceived differences, some objects became more associated with women's activities than with men's activities and vice versa. To the extent that objects denoted attributes of social space, their metaphorical roles had to change as the culture changed its use of space.

The Symbolism of Space: its Relation to Gender-based Activities and Events

Gender ideology is frequently expressed in association with the nature/culture dichotomy (Ardener 1972; Barnes 1973; Ortner 1972; Rosaldo 1987). Feminist anthropologists, using structuralist theory, have argued the presence of a universal opposition between domestic, or feminine, and public, or masculine, roles. Rosaldo's earlier work also notes the way in which sex-related uses of space effectively create social distance and thereby emphasize the boundaries between male and female activities (1974:27). Reiter wrote of the public and private domains occupied by men and women in southern France, observing a sexual geography governing the use of space (1975:256); she based her designations of social space on (a) the type of activity occurring in a given area, and (b) the gender of those associated with the activities. Reiter's analysis indicates that women's tasks and social gatherings normally occurred in private (i.e., familial) areas of the community. Men, however, operated in more public, supra-familial, formal spheres. This could be seen in their dominance of economic and political activities, and their participation in church affairs.

Men's work exists in a wider domain than does the work of women. Women's work primarily occurs within the realm of the household; kinship plays a large role in organizing household activities than it does in the outside community. Within the household, one's role is as often ascriptive as it is achieved; in the larger community, the positions of men *vis-à-vis* their economic, political, and church roles are achieved. Rieter (1975) reviewed the anthropological and historical literature, concluding that all state societies appear to organize a division between public and private sectors in which public functions are seen as masculine and private ones as feminine. Within the public sphere, men control the information, the rituals, and the personal ties concerned with group structure and alliances between groups in addition to administering economic, political, and religious affairs.

The use of space Reiter described in present-day France is analogous to the use of space in earlier Anglo-American communities: market space was public and hence masculine while household space was private and hence feminine. In my opinion, these cultural divisions were given added emphasis by parallel divisions of each of these two domains. In other words, public space was not wholly public for it also contained a private component; private space was not wholly private for it also contained a public component. Within the context of the community, household space was private. Within the context of the house, some spatial areas were more private than others. The arrangement of space within the home can be discerned by listing or observing the participants and the type of activities they engage in within particular domestic areas using either archaeological or inventory data.

In any culture where men's work areas primarily fall within family space (defined as a house and its associated grounds), formal or ritual dinners (i.e., feasts) are a major means whereby a household relates to the wider community. Feasts are times when alliances and reciprocal relations between kin and guests are negotiated or established. The use of special foods and beverages and their accoutrements at feasts is but one indication that these events fall within the masculine sphere of a household's social action. At such events, the display value of food is more important than its nutritional value; the latter is incidental to the underlying symbolism and the expression of rank (Douglas 1972).

Throughout the eighteenth century, elite men went to considerable effort to obtain prestigious dinner wares from overseas and to insure that elaborate foods were part of the dining rituals enacted under their sponsorship. In Annapolis, the prestigious and politically well-connected Calvert family served a wide range of wild and domestic birds at their table to supplement the more common beef, pork, and mutton dishes, and ate chicken more frequently than their neighbors (Reitz 1988). The wider (as demonstrated by the species list) and more extensive use (demonstrated by the minimum number of animals) of wild and domestic birds for food, and the elaborate ceramics used in their home indicate a participation in ritual dining. As members of the first national Congress meeting in 1784 in war-time Annapolis, Thomas Jefferson and James Madison also hired a French chef to insure their ceremonial meals possessed the proper flair; the staff of General George Washington made consistent efforts to procure prestigious ceramics for his war-time staff dinners (Detweiler 1982:63–80). But it is not just the effort to procure expensive tablewares or serve high-style food that by itself justifies the ascription of social dining to the masculine domain of household activity; rather, it is the degree or intensity of social display involved/expressed in the total flow of social behavior within one area of the house as opposed to another.

There is some element of display involved in everyday meals, but the degree of display intensifies with the formality of the meal, with the number or importance of the guests, and with the importance of the event that a formal meal celebrates. The nonverbal information that is conveyed in the social performance that constitutes formal dining is normally patterned and orderly. The social space occupied by this use of food has more masculine attributes than the household areas used for food storage or preparation; the furnishing and utensils of the former space are, *ipso facto*, more masculine than the furnishings and utensils of the household areas where food is stored and prepared, and where everyday food is eaten. In the social space assigned to ritual dining, what takes place belongs within the realm of domestic (and often conspicuous) consumption whereas the activities in areas where utilitarian food use is the norm are associated with the realm of domestic production.

If one wants to describe a household's social spaces in terms of the power designated to them (i.e., in terms of the relative status of people, events, and material objects associated with such spaces), there was minimal allocation of power to spaces assigned to cooking and food storage. The utensils used in these areas included the pottery vessels today known as "coarsewares" that were often purchased from local craftsmen. These areas were peripheral to the space used for ceremonial sociability; the individuals most closely associated with food production were not necessarily *ever* present in the rooms used in ceremonial food display.

Southern families who could do so removed the "working hearth" from their homes and confined cooking tasks to kitchen lean-tos, to basement kitchens, or to kitchen/slave quarters erected in the yard. Cooking was also removed from the central hearth in New England homes in the eighteenth century. Over time, instead of the central, multi-purpose familial hearth familiar to most colonists of the early years of English settlement, two or more developed: an isolated cooking hearth located within feminine social space, and hearths in parlors, chambers, offices, and so on, that supplied warmth and light, but whose fires were peripheral to food preparation. This arrangement of hearths that emerged in eighteenth-century homes created social distance. The separation of the cooking hearth from the main ceremonial eating area distanced the people and activities associated with the cooking hearth from the people and activities associated with ritual dining. The separation of social spaces formerly co-mingled also enabled a household to limit access to its display areas, thereby making entry a privilege and itself the sign of status. Doorways to these areas functioned as social thresholds. Low-status individuals such as peddlers, apprentices, servants, and African slaves were expected to enter the house and/or transact their business with household members in regions of the house and yard distant from the rooms used for entertainment and leisure activities (Glassie 1975; Neiman 1978; Upton 1988).

Some scholars argue that the rationale for the presence of outbuildings in the Southern colonies, such as kitchens, dairies, wash houses, and the like was solely economic (Walsh, personal communication). Others argue that the rationale was comfort (i.e., separating "hot" activities from cooler ones, especially in summer). Whatever the reason, by separating bound labor or slave labor from the household, the distancing of the food processing areas also separated the women of a family from the main house for significant portions of time on a daily or weekly basis. As a routine event, predictable and repetitious, the separation came to be perceived as reasonable and natural.

As the spaces where women prepared food were distanced from the area used for social display where men entertained and/or conducted their economic and political affairs, the position of women in the information networks shifted, and their access to these became constricted. To the extent that women were not actual participants in ritual dining they lost power, for their social ties with particular sets of individuals within the community became more diffuse, and their knowledge of external events became filtered and indirect. It is through such processes that otherwise ordinary events are made mysterious and individuals appear more powerful than they may actually be.

Hierarchy in Ceramic Vessels

The social scaling of activities associated with a household's activity areas provides an approach to foodstuffs that subsumes the concept of cuisine. Food can be identified with phases in the food cycle and classified according to the space and means whereby it was (1) obtained, (2) introduced into the household domain, (3) transformed from raw product into edible meal, (4) distributed, and (5) consumed. As foodstuffs pass through these phases, different implements are necessary and the individuals who handle the food or oversee its use hold different status positions related to each phase of the cycle. Although it is technically possible for a woman or a man to grow a plant, dry it, cook it, serve it, and then eat it, nevertheless, if he or she does so, the role is different at each step and accorded different status. The information in table 12.3 indicates that the more usual succession was for men to obtain food (a) if its source was distant *vis-à-vis* the home or (b) if its production in the home held the potential for sales of surpluses in distant markets. If men were instrumental in obtaining food, as is the case for most meats, then they also handled its initial processing and perhaps supervised its storage. Primarily, however, women take over the activities related to food preparation and storage (i.e., during Phase 2 of the food cycle, especially in its later steps). Food and beverages then remain within the feminine domain until they become elements in formal meals or in food served outside the home. One means of marking the different steps in the food cycle and of separating the status positions involved was a visual difference in the utensils used to move or store foodstuffs; most pottery containers appear among household utensils at points in the food cycle where women become involved. Further, variations in the ceramic utensils keep pace with the progress of foodstuffs throughout the cycle until, as food refuse, it is returned to nature.

Each era has its own core of significant symbols which express the organizing principles of a culture. Perhaps because ceramics were not readily available nor used in large quantities, they seem to have been peripheral or value-neutral in the set of meaningful symbols used to indicate hierarchy in medieval food use. Descriptions of English ceramic assemblages in British site reports (Cunningham and Drury 1986; Fox and Barton 1986) indicate that two forms – cooking pots and pitchers/jugs – were dominant at domestic English sites of the late medieval period. Starting in the sixteenth century, as cultural space was reorganized and pottery became more widely available, in addition to silver and pewter vessels, ceramic utensils also became an integral part of the symbolic inventory that surrounded the use of food in social display.

As food preparation and storage were separated from other food-related activities, the boundaries between this phase of food use and other familial activities, especially food consumption, were increasingly distinguished both by the space wherein they took place and the tools necessary to them. This had an additional impact on the way in which ceramic objects were classified: as the lines between activities were more clearly defined, the objects associated with different activities had to contain characteristic features that could be easily seen as belonging to a single phase of food use. For example, when household space was less differentiated, there was an overlap in the materials used for household pots. Differently formed vessels made of identical earthenware fabrics with similar, if not identical, glazes were used for cooking and serving food, for storing, distributing, and consuming beverages. This overlap disappeared with time. The start of the trend is readily seen in figures 12.2 and 12.3 which illustrate the increasing diversification of ceramic assemblages at an English site from 1400 to ca. 1670. Note that the trend is even more apparent in Chesapeake sites dating to 1620–50 (figures 12.4 and 12.5).

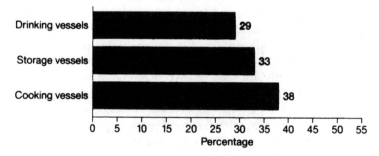

Figure 12.2 [orig. figure 10.2]   Percentage of vessel forms by functional category for assemblages
from Moulsham Street deposits dating between 1400 and 1500
(data compiled using the illustrations in Cunningham and Drury 1986).

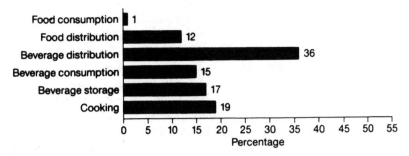

Figure 12.3 [orig. figure 10.3] Percentage of vessel forms by functional category for assemblages from Moulsham Street deposits dating to ca.1670
(data compiled using the illustrations in Cunningham and Drury 1986).

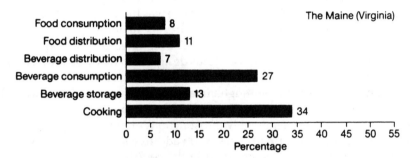

Figure 12.4 [orig. figure 10.4] Percentage of vessel forms by functional category for an assemblage from The Maine dating 1618–1626
(data based on ceramic analysis by Merry Abbitt-Outlaw and shown on minimum vessel lists in Yentsch, Bescherer, and Patrick, forthcoming).

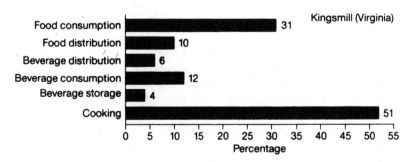

Figure 12.5 [orig. figure 10.5] Percentage of vessel forms by functional category for an assemblage from Kingsmill dating 1625–1650 (data based on ceramic analysis by Merry Abbitt-Outlaw and shown on minimum vessel lists in Yentsch, Bescherer, and Patrick (forthcoming).

Prior to New World colonization, the use of specific English vessel forms was a consequence of food use following one of two traditions: a folk tradition used in yeoman households, and an elite or courtly tradition (Mennell 1985). At harvest time, large meals prepared by yeoman households were feasts: performances illustrating the rights and obligations of the family to servants, non-resident kin, and neighbors helping with the harvest. As a rule, however, ritual dining was an occasional event in the average English household. Its use centered around rites of passage such as weddings, christenings, deaths, and/or religious holidays and fast days. In contrast, the meals of elite families were routinely used as a mechanism to display their wealth and power. In either case, different vessels symbolically associated with variations in social rank were used and in their variation provided a parallel to the variation in the use of spices, exotic foodstuffs, meat sources and cuts as well as in the complexity of the recipe, preparation time required, and availability of prepared dishes.

Divided on the basis of form, each vessel belonged to a set of similarly used vessels with status gradations expressed through material, glaze, and design motif. For example, the basic form of a tankard or plate was the same whether it was made of gold, silver, horn, pewter, or earthenware. Its material (for example, silver versus stoneware) was the first attribute which signified its position in the vessel hierarchy with further refinements in status designation made on the basis of more subtle variations in material and decoration within each basic type (i.e., stoneware vessels such as Westerwald, Nottingham, or Scratch Brown tankards were distinguishable within the stoneware class of tankards by their color, glaze, and decorative embellishments; more vivid distinctions existed among ceramic plates, and their decoration was primarily based on additive techniques).

Prestigious foods and beverages used in the courtly tradition were frequently served in special purpose vessels. Some, such as chafing dishes, were distinguished by form while others were distinguished by material, as in the case of a recipe for an Elizabethan trifle that was seasoned with sugar and ginger and then served in a "silver piece or bowl" (Wilson 1974:169). Many courtly dishes had no counterpart in the folk tradition until, in the eighteenth century, as their use trickled down and their value shifted, consumption became commonplace and the vessels associated with them became widely available. Teawares are perhaps the best example of this trend as it is encountered in the archaeological evidence left on Anglo-American sites.

The relative position of each vessel in the hierarchy indicated the relative status of the individuals involved in the production and consumption of the foods or beverages contained within it. The social principle of rank was reinforced by the physical analogy (Douglas 1986). The mechanism through which this occurred was the association, at its most basic level, of specific types of food with either food production or food consumption, i.e., with either the feminine or masculine sphere of food use. Further, the use of these principles over and over again as meals were served throughout the year reinforced the organizing principles, grounding them in events that were so ordinary and repetitious they were taken for granted, appearing as natural as the rising and setting of the sun.

How did this occur? It is my belief that initially neither men nor women were defined by the ceramics they owned. Men made pots for male and female use. Overall, medieval English pottery was probably gender-neutral or quasi-masculine. Ceramic vessels were used in undifferentiated household space, although it was space controlled by men. Men gave their cups/mugs/jugs names such as "Crumpledud," "Peregrin," and "The Grete Grubbe" (Thrupp 1962:147), thus distinguishing drinking vessels from ordinary household pots. Decorative motifs on these vessels included masculine hunting scenes and male figures (Rackham 1948). Earthenware jugs, whose spouts were decorated with masculine faces, were popular. The continuation of this tradition is visible in the faces/masks on seventeenth-century Bellarmine jugs.

Objects often acquire symbolic meaning through their association with the people who use them. It is improbable that medieval cooking pots were viewed as masculine objects for they were used by women or household servants. Cooking pots were probably not objects to which power accrued. Access to them was not limited; their use was not mysterious. They were used daily and routinely in readily accessible service rooms. From the onset, cooking vessels were either plain or had minimal decoration carved into their fabric (a subtractive process) in contrast to the drinking vessels which were decorated in additive styles as early as the fourteenth century.

There existed a division of medieval pottery, based on vessel form and decoration, wherein vessels used in food preparation and consumption were set apart from those used in beverage consumption. The boundary was not elaborately marked and consisted of basic distinctions in form and contrasting means of decoration (additive versus subtractive). The composition of the body (i.e., paste or fabric), the hue of the lead glaze (often similar despite variation in vessel form), and stylistic simplicity blurred the distinction. As a category, these pottery vessels had attributes that linked them to the natural world. The use of red, red-brown, and buff clays with lead glazes, and sometimes green or greenish-yellow decoration, created pots with varied earth tones that had a visual resemblance to the colors of earth, field, and forest, thereby setting the vessels close to nature on the culture–nature continuum. The functional association of earthenwares with the transformation of food from its raw, natural state to a cooked form reiterated their visual position on the nature–culture axis.

The metaphorical link between pottery and nature was commented on by Deetz (1983, 1988). The classificatory link between women and nature has been written about by many (see review in Ortner 1972). Ceramic decoration illustrated the intermingling of human social relationships, man–animal relationships, and the deep penetration of the natural world into the cultural domain. The decorations on earth-toned serving dishes seen in the late seventeenth century were complex and included intertwining plants, mythological monsters, and anthropomorphic animals. With the start of the eighteenth century, however, the decorative motifs change; serving dishes are moved closer to the domain of culture than nature.

Rye (1976) observed of Papuan pottery that its dark hues were more practical or heat-efficient for cooking pots, but any recognition by Englishmen of a link between cooking efficiency and color tone is difficult to establish. English archaeologists (Cunningham and Drury 1986; Fox and Barton 1986) describe finely potted vessels with white pastes found in contexts dating to the 1560s. By the eighteenth century, the technology to produce utilitarian wares in white tones had existed for more than 100 years. White slips appear on drab gray-bodied English stoneware drinking vessels by 1710. Beautifully intricate wheel-engraved, brown-dipped white stoneware mugs were reportedly made by Dwight as early as 1680–90 (Oswald et al. 1982:31). Yet stoneware cooking or storage vessels were produced in the dark-toned tradition of earlier earthenwares long into the nineteenth century.

How can one explain the persistence of dark-toned hues on cooking utensils? Thinking about the problem in terms of technological advances or market availability produces what Firth (1975:26) calls a "disjunction – a gap between the overt superficial statement of action and its underlying meaning." On the surface, the presence of dark-toned cooking vessels seems neither sensible nor necessary. The observation that there is a fairly sharp boundary between earth-toned and white-toned vessels present by the late seventeenth century that becomes increasingly well defined with time also suggests that something of greater significance than market availability is at work. Distinctive because of the sharp, simple color contrast, the division of ceramic vessel forms by ware types indicates an emergent separation of activities between Phases 2 and 3 of the food cycle that further separates Phase 4 from earlier phases.

The earth tones of seventeenth-century ceramics stand in contrast to the whiteness of later ceramic assemblages; the preference was a cultural one, although technological and economic factors also were active. Deetz (1988) was one of the first historical archaeologists to point out that pure white ceramics were available as oriental porcelain and tin-enameled cups, plates, and chargers by the early seventeenth century and that they were used in New World homes, albeit sparsely. However, in this era such vessels were not central elements within the foodways system. By ca.1680–90, the cultural preference for white vessels increases; its influence on the household of Governor William Drummond can be seen in the number of white-toned vessels from his occupational phase at Governor's Land in Tidewater Virginia (see table 12.4). At Governor's Land, earth-toned vessels were less frequently used to distribute food, consume food, consume traditional beverages, or sip tea than were their white counterparts. Looking at this assemblage in comparison with its early seventeenth-century predecessors in Virginia (deposits from The Maine, Kingsmill Tenement, Pasbehay Tenement, and from Martin's Hundred) indicated that the overall percentage of white-toned vessels was 50 percent, or double the average, 26 percent, for the earlier sites (Yentsch, Bescherer and Patrick, forthcoming).

Table 12.4 [orig. table 10.4]   Percentage of white-toned ceramics recovered from two deposits at the Drummond Site ca.1680–1710.

Functional vessel class	Percent of assemblage represented by delft or porcelain	Percent within class
Food preparation and storage	0	0
Food distribution	7	50
Food consumption	15	94
Beverage storage (bottles)	0	0
Traditional beverages	10	59
Teawares	18	100

Source: Unpublished data provided by Merry Abbitt-Outlaw and Alain Outlaw, courtesy of the Virginia Research Center for Archaeology, Historic Landmarks Commission.

The trend towards whiter vessels was accompanied by a restriction of earth-toned pottery to vessel forms used in unprestigious tasks. The increased use of the whiter wares in food distribution and consumption was also accompanied by an elaboration of individual forms through size variation (introducing a qualitative difference among, for example, plates) and through sheer number. In this the households of the gentry led the way, as can be seen in a series of tables that (a) list the vessels in terms of their primary color tone for two different sets of eighteenth-century deposits at the Calvert site in Annapolis, Maryland (where earlier governors of the Province lived)) (table 12.5) and (b) in related data that contrast the ceramic holdings of the Calvert family as recovered archaeologically with vessel forms sold by merchants in the Chesapeake (tables 12.6 and 12.7; see also Patrick 1990).

The greater elaboration in pottery and porcelain accompanied an increased spatial differentiation within houses, as described earlier. Within wealthy households, two or more social spaces were set aside: kitchens, and rooms where formal dinners were held. White-toned vessels became associated with the masculine sphere of household food use, i.e., with food used to establish and promote prestige through ceremonial display. Earth-toned vessels were dissociated from this realm of behaviour.

As symbols, ceramic vessels were part of a prestige structure associated with food use. Their differential use by various status groups was a mechanism by which one status group was set apart from another: thus to study variation in ceramic assemblages is to study the archaeology of inequality. A structural analysis is especially helpful in highlighting the way in which particular elements of the prestige structure existed and provides a framework for considering form, dominant color tone, and decoration.

The first and most obvious opposition is the duality posed by color. Glassie (1975) equates white with distance from nature, therefore with artificiality, and, following from its association with something artificial, to culture rather than

Table 12.5 [orig. table 10.5] Vessel forms represented in the preliminary minimum vessel list for the Calvert Site in Annapolis, Maryland. The list was compiled by Anne Yentsch and Karen Bescherer (Yentsch, Bescherer, and Patrick, forthcoming).

	Earth-toned vessels		White-toned vessels		Total
	N	%	N	%	N
Food processing, preparation, and storage vessels					
Dairy processing					
Milk pans	18	100	–		18
Beverage storage					
Bottles	13	87	2	13	15
Food storage					
Butter pots	29	100	–		29
Jars/crocks	56	100	–		56
Olive jars	3	100	–		3
Cooking utensils					
Baking pan	2	100	–		2
Colander	1	100	–		1
Cooking pots	5	100	–		5
Mixing bowls	11	100	–		11
Pipkins	2	100	–		2
Pudding pans	20	100	–		20
Food distribution					
Bowls, assorted		50	100	50	
Chargers/platters	0		19	100	19
Condiment jars	1	10	9	90	10
Dishes, assorted	17	30	40	70	57
Fruit baskets	–		2	100	2
Salts	–		10	100	10
Sauce boat	–		1	100	1
Saucers	–		15	100	15
Scallop shells	–		2	100	2
Tureens	–		1	100	1
Food consumption					
Porringers	4	66	2	33	6
Plates, dessert	–		2	100	2
Plates, small	–		13	100	13
Plates, soup	–		8	100	8
Plates, assorted	–		8	100	8
Plates, generic	–		102	100	102

| | Earth-toned vessels | | White-toned vessels | | Total |
	N	%	N	%	N
Beverage distribution and consumption					
Punch bowls, assorted sizes	–		75	100	75
Traditional beverage distribution					
Jugs	13	100	–		13
Jug, ornamental (bear)	–		1	100	1
Pitchers	1	20	4	80	5
Traditional beverage consumption					
Cans	2	100	–		2
Caudle pots	1	100	–		1
Drinking pots	5	100	–		5
Posset pots	–		1	100	1
Cups	1	9	10	91	11
Mugs	82	84	16	16	98
Tankards	2	11	16	89	18
Tea, coffee, chocolate					
Tea bowls and saucers	1	>1	168	<99	169
Teapots	1	7	14	94	15
Coffee or chocolate pots	–		3	100	3
Capuchins	1	33	2	66	3
Cream pots, etc.	–		4	100	4
Sugar pots, etc.	–		6	100	6
Other beverage					
Wine cups	–		2	100	2
Other					
Basins	–		12	100	12
Cosmetic jar	–		2	100	2
Drug pots or jars	–		3	100	3
Galley pots	–		28	100	28
Ginger pot	–		3	100	3
Flower pots	2	100	–		2
Chamber pots	12	57	9	43	21

Table 12.6 [orig. table 10.6] Table ceramic forms available in Chesapeake stores (1759–1775) and located at the Calvert site (ca.1720–ca.1790).[a]

Type	Calvert	Allason	Dixon	Hamilton	Hammond	Coffing
Serving						
Dish	×	×	×	×	×	×
Tureen	×		×	×		
Platter	×	×	×	×		
Salad bowl	×					
Sauce boat	×	×	×	×	×	
Butter boat plate	×		×	×	×	
Pickle stand	×			×		
Fruit dish/basket	×	×	×	×		
Mustard pot	×		×	×		
Pepper caster			×			
Table cross (cat)		×				
Salt cellar	×	×		×	×	
Teapot	×	×	×	×	×	
Coffee/chocolate pot	×		×	×		
Milk pot/cream jug	×	×	×	×	×	
Sugar bowl/dish	×	×	×	×	×	
Sugar box	×	×		×		
Slop bowl	×		×	×	×	
Punch bowl	×	×	×	×		
Punch strainer			×			
Water pitcher	×	×	×	×		
Consuming						
Dinner plate	×	×	×	×	×	×
Soup plate	×			×		
Dessert plate	×					
Twifler plate	×	×				
Breakfast plate	×		×	×		
Teacup and saucer	×	×	×	×	×	
Coffee cup/can	×	×		×		
Breakfast cup	×		×			
Cup/mug	×	×	×	×	×	
Drinking bowl	×	×	×			
Wine cup	×					
Porringer	×	×	×	×		×

[a] For these purposes, only form and not ware type is explored. Data are based on archaeological evidence for Calvert Site; annual store inventory for the shops of Allason (Falmouth, Virginia), Dixon (Port Royal, Virginia), and Hamilton (Piscattaway, Maryland); and store ledgers for Hammond (Annapolis, Maryland) and Coffing (Annapolis, Maryland).
Source: Patrick 1990.

nature. The analogy can be extended. As nature is equated with feminine properties, so then is culture equated with masculine properties (Ortner 1972). Equally useful are other binary discriminations used to analyze food: Bourdieu's (1979) formality/informality, exotic/homely, and experimental/traditional as well as Sahlins' (1976) social dimension of outer and inner.

Using Bourdieu's oppositions and noting the social space in which food vessels were used reveals that the wares found in formal dining spaces were whiter than those used in less prestigious informal contexts, where earth-toned vessels were the norm. To the extent that formal dining, social pomp, and conspicuous consumption were means of expressing power, of establishing reciprocal relationships, and of forming and strengthening alliances between households, they fell within a masculine domain. While women might participate in ritual dining and could enhance their own power through their orchestration and support of conspicuous food consumption, their benefits were merely derived; men controlled this cultural domain.

Formal designs on white-toned vessels were an important element in ritual dining. Chinese armorial porcelain is the example *par excellence* of the use of dinner wares to convey status information. Armorial porcelain was specially ordered (Howard 1974). The drawings of each coat-of-arms had to be transported from England to China where an armorial set was hand-painted as per the drawing; the porcelain was then shipped thousands of sea miles to its destination. A man whose household served food on armorial porcelain demonstrated his access to distant trade networks. But even the use of simpler, white-toned vessels such as Queen's ware cream-colored plates served to mark a family's social rank.

Using Bourdieu's analytical strategy, vessels can be ranked as experimental or traditional, exotic or homely. Earth-toned vessels were traditional. The basic continuity of form over the centuries, despite the small alterations so useful in dating sherds, is testimony of this quality. To the extent that men, as producers of pottery, permitted no radical experimentation with their form, control was retained over the domain wherein they were used/consumed. The designs that embellished earth-toned vessels were traditional English motifs; no one could associate these vessels visually with the exotic (i.e., "attractively strange or unusual"). In contrast, refined earthen and stone wares as well as porcelains often were produced in exotic, experimental forms as were many of the foods and beverages contained within them.

Sahlins' concept of "inner" refers to something closer to nature; he describes things associated with outer domains as more civilized (1976). In this context, one can interpret "more civilized" as the equivalent of "more masculine". Given the etiquette of the seventeenth and eighteenth centuries, it is appropriate to say that formal dining areas were more civilized and further from nature than kitchens, pantries, or other food preparation areas, and that this was a progressive evolution from earlier standards of civilized behavior (Elias 1939). The proliferation of knives, forks, and spoons; of specialized drinking vessels; small, medium, and large plates; and specialized serving containers such as soup tureens and sauce boats that one sees in the eighteenth century is generally taken as an indication of

Table 12.7 [orig. table 10.7]   Cooking, storing, and other ceramic forms available in Chesapeake stores (1759–1775) and located at the Calvert site (ca.1720–ca.1790).

Type	Calvert	Allason	Dixon	Hamilton	Hammond	Coffing
Cooking						
Pot	×				×	×
Pan	×				×	×
Bowl	×	×	×	×	×	×
Basin	×		×			
Pudding pan	×					
Patty pan	×		×	×		
Pie pan	×					
Colander	×					
Storing						
Jug	×	×	×	×	×	
Jar/canister	×	×	×		×	
Bottle	×	×	×	×		
Butter pot	×	×	×	×	×	
Pickle pot	×		×			
Venison pot			×			
Milk pan	×	×	×	×	×	×
Other						
Wash basin	×	×	×	×	×	
Chamber pot	×	×		×	×	
Galley pot	×					
Pill slab	×					
Tile	×					
Candlestick	×					
Flower pot	×					
Garniture	×			×		
Dolls' dish	×					

[a]   For these purposes, only form and not ware type is explored. Data are based on archaeological evidence for Calvert Site; annual store inventory for the shops of Allason (Falmouth, Virginia), Dixon (Port Royal, Virginia), and Hamilton (Piscattaway, Maryland); and store ledgers for Hammond (Annapolis, Maryland) and Coffing (Annapolis, Maryland).
Source: Patrick 1990.

"civilized dining" and is usually presumed to accompany a more elaborate table etiquette. It would be erroneous to conclude that the increased degree of gentility these items represent is symbolic of their feminization.

Other Elements of the Prestige Structure of Pottery

Variation in ceramic assemblages

In a context where the status gradations were wide-ranging, greater variety and elaboration in pottery existed. In a context where status gradations were simpler, there was less need for variation or elaboration. It is this principle that underlies the homogeneity in New England assemblages which contain much smaller quantities of delft or porcelain than those found in the South. Compare, for example, the contents of two rural Massachusetts assemblages with those from equivalent sites in the Chesapeake as shown in table 12.8. Overall there is greater use of white-toned vessels in the Chesapeake. This distinction is also visible in sherd counts: quantities at Massachusetts sites range between 3 and 15 percent of the total sherd count; quantities at Chesapeake sites range between 3 and 41 percent in the seventeenth and between 15 and 52 percent in the eighteenth century (Yentsch 1990:39, figure 6).

Southern households could be simple or highly complex, extended beyond the confines normally provided by kinship lines. In elite Southern society, food was prepared by slave cooks who were usually women (Walsh 1986, personal communication). In wealthy households, the activities associated with Phases 2, 3 and 5 of the food cycle were assigned to female servants or household slaves (female or young, adolescent males). Adolescent boys, as house slaves, might also serve food.

The use of adolescent males is important because the passage of food from preparation areas to dining areas brought food out of one domain and into another where free men who were neither kin nor household members might be present. A structuralist would say that it was appropriate for adolescent boys instead of girls to bring food into dining areas for the young men brought it out of private, intensive space where it was transformed from its raw or semi-processed natural state into an element of cuisine, and carried it into public, extensive space where it became part of social display. Their ambiguous sexual status (neither adult male nor child) paralleled the ambiguity of the transitional passage from one area to another. As exotic intermediaries, they increased the ritual value of the food. They gave to it qualities similar to those imparted by French chefs in the homes of British nobles and in the Annapolis kitchens of American statesmen like Jefferson.

Mediation between the sphere of food preparation and storage and that of food consumption was also provided by the serving utensils used to distribute food. Initially a distinction was made between utilitarian vessels used to hold liquids (German stoneware bottles and their earthenware equivalents) and those

Table 12.8 [orig. table 10.8] The representation (%) of white-toned ceramics (delft, porcelain, or white salt-glazed stoneware) in different functional categories from late seventeenth- and early eighteenth-century assemblages from coastal Massachusetts, lower Maryland, and Tidewater Virginia

	New England sites		Chesapeake sites					
Functional vessel class	Wellfleet	Howland	Utopia*	Pettus*	Compton*	Clifts IV	Hicks	Calvert
Food preparation and storage	0	0	0	0	0	0	0	0
Food distribution	7	11	33	82	25	60	24	71
Food consumption	27	47	71	97	75	66	100	100
Beverage storage (bottles)	0	0	0	0	n.a.	0	0	0
Traditional beverages	0	9	31	17	0	35	3	33
Punch bowls and teawares	100	100	n.a.	100	n.a.	100	100	99

* Denotes the late 17th-century sites.

Sources: Bragdon (1988) for New England; Outlaw and Friedlander (1989) for Compton; the remainder is based on minimum vessel lists provided in Yentsch, Bescherer, and Patrick (forthcoming). Further information on the assemblages from these sites is also provided in Yentsch (1990, 1992).

used to serve beverages; this can be seen in archaeological assemblages of the 1400s (Lewis 1978). By ca.1680 the decorative slipwares and incised graffito derivatives marked the vessels used for serving both liquids and solids. By ca.1740, the sign that one had crossed the boundary between one domain of food use and another included the visual distinction between earth-toned and white-toned vessels and other stylistic variations serving to elaborate this elemental, visual difference.

The teawares

Pottery could set apart one man from another, and one household could be distinguished from another by the quality of the ceramics used to serve those who were guests. This occurred whether or not men were present: women, in their role as hostesses, functioned as representatives of the household. Hence the teawares – Chinese porcelain, delft, and elegant salt-glazed copies of Chinese forms – did not lose their masculine association initially when used by women. By serving, a woman paid homage to her family and guests while simultaneously, by her rank, denoting the status of the household. The situation is analogous to Henry II's homage to his son which he marked by serving his son himself at the son's coronation, and it is also analogous to the manner in which young men marked the rank of their elders by serving them in medieval dining halls. As a woman's social network was formed by kinship lines, eighteenth-century women who took tea together usually were relatives or near neighbors. In almost all social situations, it was the man of the house who invited non-kin into a home, and a wife honored him by serving them.

This is demonstrated in the tea ceremony. By ca.1680, teawares began to enter the archaeological record (Yentsch 1990: figure 8; 1992: figure 9), but at this time tea was a masculine beverage. The tea ceremony, surrounded by social pomp, became a focal element in women's lives by ca.1740. Because of its association with women, some might think of the tea ceremony as feminine and hence suggest that the white-toned tea bowls, saucers, pots, and creamers used to serve it indicate that these vessels had no masculine symbolism. However, in the late seventeenth century tea was an exotic beverage consumed by elite men in tea-houses. As tea was assimilated into the household beverage system, women began to consume it and took over the role of brewing and serving it to their men, replicating the pattern of its distribution in the tea-houses.

Through the use of high-status teawares, women conveyed the social status of their household to their kin or neighbors who might visit on an informal basis and to others in the community who were invited for more formal occasions. Women increased their power by their organization of such social rituals. As the eighteenth century progressed, tea became a political symbol (Breen 1986) and a beverage whose use cross-cut the social hierarchy. As this occurred, tea pots and tea cups appeared in a variety of wares decorated in motifs associated with the folk tradition and with daily food. Whereas between 1680 and 1720 tea was a prestigious masculine beverage, as it was popularized in the mid-eighteenth century it was also feminized – a trend strongly manifested in its nineteenth-century use. Fashion was the mechanism by which teawares were transferred from one side of the oppositional binary structure to the other.

It is this which explains the short production span for agate, tortoiseshell, clouded, and green wares made by Whieldon and Wedgwood in the 1750s and 1760s. What they attempted was the transfer of earth-toned colors and the fruit/flower motifs of the earlier folk tradition to vessel forms separate from the folk tradition. Teawares were members of the masculine domain of pottery whereas the earth-toned colors and folk motifs were components in the feminine domain. The pottery these ingenious entrepreneurs created formed a mixed metaphor that carried a contradictory social message: the result was a visual insult. White salt-glazed vessels in many of the very same forms, produced in the same molds, were popular because their color and style was consistent with the symbolism associated with ceremonial food consumption. This ritual use of food involved men as individuals, and women as mothers, wives, and daughters, but not as individuals in their own right. Fashion trends in marketing, as markers of upward social mobility, were most successful when they flowed with the basic principles in the prestige structure rather than against them. Had the production of Whieldon-Wedgwood wares been delayed until the early nineteenth century, their popularity might have been greater for by that time tea was thoroughly assimilated into the folk tradition.

Cultural expressions of social inequality are often complex and may be partially masked by being situated in a context where they appear unnecessary. Teawares were objects denoting the status of a household although they were used by women. On the surface, and due in part to the fact that tea in the United States did become feminized at a later point in time, eighteenth-century teawares appear to the modern observer to wear a feminine guise. However, they were used to convey information about social rank within the household to family members and to guests through the highly formalized tea ceremony. This was a ceremony in which women played an important role, but its focus was not the feminine actors involved in it: rather, it was the conveyance of information about the household, the gathering of information about others, and the maintenance of group alliances. Hence teawares fell within the masculine domain of beverage use. Further, objects that were seemingly masculine could be used to set apart one man from another through the incorporation of feminine elements into their decoration. This follows Bloch's premise that gender symbolism may often form the basis for ideological divisions that are not gender-bound (1985).

The Metaphor of Pottery

In summary, a basic separation – an element in the social structure of each family – was the separation between men's and women's roles. Earth-toned and white-toned pottery marked this taken-for-granted separation. Simply put, men and women were not created equal. The use of white-toned vessels that were symbols associated with social display (and therefore with elite and powerful men) did not penetrate feminine space. If such vessels had done so, this would have introduced an internal inconsistency into the symbolic system by equating feminine space or, among slave owners, Afro-American space with the highest level of the social structure. The use of coarse earthenwares and stonewares in this area was, however, consistent with the social structure and its subordinate placement of those who worked in such activity areas. The use of white ceramic vessels in food preparation would have inverted the social order by equating culture with nature, men with women.

The relational statements expressed by variation in food vessels about the social hierarchy also enabled members of the culture to make statements about the use of space and the use of food by speaking of these indirectly through the metaphor of pottery. Thus the oppositions expressed in spatial boundaries between activity areas were reinforced and replicated in the division of pottery that simultaneously also substituted, metaphorically, for the different uses to which food was put. The break between two food traditions – the courtly and the folk – emphasized the two-tiered structure of the society (Yentsch 1991). The elite food tradition was built on a complex labor base, and required the use of scarce resources, elaborate utensils, and time-consuming procedures; the cooking techniques associated with haute cuisine were mysterious, for knowledge of these was restricted. The daily meals of ordinary people, on the other hand, utilized a small labor pool (often only mothers and daughters), drew on readily available foodstuffs with a seasonal base, and used procedures that minimized labor requirements. Knowledge of food preparation techniques for everyday food was passed from one generation of women to the next and might be shared outside the kin group.

The differences between the two types of food use (for social display and for daily sustenance) provided a series of visual boundaries between sets of individuals that were integral to the social organization. Man's authority over the natural world was seen to be virtually unlimited – the natural world was something he might use "for his profit or for his pleasure" (Day 1620:213, quoted in Thomas 1983:21); by creating asymmetrical relationships among individuals, relationships based on dominance and subordination, categories of people were created within the culture who might be used for profit or for pleasure. One way of establishing the legitimacy of these relationships was to situate certain of them within the natural world: one means of doing so was to define different types of activities and objects as existing closer to nature than others. This was accomplished by attributing to them qualities that were culturally defined as feminine.

The prestige structure, consisting of food and food-related objects such as pottery vessels, was not simply a division between male and female domains. It distinguished between men of different social rank, providing gradations of social worth that extended across ethnic and racial lines. It was based on the idea that qualities in an individual were defined by contiguity: that is to say, that by working in an area socially defined as closer to nature than another with tools that were perceived as belonging on the nature side of the culture-nature continuum, one also became symbolically associated with nature. Ideologically this legitimated the use or misuse of such individuals for another's profit or pleasure because it placed them lower in the hierarchy of beings, which itself was part of the political and social model for social action. This ideological division was not gender-bound, but it made use of gender symbolism in household space, in household food, and in household pottery as one of its legitimizing mechanisms.

Acknowledgements

I would like to thank Carole Carr, Jim Deetz, Conrad Goodwin, Gary Wheeler Stone, and, especially, Mary C. Beaudry and Lorena Walsh, for their helpful comments and criticisms on earlier versions of this paper. Work on the Calvert ceramics was funded, in part, by Grant RO-21482-87 from the National Endowment for the Humanities.

References

Amussen, Susan D. (1985) "Gender, Family, and the Social Order, 1560–1725." In *Order and Disorder in Early Modern England*, eds Anthony Fletcher and John Stevenson, pp. 196–217. Cambridge University Press, London.
—— (1987) *An Ordered Society: Gender and Class in Early Modern England*. Basil Blackwell, Oxford.
Ardener, Edwin (1972) "Belief and the Problem of Women." In *The Interpretation of Ritual*, ed. J. LaFontaine. Tavistock, London.
Aires, Phillipe (1962) *Centuries of Childhood*. Penguin, London.
Barnes, J. A. (1973) "Genetrix:Genitor–Nature:Culture?" In *The Character of Kinship*, ed. Jack Goody. Cambridge University Press, London.
Beaudry, Mary C. (1980) "Pot-Shot, Jug-Bitten, Cup-Shaken: Object Language and Double Meanings," Paper presented at the American Anthropological Association Meetings, Washington, D.C.
—— (n.d.) *Domestic Pursuits: Historical Archaeology of American Households*. Telford Press, Caldwell, NJ (forthcoming).
Bloch, Maurice (1985) "From Cognition to Ideology." In *Power and Knowledge* ed. Richard Fardon, pp. 21–48. Scottish Academic Press, Edinburgh.
Bourdieu, Pierre (1979) *La Distinction*. Le Minuit, Paris.
Bragdon, Kathleen (1988) "Occupational Differences Reflected in Material Culture." *Documentary Archaeology*, ed. M. C. Beaudry, pp. 83–91. Cambridge University Press, Cambridge.
Breen, Timothy (1986) "Baubles of Britain: the Meaning of Things." Paper presented at the Washington, D. C. Historical Society Meetings, March 20–21, 1986.
Cahn, Susan (1987) *Industry of Devotion: the Transformation of Women's Work in England, 1500–1600*. Columbia University Press, New York.
Cott, Nancy F. (1977) *The Bonds of Womanhood: "Women's Sphere" in New England, 1780–1835*. Yale University Press, New Haven, CT.
Cunningham, C. M. and P. J. Drury (1986) *Post-medieval Sites and Their Pottery: Moulsham Street, Chelmsford*, Chelmsford Archaeological Trust Report No. 54.
Day, John (1620) *Day's Descant* (quoted in K. Thomas (1983) *Man and the Natural World*. Allen Lane, London).
Deagan, Kathleen (1973) "Mestizaje in Colonial St. Augustine." *Ethnohistory* 20(1), 55–65.
—— (1983) *Spanish St. Augustine: the Archaeology of a Colonial Creole Community*. Academic Press, New York.

Deetz, James (1972) "Ceramics from Plymouth, 1635–1835: the Archaeological Evidence." In *Ceramics in America*, ed. Ian Quimby, pp. 15–40. Winterthur Conference Report. University of Virginia Press, Charlottesville.

—— (1977) *In Small Things Forgotten: The Archaeology of Early American Life*. Anchor Books, New York.

—— (1983) "Scientific Humanism and Humanistic Science: A Place for Paradigmatic Pluralism in Historical Archaeology." *Geoscience and Man* 23, 27–34.

—— (1988) "Material Culture and Worldview in Colonial Anglo-America." In *The Recovery of Meaning*, eds Mark P. Leone and Parker Potter, pp. 219–35.

Detweiler, Susan G. (1982) *George Washington's Chinaware*. Harry N. Abrams, Inc., New York.

Douglas, Mary (1972) "Deciphering a Meal." *Daedalus* (Winter 1972) 61–81.

—— (1986) *How Institutions Think*. Syracuse University Press, Syracuse, NY.

Elias, Norbert (1939) *The Civilizing Process: The History of Manners*. Basil Blackwell, Oxford.

Firth, Raymond (1975) *Symbols: Public and Private*. Cornell University Press, Ithaca.

Fox, Russell and K. G. Barton (1986) "Excavations at Oyster Street, Portsmouth, Hampshire, 1968–71." *Post-medieval Archaeology* 20, 31–256.

Fraser, Antonia (1985) *The Weaker Vessel*. Vintage, New York.

Glassie, Henry (1975) *Folk Housing in Middle Virginia*. University of Tennessee Press, Knoxville.

Goody, Jack (1982) *Cooking, Cuisine and Class*. Cambridge University Press, Cambridge.

Hamilton, Roberta (1978) *The Liberation of Women: A Study of Patriarchy and Capitalism*. Controversies in Sociology No. 6. George Allen & Unwin, London.

Hanawalt, Barbara A. (ed.) (1986) *Women and Work in Preindustrial Europe*. Indiana University Press, Bloomington.

Handsman, Russell (1984) "Merchant Capital and the Historical Archaeology of Gender, Motherhood, and Child Raising." Paper presented at the Council for Northeast Historical Archaeology Meetings, October 1984, State University of New York, Binghamton.

Henisch, Bridget Ann (1976) *Fast and Feast*. Pennsylvania State University Press, State Park, PA.

Howard, David S. (1974) *Chinese Armorial Porcelain*. Faber & Faber, London.

Levi-Strauss, C. (1958) *Anthropologie Structurale*. Paris (English translation, *Structural Anthropology*. Basic Books, Garden City, NY, 1963).

—— (1965) "The Culinary Triangle." *Partisan Review* 33, 586–95.

—— (1988) *The Jealous Potter* (trans. Benedicte Chorier). University of Chicago Press, Chicago.

Lewis, J. M. (1978) *Medieval Pottery and Metal-ware in Wales*. Amgueddfa Genedlaethol Cymru. National Museum of Wales, Cardiff.

Macfarlane, Alan (1988) "The Cradle of Capitalism: the Case of England." In *Europe and the Rise of Capitalism*, eds Jean Baechler, John A. Hall, and Michael Mann, pp. 185–204. Basil Blackwell, Oxford.

Mennell, Stephen (1985) *All Manners of Food*. Basil Blackwell, Oxford.

Mertes, Kate (1988) *The English Noble Household 1250–1600: Good Governance and Politic Rule*. Basil Blackwell, Oxford.

Neiman, Fraser (1978) "A Provisional Model of Culture Change in Westmorland County, Virginia." Paper presented at the Annual Meetings, Society for Historical Archaeology, San Antonio, Texas.

Nicholson, Linda J. (1986) *Gender and History: the Limits of Social Theory in the Age of the Family*. Columbia University, New York.

Norton, Mary Beth (1980) *Liberty's Daughters: The Revolutionary Experience of American Women, 1750–1800*. Little Brown & Company, Boston.

Ortner, Sherry B. (1972) "Is Female to Male as Nature is to Culture?" *Feminism Studies* 1, 5–31.

Ortner, Sherry B. and Harriet Whitehead (1982) *Sexual Meanings: The Cultural Construction of Gender and Sexuality*. Cambridge University Press, Cambridge.

Oswald, Adrian, R. J. C. Hildyard, and R. G. Hughes (1982) *English Brown Stoneware, 1670–1900*. Faber & Faber, London.

Outlaw, Alain and Amy Friedlander (1989) *The Compton Site circa 1651–1684, Calvert County, Maryland* 18CV279, prepared by Cultural Resource Group, Louis Berger & Associates (East Orange, NJ, 1989) on file at the Jefferson Patterson Park and Museum, Calvert County, MD.

Patrick, Stephen (1990) *"Round the Social Bowl:" Elite Ceramics at the Calvert Site and Other Patterns of Consumer Consumption in the Chesapeake*. M.A. thesis, American Studies Program, College of William and Mary, Williamsburg, VA.

Rackham, Bernard (1948) *Medieval English Pottery*. Faber & Faber, London.

Reed, Michael (1983) *The Georgian Triumph 1700–1830*. Routledge and Kegan Paul, London.

Reiter, Rayna R. (1975) "Men and Women in the South of France: Public and Private Domains." In *Toward an Anthropology of Women*, ed. Rayna R. Reiter, pp. 252–82. New School of Social Research, New York.

Reitz, Elizabeth (1988) "Preliminary Analysis of Vertebrate Remains from the Calvert Site in Annapolis, Maryland and a Comparison with Vertebrate Remains from Sites in South Carolina, Georgia, and Jamaica." *Calvert Interim Report No. 6* National Endowment for the Humanities Grant RO-21482-87. On file at Historic Annapolis, Inc., Annapolis, MD.

Rosaldo, Michelle Zimbalist (1974) "Women, Culture and Society: A Theoretical Overview." In *Women, Culture and Society*, eds. Michelle Z. Rosaldo and Louise Lamphere, pp. 17–42. Stanford University Press, Standford.

—— (1987) "Moral/Analytic Dilemmas Posed by the Intersection of Feminism and Social Science." In *Interpretive Social Science*, eds Paul Rabinow and William M. Sullivan, pp. 280–301 (revised edn). University of California Press, Berkeley.

Rye, O. S. (1976) "Keeping Your Temper Under Control: Materials and the Manufacture of Papuan Pottery." *Archaeology and Physical Anthropology in Oceania* 11, 106–37.

Sahlins, Marshall (1976) *Culture and Practical Reason*. Chicago University Press, Chicago.

St George, Robert B. (1982) "'Set Thine House in Order': The Domestication of the Yeomanry in Seventeenth-Century New England." In *New England Begins: The Seventeenth Century*, eds Jonathan L. Fairbanks and Robert F. Trent. Boston Museum of Fine Arts, Boston.

Schama, Simon (1987) *The Embarrassment of Riches: An Interpretation of Dutch Culture in the Golden Age*. Knopf, New York.

Schuyler, Robert L. (ed.) (1980) *Archaeological Perspectives on Ethnicity in America*. Baywood Press, New York.

Stansell, Christine (1987) *City of Women: Sex and Class in New York, 1789–1860*. University of Illinois Press, Urbana.

Thomas, Keith (1983) *Man and the Natural World*. Allen Lane, London.

Thrupp, Sylvia (1962) *The Merchant Class of Medieval London*. University of Michigan Press, Ann Arbor.

Ulrich, Laura T. (1982) *Good Wives: Image and reality in the Lives of Women in Northern New England*, 1650–1750. Alfred Knopf, New York.

Upton, Dell (1988) "White and Black Landscapes in Eighteenth-Century Virginia." In *Material Life in America, 1600–1860*, ed. Robert St George, pp. 357–69. Northeastern University Press, Boston.

Wall, Diana D. (1987) *At Home in New York: Changing Family Life among the Propertied in the Late Eighteenth and Early Nineteenth Centuries*. Unpublished Ph.D. Dissertation, Department of Anthropology, New York University, New York.

Wilson, C. Anne (1974) *Food and Drink in Britain from the Stone Age to Recent Times*. Barnes & Noble, New York.

Yentsch, Anne E. (1990) "Minimum Vessel Lists as Evidence of Change in Folk and Courtly Traditions of Food Use." *Historical Archaeology* 24(3), 26–53.

—— (1992) "Chesapeake Artifacts and Their Cultural Context: Pottery and the Food Domain." *Post-medieval Archaeology* 24 (forthcoming).

Yentsch, Anne E., Karen Bescherer, and Stephen Patrick (forthcoming) "The Calvert Ceramic Collection." *Calvert Interim Report No. 4* (Historic Annapolis Foundation, Annapolis, MD).

Yentsch, Anne and Larry W. McKee (1987) "Footprints of Buildings in Eighteenth-Century Annapolis, Maryland." *American Archaeology* 6(1), 40–51.

13

Cognitive Archaeology

Kent V. Flannery and Joyce Marcus

Praised by some and dismissed by others, 'cognitive archaeology' has become one of the latest archaeological approaches to be labelled without ever having been defined. Now comes a belated effort to define it, and to decide whether it was born of inspiration or just antipathy toward other approaches.

The decade of the 1960s saw a great upsurge in what has been called 'subsistence-settlement archaeology' – studies of prehistoric demography and changing settlement patterns, the origins of agriculture and irrigation, the human use of soils, plants and animals (Ucko & Dimbleby 1969; Ucko *et al.* 1972). The archaeological approaches associated with this upsurge were philosophically positivist and methodologically rigorous, with a heavy emphasis on material remains and a commitment to the notion that subsistence behaviour was the infra-structure of cultural systems.

It was to be expected that not all archaeologists would share this commitment, or leap upon the subsistence-settlement bandwagon. Some complained that the materialist focus of the 1960s dehumanized history, and that ways should be sought to include more of the values, ideas, beliefs, and cognitive processes that make the human species unique. By the early 1970s, one could search the American Anthropological Association's guide to anthropology departments and find occasional archaeologists who, like John Fritz and Robert Hall, listed 'cognitive archaeology' among their research interests.

Many subsistence-settlement archaeologists were distinctly lukewarm toward the notion of cognitive archaeology (Sanders 1974, 119). For some, the realm of 'ideas' was so nebulous and undocumented in the archaeological record that it could not be studied scientifically. For others, such cognitive areas as religion and ideology were epiphenomena, dependent variables so far removed from the primary variables of the subsistence economy as to be trivial and unworthy of study. Such attitudes slowed the growth of cognitive archaeology but could not prevent it entirely.

By the mid-1970s articles involving some aspect of cognition were appearing regularly in the archaeological literature. Our own first effort (Flannery & Marcus 1976) was an attempt to understand the ancient Zapotec Indians more fully by combining their cosmological beliefs with a more traditional analysis of their subsistence and settlement. We did not see ourselves as 'cognitive archaeologists', whatever that might be. We simply tried to show that one could explain a higher proportion of ancient Zapotec subsistence behaviour if, instead of restricting oneself to a study of agricultural plants and irrigation canals, one took into account what was known of Zapotec notions about the relationship of lightning, rain, blood sacrifice, and the 'satisfizing ethic'. We also stressed that we could only do so because the sixteenth-century Spanish eyewitness accounts of the Zapotec were so rich.

Despite the reservations of mainstream subsistence-settlement archaeologists, interest in cognitive archaeology continued to grow throughout the 1980s. Like Topsy in *Uncle Tom's Cabin*, however, it just 'growed' in a haphazard, unsystematic way, undefined as an area of study and clearly meaning different things to different people. To some, including the present authors, it was merely an opportunity to make mainstream archaeology more holistic whenever possible (Flannery & Marcus 1976, 383). For others, it was a reaction against what they saw as the 'vulgar materialism' of subsistence-settlement archaeology. For a third group of archaeologists, however, it took what we believe is a direction to be discouraged: it was seen as the shortcut to a kind of 'armchair archaeology' that requires no fieldwork or rigorous analysis of any kind. As a result of this shortcut, many of the worst fears of materialists have been realized; any fanciful mentalist speculation is allowed, so long as it is called 'cognitive archaeology'.

The Search for a Definition

Ironically, despite the support of a foundation, a journal, and a growing number of enthusiasts, cognitive archaeology has yet to be defined. What, in fact, is it? What subject matter does it cover? Should it be considered a separate branch of archaeology, or simply a set of topics within holistic archaeology? Is cognitive archaeology the study of epiphenomena, as many subsistence-settlement archaeologists would claim? Can it in fact be done, and if so, is it even worth doing?

Let us propose a tentative definition of the subject, one our colleagues can expand or modify as they wish. Cognitive archaeology is the study of all those aspects of ancient culture that are the product of the human mind: the perception, description, and classification of the universe (cosmology); the nature of the supernatural (religion); the principles, philosophies, ethics, and values by which human societies are governed (ideology); the ways in which aspects of the world, the supernatural, or human values are conveyed in art (iconography); and all other forms of human intellectual and symbolic behaviour that survive in the archaeological record. Note that this definition makes no mention of such common subsistence-settlement behaviours as hunting, fishing, farming, plant collecting, tool-making, and so on, although it acknowledges that human intelligence is employed in all of them. They are omitted because their inclusion would inevitably make it difficult to distinguish between 'cognitive archaeology' and 'archaeology'.

What we do in this article is restrict ourselves to four major topics listed in the paragraph above: cosmology, religion, ideology, and iconography. We begin with a definition of each, because we have noted tremendous confusion in the literature about where one topic ends and the other begins[1]. In particular, we note confusion between cosmology and religion, and between religion and ideology. The fact that there is an interface between any two of these topics does not justify blurring their definitions.

We next attempt to refute the materialist notion that any of these topics is an 'epiphenomenon'. In refutation we offer a series of studies, drawn from the literature, that suggest otherwise. These studies indicate that there may be rigorous ways to approach cognitive questions about archaeology. At the same time, we argue that such cognitive approaches can only be used when conditions are appropriate; that is, when the body of supporting data is sufficiently rich. When it is not so rich, cognitive archaeology becomes little more than speculation, a kind of bungee jump into the Land of Fantasy.

Finally, we will argue that cognitive archaeology should never become a separate branch of archaeology. If it is to be rigorous and scientific it must remain part of mainstream archaeology, something that subsistence-settlement archaeologists do to make their work more holistic, and something that they do only when the data are sufficient. Were it to be seen as a separate branch of archaeology, it would become an instant magnet for dilettantes and charlatans. When well done, cognitive archaeology makes archaeology broader and more well-rounded; poorly done, it results in some of the worst archaeology on record.

Cosmology

All cultures have a theory of the universe, or cosmos, and the rules by which it works; even twentieth-century astronomers are said to be doing cosmology when they describe 'the Big Bang'. For many cultures, of course, the cosmos includes supernatural beings which provide the linkup between cosmology and religion.

Cosmology can be defined as a theory or philosophy of the origin and general structure of the universe, its components, elements, and laws, especially those relating to such variables as space, time, and causality. How the cosmos is structured affects both religion and ideology.

Understandably, many subsistence-settlement archaeologists think that cosmology can be conveniently left to the humanists. Who cares how some ancient culture conceived of the universe? Isn't the important thing the way they used soil, water, plants, and animals to their advantage?

One answer is that the way cultures conceive of the cosmos strongly influences subsistence and settlement. Two of the clearest examples of that fact can be drawn

---

[1] Our definitions are not idiosyncratic; they are based on those offered by *Webster's Dictionary* and the *American College Dictionary*.

from J.D. Hughes' contrast between Greek and Roman attitudes toward the environment (Hughes 1975).

The Greeks, according to Hughes (1975, 48), 'saw the natural environment as the sphere of activity of the gods'. Because various gods and goddesses made their homes in the wilderness, there existed the widespread practice of setting aside a grove of trees, called an *alsos*, as a sacred area of land; alternatively, a grove called a *tenemos*, the abode of a deity, could be set aside only for worship. Hunting in such sacred groves was forbidden.

As a result of this conception of the forest's place in the cosmos, forestry in ancient Greece became the concern of the government of each *polis*. Inscriptions show that Greek states 'controlled the cutting of timber on their own territory and required replanting in some cases' (Hughes 1975, 71). To be sure, these practices were insufficient to prevent some areas of Greece from being converted to second-growth *maquis* or *garrigue*. They do, however, indicate a cosmology in which some forests were seen as an appropriate, necessary, even sacred part of the universe.

Hughes contrasts this cosmology with that of the Romans, whose attitudes toward nature he calls 'distinctly utilitarian'. He describes the Romans as 'avaricious and practical' in their use of the environment; in their cosmology 'the world [was] here for human use' (Hughes 1975, 87). Like the Greeks, the Romans had set aside some groves of trees as sacred. Unlike the Greeks, they were willing to cut down trees in such groves, sacrificing a pig and saying a prayer 'to smooth the ruffled feelings of the god or goddess . . . who lived there' (Hughes 1975, 88).

The long-term effects of a cosmology in which all plants and animals exist for human use are not hard to imagine. The Romans significantly deforested Italy and were forced to look elsewhere for timber, importing pines from the Black Sea, cedars from Lebanon, larch from the Alps, and citrus trees from North Africa. In spite of the growing shortage of local timber, state forests continued to be rented out to private exploiters (Hughes 1975, 101).

Hughes' study shows that when enough is known about the cosmology of an ancient people, one is in a better position to interpret their use of the environment. When little or nothing is known, however, as in the case of many nonliterate ancient cultures – caution is advisable. It is not likely that we will be able to 'reconstruct' ancient cosmologies for such cultures based solely on an examination of their plant and animal remains.

Religion

A religion can be defined as a specific set of beliefs in a divine or superhuman power or powers, to be obeyed and worshipped as the creator(s) and/or ruler(s) of the universe. Religions usually involve a philosophy and a code of ethics, both related to the quest for the values of an ideal life. That quest has three phases: (a) the idea itself; (b) a set of practices for attaining the values of the ideal; and (c) a theology or world view relating that quest to the universe. It is this world view that lies at the interface between religion and cosmology.

Anyone who regards religion as an epiphenomenon should read Paul Wheatley's illuminating study of overseas trade between India and Southeast Asia in the early centuries of the Christian era (Wheatley 1975). Not only does it contrast the ideals of Hinduism and Buddhism, it also shows the penetration of religion into economics and challenges the supremacy of the law of supply and demand.

According to Wheatley, the Roman emperor Vespasian (AD 69–79) prohibited the export of precious metals from the Roman Empire, aggravating a perceived shortage of gold in India. This shortage was all the more keenly felt because nomadic disturbances along the Bactrian trade route had cut off India's access to Siberian gold (Wheatley 1975, 233).

The Indians heard that gold was available on the surface of the ground in the Malay Peninsula, Java, and the lands of the South China Sea. Here lay potential for great trade, in the formalist sense of a 'demand' (in India) and a 'supply' (in Malaysia). That trade could not be realized, however, because it would have involved long ocean voyages which would bring devout Hindus into contact with *mleccha* – foreigners who, because of their different religion, were a source of pollution.

Under Hindu religion, contact with heathens was considered contaminating, especially for those of the Brahmin caste. 'The old Brahmanism had paid heed to the laws of Manu which totally prohibited such voyages [to distant areas]' and prescribed a three-year penance if the prohibition was violated (Wheatley 1975, 234). Thus it was neither a lack of sailing technology nor the presence of unfavourable economic conditions that prevented India from getting at Southeast Asia's gold; it was the Brahmin notion of ethnic purity through avoiding contact with *mleccha*.

Significantly, what turned the tide was the expansion of Buddhism, a rival religion that rejected Brahmin notions of ethnic purity and the concept of pollution through contact with foreigners. The spread of Buddhism into India thus 'did much to dispel the Hindu repugnance to travel' (Wheatley 1975, 234), opening up the sea lanes to Southeast Asia. Within a few centuries, wealthy Indian merchants were plying those lanes, bringing back to their subcontinent much more than gold.

Perhaps equally important was the impact of Indian civilization on Southeast Asia, a region that had previously been organized at the chiefdom level. Colonies of Indian traders began to spring up in Malaysia, Burma, and Java, introducing Indian concepts of kingship and nobility. What resulted was a period of 'Indianization' (Wheatley 1975, 249) during which Southeast Asia chiefdoms evolved into kingdoms whose governance was based on Indian conceptions of social order. As high-caste Indian entrepreneurs raised the level of sociopolitical complexity in Southeast Asia, the temple cities of that region became centres for the diffusion of Indian customs and beliefs.

Wheatley's study clearly shows religion's power to interfere with laws of supply and demand or 'rational' economic behaviour. It also shows how religion can provide the catalyst by which a new political ideology enters a region and guides cultural evolution. High-caste Indian merchants gained their 'gold route' and changed the course of Southeast Asian history forever; but the change might never have taken place without Buddhism's conquest of the Brahmin's fear of foreigners.

To be sure it is easier to demonstrate religion's central role through a study like Wheatley's than to provide a rigorous method for studying religion archaeologically. In an article currently in press (Marcus & Flannery 1994), we outline such a method for ethnohistorically-documented cultures like the Zapotec of ancient Mexico.

The method consists of (a) constructing a model of the ancient religion by analyzing the ethnohistoric documents; (b) isolating those elements, such as temple structures and ritual artefacts, that are likely to be preserved archaeologically (Marcus 1978); (c) undertaking an analysis of ancient temple plans and a 'contextual analysis' of ritual paraphernalia (Flannery 1976); and finally (d) comparing and contrasting the observed archaeological remains with the expected pattern derived from ethnohistory. Once again we stress that when the ethnohistoric record is lacking, far less success should be anticipated.

Ideology

Among our four categories of cognitive investigation, ideology is perhaps the most frequently confused with one of the others – often, in fact, with *all* of the others. It is useful to remind oneself that Marxism, fascism, and American democracy are all ideologies. Thus ideology falls within society and politics, not religion (although, to be sure, the lines between the three may be blurred by political movements such as Islamic Fundamentalism). Ideology may be defined as the body of doctrine, myth, and symbolism of a social movement, institution, class, or group of individuals, often with reference to some political or cultural plan, along with the strategies for putting the doctrine into operation. The point at which symbolism is used serves as an interface with iconography.

To give just one example, every archaeologist who works on the transition from egalitarian society to rank society is dealing with a change in ideology. Egalitarian societies do not simply remain egalitarian because they are poor, marginal, or underdeveloped; most have 'levelling mechanisms' that work to prevent the emergence of rank. Such societies may have numerous *acquired* differences in status, but their egalitarian ideology counteracts any tendency for such status differences to become *hereditary*, or 'institutionalized'. The emergence of hereditary ranking requires the adoption of a new ideology in which institutional élites are rationalized.

In the ethnographic literature, one of the classic treatments of the emergence of ranking is Leach's (1954) study of highland Burma. For many decades, the Kachin hill people oscillated between *gumlao* (egalitarian) and *gumsa* (rank) organization, with much of their paradigm for rank behaviour drawn from the Shan aristocracy of the nearby lowlands. Their periodic reversion to egalitarian society shows that, at least for the Kachin, the emergence of rank was not an irreversible process.

Some 25 years later Jonathan Friedman, drawing on Leach's research but adding

Meaning and Practice

a great deal of his own, presented an analysis of the ideological changes involved in the evolution of such 'Asiatic social formations' (Friedman 1979). His reconstruction of the ideological shift in Burmese societies is worth considering in some detail.

In the egalitarian groups considered by Friedman, society is composed of a series of lineages of equal prestige. Each local lineage has its own set of ancestor spirits, arranged in comparatively short genealogies of three or four generations (Friedman 1979, 41). There is also a village spirit, called a *nat*, which represents the local territory and is regarded as its 'owner'. This 'village *nat*' is conceived of as a remote ancestor of all local lineages. On a higher, more remote plane lie a series of 'celestial *nats*' which, at this egalitarian stage, can be approached by any lineage through the mediation of its own ancestors.

During the transition to rank society, the 'single most important transformation' is the monopolization of the village *nat* by a particular local lineage (Friedman 1979, 41). That local lineage is thereby converted into a chiefly lineage whose ancestors are descended from the spirit who controls all lands belonging to the community. Furthermore, the celestial *nats* are transformed as well; they are now ranked by age (following earthly rules of succession), and the chiefly lineage can now be traced back to the chief celestial *nat*, to whom it is affinally related. The head of this one élite lineage, since he is genealogically related to the spirits who control the well-being of the community, becomes a chief who serves as a mediator between the community and the supernatural. His favoured genealogical status entitles him to special privileges, which are tolerated because the old egalitarian ideology has now been superseded by an ideology of hereditary inequality.

Friedman (1979, 42) even provides us with one of the possible mechanisms by which the new ideology is made palatable to the commoner lineages of society. Under the egalitarian system, all lineages took turns in sponsoring the ritual feasts to which members of other communities were invited, and which brought acquired prestige to the hosts. During the transition to chieftainship, the emerging élite lineage – which before had only represented its community when it took its turn to play host – gradually begins to take over the job of host on a permanent basis. This élite lineage's ability to give more generous feasts is interpreted by other lineages as evidence for a closer association with the *nats*, and hence as evidence that its members are genealogically descended from higher spirits. Ironically, this 'evidence' makes use of one of the theorems of the old egalitarian ideology, namely the notion that a lineage could only afford a truly spectacular feast if smiled upon by the *nats*.

Friedman's scheme is shown in diagrammatic form in figure 13.1. In his model of the original egalitarian ideology (left) there are five lineages, all equal, living on land 'owned' by a village *nat*; the celestial *nats* hover above. What happens next (right) is an ideological change in which the village *nat* is redefined as the direct ancestor of one of the five lineages. That lineage is elevated to the status of a 'chiefly lineage', and the former village *nat* becomes the 'chief's ancestor'. Hereditary inequality emerges because one lineage's ancestors are powerful spirits, while everyone else's ancestors are mere mortals. The chief, rather than the village *nat*,

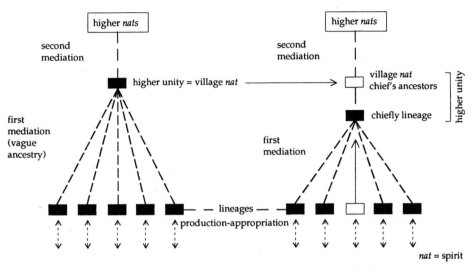

Figure 13.1 [orig. figure 1]   Friedman's model for the ideological changes that facilitate the shift from egalitarian society (left) to rank society (right) in Southeast Asia
(Redrawn from Friedman 1979, 44).

then becomes the mediator with the supernatural, and the four 'commoner' lineages derive their status from their relationship with the chief rather than from a supernatural being.

Friedman's model is an ethnographic one, but we consider it relevant to an archaeological case, namely the rise of hereditary inequality among the Zapotec of Oaxaca, Mexico (Marcus 1989). Between 1400 and 1150 BC there is no evidence for hereditary inequality in the early villages of that region. Between 1150 and 850 BC one begins to see the artistic depiction of what may be supernatural lineage ancestors equivalent to those in Friedman's model. One appears to represent 'earth' in the form of 'earthquake' or were-jaguar; the other appears to represent 'sky' in the form of 'lightning' or fire-serpent. Some degree of hereditary ranking appears during this period (documented more fully in Flannery & Marcus 1983; Marcus 1989).

As the Zapotec state formed (during the centuries leading up to 150 BC), depictions of sky and lightning became increasingly associated with the élite, while depictions of the were-jaguar faded into oblivion; 'earthquake' survived mainly as a hieroglyph in the ritual calendar. It would seem that an ideological shift, like that proposed by Friedman, accompanied the elevation of lightning's descendents to a position of pre-eminence in the Zapotec political system.

Iconography

Iconography is a subject whose definition has drifted somewhat over the years. It can refer either to the making of an icon by carving or drawing, or to the analysis of the icons themselves; today it most often refers to the analysis. (Once thought of mainly as a religious image, statue, bust, painting, or engraving, an 'icon' has also had its meaning broadened recently to include professional athletes and rock musicians.)

When archaeologists use the term 'iconography' today, they are usually referring to an analysis of the way ancient peoples represented religious, political, ideological, or cosmological objects or concepts in their art. Unfortunately, the quality of analysis is highly variable. In cases where a great deal is known about the cosmology, religion, or ideology of an ancient people – as for example, through history or ethnohistory – iconography can be a truly scientific analysis. In cases where no such background information is available, 'iconography' can turn out to be little more than science fiction. In such cases, the art of an ancient culture merely serves as a kind of neutral Rorschach blot onto which the author projects his or her own personality. The literature in Mesoamerica includes hundreds of such idiosyncratic fantasies, each of which tells us far more about the author than about the ancient culture. Almost inevitably, the authors of such studies ask us to trust their 'highly-developed intuition' in lieu of any acceptable supporting evidence for their interpretation.

Ironically, one of the best iconographic analyses of a body of Precolumbian art was done by a subsistence-settlement archaeologist, Olga Linares (1977). That is because Linares brought to her study the same kind of rigour she uses in her survey, excavation, and analysis; she relied on actual evidence rather than the 'unusually refined aesthetic sense' claimed by so many of the worst iconographers.

For her study, Linares chose decorated burial vessels from high-status cemeteries at a series of chiefly sites in the central Panamanian provinces (Veraguas, Coclé, Herrera, Los Santos). These cemetery sites spanned the period AD 500–1500, with the latest of them falling at the time of the Spaniards' arrival in Panama (Lothrop 1937; 1942). Linares was therefore able to use eyewitness accounts of sixteenth-century Panamanian chiefdoms in her analysis, including documents by Gonzalo Badajoz (in Andagoya 1865), Gaspar de Espinosa (1864; 1873), Bartolomé de Las Casas (1951), and Gonzalo Fernández de Oviedo y Valdés (1851–1855).

Many cemetery vessels are painted in a flamboyant, polychrome style, with naturalistic animal representations. Their open shapes and their placement in the ground suggest that the motifs were meant to be seen from above by funeral participants or graveside mourners. The great intrinsic value of the vessels is suggested by the fact that some were later removed from one grave to be placed in another, or even deliberately destroyed in what could be acts of status competition.

Four main lines of information were used in Linares' study: (1) ethnohistoric accounts of sixteenth-century Panamanian chiefdoms; (2) knowledge of animal species diversity in the Panamanian tropics; (3) primary archaeological data on the context of the graves and the burials they contain; and (4) the range of themes and/or motifs painted on the pottery vessels.

Ethnohistory tells us that sixteenth-century Panamanian chiefdoms featured a high level of warfare or raiding, with intense competition for positions of leadership. Painted motifs and special tattooing were applied to the body of important individuals as badges of rank and bravery. Warriors fighting under a single chief wore a special motif to distinguish them from warriors fighting under rival chiefs. Such warriors were also buried with helmets, a wide range of weapons, and other military paraphernalia.

The central Panamanian art style was based on a rich symbolic system, using animal motifs as metaphors to express the qualities of bravery and aggression desired in both chiefs and warriors. Linares noted that plants were rarely depicted, and reasoned that the attributes of certain animals were being used to communicate the rank and bravery of the buried warriors. She pointed out that species diversity in the humid tropics is significantly higher than in temperate zones, facilitating an artist's selection of animal species thought to have the desired qualities while ignoring others. Tropical species have evolved complex and varied interspecific and intraspecific patterns of interaction, including predation, commensalism, mimicry, and elaborate signalling systems. Such animal behaviour mirrors the complexity of human behaviour, providing abundant raw material for symbolism and its iconographic expression.

Once Linares turned to the specific animals used on the burial vessels of the Panamanian chiefdoms, she noted that there had been careful selection of those which reflect the aggressive values of the warrior. Some are man-eaters, some

Table 13.1 [orig. table 1]   Behavioural qualities of animals depicted in the funerary art of Panamanian chiefdoms. (Adapted from Linares 1977).

Category of Animal	Significant Attributes
Crocodiles	Potentially man-eating
Large felines (puma, jaguar)	Potentially man-eating
Sharks	Potentially man-eating
Stingrays	Potentially dangerous
Needlefish	Potentially dangerous
Scorpions	Capable of stinging
Crabs	Capable of pinching
Guans/Curassows	Notably belligerent
Hawks	Predatory
Turtles	Defended by a hard shell
Armadillos	Defended by a hard shell
Squid	Defend themselves with ink
Poisonous snakes	Potentially dangerous
Poisonous toads/frogs	Potentially dangerous
Toxic marine worms	Potentially dangerous

predators, some belligerent fighters, while others bite, sting, or have toxic defences. For example, Parita Polychrome designs often feature a predator and its prey – the hammerhead shark and the stingray – with the former known to feed on the latter. Pottery from Sitio Conte and other sites in Coclé, Herrera, Veraguas, and the Azuero Peninsula featured not only sharks and rays, but also crocodiles, raptorial birds, and crabs. Some of the most common birds were guans and/or curassows, large gallinaceous birds which are notoriously ill-tempered and whose males often fight furiously among themselves (table 13.1). The artistic depiction of each animal emphasizes precisely those organs or body parts involved in predatory or defensive activities such as biting, clawing, stinging, and so forth.

As significant as those animals depicted on funerary vessels were those not represented. Prey species and animals with soft body parts, such as agoutis, pacas, rabbits, sloths, monkeys, opossums, iguanas, and most fish were essentially ignored by the artist, even though they were among the animals commonly eaten (and present in middens). These animals, despite their economic importance to the Panamanian chiefdoms, simply did not reinforce the values of bravery, fighting ability, rank, or warrior status desired by the painters of funerary vessels. Moreover, body parts of many of the aggressive animals depicted iconographically – such as shark's teeth and stingray spines – were themselves included in the same graves. Linares concluded that in the cognized world of the Panamanian chiefdom, animals had been carefully chosen from the diversity of tropical species in order to communicate those qualities most admired in the chief and his warriors.

We have chosen Linares' study as our example of how archaeological iconography should be done for several reasons. Among other things, it demonstrates that iconography is not some esoteric skill that must be employed by a group of investigators different from those who do subsistence-settlement archaeology. Iconography works just fine when it is analytical and draws on a wide range of social and natural sciences. In turn, this suggests that the 'special gifts' claimed by many iconographers may be no more than a smokescreen designed to discourage closer examination of their reasoning.

Summary and Conclusions

In this paper we have considered four categories of human intellectual activity – cosmology, religion, ideology, and iconography – that could be considered appropriate subjects for cognitive archaeology. Those four categories do not by any means exhaust the subject matter of the field. We do think, however, that our four chosen topics cover a great deal of what passes today for cognitive archaeology.

Do we really believe that archaeologists can work on these topics? Yes, but only under the appropriate circumstances and with the appropriate rigour. When a great deal of background information is available – as, for example, among the sixteenth-century Aztec or New Kingdom Egyptians – it makes sense to reconstruct the cosmology and religion of those people. When almost no background knowledge is available, as for the aceramic Neolithic, such reconstruction can border on science fiction. That is when every figurine becomes a 'fertility goddess' and every misshapen boulder a 'cult stone'.

Are cosmology, religion, ideology, and iconography mere epiphenomena, unworthy of scientific study? We hope we have shown the opposite. We hope we have shown that cosmology affects the way the natural environment is used, that religion can promote or inhibit commerce with foreigners, that ideology must change before rank society can evolve, and that iconography can be used to reinforce the militaristic values of competing chiefdoms. Those topics cannot be dismissed out of hand by subsistence-settlement archaeologists.

On the other hand, we understand why many subsistence-settlement archaeologists are sceptical of cognitive archaeology. No approach has greater potential for dilettantism, flights of fancy, charlatanism, and intellectual laziness. No one is likely to make up a fictitious plant assemblage from a site, but we see fictitious religions, ideologies, and cosmologies made up on the spot in both the New and Old Worlds.

Subsistence-settlement archaeology requires a lot of work, much of it tedious and time-consuming: strenuous surveys, careful and extensive excavations, fine screening and flotation, painstaking identification of plant and animal remains, and so on. If cognitive archaeology can be done with the same careful, painstaking effort as subsistence-settlement archaeology, few will have any doubts about it.

Unfortunately, the cognitive route is frequently chosen by those who, while wishing to call themselves archaeologists, do not have the patience for the work described above. Searching for a way around the rigour and tedium, they have seized upon cognitive archaeology as a shortcut. Worse still, they often see it as a prestigious shortcut, one that relies on 'brilliance', 'insight', or 'intuition' rather than hard work. They would like us to believe that they don't have to survey, dig, or analyze archaeological remains because they have 'special gifts' denied the rest of us. We, on the other hand, suspect that they don't survey, dig, or analyze because they aren't concerned with what actually happened in prehistory.

When we see cosmology derived solely from the alleged orientation of a building to a particular star, when we see an entire ideology reconstructed from the style of a carving, and when we see ancient religion reconstructed from a handful of figurines or the red dado painting on the wall of a shrine, we have a right to be sceptical. Equally troubling is the notion – clearly subscribed to by some self-styled 'cognitive archaeologists' – that the quality of a theory is to be measured by its style and flair, rather than the extent to which it is grounded in evidence.

It is for all these reasons that we believe cognitive archaeology should not be a separate branch of archaeology. The study of cosmology, religion, ideology, and iconography, and other products of the ancient mind, should simply be a task that the well-rounded archaeologist takes on as a matter of course – when it is appropriate.

Do we then need cognitive archaeology? Yes, but as a way of making mainstream archaeology more holistic, rather than creating an esoteric subdiscipline. The biggest challenge facing cognitive archaeology is to become anchored as firmly in the ethnographic, historic, ethnohistoric, and archaeological records as the more subsistence- and settlement-based aspects of archaeology. Like the New Archaeologists of 25 years ago, aspiring cognitive archaeologists should heed the advice of Jesse D. Jennings (1968, 329): 'At all costs, all archaeologists need to remember that, like Antaeus, they must continue to "touch the earth" or they will lose their strength.'

References

Andagoya, P., 1865. *Narrative of the Proceedings of the Pedrarias Davila in the Provinces of Tierra Firme or Castilla del Oro, and the Discovery of the South Sea and the Coasts of Peru and Nicaragua*, trans. C.R. Markham. (Hakluyt Society 34.) London: Hakluyt Society.

Espinosa, G. de, 1864. Relación hecha por Gaspar de Espinosa, Alcalde Mayor de Castilla del Oro, dada a Pedrarias de Avila . . ., in *Colección de Documentos del Archivo de Indias*, Tomo II. Madrid: Imprenta Española, 467–522.

Espinosa, G. de, 1873. Relación e proceso quel Lic. Gaspar Despinosa, Alcadale mayor, hizo en el viaje . . ., in *Colección de Documentos Inéditos del Archivo de Indias*, Tomo XX. Madrid: Imprenta del Hospicio, 5–119.

Fernández de Oviedo y Valdés, G., 1851–55. *Historia general y natural de Las Indias, Islas y Tierra Firme del Mar Océano.* 4 vols. Madrid: Imprenta de la Real Academia de la Historia.

Flannery, K.V., 1976. Contextual analysis of ritual paraphernalia from formative Oaxaca, in *The Early Mesoamerican Village*, ed., K.V. Flannery. New York (NY): Academic Press, 333–45.

Flannery, K.V. & J. Marcus, 1976. Formative Oaxaca and the Zapotec cosmos. *American Scientist* 64, 374–83.

Flannery, K.V. & J. Marcus (eds.), 1983. *The Cloud People, Divergent Evolution of the Zapotec and Mixtec Civilizations.* New York (NY) & San Diego (CA): Academic Press.

Friedman, J., 1979. *System, Structure and Contradiction: The Evolution of 'Asiatic', Social Formations.* (Social Studies in Oceania and South East Asia 2.) Copenhagen: The National Museum of Denmark.

Hughes, J.D., 1975. *Ecology in Ancient Civilizations.* Albuquerque (NM): University of New Mexico Press.

Las Casas, B. de, 1951. *Historia de las Indias.* 3 vols. Mexico: Fondo de Cultura Económica.

Linares, O.F., 1977. *Ecology and the Arts in Ancient Panama: On the Development of Social Rank and Symbolism in the Central Provinces.* (Studies in Pre-Columbian Art & Archaeology 17.) Washington (DC): Dumbarton Oaks.

Lothrop, S.K., 1937. *Coclé: An Archaeological Study of Central Panama.* Part I. (Memoirs of the Peabody Museum of Archaeology and Ethnology, Harvard University VII.) Cambridge (MA): Peabody Museum.

Lothrop, S.K., 1942. *Coclé: An Archaeological Study of Central Panama.* Part II. (Memoirs of the Peabody Museum of Archaeology and Ethnology, Harvard University VIII.) Cambridge (MA): Peabody Museum.

Marcus, J., 1978. Archaeology and religion: a comparison of the Zapotec and Maya. *World Archaeology* 10, 172–91.

Marcus, J., 1989. Zapotec chiefdoms and the nature of formative religions, in *Regional Perspectives on the Olmec*, eds. R.J. Sharer & D.C. Grove. (School of American Research Advanced Seminar Series.) Cambridge: Cambridge University Press, 148–97.

Marcus, J. & K.V. Flannery, 1994. Zapotec ritual and religion: an application of the direct historical approach, in *The Ancient Mind*, eds. C. Renfrew & E.B.W. Zubrow. Cambridge: Cambridge University Press.

Sanders W.T., 1974. Chiefdom to state: political evolution at Kaminaljuyu, Guatemala, in *Reconstructing Complex Societies: An Archaeological Colloquium*, ed. C.B. Moore. Cambridge (MA): MIT Press, 97–121.

Ucko, P.J. & G.W. Dimbleby (eds.), 1969. *The Domestication and Exploitation of Plants and Animals*. London: Duckworth.

Ucko, P.J., R. Tringham & G.W. Dimbleby (eds.), 1972. *Man, Settlement and Urbanism*. London: Duckworth.

Wheatley, P., 1975. Satyanrta in Suvarnadvipa: from reciprocity to redistribution in ancient southeast Asia, in *Ancient Civilization and Trade*, eds. J.A. Sabloff & C.C. Lamberg-Karlovsky. Albuquerque (NM): University of New Mexico Press, 227–65.

14

Style and the Design of a Perfume Jar from an Archaic Greek City State

Michael Shanks

An Aryballos

The pot (figures 14.1A and B) remains, placed upon a shelf in a museum of fine art (Boston), numbered (95.12). It is small, less than 7.5cm high, and carries upon its surface two friezes of finely-drawn animals, birds, and human figures. The shape and size mark the pot as what is conventionally termed an *aryballos*. The small size of such *aryballoi* means that they held only little oil. It may be supposed therefore that the oil was special, expensive, or rare, probably perfumed. This was a perfume jar (Payne 1931:3–4; Cook 1966:232–3).

Proto-Korinthian Style

With the size and shape, the hard, smooth and pale clay fabric indicate that the pot is Korinthian and of the seventh century BC. Specifically it is of the *style* or industry proto-Korinthian. The boundaries and coherence of this 'industry' were set and established by Johansen in his work *Les Vases Sicyoniens* (1923). He gathered and coordinated pots of such shape and fabric, noted their occurrence in excavated deposits with other vessel forms, defined a set of stylistic points which united them. He also proposed a chronological sequence to the shape of *aryballoi* – from early and 'paunchy' to late and pointed or 'piriform' through middle of ovoid shape. Most of the pots that Johansen dealt with were from early Greek colonies in Italy, but he considered this coherent stylistic group to have been manufactured in the north-east Peloponnese of southern Greece, at Sikyon; hence the title of his book.

Payne (1931) accepted Johansen's grouping and synthesis but saw the stylistic similarities with what was known to be later Korinthian pottery to be too great to allow there to be different manufacturing centres. He took the animal friezes, decorative devices, and distinctive fabric to be early Korinthian ware, or rather proto-Korinthian. These *aryballoi* were made in Korinth.

Johansen and Payne (1933) sketched the lineaments of proto-Korinthian *style*.

Figures 14.1A and B [orig. figure 1a and b].

The work of traditional classical archaeology has added little in the way of refinement of the sense, usually and largely intuitive, of this style. The earlier chronological schemes of its development have been much debated, modified, even challenged (see the extensive summary and discussion in Neeft 1987, passim). Such debate has been a major concern of early Hellenic specialists. First, because chronological sequence is thought to be of primary importance in making sense of the cultural remains of the past; it also lends an appearance of historical substance to the classificatory archaeology – the passing of history, even if without any content or narrative. Second, the distinctive shapes and proposed clear sequence from fat and globular to pointed makes the *aryballos* a good index of the relative chronology of the context within which it was found. And *aryballoi* like the one which concerns me here have consistently been found in the cemeteries of early Greek colonies in Sicily and southern Italy. Absolute dates of foundation seem calculable for some colonies from references in later Greek authors, particularly Thucydides. So proto-Korinthian provides a chronological schema for the late eighth and seventh centuries BC, and one which is so useful because *aryballoi* turn up all over the Greek world, enabling cross-referencing of disparate stylistic groupings and local relative sequences (the classic pioneering work was presented by Payne 1931).

Ceramic art histories have recounted over and over again, and with more or less eloquence, the features and innovations of Korinthian pottery (for example Cook 1966). Pots made in Korinth in the earlier eighth century were decorated in a linear and restrained geometric canon (figure 14.2). But there then occurred the birth of a new style, or rather a radical transformation of geometric. It is called orientalising. On some pots the austerity of the geometric is abandoned for swirling and animated designs, and with some features apparently borrowed from designs found in the east; hence the terms orientalising. These include floral decoration (lotus and palmette), some mythical creatures (such as a new form of sphinx), ways of drawing others (such as lions), certain 'stock' scenes (the lion hunt, for example), and some geometric traits (rays at the base of a pot). The account of the orientalising movement, with its stylistic diffusion (supposed according to detailed comparison of artefacts from Greece and abroad) and the creative adaptation of Greek 'artists', is an exemplary aspect of classical art history (see for example Boardman 1967:73–108; Akurgal 1968; Hurwit 1985; cf. Coldstream 1968 and 1977:ch. 15; Carter 1972). The *aryballos* with which I began is in the orientalising style, with its figures, animals, and rays below. It is part of Payne's 'first black figure style' (1933), where detail is added to figures by scratching through the painted slip. Proto-Korinthian incised black figure decoration: adopted by the potters of Attika to the north, it developed into Attic Red Figure, the acme of achievement in ancient Greek ceramic art.

So, archaic proto-Korinthian is, in the accounts of art history, a key style in the emergence of the classical, indeed in the development of representations of bodily form. The *aryballos* in Boston is representative of its style which provides its artistic credentials. It is not just any old pot but fits into the story of the emergence of the classical.

Figure 14.2 [orig. figure 2].

These narratives of art history involve the ascription of value. Artefacts are evaluated according to their judged place in stylistic development. There is a search for those pieces which mark the changes – great works, or works of creative innovation. They are the works of 'artists', those who set the pace and sketch the character of stylistic growth.

The Connoisseurs

So this little *aryballos* bears the marks of its style. The archaeologist as connoisseur delves into the particularities of style, noting the rendering of figure detail, shapes, forms, and subject matter, surmising that different artists, otherwise anonymous, could be distinguished on this basis. John Beazley, in his work on Attic Black and Red Figure, pioneered such an approach in classical archaeology (see Kurtz 1985; von Bothmer 1987). He has been the model or reference for much work on proto-Korinthian figure pottery since Payne's book *Necrocorinthia* (1931); there have been produced lists of pots and sherds claimed to be of the same stylistic school, or of the same artist's hand, masters and pupils traced in the evolution of style.

This *aryballos* has been attributed to the 'Ajax' painter (Dunbabin and Robertson 1953:176; Amyx 1988:23–4; Benson 1989:43–4; and others). This artist-potter is so named after another *aryballos* in Berlin (number 3319) upon which is a figured scene which includes a man lying upon a sword which apparently runs through his body. This is taken to be Ajax, the epic hero, who committed suicide in such a way (Johansen 1923:144). The *aryballoi* of the Ajax painter (four or more depending upon connoisseur) have common features such as cabling upon handles, neck ornament, and particularly figure form – quite full-bodied with distinctive long arms at an acute angle at the elbow, hair-styles and beards incised cross-wise.

In the attribution of pots to different artists, the archaeologist, as connoisseur, gains familiarity with the minute and particular detail of each pot: hair-styles, lions' paws, and lotus petals. The task is to identify diagnostic traits. Stylistic attribution depends upon a symptomatic logic (Ginzburg 1983): particular stylistic traits are conscious or unconscious symptoms of a painterly hand. To this concept of painterly hand the *aryballos* is subordinated and referred. This *aryballos* is 'lucky' and diagnosis can be made. But for many, indeed the majority of proto-Korinthian pottery, there are too few diagnostic stylistic traits and no attribution can be made. These pots seem somehow less than the *aryballoi* of the Ajax painter; they have no hope of diagnosis; they contain no trace of that which would explain them, their originator or author. In having fewer stylistic traits they are less 'artistic'. Attribution, the work of the connoisseur, accords value.

The procedures of stylistic attribution are ill-defined; much is to do with intuition arising from long-term handling and reading around the material; it depends on becoming aware of the ineffable qualities of design and manufacture. The non-verbal component accounts for the absence in almost all listings of explanation for particular attributions; seeing the pots together is argument for their affiliation. The idea of visual rather than verbal argument is an attractive one, given the character of archaeological materials, but the esoteric expertise of the connoisseur, which is founded on the rare facility of being able to study a body of disparate and often obscure material over decades without any immediate return, is open to the charge of elitism. The connoisseur senses the essence of style on the basis of expertise and familiarity with the material; the rest of us have little ground for empirical disagreement. There is also the charge of ethnocentrism and cultural imperialism. The Classics connoisseur roams the museum vaults and auction rooms of the 'cultured' world (at least through publication), seeking the bearers of *style*, but without reference to social, political, or historical context, only that of his own academic evaluation (Elsner 1990; on attribution see Friedlander 1943; and also discussion in Whitley 1991:15–17).

Expertise and practical knowledge gained through familiarity are conceivably valuable, but the lack of rigour, lack of quantitative definition and absence of reflection on the theoretical and philosophical assumptions of stylistic attribution (such as the categories of style and artistic personality in relation to social and historical change) are disconcerting. Some of the artists' hands do seem reasonable: the figure drawing and choice of design elements of the pots attributed to this Ajax painter seem to form a coherent unity, but only of four pots (Dunbabin and Robertson do list more: 1953:176). However, for proto-Korinthian pottery, it is clear that stylistic attribution does not work. Between the three main listings (those of Dunbabin and Robertson (1953), Amyx (1988), and Benson (1953 and 1989), there is agreement on hardly more than one in four pots. Some disagreement is reasonable, but how expert are the experts? How refined are their sensibilities? And if stylistic attribution is such a subjective exercise, on what basis have these people been authorised the luxury of cultivating their expert opinion?

And just what do the stylistic groupings represent? I have indicated how some are prepared to think of relationships between masters and apprentices or schools of followers. The chapter headings and discussion of proto-Korinthian by Amyx (1988), and Benson's discussion of the painters of the middle phase of proto-Korinthian (1989: especially 38–40) clearly indicate that they believe in the notion of artistic and creative personality. But it does not really matter. Stylistic attribution has little bearing on anything other than the discourse of style to which it belongs. After the conspicuous success of Beazley in simply gathering a vast amount of material in listings, searching for the affiliation of idiosyncrasy of style was, and for some still is, the practice required of the ceramic expert. To manage the particularity of style in this way is a credential of the discipline; it shows that you are one of the cognoscenti. More seriously, the concepts of style and artist, at the root of such practices, are idealist. The hand or mark of the pot painter is meaningful only in relation to the art style to which it contributes (see again, for example, Benson (ibid.) on middle proto-Korinthian). In this it does not matter how they are conceived (as personalities or workshops), because they are abstract constructions. The *Style* exists in relation to the artistic efforts of potters who commune with it through their struggling with form and decoration, concept and content in the figured scene. The overarching whole of *Style*, beyond the mainly incidental act of the potter, allows teleological explanation: a painter or pot may be

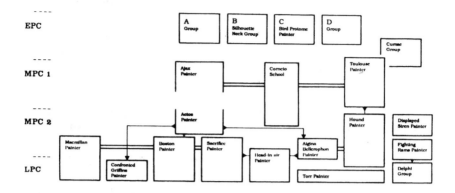

The Connoisseur's choice: painters and workshops of proto-Korinthian,
after Dunbabin and Robertson (1953)

Phases: early (EPC) to late (LPC) proto-Korinthian
Strong (workshop) association: ■
Influence: ▶

Figure 14.3 [orig. figure 3]   The connoisseur's choice.

explained, evaluated, or given significance by its contribution to the future, to what
is to come in the *Style*. In this way style is largely detached from the social and
political reality of people; though there is Art History – the evolutionary
momentum and cycles of *Style* (figure 14.3) (Cf. Whitley (1987) on idealism and
classical archaeology).

Iconography and Meaning

There are studies of the iconography of proto-Korinthian which also display a
concern with the fine particularities of the rendition of detail and figure. Johansen's
work of 1923 included much description of the variety and type of things painted
upon his proposed style. Strictly speaking, iconography is merely descriptive, and
need not be restricted to any one style: there are studies of the depiction of griffons,
sphinxes, centaurs, lions, panthers, all of which are to be found within other styles
of decoration as well as proto-Korinthian (a selection: Arnold 1972; Benton 1961;
Bosana-Kourou 1979; Delplace 1980; Schiffler 1976; Schmitt 1966). Types are
defined and classifications proposed, lines of development induced or deduced.
The meaning of the things painted upon the pots is secondary to iconographic
work.

And so to meaning. Something seems to be happening in the scene upon this
aryballos. A man-animal or centaur is confronting a swordsman who brandishes
something which is not immediately recognisable. Behind the monster is a stand
for a *krater* or *dinos* (mixing bowls) with four birds of prey. Another animated
swordsman and various 'decorative' devices complete the scene. Is this the

depiction of some story or myth? This is the question posed of all figured scenes by conventional art history. The sense of style is to be found in narrative or myth (known from literary and epigraphic references). Something seems to be happening so there is the potential of discovering sense; whereas the frieze of animals upon the shoulder of this *aryballos* seems more mundane, merely a frieze – what narrative can there be? Sense and meaning are thus contrasted with the decorative. For this particular *aryballos* there has been considerable discussion of possible myth represented. Much has been made of the object in the hand of the figure opposing the monster, whether it is a thunderbolt, the weapon of god Zeus, who is facing some enemy of his (Johansen 1923:145–7; Buschor 1934:128–30; Fittschen 1969: especially 119–23; and others).

Pottery in Context

But what of the historical moment of the *aryballos* in Boston by the Ajax painter? From meagre literary references it is known that Korinth underwent a social revolution in the seventh century BC (for the ancient history of revolution and tyranny see Andrewes 1956; for an historical commentary on Korinth see Salmon 1984: chapters 3 and 15). How, if at all, may this have affected the production of vessels such as these? This *aryballos* was found in uncertain circumstances, but as I have already mentioned, many are found in sanctuaries and cemeteries west of Korinth. The Korinthian aristocratic oligarchy is noted as having been interested in trading and colonising ventures. So perhaps proto-Korinthian style and its distribution are to do with the economics of aristocracy in the early-Korinthian city state. This has usually been stated in descriptive and narrative terms of export trade: the late eighth and seventh century Korinthian trade in ceramics dominated the Greek west. This is the usual and simple point of contact between art history and ancient history (Salmon 1984:74f, 92–116: passim, and 148–54 for an historian's account).

Some recent approaches to early-Hellenic pottery stress the importance of social context in understanding and explaining style. Coldstream (1983) has applied the traditional archaeological concept of culture (relating clusters of similar artefacts to 'cultures' or peoples on the assumption that style reflects identity and inter-action) to pottery decorated in the Geometric style. Variations in eighth-century geometric he associates with the emergence of the city states, many developing their own version of the Geometric in asserting identity and unity.

In a more-sophisticated development of the idea that style relates to site of production, Morgan and Whitelaw (1991) have investigated variability in the decoration of Geometric pottery produced in and around Argos. They argue that pottery functions as a medium and index of interaction, and so reflects and takes part in changing relations of dominance by the main city state, Argos.

Whitley too deals with the function of style in his studies of Attic Geometric (1991) and orientalising proto-Attic pottery (forthcoming). He reasserts the necessity of relating 'art' to social context. Given that most Attic Geometric pottery is found in graves, Whitley undertook a large-scale cluster and multivariate statistical analysis of pots and other artefacts deposited with the dead in Dark-Age and early-Archaic Attika. He aimed to define the patterning in the cemeteries (certain pots being regularly associated, or not, with others and with other artefacts on the basis of type, decoration, and form of mortuary treatment). He correlated the patterning he claimed to find with early-Attic 'society' under the proposal that the treatment of the dead is to do with the organisation of society. His contention is that changes in the design of geometric pottery are to do with the changing social hierarchies in Attika; style was used to mark social status, expressing social personae. This, for Whitley, stands also for the later proto-Attic sequence. (For a detailed review and critique of these recent approaches of Morgan and Whitelaw, Whitley, and others, see Shanks 1992).

In an approach with closer ties to traditional art history, Boardman (1983:15–24) has attempted to explain particular figurative and abstract elements of Geometric pottery from Argos as icons of the city and people which produced them. He notes references in literature to the horses and waters of Argos and relates these to pictures of horses, fish, water, and fishing water birds upon the pots.

More generally, Snodgrass (1980; 1982; 1987; for a review of debate see Boardman 1983:23–33) has interpreted the figured scenes on Attic late-Geometric pottery as reflecting a social ethos which valued the heroic, and which is also visible in other manifestations of material culture. Osborne (1989) has given an historical account of changing social and ideological conceptions on eighth and seventh-century Attika, concerning the growth of the *polis* and general structural characteristics of burial, religious activity, settlement pattern, and artistic style. He has explained Geometric and Attic pottery in terms of the structure of their decoration and form reflecting deep and general social outlooks. From regularity, order without subordination, juxtaposition without connection, and a world taken for granted in the Geometric, to: questions posed (about life, death, and myth), challenges set by the style of proto-Attic.

I may also mention approaches to later Black and Red Figure which draw inspiration from structuralist analysis. Pot illustration can be interpreted as the articulation of deep cultural dispositions and systems of values regarding, for example, sexuality, domestic life, the conceptual world of the city and its environs (see the now classic volume *Cité des Images* 1984 and the monumental Schnapp 1987).

These treatments of pottery in social context provide and promise much richer accounts of ceramic style in Archaic Greece and earlier. There are however, as yet, no approaches to proto-Korinthian along these lines and to which I might refer; I am being led away somewhat from the perfume jar with which I began this essay.

The Particular and the General, and the Fallacy of Representation

The *aryballos* carries a considerable burden. For the aficionado it represents an origin of representative art in the western classical tradition, a source of that which is recognised as classical Greek. Its 'orientalising' style mediates the east and an emerging Greek (and European) identity. For the connoisseur there is the mark of the artist's style too, hints of workshop masters, the bearers of the movement of artistic style. The *aryballos* rests on a heap of discursive debris, a cumulative sweep of discussion over the last century. It is, with many others, a supreme object of classical discourse, albeit in the byways of scholasticism. Lists of pots attributed to painters by the connoisseurs repeat every (or as many as are known) mention and discussion of the *aryballos*; the pot seems held in a web of citation. What more can be said?

Traditional classical archaeology seems to focus on the particularity of this *aryballos*, attributing it to a style, identifying its date to within a decade through stylistic comparison, appreciating its relation to the development of style, recognising its subject matter, and even the mark of its maker. But in all of this the pot is, in fact, subsumed beneath something other than itself: it requires relating to chronology, style, and workshop, and the sense of its figured decoration is found in the body of Greek myth. Though the terms of close description (so characteristic of classical archaeology), both analytic and evaluative, seem to represent direct and intimate contact, not merely empirical but also affective and aesthetic, the *aryballos* is epiphenomenal. It *represents* something else, which is often general and abstract.

And those approaches to style that would place the pottery in social context can mark the particular artefact as ephiphenomenal. Artefacts are taken to signify cultural belonging; pots are considered as representing social interaction; style is explained by its social function, expressing rank or social status. The artefact becomes a by-product of social practice or behaviour. The primary terms are society, culture, hierarchy, rank; the artefact expresses, reflects, signifies, or engages with the something else which gives it significance or meaning.

When the artefact is considered thus as representative, analysis of style becomes a search for pattern (which represents), a specification of characteristics or attributes which constitute style, a symptomatic logic, finding traces of that other which is desired – the person of the maker, the artistic hand, the story, the society. It is a desire for that other which can never be had, the dead and lost artisan, the society no more; absent origins. Time has passed; the person is torn away. But the thing remains, the *aryballos* in the museum case, worn, scratched, surviving in its materiality, its particularity. And its 'artistic' character, the autonomy of the particular look it gives, the complexity of an aesthetic response which is evoked (and is this not its 'art'?), draws more attention to the dialectic which lies at the heart of the archaeological – that between the particular and the general.

Contemporary desire can be a forgetting of the loss, effacing this dialectic. It is the *fallacy of representation*, that the style of something represents. Style, conceived as a medium of description, and with associated studies of classification and typology, is abstract(ed) from social context, and ultimately meaningless. (What do the lists of painters of pots tell us? What does it mean to say that this *aryballos* is by the Ajax painter?) With style as an attribute of an object, a pattern to be discovered, what explains the particular object(ivity) beneath the attribute and beneath the pattern? (Just what *is* this *aryballos*?)

The *aryballos* is what is left of the past, its materiality. It is not a secondary manifestation of something more primary, or material, or real – the lost potters and their society. Concomitantly, the style of this *aryballos* is not an attribute; style is the way something is done (Hodder 1990: especially 44–6). Style, as medium of action, is production (to form and to decorate), distribution and consumption; a process of writing (Tilley 1990; Tilley 1991), and of making (see the papers and discussion in *Archaeological Review from Cambridge* 9 1990: Technology in the humanities). To think of style is to consider design, acts of transformation, and the form they take: clay taken by potter, painted pictures applied, pot chosen and taken, exchanged, consumed; acts of production, creation, looking, travel, rituals of death and dedication. I would move from a conception of attributes upon a pot, to association and displacement, following lines of suggestion and affiliation within the *aryballos* through design, form, and decoration. These are cycles of *interpretation*, interpretations of material and form in the life-cycle of the artifact, its movement through production to consumption, deposition and reconsumption, collection (for this *aryballos*, in the nineteenth century for a museum of art) (on the primacy of the interpretive act, reference and affiliation see Shanks 1990 and 1991).

I need to show what I mean. I will return to the *aryballos* with which I began.

Fine Accomplishment, and Risk

The *aryballos* is an accomplished piece. Recognisably fine is the ceramic fabric, Korinthian in its smooth, consistent, and regular colour and texture. Slips, applied by brush, were turned to contrasting dark by a clever, careful, and necessarily practised manipulation of kiln and firing environment (Noble 1988). Clay body and slip required very precise preparation too, especially at Korinth, given the quality of the local clay (Farnsworth 1970). The labour and control used to produce proto-Korinthian pottery was that commonly employed to produce fine ware in Greece generally in the first millenium BC, from proto-Geometric pottery style to Red Figure and beyond. The potters of proto-Korinthian were staying with a wider and old tradition of fineware manufacture.

The appearance is highly regulated; the workmanship is of the sort where achievement seems to correspond closely with the idea (of its design): lines are fine, precise, and regularly spaced, and there appears to be control over shape and height too. There is a sense of 'prototype' (Miller 1985; Boast 1990: passim) or concept of 'right shape' behind the easily recognisable *aryballos* (and other shapes too). As with Geometric Korinthian, proto-Korinthian pots were decorated on a banding wheel (a turntable), and often with a multiple brush. This affords a good degree of certainty that the desired result could be achieved: regulated linearity. Geometric is the product of a workmanship of certainty (see Pye 1980 on workmanship).

There is a difference which marks the beginning of proto-Korinthian. The figured *aryballos* here was drawn upon free-hand and then the surface was scratched or incised. It displays immense control. But whereas the painter of geometric decoration (which continues to be produced alongside figurative, when it is known as sub-geometric) must have been quite certain of achieving the desired appearance, the precision and regulated accomplishment of figured scenes such as these were achieved at risk of the painter's hand or brush slipping, and they depended largely on the painter's individual care, judgement, and dexterity (as opposed to the traditional and shared technology of banding wheel and multiple brush).

I propose that such risk on the part of the potter is a significant reason for the development of figured proto-Korinthian. The figures are painted free-hand with silhouette and outlined features. A mistake in painting could be corrected perhaps – the oxide slip wiped off. But the incision through the applied slip into the body of the pot was a scar that could not easily be removed. (Whether the idea of incision came from metalworking, as is usually mentioned, is irrelevant.) Incision marks decision, finality, and risk of spoiling the work's regulated surface and decoration. It also heightens the appearance of regulation, with its ability to render every fine detail.

Proto-Korinthian opens space in the Geometric linear field for figured designs, such as on this *aryballos*, which are intricate and complex. But a great increase in time and labour expenditure is perhaps not involved. Painters who have acquired the skills necessary for figured painting in miniature are needed, as are new fine brushes, but the designs within the small linear bands opened on the pots, with their predominantly 'confident' line (few breaks, hesitation, signs of holding back), were probably quick to produce. Many indeed are 'hasty' and 'free'. The workmanship of risked hand and brush is new, but occurs within a frame (literally) of dependable technological and technical practice and knowledge.

Proto-Korinthian is mainly a miniature style: there are many figured *aryballoi*, and few figured pieces over 20cm high. Held in the palm of the hand, or between finger and thumb, the designs upon this *aryballos* are at the threshold of visibility. The figured scenes particularly invite scrutiny and recognition of the accomplishment of precision and regulation, and so by contrast the new mode of painting. This is the significance of miniaturism. Why do the pot painters of Korinth move to a workmanship of risk in producing the figured designs, and particularly in comparison with the high regulation and conservatism (little experiment and variety) of Korinthian Geometric? I argue that the risk of proto-Korinthian workmanship was adopted because it suited the representation of scenes with a particular range of subject matter.

To the main scene upon the *aryballos*.

(From now on I will be making reference in quantitative terms to pots classed as proto-Korinthian. I assume nothing about the meaning of this designation, and accept only that such pots were probably made in Korinth from about 720 to 640 BC. The short interpretation I present of this *aryballos* from a museum in Boston is rooted in a sample of 1930 well-published and complete pots which I have been working with over the last four years. This comprises all figured pots known to me, and those which have geometric or linear decoration (sub-geometric proto-Korinthian) from the main sites of discovery. I have divided the sample into earlier and later according to gross changes in the design of *aryballoi* (rather than the stylistic criteria of most conventional accounts) which seem to be stratigraphically secure. For full details: Shanks 1993a).

Men in a Scene

Two figures, armed and male, appear with a horse-man and an artefact with birds. Of 366 human or part-human figures which appear upon such pots, only six are definitely female, apart from the sphinxes (which have no sexual features). This is a male imagery, dominated by the masculine, I propose.

There are thirty five types of figure found on earlier proto-Korinthian pots, as is this one. This variety decreases as three-quarters of all later figures are either fighting armoured soldiers (hoplites), riders, or sphinxes.

Here the centaur is not so much fighting the swordsman as standing in antithesis: the postures mirror each other. In spite of all the discussion of mythical subject matter it is not really feasible to describe the whole scene as a narrative, other than in the most general sense of an illustration of a conflict by a tripod with attendant birds of prey and a mobile naked swordsman. The geometric devices give some clues as to the structure of the scene, suggesting connections between the human elements (hooks), in contrast to the antithesis of man and monster. But many scenes on earlier pots are as fluid and indeterminate in their references, antitheses, juxta-postions, and sequences of figures, animals, and other devices. Most scenes involving people on later pots are immediately comprehensible or thematic, as a fight, hunt, race, or procession (64 per cent of the friezes).

Tripod Stands, Heads and Flora

The object behind the centaur and in front of the swordsman is a stand, ceramic most probably, for a *lebes* or *dinos*, a bowl for mixing wine, and appropriate to the (aristocratic) symposium, drinking party. They are analogous to the bronze caul-drons and bowls set upon tripods or conical stands. Such artefacts have a known lineage reaching back to Mycenaean times. They sometimes had griffon (or siren) *protomes* on the rims, or large annular handles. Many have been found dedicated in the sanctuaries of Olympia and Delphi. They are known to have been prizes in the games (aristocratic again). (See the convenient and illustrated summaries in Hampe and Simon 1981:111f; Coldstream 1977: especially 334–8 and 362–5; also Benton 1935; Schweitzer 1969: chapter 7.)

Seven earlier pots show tripods or bowl-stands. Apart from the swords, weaponry, and armour of soldiers, and the bridles of horses, these are the only arte-facts depicted. They are thus marked out as special. Their dedication in sanctuaries and their award as prizes at the games also mark them out as special artefacts – *agalmata* – with value fit for a hero or god, mediating mortality and divinity (Gernet 1981).

The seated birds upon this *aryballos* do not appear to be attachments to the *dinos*, but rather live birds of prey resting upon the artefact. Other pots do show bird or avian *protome* attachments. Of seven pots with tripods or stands, five associate them in some way with birds.

On a *pyxis* (box) from the sanctuary of Artemis Orthia at Sparta (figure 14.4; Johansen 1923: plate 24.3) an object in an animal scene appears to be a stand, but instead of *protomes* there emerge two plant-like growths (cf. Robertson 1948:48–9). The floral ornaments on an *aryballos* in the British Museum (1969: 12–15.1; figure 14.5) almost look like tripods. Three of these tripod stands are associated with exotic (eastern-derived) floral ornament. Free standing in the friezes, they are very stylised (lotus, palmette, and tree-like derivations) and contribute to paratactic sequences, that is sequences of (juxtaposed) items which seem to have little syntactic or narrative connection. Of the eight examples of flora in the sample which do not occur on their own, five are associated with birds.

Figure 14.4 [orig. figure 4]   Sparta: Artemis Orthia (50).

Figure 14.5 [orig. figure 5]   *British Museum 1969, 12–15.1 (8).*

Avian heads or *protomes* appear in line of repetition on six pots (figure 14.6) (like birds lined on later Geometric and proto-Korinthian sub-geometric vessels). On the shoulder of another *aryballos* from Pithekoussai (figure 14.6; Lacco Ameno 168268; Neeft 1987: List 33.A.1) freely-drawn designs look like bird *protomes* crossed with triangular stands.

An aryballos in Naples (361)

Lacco Ameno 168268 (360)

Naples 128296 (11)

Brussels A2 (17)

Figure 14.6 [orig. figure 6].

An *aryballos*, probably earlier, shows crested helmets and other objects which Snodgrass interprets as shields (1964: figure 14). These are the only other artefacts detached from people on earlier proto-Korinthian vessels in the sample. They too are associated with flying birds (of prey).

Helmets, heads, *protomes*. An *aryballos* in Brussels (A2; figure 14.6; Johansen 1923: fig. 42) provides another variation. On the shoulder is a line of winged male human *protomes*. Beneath is a scene of a tree-like floral flanked by three birds, two in contact with winged and helmeted *protomes*, crests growing from helmeted heads.

The tripod *agalma*, special object, gift to the gods, prize in the games, convivial bowl from which may be taken wine for the (lord's) cup; bird heads; birds; floral decoration; helmet heads growing crests and spread wings (consider figure 14.7). Strangeness and the exotic. The exotic marks the beginning of (orientalising) proto-Korinthian: motifs from the east. Geometric zig-zag friezes become lotus and palmette, standing in sequence with birds and stars. Some potters of the *oinochoai* (jugs) known as the 'Cumae Group' (e.g. listed by Dunbabin and Robertson

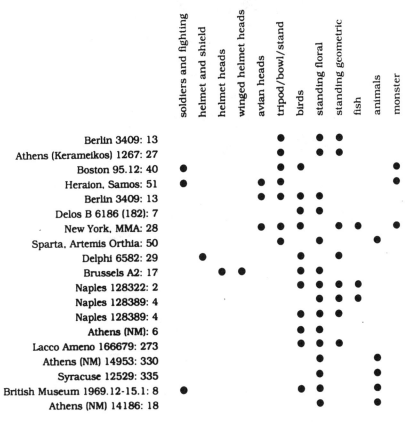

	soldiers and fighting	helmet and shield	helmet heads	winged helmet heads	avian heads	tripod/bowl/stand	birds	standing floral	standing geometric	fish	animals	monster
Berlin 3409: 13						●		●	●			
Athens (Kerameikos) 1267: 27						●		●	●			
Boston 95.12: 40	●					●	●					●
Heraion, Samos: 51	●				●	●						●
Berlin 3409: 13					●	●	●	●				
Delos B 6186 (182): 7						●	●					
New York, MMA: 28				●	●	●		●	●		●	●
Sparta, Artemis Orthia: 50						●		●		●		
Delphi 6582: 29			●			●		●				
Brussels A2: 17				●	●	●	●					
Naples 128322: 2						●	●		●	●		
Naples 128389: 4							●	●		●		
Naples 128389: 4						●	●	●				
Athens (NM): 6						●	●					
Lacco Ameno 166679: 273						●	●	●				
Athens (NM) 14953: 330							●				●	
Syracuse 12529: 335							●				●	
British Museum 1969.12-15.1: 8	●						●	●			●	
Athens (NM) 14186: 18							●				●	

Figure 14.7 [orig. figure 7] Tripod stands, birds, heads, and flora: some associations occurring in earlier proto-Korinthian.

1953:174) took the previously linear field of pot belly into their hands with line-stem swirls and geometric-like lotus. Elsewhere tripods grow bird-heads, lotus-palmettes stand like tripods and grow with cabling stems into the grand garlands on the shoulders of later *aryballoi* (figure 14.6; figure 14.8).

Visual play or tropes; the risk of free-hand painting; and the variety and surprise of juxtaposed people, soldiers, animals, birds, the exotic: these are the creative elements of earlier proto-Korinthian. This is no longer apparent in later scenes. The floral becomes the slick, intricate, and luxurious displays on the shoulders of *aryballoi* (figure 14.8), and dot rosettes in some animal friezes. There are two later pots which carry depictions of tripod stands. Both are in race scenes (figure 14.8), (the vessels presumably as prizes, symbols of contest). The only other artefact is a net in a hare hunt.

Figure 14.8 [orig. figure 8]   From the Athenaion, Syracuse (77).

Monsters: Identity, Integrity, Violence, Dismemberment

Monsters such as the centaur upon this pot are found not infrequently in proto-Korinthian (one in twelve figures is a monster). They are formed by the incongruous assembly of animal, bird, and human bodies, heads, and limbs or wings. In the mixing-up of different parts, the monsters deny difference. And on this basis the monsters are equivalent, many variations on sphinx, siren, griffon, centaur, chimaira; animal, bird, and person. A disordered loss of difference is intimately related to violence, because order and peace depend on difference: equilibrium may lead to violence in an attempt to establish a preponderance of one over another, whether it is good over evil, the hero and his enemy, or a boundary between pure and impure (Girard 1977:51).

On this *aryballos* the swordsman opposes a centaur and its denial of integral human form. But the centaur is part human. Horses too are, with only ten exceptions (out of 94), always shown bridled and ridden or harnessed to chariots, associated with men. The centaur has something of the swordsman: both hold the staff, and the brandished staffs or weapons mirror each other. There is an ambiguity or dialectical tension in the antithesis. Behind the pair is a tripod stand. If equivalence and equilibrium can lead to violence (the mobile swordsman behind),

Figure 14.9 [orig. figure 9]   Berlin 3773 (68).

then may justice appropriately be imbalance, winners and losers, the outcome of this conflict? The prize for the winner?

Mediation and contest: the two later scenes which feature tripods, stands, and kraters (Taranto 4173 and from the Athenaion, Syracuse, figure 14.8) are both races, as I have mentioned: horses on one, chariots on another, race towards robed figures – the judges? On one a sphinx stands in attendance. Of the ten unarmed and long-robed figures in the sample, six can be interpreted as being in a position of mediation. Of these, two on earlier pots hold wreaths.

Between monsters and people are *protomes* or severed heads without bodies. Play on the connection or separation of head and body is brought to maximum visibility in the *aryballoi* (later) which have modelled human and lion heads on *aryballos* bodies (figure 14.9). Instead of monstrous bodies, the lion and human heads grow from ceramic bodies (earth transformed) containing perfumed oil (of scented flora?). Some of the tripod stands grow *protomes* too, of avian creatures, their ceramic or bronze body container for wine (another transformed fruit of floral product). Heads, birds, body form, and now manufacture, transformation of the material, grown, cultivated, and wild.

Violence: the Animal within the Body

Violence and confrontation, perhaps arbitration through conflict, is a theme of this *aryballos*. Violence is a major part of proto-Korinthian imagery. Out of 238 people figures (65 per cent) 115 are armed or fighting. Animals are hunted, lions roar and attack, goats butt each other, boars and bulls oppose lions. Out of 184 (55 per cent) 102 human figures on later pots are hoplites, heavily armed with helmet, shield, spear(s), and sometimes sword and body armour. All except one are fighting or dying (figure 14.10).

In contrast to the swordsmen here, hoplites are anonymous within helmet, armour, and behind shield. The swordsman's dynamic upon this *aryballos* is in his angled limbs. The hoplite's shield and spear are the focus of his energy. Only the hoplite shields mark difference, but one of bird and animal devices. In contrast to the *protomes* and monsters of dismemberment and incongruous assembly, the physique of the heavy infantryman is held together and defended by the talismans of his identity – the weaponry. The hoplite looks like another and another. In the fighting formation the armoured soldier's helmeted head has a closer functional connection to the head of his fellow hoplite than it does to his own torso or greaved calf (a line of *protomes*). In the phalanx formation, bodies unite and their integration fears disruption and break up (hoplites caught alone die easily). The formation and the equipment forms new, centred bodies, and provides identity. The hoplite's armour and shield hold him together, but he does face violence and risks death, risk dismemberment and monstrous chaos.

Animals such as those on the shoulder of this *aryballos* appear on the pots in great numbers and the soldier may conceive of himself as a lion, or one of the other wild creatures pictured on the pots (lions, boars, bulls, rams, and stags comprise

Figure 14.10 [orig. figure 10] Louvre CA 931 (75).

90 per cent of animals shown on later pots). The juxtaposition of the two friezes upon this *aryballos* may suggest some analogy between animal and human worlds. Animal metaphor is prevalent in Homeric epic where the lion is the animal mirror of the hero (see Schnapp-Gourbeillon 1981). But animals and lions are of another order. Animals are like, and unlike humans; (the swordsman and centaur in dialectical tension). Lions rage and fight like the hero, but animals are animated, complex, varied, changeable, and unpredictable. This is especially true of those wild and dangerous animals which figure on the pots. Opposed to order and domestication, they are a threat to the societal man of culture. So I might say that the death risked through violence does not oppose life (the figures on the pots are animated precisely through violence: see Carter 1972:38–9); death is opposed to the consciousness of life, and this is of culture, involving life-style, and is a negation of the animal.

But the soldier in the fight leaves order and security behind (the ceramic stand as arbitrated order) to risk the otherness of death (the otherness of the man-animal). Violence allows the soldier to find identity with his bestial interior while avoiding being devoured by it. War animates the dead within him. The fighting man is both hunter and hunted (scenes of animal hunts, animal attacks on people, soldiers fight among wild animals). Finding the identity of his self in hunting and fighting the 'other'.

The wild animals themselves are brought into a regulated code, particularly on later larger vessels. These animal friezes stylise and de-animate their animals, lined up in formal sequence.

Heads and bodies, helmets, armour, spears, and stabbing; human, avian, animal, and monstrous; torn, mixed, stylised. The major focus of proto-Korinthian iconography comes to be bodily form (cf. Schnapp (1988) on Greek art generally) and the body, in my argument, is a primary site for the aesthetic ethos of violence and war. To depict such an ideology was a reason for proto-Korinthian.

The Lord, His Enemies, and Sovereign Identity

> It is not in giving life but in risking life that man is raised above the animal: that is why superiority has been accorded in humanity not to the sex that brings forth but to that which kills.
>
> —*Simoné de Beauvoir*

The figured scenes on pots such as this one represent a world of imagery which is antinomial to that gendered feminine. Of 4,104 animals in the sample only nine are drawn as being of female sex (some deer without antlers are of indeterminate sex and age; birds appear in different species, but again of indeterminate sex). There is no reference to sexual reproduction, or ageing (apart from the possible young deer); there is only the fertility of repetition. Dogs and horses are the main representative of domestic animals upon the pots. One accompanies the hunt, the other war, and races in the contests of those who can afford them. Horses are beyond the wealth of the small-holder. Dogs do not appear with men in proto-Korinthian imagery (of 2,390 dogs, only seven are in scenes with a man).

The domestic, the world of agriculture, the *oikos* (household), food and nutrition, sexual reproduction are conspicuously missing from the proto-Korinthian world peopled by men. Instead there is violence, confrontation, and contest, defining self in the face of some thing other. The scenes also speak of display: the elaborate floral and geometric pattern, helmet crests, shield devices in war. And the pot forms themselves: perfume jars, expensive (? only tiny pots), scents of seduction (antinomial to the order of reproductive marriage; see Detienne 1972 and 1977), cups and accoutrements to drinking wine, some pots displaying themselves with fine figured work.

The identity of the lord: striving for recognition to improve himself over another through his qualities. In this men are opposed to each other and to the other; and it tends to violence. It also means that risking life is the means to gain identity. To deny an attachment to mere life (the household, family, nutrition, reproduction), to a particular self which is their self, is the attempt to reconstruct an identity for themselves which is in itself, separate, of another order, the heroic, the divine.

Life then is subordinate to the *life-style* of the fighting lord. His life is one of living pleasure (oiled with perfume, drinking from the cup). A pure consumption of goods produced by subordinate classes. Life-style: gifts, wine, contest, perfume.

And violence. Risking death on the battlefield or in the hunt, risking and surviving for recognition by the herd of others. War becomes luxury, wealth, and festival (nodding crests, shield devices, pipers; decorative and floral devices in the visual field of the scene on this *aryballos*). Violence is excess (the cost of the weaponry, horses, time, and risk; a new and exotic visual order of style); the domestic (absent) is sufficiency. The risk is about transgression: violence as transgression of the law which is against murder because vengeance and blood feud result. (Transgression of the Geometric canon of style). But transgression asserts the identity of a self which refuses prohibition and survives, and this reward is accessible only to those of wealth who may fight the risk and display their sovereignty.

(But even in its miniature insignificance, proto-Korinthian style takes this step at the hand of the potter.)

This masculine order is, I argue, a complex mediation of themes referenced by the pots.

masculine	feminine
war	*oikos*
luxury	nutrition
otherness and risk	the domestic
death	reproduction
transgression	law and convention
identity	loss of self
integral creatures	monsters
integration and formation	dismemberment
animals as reflections	animals as strange
sovereignty	subordination

Mediating elements are violence, conflict and confrontation, the body or form (of people, of animals, of monsters, of flowers).

The *Aryballos*, Cemetery, and Sanctuary

This *aryballos* is recorded as bought in Korinth; the museum notes give no more detail. Most *aryballoi* have been found in sanctuaries and cemeteries. They contained perfumed oil, in all probability. Given also the shape of the iconographic discourse I have sketched, this is appropriate to sanctuary or cemetery. Perfume is a substance which comes between:

masculine	feminine
exotic flowers, wild spices	agricultural oil
seduction	marriage

Spices and perfumed scent of sacrifice mediate humanity and divinity. The imagery, about death, transgression, and an absence of reproduction, mediates that which is other and that which is self. Gift from humanity to divinity, or placed in the grave of a family member. And oils of perfume are of the world, not of ordered reproductive sexuality, but that of seduction (Detienne 1972 and 1977: passim).

Risk, Ideology, and a Korinthian Potter

The scenes of animals, birds, people, and exotic ornament were a distinct contrast with the preceding (and often contemporary) geometrically-covered pot surface. New pot shapes, the *aryballos* particularly, were (re)introduced by potters. With a celebration of a workmanship of risk within controlled limits of conventional linear banding, the potters painted free-hand silhouette and outlined figures. Incision added another element of display of dexterity and regulated precision. In figured earlier proto-Korinthian, potters played on old subject matter, transforming Geometric water birds, retaining wavy-line snakes, but expanded on geometric with elaboration, and introduced rich exotic flora. New themes of violence, soldiering, the animal and avian worlds, monsters and strangeness, symbols of the special are juxtaposed in parataxis in the open linear field. The logical connections and lines of connotation between the themes conforms with what becomes clearer later. It is a loose and hazy flow around a special world which is antinomial to marriage, reproduction, and the domestic. There is some play with transforming designs: standing tripods through *protomes*, standing florals through cabled garlands. The introduction of incision is play on figuration.

The variety of figures on earlier pots is greater than that seen later, and even with the predominantly linear sub-geometric *aryballoi*, there are few coherent classes of decoration. There is clearly an explicit conception, size, and look of the *aryballos* – the way it should be. This conception, or prototype, is provided with slight variations of decoration, producing uniqueness in conformity with the generic *aryballos*. The figured pots, such as this *aryballos*, are at the extreme of such a scale.

I emphasise the workmanship of risk allied to an iconography which in its juxtaposed elements sets up questions and sparks off lines of association, rather than providing clear ideological messages (cf. Osborne on proto-Attic pottery: 1989:318). This means that the risk, ambiguity, and elaboration of form and figure are more of an affirmation of the potter's creative self.

Risk in mode of production and execution, convention transgressed; risk and transgression too in the content of ideological meaning: the life-style of the hero. The analogy may well have appealed to potters themselves, to those who were to take the potters abroad from Korinth, and to those who acquired them as gifts to gods or for the dead (consciously or unconsciously). I argue that the connection between the figured scenes, technique, ideology, and deposition is a significant one: proto-Korinthian was invented as a means of expressing a particular visual ideology. But it cannot be claimed that the style was anything more than a *marginal* play with figured scenes: there are too few pots with figured decoration (on the scale of Korinthian pottery production see the comments in Salmon 1984:101f.). Nor do the pots represent a powerful ideological argument for an ethical order of aristocratic masculinity. The imagery is often restrained, ambiguous, 'open' to interpretation. The pots figured of risk and transgression communicate a few potters (perhaps with commissioning others) experimenting with an expression of 'individual' identity and aspiration to aristocratic masculinity.

Most pots of later proto-Korinthian are still linearly decorated, but there is not the variability around decorative model as there is on earlier *aryballoi*. Neeft (1987) found it possible to classify over 925 later *aryballoi* into 48 groups on the basis of gross decorative features, and most of these classes are variations on dog friezes, dot rosettes, and linear banding. The linearity continues the backward and conventional reference – *aryballoi* in accordance with traditional manner of finish and decoration, but with a brief and restrained reference to the hunt through the coursing domesticated hounds. In the figured scenes structure is much clearer, as is communication of the ideological components of violence, excess, and the mediation of the animal in a world of aristocratic masculinity. The scenes set fewer overt questions. Exotic flora are contained within controlled shoulder garlands. Animals are marshalled and regulated; there is less use of incongruous juxtaposition. Both earlier and later proto-Korinthian display an excess over the linear Geometric. The earlier pots may look closer to Geometric, but later figured scenes are more regulated and formulaic.

Against a background of conservative pottery design, proto-Korinthian figured was an experiment with a risked potter's hand in an ideological field of aristocratic life-style and value. It is very unlikely that this was the culture of the potter, yet an iconographic medium was adapted to express it, perhaps to achieve the 'sale' of the ware (structures of the archaic Korinthian economy), and probably because of the conceptual and ideological constraints of stylistic expression which were already existing. The potter's own class background is perhaps retained in the earlier play on themes and design which questions and opens space rather than expresses with ease and clarity, but the ideology of the decisive hand and risk of creative self and integrity in the fine miniature brush work and incision can be interpreted as within the bounds of the depicted conceptual world. This is more evident in the later tamed scenes.

In spite of the supposed emergence of the Korinthian *polis*, its citizen and hoplite community, and a political revolution in the mid-seventh century (a narrow and exclusive aristocratic oligarchy expelled), there is little evidence in proto-Korinthian for attempts to represent any of the new values and aspirations of the *polis* (for such see Vernant 1962; Snodgrass 1980; and cf. Morris 1987). Instead, there is visible a process of refining the expression of themes surrounding the antinomies of an (aristocratic) masculine identity. I will end with this open question of the historical character of the style proto-Korinthian.

Some Remarks on Wider Themes

I have tried to give some impressions of an interpretive dialogue with this *aryballos*, following lines of reference and affiliation suggested by its particular design. I can only mark some beginnings, given this limited context of an essay in a journal. I have raised more questions than I have addressed. There is the issue of the 'creativity' or agency of the proto-Korinthian potters, notions of the individual expression of a potter (given the argument for a workmanship of risk) with respect to ideological structures of aristocratic meaning (of iconography) and structures of stylistic expression. I have omitted considering workshop organisation, possible models of the economics of design and 'commissioning' of particular iconographies, and stories of 'trade', travel, and exchange. And I have not elaborated on the particularity and variability of the contexts of the consumption and deposition of proto-Korinthian pottery. The references to aristocratic masculinity and the change in design from early to later could clearly be implicated in what is known of the social and cultural changes of seventh-century aristocratic Korinth.

In the outline of meaning and ideology I deliberately avoided reference to literary sources. The purpose was to make clear my avoidance of what I termed the fallacy of representation – reducing this *aryballos* to a representation of something other, in this case ideas and a conceptual world derived from literature. But this avoidance is artifical; I will be presenting such relationships and contexts of iconography elsewhere (Shanks 1993a).

I hope to have shown that the chronological aspirations of traditional classical archaeology, working through the notion of style as descriptive attribute, are almost irrelevant to a study such as that presented in outline here (see the comments by Beard 1991:17–8). Such aspirations, to provide a fine-grained absolute and relative chronology to stylistic development, are largely the legacy of an identification of date and history – a pseudo-historiography. I reiterate too that classical archaeology has, in its aspiration to art history, paid little or no attention to the social form of its main type of evidence – material culture. (There are important exceptions to this omission.) Indeed I would hope to raise the question of the relation of style, chronology, and history (see the comments by Morris 1987:17 and chapter 9 passim). The design of an *aryballos* such as this resonates with pasts, presents, and futures: looking back to certainties and securities of manufacturing technologies, and to the Geometric; and in comparison with sub-geometric decoration, its imagery appears as radical departure. Proto-Korinthian style refers to time far wider than its date. And these references to time are more than reflections of the quality of a pot painters art: being avant-garde or dyed-in-the-wool Geometric.

I also make mention of aspects of the long-term. The potters of proto-Korinthian were working with an expressive vocabulary, conventions of design, which has a considerable range of time and space. This use of animal imagery and metaphor is, of course, found in Minoan and Mycenaean, as well as Near-Eastern design. And I place particular stress on the ideological structure of proto-Korinthian style, with its contrasts of death and reproduction, otherness and the domestic. The political success of an articulation of such themes, the shifting refinements of definition of masculinity and aristocratic power, are with us still today. The oppositions of wild and domestic, origins of ideologies of home in earlier prehistory are discussed by Ian Hodder (1990a).

This *aryballos* is a particular articulation of references to time and space. This unity is the 'historical moment' of the *aryballos* (Shanks 1993b; on temporality and material culture see Shanks and Tilley 1987: chapter 5; and comments in Hodder 1990b). Narratives are implied which are far richer and more subtle than those of the development of Greek classicism.

I have not addressed directly the subject of proto-Korinthian as the orientalising moment of Greek art. Conventional accounts (such as Boardman 1967; Akurgal 1968; and Cook 1966:46f; see also Coldstream 1977: chapter 15; and Carter 1972) all rely on notions of style as having a unity, identity, and authenticity. Style, as a cultural attribute, can be identified as 'Greek' or 'Eastern', and diffusion and influence plotted. Explaining the reception in Greece of some eastern stylistic traits and not others becomes a question of abstract stylistic diffusion, with some eastern style 'suiting' the Greek; and a question of cultural vigour, of Greeks who were of such artistic vigour that they could be selective in doing what they would with the style of the east. Given the complexities of stylistic behaviour, any easy elision of style and ethnicity is a hazardous one (see Shanks and Tilley 1987b; chapter 4; and Conkey and Hastorf 1990: passim). I would also reject an explanation of orientalising as related to abstract principles of style and ethnicity on the grounds that 'culture', as a very contentious concept, is not an ethnic attribute which can be characterised as stable or authentic. I argue against a conception of cultural identity which, on an organic analogy, involves notions of wholeness, spread, growth, roots, and stable existence in a definable locality. Such a concept does not take account of historical practices of compromise, invention, revival, and adaptation (see for example Clifford 1988: chapter 12; and discussion in Shanks 1991: part 3; also Shanks and Tilley 1987a: chapter 7; and 1987b: chapter 4; see Hebdige 1979; and 1988 for analogous argument and illustration for contemporary culture; Miller (1987) on the dialectic of production and consumption actively recreating culture). The conventional accounts of classical art history omit such social context, and refer only to a descriptive background of possible cases of actual social contact between the Greeks and the east, or to possible mechanisms, such as traded items, of the diffusion of cultural attributes (see the comments and argument in Whitley forthcoming).

I have indicated also how conventional explanation is rooted in principles of valuation which are largely taken for granted and left unexamined: a pot is evaluated according to its artistic worth or degree of contribution to the development of *Style*. The evaluation measures pertain to particular academic and cultural discourses of ethnic vitality (Greeks as proto-Europeans) and artistic excellence. Of course, these issues have recently been highlighted by Martin Bernal's *Black Athena* (1989 and 1991) and ensuing discussion (*Arethusa* Special Issue 1989; *Journal of Mediterranean Archaeology* 3 1990; see also my review of Bernal in *History Today*; forthcoming).

The interpretation of style as ways of doing, as design, with immediate reference to social and political resonance can, I hope to have shown, produce different narratives: here I have argued that orientalism belongs with an experiment in articulating an aristocratic and masculine discourse. I also emphasise the importance of gender. This is clearly acknowledged in some cultural studies of the ancient world (for example, see papers and references in Blok and Mason 1987, and also DuBois 1988), and in some studies of the iconology of later Attic pottery (such as, again, the volume *Cité des images*). But, as yet, there is little recognition in early Hellenic archaeology of the possible roles of gender positioning in the development of the city state (see my comment (Shanks 1992) on the social archaeologies of Whitley (1991) and Morris (1987)).

A tension between the particular and the general, with which I have tried to work, is often translated in the terms of theory as the interplay between individual agency and structure. I avoid a technical discussion here, but mention that in reconciling the two I think the aim should not be social reconstruction in the sense of subsuming the particulars of material culture beneath overarching social process or change (perhaps involving ascription to broad categories such as state formation and the *polis*, or cross-cultural social typologies). Chris Tilley and I have argued at length against such social archaeology (1987a: chapter 6; 1987b) and the problems entailed of explaining the particular forms that material culture may take by referring to an 'expression' of social logic. Instead we may rather hope to interpret and understand the (social) *practices* which the design of particular items of material culture implies. To avoid the fallacy of representation, I would propose that the design of *aryballos*, such as that with which I have been concerned, is a material part of what it may be showing us. Archaic Korinthian society, ideologies, aspirations of potters or of citizens are not experienced now or then directly and in themselves (what would their reality be?). They appear sphinx-like in the riddles of the object, its design. (For reflection on this philosophy of the material artefact see Shanks and Tilley 1987a; Miller 1987; and Shanks 1991.) There is no 'Greek' history out there; there is no origin of western European culture to be found. There are only the tattered residues of times past, still clinging on now. All else is created, emergent in our dialogue with these material remains.

Acknowledgements

Thanks again to Anthony Snodgrass and Ian Hodder for help and encouragement with my work. Special thanks go to Alain Schnapp for his interest and for setting up my stay here in Paris, courtesy, especially, of the Maison des Sciences de l'Homme.

References

Akurgal, E., 1968. *The Birth of Greek Art*. London: Methuen.
Amyx, D. A., 1988. *Corinthian Vase Painting in the Archaic Period*. Berkeley: University of California Press.
Andrewes, A., 1956. *The Greek Tyrants*. London: Hutchinson.
Archaeological Review from Cambridge 1990. 9.1 (Technology in the humanities).
Arnold, R., 1972. The Horse-Demon in Early Greek Art and his Eastern Neighbours. Ph.D. Dissertation: Columbia University.
Beard, M., 1991. Adopting an approach. In T. Rasmussen and N. Spivey (eds), *Looking at Greek Vases*. Cambridge: Cambridge University Press.

Benson, J. L., 1953. *Die Geschichte Der Korinthischen Vasen.* Basel: Benno Schwabe.

Benson, J. L., 1989. *Earlier Corinthian workshops: a Study of Corinthian Geometric and Protocorinthian Stylistic Groups.* Amsterdam: Allard Pierson.

Benton, S., 1961. Cattle egrets and bustards in Greek art. *Journal of Hellenic Studies* 81:44–55.

Bernal, M., 1987 and 1991. *Black Athena.* Volumes 1 and 2. London: Free Association.

Blok, J., and P. Mason, 1987. *Sexual Asymmetry: Studies in Ancient Society.* Amsterdam: Gieben.

Boardman, J., 1967. *Pre-classical: from Crete to Archaic Greece.* Harmondsworth: Penguin.

Boardman, J., 1983. Symbol and story in Geometric art. In W.G. Moon (ed.), *Ancient Greek Art and Iconography.* Madison: University of Wisconsin Press.

Boast, R., 1990. The categorisation and design systematics of British Beakers: a reassessment. Ph.D. dissertation: Cambridge.

Bosana-Kourou, P., 1979. The sphinx in early Archaic Greek art. Ph.D. dissertation: Oxford.

Buschor, E., 1934. Kentauren. *American Journal of Archaeology* 38:128–32.

Carter. J., 1972. The beginning of narrative in the Greek Geometric period. *Annual of the British School at Athens* 67:25–58.

La cité des images: religion et société en grèce antique. 1984. Paris: Nathan.

Coldstream, J. N., 1968. *Greek Geometric Pottery: a Survey of Ten Local Styles and their Chronology.* London: Methuen.

Coldstream, J. N., 1977. *Geometric Greece.* London: Benn.

Coldstream, J. N., 1983. The meaning of the regional styles in the eighth century BC. In R. Hagg (ed.), *The Greek Renaissance of the Eighth Century BC.* Stockholm.

Conkey, M. and C. Hastorf (eds), 1990. *The Uses of Style in Archaeology.* Cambridge: Cambridge University Press.

Cook, R. M., 1966. *Greek Painted Pottery.* London: Methuen.

Delplace, C., 1980. *Le griffon de l'archaisme at l'époque impériale.* Brussels.

Detienne, M., 1972. *Les jardins d'Adonis.* Paris: Gallimard.

Detienne, M., 1977. *Dionysos mis à mort.* Paris: Gallimard.

DuBois, P., 1988. *Sowing the Body: Psychoanalysis and Ancient Representations of Women.* Chicago: Chicago University Press.

Dunbabin, T. J., and M. Robertson, 1953. Some Protocorinthian vase painters. *Annual of the British School at Athens* 48:172–81.

Elsner, J., 1990. Significant details: systems, certainties and the art historian as detective. *Antiquity* 64.

Farnsworth, F., 1970. Corinthian pottery: technical studies. *American Journal of Archaeology* 74:9–20.

Fittschen, K., 1969. *Untersuchugen zum Beginn der Sagendarstellungen bei den Greichen.* Berlin: Bruno Hessling.

Friedlander, M. J., 1943. *On art and connoisseurship* (trans Borenius). London: Bruno Cassirer.

Gernet, L., 1981. 'Value' in Greek myth. In R.L. Gordon (ed.), *Myth, Religion and Society.* Cambridge: Cambridge University Press.

Ginzberg, C., 1983. Morelli, Freud and Sherlock Holmes: clues and the scientific method. In U. Eco and T. Sebeok (eds), *The Sign of Three.* Bloomington: Indiana University Press.

Girard, R. 1977. *Violence and the Sacred* (trans Gregory). London: John Hopkins.

Hampe, R. and E. Simon, 1981. *The Birth of Greek Art: from the Mycenean to the Archaic Period.* London: Thames and Hudson.

Hebdige, D., 1979. *Subculture: the Meaning of Style.* London: Methuen.

Hebdige, D., 1988. *Hiding in the Light.* London: Routledge.

Hodder, I., 1990a. *The Domestication of Europe.* Oxford: Blackwell.

Hodder, I., 1990b. Style as historical quality. In M. Conkey and C. Hastorf (eds), *The Uses of Style in Archaeology*. Cambridge: Cambridge University Press.

Hurwitt, J. M., 1985. *The Art and Culture of Early Greece 1100–480 BC*. Ithaca: Cornell University Press.

Johansen, K. F., 1923. *Les vases Sicyoniens*. Paris: Champion. Copenhagen: Branner.

Kurtz, D. C., 1985. Beazley and the connoisseurship of Greek vases. In *Greek Vases in the J. Paul Getty Museum*. Malibu.

Miller, D., 1985. *Artefacts as Categories*. Cambridge: Cambridge University Press.

Miller, D., 1987. *Material Culture and Mass Consumption*. Oxford: Blackwell.

Morgan, C. and T. Whitelaw, 1991. Pots and politics: ceramic evidence for the rise of the Argive state. *American Journal of Archaeology* 95:79–108.

Morris, I., 1987. *Burial and Ancient Society: the Rise of the Greek City State*. Cambridge: Cambridge University Press.

Neeft, C. W., 1987. *Protocorinthian Subgeometric Aryballoi*. Amsterdam: Allard Pierson.

Noble, J. V., 1988. *The Techniques of Attic Painted Pottery* (revised edition). London: Thames and Hudson.

Osborne, R., 1989. A crisis in archaeological history? The seventh century BC in Attica. *Annual of the British School at Athens* 84:297–322.

Payne, H. G. G., 1931. *Necrocorinthia*. Oxford: Clarendon.

Payne, H. G. G., 1933. *Protokorinthische Vasenmalerei*. Berlin: Keller.

Pye, D., 1980. *The Art of Workmanship*. London: Royal College of Art.

Robertson, C. M. 1948. Excavations in Ithaca V: the Geometric and later finds from Aetos. *Annual of the British School at Athens* 43:60–113.

Salmon, J. B., 1984. *Wealthy Corinth: a History of the City to 338 BC*. Oxford: Clarendon.

Schiffler, B., 1976. *Die Typologie des Kentauren in Antiken Kunst vom 10 bis zum Ende des 4 Jh. v. Chr.* Frankfurt and Bern: Lang.

Schmitt, M., 1966. Bellerophon and the chimaera in Archaic Greek art. *American Journal of Archaeology* 70:341–347.

Schnapp, A., 1987. *La duplicité du chasseur*. Doctorat d'Etat. Lille Theses.

Schnapp, A., 1988. Why did the Greeks need images? In J. Christiansen and T. Melander (eds), *Ancient Greek and Related Pottery*. Copenhagen.

Schnapp-Gourbeillon, A., 1981. *Lions, heroes, masques: les représentations de l'animal chez Homère*. Paris: Maspero.

Schweitzer, B., 1969. *Die geometrische Kunst Griechenlands*. Köln: M. du Mont Schauberg.

Shanks, M., 1990. Interpretation in archaeology. In R. Francovich et al. (eds), *Il ciclo di lezioni sulla ricerca applicata in campo archaeologica*. Firenze: Edizioni all'insegna del giglio.

Shanks, M., 1991. *Experiencing the Past: on the Character of Archaeology*. London: Routledge.

Shanks, M., 1992. Some recent approaches to style and social reconstruction in classical archaeology. *Archaeological Review from Cambridge* 11.

Shanks, M., 1993a. *Art and the Rise of the Greek City State*. London: Routledge.

Shanks, M., 1993b. The forms of history. In I. Hodder and M. Shanks (eds), *Interpreting Archaeologies*. London: Routledge.

Shanks, M., forthcoming. A review: Bernal: Black Athena (vols 1 and 2). *History Today*.

Shanks, M., and C. Tilley, 1987a. *Reconstructing Archaeology*. Cambridge: Cambridge University Press.

Shanks, M., and C. Tilley, 1987b. *Social Theory and Archaeology*. Cambridge: Polity.

Snodgrass, A., 1964. *Early Greek Armour and Weapons*. Edinburgh: Edinburgh University Press.

Snodgrass, A., 1980a. *Archaic Greece: the Age of Experiment*. London: Dent.

Snodgrass, A., 1980b. Towards the interpretation of the Geometric figure scenes. *Mitteilungen des deutschen archäologischen Instituts, Athenische Abteilung* 95:51–8.

Snodgrass, A., 1982. *Narration and Allusion in Archaic Greek Art.* Eleventh J. L. Myres Memorial Lecture. London: Leopards Head.

Snodgrass, A., 1987. *An Archaeology of Greece: the present state and future scope of a discipline.* Berkeley: University of California Press.

Tilley, C. (ed.), 1990. *Reading Material Culture.* Oxford: Blackwell.

Tilley, C., 1991. *Material Culture and Text: the Art of Ambiguity.* London: Routledge.

Vernant, J. P., 1962. *Les origines de la pensée Grecque.* Paris: Presses Universitaires de France.

Von Bothmer, D., 1987. Greek vase painting: 200 years of connoisseurship. In *Papers on the Amasis Painter and his World.* London: Thames and Hudson.

Whitley, J., 1987. Art history, archaeology and idealism: the German tradition. In I. Hodder (ed.), *Archaeology as Long Term History.* Cambridge: Cambridge University Press.

Whitley, J., 1991. *Style and Society in Dark Age Greece.* Cambridge: Cambridge University Press.

Whitley, J., forthcoming. Protoattic pottery: a contextual approach. In I. Morris (ed.), *Classical Greece: Ancient History and Modern Archaeology.* Cambridge: Cambridge University Press.

15

The Living, the Dead and the Ancestors: Neolithic and Early Bronze Age Mortuary Practices

John C. Barrett

The Archaeology of Death

If we are to make sense of the considerable variation in our Neolithic and Bronze Age mortuary data we must be clearer about the procedures used in its analysis. Renfrew has argued that archaeologists should move beyond description and reconstruction to grasp the possibility of explaining the past (Renfrew 1982 & 1984:3ff). This much may be agreed, even if we have only now begun to understand the problems of site formation, making reconstruction a more reliable task. But if we accept that the methodological procedures of reconstruction can be developed we are still faced with the question of what constitutes an explanation.

Renfrew (and others) have argued that our explanations should be concerned with classes of events or general processes, such as 'state formation' or 'the origins of agriculture' (Renfrew 1982). In other words, explanation seeks out the cross cultural process which lies behind empirical regularities. In our case it means that a cross cultural explanation should be possible for variations in mortuary practices. Only in this way, implies Renfrew, can the archaeologist avoid a type of historical particularism which has no general validity and therefore no scientific value. I wish to demonstrate something of the weakness in such an argument and show that, in the particular case of mortuary variability, no general explanation is possible. Instead explanation must take account of the specific historical conditions under which those people acted who made the histories we study. This does not lead to a dead end of historical particularism. To claim that such a thing exists misunderstands the nature of historical scholarship.

Many recent reviews of the archaeological study of mortuary practices place the publications of Saxe (1970) and Binford (1971) at the centre of the current 'conceptual framework' (Tainter 1978; Chapman and Randsborg 1981; O'Shea 1984). Certainly the 'New Archaeology' marks a dislocation in the history of mortuary studies, for it was here that mortuary variability was no longer seen as an expression of cultural belief but rather as a reflection of the organisational principles of the social system itself.

The underlying principle employed by Binford and Saxe was that the treatment of the corpse depended upon the selection and the marking of a number of the social identities which an individual had achieved in life. That selection was made by those who accepted certain social responsibilities towards the deceased. If we consider the social system as comprising a system of roles and statuses, each of which has a call upon particular obligations, then the formal organisation of burial (described by the range of symbolism and the degree of energy input) supposedly mirrors the formal organisation of the social system. Various ethnographic tests were carried out to support the cross cultural generalisation that social complexity will be matched by mortuary complexity (Binford 1971).

If the argument is accepted a number of methodological issues still remain, and O'Shea has been concerned to follow these through in a specifically archaeological treatment of the data. They include problems of recognising the distinction between 'vertical' divisions of rank and 'horizontal' divisions of status, understanding the historical development of symbolism in a single cemetery, and a more detailed consideration of the formation processes affecting the archaeological record itself (O'Shea 1981 & 1984). But beneath these methodological issues lie more fundamental questions.

We cannot proceed by analysing the organisational form of mortuary data to reveal the form of the social system, and then use the form of the social system to explain the form of the burial data. For example, in his 'hypothesis 8' Saxe states that formal disposal areas may be maintained by particular corporate groups whose claim to the use or control of crucial but restricted resources depended upon lineal descent from the dead (Saxe 1970:119). In archaeology this idea has tended towards circularity; cemeteries are taken to indicate the existence of corporate groups, the need for corporate groups to establish control over 'critical resources' is then assumed (Chapman 1981) and the cemeteries are seen to result from the need to legitimate that claim.

If explanations involve linking general principles to particular cases it is hardly adequate simply to describe the particular in terms of the general. As Hodder has noted, the specific character of the mortuary remains, cemetery architecture and so forth cannot be dealt with in these terms (Hodder 1984:52). Archaeologists often appear trapped in describing the same types of social system by reference to different sets of archaeological material. This has become the basis of so much cross cultural generalisation and model building that the past becomes increasingly uninteresting as we move from one study to the next.

To build an alternative we must recognise that social systems are constructed out of particular social practices. These practices take place within the specific cultural and historical conditions they maintain. Archaeological evidence can tell us something about the way such practices were maintained over time, contributing towards the reproduction of one social system (Barrett 1987). Corporate groups do not *do* anything. They result from institutionalised practices by which people maintain relations of affinity, obligation and enmity, thereby controlling access to certain material and human resources. As Parker Pearson has said, "the reconstruction of social organisation through the identification of roles . . . can be challenged by the theoretical stance that social systems are not constituted *of* roles but *by* recurrent social practices." (1982:100).

Mortuary rituals are particular types of social practices and we must examine the way they were enacted by the living around the corpse and the grave. The dead do not participate in their own funeral, nor is the entire essence of the social system mapped out by this single practice. Instead death precipitates a requirement for the living to renegotiate certain of their own relations of affinity and obligation. This they may do with reference to the dead, ancestors and gods. The corpse, and the way it was treated, presents a powerful symbolic medium by which the transition from life to death can be represented, a process during which the living reconsider their own legitimate claims of social position and inheritance.

The Archaeology of Ritual

Cultural archaeology seems to have assumed that human action was determined by a received cultural doctrine. However humans are inventive in the formation and maintenance of particular practices. They act in, and upon, a world which is already culturally formed. Their actions are both structured by their experiences of that world and in turn those actions structure their own conditions. By such reflexive monitoring of action the fabric of a social and cultural existence is constructed, including the knowledge people have of the conditions and aims of their actions. Knowledge here is meant to include a practical day to day knowledge of 'how to go on' as well as a discursive awareness whereby the cultural conditions of the world can be brought to mind.

Different practical knowledges therefore exist, but people are able to combine those practical experiences within dominant readings of the wider, cultural regularities of their world. Bloch has recently argued that anthropological work, particularly that of V. Turner, shows that ritual often plays a central role in building these forms of shared discursive knowledge (Bloch 1985; Turner 1967). It is during rituals that fundamental cultural regularities are exposed to participants and observers, because it is during rituals that transitions across social categories are achieved. This means that the categories have to be defined, transgressed and then redefined (Turner 1969).

These ideas have two important implications for archaeology:

1   Ritual is made up of actions, not things. There are no such things as 'ritual sites' or 'ritual objects'. The places where rituals may be enacted and the artefacts used will also have been encountered in the daily routines of life (including the avoidance of sacred ground). The selections of specific times, places and artefacts for ritual dramas are the means by which people draw diverse experiences towards a dominant reading of cultural order. We have to allow for the ambiguities which run through the material world rather than attempt to recover a single meaning for some element of archaeological remains. Hodder has suggested that the megalithic monuments of western Europe "had symbolic associations and meanings and this meaningful context must be considered." He goes on to argue that formal similarities indicate that the tombs

"referred symbolically to earlier and contemporary houses in central Europe" (Hodder 1984:53). But meaning is not inherent in the shape of the tomb nor in the house. It is constructed out of people's occupancy, their practical experience, of that architecture. Hodder has not demonstrated how those experiences can be retrieved archaeologically.

2   Particular types of archaeological deposit do not necessarily reflect the occurrence of ritual activity. Archaeologists regularly equate 'ritual' with deposits which they regard as 'symbolic'. But symbolism pervades all areas of life, and it is meaningless to assign ritual to cover all non-mechanical actions (Goody 1961). Daily activities may be organised with reference to ever present gods and ancestors, they may maintain ideas of cultural purity, or they may express divisions of status between the living. The organisation of sites and archaeological deposits are therefore likely to be structured according to particular cultural values without deriving from ritual practices.

Mortuary Rituals

Mortuary rituals are taken here to be those rituals which construct passages between life and death. They may include the passage of human burial, or the intervention of ancestors in the world of the living and they may draw upon ideas of death and rebirth (Bloch and Parry 1982). We must distinguish between ancestor rituals and funerary rituals because human remains may be employed in both. As Kinnes has argued human remains do not simply imply burial (Kinnes 1975:17).

1   *Ancestor rituals* establish the presence of ancestors in rites concerned with the living. Amongst the places and symbols used may be funerary architecture and the bones of the dead. Ancestor rituals may also play a part in the rites of burial.

2   *Funerary rituals* are specifically concerned with human burial. Within this context we can distinguish between inhumation, secondary burial (by which I do *not* mean the perceived order of interment in a barrow or grave) and cremation, depending upon the particular form the 'rite of passage' takes. Van Gennep (1960) recognised a threefold division in rites of passage into rites of separation, rites of liminality and rites of incorporation. The first and last are moments of cultural stability, separated by the transformation of the liminal period. Turner has developed this observation and examined the way each stage in the ritual process may be marked out by different forms of symbolism.

Archaeologists do not observe the entire sequence of a burial rite. In the case of inhumation the liminal period may terminate as the body is placed in the grave; the body is incorporated into death as the mourners return to the living. Symbolism associated with the liminal transformation of the body, and the segregation of the mourners, may therefore be carried over into the grave and thus preserved archaeologically. Such symbolism may include the adornment of the corpse (not to be confused with the dress of the living *contra* Pader 1982), an adornment which forms the basis for some of our 'richer' grave assemblages (Barrett 1985:104). With these ideas in mind it is obviously important to distinguish carefully between objects found within and those placed outside a coffin; for these different sets of material are likely to derive from different moments of the ritual process.

Secondary burial (Hertz 1960; Huntington & Metcalf 1979:13) involves a lengthy liminal period with the corpse being buried or stored before being recovered and reinterred at the close of the burial process. These final rites may be separated spatially from the places associated with liminality. A similar separation may be achieved by cremation. Here the rites of incorporation may commence with the lighting of the funeral pyre, only to be completed by the collection and sorting of the ashes and their final dispersal or burial. The separation of rites of incorporation from the earlier rites of liminality in both secondary burial and cremation may be great enough to ensure that the symbolism associated with liminality is discarded by the time deposits finally enter the 'archaeological record'. The methodological implication is to prevent comparisons between inhumation and cremation assemblages, for we are not comparing like with like.

These different rites also structure the topographical relationships of death in different ways. Whilst inhumation appears to fix both the place and the moment at which the transition of death is arrested for both the mourners and the corpse at the grave with its infilling, secondary burial and cremation establish a topo- graphical separation between rites of liminality and the final rites of incorporation. The place of transition is separated from that place at which the ritual sequence as a whole is brought to a close. These differences are important for any consider- ation of funerary ritual which is concerned with the way the mourners use the process to construct their relation with the dead and ancestors. It is by the construc- tion of these passages between life and death, within an architectural and topographical framework which may be constantly reused, that certain lines of inherited authority are preserved or challenged.

Neolithic and Early Bronze Age Mortuary Practices

It has been a commonly agreed convention that the late Neolithic witnessed a change in mortuary rituals, with a shift away from 'communal burial' towards a 'single-grave tradition'. Alongside this other trends have been identified, including the construction of round, in place of the earlier long, mounds, and the inclusion of 'grave goods' in the mortuary rituals. These changes, recognised in the nineteenth century (Thurnam 1869 & 1872), came to be taken as a distinct horizon of cultural discontinuity associated with the introduction of beakers (Abercromby 1912).

The abandonment of this apparent cultural horizon arose from the desire to break with cultural explanations, and with the empirical realisation that the sequence of material is more complex. Radiocarbon dates have lengthened the timescale of the period, loosening those cultural horizons which were simply artefacts of a short chronology (c.f. Piggott 1954, Fig. 64; Burgess 1980:37–78). At the same time round barrows are now recognisable in the Neolithic (Kinnes 1979), and the division between 'communal' and 'single grave' traditions can no longer be held as an adequate description of Neolithic and Bronze Age mortuary practices (Petersen 1972; Burgess and Shennan 1980; Thorpe 1985). As I have argued, however, little is gained if having recognised the complexity of these data, if we are forced to depict them as general patterns to facilitate their explanation. If we no longer accept descriptions and explanations in terms of cultural norms we should be equally critical of description and explanations in terms of social norms.

We must confront the full diversity of our data. This is only possible with the aid of a theoretically competent framework designed to expose the nature of specific practices. I have attempted to outline some of the general principles which guide mortuary practices. The development of these general principles along with an investigation of specific data should lead to the construction of historical syntheses.

In many parts of Britain Neolithic mortuary rituals left little or nothing in the way of archaeologically identifiable monuments or deposits. It is certainly true that a mound is not an invariable feature of mortuary activity (Kinnes 1975), and mortuary rituals clearly occurred amongst other activities on some sites (Mercer 1980). Archaeological sites were part of an architectural landscape. These landscapes were inhabited through different cycles of activity, each defined as particular temporal and geographical occurrences. Sites were the focus for some activities, guiding the way they were structured. Sites were permanent only in the physical sense of their material existence. No site was permanent in the way it was inhabited through different social practices, for practices began and ended as people passed through these landscapes.

We know little about the way the vast majority of those who died were treated during the Neolithic, but a few human remains were incorporated in some of the architectural forms which survive. The places selected for such deposits were never arbitrary, they were located in a landscape already structured by routine and ritual cycles. Through their inclusion in this timespace matrix of activity, mortuary rituals may have played a part in constructing a particular, dominant meaning out of more routine practices. These mortuary rituals may have included rites of burial, but seem more often concerned with the relocation and veneration of ancestral remains. The architecture often defines an area or areas in which human remains may be located, the paths of access in and out of those areas and the focal point(s) where the entire architectural form could be considered and incorporated within particular ritual and ceremonial practices. Kinnes has demonstrated how different architectural elements may be combined to satisfy such requirements (Kinnes 1975, 1981) and Fleming has stressed the importance of considering the focal stage presented by the cairn or mound (Fleming 1972, 1973).

At Gwernvale, south Wales (figure 15.1), on a terrace overlooking the river Usk to the south and overlooked itself on the north by a 700m rocky summit, an area of cleared ground had seen repeated visits by hunting parties moving along the upper reaches of the valley (Britnell and Savory 1984). Here on the margins of the cultivated land two, possibly three, small timber buildings were erected, not all of which were necessarily contemporary. Occupying the site of earlier middens one of these buildings was aligned upon a natural stone monolith. Whatever use

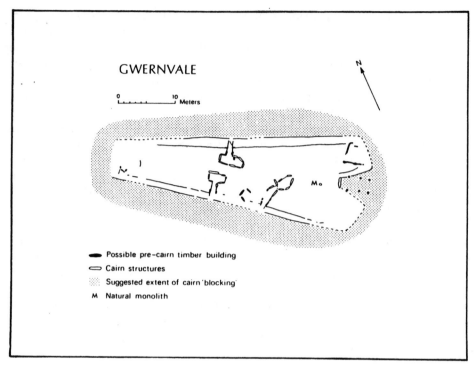

Figure 15.1 [orig. figure 3.1]   *(after Britnell & Savory 1984).*

was made of these buildings and the clearing itself, pottery, quernstones, flints and carbonised grain ultimately accumulated around them.

It was from these activities that the architectural elements of a chambered cairn also came to be constructed. An orthostat was erected to the west of one building, between it and the monolith. This stone preserved one focal axis of activity, and ultimately formed the eastern façade of the cairn. Cairn material was piled behind this stone and built out to form hornworks around the still standing timber building. The cairn mound ran westwards to enclose three separately constructed chambers, two of which opened towards the river on the south and one towards the valley side on the north. The cairn was surrounded by a revetment wall.

This process of integrating specific activities to produce a monumental form is similar to the sequence recently outlined for the Hazleton North long cairn (Saville 1984). Initial activity is represented by hearths, flints and midden deposits (figure 15.2). Two orthostatic chambers were constructed independently, facing north and south and lying to the east of a midden of flint, pottery, bone, quernstone fragments and carbonised seeds. The cairn was then constructed from rubble derived from two flanking quarries. Dumps of rubble were built up and revetted by dry-stone walling. They ran west and east from the northern chamber before returning to enclose the southern chamber (Saville 1984, Fig. 3). At the western end of the cairn a broad façade was formed, at a point already marked by earlier activity. The whole cairn was again enclosed by a revetment wall.

In both these cases the cairn and chambers are the material product of a prolonged sequence of activity. As the monuments were constructed so those activities which took place around them would have accommodated their existence, perhaps becoming more formalised in their execution. Ultimately they would have made some reference to the mortuary deposits which came to be included within the cairns. The architectural form of each resulting cairn is complex; access to the various chambers is displaced one from the other, and the long axis of each cairn and the façade establishes a separate architectural focus away from the chamber entrances. The lack of any permeability (paths of access) between these various architectural elements might suggest that each was employed separately, otherwise a processional path would have been the only means by which each element could be linked during a single ritual (c.f. Hillier & Hanson 1982). In the case of Gwernvale, Britnell argues that the outer revetment wall was built across the entrances to the chambers, necessitating its dismantling to gain access (Britnell and Savory 1984:47). This alone might imply an infrequent movement into the chambers.

The use of each monument and its surrounding ground can therefore be

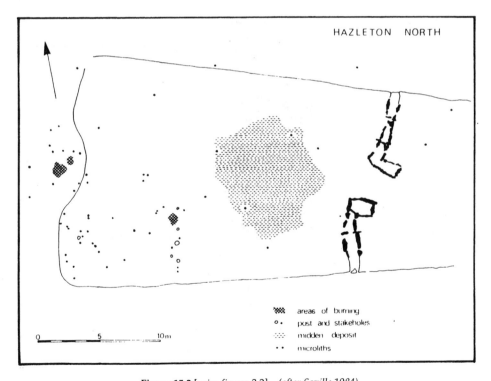

Figure 15.2 [orig. figure 3.2] *(after Saville 1984).*

represented in terms of different occupancies of time and space. These included the incorporation of the monument in the routine landscapes of daily activity; forecourt ceremony and ritual where the mortuary deposits lay hidden in the 'back space' of the chambers; mortuary rituals where ancestral remains were recovered or the dead were incorporated within the chamber; and perhaps processional rituals where each element of the monument was visited in turn.

An architectural practice which established these spatial distinctions of separate access around the cairn contrasts strongly with a monument such as West Kennet (figure 15.3) where the chambers were originally accessible through the façade (Piggott 1962). We know little about the history of the West Kennet mound, for example the status of the dry-stone walling abutting stones 7 and 36 is unknown. Beyond these stones lay a deep façade (figure 15.3 façade 1). Although a distinction of front/back space is maintained by this façade (i.e. forecourt/chambers) it was possible, although not always necessary, for rituals and ceremonies to unite observers in the forecourt with the spaces behind by means of a procession. The redesign of this façade, beginning with the erection of stones 44 and 46, and then stones 43, 45 and 47 producing a second, massive, façade prevented further access

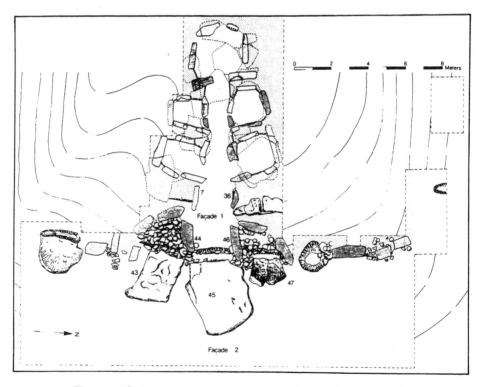

Figure 15.3 [orig. figure 3.3]   West Kennet, structures at the eastern end
(after Piggott 1962).

to these chambers which had themselves been infilled and blocked (Thomas & Whittle 1986).

Many writers have divided the architectural traditions of Neolithic mortuary monuments between the stone structures of western Britain and the non-megalithic monuments of the east. The different building materials mediated between architectural intentions and the resultant form. In this process the world was crafted within the limits of its own physical conditions. Earlier writers have sometimes proposed that a single cultural rule determined the building plan achieved using different materials, or that the architectural form established in one material led to its skeuomorphic representation in another. But such attempts as Ashbee's to identify the wooden counterparts of megalithic chambers mis-understands the recursive process which links knowledgeable action, its material conditions and its results (Ashbee 1970). The processes by which locations were selected, construction undertaken, and the monuments employed in routine or ritual activities, resulted from people's practical experience, evaluation and control over the conditions within which they acted. There is always an interplay between motivation, material conditions and execution.

The non-megalithic monuments known in southern and eastern Britain also display a long constructional history. Again the early phases can display a separation between forecourts and mortuary structures. At Street House, Loftus (Vyner 1984), a double row of timbers ran westwards towards a continuous timber façade. Behind this lay an embanked mortuary structure to the west of which a kerbed platform was built (figure 15.4B). Each element would have been approached separately for no internal path linked the forecourt area to the enclosures behind the façade. At Nutbane (Morgan 1959) a more complex set of forecourt buildings was identified (c.f. Kinnes 1981, Fig. 6:7), these were ultimately separated from the mortuary structure by a single timber barrier (figure 15.4A). This mortuary structure was itself fenced off in a late stage of its history.

A number of forecourt buildings have been recognised elsewhere (Atkinson 1965; Ashbee 1966; Manby 1976) but none presuppose direct access from such buildings to the adjoining mortuary structures. Occasionally, as in the case of Skendleby (Phillips 1936), the mortuary structure may be displaced from the façade and forecourt.

No single use or purpose can be assigned to these monuments. The inclusion of groups of human bone certainly does not make them 'burial monuments'. Burial and ancestor rites may have taken place during history of a site's use, but even the activities appear unattested at South Street and also, seemingly, at the Beckhampton Road and Windmill Hill long barrows (Ashbee, Smith & Evans 1979).

Each architectural form came into being out of the execution of a far wider range of activities and rituals, only some of which need leave a direct archaeological signature (c.f. Kinnes 1981:84). The archaeological site, with its sequence of deposits and architectural modifications, is the objective realisation of the history of these different ritual and routine practices. The evolution of each monument was not a matter of forward planning. Nor was it the laborious application of successive cultural rules resulting in a typological sequence of tomb morphologies. Instead

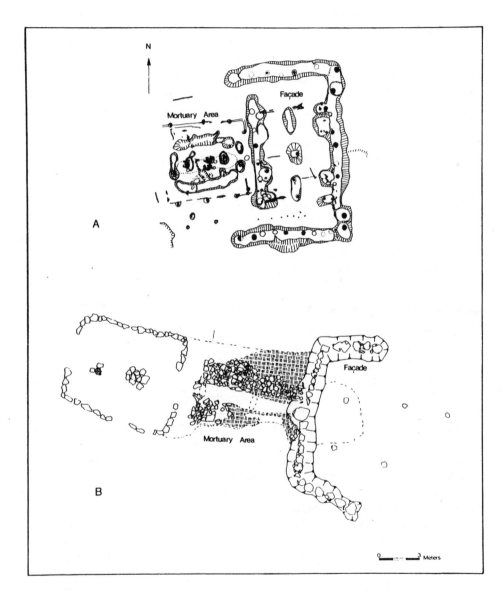

Figure 15.4 [orig. figure 3.4]   Mortuary and façade structures at (A) Nutbane and (B) Street House *(after Morgan 1959 & Vyner 1984).*

these histories were made by the reconstitution of a seemingly timeless order in Neolithic life. People inhabited these particular foci as part of their daily and seasonal landscapes, reaffirming relations and obligations one to another. That reaffirmation may have been demanded by a death, or through the labour of harvesting, but it was possible because an accepted order between people and things could be built out of these various experiences. The discovery of such an order was partly facilitated by the symbolic resources stored in the architecture of these monuments. As they were occupied and acted upon, so they guided those actions and their own structural modifications. As the mound came to be built up over the earlier timber buildings at Nutbane different deposits of material were placed in the different sections of the structure (Morgan 1959, Figs. 4 & 5). A similar distinction in building materials was traced in the low capping placed over the burnt mortuary structure and the platform at Street House (Vyner 1984, Fig. 10).

New obligations or challenges to a dominant authority would have required different readings of the cultural order, and these resources would have had to have been rethought and remodelled. The reforming of the West Kennet façade and the infilling of the chambers removed the space and contents of these chambers from further contemplation. This was not the abandonment of the monument but a shift in the focus of activities, ancestral remains could no longer be recovered and the dead could no longer be carried through to join them. By this act these once crucial symbolic resources were no longer available for direct intercession in the rituals played out in front of the monument, they became a hidden background of authority which would slowly have slipped from the collective awareness.

Establishing new codes of authority, capturing new obligations and challenging earlier practices, all are procedures of social reproduction and transformation. Shifts in the dominant symbolism of certain practices seem to characterise the use of the monuments we have been discussing. These changing practices effected the means by which burial and ancestor rituals were integrated within the use of the various monuments. The burial rituals appear to vary between sites, and in the history of a single site. They include inhumation, secondary burial and cremation.

Given this variation, and given the recognition that round barrows also contain multiple deposits (Peterson 1972), the nature of the distinction between the classic 'Neolithic' and 'Bronze Age' mortuary practices has become unclear. I wish now to demonstrate that certain changes do occur at the end of the third millennium BC affecting some aspects of mortuary practice. It is necessary, however, to stress that the mortuary deposits contained in all these monuments represent only a small proportion of the dead. It is a common fault of almost every approach to these data to assume that they represent the full pattern of the way the dead were treated (c.f. Fraser, Kinnes & Hedges 1982). The reason for such an assumption is never argued and it is simply not supported by the attempts to establish demographic projections on the basis of the mortuary data (Atkinson 1968, 1972).

We must begin from the perspective of landscape and architecture, and an understanding of the movement of people in time and space. I have argued that the megalithic and non-megalithic monuments of the late fourth and third millennia BC represented architectural foci in landscapes of timespace. Here we find the occasional enactment of ancestor and burial rituals. By the second millennia BC new foci for such rituals emerged and the architectural framework which encompassed them was differently structured. I do not mean by this that the difference is simply a matter of form (round mounds rather than long mounds) but that the sequences of construction, paths of access, and the primacy given to certain rituals were all transformed. The occupancy of these new foci and the transformation of the ritual procedures therefore represent the emergence of new areas of social practice at the end of the third millennium BC (Braithwaite 1984).

I will explore these changes through the example of a single barrow, Amesbury G.71 (Christie 1967). This mound was part of a linear barrow cemetery and survived to a height of 2.5m. The publication presented the history of the site in terms of three phases, the sequence offered here is based upon a rereading of that report and deals with the major constructional and burial sequence in terms of four periods. Each period contained a number of structural phases (figure 15.5).

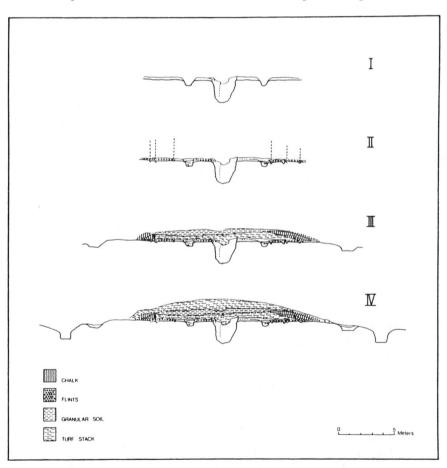

Figure 15.5 [orig. figure 3.5]   Amesbury G.71, suggested structural sequence
(after Christie 1967).

Period I. A ring ditch some 8m in diameter was dug, within which lay a semi-circular setting of stakes. At the centre was a grave, seemingly containing an adult inhumation. This grave was subsequently reopened cutting a new grave to a depth of 2m. The inhumation of an adult male, possibly in a coffin, was placed on the bottom of the grave. Chalk blocks were put around the burial and the grave infilled with chalk rubble. This infilling contained the disturbed bones of the earlier inhumation. A combined sample of wood from the grave gave a radiocarbon date of 2010±110BC (NPL–77).

Period II. A circle of stakes was erected around the outer lip of the earlier ring ditch and a second double stake ring of 13m diameter around this. A spread of chalk, possibly derived from the grave digging, or from a further re-excavation into the top of the grave, covered the earlier ditch and the ground surface within the outer stake circles.

Period III. When the stake circle was no longer standing a turf mound *c.* 13m in diameter was raised over the entire area. A kerb of flint nodules surrounded the turf stack and a layer of chalk, derived from an encircling ditch, was thrown up over the flints and the edge of the mound. A 2.5m wide berm separated the mound from the ditch. This mound came to be used as a platform, and a spread of chalk on the south side seems to mark one line of access onto the platform. A number of graves were dug down through this elevated surface. They include: 1) The contracted inhumation of an adult female accompanied by a perforated stone bead. 2) The contracted inhumation of a child accompanied by a wooden object lying beside the legs. Over the top of this grave, on the surface of the platform, lay a concentration of flint nodules (some struck) and a few animals bones. 3) The flexed inhumation of a child accompanied by a Food Vessel placed in front of the body and the lower part of a red deer antler. 4) The contracted inhumation of an 18 month old child lay at the base of the turf mound. No grave pit was observed and it is possible that this burial was included in the mound construction. A large flint lay by its head and a layer of carbonised material lay in front of its head and arms. 5) The cremated remains of an adolescent and child placed beneath an inverted Enlarged Food Vessel in a shallow scoop in the turf stack. 6) The cremated remains of a young adult were placed in a shallow scoop in the top of the turf stack.

A large fire had been built towards the centre of the platform, this may have been a cremation pyre. A radiocarbon date of 1640±90 BC (NPL–75) was obtained for charcoal from this area. A single post had been driven into the mound near this fire setting and an irregular ring of stakes was erected on the chalk bank around the edge of the platform. A mixture of soil and chalk was finally spread over the platform. It contained sherds of an Enlarged Food Vessel, an unburnt human bone, a scatter of cremated bone and three perforated stone beads. A small amount of flint knapping debris lay above the primary silts of the ditch in the southeast quadrant.

Period IV. A second turf stack was erected over the top of the mound, thus covering the platform. Around this a new ditch, 29m in diameter was dug, chalk from which was thrown up around the edge and onto the top of the mound. Further burials were then placed in the mound and into the silted ditch. These include: 1) A cremation beneath an inverted Collared Urn dug into the chalk capping. 2) A cremation, associated with a razor and beneath an inverted Biconical Urn, dug into the mound. 3) An adult inhumation in a shallow grave towards the top of the mound (the excavator believed this to be post-Roman). 4) The contracted inhumation of a child in the upper silting of the ditch. 5) The contracted inhumation of an adult male with trephined skull, placed in the upper silting of the ditch. The skull was surrounded by flecks of charcoal and covered by a large mound of flints. 6) The contracted inhumation of an adolescent in a grave dug into the upper silts of the ditch. This was covered by large flints with a number of struck flakes placed under the head. 7) The cremation of an adult male buried in a Bucket Urn in the ditch. 8) The cremations of an adult female and infant in a Globular Urn buried in the ditch. 9) Fragments of an adult cremation buried above (8) and probably associated with a Bucket Urn. 10) Cremated bone and ash placed in a flint-lined pit dug into the ditch. 11) The cremation of a young adult in a pit lined by flint nodules dug into the ditch. 12) The cremation of a child in a shallow pit dug into the ditch.

The burial deposits from the ditch were clustered in the southeast quadrant, and a scatter of cremated bone was also recovered from this area. Sherds of additional urns were also found in the southeast and northeast ditch quadrants. In the northeast, and over the upper silts of the ditch, lay a quantity of knapping debris.

Circular mounds, covering a variety of burial and ancestral deposits, begin to appear from the third millennium onwards (Kinnes 1979). The one feature common to all such monuments is that they have a single focal point at their centre. In Amesbury G. 71 the focal point is originally defined by a grave which is re-opened and a new burial inserted. In its earliest development there is little sign of a covering mound. The circular form is preserved when a mound is erected, and this mound elevates activity within the ditched area above that of the surrounding ground surface. Burials are dug into the platform and a fence erected around it. Finally the form of the mound is maintained but burial activity shifts to focus upon the periphery with a number of deposits being dug into the ditch. A high proportion of these burials are cremations.

A series of contrasts can be drawn between this architectural development and that outlined for the megalithic and non-megalithic monuments. The single focal point contrasts with the multiplicity of foci presented by the long mounds, and that focus is now placed *within* the monument. The focus, and thus the entire monumental development, is defined by burial rituals in the earliest stages of the monument's development. A recall of ancestral deposits was still observed with the reopening of the grave but entry into the monument required re-excavation for there were no open passages and chambers. But burial now structures and dominates the organisation of the monument rather than being included within an architectural form structured around other practices. Indeed we seem to be observing a monument which is at times specifically concerned with burial, something which cannot be claimed for the Neolithic mounds. By the later phases of its history the importance of the central deposit is maintained, but now by acts of avoidance. Burials, often cremations, were placed on the periphery of the mound in the ditch. The early graves meant that the point of transition with death defined the topography of the monument, but ultimately that point of transition is shifted away to the new location of a cremation pyre. The final deposition of cremated remains is fixed at a specifically subsidiary position within the spatial hierarchy of the mound.

Conclusion

In some areas of Britain mortuary practices can be observed archaeologically to have followed particular lines of development during the Neolithic and Early Bronze Age. By the third millennium a number of buildings had been established which reserved spaces for various mortuary and ritual activities. It seems likely that a particular emphasis was placed upon ancestral rites, and that burial rites often go unattested. Because human bones may relate to both types of rite, detailed taphonomic and stratigraphic analysis is required for all bone deposits in an attempt to disentangle which processes of deposition may have been at work. If the emphasis upon ancestral rites is accepted, then this helps to explain the architectural form of many of these monuments with their chambers and passages allowing access to the mortuary remains. Such monuments therefore allowed mortuary rites to be integrated within a wider sphere of ritual and routine activities; it was not the mortuary rites alone which structured the form of the architecture.

The apparent changes which have long been observed in the mortuary practices at the end of the third millennium can still be accepted. But these are not changes in burial practice, from communal to single grave, but the appearance of burial for the first time on a large scale in the archaeological record. Now the burial rites for some people actually appear to have instigated the foundation of monuments. But these monuments, at first small mounds, sometimes with encircling ditches and fences, were solid 'sculpture' (Zevi 1957) within the landscape. Further use for burial required them to be broken open by re-excavation. As some mounds were enlarged the graves were not re-opened but burials were placed instead in the mounds above the earlier burials. Finally the place of the monument shifts within the scheme of ritual practice as an increasing emphasis is placed upon cremation and the peripheral location of burial around the edge of some mounds.

These practices maintained or developed particular lines of authority and inheritance between the living, lines of authority which could be drawn upon in other fields of social action. To develop these approaches we must develop detailed regional analyses which attempt to build syntheses out of all the available data which relate to these different fields. In this way we may learn something about the processes of social reproduction without recourse to general, and spurious, models of social totalities.

Acknowledgements

A number of people commented upon earlier work which contributed towards this paper including Richard Bradley, Ann Clark, Ian Kinnes and Nicholas Aitchison. I have also benefited from detailed discussions with Pamela Graves and Colin Richards whilst preparing this paper. Julian Thomas kindly let me read his and Alasdair Whittle's paper on West Kennet before publication. I must also thank those Glasgow students who worked with me on the Mortuary Practices, course. Alison McGhee prepared figure 15.1 [orig. figure 3.1] and Lorraine McEwan figures 15.2–5 [orig. figures 3.2–5].

References

Abercromby J. 1912 *A Study of the Bronze Age Pottery of Great Britain and Ireland and its Associated Grave Groups.* Vol. 1. Oxford.

Ashbee P. 1966 The Fussell's Lodge Long Barrow. *Archaeologia* 100:1–80.

Ashbee P. 1970 *The Earthen Long Barrow in Britain.* London.

Ashbee P., Smith I.F. & Evans J.G. 1979 Excavation of three long barrows near Avebury, Wiltshire. *Proc. Prehist. Soc.* 45:207–300.

Atkinson R.J.C. 1965 Wayland's Smithy. *Antiquity* 39:126–133.

Atkinson R.J.C. 1968 Old mortality: some aspects of burial and population in Neolithic England. In J.M. Coles & D.D.A. Simpson (eds) *Studies in Ancient Europe.* Leicester, pp. 83–93.

Atkinson R.J.C. 1972 Burial and population in the British Bronze Age. In F. Lynch & C. Burgess (eds) *Prehistoric Man in Wales and the West,* Gloucester, pp. 107–116.

Barrett J.C. 1985 Hoards and related metalwork. In D.V. Clarke, T.G. Cowie & A. Foxon (eds) *Symbols of Power.* Edinburgh, pp. 95–106.

Barrett J.C. 1987 Fields of discourse: reconstituting a social archaeology. *Critique of Anthrop.* 7(3):5–16.

Binford L.R. 1971 Mortuary practices: their study and potential. In J.A. Brown (ed) *Approaches to the Social Dimensions of Mortuary Practices.* Memoir 25 Soc. American Archaeol, pp. 6–29.

Bloch M. 1985 From cognition to ideology. In R. Fardon (ed) *Power and Knowledge: anthropological and sociological approaches.* Edinburgh, pp. 21–48.

Bloch M. & Parry J. 1982 (eds) *Death and the Regeneration of Life.* Cambridge.

Braithwaite M. 1984 Ritual and prestige in the prehistory of Wessex *c.* 2,200–1,400 BC: a new dimension to the archaeological evidence. In D. Miller & C. Tilley (eds) *Ideology, Power and Prehistory.* Cambridge, pp. 92–110.

Britnell W.J. & Savory, H.N. 1984 *Gwernvale and Penywyrlod: two Neolithic long cairns in the Black Mountains of Brecknock.* Cambrian Archaeol. Monograph 2.

Burgess C. 1980 *The Age of Stonehenge.* London.

Burgess C. & Shennan S. 1976 The Beaker phenomenon, some suggestions. In C. Burgess & R. Miket (eds) *Settlement and Economy in the Third and Second Millennia BC.* Oxford, pp. 309–327.

Chapman R. 1981 The emergence of formal disposal areas and the 'problem' of megalithic tombs in prehistoric Europe. In R. Chapman, I, Kinnes & K. Randsborg (eds) *The Archaeology of Death.* Cambridge pp. 71–81.

Chapman R. & Randsborg K. 1981 Approaches to the archaeology of death. In R. Chapman, I. Kinnes & K. Randsborg (eds) *The Archaeology of Death.* Cambridge, pp. 1–24.

Christie P.M. 1967 A barrow-cemetery of the second millennium BC in Wiltshire, England. *Proc. Prehist. Soc.* 33:336–366.

Fleming A. 1972 Vision and design: approaches to ceremonial monument typology. *Man* (NS) 7:57–72.

Fleming A. 1973 Tombs for the living. *Man* (NS) 8:177–93.

Fraser D., Kinnes I. & Hedges J. 1982 Correspondence: the archaeology of Isbister. *Scottish Archaeol. Review* 1:144–148.

Goody J. 1961. Religion and ritual: the definitional problem. *British J. Sociol.* 12:142–164.

Hertz R. 1960. A contribution to the study of the collective representation of death. In R. Hertz, *Death and the Right Hand*. London.

Hillier W.R.G. & Hanson, J. 1982 *The Social Logic of Space*. Cambridge.

Hodder I. 1984. Burials, houses, women and men in the European Neolithic. In D. Miller & C. Tilley (eds) *Ideology, Power and Prehistory*. Cambridge, pp. 51–68.

Huntington R. & Metcalf P. 1979 *Celebrations of Death*. Cambridge.

Kinnes I. 1975 Monumental function in British Neolithic burial practices. *World Archaeol.* 7:16–29.

Kinnes I. 1979 *Round Barrows and Ring-ditches in the British Neolithic*. British Museum Occas. Papers 7.

Kinnes I. 1981 Dialogues with death. In R. Chapman, I. Kinnes & K. Randsborg (eds) *The Archaeology of Death*. Cambridge, pp. 83–91.

Manby T.G. 1976 Excavation of the Kilham long barrow, East Riding of Yorkshire. *Proc. Prehist. Soc.* 42:111–159.

Mercer R. 1980 *Hambledon Hill: a Neolithic landscape*. (Edinburgh).

Morgan F. de M. 1959 The excavation of a long barrow at Nutbane, Hants. *Proc. Prehist. Soc.* 25:15–51.

O'Shea J. 1981 Social configurations and the archaeological study of mortuary practices: a case study. In R. Chapman, I. Kinnes & K. Randsborg (eds) *The Archaeology of Death*. Cambridge, pp. 39–52.

O'Shea J. 1984. *Mortuary Variability: an archaeological investigation*. London.

Pader E.-J. 1982 *Symbolism, Social Relations and the Interpretation of Mortuary Remains*. Oxford.

Parker Pearson M. 1982 Mortuary practices, society and ideology: an ethnoarchaeological study. In I. Hodder (ed) *Symbolic and Structural Archaeology*. Cambridge, pp. 99–113.

Petersen F. 1972 Traditions of multiple burial in later Neolithic and early Bronze Age England. *Archaeol. J.* 129:22–55.

Phillips C.W. 1936 The excavation of the Giant's Hill long barrow, Skendleby, Lincolnshire. *Archaeologia* 85:37–106.

Piggott S. 1954. *The Neolithic Cultures of the British Isles*. Cambridge.

Piggott S. 1962 *The West Kennet Long Barrow Excavations, 1955–56*. London.

Renfrew C. 1984 *Approaches to Social Archaeology*. Edinburgh.

Renfrew C. 1972 Explanation Revisited. In C. Renfrew, M.J. Rowlands & B.A. Segraves (eds) *Theory and Explanation in Archaeology*. London, pp. 5–23.

Saville A. 1984 Preliminary report on the excavation of a Cotswold-Severn tomb at Hazelton, Gloucestershire. *Antiqu J.* 64: 10–24.

Saxe A.A. 1970 *Social Dimensions of Mortuary Practices*. Michigan.

Tainter J.A. 1978 Mortuary practices and the study of prehistoric social systems. *Advances in Archaeol. Method & Theory* 1:105–141.

Thomas J. & Whittle A. 1986 Anatomy of a tomb: West Kennet revisited. *Oxford J. Archaeol.* 5:129–156.

Thorpe I.J. 1985 Ritual, power and ideology: a reconstruction of earlier Neolithic rituals in

Wessex. In R. Bradley & J. Gardiner (eds) *Neolithic Studies: a review of some current research.* Oxford, pp. 41–60.

Thurnam J. 1869 & 1872 On Ancient British barrows, especially those of Wiltshire and adjoining counties. *Archaeologia* 42:161–244 & 43:285–544.

Turner V. 1967 *The Forest of Symbols: Aspects of Ndembu Ritual.* London.

Turner V. 1969 *The Ritual Process: structure and anti-structure.* New York.

Van Gennep A. 1960 *The Rites of Passage.* London.

Vyner B.E. 1984 The excavation of a Neolithic cairn at Street House, Loftus, Cleveland. *Proc. Prehist. Soc.* 50:151–195.

Zevi B. 1957 *Architecture as Space.* New York.

Part VI

Feminist and Gender Archaeologies

Understanding Sex and Gender

Feminism embodies a basic political commitment to confronting and eliminating the androcentrism in Western society. In the last twenty years, a large corpus of literature has developed spanning the arts and humanities, social and natural sciences that explores the multiple effects of this bias, including equity issues. However, feminism is more than a women's rights movement. It consists of a series of diverse discourses that together have made significant theoretical contributions to a wide range of issues central to philosophy and the social sciences, issues such as power and politics, the intersections of gender, race, class, and sexuality. The results often challenge all aspects of how we think about and practise science.

The theoretical topic most commonly associated with feminist anthropology is gender. This is a problematic attribution since feminist scholarship has contributed to the exploration of, for example, the anthropology of self, the body, and representation. Also, the study of biological differences between the sexes, and sex-based social roles, is not now and never has been restricted to feminists. This being said, it is true that gender has been a topic of considerable interest to many feminists. One of the most important contributions is the decoupling of biological sex and social roles. Cross-cultural anthropological data have been effectively used to demonstrate that there is no uniform relationship between sex and gender roles and that the term gender is best reserved for the socially constructed identities related to, but not determined by, biological sexual differences (Ortner and Whitehead 1981; Moore 1988). This move opens up the possibility of multiple genders, beyond simply male and female, for analysis and interpretation.

However, as we shall see, the simple equations of "gender equals the sociocultural" and "sex equals the biological" are themselves open to criticism. Issues such as the stability of gender in a person's life, its meaning for different groups within society, and the social construction of "biological" sex are being brought into the field of study. Thus the area of "gender relations" is diffuse, multidimensional, and changing. Anthropologists and archaeologists alike have generally inferred gender roles on the basis of modern Western assumptions about the division of labor. This has given rise to the popular "Man-the-Hunter/Women-the-Gatherer" model (Dahlberg 1981; Lee and DeVore 1968). In archaeology, the critical theorizing of such inferences has led to three projects, one seeking to explore how contemporary gender ideologies influence our interpretations of the past, another concerned to understand the operation of gender in past political economies, and still another focusing on the status of women in the profession. But before discussing these projects it is appropriate to discuss the historical context of the emergence of feminist archaeologies.

Feminist Archaeologies

The first widely read feminist piece in Anglo-American archaeology was published in 1984 by Meg Conkey and Janet Spector (Conkey and Spector 1984). This review article was essentially a call to arms, an attempt to introduce gender as a legitimate topic of archaeological research and to draw attention to the status inequalities of women in the profession. Contemporaneous with this was Joan Gero's (1983, 1985) work on how our Western ideological construction of womanhood affects the research and funding opportunities of women in archaeology and the sciences. Her results pointed to clear discrepancies in the funding of male and female scholars by the National Science Foundation (see the responses by Yellen 1983). In 1988 Gero and Conkey organized the Wedge Conference as the first group effort to explore how a consideration of women and production might affect interpretations of prehistory (Gero and Conkey 1991).

In the 1990s, there has been a proliferation of studies inspired by this research, running the gamut from empirical to idealist, positivist to hermeneutic. Special symposia and sessions at professional meetings are routinely devoted to feminist issues (see the edited volumes by Claassen 1992, 1994; Nelson, Nelson, and Wylie 1994; Siefert 1991; Walde and Willows 1991). Special committees and workgroups have been established within the professional associations (e.g. the Society for American Archaeology's Committee on the Status of Women in Archaeology). This interest in feminism and gender research is paralleled in other countries, particularly in England (e.g. Braithwaite 1982; Gibbs 1987; Gilchrist 1993; Moore 1982), Norway (e.g. Dommasnes 1982, 1990; Engelstad 1986), and Australia (e.g. du Cros and Smith 1993).

Wylie (1991, **chapter 16**) has recently evaluated the emergence of an archaeology of gender. She suggests that it has been delayed because processual archaeology and its positivist methodology regarded "ethnographic" variables such as gender as scientifically inaccessible. While this may indeed explain part of the situation in the United States and Canada, it does not appear to apply to those contexts where processual archaeology has had less influence. In continental Europe, the ex-Soviet Union, China, and Latin America a series of male-dominated archaeologies also exist and these have not been significantly concerned to develop feminist perspectives (an exception being Norway with perhaps the earliest moves toward feminist archaeology, see Dommasnes 1990). This observation suggests that androcentrism and archaeology are linked in ways which crosscut theoretical frameworks and national boundaries.

There is a close connection between postprocessual archaeology and feminist and gender archaeologies. Both have developed similar critiques of processual archaeology. Both challenge the essentialist and foundationist basis of positivism and both turn to relational identities and versions of hermeneutics. But to say this, is to ignore the significant role that feminism has played in the early formation of postprocessual archaeology. In particular, feminists have bridged archaeology and ethnoarchaeology and explored questions such as the gendered use of space (Donley 1982; Moore 1982), agency and ritual practice (Braithwaite 1982, 1984), ideology and power (Wellbourn 1984), material order and classification (Sørenson 1987), gender in social context (Gibbs 1987; Williams 1987). An issue of the *Archaeological Review from Cambridge* (vol. 7, 1988) was devoted to "Women and Archaeology." This contribution has not been widely acknowledged within postprocessual archaeology. And indeed, as Engelstad (1991) and Smith (1994) have argued, postprocessual archaeology can be as closed as positivist archaeology to feminist issues.

Feminist archaeologies are often criticized because of their overt political focus. After all, so the argument goes, how can the mixture of politics and science produce good science? This position, however, depends upon a particular model of science in which knowledge is produced for its own sake and the process of knowledge production is unaffected by anything other than scientific questions. This view of knowledge production is now regarded as deeply problematic since knowledge cannot be separated from human interests. (Barnes 1977, Outhwaite 1983). Science is a social practice, and there is no contradiction in being a feminist and a good scientist. Indeed, as Harding (1986) argues, it is necessary to be a feminist to do good science because to do otherwise is to introduce bias. In addition, feminist approaches have the potential to ask new questions of the data, to identify gaps in established theories, to question assumptions that would not otherwise be questioned. Longino (1990) develops an argument for the most inclusive science possible suggesting that such a move requires creating a new social and political reality.

Gender and Biology

The question of gender and biology reveals some of the differences between positivist and postpositivist approaches. Positivist scholars tend to regard the two as synonymous with biological sex determining gender. In this case, studying gender means identifying biological women and men in prehistory. Postpositivist scholars see gender and sex as social constructs. This kind of analysis involves reconstructing gender dynamics through the analysis of specific historical contexts. Both of these approaches are stimulating research into previously unexplored areas.

Advocates of the gender-as-biology approach are exploring empirical questions related to identifying biological women and differential diet, disease, and mortality rates between the sexes. Two main techniques are used to identify women archaeologically. The first uses internal or contextual evidence. Typically this approach starts with osteological evidence in burials) depictions of women in iconography, or in the case of historical archaeology texts can be used. An example of this type of work is Hastorf's (**chapter 17**) study of isotopic values obtained from male and female skeletons. The second technique used to identify women involves ethnographic analogy. The cross-cultural or direct historical association between men and women and particular tasks is evaluated. Thus, on the whole it is the case that hand-made pots are often made by women. Sherratt (1981) uses ethnographic evidence that men tend to do the ploughing in small-scale societies to argue for increased power for men with the adoption of the plough in prehistoric Europe. Clearly the use of ethnographic analogy in this way is fraught with difficulties, and some writers prefer not to assume that the role of women in ethnographies can be projected back into the past.

The gender-as-social approach focuses on gender relations as contingent and contextual. In a recent review, Conkey and Gero (1991, p. 8) see gender as a constitutive element of human social relations based upon culturally ascribed similarities and differences between and among males and females. They regard gender not as a fixed state determined at conception, but rather as a fluid category always in the process of being contested and negotiated. The implications of this statement are profound; for each society and time period of interest the relationships between biology and gender must be independently demonstrated (Joyce 1992). In many (and perhaps all) societies, there are more than two genders (e.g. the Zuni man/woman or the plains berdache), and gender may have very different meanings at different ages and in different social contexts. Sexual relationships between older and younger men or between women also need to be brought into consideration (e.g. Yates 1993). Overall, sex and gender are components of many social relationships. Gender may be the central structuring principle of human social and cultural life, the ground upon which everything else is built.

Part of the confusion about gender stems from these different definitions. Some scholars, as we have seen, start with a biological definition of two sexes and oppose these to two culturally constructed genders. From this perspective archaeological analysis proceeds from osteological analysis of the sexes of bodies in graves. We can then look for the material culture correlates of the biological distinction. But in such studies it is taken for granted that sex is biological, whereas gender is cultural, a social construct. However, as Yates (1993) has argued, even our definition of biological sexual differences is to some degree cultural. There is a biological continuum from "male" to "female" on a number of different dimensions. Which dimension we emphasize and which boundary line we choose is partly cultural. As Foucault's (1981) "History of Sexuality" demonstrates, "sex" is not given, but is produced in particular historical contexts. The realization that there is no prediscursive "sex" undermines any simplistic notion that the study of past gender can begin on the sure ground of osteological differences between male and female. Rather, the biological is only one of many components in the cultural construction of sexuality and social relations.

Gender Ideologies and Bias

The study of gender in archaeology has two related concerns. The first is the evaluation of our standard assumptions and models to show how they reflect the dominant political ideology, which systematically ignores and marginalizes women in the present (gender ideologies). The second is to show how these models have been used to exclude women in interpretations of the past (gender bias). There is a reflexive relationship between gender ideologies and bias such that conceptions about past gender roles based on present gender roles are used to legitimize those same gender roles in the present.

The first exploration of how contemporary views of gender affect women in archaeology was an article by Joan Gero (1985) in which she exposed what she called the "woman-at-home ideology." This is the stereotypical view of female archaeologists in the laboratory or museum, specializing in artifact analysis, constructing typologies, seriating, in contrast to the male archaeologist in the field collecting data, leading a crew; she "does the archaeological housework," he "brings home the data raw." Gero shows that although fieldwork, museum work, and laboratory work are all necessary in doing archaeology, the discipline does not value them equally. Fieldwork is the privileged activity, and as Gero's survey of doctoral dissertations shows, it is the domain of males. In a more recent study, Gero and Root (**chapter 20**) have examined the ways in which women are represented in the pages of the *National Geographic*. They find that women are rarely depicted, but in those cases where they are shown they are depicted as passive observers and never engaging in the activities that constitute field excavation.

There has been a widespread assumption within the social sciences that men and women can be associated respectively with public and private, wild and domestic, culture and nature. The most obvious example in archaeology is the assumption that in the distant past men were the hunters and women the gatherers and, additionally, that hunting was more important in the development of technologies and society. But there are many other examples, from the ideas that women made the pots and were largely confined to the domestic sphere to the idea that they were passive objects or commodities in exchanges of prestige goods. Such associations involve a view of women as having a universal and unchanging essence, true for all cultures at all times and places. These associations constrain analysis in particular ways, shutting off variability and denying women an active role in the past. It is precisely these assumptions which should be the basis of critique and evaluation.

Sometimes the critique of gender bias makes use of ethnographic evidence to show that the associations between men, women, and particular tasks are not invariable. Rice (1991) has studied cross-cultural accounts of pottery production to determine its relation to gender roles. Her results show that there is considerable variability, although statistically speaking ceramics are predominantly made by women. Gero (1991) has addressed why stone-tool manufacture is commonly gendered male in archaeological interpretations. She cites ethnohistoric data from Australia, Africa, and the United States to demonstrate that women have been observed making stone tools. Indeed, it is difficult to identify universal categories because women's experiences are varied and multi-leveled. Who counts as a male or female is a social construct that varies across cultures. These studies indicate that gender attributions cannot be assumed and must be carefully built up in each particular context.

At other times, the critique of gender bias reveals logical problems in androcentric arguments. Thus Gero (1985) points out that when pestles are found in female burial contexts they are interpreted as evidence for grinding and food processing, but when they are found in male burial contexts they are interpreted as evidence for the production of tools. Why are males assumed to be the tool makers and females the tool users? Likewise, Watson and Kennedy (1991) note that women are often assumed to have been wild-plant gatherers. But when it comes to the domestication of plants, it is assumed that men played a dominant role. Is it not more likely, they ask, that the female plant gatherers were the active agents in the domestication of plants? These cases indicate how deeply ingrained gender bias is in archaeology to the point that arguments are unconsciously made to accommodate it.

Current research is beginning to explore the different roles held by men and women in specific cultural contexts. New studies suggest that gender may not necessarily be stable and may in fact change with the age of the individual. Some scholars also are beginning to explore the intersection of gender with race, class, and ethnicity. This is the direction taken by many feminist sociologists (e.g. Butler 1990, 1993; Grosz 1994). These latter variables tend to create lines of differentiation that can cut across gender (see Wylie 1991 for a discussion of this issue in archaeology). Gender is one part of the complex process of forming a self-identity. Women or men in different classes or ethnic groups may have very different constructions of themselves – the term "woman" may hide very different life experiences, access to resources and so on. It is inadequate simply to study "women" or "men" as if these formed unified categories.

The Political Economy of Gender

Gender is inextricably intertwined with topics of longstanding concern in archaeology such as trade and exchange, craft specialization, household economies, the division of labor, and state formation. At present, however, there is no single theory of gender beyond the broad recognition that it plays a significant structuring role in social life. There is no clear consensus on how gender should be weighted in these different areas. Some approaches regard gender as fundamental to the political economy, while others treat it as secondary. This may, in fact, be appropriate since the meaning of gender should be expected to vary among different societies at different times and places.

One set of archaeological gender theories concerns the so called "Origins" debates. There has been considerable interest in the role of gender in the origins of culture and hominid behaviour. Zihlman (1981, 1989, 1991) has explored the division of labor and McBrearty and Moniz (1991) have challenged a number of assumptions about hunting, tool use and sex roles, arguing that there are no necessary correlations to be found. There is also an interest in the role of gender in domestication and the origins of agriculture. Ehrenberg (1989) argues that women were responsible for the invention of agriculture in the Near East, and Watson and Kennedy (1991) have argued that women actively developed the varieties of maize in the Eastern Woodlands. These approaches are valuable because they contribute to a questioning of received assumptions about gender, but they themselves can be criticized for accepting overarching and simplistic definitions of gender, and for accepting the premise of the Origins debate, namely that there was a first tool user or a first farmer (see Part V). From a feminist perspective, Conkey and Williams (1991) regard the obsession with Origins as grounded in a unitary and progressive evolutionism which amounts to a validation of the status quo, of the way things are today.

There has also been considerable discussion of the role of gender in the rise of the state (Silverblatt 1978, 1991). For example, Gailey (1987) has argued that state formation involves the political subordination of a majority of the population by a non-producing elite class. Because women are both producers and reproducers, they represent a potential source of autonomy and resistance. For this reason, their labor is quickly appropriated and channeled. This thesis is supported by Hastorf's (**chapter 17**) study of how the expansion of the Inka empire affected the roles of Sausa women and men of Peru. The differences between female and male diets increase as men are drawn into a state economy of labour in exchange for maize beer consumption. But as Brumfiel (1991) shows in her study of women's production of food and weaving in Aztec Mexico, women often do have diverse and multifaceted roles in complex societies. A simple account of increased subordination will often not be satisfactory. A fuller consideration of the historical contexts within which women negotiated their identities and statuses is needed.

There is a growing recognition that gender is not a thing but a process (Conkey and Gero 1991, p. 9). Gender cannot be described in essentialist terms as a given, static and intransient. Rather, it is embedded within status, class, ethnicity and race. As such, an understanding of the role of gender leads to a wider consideration of social dynamics. Indeed, some feminist archaeologists have turned their attention beyond gender itself, and have explored the development of new theories of the body and the self, have developed a critique of the archaeological discourse on power, ideology and the body, and have explored issues of representation and problems evident in the science of archaeology as a whole. Meskell (1996) has argued that Cartesian oppositions of mind and body underlie the burgeoning archaeological discourse on the body (see Part V). Her alternative, feminist approach is concerned to avoid issues of power and domination of the body and to replace these with a more experiential and integrated view of individuals.

In some ways, this diversity recapitulates some of the diversity expressed within other postprocessual approaches. However, the theories of gender cannot easily be equated with other theoretical trends in the discipline. Approaches to the archaeology of gender at the same time encompass and extend beyond current archaeological theories. Some link gender to evolutionary theories about, for example, the role of women in the rise of the state, while others associate it with theories of agency and the recovery of past lived experience. The political focus of feminist archaeologies closely parallels the critical-theory approaches in archaeology and the call for a value-committed archaeology (see Part VII), particularly in the questioning of existing power relations. However, there are important differences dealing with the constitution of self, social identity, and representation that are not addressed by these other approaches.

Lived Experience

Some feminists, critical of the standard positivist processual archaeology, have been inspired by recent developments in poststructuralism, in particular the decentering of the subject and the emphasis on the construction of meaning. Feminist archaeologists, and poststructuralists in general, tend to be wary of universals and essentials since these are so often defined in androcentric terms. But feminists also tend to argue that poststructuralism's emphasis on the surface and on language threatens to undermine the reality of different experiences. Poststructuralism thus appears apolitical – or rather it elevates a dichotomized concern with language over experience. For this reason a number of feminists advocate the reconstruction of past lived experiences as a means of creating a more holistic picture of past individuals. They also argue that such representations open up the past to critique and involvement. This move is similar in some respects to the phenomenology of the postprocessual archaeologists interested in the archaeology of body and practice (see Part V).

Some feminists are experimenting with narrative approaches to provide a more informed view of the past. They show that traditional archaeological writing is not neutral, but rather embodies an androcentric perspective. The sterile prose of science writing is complicit in the process of creating hierarchy and excluding women and other non-privileged groups. They also note that reducing people to systems that passively adapt to changes in the environment effectively dehumanizes the past. In response many scholars argue for alternative ways of writing that allow for the possibility of empathy and recreation of lived experiences. The issue of representation is seen as crucial since it is in modes of representation that dominating and excluding visions are hidden. Similar points have been made about writing in archaeology in general (e.g. Hodder 1989; Tilley 1989), but the feminist discussion is a central part of this debate and certainly the most exciting developments have been in this area.

An example of this approach is Janet Spector's (**chapter 18**) reconstruction of the lives of two Dakota women, Blueberry Woman (*Ha-za*) and her daughter, One-Who-Talks-to-Iron (*Mazo okiye win*) during the missionary period. Using the act of losing an awl as a touchstone, Spector conjures up the sense of loss that is associated both with the onset of womanhood in Lakota society and with the transition to a new way of life where men farmed, a role traditionally held by women. This way of writing effectively creates a feeling of empathy or connectedness with past people that is made all the more profound because we know the rest of the story. We know how the Lakota were subdued and placed on reservations, we know how their religion was banned, and we know how their traditional lifeways were transformed. Another example is Tringham's (1991) dialogue about the interpretation of the Neolithic site of Opovo, and her evocative reconstruction of the burning of one of the houses.

A common criticism of narrative approaches is that they are fictions, that the past existed and our job is to be as objective as possible in writing about it. But this view cannot be sustained since the past only exists through its "telling" or "writing." In one sense, there is no difference between a scientific "descriptive" site report and Spector's narrative since both represent an account, both are grounded in particular forms of discourse. Indeed, Spector (1993) has shown that even a catalogue of the finds from her site would normally included biases and assumptions – for example, the metal parts of an awl might be classified prominently as foreign, indicating colonial contact. Farther down in the supposedly neutral catalogue would come the awl handle – made of bone, locally produced and of little interest. Even a catalogue is a "story" (cf. McMullin and Handsman 1987). However, there are important differences between the stories told by archaeologists and those told by non-archaeologists, the most important being a commitment to the archaeological data in all its ambiguity and complexity. Archaeological narratives must be congruent with the network of resistances posed by data.

A more serious objection has to do with the audiences of narrative representations. To whom are they accountable? – the archaeological profession, the general public, women, or the descendants of the people being written about? Spector (1993) explicitly discusses the tensions that emerged at different times during her research project, tensions between her commitment to these different interest groups. She admits to becoming aware of her privileged status by race and profession. She talks of making presentations to the Wahpeton community in Little Rapids and sharing her work with them, and of their reactions to her. This kind of self-reflection occasioned by an encounter with an indigenous people, not as "the Other" (Part VIII) but as distinctive individuals with real interests, sets the stage for productive dialogues and communication.

The advantages of narrative approaches are that they can open up the past to being peopled by sentient human beings. They can allow us to see just how material culture is implicated in how individuals constructed themselves as social beings through experience and daily life. This approach, aligned with other developments in postprocessual archaeology, is an important step forward. But we also need to remain critical. The narratives we construct need to be open to evaluation on both empirical and political grounds. It is certainly possible in Spector's (1993) fuller account to evaluate aspects of her narrative in relation to the archaeological and ethnographic evidence. It should also be possible to determine the repercussions of her decision to write this narrative, in the political dynamics of the Wahpeton community. Indeed, Spector relates that some members of the community saw her work as a positive contribution and were inspired to share with her stories that they recalled from their childhood.

Equity Issues

An issue that should be of concern to all archaeologists is the status of women in the profession. In the last ten years, women and men alike have begun to question the ways gender bias has affected the careers of women. What impact has gender had on promotion and tenure decisions? How does it affect the granting process? What opportunities are there for redressing this bias? In addition to the exploration of gender ideology and bias (see above), there are two directions currently being pursued.

The first has been to gather and interpret statistics on women in the profession. In the first study of its kind, Gero (1983) compiled data on the distribution of National Science Foundation (NSF) grants to male and female applicants from fiscal year 1978–81. Her results showed a strong bias in favor of male fieldwork projects. Yellen (1991) has provided additional data for fiscal year 1989 to show that women twelve years or more beyond their PhD are less successful than their male counterparts in gaining NSF grants. Carol Kramer and Barbara Stark (1988) compiled the first study of the distribution of women in departments of anthropology at the graduate and faculty levels. Their results suggest that female graduate students are either slower to receive the PhD than their male counterparts, or they are leaving their graduate programs at proportionally higher rates, or both. Their statistics also show that women are underrepresented on the faculties in their sample of thirty major universities, never accounting for more than 15 percent. Significantly, in 1991 the Society for American Archaeology reactivated its Committee on the Status of Women to monitor these issues and Alison Wylie and Sarah Nelson organized an American Anthropological Association symposium and workshop on equity issues for women in archaeology (Nelson, Nelson, and Wylie 1994).

Although the results of this research are only now beginning to appear, they show just how deeply inequities pervade all aspects of archaeology. Areas studied include publishing (Beaudry and White 1994; Victor and Beaudry 1992), areal speciality (Ford 1992; Ford and Hundt 1994), analytical speciality (Gifford-Gonzales 1994), and cultural-resource management (Garrow et al. 1992; Whittlesey 1992). In addition, questions of dual-career couples (Nelson and Crooks 1991) and chilly-climate workplace issues (Parezo and Bender 1994; Wylie 1994) are being explored. A contemporaneous professional evaluation with somewhat different emphases and foci is taking place in Norway (Engelstad et al. 1994), Britain (Cane et al. 1994), Australia (Beck 1992; du Cross and Smith 1993; Hope 1994), Argentina (Bellelli et al. 1994), Spain (Diaz-Andreu and Gallego 1994), and Canada (Kelley and Hill 1991). The results of these studies and of studies currently underway will have a major effect on the shape of world archaeology.

The second direction has been to turn to individual women's biographies to better appreciate the challenges faced by early women archaeologists in the profession (see the contributions to Claassen 1992). An example of this is Rosemary Joyce's (**chapter 19**) study of Dorothy Hughes Popinoe, an early twentieth-century pioneer archaeologist working in Central America. In a striking postmodern style, she juxtaposes the voices of Dorothy, Wilson Popinoe (her husband), and Alfred Tozzer in a narrative that uses the Garden of Eden as a central allegory. The entire piece revolves around the fact that Dorothy died eating a poisonous *akee* fruit, "the forbidden fruit of knowledge." Through her writing style, Joyce creates a sense of the interconnections between the different personalities that together had major influences over Dorothy's career. The nuances of and conflicts between Dorothy's multiple roles as wife, mother, and researcher are all brought out. What is especially telling is how the major accomplishments of her career are reinterpreted by the professional archaeological establishment in her absence.

These studies of the status of women in archaeology demonstrate some of the ways women have experienced and still experience discrimination. What we still don't fully understand are the larger structures that maintain and reproduce these biases. What are the social dynamics between male and female students in graduate school? What kinds of associations do they form? Is sexual harassment more prevalent in academic settings or in fieldschool contexts? Nor have we studied how archaeology fits in with the androcentrism expressed in other academic professions. How does archaeology compare with the sciences, like geology, which also have a fieldwork component? How does it compare with the laboratory sciences? Finally we still don't fully understand the relationships between these biases and the androcentrism characteristic of Western society in general. Has archaeology adopted a more or less restrictive view of gender roles than exists in society in general? Clearly more studies are needed.

Conclusion

The emergence of feminist archaeologies and archaeologies of gender is one of the most significant theoretical developments in recent years. It is clear that the feminist debates are contributing significantly to wider discussion in archaeology and the social sciences about methods and theories dealing with lived experience. These new theories are providing new considerations of agency, structure, meaning, and power; some of these are issues not raised by other postprocessual approaches.

As discussed above, there is no one feminist archaeology or single archaeological theory of gender. It might be argued that "gender" is simply a category, like "settlement" or "ranking", and thus we should not necessarily expect any theoretical coherence – rather, the full range of theories can be applied. However, because of the value-committed nature of feminist discussion there is undoubtedly a theoretical direction which extends the range of debate within the discipline. Thoroughly radical positions are being taken in important areas, especially the critique of positivism and the attempt to replace a dichotomous with an inclusive science; the area of representation and writing; and new theories of the body, the self, and identity. And it is from feminist archaeology that the most thorough-going critiques of essentialism may stem.

The concern with individuals and lived experience is perhaps part of a wider emphasis in feminist discourse on persons (Moore 1994) and on constructing a more peopled past. A move from structures to interpersonal relations is summarized by Conkey and Gero (1991, p. 15). "An engendered past replaces the focus on the remains of prehistory with a focus on the people of prehistory; it rejects a reified concept of society or culture as an object of study, does away with the "earliest", "biggest", the "best" examples of prehistoric forms, and concentrates instead on the continuities and dialectics of life, the interpersonal and intimate aspects of social settings that bind prehistoric lives into social patterns." This move challenges the foundational premises of standard processual archaeology and opens up new possibilities for understanding the past, even though it might be criticized for straying close to an essentialist argument that gender is largely confined to the interpersonal.

By virtue of the political structure of Western archaeology, feminism shares a connection to the concerns of marginalized people worldwide and an interest in the possibility of creating a more democratic archaeology (see Parts VII and VIII). But curiously it has had mixed success in reaching out to women in Third World contexts. One reason may be that feminism is often perceived by non-Western women as a part of the colonialist, national, and imperialist enterprise, as discussed by Trigger (**chapter 23**). When indigenous women are instructed to acknowledge and confront the gender-based inequalities they face in their homes, their response is often – what business is it of yours how I choose to live my life? The problem here is that gender relations are embedded in larger social and political formations, and changes in gender relations cannot be easily accomplished without corresponding changes in those structures.

References

Archaeological Review from Cambridge, vol. 7, 1988.

Barnes, Barry 1977. *Interests and the Growth of Knowledge*. London.

Beaudry, M. and White, J. 1994. Cowgirls with the blues: a study of women's publications and the citation of women's work in *Historical Archaeology*. In Claassen, C. (ed.) *Women in Archaeology*. Philadelphia, pp. 138–58.

Beck, W. 1992. Women and archaeology in Australia. In Claassen, C. (ed.) *Women in Archaeology*. Philadelphia, pp. 210–18.

Bellelli, C., Beron, M. and Scheinsohn, V. 1994. Gender and science: demystifying Argentine archaeology. In Nelson, M. C., Nelson, S. M. and Wylie, A. (eds) *Equity Issues for Women in Archaeology*. Archaeological Papers of the American Anthropological Association No. 5. Washington D.C., pp. 131–7.

Braithwaite, M. 1982. Decoration as ritual symbol: a theoretical proposal and an ethnographic study in the southern Sudan. In Hodder, I. (ed.) *Symbolic and Structural Archaeology*. Cambridge, pp. 80–8.

Braithwaite, M. 1984. Ritual and prestige in the prehistory of Wessex c.2,200–1,400BC: a new dimension to the archaeological evidence. In Miller, D. and Tilley, C. (eds.) *Ideology, Power and Prehistory*. Cambridge, pp. 93–110.

Brumfiel, E. 1991. Weaving and cooking: women's production in Aztec Mexico. In Gero, J. and Conkey, M. (eds) *Engendering Archaeology*. Oxford, pp. 224–54.

Butler, J. 1990. *Gender Trouble: Feminism and the Subversion of Identity*. London.

Butler, J. 1993. *Bodies that Matter: On the Discursive Limits of "Sex"*. London.

Cane, C., Gilchrist, R. and O'Sullivan, D. 1994. Women in archaeology in Britain: three papers. In Nelson, M.C., Nelson, S.M. and Wylie, A. (eds) *Equity Issues for Women in Archaeology*. Archaeological Papers of the American Anthropological Association No. 5. Washington D.C., pp. 91–7.

Claassen, C. 1992. (ed.) *Exploring Gender through Archaeology*. Madison.

Claassen, C. 1994. (ed.) *Women in Archaeology*. Philadelphia.

Conkey, M. and Gero, J. 1991. Tensions, pluralities and engendering archaeology. In Conkey, M. and Gero, J. (eds) *Engendering Archaeology*. Oxford, pp. 3–30.

Conkey, M. and Spector, J. 1984. Archaeology and the study of gender. In Schiffer, M. (ed.) *Advances in Archaeological Method and Theory* 7, 1–38.

Conkey, M. with Williams, S. 1991. Original narratives: the political economy of gender in archaeology. In DiLeonardo, M. (ed.) *Gender at the Crossroads of Knowledge*. Berkeley, pp. 102–39.

du Cros, H. and Smith, L-J. (eds) 1993. *Women in Archaeology: A Feminist Critique*. Australian National University, Canberra.

Dahlberg, F. (ed.) 1981 *Woman the Gatherer*. New Haven.

Diaz-Andreu, M. and Gallego, N. 1994. Women in Spanish archaeology. In Nelson, M.C., Nelson, S.M. and Wylie, A. (eds) *Equity Issues for Women in Archaeology*. Archaeological Papers of the American Anthropological Association No. 5. Washington D.C., pp. 121–30.

Dommasnes, L.H. 1982. Late Iron Age in western Norway: female roles and ranks as deduced from the analysis of burial customs. *Norwegian Archaeological Review* 15, 70–84.

Dommasnes, L.H. 1990. Feminist archaeology: critique or theory building? In Baker and Thomas (eds) *Writing the Past in the Present*. St. David's University College, Lampeter, pp. 24–31.

Donley, L. 1982. House power: Swahili space and symbolic markers. In Hodder, I. (ed.) *Symbolic and Structural Archaeology*. Cambridge.

Ehrenberg, M. 1989. *Woman in Prehistory*. British Museum Publications, London.

Engelstad, E. 1986. Gender studies – a Stone Age perspective. *Kontakstencil* 28–9, 54–69.

Engelstad, E. 1991. Images of power and contradiction: feminist theory and post-processual archaeology. *Antiquity* 65, 502–14.

Engelstad, E., Mandt, G. and Naess, J-R. 1994. Equity issues in Norwegian archaeology. In Nelson, M.C., Nelson, S.M. and Wylie, A. (eds) *Equity Issues for Women in Archaeology*. Archaeological Papers of the American Anthropological Association No. 5. Washington D.C., pp. 139–45.

Ford, A. 1992. Women in Mesoamerican archaeology: why are the best men winning? In Claassen, C. (ed.) *Women in Archaeology*. Philadelphia, pp. 159–72.

Ford, A. and Hundt, A. 1994. Equity in academia – why the best men still win: an examination of women and men in Mesoamerican archaeology. In Nelson, M.C., Nelson, S.M. and Wylie, A. (eds) *Equity Issues for Women in Archaeology*. Archaeological Papers of the American Anthropological Association No. 5. Washington D.C., pp. 147–56.

Foucault, M. 1981. *The History of Sexuality. Volume 1: An Introduction*. London.

Gailey, C.W. 1987. *Kinship to Kingship*. Austin.

Garrow, B.A., Garrow, P.H. and Thomas, P.A. 1992. Women in contract archaeology. In Claassen, C. (ed.) *Women in Archaeology*. Philadelphia, pp. 182–201.

Gero, J.M. 1983. Gender bias in archaeology: a cross-cultural perspective. In Gero, J.M., Lacey, D.M. and Blakey, M.L. (eds) *The Socio-Politics of Archaeology*. Department of Anthropology, University of Massachusetts, Research Report No. 23. Amherst, pp. 51–7.

Gero, J.M. 1985. Socio-politics and the woman-at-home ideology. *American Antiquity* 50, 342–50.

Gero, J.M. 1991. Genderlithics. In Conkey, M. and Gero, J.M. (eds) *Engendering Archaeology*. Oxford, pp. 163–93.

Gero, J.M and Conkey, M. 1991. (eds) *Engendering Archaeology*. Oxford.

Gibbs, L. 1987. Identifying gender representation in the archaeological record: a contextual study. In Hodder, I. (ed.) *The Archaeology of Contextual Meanings*. Cambridge, pp. 79–89.

Gifford-Gonzalez, D. 1994. Women in zooarchaeology. In Nelson, M.C., Nelson, S.M. and Wylie, A. (eds) *Equity Issues for Women in Archaeology*. Archaeological Papers of the American Anthropological Association No. 5. Washington D.C., pp. 157–71.

Gilchrist, R. 1991. Women's archaeology? Political feminism, gender theory and historical revision. *Antiquity* 65, 495–501.

Gilchrist, R. 1993. *Gender and Material Culture: The Archaeology of Religious Women*. London.

Grosz, E. 1994. *Volatile Bodies: Toward a Corporeal Feminism*, Bloomington.

Harding, S. 1986. *The Science Question in Feminism*. New York.

Hodder, I. 1989. Writing archaeology: site reports in context. *Antiquity* 63, 268–74.

Hope, J. 1994. On the margin: women, archaeology, and cultural heritage – an Australian case study. In Nelson, M.C., Nelson, S.M. and Wylie, A. (eds) *Equity Issues for Women in Archaeology*. Archaeological Papers of the American Anthropological Association No. 5. Washington D.C., pp. 105–13.

Joyce, R.A. 1992. Images of gender and labor organization in classic Maya Society. In Claassen, C. (ed.) *Exploring Gender Through Archaeology: Selected Papers from the 1991 Boone Conference*. Monographs in World Archaeology No. 11 Madison, pp. 3–70.

Kelley, J. and Hill, W. 1991. Relationships between graduate training and placement in Canadian archaeology. In Walde, D. and Willows, N.D. (eds) *The Archaeology of Gender: Proceedings of the 22nd Annual Chacmool Conference*. The Archaeological Association of the University of Calgary, Calgary, pp. 195–200.

Kramer, C. and Stark, B. 1988. The status of women in archaeology. *Anthropology Newsletter* 29, 1, 11–12.

Lee, R.B. and DeVore, I. (eds) 1968. *Man the Hunter*. Chicago.

Longino, H. 1990. *Science as Social Knowledge: Values and Objectivity in Scientific Inquiry*. Princeton.

McBrearty, S. and Moniz, M. 1991. Prostitutes or providers? Hunting, tool use, and sex roles in earliest Homo. In Walde, D. and Willows, N.D. (eds) *The Archaeology of Gender: Proceedings of the 22nd Annual Chacmool Conference*. The Archaeological Association of the University of Calgary, Calgary, pp. 71–81.

McMullin, A. and Handsman, R. 1987. (eds) *A Key to the Language of Woodsplint Baskets*. American Indian Archaeological Institute, Washington, Connecticut.

Meskell, L. 1996. The somatisation of archaeology: institutions, discourses, corporeality. *Norwegian Arch. Review* 29, 1.

Moore, H. 1982. The interpretation of spatial patterning in settlement residues. In Hodder, I. (ed.) *Symbolic and Structural Archaeology*. Cambridge, pp. 74–9.

Moore, H. 1988. *Feminism and Anthropology*. Cambridge.

Moore, H. 1994. *A Passionate Difference: Essays in Anthropology and Gender*. Bloomington.

Nelson, M. and Crooks, D.L. 1991. Dual anthropology career couples: different strategies and different success rates. In Walde, D. and Willows, N.D. (eds) *The Archaeology of Gender: Proceedings of the 22nd Annual Chacmool Conference*. The Archaeological Association of the University of Calgary, Calgary, pp. 220–5.

Nelson, M., Nelson, S. and Wylie, A. 1994 (eds) *Equity Issues for Women in Archaeology*. Archaeological Papers of the American Anthropological Association, No. 5. Washington D.C.

Ortner, S. and Whitehead, H. 1981. *Sexual Meanings: The Cultural Construction of Gender and Sexuality*. Cambridge.

Outhwaite, W. 1983. *Concept Formation in Social Science*. London.

Parezo, N. and Bender, S. 1994. From glacial to chilly climate: a comparison between archaeology and socio-cultural anthropology. In Nelson, M.C., Nelson, S.M. and Wylie, A. (eds) *Equity Issues for Women in Archaeology*. Archaeological Papers of the American Anthropological Association No. 5. Washington D.C., pp. 73–81.

Rice, P. 1991. Women and prehistoric pottery production. In Walde, D. and Willows, N.D. (eds) *The Archaeology of Gender: Proceedings of the 22nd Annual Chacmool Conference*. The Archaeological Association of the University of Calgary, Calgary, pp. 436–43.

Sherratt, A. 1981. Plough and pastorialism: aspects of the secondary products revolution. In Hodder, I., Isaac, G. and Hammond, N. (eds) *Pattern of the Past*. Cambridge, pp. 261–305.

Siefert, D.J. 1991. Gender in historical archaeology. *Historical Archaeology* 25, 4, 1–5.

Silverblatt, I. 1978. Andean women in the Inca Empire. *Feminist Studies* 4, 36–61.

Silverblatt, I. 1991. Interpreting women in states. In diLeonardo, M. (ed.) *Gender at the Cross-roads of Knowledge*. Berkeley, pp. 140–71.

Smith, L. 1994. Heritage management as postprocessual archaeology. *Antiquity* 8, 300–9.

Sørensen, M-L. 1987. Material order and cultural classification. In Hodder, I. (ed.) *The Archaeology of Contextual Meanings*. Cambridge, pp. 90–101.

Spector, J. 1993. *What this Awl Means*. St Paul.

Tilley, C. 1989. Discourse and power: the genre of the Cambridge Inaugural Lecture. In Miller, D., Rowlands, M. and Tilley, C. (eds) *Domination and Resistance*. London, pp. 41–62.

Tringham, R. 1991. Households with faces. In Gero, J. and Conkey, M. (eds) *Engendering Archaeology*. Oxford, pp. 93–131.

Victor, K.L. and Beaudry, M.C. 1992. Women's participation in American prehistoric and historic archaeology: a comparative look at the journals American Antiquity and Historical Archaeology. In Claassen, C. (ed.) *Exploring Gender through Archaeology: Selected Papers from the 1991 Boone Conference*. Madison, pp. 11–22.

Walde, D. and Willows, N.D. 1991. (eds) *The Archaeology of Gender: Proceedings of the 22nd Annual Chacmool Conference*. The Archaeological Association of the University of Calgary, Calgary.

Watson, P.J. and Kennedy, M.C. 1991. The development of horticulture in the Eastern Woodlands of North America: woman's role. In Gero J. and Conkey, M. (eds) *Engendering Archaeology*. Oxford, pp. 255–75.

Welbourn, A. 1984. Endo ceramics and power strategies. In Miller, D. and Tilley, C. (eds) *Ideology, Power and Prehistory*. Cambridge, pp. 17–24.

Whittlesey, S.M. 1992. Academic alternatives: gender and cultural resource management. In Claassen, C. (ed.) *Women in Archaeology*. Philadelphia, pp. 202–9.

Williams, S. 1987. An archaeology of Turkana beads. In Hodder, I. (ed.) *The Archaeology of Contextual Meanings*. Cambridge, pp. 79–89.

Wylie, A. 1991. Gender theory and the archaeological record: why is there no archaeology of gender? In Gero, J. and Conkey, M. (eds) *Engendering Archaeology*. Oxford, pp. 31–54.

Wylie, A. 1994. The trouble with numbers: workplace climate issues in archaeology. In Nelson, M.C., Nelson, S.M. and Wylie, A. (eds) *Equity Issues for Women in Archaeology*. Archaeological Papers of the American Anthropological Association No. 5. Washington D.C., pp. 65–71.

Yates, T. 1993. Frameworks for an archaeology of the body. In Tilley, C. (ed.) *Interpretative Archaeology*. London, pp. 31–72.

Yellen, J. 1983. Women, archaeology, and the National Science Foundation. In Gero, J.M., Lacey, D. M. and Blakey, M. L. (eds) *The Socio-Politics of Archaeology Department of Anthropology*, University of Massachusetts, Research Report No. 23. Amherst, pp. 51–7.

Yellen, J. 1991. Women, archaeology, and the National Science Foundation: An analysis of fiscal year 1989 data. *Society for American Archaeology Bulletin* 9 (1).

Zihlman, A. 1981. Women as shapers of the human adaptation. In Dahlberg, F. (ed.) *Woman the Gatherer*. New Haven, pp. 75–120.

Zihlman, A. 1989. Woman the gatherer: the role of women in early hominid evolution. In Morgen, S. (ed.) *Gender and Anthropology: Critical Reviews for Research and Teaching*. American Anthropological Association, Washington, pp. 21–40.

Zihlman, A. 1991. Did Australopithecenes have a division of labor? In Walde, D. and Willows, N.D. (eds) *The Archaeology of Gender: Proceedings of the 22nd Annual Chacmool Conference*. The Archaeological Association of the University of Calgary, Calgary, pp. 64–70.

16

The Interplay of Evidential Constraints and Political Interests: Recent Archaeological Research on Gender

Alison Wylie

It is a striking feature of North American archaeology that there is very little in print advocating or exemplifying a feminist approach to archaeology; certainly there is nothing comparable to the thriving traditions of feminist research on women and gender that have emerged, in the last twenty years, in such closely aligned fields as sociocultural anthropology, history, various areas in the life sciences (including evolutionary theory), classics, and art history. The first paper to explore systematically the relevance of feminist insights and approaches for archæology was published in 1984 by Conkey and Spector, and the first collection of essays dedicated to reporting original work in the area has just appeared (Gero and Conkey, *Engendering Archaeology: Women and Prehistory*, 1991).[1] This collection is the outcome of a small working conference convened in South Carolina in April that had been raised by Conkey and Spector in 1984. Its organizers, Gero and Conkey, were concerned that, in the four years since the appearance of this paper, very little work had appeared, or seemed imminent, that took up the challenges it posed (see Gero and Conkey 1991: xi–xiii). They approached colleagues who represented a wide range of research interests in prehistoric archaeology and asked if they would be willing to explore the implications of taking gender seriously as a focus for analysis in their fields; most had never considered such an approach and

---

[1] There has been some important exploration of feminist themes in other connections, for example, in problem- or region-specific literatures where a developed anthropological and historical interest in the status and roles of women is extended to archaeology (see, for example, Barstow 1978; Kehoe 1983; Spector 1983). This is especially evident in historical archaeology where individual studies of women and gender in various historical contexts have appeared on Society for Historical Archaeology meeting programs since at least the mid-1980s, giving rise, in the last several years, to at least one session a year dedicated to research in this area. In addition, some postprocessual critics of the new archaeology have advocated feminist initiatives as an example of the sort of politically engaged approach they endorse (e.g., Hodder 1982, 1985, 1986:159–161; Shanks and Tilley 1987a: 246), although not many of them have undertaken sustained work in the area. Important exceptions are some of the contributions to Miller and Tilley's (1984) collection, *Ideology, Power and Prehistory* (for example, Hodder 1984b, and Braithwaite 1984) and to Gathercole and Loenthal's (1989) World Archaeology Congress Collection, *The Politics of the Past*.

had no special interest in feminist initiatives, but agreed to see what they could do. In effect, Gero and Conkey commissioned a series of pilot projects on gender that they hoped might demonstrate the potential of research along the lines proposed by Conkey and Spector in 1984.[2]

Between the time of this initial conference and the appearance of *Engendering Archaeology*, many of the papers prepared for discussion in South Carolina were presented in a session on gender and archaeology at the annual meeting of the Society for American Archaeology in April 1989; they drew a substantial and enthusiastic audience, to the surprise of many of the participants. But most significant, one much more public conference, the 1989 Chacmool conference held the following November at the University of Calgary, took "The Archaeology of Gender" as its focal theme. It drew *over 100* contributions on a very wide range of topics, all but four of which (the invited keynote addresses) were submitted, directly or indirectly, in response to an open call for papers (most will appear in Walde and Willows [1991]).[3] So despite the fact that little more than Conkey and Spector's 1984 paper was in print at the time the Chacmool conference was being organized and the SAA session presented, an awareness of the issues they raised and an enthusiasm about the prospects for archaeological work on gender seem to have had taken hold across the length and breadth of the field.[4]

This precipitous emergence of broadly feminist initiatives raises a number of questions. First are questions about the development itself: Why has there been no

---

[2] By way of comparison, I was intrigued to learn that a group of Norwegian archaeologists had organized a conference called, "Were They All Men?", in November 1979 – the proceedings were not published until 1987 (Bertelsen et al. 1987) – and that a group called "Norwegian Women in Archaeology" (the acronym is KAN in Norwegian) has been meeting and producing a journal, *KAN*, since 1985. In the same year as the Gero/Conkey conference, a special issue of *Archaeological Review from Cambridge* was produced on "Women and Archaeology" (Spring 1988), based in part on the "Cambridge Feminist Archaeology Workshops" in 1987–1988 and on presentations made at the annual Theoretical Archaeology Group Conferences held in the United Kingdom in 1987 (with antecedents in 1982 and 1985; see Arnold et al. 1988:1). In addition, a synthetic overview of the evidence pertaining to women and gender in European prehistory appeared in 1989, *Women in Prehistory* (Ehrenberg 1989).

[3] I say direct and indirect because some of those who participated undertook to organize special-topic sessions in response to the call for papers and solicited contributions from others who may not have seen the call for papers or planned to attend on their own. The number of contributions ultimately included in the program represents a substantial increase over the level of participation seen in previous years on more mainstream topics, e.g., long-distance trade, ethnicity, lithics and faunal analysis, and ecological models. However, in a paper that provides a content analysis of the abstracts contributed to "The Archaeology of Gender," Kelley and Hanen (1992) argue that the response to the 1989 call for papers is within the range expected given a general pattern of increase in the size of the Chacmool conference over the years. It is striking, nonetheless, that, given the dearth of published material in the area, a gender-focused conference would have maintained the rate of increase seen in previous years; several of the organizers indicated, in discussions about the genesis of the conference, that the momentum of the Chacmool institution itself had not always assured an increase in attendance (i.e., they could cite at least one previous topic that was specialized enough that participation had dropped relative to past years), and that the enthusiasm generated by their topic was quite unexpected, by both its supporters and its critics.

[4] In fact, as Kelley and Hanen (1992) argue, some subfields and specialties were more heavily represented than others at the Chacmool conference; for example, they note that papers tended to cluster in

sustained interest before now in women and gender as subjects of archaeological inquiry and/or in scrutinizing the interpretive assumptions routinely made about women and gender in extant practice?; and, why is such an interest emerging at this juncture? These are questions I have addressed elsewhere (Wylie 1991a, 1991b), but which bear brief discussion here as a basis for considering a second set of issues to do with the implications of embracing, or tolerating, feminist approaches. For many I believe the real question raised by these developments is not why research on gender is emerging (only) now, but why it should ever emerge. The genre of question posed in this connection is, "why do we need it?"; "what does it have to offer?" or, more defensively, "why should we take any of this seriously?" (after Wylie 1991b). Often the most dismissive responses reflect, not just uneasiness about feminist initiatives, but a general wariness about intellectual fads and fashions. Given the rapid emergence of the scientific new archaeology, displacing so-called "traditional" modes of practice, and now the equally dramatic reaction against the new archaeology and the emergence of a plethora of warring anti- or postprocessualist and critical alternatives, many are deeply weary of debate. Renfrew's review of "isms" of our time (Renfrew 1982:8) and the challenge Watson (in Watson and Fotiadis 1990) issue to the advocates of some of these "isms" to deliver the goods, as it were, convey a sense of alarm at the instability of this succession of research programs. Viewed in this light, the call to study women and gender may seem especially tenuous, even self-destructive.

I want to argue that a feminist perspective, which questions entrenched assumptions about women and gender and directs attention to them as subjects of inquiry, promises to substantially enhance the conceptual and empirical integrity – the "objectivity," properly construed – of archaeological inquiry. To this end, I consider how feminist initiatives have arisen and how the debate over "isms" has unfolded such that they might be viewed with particular scepticism. I offer general arguments against this scepticism, questioning the terms of abstract debate from which it derives, and then turn, in the final section, to an analysis of several examples of the new research on gender, drawn from *Engendering Archaeology* (Gero and Conkey 1991), which illustrates how evidential considerations can challenge and constrain political and theoretical presuppositions, even where these constitute the encompassing framework of inquiry.

time periods closer to the historic (Kelley and Hanen 1992). Nonetheless, they note that the geographical distribution of archaeological subjects was very broad, with no evident clustering by field area, and with a representation of topics ranging from evolutionary theory and research on early hominids, through various problem areas and periods in prehistory, to ethnoarchaeology and ethnohistory, as well as historical archaeology. In addition, there was a full-day session on the status of women in archaeology.

Why Now? Why Ever?

Why is the Archaeology of Gender Emerging Only Now?

Where the preliminary questions – "why not before now?" and, "why now?" – are concerned, my thesis is that a number of factors have been relevant both in forestalling and in precipitating these developments in archaeology, similar to the situation described by Longino (1987) and by Longino and Doell (1983) for the life sciences.[5] The conceptual and methodological commitments of scientific, processual archaeology have tended to direct attention way from what Binford (1983, 1986a, 1989: 3–23, 27–39) has vilified, in his most uncompromising defenses of processual approaches, as "ethnographic," internal variables; gender dynamics, which would be included among such variables in most analyses, are just one example of the sort factor he considers explanatorily irrelevant and scientifically inaccessible (for a more detailed analysis, see Wylie [1991a:35–38]). While anti- and postprocessual challenges to this general orientation have certainly been crucial in opening a space for the development of an interest in gender, among other symbolic, ideational, social, and broadly "ethnographic" dimensions of the cultural past, it is striking that none of the chief exponents of postprocessualism have done a great deal to develop a feminist analysis of archaeological method or theory (see Note 1). Indeed, as Ericka Engelstad (1991) argues, they have largely avoided any sustained reflexive critique of their own proposals and practice, with the result that these remain resolutely androcentric. Moreover, postprocessualists had established the need for work on variables like gender fully a decade ago, and yet there was no sustained archaeological work on gender, per se, and no serious consideration of the implications for archaeology of feminist research in other fields, until the last few years. Given this, I suggest that social and political (i.e., "external," non-cognitive) factors must play a central role in the emergence of an interest in gender at this juncture.

To be more specific, it would seem plausible, given the experience reported in other disciplinary contexts, if the prepardness to consider questions about gender, and in some cases, the willingness to champion research that addresses them, did not have to do with the influence of explicitly political, feminist thinking on practitioners in the field (Wylie 1991b).[6] In most cases I expect this influence will be only

---

[5] Longino argues persuasively that, although androcentrism pervades the social and life sciences, the form it takes, and the sources from which it derives in any given field of research, will be diverse and often quite specific to the intellectual agenda and history of the field: single-factor and widely generalized accounts of the nature or roots of androcentrism across the sciences are inherently implausible (Longino 1987:61). She argues, more specifically, that it will be necessary to understand the "unstated and fundamental assumptions [of a particular field or research tradition] and how they influence the course of inquiry" (Longino 1987:62) in order to respond effectively to androcentric bias.

[6] What follows is a sketch of processes that I believe may underly the recent emergence of a visible interest in questions about women and gender, and in feminist initiatives, among North American archaeologists. The sketch itself is developed in more detail elsewhere (Wylie 1991b), but it remains to be filled in; I have recently undertaken a survey and a series of interviews that I hope will make it

indirect; whether many practitioners identify as feminists or are in any sense sympathetic to feminism, a great many will have been affected by a growing if still liminal appreciation of women's issues, starting with equity issues, that grows out of second-wave feminist activism and has become evident, in recent years, in the discourse and practice of archaeologists.[7] No doubt this is closely tied to the demands for equity they face as members of academic institutions, consulting businesses, and government agencies, and to resulting changes in the representation, roles, and status of women in these larger institutional contexts. But however they arise, and however welcome or unwelcome they may be, as these changes enforce some level of awareness of gender politics in contemporary contexts they also produce (in some) a growing awareness that gender is not a "natural," immutable given, an insight which is seen by many as the pivotal discovery of feminist theory (Flax 1987; Harding 1983). And (in some) this has influenced, in turn, scholarly thinking about the subjects of archaeological study. Whatever their political commitments, they may begin to question entrenched assumptions about sexual divisions of labor and the status of women in prehistory, and to consider previously unexplored questions about the diversity of gender structures in prehistoric contexts, about the significance of gender dynamics in shaping past cultural systems, and about the origins and emergence of contemporary and/or ethnohistorically documented sex/gender systems.

In some cases the influence of feminist thinking has been direct. For example, both organizers of the South Carolina Conference have long been active on issues to do with the status of women in archaeology. Gero has published a number of groundbreaking articles on these issues and been actively involved in promoting research on the political dynamics, including the gender dynamics, of the discipline (Gero 1983, 1985, 1988). And Conkey was a member of the American Anthropological Association (AAA) Committee on the Status of Women from 1974 (chair in 1975–1976) in which capacity she was drawn into the organization of a panel for the 1977 AAA meetings on gender research in the various subfields of anthropology. Charged with presenting a section on archaeological research on gender, Conkey confronted the dearth of literature in the area; for the most part she found that "women [and gender] were considered by chance rather than by design," if they were considered at all (M. Conkey, personal communication 1991). In these connections both organizers were drawn into contact with feminists working in other fields, especially socio-cultural anthropology, and were aware of the insights, both critical and constructive, that had resulted from the systematic investigation of questions about the status, experience, and roles of women in their

possible to give a fuller account of how those who organized and contributed to the groundbreaking archaeological conferences on gender in North America came to be involved in research in this area.

[7] As indicated, these concerns were well represented on the program of the Chacmool conference, which included a full-day session on the status of women in the discipline (see contributions to Walde and Willows [1991]), and have been articulated in a number of analyses of women's status in archaeology that have appeared in the last decade (e.g., Gero 1983, 1985, 1988; Kramer and Stark 1988; Wildeson 1980).

various research fields. It was quite explicitly this exposure to, and engagement in, feminist discourse outside archaeology that led them to question the assumptions about gender underlying archaeological theorizing and to see both the need and the potential for a focused program of feminist research in archaeology. As they came to question the assumptions about gender that underpin *contemporary* sex roles, they came to see that these same assumptions infuse the theories about other people's lives they were engaged in constructing as archaeologists. In organizing events and publications that they hoped would generate wider interest among archaeologists in questions about gender they, and, specifically, the feminist commitments that had come to inform their own work, have been instrumental in mobilizing the latent grass-roots interest in these questions that now seems widespread, even among archaeologists who would never identify as feminists and have had no contact with feminist research in other contexts. On this account it is, most simply, the experience of women and, more important, the emerging feminist analysis of this experience, which figures as a key catalyst (both directly and indirectly) for skepticism about entrenched conceptions of women and gender and for research in this area as it is now emerging in archaeology.

Relativist Implications

But if this is the case – if the new research on gender is motivated and shaped, at least in part, by explicitly feminist commitments – does it not follow that it is to be identified and, for many, dismissed, with the extreme anti-objectivist positions defended by postprocessualists? Does it not exemplify precisely the sort of partisan approach to inquiry that they endorse, and that Binford (1989:32), for example, has condemned as conceptual "posturing"? To be more specific, if political interests are allowed to set the agenda of archaeology, do they not irrevocably compromise the commitments to objectivity and value neutrality – most broadly, the commitment to settle empirical questions by appeal to the "world of experience" (Binford 1989:27; see also Binford 1982:136), rather than to prejudgments or sociopolitical interests – that stand as a hallmark of science? And in this case, what credibility can such inquiry claim on its own behalf; are its results not as limited and biased as those they are meant to displace? Perhaps more disturbing, if an explicitly partisan feminist standpoint reveals the partiality (the unacknowledged standpoint specificity) of our best existing accounts of the past and brings into view a different past, or new ways of understanding the past, does it not follow that any number of other standpoints might do the same? And in this case, what is to stop the proliferation of conflicting views of prehistory and, with this, a slide into extreme standpoint relativism according to which the credibility of each of these "versions" is strictly context or perspective and interest specific?

Such conclusions only follow, I argue, if you accept the sharply polarized terms in which much current debate about the aims and status of archaeology has been cast, and assume that any critique of objectivist ideals, any break with the scientific canons of processual archaeology (originally construed in rigidly positivist terms), leads irreovacably to what Trigger (1989:777) calls "hyperrelativism." This oppositional response to questions about the standards and goals of inquiry is not unique to archaeology; on Trigger's account the social sciences as a whole are marked by

> *an increasingly vociferous confrontation . . . between, on the one hand, an old-fashioned posi-tivist certainty that, given enough data and an adherence to "scientific" canons of interpretation, something approximating an objective understanding of human behavior can be achieved . . ., and on the other hand, a growing relativist scepticism that the understanding of human behavior can ever be disentangled from the interests, prejudices, and stereotypes of the researcher.* [Trigger 1989: 777; see also Bernstein (1983); Wylie 1989b]

On the former view, the aim of producing "objective" knowledge – knowledge which is credible, "true", transhistorically and cross-contextually, not just given a particular standpoint (Bernstein 1983:8–25) – can be realized if researchers scrupu-lously exclude all "external," potentially biasing (idiosyncratic or contextually specific) factors from the practice of science, so that judgements about the inade-quacy of particular knowledge claims are made solely on the basis of "internal" considerations of evidence, and of coherence and consistency. Positivist/empiri-cist theories of science, including those that influenced North American archaeology in the 1960s and 1970s and are still evident in archaeological thinking, made much of a distinction between the context of discovery, in which such "external" factors might be given free reign, and the context of verification or confirmation in which the fruits of creative speculation, however inspired or shaped, would be subjected to rigorously impartial testing against (independent) evidence; the body of empirical "facts" deployed as evidence was presumed to be the stable foundation of all (legitimate, nonanalytic) knowledge, and was, in this capacity, the final arbiter of epistemic adequacy.[8]

It is by now commonly held that this view of knowledge production (specifically scientific-knowledge production) is deeply problematic. The sharp distinction between the contexts of discovery and verification, and "foundationalist" faith in facts as the source and ground of legitimate knowledge, has broken down in face of a number of challenges. Even the proponents of a robust (empiricist/positivist) objectivism had, themselves, long acknowledged that all available evidence (some-times even all imaginable evidence) routinely "underdetermines" interesting knowledge claims about the world, that is, evidence rarely entails or supports a unique explanatory or interpretive conclusion and eliminates all potential rivals (for a summary, see Laudan and Leplin [1991]; Newton–Smith [1981]; Suppe [1977]). Furthermore, the analyses of "contextualist" theorists (e.g., Hanson 1958; Kuhn 1970) suggests that the facts, data, or evidence against which theoretical constructs are to be tested are all too intimately connected with these constructs to stand as a secure and autonomous "foundation" of knowledge; data are, famously,

---

[8] For a summary of the main tenets of this position see Suppe (1977), and for a classic example of their application to the social sciences, see Rudner (1966). Gibbon (1989) provides an excellent account of their incorporation into archaeology.

"theory laden." This opens up considerable space for the insinuation of "external" interests and values into the processes of both formulating and evaluating empirical knowledge claims. Indeed, sociologists of science have argued, on the basis of innumerable detailed studies of the practice (rather than just the products) of science, that "facts" are as much made as found and that judgements about their evidential significance are radically open.[9] The most thoroughgoing "social constructivists" among them maintain that facts, and the theoretical claims they are used to support, are equally a product of the local, irreducibly social and political, interests that inform the actions and interactions of scientific practitioners in particular contexts; in their most radical moments, they seem to suggest that scientists quite literally create the world they purport to know (see Woolgar's [1983:244] discussion of the range of positions at issue here). It seems a short step from the original contextualist and constructivist arguments against naive objectivism and foundationalism to the conclusion that cognitive anarchy is unavoidable; "anything goes" in the sense (not intended by Feyerabend [1988:vii, 1–3]) that virtually any knowledge claim one can imagine could, in principle, find some perspective or context in which it is compelling, and that there are no overarching grounds for assessing or challenging these context-specific judgments.

In an archaeological context, the outlines of this reaction emerge in some anti- or postprocessual literature. The point of departure is typically a "contextualist" argument to the effect that, where archaeological data must be theory laden to stand as evidence, it is unavoidable that archeologists have always, of necessity, actively *constructed* (not reconstructed, recaptured, or represented) the past, no matter how deeply committed they may have been to objectivist ideals. In some of his early critical discussions, Hodder insists, in this connection, that any use of archaeological data as test evidence is mediated by "an edifice of auxiliary theories and assumptions which *archaeologists have simply agreed not to question*" (Hodder 1984a:27, emphasis added); evidential claims thus have nothing but conventional credibility. In short, archaeologists literally, "create 'facts' " (Hodder 1984a:27). From this it follows that archaeologists are "without any ability to test their reconstructions of the past" (Hodder 1984a:26); as Shanks and Tilley put the point four years later, "there is literally nothing independent of theory or propositions to test against . . . any test could only result in tautology" (Shanks and Tilley 1987b:44, 111). As a consequence, archaeological data, test evidence, and interpretive claims about the past must be regarded as all *equally* constructs: "knowledge consists of little more than the description of what has already been theoretically constituted" (Shanks and Tilley 1987a:43; see also 1987:66). "Truth is" they declare, "a [mobile] army of metaphors" (Shanks and Tilley 1987b:22). More specifically, Shanks and Tilley argue that what counts as true or plausible, indeed, what counts as "fact" in any relevant sense, is determined by contextually specific interests: individual,

[9] For a classic case study that was widely influential in supporting this position, see Latour and Woolgar (1986), and for further discussion, see Knorr and Mulkay (1983) and Latour (1987). One of the most uncompromising advocates of a strong constructivist view has been Pickering (1984, 1989), although he sometimes distances himself from some even more radical constructivists (Pickering 1987).

micropolitical interests, as well as class interests, broadly construed. It is thus unavoidable that archaeology is a thoroughly and irredeemably political enterprise, one which is engaged in creating a past thought expedient for, or dictated by, present interests (Shanks and Tilley 1987b:209–212, but see also 192–193). And where there are no independent factual resources with which to counter the influence of "external" factors – where pretensions to objectivity can only be, on their account, a masking of the effects of these influences – Shanks and Tilley advocate self-consciously political reconstruction of the past(s) thought necessary for "active intervention in the present" (Shanks and Tilley 1987b:103). In this vein, Hodder (1983:7) once enjoined archaeologists to avoid "writ[ing] in the past" for others, or for societies in which they are not themselves prepared to live.

The process of polarization described by Trigger (1989:777) is complete when objectivists, reacting against what they consider the manifestly untenable implications of "hyperrelativism," insist that there *must* be "objective foundations for philosophy, knowledge, [and] language" (Bernstein 1983:12); they reject out of hand the critical insights that arose, originally, from the failure of objectivist programs cast in a positivist/empiricist mold, and renew the quest for some new Archimedean point, some "stable rock upon which we can secure our lives," and our knowledge, against the insupportable threat of "madness and chaos where nothing is fixed" (Bernstein 1983:4; see also Wylie 1989b:2–4). Just such a turn is evident, in the context of archaeological debate, in the exceedingly hostile counterreaction of (some) loyal processualists: in the caricatures in terms of which the positions of anti- and postprocessualists are assessed and rejected (e.g., in Binford's [1989:3–11] "field guide" and discussion of "yippie" archaeology; and in R. Watson's [1990] treatment of Shanks and Tilley); in uncompromising restatements of the central doctrines of processualism (e.g., by Binford 1983:137, 222–223; and by Renfrew 1989–39; for fuller analysis of Binford's position, see Wylie [1989a:103–105]); and in the frequent accusations, on both sides, that the opposition has simply missed the point, that they indulge in "wafting . . . [red herrings] in front of our noses" (Shanks and Tilley 1989:43; Binford 1989:35; see discussion in Wylie [1992]).

It is clear where feminist research initiatives will be placed in the context of debates such as these. In the past two decades, feminist-inspired research across the social and life sciences has provided strong substantive grounds for questioning the "self-cleansing" capacity of scientific method – they have identified myriad instances of gender bias that have persisted, not just in instances of "bad science," but in "good" science, "science as usual" – and frequently they have done this by bringing to bear the distinctive "angle of vision" afforded by various feminist and, more generally, women's perspectives (for a summary see Wylie [1991a:38–44]). In this, feminist researchers have made clear (sometimes unintentionally) the theory- and interest-laden, contextual, and constructed nature of scientific knowledge. Where debate is polarized in the manner described by Trigger (1989), some argue that the move to embrace a radically deconstructive, postmodern standpoint is irresistible; it is the logical outcome of their critiques (see Harding 1986).

But are the polarized options defined in the context of these debates the only ones open to archaeologists or other social scientists who have been grappling with an acute awareness "of how fragile is the basis on which we can claim to know anything definite about the past or about human behavior" (Trigger 1989: 777)? More specifically, is the radically anti-objectivist stance endorsed, most strongly, by Shanks and Tilley the only alternative to uncompromising faith in the foundational nature of "facts" and the capacity of the "world of experience" to adjudicate all "responsible" claims to knowledge? In fact, as has been noted by virtually every commentator on their work, both sympathetic and critical (e.g., see comments published with Shanks and Tilley [1980]; Wylie 1992), Shanks and Tilley are not consistent, themselves, in maintaining a radically deconstructive position. Indeed, this ambivalence is a consistent feature of anti- or postprocessual literature. As early as 1986, Hodder had substantially qualified his earlier position (1983), insisting that, although "facts" are all constructs, they derive from a "real world," which "does constrain what we can say about it" (Hodder 1986:16). He has recently urged what seems a rapprochement with processualism, and endorsed a "guarded commitment to objectivity" (Hodder 1991:10). Although Shanks and Tilley (1987a:192) indicate distaste for this attempt to "neutralize and depoliticize" archaeological inquiry, they themselves hasten to add, in the same context, that they "do not mean to suggest that all pasts are equal" (Shanks and Tilley 1987a:245); there is a "real" past (Shanks and Tilley 1987a:110), moreover, archaeological constructs are to be differentiated from purely fictional accounts of the past by the fact that they are constrained by evidential considerations ("data represents a network of resistances") that can "challenge what we say as being inadequate in one manner or another" (Shanks and Tilley 1987a:104). The turn away from an uncompromising constructivism seems to come, in every case, at the point where anti- or postprocessualists confront the problem that radical constructivism (or, its "hyperrelativist" implications) threatens to undermine their own political and intellectual agendas as much as it does those they repudiate.

It is striking, in this connection, that many *feminists* working in the developed traditions of feminist research outside archaeology are likewise deeply "ambivalent" about the relative implications that are sometimes seen to follow from their own wide-ranging critiques of objectivism (see Lather 1986, 1990; Fraser and Nicholson 1988). For example, despite endorsing postmodern approaches, the feminist philosopher of science, Sandra Harding, argues that we cannot afford to give up either the strategic advantages that accrue to more conventional modes of scientific practice – in effect, feminist uses of the tools of science – or the emancipatory vision embodied in postmodern transgressions of these "successor science" projects (Harding 1986:195; see Wylie 1987). Others (like biologist Fausto-Sterling [1985]) quite clearly want to preserve the option of defending feminist insights as *better* science in quite conventional terms, and a great many social scientists routinely privilege "facts" of some description – often as the grounds for conclusions about the gender-biased nature of the theories they criticize – even when they insist that facts cannot be treated as stable, given "foundation" of knowledge (for a more detailed account, see Wylie [1991c]). One commentator from political science, Mary Hawkesworth (1989:538), takes the even stronger position that "the feminist postmodernists' plea for tolerance of multiple perspectives is altogether at odds with feminists' desire to develop a successor science that can refute once and for all the distortions of androcentrism" (Hawkesworth 1989:538). She clearly hopes that feminism has not reached "such an impasse that its best hope with respect to epistemological issues is to embrace incompatible positions and embed a contradiction at the heart of its theory of knowledge" (Hawkesworth 1989: 538).

I myself find inescapable the suspicion that strong constructivist and relativist positions embody what seems patently an ideology of the powerful. Only the most powerful, the most successful in achieving control over their world, could imagine that the world can be constructed as they choose, either as participants or as observers. Any who lack such power, or who lack an investment in believing they have such power, are painfully aware that they negotiate an intransigent reality that impinges on their lives at every turn. Certainly, any serious attempt to change inequitable conditions of life requires a sound understanding of the forces we oppose; self-delusion is rarely an effective basis for political action. It is, then, precisely their political commitment to the emancipatory potential of feminism – their commitment to learn about how gender structures operate so that they can act effectively against the inequities that these structures perpetuate – that enforces, for many feminist practitioners and theorists, as much scepticism about extreme relativisms as about the (untenable) objectivism that has so long masked andro-centric bias in the social and life sciences (this point is acknowledged in Hodder [1991]). They are persistently forced back from either of the extremes that emerge in abstract debate by a clear appreciation of how intransigent are the practical, empirical constraints binding on both inquiry and activism. A similar turn is evident in postpositivist philosophy of science; the critical insights of "contextual-ists" and "constructivists" are by now incontrovertible, where directed against "received view" positivism and empiricism (Suppe 1977), but the positions that have carried these critiques to an extreme have proven as untenable as those they displace. Consequently, there has been considerable interest in making sense of how, exactly, data come to be "laden" with theory, such that it acquires evidential significance through rich interpretive construction, and yet still has a capacity to surprise, to challenge settled expectations (see, e.g. Shapere [1985] on the constitu-tion of "observations" in physics, and Kosso [1989] on observation in science generally; see also the recent work on experimental practice, e.g., Galison [1987]; Hacking [1983, 1988]; for further discussion of how this bears on archaeology, see Wylie [1990]).

Where feminist initiatives in *archaeology* are concerned, the encompassing philo-sophical problem at issue is precisely that which has attracted attention in recent postpositivist history and philosophy of science, and of feminist theorists in many contexts, viz., that of how we can conceptualize scientific inquiry so that we recog-nize, without contradiction, *both* that knowledge is constructed and bears the marks of its makers, *and* that it is constrained, to a greater or lesser degree, by con-ditions that we confront as external "realities" not of our own making. I want to argue that just this sort of mediating position is emerging in and through the new archaeological work on gender. It is political and should be aligned with antiprocessualist approaches insofar as it repudiates narrow objectivism of a positivist/scientific cast. But it is not altogether assimilable to, indeed, it embodies a serious, politically and epistemically principled critique of, the more extreme claims associated with post-processualism. That is to say, social and political factors are crucial in directing attention to questions about gender but, at least in the case of the South Carolina conference, which I will take as the focus of my analysis here, these do not account for the successes of the research they inspire or inform. It is the substantive results of this research that make it a serious challenge to extant practice, and these results are to a large degree autonomous of the political motivations and other circumstances responsible for the research that produced them.

"Engendered" Archaeology

The results of the preliminary investigations reported at the South Carolina conference are remarkable in a number of respects. Most of the contributors reported that they began with serious reservations about the efficacy of the approach urged on them by Gero and Conkey; they did not see how questions about gender could bear on research in their fields or subfields, given that they had never arisen before.[10] But even the most skeptical conceded that attention to such questions did result in quite striking "discoveries" of gender bias in existing theory and in clear evidence of gender-related variability in familiar data bases that had been completely overlooked.

One especially compelling critical analysis, due to Watson and Kennedy (1991), exposes pervasive androcentrism explanations of the emergence of agriculture in the eastern United States. Whatever the specific mechanisms or processes postulated, the main contenders – Smith (1987) and proponents of coevolutionary models that postulate a local, independent domestication, and Prentice (1986), among those who support a diffusionist model – all read women out of any active, innovative role in developing cultigens, even though it is commonly assumed that women are primarily responsible for gathering plants (as well as small game) under earlier foraging adaptations, and for the cultivation of domesticates once a horticultural way of life was established. Prentice does attribute some degree of initiative to members of Archaic period societies for adopting imported cultigens, but he identifies this firmly with the authority and magical/religious knowledge of shamans, who are consistently referred to as male (Prentice 1986, as cited in Watson and Kennedy 1991:263). It was their role as "high-status" (commerce-oriented) culture brokers that would have ensured the success of an agricultural

---

[10] Indeed, Tringham reports considerable resistance to the idea of the conference: "I was taken kicking and screaming to the conference 'Women and Production in Prehistory' in the marshes of South Carolina, convinced that gender differences were not visible in the archaeological record, least of all in the architectural remains of deep prehistory, with which I was most concerned" (Tringham 1991:93).

innovation, once introduced, and it was they, Prentice maintains, who "would have had the greatest knowledge of plants" (Prentice 1986, as cited in Watson and Kennedy 1991:263), and the motivation to cultivate and domesticate them. To be more specific, it was the knowledge they would have developed of plants for ritual purposes, and their interest in securing a source of rattles and exotic medicine, that led to the introduction of tropical gourds (*Cucurbita*) and, subsequently, to the development of indigenous cultigens in the Eastern Woodlands. In effect, women passively "followed plants around" when foraging, and then passively tended them when introduced as cultigens by men.

The dominant alternative, as articulated by Smith (1987), postulates a process whereby horticultural practices emerged as an adaptive response to a transformation of the plant resources that occurred without the benefit of any deliberate human intervention. At most, human patterns of refuse disposal in "domesti-ocalities," and the associated disturbance of the environment around base camps and resource-exploitation camps, would have unintentionally introduced artificial selection pressures that generated the varieties of indigenous plants that became domesticates. On this account "the plants virtually domesticate themselves" (Watson and Kennedy 1991:262) , and women are, once again, assumed to have passively adapted to imposed change.

Watson and Kennedy make much of the artificiality of both models. Why assume that dabbling for ritual purposes would be more likely to produce the knowledge and transformations of the resource base necessary for horticulture than the systematic exploitation of these resources (through foraging) as a primary means of subsistence (Watson and Kenney 1991: 268)?[11] And why deny human agency altogether when it seems that the most plausible ascription of agency (if any is to be made) must be to women (Watson and Kennedy 1991:262–264)? Watson and Kennedy make a strong case against the presumption, central to the coevolution model, that cultural change as extensive as adopting or developing domesticates could plausibly have been an "automatic process" (Watson and Kennedy 1991:266–267), and observe that they are "leary of explanations that remove women from the one realm that is traditionally granted them, as soon as innovation or invention enters the picture" (Watson and Kennedy 1991:264). Their assessment is that both theories share a set of underlying assumptions, uncritically appropriated from popular culture and traditional anthropology, to the effect that women could not have been responsible for any major culture-transforming exercise of human agency (Watson and Kennedy 1991:263–264).

In a constructive vein, a second contributor who works on Prehispanic sites in the central Andes, Hastorf, drew on several lines of evidence to establish that gendered divisions of labor and participation in the public, political life of Prehispanic Sausa communities were profoundly altered through the period when the Inka extended their control in the region; that is, the household structure and gender roles encountered in historic periods cannot be treated as a stable,

---

[11] Indeed, why assume that shamans were men?

"traditional" feature of Andean life that predates state formation (Hastorf 1991:139). In a comparison of the density and distribution of plant remains recovered from household compounds dating to the periods before and after the advent of Inka control, Hastorf found evidence of both an intensification of maize production and processing, and of an increase in the degree to which female-associated processing activities were restricted to specific locations within the sites over time. In addition, she reports the results of stable-isotope analysis of skeletal remains recovered from these sites,[12] comparing male and female patterns of consumption of meats, and various plant groups (mainly tubers and quinoa, and maize). Although the lifetime dietary profiles of males and females are undifferentiated through the period preceding the advent of Inka control in the valley, she finds evidence, consistent with the results of the paleobotanical analysis, that the consumption of maize increased much more dramatically for (some) men than for any of the women, at the point when evidence of Inka presence appears in the valley (Hastorf 1991:150). Given ethnohistoric records that document Inka practices of treating men as the heads of households and communities, drawing them into ritualized negotiations based on the consumption of maize beer (*chicha*) and requiring them to serve out a labor tax that was compensated with maize and *chicha*, she concludes that, through this transitional period, the newly imposed political structures of the Inka empire had forced a realignment of gender roles. Women "became the focus of [internal, social and economic] tensions as they produced more beer [and other maize foodstuffs] while at the same time they were more restricted in their participation in the society" (Hastorf 1991:152); indeed, their increased production was an essential basis for the political order imposed by the Inka, an order that drew male labor and political functions out of the household.

Similar results are reported by Brumfiel (1991) in an analysis of changes in household production patterns in the Valley of Mexico through the period when the Aztec state was establishing a tribute system in the region. She argues, through analysis of the frequencies of spindle whorls, that fabric production, largely the responsibility of women (on ethnohistoric and documentary evidence), increased dramatically in outlying areas but, surprisingly enough, decreased in the vicinity of the urban centers as the practice of extracting tribute payments in cloth developed. On further analysis, she found evidence of an inverse pattern of distribution and density in artifacts associated with the production of labor-intensive and transportable (cooked) food based on the use of tortillas; the changing proportion of griddles to pots suggests that the preparation of griddle-cooked foods increased near the urban centers and decreased in outlying areas, where less-demanding (and preferred) pot-cooked foods continued to predominate. She postulates, on this basis, that cloth may have been exacted directly as tribute in the hinterland, while populations living closer to the city center intensified their production of

---

[12] These were analyses undertaken by DeNiro at the University of California–Los Angeles (Hastorf 1991:153).

transportable food so that they could take advantage of "extra-domestic institutions" in the Valley of Mexico (Brumfiel 1991:243) – markets and forms of production that "drew labor away from the household context" (Brumfiel 1991:241) – that required a mobile labor force. In either case, Brumfiel points out, the primary burden of (directly or indirectly) meeting the tribute demands for cotton and maguey cloth imposed by Aztec rule was shouldered by women and was met by strategic realignments of their household labor. Where the Aztec state depended on such tribute to maintain its political and economic hegemony, its emergence, like the spread of the Inka state, as studied by Hastorf, must be understood to have transformed, and to have been dependent on a transformation of, the way predominantly female domestic labor was organized and deployed.

Finally, several contributors considered assemblages of "artistic" material, some of them rich in images of women, and explored the implications of broadening the range of conceptions of gender relations that inform their interpretation. Handsman undertook a critical rethinking of the ideology of gender difference, specifically, the "male gaze" (Handsman 1991:360), that infused a British exhibition of "The Art of Lepenski Vir" (Southampton, 1986), a Mesolithic site along the Danube River dating to the sixth millennium B.C. Where this "art" is represented as the product of men who "were not ordinary hunter-gatherers" (Handsman 1991:332), while the women of Lepenski Vir are treated exclusively as their subjects (Handsman 1991:335), Handsman objects to the ways in which this exhibit, and archaeological discourse generally, is "productive and protective of [hierarchical relations between men and women] inside and outside the discipline" (Handsman 1991:334), especially where it represents these hierarchies as timeless and natural, as "a priori, as a constant and universal fact of life" (Handsman 1991:338). In short, he challenges the notion that gender (or "art") can be treated in essentialist terms in this or in any context. In countering the uncritical standpoint of the exhibit, Handsman explores several interpretive strategies by which "relational histories of inequality, power, ideology and control, and resistance and counter-discourse" might be explored, where gender dynamics are concerned (Handsman 1991:338–339). And in the process, he points to a wide range of evidence – features of the "artistic" images themselves, differences between them and other lines of evidence, and associations with architectural and artifactual material that (could) provide them context – that constitute "clear signs" (Handsman 1991:340) of complexities, contradictions, "plurality and conflict" (Handsman 1991:343), which undermine the simple story of natural opposition and complementarity told by the exhibit.

In a similar vein, Conkey has developed an analysis of interpretations of paleolithic "art," especially the images of females or purported female body parts, in which she shows how "the presentist gender paradigm" (Conkey with Williams 1991:13) – the contemporary ideology of gender difference that represents current definitions and relations of men and women as "a matter of bipolar, essential, exclusive categories" (Handsman 1991:335), locked in stable and predetermined relations of inequality – has infused most reconstructions of Upper Paleolithic 'artistic' life," yielding accounts in which "sexist 20th century notions of gender and sexuality are read into the cultural traces of 'our ancestors' " with remarkable disingenuity (Conkey with Williams 1991:13)[13] She concludes that whatever the importance of these images and objects, it is most unlikely that they were instances of either commodified pornography or "high art," as produced in contemporary contexts, which is indeed how many treatises on such images consider them (see also Mack 1990). Moreover she, like Handsman, urges that we scrutinize the ideological agenda that lie behind the quest for closure in such cases, viz., the compulsion to naturalize those features of contemporary life most crucial to our identity as human and cultural beings, by tracing them back to our "origins" (as human and cultural).

None of these researchers, not even Handsman who moves furthest in the direction of a deconstructive (postprocessual) stance, considers their results merely *optional*, standpoint-specific alternatives to the androcentric models and paradigms they challenge. They purport to *expose error*, to demonstrate that formerly plausible interpretive options are simply false (empirically) or untenable (conceptually), and to improve on previous accounts. Watson and Kennedy (1991:267–268) draw attention to a straightforward contradiction implicit in much current theorizing about the emergence of horticulture in the Eastern Woodlands: Women are persistently identified as the tenders of plants, whether wild or under cultivation, and yet are systematically denied any role in the transition from foraging to horticulture, whatever the cost in terms of theoretical elegance, plausibility, or explanatory power. Hastorf, and Brumfiel, bring into view new facts about the structure of otherwise well-understood data bases that call into question, not just the conceptual integrity but also the empirical adequacy of otherwise credible models of the political and economic infrastructure of states in Mesoamerica and the Andes. Brumfiel advances, on this basis, an alternative model that effectively fills (some of) the gaps and solves (some of) the puzzles she exposes as problematic for extant theories. And Handsman, and Conkey, argue that, although the artistic traditions they deal with are enormously rich and enigmatic, some interpretive options, including many that accord with the assumptions about gender taken for granted in our own contemporary societies, are simply unsustainable. Although the quest for closure, for one right answer, may be misguided when dealing with this sort of material, it does not follow that "anything goes."

Evidential Constraints

In all of these cases, the results – both critical and constructive – turn on the appraisal of constraints imposed by, or elicited from, various kinds of relevant evidence. This is significant inasmuch as it suggests that however thoroughly mediated, or "laden," by theory archaeological evidence may be, it routinely turns

---

[13] This paper was not Conkey's contribution to the South Carolina conference, but several of its main points were discussed in this context.

out differently than expected; it generates puzzles, poses challenges, forces revisions, and canalizes theoretical thinking in ways that lend a certain credibility to the insights that sustain objectivist convictions. Consequently, while we cannot treat archaeological data or evidence as a given – a stable foundation – it is by no means infinitely plastic. It does, or can, function as a highly recalcitrant, closely constraining, "network of resistances," to use the terms of Shanks and Tilley's (1987a:104) discussion. What we need now is a nuanced account of *how* data are interpretively laden such that, to varying degrees, they can stand as evidence for or against a given knowledge claim. Such an account has not been developed by Shanks and Tilley, or by Hodder, even though they are themselves manifestly ambivalent about their strongest constructivist claims. Their response has been to juxtapose with claims about the radical instability of all evidence and the vicious circularity of all empirical testing, counterclaims to the effect that archaeological data can (and sometimes do) decisively resist theoretical appropriation. But, with the exception of Hodder's (1991) most recent discussion, they do not then reassess their original constructivist assertions. The result is incoherence.

The point of departure for an account that could make sense of these contradictory insights must be the now-familiar thesis that the empirical evaluation of knowledge claims, including claims about the past, is never a "lonely encounter of hypothesis with evidence" (Miller 1987:173). Evidential relevance is constructed as a three-place relation (Glymour 1980); archaeologists inevitably constitute data as evidence or, ascribe it "meaning" (Binford 1983) as evidence of specific events or conditions in the past, by means of linking hypotheses and interpretive principles. The key to understanding how evidence (as an interpretive construct) can constrain is to recognize, first, that the content and use of these linking principles is, itself, subject to empirical constraint and, second, that a great diversity of such principles figure in any given evidential argument. The credibility of these principles is by no means necessarily a matter of convention, but can often be established empirically and quite independently of any of the theories or assumptions that inform archaeological theorizing (i.e., the theories that might be tested against interpretively constituted evidence). Their independence from one another further ensures that error in any one line of interpretation may be exposed by incongruity with others that bear on the same (past) subject. Archaeologists thus exploit a great variety of evidence when they evaluate knowledge claims about the past; not just different kinds of archaeological evidence, but evidence from a wide range of sources, which enters interpretation at different points, and which can be mutually constraining when it converges, or fails to converge, on a test hypothesis.

In the cases considered here and, indeed, in most archaeological interpretation, claims about the past are invariably shaped by an encompassing theory, or at least by some set of precepts about the nature of the cultural subject, which can also inform the interpretation of archaeological data as evidence for or against these claims. When the theoretical framework is closely specified, a structurally circular interdependence between test evidence and test hypotheses can emerge, i.e., where the test hypothesis in question derives from a theory about cultural dynamics that also supplies the linking principles used to interpret the data as evidence for or against this hypothesis. It is presumably circularity of this sort that led post-processualists to declare that archaeologists quite simply "create facts" (Hodder 1984a:27), and that testing is inevitably futile, being viciously circular.

When practice is examined more closely, however, I suggest that any examples of full-fledged circularity that antiprocessualists might cite fall at one end of a continuum of types of interpretive inference, most of which do not sustain radically pessimistic judgments about the indeterminacy of archaeological inference and hypothesis evaluation. Even when the threat of self-validating circularity is realized, which is, in part, what Watson and Kennedy (1991) object to in explanations for the emergence of horticulture in the eastern United States, it is often possible, as they demonstrate, to establish evidential grounds for questioning the assumptions that frame both the favored hypothesis and the constitution of data as supporting evidence. Sometimes even data used to support the hypothesis can play this role. A traditional model of gender relations, underpinned by sexist assumptions about the nature and capabilities of women, infuses the interpretations of archaeological data that Watson and Kennedy consider, ensuring that, inevitably, these data will be seen as evidence of a "natural" division of labor in which women are consistently passive and associated with plants. Nevertheless, this does not (also) ensure that the record will obligingly provide evidence that activities identified as male in the terms of this model mediated the transition from a foraging to a horticultural way of life, however strong the expectation (on this model) that they must have. Where Smith's coevolution hypothesis is concerned, Watson and Kennedy point out that a very large proportion of the activities around "domestilocalities," which he cites as causes of the disturbances that would have transformed the weedy plant species into indigenous domesticates, were the activities of women, given (for the sake of argument) the traditional model they find presupposed by his account (Watson and Kennedy 1991:262).

But even if the interpretation of archaeological data as evidence is so "over-determined" by orienting presuppositions that tensions and contradictions such as these never arise, critiques of these presuppositions – including critiques of the linking principles used to establish the evidential significance of specific data, as well as of the central tenets of the encompassing conceptual framework – may be based on independent evidence, that is, evidence generated outside the (archaeological) context to which these presuppositions are applied, evidence established in the "source" contexts from which interpretive linking principles are drawn. Watson and Kennedy make effective use, in this connection, of background (botanical) knowledge about the range and environmental requirements of the relevant varieties of maize to argue that many of the contexts in which they appear prehistorically are far from optimal (indeed, "inhospitable," "adverse"; Watson and Kennedy [1991:266]). Hence, it is not altogether plausible that they could have arisen under conditions of neglect; it is "more plausible" that humans knowledgeable about these plants (e.g., women foragers) must have taken a role in their cultivation and development. When Watson and Kennedy call into question the proposal that male shamans must have played this role (due to Prentice [1986]), they indicate some appreciation that the traditional model of sexual divisions of labor, which they find implicit in all the hypotheses they consider and accept for the sake of argument, is itself profoundly problematic given ethnographic evidence of foraging practices and the (gendered) distribution of botanical information among members of foraging societies (Watson and Kennedy 1991:256–257, 268). Over the past three decades, feminist anthropologists have documented enormous variability in the roles played by women, in the degrees to which they are active rather than passive, mobile rather than bound to a "home base," and powerful rather than stereotypically dispossessed and victimized.[14] All of this decisively challenges any presupposition that women are inherently less capable of self-determination and strategic manipulation of resources than their male counterparts. Where independent botanical and ecological information provides a basis for calling into question specific interpretive principles (i.e., concerning the import of data bearing on the spatiotemporal distribution of early maize varieties in the eastern United States), these ethnographic data challenge the credibility of the interpretive framework itself, rendering suspect any interpretation that depends on such an assumption, quite independently of archaeological results.

Straightforward circularity is generally not the central problem in archaeological interpretation, however. Given the state of knowledge in the relevant fields, explanatory hypotheses about particular past contexts, and the linking principles deployed to interpret the record of these contexts, are rarely integrated into a single, unified, encompassing culture theory; indeed, given the complexity of most archaeological subjects, it is almost unimaginable that a single unified theory (e.g., of cultural systems) would have the resources to provide both the necessary explanatory hypotheses and the grounds for testing them (i.e., the relevant linking principles) in a given archaeological context. Despite disclaimers, analogical inference is generally the basis for ascribing evidential significance to archaeological data, and here the worry is usually underdetermination, not overdetermination. Nevertheless, as in the case just described, analogical inference is subject to two sets of evidential constraints that can significantly limit the range of evidentially viable options: those determining what can be claimed about the analog based on knowledge of source contexts and those deriving from the archaeological record that determine its applicability to a specific subject context (Wylie 1985). In linking women with the use of spindle whorls in weaving, and with the use of pots and griddles in food preparation, Brumfiel (1991) relies on a direct historic analogy that postulates that the same sorts of food and cloth production were involved in archaeological as in ethnohistoric contexts (given a judicious reading of codices dating to the sixteenth century; Brumfiel [1991:224–230, 237–239, 243–245]); this is, in turn, the basis for postulating further limited similarities in the relations of production where gender is concerned. Similarly, archaeologists dealing with evidence of horticultural lifeways routinely postulate a division of labor in which women are primarily responsible for agricultural activities, but they base this not

---

[14] For an early series of arguments to this effect, see the contributions to *Women, Culture, and Society* (Rosaldo and Lamphere 1974), and for contemporary reviews and assessments see *Feminism and Anthropology* (Moore 1988) and Mukhopadhyay and Higgins (1988).

on an appeal to the completeness of mapping between source and subject, which Brumfiel's case illustrates, but on the persistence of this association across historically and ethnographically documented contexts, however different they may be in other respects (see, for example, Ehrenberg's discussion of the ethnographic bases for assuming these correlates; Ehrenberg [1989:50–54, 63–66, 81–83, 90–105]).

In these cases, evidence of extensive similarity (the completeness of mapping) between source and subject contexts, and of reliable correlation between clusters of attributes in source contexts, suggests that the linkage postulated between archaeologically observed material and its inferred functional, social, ideational, or other significance is not entirely arbitrary. To be specific, this kind of source-derived information constitutes evidence that the general association of women with the foraging of plant resources and with horticulture, and their local association with cooking and weaving in Aztec contexts, is to some (specifiable) degree nonaccidental; it is at least preliminary evidence that an underlying "determining structure" links the artifactual material in question to specific functions, gender associations, or activity structures securely enough to support an ascription of the latter attributes to the archaeological subject (for the details of this analysis, see Wylie [1985, 1988]).[15] A change in background knowledge about the sources, as much as in what archaeologists find in the record, can decisively challenge these interpretive claims. Where the feminist research on foraging societies (mentioned above) calls into question all aspects of the assumption that women passively "followed plants around" (as Watson and Kennedy characterize the traditional model), indeed, where it provides evidence that the "gathering" activities of women often include the hunting of small game, it becomes necessary to reconsider simplistic interpretive assumptions to the effect that "hunting" artifacts are indicative of the presence or activities of men. But most important, when the linking principles used to "ascribe meaning" to archaeological data as evidence are uncontested – when their credibility is well established and independent of any of the hypotheses that archaeologists might want to evaluate – archaeological evidence can very effectively stabilize the assessment of comprehensively different claims about the cultural past.[16] The power of the challenge posed by Brumfiel to extant models of the economic base of the Aztec empire depends on precisely this. Her identification of spindle whorls, and pots and griddles, with cloth and food production by women is unproblematic for any she might engage in debate and wholly independent of both the hypotheses she challenges and those she promotes. Hence, when she shows that variability inheres in these data that cannot be accounted for on standard models *when interpreted in these shared terms*, she establishes a challenge that is by no means an artifact of the feminist standpoint that led

---

[15] The notion of "determining structures" derives from an analysis of analogical inference due to Weitzenfeld (1984) and refers to any systematic relation of dependence (functional, rule related, as well as causal); it does not imply a commitment to uniformitarianism or any strong or specifically causal sort.

[16] This argument is developed in more detail, with reference to proposals for the development and use of middle-range theory, in Wylie (1992).

(directly or indirectly) to her analysis, or that is compelling only for those who share a feminist understanding of gender relations.

Insofar as analogical inferences often allow considerable scope for (independent) empirical assessment, they fall into the middle ranges of a continuum of types of inference, where degrees of insecurity and the potential to be systematically insulated from critique (as in the case of vicious circularity) are concerned. The limiting case on this continuum of theory-ladening inferences – the ideal of security in the ascription of evidential significance to data – are instances where archaeologists can draw on completely independent, nonethnographic sources for biconditional linking principles (laws or law-like principles) that specify unique causal antecedents for specific components of the surviving record.[17] Among the cases considered here, Hastorf's use of the analysis of bone composition comes closest to the ideal. If the background knowledge deployed in stable-isotope analysis is reliable (and this is always open to critical reassessment) it can establish, in chemical terms, what dietary intake would have been necessary to produce the reported composition of the bone marrow recovered from archaeological contexts. And where this can be linked, through paleobotanical analysis, to the consumption of specific plant and animal resources, it can underwrite the inference of dietary profiles that is very substantially independent of, and can seriously challenge (can provide a genuine test of), any interpretive or explanatory presuppositions about subsistence patterns and/or social practices affecting the distribution of food that archaeologists might be interested in testing. The independence and security of linking arguments based on background knowledge of this physical, chemical, bioecological sort is exploited in many other areas: in morphological analyses of skeletal remains that provide evidence of pathologies and physical stress; in radiocarbon, archaeomagnetic, and related methods of dating; and in some reconstructions of prehistoric technology and paleoecology, to name a few such examples. As the degree of independence between linking principles and test hypotheses or framework assumptions evident in these cases is approximated, archaeologists secure a body of evidence that establishes provisionally stable parameters for all other interpretation and a stable basis for piecemeal comparison between contending claims about the cultural past (a further analysis of independence is developed in Wylie [1990]). Something along the lines of these limiting cases constitute the ideal on which Binford bases his arguments for middle-range theory (e.g., Binford 1983:135, 1986b:472).

It is important to note, however, that the import of this sort (i.e., evidence that is constituted on the basis of extremely reliable, deterministic, and independent linking principles) is often very limited, taken on its own. As indicated, Hastorf

---

[17] Biconditional laws take the form, "if and only if," specifying antecedent conditions that are both necessary and sufficient to produce the effects or outcome in question. In an archaeological context, a linking principle of this sort would specify past activities or events that had to have occurred for a particular archaeological record to have resulted, and it would exclude any other possible antecedents. Something along the lines of these limiting cases constitute the ideal on which Binford bases his arguments for middle-range theory (e.g., Binford 1983:135, 1986b:472).

must rely on a number of collateral lines of evidence to establish that the anomalous shift in diet evident in male skeletons was likely due to increased consumption of maize beer, to link this to the advent of Inka-imposed systems of political control in the valley, and to draw out the implication that this political transformation depended on a profound restructuring of gender relations at the level of the household. Indeed, this reliance on multiple lines of evidence is an important and general feature of archaeological reasoning; archaeologists rarely ascribe evidential significance to items taken in isolation. But this is not necessarily cause for despair. In such cases the security of archaeological evidence depends not just on the credibility of particular linking principles, taken in isolation, or on their independence from the test claims they are used to support or refute, but also, and crucially, on the independence *from one another* of the various linking principles used to establish diverse lines of evidence bearing on these claims. That is to say, where the constraints inherent in the relation between evidence and hypothesis operate on *a number of different vertical axes* (i.e., running from different elements of the data base, via a range of linking hypotheses, to the claims in question), a network of "horizontal" constraints comes into play between the lines of inference by which various kinds of data, bearing on a particular past context, are interpreted as evidence of this context. If diverse evidential strands all converge on a given hypothesis – if you can use different means to triangulate on the same postulated set of conditions or events – then you may be able to provide it decisive, if never irreversible, support simply because it is so implausible that the convergence should be the result of compensatory error in all the inferences establishing its evidential support (for philosophical discussion of these considerations, see Kosso [1988:456]; Hacking [1983:183–185]).

Like Hastorf, Brumfiel operates under this sort of constraint when she shows that independently constituted lines of evidence concerning both cloth and food production converge on the counter-hypothesis that change in the organization of domestic labor was a key component in establishing the economic basis for the Aztec empire. This convergence is a strong argument for her account precisely because it cannot be counted on. Even when, taken separately, each line of evidence relevant to a particular model of past events or conditions of life enjoys strong collateral support (i.e., from the sources that secure the linking principles on which they depend), undetected error or weakness may become evident when one line of evidence persistently runs counter to the others, when dissonance emerges among lines of interpretation; the failure to converge on a coherent account makes it clear that error lies somewhere in the system of auxiliary assumptions and linking principles, however well entrenched they may be. In the extreme, which might be represented by the sorts of cases Handsman and Conkey consider (i.e., interpretations of "artistic" images and traditions), persistent dissonance may call into question the efficacy of *any* interpretive constitution of the data as evidence. Ultimately, there may be no determinate fact of the matter where the symbolic import of gender imagery is concerned or, as Conkey suggests, we may have to conclude that we simply are not (and may never be) in a position to determine what the fact of the matter is in such cases. It is, paradoxically, the fragmentary nature of the archaeological record that is its strength in setting up evidential constraints of these sorts, even in establishing the limits of inquiry.

The key point to be taken from reflection on these examples of gender research in archaeology is that although archaeological data stand as evidence only under (rich) interpretation, the process of interpretation – of ladening data with theory so that it has evidential import – is by no means radically open ended. The linking principles and background knowledge that mediate the constitution of data as evidence are by no means necessarily or inherently arbitrary conventions, as Hodder (1984a:27) once suggested. Values and interests of various kinds do play a crucial role not just in setting the agenda of archaeological inquiry – determining what questions will be asked – but in determining what range of interpretive and explanatory options will be considered fruitful or plausible; in this they shape not just the direction, but also the content and outcome of archaeological research. But this does not mean that such "external" influences determine the shape of inquiry seamlessly, or irrevocably; they can be very effectively challenged on conceptual and empirical grounds, as has been demonstrated repeatedly by feminist social scientists over the past two decades, and by the critical analyses described here. It is significant, however, that the impetus for reassessing a discipline's "taken-for-granteds," at all levels (i.e., at the level of specific interpretations and linking principles, as well as at that of broad framework assumptions), very often comes from those who bring to bear a standpoint, a socially and politically defined "angle of vision," that differs from that typical of the established status quo in a field (whatever form it takes). It is precisely a shift in the values and interests informing the work of these critics that directs their attention to new questions, which throws into relief gaps and incongruities in established theories, and which leads to a questioning of settled judgements of plausibility that have otherwise never been challenged (see Longino 1990). And while the insights that result from such a turn, for example, from the work of those who bring to bear a feminist perspective, are always themselves open to further critique – as feminist discussions of class and ethnic, cultural, and racial difference have made clear, they have their own limitations – it is not the case that they are on the same footing, in this respect, as the (partial) perspectives they critique and sometimes displace. Once our understanding is expanded (indeed, many argue, transformed) so that it takes women and gender fully into account, there is no return to the traditional androcentric models described by Watson and Kennedy; the process of inquiry is, in this sense, open-ended, but it is not anarchic.

Conclusion

Although it can no longer be assumed that there is one set of standards or reference points to which all models, hypotheses, and claims can be referred – there is no "transcendental grid" (Bernstein 1983; Wylie 1989b) – at any given time, there will be a number of stable, shared evidential reference points that can be exploited piecemeal in the comparison and evaluation of contending claims, and these can sometimes yield "rationally decisive" (Bernstein 1983), if never final, conclusions. This means that, at least sometimes, it is plausible to say that we have quite literally "discovered" a fact about the world, or that we have shown a formerly plausible claim to be "just false." Such claims are established by a good deal of politically motivated, explicitly feminist research, including that which has begun to emerge in archaeology; the critical analysis by Watson and Kennedy, and the constructive proposals of Hastorf, and of Brumfiel, are cases in point. In other cases the outcome of inquiry is more equivocal. As Handsman, and Conkey, illustrate, sustained investigation may lead us to question basic assumptions about the existence and the accessibility of certain "facts" about a given subject domain. In short, there is a whole continuum of inferences, ranging from the viciously circular, through analogical and other forms of ampliative inference, to the nearly deductive naturalistic inferences favored by Binford, that manifest enormously different degrees of security and open-endedness; none of these parts should be read for the whole.

I suggest, then, that the question of what epistemic stance is appropriate – whether we must be relativists or objectivists, or postprocessualists – should be settled locally, in light of what we have come to know about the nature of specific subject matters and about the resources we have for their investigation. We should resist the pressure to adopt a general epistemic stance appropriate to all knowledge claims. The ambivalence expressed by Harding (1986) and inherent in the contradictory impulses evident in postprocessualism is well founded, but need not lead us to build inconsistencies into the core of our epistemology and practice.

If these general points are accepted, it follows that feminist research, including feminist research in archaeology, is not "political" in any especially distinctive or worrisome sense (Wylie 1991b). Sociopolitical factors are key in explaining how and why it has arisen at this point, but the results of inquiry are not the "over-determined" products of (viciously) circular inference that takes, as both point of departure and conclusion, the political conviction from which it draws inspiration. In fact, if any general lesson is to be drawn from reflection on feminist practice, it is that politically engaged science is often much more rigorous, self-critical, and responsive to the facts than allegedly neutral science, for which nothing much is at stake.

Acknowledgements

The research resulting in this paper has been supported by a three-year research grant from the Social Sciences and Humanities Research Council of Canada and was undertaken while on sabbatical leave from the University of Western Ontario, as a "visiting scholar" in the Department of Anthropology at the University of California at Berkeley. I am deeply indebted to my colleagues at Berkeley, who have provided an enormously stimulating and supportive environment in which to work, as well as to a large number of others who commented on earlier drafts of this paper when I read it in the various contexts that sabbatical leave allowed me to visit during the academic year 1990–1991. I particularly appreciated the spirited discussions in which I was engaged by participants in the Australian conference, "Women in Archaeology," by members of the Departments of Archaeology at

Cambridge University and at the University of Southampton, by Norwegian archaeologists affiliated with the University of Tromsø and with Tromsø Museum, and with the Universities of Bergen and Oslo, by Fellows of the Boston University Humanities Foundation, and by the anthropologists, philosophers, and women's studies students and faculty to whom I spoke at Arizona State University, the University of California at Berkeley, and the University of Calgary. Finally, this paper would not have been possible without generous input from those who have been centrally involved in the developments I have taken as my subject. It is with gratitude and admiration that I dedicate this paper to all of those who have pioneered the exploration of feminist initiatives in archaeology. Although I know many of them take very different positions than I do on various of the issues I have raised, I hope they can, nonetheless, find something of value in the foregoing discussion.

References Cited

Arnold, K., R. Gilchrist, P. Graves, and S. Taylor (editors) 1988. Women in Archaeology. *Archaeological Review from Cambridge* 7(1):2–8.

Barstow, A. 1978. The Uses of Archaeology for Women's History: James Mellaart's Work on the Neolithic Goddess at Çatal Hüyuk, *Feminist Studies* 4(3)7–17.

Bernstein, R.J. 1983. *Beyond Objectivism and Relativism: Science, Hermeneutics, and Praxis*. University of Pennsylvania Press, Philadelphia.

Bertelsen, R., A. Lillehammer, and J. Naess (editors) 1987. *Were They All Men?: An Examination of Sex Roles in Prehistoric Society*. Arkeologist museum i Stavanger, Stavanger, Norway.

Binford, L.R. 1982. Objectivity – Explanation – Archaeology 1981. In *Theory and Explanation in Archaeology*, edited by C. Renfrew, M.J. Rowlands, and B.A. Segraves, pp. 125–138. Academic Press, New York.

1983. *Working at Archaeology*. Academic Press, New York.

1986a. Data, Relativism, and Archaeological Science. *Man* 22:391-404.

1986b. In Pursuit of the Future. In *American Archaeology Past and Future*, edited by D.J. Meltzer, D.D. Fowler, and J.A. Sabloff, pp. 459-479. Smithsonian Institution Press, Washington, D.C.

1989. *Debating Archaeology*. Academic Press, New York.

Braithwaite, M. 1984. Ritual and Prestige in the Prehistory of Wessex c. 2200–1400 BC: A New Dimension to the Archaeological Evidence. In *Ideology, Power, and Prehistory*, edited by D. Miller and C. Tilley, pp. 93–110. Cambridge University Press, Cambridge.

Brumfiel, E.M. 1991. Weaving and Cooking: Women's Production in Aztec Mexico. In *Engendering Archaeology: Women and Prehistory*, edited by J.M. Gero and M.W. Conkey, pp. 224–251. Basil Blackwell, Oxford.

Conkey, M.W. and J.D. Spector 1984. Archaeology and the Study of Gender. In *Advances in Archaeological Method and Theory*, vol. 7, edited by M.B. Schiffer, pp. 1–38. Academic Press, New York.

Conkey, M.W., with S.H. Williams 1991. Original Narratives: The Political Economy of Gender in Archaeology. In *Gender at the Cross-roads of Knowledge: Feminist Anthropology in the Post-Modern Era*, edited by M. di Leonardo. University of California Press, Berkeley, in press.

Ehrenberg, M. 1989. *Women in Prehistory*. University of Oklahoma Press, Norman.

Engelstad, E. 1991. Images of Power and Contradiction: Feminist Theory and Post-Processual Archaeology. *Antiquity* 65: 502–514.

Fausto-Sterling, A. 1985. *Myths of Gender: Biological Theories About Men and Women.* Basic Books, New York.

Feyerabend, P. 1988. *Against Method.* 2nd ed. Verso, London.

Flax, J. 1987. Postmodernism and Gender: Relativism in Feminist Theory. *Signs* 12:621–643.

Frazer, N., and L.J. Nicholson 1988. Social Criticism without Philosophy: An Encounter Between Feminism and Postmodernism. *Communications* 10:345–366.

Galison, P. 1987. *How Experiments End.* University of Chicago Press, Chicago.

Gathercole, P., and D. Lowenthal 1989. *The Politics of the Past.* Unwin Hyman, London.

Gero, J.M. 1983. Gender Bias in Archaeology: A Cross-Cultural Perspective. In *The Socio-Politics of Archaeology,* edited by J.M. Gero, D.M. Lacy, and M.L. Blakey, pp. 51-58. Research Report No. 23. Department of Anthropology, University of Massachusetts, Amherst.

1985. Socio-Politics and the Woman-at-Home Ideology. *American Antiquity* 50:342–350.

1988. Gender Bias in Archaeology: Here, Then and Now. In *Feminism Within the Science and Health Care Professions: Overcoming Resistance,* edited by S.V. Rosser, pp. 33–43. Pergamon Press, New York.

Gero, J. M., and M.W. Conkey (editors) 1991. *Engendering Archaeology: Women and Prehistory.* Basil Blackwell, Oxford.

Gibbon, G. 1989. *Explanation in Archaeology.* Basil Blackwell, New York.

Glymour, C. 1980. *Theory and Evidence.* Princeton University Press, Princeton, New Jersey.

Hacking, I. 1983. *Representing and Intervening.* Cambridge University Press, Cambridge.

1988. Philosophers of Experiment. *PSA 1988,* vol. 2, edited by A. Fine and J. Leplin, pp. 147–156. Philosophy of Science Association, East Lansing, Michigan.

Handsman, R. 1991. Whose Art Was Found at Lepenski Vir?: Gender Relations and Power in Archaeology. In *Engendering Archaeology: Women and Prehistory,* edited by J.M. Gero and M.W. Conkey, pp. 329–365. Basil Blackwell, Oxford.

Hanson, N.R. 1958. *Patterns of Discovery.* Cambridge University Press, Cambridge.

Harding, S. 1983. Why Has the Sex/Gender System Become Visible Only Now? In *Discovering Reality: Feminist Perspectives on Epistemology, Metaphysics, Methodology and Philosophy of Science,* edited by S. Harding and M.B. Hintikka, pp. 311–325. D. Reidel, Dordrecht, Holland.

1986. *The Science Question in Feminism.* Cornell University Press, Ithaca.

Hastorf, C.A. 1991. Gender, Space, and Food in Prehistory. In *Engendering Archaeology: Women and Prehistory,* edited by J.M. Gero and M.W. Conkey, pp. 132–159. Basil Blackwell, Oxford.

Hawkesworth, M.E. 1989. Knowers, Knowing, Known: Feminist Theory and Claims of Truth. *Signs* 14:533–557.

Hodder, I. 1982. *Symbols in Action.* Cambridge University Press, Cambridge.

1983. Archaeology, Ideology and Contemporary Society. *Royal Anthropological Institute News* 56:6–7.

1984a. Archaeology in 1984. *Antiquity* 58:25–32.

1984b. Burials, Houses, Women and Men in the European Neolithic. In *Ideology, Power, and Prehistory,* edited by D. Miller and C. Tilley, pp. 51–68. Cambridge University Press, Cambridge.

1985. Post-processual Archaeology. In *Advances in Archaeological Method and Theory,* vol. 8, edited by M.B. Schiffer, pp. 1–25. Academic Press, New York.

1986. *Reading the Past: Current Approaches to Interpretation in Archaeology.* Cambridge University Press, Cambridge.

1991. Interpretive Archaeology and Its Role. *American Antiquity* 56:7–18.

Kehoe, A. 1983. The Shackles of Tradition. In *The Hidden Half: Studies of Plains Indian Women*, edited by P. Albers and B. Medicine, pp. 53–73. University Press of America, Washington, D.C.

Kelley, J., and M. Hanen 1992. Gender and Archaeological Knowledge. In *Metaarchaeology*, edited by L. Embree. Boston Studies in Philosophy of Science. Reidel, Holland, in press. Ms. 1991.

Knorr, K., and M. Mulkay (editors) 1983. *Science Observed: Perspectives on the Social Study of Science*. Sage Publications. London.

Kosso, P. 1988. Dimensions of Observability. *British Journal of Philosophy of Science* 39:449–467.

1989. Science and Objectivity. *Journal of Philosophy* 86:245–257.

Kramer, C., and M. Stark 1988. The Status of Women in Archaeology. *American Anthropological Association Newsletter* 29(9):1, 11–12.

Kuhn, T.S. 1970. *The Structure of Scientific Revolutions*. 2nd ed. University of Chicago Press, Chicago.

Lather, P. 1986. Issues of Validity in Openly Ideological Research: Between a Rock and a Soft Place. *Interchange* 17(4):63–84.

1990 Postmodernism and the Human Sciences. *The Humanist Psychologist* 18:64–83.

Latour, B. 1987. *Science in Action*. Harvard University Press, Cambridge.

Latour, B., and S. Woolgar 1986. *Laboratory Life: The Construction of Scientific Facts*. Princeton University Press, Princeton, New Jersey.

Laudan, L., and J. Leplin 1991. Empirical Equivalence and Underdetermination. *Journal of Philosophy* 88:449–472.

Longino, H.E. 1987. Can There Be a Feminist Science? *Hypatia* 2:51–65.

1990 *Science as Social Knowledge*. Princeton University Press, Princeton, New Jersey.

Longino, H.E., and R. Doell 1983. Body, Bias, and Behavior: A Comparative Analysis of Reasoning in Two Areas of Biological Science. *Signs* 9:206–227.

Mack, R. 1990. Reading the Archaeology of the Female Body. *Qui Parle* 4:79–97.

Miller, D., and C. Tilley (editors) 1984. *Ideology, Power, and Prehistory*. Cambridge University Press, Cambridge.

Miller, R. 1987. *Fact and Method: Explanation, Confirmation and Reality in the Natural and Social Sciences*. Princeton University Press, Princeton, New Jersey.

Moore, H.L. 1988. *Feminism and Anthropology*. Polity Press, Cambridge.

Mukhopadhyay, C.C., and P. J. Higgins 1988. Anthropological Studies of Women's Status Revisited: 1977–1987. *Annual Review of Anthtropology* 17:461–495.

Newton–Smith, W.H. 1981. *The Rationality of Science*. Cambridge University Press, Cambridge.

Pickering, A. 1984. *Constructing Quarks: A Sociological History of Particle Physics*. Edinburgh University Press, Edinburgh.

1987. Essay Review: Forms of Life: Science, Contingency and Harry Collins. *British Journal for the History of Science* 20:213–221.

1989. Living in the Material World: On Realism and Experimental Practice. *The Uses of Experiment: Studies in the Natural Sciences*, edited by D. Goodings, T. Pinch, and S. Schaffer, pp. 275–297. Cambridge University Press, Cambridge.

Prentice, G. 1986. Origins of Plant Domestication in the Eastern United States: Promoting the Individual in Archaeological Theory. *Southeastern Archaeology* 5:103–119.

Renfrew, C. 1982. Explanation Revisited. In *Theory and Explanation in Archaeology*, edited by C. Renfrew, M.J. Rowlands, and B.A. Segraves, pp. 5–23. Academic Press, New York.

1989. Comments on Archaeology Into the 1990s. *Norwegian Archaeological Review* 22(1):33–41.

Rosaldo, M.Z., and L. Lamphere (editors) 1974. *Women, Culture, and Society*. Stanford University Press, Stanford.

Rudner, R. 1966. *Philosophy of the Social Sciences*. Prentice Hall, Englewood Cliffs, New Jersey.

Shanks, M., and C. Tilley 1987a. *Re-constructing Archaeology*. Cambridge University Press, Cambridge.

　　1987b. *Social Theory and Archaeology*. Polity Press, Cambridge.

　　1989. Archaeology Into the 1990s; Questions Rather Than Answers. Reply to Comments on Archaeology Into the 1990s. *Norwegian Archaeological Review* 22(1):1–14, 42–54. (With comments, pp. 15–41.)

Shapere, D. 1985. The Concept of Observation in Science and Philosophy. *Philosophy of Science* 49:485–525.

Smith, B.D. 1987. The Independent Domestication of the Indigenous Seed-Bearing Plants in Eastern North America. In *Emergent Horticultural Economies of the Eastern Woodlands*, edited by W. Keegan, pp. 3–47. Occasional Paper No. 7. Center for Archaeological Investigations, Southern Illinois University, Carbondale.

Spector, J.D. 1983. Male/Female Task Differentiation Among the Hidatsa: Toward the Development of an Archaeological Approach to the Study of Gender. In *The Hidden Half: Studies of Plains Indian Women*, edited by P. Albers and B. Medicine, pp. 77–99. University Press of America, Washington, D.C.

Suppe, F. 1977. *The Structure of Scientific Theories*. 2nd ed. University of Illinois Press, Urbana.

Trigger, B.G. 1989. Hyperrelativism, Responsibility, and the Social Sciences. *Canadian Review of Sociology and Anthropology* 26:776–797.

Tringham, R.E. 1991. Households with Faces: The Challenge of Gender in Prehistoric Architectural Remains. In *Engendering Archaeology: Women and Prehistory*, edited by J.M. Gero and M.W. Conkey, pp. 93–131. Basil Blackwell, Oxford.

Walde, D., and N. Willows (editors) 1991. *The Archaeology of Gender*, Proceedings of the 22nd Annual Chacmool Conference. The Archaeological Association of the University of Calgary, Calgary, in press.

Watson, P.J., and M. Fotiadis 1990. The Razor's Edge: Symbolic-Structuralist Archaeology and the Expansion of Archaeological Inference. *American Anthropologist* 92:613–629.

Watson, P.J., and M.C. Kennedy 1991. The Development of Horticulture in the Eastern Woodlands of North America: Women's Role. In *Engendering Archaeology: Women and Prehistory*, edited by J.M. Gero and M.W. Conkey, pp. 255–275. Basil Blackwell, Oxford.

Watson, R.A. 1990. Ozymandias, King of Kings: Postprocessual Radical Archaeology as Critique. *American Antiquity* 55: 673–689.

Weitzenfeld, J.S. 1984. Valid Reasoning by Analogy. *Philosophy of Science* 51:137–149.

Wildeson, L.E. 1980. The Status of Women in Archaeology: Results of a Preliminary Survey. *American Anthropological Association Newsletter* 21(5):5–8.

Woolgar, S. 1983. Irony in the Social Study of Science. In *Science Observed: Perspectives on the Social Study of Science*, pp. 239–266. Sage Publications, London.

Wylie, A. 1985. The Reaction Against Analogy. In *Advances in Archaeological Method and Theory*, vol. 8, edited by M.B. Schiffer, pp. 63–111. Academic Press, New York.

　　1987. The Philosophy of Ambivalence: Sandra Harding on *The Science Question in Feminism*. *Canadian Journal of Philosophy* (supplementary volume) 13:59–73.

　　1988. "Simple" Analogy and the Role of Relevance Assumptions: Implications of Archaeological Practice. *International Studies in the Philosophy of Science* 2(2):134–150.

　　1989a. Matters of Fact and Matters of Interest. In *Archaeological Approaches to Cultural Identity*, edited by S. Shennan, pp. 94–109. Unwin Hyman, London.

1989b. Archaeological Cables and Tacking: The Implications of Practice for Bernstein's "Options Beyond Objectivism and Relativism." *Philosophy of the Social Sciences* 19:1–18.

1990. The Philosophy of Archaeology: Varieties of Evidence. Paper presented at the Annual Meeting of the American Philosophical Association Meetings, Eastern Division, Boston.

1991a. Gender Theory and the Archaeological Record: Why Is There No Archaeology of Gender? In *Engendering Archaeology: Women and Prehistory*, edited by J.M. Gero and M.W. Conkey, pp. 31–54. Basil Blackwell, Oxford.

1991b. Beyond Objectivism and Relativism: Feminist Critiques and Archaeological Challenges. In *The Archaeology of Gender*, Proceedings of the 22nd Annual Chacmool Conference, edited by D. Walde and N. Willows. The Archaeological Association of the University of Calgary, in press.

1991c. Reasoning About Ourselves: Feminist Methodology in the Social Sciences. In *Women and Reason*, edited by E. Harvey and K. Okruhlik. University of Michigan Press, Ann Arbor, Michigan, in press.

1992. On "Heavily Decomposing Red Herrings": Scientific Method in Archaeology and the Ladening of Evidence with Theory. In *Metaarchaeology*, edited by L. Embree, Boston Studies in the Philosophy of Science, Reidel, Holland, in press. Ms. 1991.

17

Gender, Space, and Food in Prehistory

Christine A. Hastorf

Introduction

If we take "gender" to mean socially constructed male and female categories, can we study gender relations in the archaeological record? Can studies of food systems and how people interact via the food they eat and discard lead us to new understandings of how human social relations operated in past cultures? Many scholars have proposed that there is a direct relationship between food systems and social relations, just as economic relations are part of food production (Bourdieu 1979; Douglas 1984; Mead 1943; Sahlins 1972). I propose that since the use and distribution of food can express political, social, and economic relations as well as nutrition, it also expresses the development and maintenance of gender relations in the past. To initiate this pilot study, I present several archaeological approaches that link food and culture.

While paleoethnobotanical data should be able to be linked to women's activities in the past with sufficient supporting evidence, it has rarely been used to discuss women's or men's roles in past societies. Plant remains are often considered a poor data set and therefore not important in most archaeological investigations. This might be related to the current, unspoken assumption that women's activities are commonly linked to plants and cooking and therefore are not of importance in the study of "larger" issues. Although the ethnographic literature often shows women playing some role in these domains, these activities are not always women's work. No matter whose domain the kitchen is, however, the expression of relations between men and women necesssarily operate wherever food is produced, prepared, served, or disposed. The study of food remains should inform us about the development and maintenance of gender relations which, in turn, should improve our interpretation of food deposits.

To find interpretable links between foods systems and social relations I begin by examining some ethnographic relationships between food and gender in the realms of economics as well as politics. I then focus on interpretations of food and diet in the archaeological record with special reference to paleoethnobotanical data. Here I propose two complementary approaches. First I explore spatial distributions of food deposited and/or stored as they reveal the roles of men and women through the use of space. I assume that food remains can, in their spatial distribution, portray aspects of social relations within the residential house (Ardener 1981: 12). In the second approach I look at dietary intake of males and females to understand how access to different foods might signify different social positions. Both approaches are illustrated using botanical distributions in domestic compounds and burial data for the Sausa, a group in the central Andes of Peru.

Studies of gender in the prehistoric record have concentrated on female burials that can be sexed, on female imagery in paintings or figures (Gibbs 1987; Pollock, this volume), on artifactual associations and ethnographic analogies (Marshall 1985), or on spatial patterning of gender associated activity areas (from artifacts) in structures (Clarke 1972; Flannery and Winter 1976). Gender identification in material distribution is one of the challenging goals for archaeological research, for the data must be linked before the meanings of the distributions can be considered or the tasks can be discussed in terms of control and social interaction. Ethno-archaeological studies that describe the contents of domestic areas could be productive in linking gender relations and artifact distributions as long as care is taken in interpretation (Gould 1978; Gnivecki 1987; Kent 1984, 1987; Kramer 1979). Yet almost none of these ethnoarchaeological studies have considered plant deposition let alone gender.

Food and Gender

Gender is created out of more general relations within the family through division of labor, differential access to goods, social negotiation, production, and reproduction. All are created from cultural ideas and cultural symbols that are seen in the use and placement of material items in space within the residential house (Ardener 1981; Bourdieu 1973; Cunningham 1973). Hence, if gender is created in the residence, then food should be a significant medium for determining and maintaining gender relations. Food and eating are central to these processes, as ethnographies about gender and family relations are often about food. Durkheim (1961) and Radcliffe-Brown (1977) note that most social activities center on food, and both functionalists (Malinowski (1961) and structuralists, (Lévi-Strauss 1988) have written about the importance of food, its categorization, and preparation. Hartmann (1981) suggests that the creation of gender developed out of the division of labor in food production. More than a necessary nutritional requirement to keep living things alive, food is a focus of social interaction for family and community as seen in the many cultural dimensions in which food is central; in food procurement and distribution, in exchange, tribute, as well as in food taboos (Goody 1982). While each food-related activity can be associated with specific implements and activity areas, linking these tasks to a gender is not easy or universal.

In ethnographically documented contexts, women are often reported to be in charge of the preparation and serving of food (Afshar 1985; Friedl 1975). In many cases, women's power surrounds the distribution of food. Because of this, women are regularly associated with hearths, grinding equipment, cooking pots, and processing food (in the New World see Cushing 1920; Hayden and Cannon 1984; Weismantel 1988). They can also regularly be associated with the refuse from cooking, hearth ash, and food rubbish (Hodder 1987; Moore 1986). Female involvement with production and storage, however, is more variable, especially in their control of the means of production and the yields, both *de facto* and *de jure*. It is in just these spatial distributions of production/storage and preparation/disposal that I hope to find social relationships. I am concerned therefore not so much with linking a gender with an activity, as much as gaining evidence of differential control in how the activities are performed.

Material correlates for women's positions in a society may be evident from spatial distributions such as boundedness of work spaces and material deposits (Ardener 1981; Arnold 1989; Kus and Raharijaona n.d.). When women can be linked to artifacts and activities in specific cultural settings, the artifactual distributions may suggest social relationships among members of a residence but also in the greater society. Patterns of artifactual distribution in space perhaps might provide a way to view the daily life of social relations. Let us begin with a few ethnographic examples before focusing on the Andes.

Several studies of societies where women enjoy some degree of economic independence show a pattern of spatially discrete storage of goods. Among the Kofyar of the Nigerian Jos Plateau, for instance, women control all the food they have grown, storing it in their own houses and selling it as they wish (Netting 1969). This is also seen on the coast of Tanzania where Caplan (1984) found that women retain their private property and their own income in marriage. Here, both partners have their own resources which are kept separate, exchanging goods and labor when needed. Women's control over resources gives them power and is reflected materially through controlled and restricted access to storage space.

An example of space, women, and relations, is seen in the ethnographic study among the Marakwet by Henrietta Moore (1986) where she claims that opposing gender interests are manifested in the spatial locations of food preparation, refuse deposition, and food storage. Control and restrictions in these areas defines and provides social meaning for the Marakwet. The female domain of control is restricted within discrete locations of the residence, centered around the hearth and associated with specific food-related objects such as ash and chaff refuse (while animals and animal dung are male). Women are in control of the harvest, the stores, and the provisioning of food, but this constitutes little status or value in the larger society. Women, subordinate to men, are considered dangerous in that they can destroy the social unit and are instructed and constrained in how they dispose of house refuse such as ash from the fire. Moore's study shows how the spatial distribution of objects in the home is the product of as well as constitutes gender relations in that society.

Another approach to gender through food is through investigations of specific foods, their meanings, and their uses over time. Food symbolism and meaning depend on the cultural setting, who prepared the food, how it was prepared, who served it, and what it was served with (Lévi-Strauss 1988). In every society plant foods have specific connotations. Some foods may change meanings by context, while other foods may have a constant meaning throughout all contexts. Specific foods, their uses, and associations communicate, reaffirm, and aid in the construction of the cultural system, acting as a system of signs containing social messages (Barthes 1973). Thus, the meal as a group of food types portrays a set of meanings that the viewer and consumer internalize through repetition. In this way, dietary practices become a collective tradition that maintains and reinforces the culture by the co-occurence of material artifacts. This should allow us to link certain prehistoric food remains with certain meanings.

How can we learn about internal contestation through food use? One avenue is to study the use and restriction of highly symbolic foods. Although Douglas (1966) writes mainly of sexual taboos this can include taboos of food, for hunger and sex are two powerful drives that often become of locus of power and control. Food restrictions circumscribe and maintain boundaries in marginal, dangerous, or socially sensitive arenas, often relating to the act or results of sex (1966: 127). Douglas proposes a dichotomy of cultural dynamics surrounding sex (and food). In cultures where the males have fairly clear control over the social relations and moral codes (including power over the sexuality of women and their marriage), such as among the Walbiri of Central Australia, food and sex taboos tend to be absent (Douglas 1966: 141). Social relationships are controlled directly by the males as subordinate subgroups (females) do not have avenues to contest (Goodale 1971; Hiatt 1965).

On the other hand, in cultures where dominance is contested, Douglas notes that ambiguous and contested power between genders is often translated into food taboos that involve restrictions on specific foods. These groups may have taboos on food consumption, on certain activities (speech), and on timing of sexual activity (abstinence during menstruation), thus delimiting areas of control (e.g. the Enga or Wamira of New Guinea). In this way, women have some control over themselves but it is bounded (Hamilton 1981). If there are gender differences in consumption restrictions we might be able to link them to social contestation. Certain subgroups are constantly at odds with each other and so rules are made (and challenged) in an attempt to maintain control over what is considered important.

Relating food use to contestation between genders, Miriam Kahn (1986) studies gender expression through food consumption amongst the Wamira of New Guinea. She found that food, especially certain highly valued types of food (sea food and oily food), expresses and manipulates social relationships and tensions between men and women. Both food and sex are acknowledged as creative forces for the Wamira and must be controlled to maintain society. One of the fundamental issues that gives Wamira women independence is the power they derive from their creative potential through childbirth. Women gain this position naturally while men must achieve an equivalent procreative power. This power is created and controlled through rituals of masculinization and food restrictions for males and females – but mainly females! (Kahn 1986: 149; Newman 1965). The male procreative rituals revolve around food. Taro for men is analogous to children for women. In producing taro, men claim they gain productive forces like women.

There are a series of food taboos surrounding childbirth for the Wamira. Men who are cultivating taro and women who are pregnant or nursing are not allowed to eat foods that might cause the "fetus" to slip; salty foods (sea food), greasy foods (pork), or coconut cream, all are highly prized foods (Kahn 1986: 116). This of course makes female food restrictions much more extensive then males, as pregnancy lasts for nine months and nursing after birth continues for well over a year, whereas taro cultivation happens only in short spurts, a day or two at a time (Kahn, personal communication). There are different levels of consumption between males and females of these prized foods.

Restrictions of and contradictions in power between the genders are complex and operate on many levels. Yet, with careful study, I hope to begin to infer social negotiations similar to these examples in the archaeological record from spatial distribution of or access to certain food items. Ethnographic studies suggest that we might be able to see different spatial patterning of artifacts, in storage contexts, in food preparation loci (surrounding hearths), in refuse disposal areas, in or near the domestic structures (Bourdieu 1973; Kus and Raharijaona n.d.; Moore 1986; Sikkink 1988; Vogt 1969), and in different diets (Douglas 1966; Kahn 1986). As they change over time we can see shifts in the relative control of space and diet.

We can begin to propose links that exist in many societies between gender relations, spatial distributions, and food taboos. Relating these issues to archaeology, the problem becomes which artifact distributions imply meaningful interpretation of control or contestation? If one assumes that gender is a structuring principle in human life and is reaffirmed through practice (Barthes 1973), the material aspects of gender relations *should* be present in archaeological assemblages.

The Pre-Hispanic Sausa of Peru

Cultural Background

Although there are many relevant studies in Andean society that pertain to women's positions and their social negotiations (Bourque and Warren 1981; Silverblatt 1987; Skar 1981), I briefly mention only a few social traits that I think could be particularly illustrative in a study of pre-Hispanic Andean gender relations. While there are indications that women have not been equal to men in all domains, especially in political realms, there are suggestions that women were not always so subordinated as they are today.

Today dual complementarity, a division into two parts, is important in highland life (Bastien 1978; B.J. Isbell 1987). It is tempered by inequality within the division between upper/right/male and, lower/left/female. This symbolically places the woman as the lesser partner, suggesting the female has her own sphere of influence but that it is smaller and less valued than the male. These dualities are present in many aspects of social life seen spatially in communities and village plans (Bastien 1978; Skar 1981). In some regions, females pass on land-use rights or animals to their female children, and men do the same to male children. This bilateral inheritance and parallel descent gives autonomy to women within their household, as both males and females gain their own resources and membership in their same-sex parent's *ayllu* (Arnold 1989; Zuidema 1973, 1977: 240). It is through this connection to the *ayllu*, political units with territory control, that each individual holds rights to the means of production.

Andean society is clearly gendered, but it is also dependently reciprocal. This is so in domestic as well as cosmological realms. There is a sexual division of labor in the household but it is flexible (Harris 1982). Different people completing tasks lead to different valuation of the tasks. For many agricultural tasks, men and women work together, often completing the same activities. On the other hand, there are also some clearly gendered aspects to agriculture, that reflect differential control. Today, women are in charge of the seeds and the planting of the seeds. Men, on the other hand, must plow. In some areas, women are in charge of processing and storing the harvest, thus they have control over the produce for consumption and sale (Arnold 1989; S. Radcliffe, personal communication; Skar 1981: 41). Andean women make decisions about the kitchen and the storage areas, located in the roofed structures off the patios. Ethnohistoric documents mention tasks that are associated with highland women (Cobo 1964; Garcilaso 1960; Murra 1980; Moria 1946). These include weaving, spinning, cooking, brewing *chicha* (maize beer), planting seeds, child rearing, hoeing, weeding, and carrying water (Arriaga 1968: 33–5; Cobo 1964; Garcilaso 1960; Guaman Poma 1956).

There is little information about the wider network of women. Women are known to be curers as well as traders who travel (G. Delgado, personal communication). Today they are often sellers in the local markets, though these did not exist before the conquest. Women have close contact with their kin group and members of their *ayllu*, rarely moving far from their family's home with marriage. Today they rarely hold political office. There are hints in the ethnohistoric documents, however, that Andean women occasionally held political positions during Inka times (Espinoza Soriano 1978: 338; Oberem 1968). Perhaps the choosing of local leaders (*curacas)* from certain lineages resulted in the occasional circumstances where a woman was the next person in line. Silverblatt (1987: 19) comments that the scant evidence of female political leaders in the documents may be because the Spanish chroniclers did not recognize the female leaders.

Males have discrete tasks as well: plowing, loading the pack animals, and organizing transports of the crop to the house. During Inka times, men were obliged to be warriors and complete state *mit'a* labor away from their homes (Guaman Poma 1956). Today, once married, men are responsible for the household labor tax owed to the community (*faena*), they often are the traders, hold the community political offices, and leave periodically for work (B.J. Isbell 1978; Skar 1982). And, so, highland men operate more in the sphere outside the home than women.

As Silverblatt (1987) has suggested, the social restructuring that began with the Inka conquest was amplified by the Spanish, diminishing the social position of women in Andean society. What we see today is that Andean women exercize their power and influence from within the household, over familial issues.[1] Has the social position of women altered over time and can we track it?

The pre-Hispanic data

The material used in this study comes from the intermontane central Andes, where the Upper Mantaro Archaeological Research Project (UMARP) has been investigating the pre-Hispanic Sausa, a subgroup of the Wanka (Earle et al. 1980, 1987; Hastorf et al. 1989). The Sausa's ancestors have been residing for several thousand years in an area of the northern part of the intermontane Mantaro Valley where there is an array of indigenous crops that are produced including maize (*Zea mays*), Andea tubers (potato *Solanum tuberosum*, oca *Oxalis tuberosa*, ulluco *Ullucus tuberosus*, and mashua *Tropeaolum tuberosum*), quinona (*Chenopodium quinoa*), and legumes (tarhui *Lufinus mutabilis* and beans *Phaseolus vulgaris*). Of particular note are the many historic and modern references that describe the sacred and ritual importance of maize (Rowe 1946; Murra 1960; Rostworowski 1977:240; Morris 1978). Maize is often converted into beer (*chicha*) and is consumed at all ritual, political, and social meetings (Skar 1981). We know that the Inka focused much of their agricultural work projects on increasing maize production (Murra 1982). Potatoes, the other highland staple, although an important component in the Andean diet, do not have the symbolic value of maize. The other crops are vegetable-like and supplement these two staples.

We have excavated domestic compounds dating back to at least the Early Intermediate Period (AD 200–600). These pre-Hispanic compounds are composed of one or more circular structures entering onto a curved walled courtyard area. The walls and internal divisions throughout all eras suggest that residents desired to divide their space into different units where different activities could occur. Ethnographic and archaeological evidence indicates that the range of domestic activities in the compounds has continued to be the same.

Much of our research has focused on the later pre-Hispanic record, just before the Inka, Wanka II (AD 1300–1460) and during Inka control, Wanka III (AD 1460–1532). In Wanka II times the local population seemed to have been organized into politically differentiated groups numbering in the thousands. This organization is inferred from the settlement pattern, artifact distribution, and agricultural

---

[1] Although the use of the concept household has been correctly criticized in many parts of the world (Moore 1988: 54), it actually works quite well in the Andes for the working unit based in a residential compound, as community work is organized by household.

systems at large centers and small associated satellites (LeBlanc 1981; Hastorf 1990a).

In the Wanka III times, the Sausa society was transformed through imperial conquest and incorporation into the Inka state (D'Altroy 1981, 1987; D'Altroy and Earle 1985; Espinoza Soriano 1971; Murra 1980). As part of this transformation the population returned to small valley settlements. We know that the Inka restricted access to some goods such as silver, while influencing crop production and consumption of some crops (Hastorf 1990b). What were the dynamics of social relations in the Wanka II and the Wanka III home? Was there a differential impact on men and women with the Inka arrival? How did women's social position change?

The spatial distribution of artifacts

This is an application of the idea that artifact distributions, reflecting processing, consumption, and disposal, either at refuse dumps or in activity areas, are linked to gender relations. From a modern household study in the central Andes, we learn that certain locations are used in specific ways by individuals while other multipurpose zones can be used by any member of the household such as "ungendered" patio areas (Sikkink 1988). Some tasks concentrate in specific locations indoors; cooking, eating, storage, ritual offerings, and sleeping, while others occur anywhere, such as tool production, mending, and processing. The artifactual evidence supports this behavioral evidence, although it is not a simple relationship. The plant distributions collected by Sikkink are patterned. Charred seeds are less dense where many different activities occurred, in the patios and in outer walled enclosures, with more charred material deposited in the more specialized activity areas such as the kitchen and the storage areas, both of which today are located inside the structures or the refuse-compost piles in the walled patios. Taxa diversity is greatest in the kitchen, with charred food remains most highly concentrated in the cooking areas, it is less dense in the storage areas (Lennstrom and Hastorf forthcoming). From what we know about the Andean house, women are closely connected with food preparation and storage. These "female" activities are directly reflected in botanical data, hearth, food processing, and storage locations.

We cannot infer too much from Sikkink's three households with respect to gender relations, but it is intriguing to note that the one household with a female head had crop seeds more frequently in patio locations as well as inside her kitchen structure. It is possible, given the type of relationships between food and gender discussed above, that this family has less need to control the preparation and deposition of food because there is no contestation between genders, with no male head of the household. So, one might propose in the Andes that restricted crop distributions reflect more constraints on female activities, while less restrictions on the distributions would suggest less social (gendered?) pressure to contain crops to specific activity areas.

To initiate a study of the distribution of plant remains and how the use of space informs us about gender, I present paleoethnobotanical data from two pre-Hispanic compounds. I assume that paleoethnobotanical data in general reflects production rather than consumption (Dennell 1976). The Wanka II compound, J7 = 2, is from the 25 ha single occupation knolltop site of Tunánmarca. The Wanka III compound, J54 = 2, is from the 33 ha site of Marca some 4 km from Tunánmarca on a lower hilltop (Earle et al. 1987). These compounds were chosen because they are well preserved, have evidence of domestic occupation, are well dated, and much of each compound has been excavated. Both compounds display evidence of single occupation, with two floors in only one structure at J7 = 2 (structure 6). J7 = 2 is a large enclosed six-structure compound, centrally located on the site with no evidence of rebuilding over the some 100 years of occupation (Earle et al. 1987: 23). Three structures contained hearths, each with an above average density of food remains and grinding stones. J54 = 2 is smaller with one only well-associated structure and one hearth in the southeastern corner of the patio. The Wanka III occupation would have only been used for approximately 70 years and there is no evidence of rebuilding in this compound.

I plotted the botanical domestic food taxa from all 88 soil samples collected throughout the J7 = 2 compound (figure 17.1 with figure 17.2 displaying the sample number locations) and 68 samples from J54 = 2 (figure 17.3, with figure 17.4 displaying the sample locations; see table 17.1 for raw counts). The charred

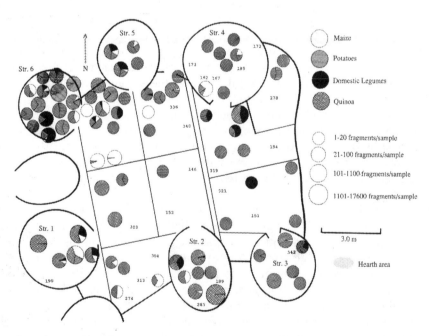

Figure 17.1 [orig. figure 5.1]   Patio J7 = 2 on Tunánmarca with the four adjusted food plant frequencies represented in pie charts. Soil sample locations plotted as pie charts or numbers. Numbers are samples that have no food crops.

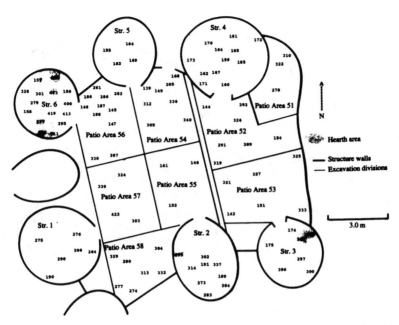

Figure 17.2 [orig. figure 5.2]   Patio J7 = 2 Tunánmarca with soil sample locations plotted by the flotation number.

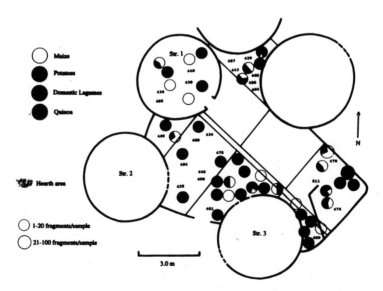

Figure 17.3 [orig. figure 5.3]   Patio J54 = 2 on Marca with the four adjusted food plant frequencies represented in pie charts. Soil sample locations plotted as pie charts or numbers. Numbers are samples that have no food crops.

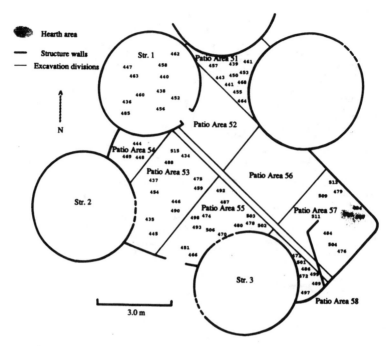

Figure 17.4 [orig. figure 5.4]   Patio J54 = 2 on Marca with soil sample locations plotted by the
flotation number.

plant remains are from point provenienced soil samples that were separated out
by water flotation (see Earle et al. 1987 for a description of the procedure). The pie
charts on figures 17.1 and 17.3 are generated from specimen counts adjusted to a
standardized weight of 6 kg. Samples where there were no botanical remains
have their flotation sample number. The pie diagrams come in four sizes, illustrating increasing densities of the food remains. This provides the relative
presence of the food crops across each compound as well as a picture of their
relative densities. While these pie charts are biased in a number of ways, there
should be little post-depositional effect as each site was abandoned rapidly and
the walls were pushed over, covering the domestic areas and protecting them
from the elements. Each crop has its own rate of deterioration and likelihood of
survival which should be kept in mind when viewing the data (Schiffer 1976). The
soft tissue in tubers degrade most quickly, while maize, legumes, and quinoa are
more durable.

At J7 = 2 in figure 17.1 the density of charred plants is much higher and more
diverse in the structures than in the patio areas (larger pie diagrams). This is the
pattern for the charred remains in modern household examples (Sikkink 1988).
This pattern can be partially explained by the hearth locations, found only in the
structures. In the patios, rubbish-compost piles, processing, and industrial activity

Table 17.1 [orig. table 5.1]   Charred agricultural product counts from J7=2 and J54=2 by flotation sample number. Counts made from 6 kgs of soil per sample.

No.	Maize	Potato	Quinoa	Legumes	No.	Maize	Potato	Quinoa	Legumes
139	0	0	14	1	264	7	2	25	14
142	0	0	2	0	273	2	0	29	0
144	0	5	0	3	274	0	0	0	0
145	0	0	4	3	275	0	0	133	1
146	0	0	0	0	276	13	2	56	24
147	0	0	1	0	277	1	0	1	0
148	1	0	0	0	278	0	0	0	0
149	0	1	2	0	279	0	25	10	0
151	0	0	0	0	280	0	0	1	0
152	0	0	0	0	281	0	0	10	0
154	0	0	0	0	282	0	0	12	0
155	3	4	10	6	283	0	0	0	0
156	1	50	4	0	284	2	90	17465	0
157	0	14	2	0	285	2	4	45	0
158	0	9	2	0	286	1	29	9	0
159	0	0	7	0	287	225	0	5	0
160	0	0	1	0	288	41	21	45	1
161	0	4	0	0	289	0	0	3	0
162	0	0	0	0	290	3	0	33	2
164	0	3	0	0	291	0	0	3	0
165	1	1	3	0	292	0	0	48	37
167	0	0	0	0	295	0	9	14	0
168	0	0	2	0	297	0	0	2	0
169	0	0	1	0	298	2	112	96	39
170	0	0	2	0	299	0	0	19	9
171	48	5	13	0	300	0	0	1	0
172	0	0	0	0	301	2	5	8	3
173	0	0	0	0	302	0	6	51	2
174	1	0	22	0	303	0	0	0	0
175	0	2	14	0	304	0	0	0	0
177	0	4	1	0	305	0	0	1	0
181	0	0	5	0	307	0	0	3	13
182	4	15	26	24	310	0	0	1	0
184	1	2	5	0	311	2	1	12	37
185	0	0	0	0	312	1	0	0	0
186	0	0	12	0	313	0	0	0	0
187	21	10	18	3	314	2	0	3	0
188	1	4	2	1	319	0	0	0	0
189	0	0	0	0	321	0	0	0	0
190	0	0	0	0	322	0	7	5	0

No.	Maize	Potato	Quinoa	Legumes	No.	Maize	Potato	Quinoa	Legumes
324	0	1	2	0	456	12	0	0	0
325	0	0	13	0	457	0	0	0	0
326	0	1	3	6	458	1	0	0	0
327	0	0	0	3	459	0	1	2	2
328	3	1	3	0	460	5	0	0	0
329	2	0	9	0	461	1	0	2	5
330	65	2	3	0	462	0	3	1	0
332	2	0	1	0	463	0	1	1	1
333	0	0	3	0	464	0	0	0	0
336	0	0	0	0	466	1	2	16	0
337	0	0	14	0	468	0	0	0	0
339	0	0	38	0	469	0	0	0	0
340	0	0	0	0	470	0	0	2	0
342	0	0	0	0	471	3	0	0	0
396	0	0	22	0	472	0	0	4	0
400	2	5	24	1	474	2	0	2	0
407	0	0	7	2	475	0	0	0	0
413	2	0	3	0	476	0	0	0	0
419	0	37	32	1	478	0	0	2	0
422	0	0	20	0	479	0	0	0	0
423	1	989	79	1	480	1	0	2	2
					484	1	0	4	0
					485	0	0	0	0
		J54=2			486	0	0	1	0
					487	0	0	5	0
434	0	0	0	0	488	0	0	0	0
435	0	0	0	0	489	0	0	0	0
436	0	0	0	0	490	0	0	0	0
437	0	0	1	0	492	0	0	1	0
438	0	0	0	0	493	0	0	1	0
439	0	0	0	0	494	0	0	36	0
440	0	0	0	0	497	0	0	3	0
441	1	1	1	0	498	0	0	2	0
443	0	0	0	0	499	3	0	0	0
444	0	0	2	1	500	0	0	5	3
445	0	0	1	0	501	0	0	2	0
446	0	0	0	0	502	3	0	0	3
447	3	1	1	0	503	1	0	0	0
448	10	1	0	3	504	2	0	3	0
450	2	1	1	0	506	1	0	0	0
451	0	0	0	0	507	0	0	5	0
452	0	0	2	1	509	4	2	1	0
453	0	0	1	0	511	0	0	0	0
454	0	0	0	0	512	18	0	1	6
455	0	0	0	0	515	0	0	9	0

waste could have been burned, but it would have occurred more sporadically since no discrete hearths were found in the patio.

Dense and diverse food clusters in the J7 = 2 structures suggest that the houses were zones of use, storage, and deposition. This is seen in the higher tuber presence in structures 5 and 6, with more of everything in structure 1. The plant, artifact, and human bone deposits in structure 1 are jumbled up, suggesting that it might have been a dump or compost area (Kadane and Hastorf 1988). Hearths in structures 2, 3, and 6 each have an above average density of food remains and grinding stones (Earle et al. 1987). Structure 4 has the least amount of charred food and other plant matter with no hearth, but it does have a lot of animal dung (presumably used for fuel). Based on an array of artifactual data from the structures, I infer that the structures were used primarily for cooking, eating, sleeping, food and fuel storage, and some refuse, especially ash disposal, today retained for fertilizer (Earle et al. 1987: 23–4). This makes structures the likely candidates for womens' domains. I conclude then that at least four of these structures would have been primarily a female domain.

The densities in figure 17.1 show that the botanical taxa are not evenly distributed throughout the patio as there are some dense clusters in individual locations. Yet crops are found in 77 per cent of the patio samples. Samples without crops predominate in the center of the patio where more foot traffic would occur (identified by sample numbers). Plant food remains occur throughout the patio. With more tubers in the north and more maize in the west, crops seemed to spill out from the structures, as the densest crops cluster outside of structures 4, 5, and 6, and at the compound entrance. Maize tends to be found in the patio area. Because maize is such a special and sacred crop and is relatively uncommon in this cultural phase (Hastorf 1990b), the maize in the patio suggests group efforts at food processing (such as beer production) and/or group consumption.

The patio data suggest that the space was used for many different activities including tool manufacture, processing, preparation, metal production, and midden deposits, but not for everyday cooking and food storing. It is along the patio walls where most of the lithics and ceramics were found. While this area is multipurpose, women's activities are present as crop processing remains are scattered throughout the patio.

Looking at the next phase illustrated by J54 = 2, figure 17.3 displays a slightly different picture. First of all, the plant diversities and densities are lower. Despite regular sampling, the one structure definitely in the compound did not yield many plant remains, as only 63 per cent of the samples contained crops. Unlike the samples in the J7 = 2 structures, these samples are not very mixed but contain pure plant taxa with an unusual dominance of maize, as three of the samples are 100 per cent maize.

The pie diagrams show more maize in this Wanka III compound than is present in the Wanka II compound, especially in the one structure. There are however almost no potatoes, the Andean staple. Relative to the earlier compound, this gives us a sense of more maize processing and of concentrated activities with little burning in the structure. It is very possible also that the most common form of maize consumption is as beer.

In the J54=2 patio, there is also a very low density of plant matter scattered across the compound, with the greatest densities in the corners of the patio, near the compound entrance, and in the walled-off corner where the hearth is. The hearth area in the patio suggests that the occupants were cramped for discrete activity zones, creating a makeshift structure in the corner for food preparation and eating. Again, there are no potatoes in this walled-in zone. In general, the patio crop remains seem restricted in clusters up against the compound walls. Only 57 per cent of the patio samples contained crop remains in contrast to 77 per cent of the Wanka II patio samples. While this is only one example from each phase, it begins to suggest that there was more restriction in crop deposition in this Wanka III patio when compared to the Wanka II patio distributions.

Using Sikkink's (1988) modern study as a comparison, one would expect charred food plants in the cooking area, the processing area, and the compost/ash dump areas; other activity area or generalized space should not yield as many crop remains. Clustered remains might suggest a more designated use of space or more regular/intensive activity. Food remains commonly scattered throughout a residence suggests that it might not have been important to keep the burned hearth and refuse remains in discrete locations.

The dense pre-Hispanic botanical distributions around the hearths and ash pits links the greatest amount of charred crop remains to the female domain. Crop plant refuse is not restricted to these areas however, as it is distributed both within all structures and throughout the patio, though this is more evident in the Wanka II patio. This lack of discrete spatial deposition in the J7=2 patio and structures (see especially structure 1 at J7=2 as constrasted with structure 1 at J54=2) might suggest less strain between individuals or genders during that time when compared to the Wanka III patio. If we assume that an increase in control over the daily household activities is tied to more constraints on individuals, including women, this relationship might have been changing during the Wanka III times.

Being bold for a moment and perhaps over-interpreting this information, I would propose that we might be seeing an increased circumscription of female activities in the Inka phase of Sausa life. In addition dense but restricted Wanka III maize distributions also suggest increased intensification of female processing labor, representing an escalation of women's labor to support social-political activities, which are predominantly male activities.

Access to specific foods

The second approach to gender relations through food investigates food consumption, access, and meaning. Food communicates, reaffirms, and builds a cultural "way of life". In every society plant foods have specific connotations. It is the recurring use of food items and their contexts that gives certain foods meaning, become a collective tradition that maintains and reinforces the cultural order.

Here I look at Sausa food use and meanings through dietary evidence, using stable isotopic[2] analyses of sexed skeletons from the Wanka II and III phases. Stable isotopic analysis, as Murray and Schoeniger (1988) and Price (1989) demonstrate, provides an important method for studying gender and class through dietary differences. Isotope values for individuals reflect a cumulative picture of food consumption.

The consumption data from Wanka II and III human skeletal material are presented as stable carbon and nitrogen isotope delta values, calculated from geochemical procedures (DeNiro 1987; van der Merwe 1982). There are many aspects of biochemical isotopic research that are still in the process of refinement due to the problems of contamination and diagenetic changes in the amino acids from which the isotopes are measured. Tests on the samples completed thus far demonstrate that they are valid (M. DeNiro, personal communication).

The way to interpret isotope values from extracted bone collagen is to plot each sample's delta values in relation to the ideal values for the major food types, illustrated by the boxes in figures 17.5 and 17.6. Each box represents the isotopic values of the biochemical plant group assessed from modern regional plants. The right C4 box reflects the range of stable isotopic values for a pure C4 (maize) diet, ranging between -8.5 to -11.00 parts per mil (thousand). The left C3 box reflects 100 per cent non-leguminous C3 plant (tubers, quinoa) consumption, with a range between -22.00 and -28.00 parts per mil. For the Sausa, the farther right along the horizontal axis the more maize was consumed, the farther left, the less maize and the more tubers and quinoa.

Meat consumption is also reflected in the isotope values. Animals are not as easy as plants to place on an isotopic chart because their diet can vary. Overall, camelids were the dominant animal food source for the pre-Hispanic Sausa (Earle et al. 1987:86; Sandefur 1988). In general, the delta N values below 10.5 parts per mil reflect a terrestrial herbivorous diet, while above 10.5 is a terrestrial carnivorous diet. For the animals in this region, the delta C value reflects grazers towards the C4 end versus browsers towards the C3 values. The camelid (*Llama* spp.) values reflect a mixed herbivorous diet of grazing and browsing with a delta C

---

[2] Isotopes are varieties of elements with different amounts of neutrons. They occur in living systems in different ratios due to different reaction times when the isotope ratios of the products are different from the ratios of the reactants. The two stable isotopes in this study are nitrogen and carbon. Among terrestrial plants, carbon isotopes can separate C4 (tropical grasses), C3, and CAM plants. The nitrogen isotope is more complex, but in terrestrial situations nitrogen isotopes can separate nitrogen-fixing plants (legumes) from non-legumes, as well as identifying 3 to 4 parts per mil enrichment up the food chain (Schoeniger and DeNiro 1984). From experimental data, it has been shown that different plant foods have different isotope ratios (DeNiro and Epstein 1978, 1981; DeNiro and Weiner 1988). Hence, all animals take up the isotopic ratios of the food they consume, making it possible to infer from skeletal collagen, for example, what the average lifelong diet was for the individual under investigation (van de Merwe and Vogel 1977). These isotopic values are notated as delta values in parts per mil (thousand), or as the difference in the amount of 13C isotope to 12C isotope or 15N isotope to 14N isotope. These two isotopic ratios can then be graphed together to show values that correlate to food types.

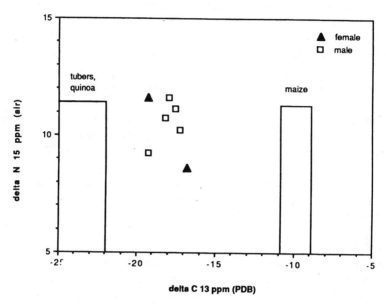

Figure 17.5 [orig. figure 5.5]   Carbon and nitrogen isotopic values for Wanka II adults.

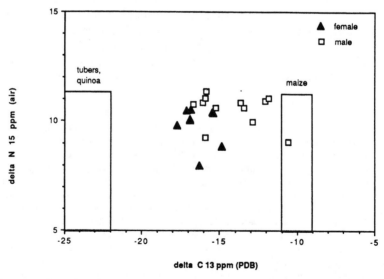

Figure 17.6 [orig. figure 5.6]   Carbon and nitrogen isotopic values for Wanka III adults.

values reflect a mixed herbivorous diet of grazing and browsing with a delta C value around –17 parts per mil. The human isotopic values suggest that animal meat was a portion of the Sausa diet, decreasing slightly the amount of maize consumption.

When we view the isotopic values of the sexed burials from the Wanka II and Wanka III time periods, we see intriguing social and political results. Figure 18.5 presents the Wanka II sexed adult delta values. Unfortunately to date, there are only seven skeletons that could be unquestionably sexed from good Wanka II contexts, two females and five males. This makes the discussion of these data very tentative. The mean male delta C value is -18.03, and the mean female value is –18.01, suggesting no difference between male and female diets in the Wanka II times.

This Wanka II diet parallels the local production data, as one of mainly tubers and quinoa with a lesser amount of maize (Hastorf 1990a). In addition, the isotope data suggest that men and women were *not* consuming plant food differentially, including maize. This is of particular interest because maize is often consumed in the form of *chicha*, the crop of ritual and political gatherings, suggesting that both genders participated equally in ritual, community, and political events though this was done with women's labor (Skar 1981). What was processed seems to have been shared.

With the Inka's entrance into Sausa society, the diets changed. There are 21 human skeletons from good Wanka III contexts (figure 17.6), 9 females and 12 males. One can immediately see the delta C value differences between males and females. Whereas the female population has a mean delta C value of –16.41, the males have a mean value of –14.18. Both have more maize in their diet than before, but 50 percent of the male diets are significantly enriched in maize beyond the female diets. While the female data suggests a diet similar to the Wanka III botanical production data (a fairly even mix of tubers/quinoa, and maize, Hastorf 1990b), the male diet is 1.5 parts per mil enriched in maize. This enrichment suggests that under the Inka hegemony, while the women were producing more *chicha*, it was only certain men in the Sausa community who were consuming more maize outside the house and the community food exchange networks. Additionally, most males also have higher delta N values than females, suggesting increased meat consumption as well. The diets of the two genders were no longer the same. This is of special interest since there is no difference between the two identified economic classes of this time period (Hastorf 1990b).

Differential consumption could have taken place in the home, in the community, or on state business. Supporting evidence suggests that this was stimulated by the Inka's new political organizations, including state work parties as well as increased local political negotiations among the Sausa themselves (D'Altroy and Earle 1985; Murra 1980; Rowe 1982: 110; Salomon 1986). Because there was no unifying regional organization before the Conquest, the Inka had to create one. In particular, Rowe (1982) notes from native testimony that the Inka had to create a regional government for the Wanka (Levillier 1940: 19–20). This suggests that the Sausa were incorporated into the Wanka regional system of political hierarchies based on existing principles like exchange and mutual obligation. This political sphere would have included gatherings, rituals, and obligatory work forces, hence more meat and maize beer consumption for the participants, and more *chicha* production. The isotopic data suggests that this participation was for Sausa men rather than for Sausa women. While the women were working harder producing beer, they did not join in the extra-house political consumption. In this way we again see how the women's position outside the home was more restricted in the Wanka III times.

A hallmark of the Inka state was the obligatory *mit'a* labor tax that generated surplus production. All populations worked periodically for the Inka throughout the year in their home territories (LeVine 1987: 15). Although there is agreement that the taxation was levied on the married male household-head, there is some debate about exactly who completed the labor. For certain specialized tasks like state *chicha* brewing or weaving, women were moved into Inka centers (Morris 1982). The most common *mit'a* services were considered male tasks: agriculture and military service, often taking men away from the home for short periods.

As part of the Andean ethic of exchange, the state institutionalized a symbolic exchange for the *mit'a* work by feeding laborers. One chronicler, Vilca Cuitpa, gives us a typical example of this stating that those who worked for the Inka were fed "meat and maize and cornbeer" (Murra 1982: 256). Therefore it seems that males actually did complete most of what was labelled *mit'a* service, by receiving more maize in their diet. These activities separated the two genders physically, politically, and symbolically.

The symbolism of maize and the differential access to it seem to have played an important role in the construction of gender during the period of the Inka state. Through maize we see how women became the focus of tensions as they produced more beer while at the same time they were more restricted in their participation in society. The isotopic and ethnohistoric data also suggest that during Inka rule, the Andean women's political position diminished. This seems to have been initiated not through specific internal politics within the Sausa, but through the newly imposed state political structures. At the same time, the Sausa women probably did not lose their means of domestic production at home. Surely these dynamics altered the gender relations in the Sausa community.

Summary

By studying the shifts in material over time, we can begin to make women and men visible in the archaeological record, albeit in this case it is watching women's political position diminish as they focus on the domestic sphere. From these independent data sets related to food, we can begin to see the change in women's position in an Andean community. Overall, with the entry of the Inka state, women, while maintaining autonomy in some domestic tasks, probably were under more social strain. Interestingly enough, the two approaches complement each other and provide a picture of changing social relations. Exploratory as these examples are, I hope they illustrate a potential for the study of social relations in the archaeological record through the dynamics of food.

Although much is left unexplained in these archaeological examples, I have tried to demonstrate the importance of food in the study of social and gender relations in prehistory and in particular, women in the Andes. Two approaches are proposed, one focusing on the spatial distribution of material within domestic settings and its reflections of interpersonal negotiation and control. The second approach is to look at gender relations through differential access to food. More specifically, I attempted to test the usefulness of these approaches by presenting first, Andean food systems and botanical frequencies within domestic compounds, and second, skeletal evidence for gender differences in diet.

With conscious effort, both ethnographically and archaeologically, I think much can be gained through the study of boundedness and control over things and space, especially viewing changes in spatial distributions over time. Great care must be taken labelling genders with artifacts, activities, and foodstuffs in the archaeological deposits however.

Food systems, in many ways, are the bases of societies, essential to sustenance, division of labor, control, and social symbolism. Despite our archaeological fascination with how people got their food, we must not miss the ability of food to inform us about the equally important cultural dynamics. The use of botanical data has its limitations, but it also has important potential to view social and political relations. Paleoethnobotanical data should not be confined only to what people ate, but should help in investigating broader social and political relationships. My goal in this paper was to try to provide a new perspective from which to study gender in prehistory, using such unlikely data as charred plant remains. In the archaeological examples from Peru, I hope that the connection between food, gender, access, and control has been sufficiently highlighted to attract the attention of other investigators.

Acknowledgements

I would like to thank very much both Joan Gero and Meg Conkey for inviting me to participate in the Women and Gender in Prehistory conference. It was challenging and very exciting. I wish to thank Michael DeNiro for the stable isotope analysis completed at UCLA, and Heidi Lennstrom, along with the members of the Archaeobotany Laboratory at the University of Minnesota, for help in plant analysis and especially the graphics. The field and laboratory research has been supported by the National Science Foundation grants BNS 8203723 and BNS 8451369. Part of the data analysis was completed while a fellow at the Center for the Advanced study in the Behavioral Sciences, with partial support by BNS 8411738. Special thanks goes to the Instituto Nacional de Cultura for allowing us to excavate and study in the Mantaro region and to export the macrobotanical and bone data for these analyses. This paper, being an experiment for me, was helped greatly by the comments discussions, and encouragements of Meg Conkey, Russ Handsman, Ian Hodder, Beth Scott, Janet Spector, and Patty Jo Watson. All of the analysis and conclusions however are my own responsibility. This paper is dedicated to Rosalyn Hoyt who struggled long and hard to gain some control of her life in a man's world.

References

Afshar, Haleh, ed. (1985). *Women, Work, and Ideology in the Third World*. New York: Tavistock.

Ardener, Shirley, ed. (1981). *Women and Space*. London: Croom Helm.

Arnold, Denise (1989). "The House as a Dungheap, the House as Cosmos: The Aymara House in its Social Setting." Lecture at the Centre of Latin American Studies, Cambridge, England (February 2, 1989).

Arriaga, Father Pablo José de (1968). *The Extirpation of Idolatory in Peru* [1621], Tr. L. Clark Keating. Lexington: University of Kentucky Press.

Barthes, Roland (1979). "Toward a Psychosociology of Contemporary Food Consumption." In *Food and Drink in History*, R. Forster and O. Ranum, eds. Baltimore: Johns Hopkins University Press.

Bastien, Joseph W. (1978). *Mountain of the Condor*. Prospect Heights, IL: Waveland Press.

Bourdieu, Pierre (1973). "The Berber House." In *Rules and meanings*, M. Douglas, ed. Harmondsworth: Penguin Books, 98–110.

   (1979) *La distinction, critique social de jugement*. Paris: Éditions de Minuit.

Bourque, Susan C. and Kay Barbara Warren (1981). *Women of the Andes*. Ann Arbor: University of Michigan Press.

Caplan, Patricia (1984). "Cognatic Descent, Islamic Law and Women's Property on the East African Coast." In *Women and Property, Women as Property*, R. Hieschon, ed. London: Croom Helm, 23–43.

Clarke, David L. (1972). "A Provisional Model of an Iron Age Society." In *Models in Archaeology*, D.L. Clarke, ed. London: Methuen, 801–70.

Cobo, Bernabe (1964) *Historia del nuevo mundo* [1653], 2 vols. Madrid: Bibloteca de autores Espanoles.

Cunningham, Clark E. (1973). "Order in the Atoni House." In *Right and left*, R. Needham, ed. Chicago: University of Chicago Press, 204–38.

Cushing, Frank (1920) *Zuni Breadstuff*. Washington: Smithsonian Institution.

D'Altroy, Terence N. (1981). "Empire Growth and Consolidation: the Xauxa Region of Peru under the Incas." Ph.D. dissertation, Department of Anthropology, UCLA. Ann Arbor: University Microfilms.

   (1987). "Transitions in Power: Centralization of Wanka Political Organization under Inka Rule." *Ethnohistory* 34(1): 78–102.

D'Altroy, T.N. and T.K. Earle (1985). Staple Finance, Wealth Finance, and Storage in the Inka Political Economy. *Current Anthropology* 25(2): 187–206.

Dennell, Robin W. (1976). "The Economic Importance of Plant Resources Represented on Archaeological Sites." *Journal of Archaeological Science:* 1: 257–65.

DeNiro, Michael J. (1987). "Stable Isotopy and Archaeology." *American Scientist* 75: 182–91.

DeNiro, M.J. and S. Epstein (1978). "Influence of Diet on the Distribution of Carbon Isotopes in Animals." *Geochimica et Cosmochimica Acta* 42: 495–506.

   (1981). "Influence of Diet on the Distribution of Nitrogen in Animals." *Geochimica et Cosmochimica Acta* 45: 341–51.

DeNiro, M.J. and S. Weiner (1988). Chemical, enzymatic, and spectroscopic characterization of collagen and other organic fractions in prehistoric bones. *Geochimica et Cosmochimica Acta* 52: 2197–2206.

Douglas, Mary (1966). *Purity and Danger: An Analysis of Concepts of Pollution*. New York: Praeger.

   ed. (1984). *Food in the Social Order*. New York: Russell Sage Foundation.

Durkheim, Émile (1961). *The Elementary Forms of the Religious Life* [1912]. New York: Collen Books.

Earle, T.K., T. D'Altroy, C. LeBlanc, C. Hastorf, and T. LeVine (1980). "Changing Settlement Patterns in the Yananmarca Valley, Peru." *Journal of New York Archaeology* 4(1).

Earle, T.K., T. D'Altroy, C. Hastorf, C. Scott, C. Costin, G. Russell, and E. Sandefur (1987). *Archaeological Field Research in the Upper Mantaro, Peru 1982–1983: Investigations of Inka Expansion and Exchange.* Institute of Archaeology, UCLA, Monograph 28.

Espinoza Soriano, Waldemar (1971). "Los huancas, aliados de la conquista." *Anales científicos de la universidad de centro del Peru* 1: 3–407.

(1978). "Dos casos de senorialismo feudal en el imperio Inca." In *Los modos de produccion en el imperio de los Incas,* W. Espinoza Soriano, ed. Lima: Mantaro-Grafital, 329–56.

Flannery, Kent and Marcus Winter (1976). "Analyzing Household Activities." In *The Early Mesoamerican Village,* K. Flannery, ed. New York: Academic Press.

Friedl, Ernestine (1975). *Women and Men: An Anthropologist's View.* New York: Holt, Rinehart & Winston.

Garcilaso de la Vega, "El Inca" (1960). *Commentarios reals de los Incas* [1609], 3 vols. Jose Durand, ed. Lima: Universidad Nacional Mayor de San Marcos.

Gibbs, Liv (1987). "Identifying Gender Representation in the Archaeological Record: A Contextual Study." In *The Archaeology of Contextual Meanings,* I. Hodder, ed. Cambridge: Cambridge University Press, 79–89.

Goodale, Jane (1971). *Tiwi Wives.* Seattle: University of Washington Press.

Goody, Jack (1982). *Cooking, cuisine, and class.* Cambridge University Press.

Gould, R.A., (ed.) (1978). *Explorations in Ethnoarchaeology.* Albuquerque: University of New Mexico Press.

Gnivecki, Perry (1987). "On the Quantitative Derivation of Household Spatial Organization from Archaeological Residues in Ancient Mesopotamia." In *Method and Theory for Activity Area Research,* S. Kent, ed. New York: Columbia University Press, 176–235.

Guaman Poma de Ayala, Felipe (1956–7). *La nueva cronica y buen gobierno* [1613], 3 vols. Tr. into modern Spanish by Luis Bustios Galvez. Lima: Editorial Cultura.

Hamilton, A. (1981). "A Complex Strategical Situation: Gender and Power in Aboriginal Australia." In *Australian Women: Feminist Perspectives.* N. Grieve and P. Grimshaw, eds. Oxford: Oxford University Press, 69–85.

Harris, Olivia (1982). "Labour and Produce in an Ethnic Economy, Northern Potosi, Bolivia." In *Ecology and Exchange in the Andes,* D. Lehmann, ed. Cambridge University Press, 70–96.

Hartmann, Heidi (1981). "The Family as the Locus of Gender, Class, and Political Struggle: The Example of Housework." *Signs* 6(3): 366–94.

Hastorf, Christine A. (1990a). A path to the heights: The negotiation of political inequality. In *Political evolution and the communal mode.* Edited by S. Upham, Cambridge University Press.

(1990b). "The Effect of the Inka State on Sausa Agricultural Production and Crop Consumption." *American Antiquity* 55(2): 262–90.

Hastorf, C., T. Earle, H.E. Wright, L. LeCount, G. Russell, C. Costin, and E. Sandefur (1989). "Settlement Archaeology in the Java Region of Peru: Evidence from the Early Intermediate Period through the Late Intermediate Period: A Report on the 1986 Field Season." *Andean Past* 2: 81–129.

Hayden Brian, and Audrey Cannon (1984). *The Structure of Material Systems: Ethnoarchaeology in the Maya Highlands.* Washington: Society for American Archaeology.

Hiatt, L.R. (1965). *Kinship and Conflict.* Canberra: Australian National University.

Hodder, Ian (1987). "The Meaning of Discard: Ash and Domestic Space in Baringo." In *Method and Theory for Activity Area Research*, S. Kent, ed. New York: Columbus University Press, 424–48.

Isbell, Billie Jean (1978). *To Defend Ourselves*. Austin: Institute of Latin American Studies, University of Texas.

Isbell, William (1978). "Cosmological Order Expressed in Prehistoric Ceremonial Centers." *Actes XII Congrès International des Americanestes* 9: 269-99. Musée de l'Homme, Paris.

Kadane, Joseph B. and Christine A. Hastorf (1988). "Bayesian Paleoethnobotany." In *Bayesian Statistics III*, J. Bernards, M. DeGroot, D.V. Lindley, and A.M.F. Smith, eds. Oxford: Oxford University Press, 243–59.

Kahn, Miriam (1986). *Always Hungry, Never Greedy*. Cambridge: Cambridge University Press.

Kent, Susan (1984). *Analyzing Activity Areas: An Ethnoarchaeological Study of the Use of Space*. Albuquerque: University of New Mexico Press.

(ed.) (1987). *Method and Theory for Activity Area Research*. New York: Columbia University Press.

Kramer, Carol, ed. (1979). *Ethnoarchaeology*. New York: Academic Press.

Kus, Susan and Victor Raharijaona (n.d.). "Domestic Space and the Tenacity of Tradition among some Betsileo of Madagascar." In *Architecture and the Use of Space – An Interdisciplinary Cross-cultural Study*, S. Kent, ed. MS in author's possession.

LeBlanc, Catherine (1981). "Late Prehispanic Huanca Settlement Patterns in the Yanamarca Valley, Peru." Ph.D. dissertation, Department of Anthropology, UCLA. Ann Arbor: University Microfilms.

Lennstrom, H. and C.A. Hastorf (forthcoming). "Homes and Stores: A Botanical Comparison of Inka Storehouses and Contemporary Ethnic Houses." In *Storage in the Inka Empire*, Terry Y. LeVine, ed. University of Oklahoma Press.

Levillier, Roberto (1940). *Don Francisco de Toledo, supremo organizador del Peru: su vida, sub obra (1515–1582), Tomo II, Sus informaciones sobre los Incas (1570-1572)*. Buenos Aires: Espasa-Calpe.

LeVine, Terry Yarov (1987). "Inka Labor Service at the Regional Level: Functional Reality." *Ethnohistory* 34(1): 14–46.

Lévi-Strauss, Claude (1988). *The Origins of Table Manners*. New York: Harper & Row.

Malinowski, Bronislaw (1961). *Argonauts of the western Pacific* [1922]. New York: E.P. Dutton.

Marshall, Yvonne (1985). "Who Made the Lapita Pots? A Case Study in Gender Archaeology." *The Journal of the Polynesian Society* 94(3): 205–33.

Mead, Margaret (1943). *The Problem of Changing Food Habits, 1941–1943*. Washington: National Academy of Sciences, National Research Council, Bulletin 108.

Moore, Henrietta (1986). *Space, Text and Gender*. Cambridge: Cambridge University Press.

(1988). *Feminism and Anthropology*. Cambridge: Polity Press.

Morris, Craig (1978). "The Archaeological Study of Andean Exchange Systems." In *Social Archaeology*, C. Redman et al., eds. New York: Academic Press, 315–27.

(1982). "Infrastructure of Inka Control in the Central Highlands." In *The Inca and Aztec States*, G.A. Collier, R.I. Rosaldo, and J.D. Worth, eds. New York: Academic Press, 153–71.

Moria, Martin de (1946). *Historia del origen y geneologia real de los Incas [1590]*. C. Bayle, ed. Madrid: Consejo superior de investigaciones científicas, Instituto Santo Toribio de Mogrovejo.

Murra, John V. (1960). "Rite and Crop in the Inca State." In *Culture in History*, S. Dimond, ed. New York: Columbia University Press.

(1980). *The Economic Organization of the Inka State*. Ph.D. dissertation, 1955 Greenwich, CT: JAI Press.

(1982). "The Mit'a Obligations of Ethnic Groups to the Inka State." In *The Inca and Aztec States*, G. A. Collier, R. I Rosaldo, and J. D. Wirth, eds. New York: Academic Press, 237–62.

Murray, M. L. and M. J. Schoeniger (1988). "Diet, Status, and Complex Social Structures in Iron Age Central Europe: Some Contributions of Bone Chemistry." In *Tribe and Polity in Prehistoric Europe*, D.B. Gibson and M.N. Gelselowitz, eds. New York: Plenum Press, 155–76.

Netting, Robert McC. (1969). "Women's Weapons: The Politics of Domesticity among the Kofyar." American Anthropologist 71: 1037–45.

Newman, Philip (1965). *Knowing the Gururumba*. New York: Holt, Rinehart & Winston.

Oberem, Udo (1968). "Amerikanistische Angaben aus Dokumenten des 16. Jahrhunderts." *Tribus* 17: 81–92.

Price, T. Douglas ed. (1989). *The Chemistry of Prehistoric Human Bone*. Cambridge University Press.

Radcliffe-Brown, A.R. (1977). *The Social Anthropology of Radcliffe-Brown*, A. Kuper, ed. Boston/London: Routeledge & Kegan Paul.

Rostorowski de Diez Canseco, Maria (1977). *Etnia y sociedad*. Lima: Instituto de Estudios Peruanos.

Rowe, John Howland (1946). "Inca Culture at the Time of the Spanish Conquest." *Handbook of South American Indians*, Bureau of American Ethnology, Bull. 143(2): 183–330.

(1982). "Inca Policies and Institutions Relating to Cultural Unification." In *The Inca and Aztec States*, G.A. Collier, R.I. Rosaldo, and J.D. Wirth, eds. New York: Academic Press, 93–118.

Sahlins, Marshall (1982). *Stone Age Economics*. Chicago: Aldine.

Sandefur, Elsie (1988). "Andean Zooarchaeology: Animal Use and the Inka Conquest of the Upper Mantaro Valley." Ph.D. Dissertation, UCLA, Archaeology Program. Ann Arbor: University Microfilms.

Salomon, Frank (1986). *Native Lords of Quito in the Age of the Incas*. Cambridge: Cambridge University Press.

Schiffer, Michael (1976). *Behavioral Archaeology*. New York: Academic Press.

Schoeniger, M.J. and M.J. DeNiro (1984). "Nitrogen and Carbon Isotopic Composition of Bone Collagen from Marine and Terrestrial Animals." *Geochimica et Cosmochimica Acta* 48: 625–39.

Sikkink, Lynn (1988). "Traditional Crop-processing in Central Andean Households: An Ethnoarchaeological Approach." In *Multidisciplinary Studies in Andean Anthropology*, V. J. Vizthum, ed. Ann Arbor: Michigan Discussions in Anthropology 8, 65–87.

Silverblatt, Irene M. (1987). *Moon, Sun, and Witches*. Princeton: Princeton University Press.

Skar, Harold O. (1982). *The Warm Valley People*. New York: Columbia University Press.

Skar, Sarah L. (1981). "Andean Women and the Concept of Space/time." In *Women and Space*, S. Ardener, ed. London: Croom Helm, 35–49.

van der Merwe, Nick J. (1982). "Carbon isotopes, Photosynthesis, and Archaeology." *American Scientist* 70: 209–15.

van der Merwe, Nick J. and J.C. Vogel (1977). "Isotopic Evidence for Early Maize Cultivation in New York State." *American Antiquity* 42: 238–42.

Vogt, E. Z. (1969). *Zinacantan: A Maya Community in the Highland of Chiapas*. Cambridge, MA: Belknap Press.

Weismantel, Mary (1988). *Food, Gender, and Poverty in the Ecuadorian Andes*. Philadelphia: University of Pennsylvania Press.

484 *Feminist and Gender Archaeologies*

Zuidema, R. Tom (1973). "Kinship and ancestor cult in three Peruvian communities. Hernandes Principe's account of 1622." *Bulletin de l'Institut Français d'Études Andines* 2: 16–33.
(1977). "Inca Kinship." In *Andean Kinship and Marriage*, R. Bolton and E. Mayer, eds. Washington: American Anthropological Association, Special Publ. 7, 240–81.

18

What This Awl Means: Toward a Feminist Archaeology

Janet D. Spector

Introduction

I have been trying to delineate the parameters of an explicitly feminist archaeology since the early 1970s when scholars in socio-cultural anthropology and other fields began new theoretical, historical, and cross-cultural research on gender. This has been a complex task given the continuing evolution of feminist scholarship over the past two decades.

During this time we have increasingly laid bare the full ramifications of the fact that, until very recently, the production and distribution of western, academic knowledge has been dominated almost exclusively by white, western, middle-class men socialized in cultures that systematically discriminate on the basis of gender, race, and class. Early feminist studies documented bias in the treatment of women both as students and workers within academic professions and as subjects of scholarly inquiry.

Critics working across the disciplines demonstrated that the perceptions and experiences of women were too often ignored, trivialized, peripheralized, or stereotyped. Studies about "man" claiming to be gender-inclusive were shown to be gender-specific in that researchers focused disproportionate attention on the experiences, accomplishments, and social lives of men as if they represented all members of a given group (Minnich 1982).

Archaeology has been no exception. Feminist critiques of this field revealed pervasive androcentric bias (Conkey and Spector 1984, Gero 1985, Spector and Whelan 1989). In addition to presenting "man" as the measure, archaeologists all too often project culturally specific, contemporary notions about the roles, positions, activities, and capabilities of men and women onto the groups they study. Such projections implicitly suggest that gender arrangements have been static and unvarying regardless of temporal or cultural contexts.

My first response to this exposure of androcentrism was to try to develop a strategy for studying gender archaeologically. The key questions for me were: precisely how and what can we learn about men and women based on archaeological traces of their activity patterns, social relations and beliefs? What are the material dimensions of gender systems? Which of these might enter and be preserved in the archaeological record? Can contemporary researchers recognize and interpret such indications of gender given the historical and cultural distance between us and the people we study?

Developing methods to study gender archaeologically seemed an essential prerequisite for the systematic revision or replacement of androcentric treatments of the past. By the late 1970s, drawing on feminist scholarship about gender along with approaches in ethnohistory and ethnoarchaeology, I proposed a "task differentiation" framework for the archaeological study of gender (Conkey and Spector 1984: 24–7; Spector 1983). Then, in 1980, I initiated a research project about nineteenth-century Eastern Dakota people living at the Little Rapids site in Minnesota which promised to yield archaeological and related documentary information suitable for actually testing the potential of the task differentiation approach.

As work on this project progressed I again returned to the core issue in feminist criticism: the ramifications of excluding groups from the production and distribution of knowledge. That interest was refueled in 1985 when, for the first time in my 20-year career of research in the Great Lakes region, I began an active collaboration with Indian people on a field project. This experience stimulated me to think more deeply about what it might mean to *do* a more inclusive feminist archaeology. The initial feminist critique exposed androcentrism, argued for the importance of including women both as researchers and as subjects of study, and demonstrated the significance of gender as an analytical category. More recent feminist criticism addresses issues of difference and diversity among women (e.g. by race, class, age) and cautions against universalistic notions of generic "women" and the privileging of experiences and perspectives of white, western women (see Moore 1988: 186–98).

I began to think more concretely about the ramifications of including Indian people in the production of archaeological knowledge about their histories and cultures. How will this affect the ways we set our research agendas, organize field projects, treat archaeological materials? How would their inclusion shape the ways we generate, express and present our understandings of the past or the audiences we write for? In other words, how would an inclusive feminist approach transform the character of archaeological practice beyond incorporating gender as a significant legitimate area of study?

As these issues captured more of my attention and interest, I began to re-orient my thinking about Little Rapids and the way I wanted to portray the people whose cultural landscapes were unearthed at "Inyan ceyake atonwan" (Village at the Rapids), as the site is known in the Dakota language. Through the task differentiation framework I had learned a great deal about nineteenth-century Dakota gender arrangements. The challenge then became to find a way to write about what life was like for the people at Little Rapids. I wanted to keep my focus on women and gender but I also wanted to respond to my increasing awareness about the problematical portrayal of Indians in archaeology, problems I believe are aggravated by conventional norms of writing archaeology.

In this paper I discuss the evolution of my thinking about feminist archaeology as I shifted my attention from methodological issues to a concern with the presentation of archaeological knowledge. The interpretive narrative "What this Awl Means" presented later in this essay, was inspired by a small, inscribed antler awl handle we found in a midden at Little Rapids in 1980. I am certain that this one tool conveyed a great deal of information about the accomplishments of the woman who used it to her nineteenth-century Dakota contemporaries. It became an important material symbol to me as well, long after her death, leading me to unexpected insights about aspects of Dakota gender arrangements and about the depth and the transforming nature of the feminist critique of academic scholarship.

The Task Differentiation Approach to an Archaeology of Gender

When I initiated work at Little Rapids in 1980, I hoped to use the site material and related written records to test the task differentiation approach I'd developed in the mid 1970s to study gender archaeologically (Conkey and Spector 1984, Spector 1983). In designing that approach, I tried to take into account some of the complexities of gender revealed in then current feminist anthropology and the complexities of the archaeological record. Both considerations seemed essential for generating new methods for an archaeology of gender which avoids simplistic projections of present notions about gender into the past.

I thought that the best way to proceed was to examine relationships between material and non-material aspects of gender in known or documented cases where we could learn about gender specific tasks, behaviors, and beliefs *and* their material/spatial dimensions. I emphasized task patterns assuming that these would have definable material dimensions and that the linkages between activities, spaces, and materials would influence the character of archaeological sites of any given group.

Working with a team of graduate and undergraduate research assistants to explore such correlations, I analyzed several different Indian groups as described in selected historical and ethnographic sources. For each group we examined women's and men's activity patterns on a task by task basis focusing on: the social composition of task groups, the frequency, duration, and season of task performance, the environmental and community (or site) location of various tasks, and the artifacts, structures and facilities associated with each task.

We highlighted those particular dimensions of task performance because they seemed to be most directly related to the formation of archaeological sites. In combination they would determine or significantly influence the frequency, variations and spatial distributions of materials, facilities, and/or structures at sites. A multi-dimensional approach also underscores the complexity and potential variability of gendered divisions of labor challenging simplistic and often androcentric notions about activities like hunting, gathering, foraging, farming, and child-rearing. Too often archaeologists treat these as single, indivisible entities rather than multi-task activities which could be organized in varied ways.

I hoped that with sufficient study we would be able to see relationships between people's task differentiation systems described in the written records and their sites. If so, with comparative studies, I thought we could eventually isolate some material regularities or patterns about different types of task systems which then could be identified archaeologically. This would place us in a better methodological position to study gender for undocumented groups living in more remote time periods.

I was encouraged by the results of our initial studies. Though the written records for the groups we examined often were partial and androcentric, the framework did illuminate and help organize detailed, empirical information about men's and women's activity patterns. This enabled us to compare their technical knowledge and skills, mobility patterns, use of resources, equipment, materials and space, and the general tempo of their lives. The volume of data generated through the task differentiation framework helps undermine androcentric stereotypes about "the" sexual division of labor and its consequences.

The approach also reinforces a point made by many feminist scholars but not yet incorporated into archaeology: in order to adequately understand processes like culture change, contact, or conflict we have to engender our analyses. Men and women may experience any of these areas differently, depending at least in part on the character of their task differentiation system.

What I could not do in my initial studies was examine which aspects of a given task system might be expressed archaeologically and which parts would be essentially inaccessible. For that I needed some site specific data and the Little Rapids site seemed appropriate. By 1986, after completing four seasons of fieldwork and six years of archival research, I had assembled a large sample of archaeological and documentary materials of known cultural affiliation and time period. The evidence shows that the portion of Little Rapids we sampled was occupied during the summer months in the 1940s by a community of Wahpeton people, members of one of the seven Dakota "council fires" or divisions.

In 1987 I began to write up the results of my Eastern Dakota task differentiation investigations using Little Rapids as a case study. Although both the ethnohistoric and archaeological records were partial and fragmentary, I had enough information to organize and analyze within the specifications of the task framework.

I started with two sets of data: the Little Rapids site information mapped, sorted, identified, and counted, and the documentary evidence about Eastern Dakota task patterns and other features of their gender system. I had organized the documentary material into a series of tables with titles like: "Gender-Specific Task Inventory: Women/Men"; "Task Seasonality"; "Task Materials: Women/Men"; "Men's and Women's Material Inventory". Though most written accounts were authored by Euro-American men, I also had eyewitness accounts from several women and the books of Dr Charles Eastman, a Wahpeton man who described his childhood experiences in the mid 1800s (Eastman 1971).

The sources were consistent and often quite detailed in their descriptions of the activity patterns of Eastern Dakota men and women, although authors certainly differed in their attitudes about the Dakota system of dividing labor and especially about the volume of work performed by women compared to men (Eastman 1971; Eastman 1853; Pond 1986; Riggs 1893; Schoolcraft 1851-4). Philander Prescott, who was married to a Dakota women, described their division of labor like this:

> *The men hunt a little in summer, go to war, kill an enemy, dance, lounge, sleep, and smoke. The women do everything – nurse, chop wood, and carry it on their backs from a half to a whole mile; hoe the ground for planting, plant, hoe the corn, gather wild fruit, carry the lodge, and in winter cut and carry the poles to pitch it with; clear off the snow, etc., etc.; and the men often sit and look on. (Prescott 1852: 188)*

Early chroniclers repeatedly and in varying tones of approval or disapproval described the strength and "industry" of Dakota women. Given the task system described in historical records, it is likely that most of the materials we recovered at Little Rapids were manufactured, produced and/or used by women. With the exception of actually killing deer, birds, and muskrat – which the men did – women were responsible for most other resource procurement and processing tasks. They planted and tended the corn, made, repaired, and decorated clothing and most artifacts, built and repaired household equipment, structures and facilities. Men quarried catlinite that was used for pipes and other objects, and only men were explicitly associated with the guns, traps, and iron rat spears procured through the fur trade. But the vast majority of goods and equipment made and/or used by the Dakota, regardless of the source of origin (locally produced or acquired through the fur trade), were associated with women. The Little Rapids assemblage undoubtedly reflects this.

At Little Rapids we had recovered evidence of numerous resource procurement, processing and storage activities, signs of manufacturing clothes, tools, ornaments, and ammunition, and some evidence of rituals and housing. By organizing documentary information about men's and women's activity patterns within the specifications of the task differentiation framework, we could link specific elements of the archaeological assemblage to Wahpeton men and women.

Yet as I continued to work with this approach to the Little Rapids materials, at the same time reflecting about my experiences working with descendents of people who had lived at Little Rapids, I became increasingly dissatisfied with the task framework. It had "worked" to organize documentary and archaeological information about gender in an orderly way. But it also inhibited my ability to express what I'd learned through a variety of sources about the Wahpeton men, women, and children who had lived at Little Rapids during a particularly disruptive period of their history when American colonial expansion was rapidly accelerating in Minnesota.

Like other archaeological taxonomic schemes, the task differentiation framework generates distanced, generic, and lifeless descriptions. Working with Dakota people had heightened my awareness of the problematic portrayals of Indian people in archaeological literature. Like earlier nineteenth-century documents, contemporary site reports and monographs typically reinforce Eurocentric stereotypes and images. While the task differentiation framework draws attention to gender it does not alter the way we present knowledge of the past. I wanted to become more attentive to the explicit and implicit images I conveyed in my writing about the Wahpeton people at Little Rapids. I abandoned my case study of task differentiation and began to experiment with a new way of presenting the archaeological and ethnohistoric knowledge I had acquired.

Toward a More Inclusive Feminist Archaeology

After publishing some of the results of the first three field seasons of work at the site (Spector 1985), I realized it was critical for me to involve Dakota people in the project, particularly in light of my feminist criticisms of archaeology. What had become clear to me by then was that the same general problem that afflicted archaeology with respect to women also applied to the situation of Indian people (see Martin 1987, McNickle 1972, Trigger 1980). Their exclusion from the production of academic knowledge about Indian histories and cultures resulted in the same types of distortions and stereotyping as the exclusion of women had in terms of understanding gender historically and cross-culturally. In a fundamental sense, given the role of scholarship in the acculturation process, these exclusions and distortions perpetuate both sexism and racism.

As I started planning in the 1986 field season at Little Rapids, I actively enlisted Dakota participation in the project so that their visions, voices, and perspectives could be incorporated. Fortunately, I met Dr Chris Cavender, an educator and scholar of Dakota history and culture. As it turned out, Chris is related to Mazomani, a Dakota leader who lived at Little Rapids during the early to middle nineteenth century, through his mother, Elsie Cavender. She had been raised by Isabel Roberts, Mazo okiye win, the daughter of Mazomani and Ha-za win. This family connection to the site clearly prompted Chris Cavender's willingness to work with me.

We were able to secure funding for an interdisciplinary, team-taught field program at Little Rapids including myself, Chris, and his aunt, Carolynn Schommer, a Dakota language instructor at the University of Minnesota (as well as Professor Ed Cushing, an ecologist, and Professor Sara Evans, an historian). The field experience that summer was immeasurably enriched and transformed by the participation of Dakota people. Through Chris and Carrie, we met other Dakota people and learned about new sources of information about their history and culture. These experiences and relationships profoundly influenced my appreciation for and understanding of the Eastern Dakota and my decisions about how I wanted to present their past as I wrote about Little Rapids.

After that field experience I became particularly self-conscious about the ways I had learned to write about Indian people, their material culture, and their sites. Though the task differentiation framework had deepened my understanding of gender and how it might be investigated archaeologically, it did not provide an appropriate structure or format for presenting what I'd learned about Dakota men and women.

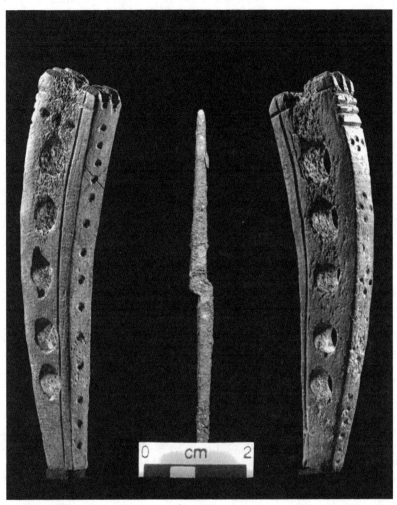

Figure 18.1 [orig. figure 14.1]   A metal tip and two views of the inscribed awl handle from the Little Rapids site.
(Photo by Diane Stölen).

As a way to engage differently with the material, I turned my attention to a small antler awl handle we'd found at Little Rapids in 1980 (figure 18.1). I had been drawn to this small, delicate handle since the day we found it buried 20 cm beneath the ground surface along with deposits of ash, broken and lost artifacts, and the remains of plants and animals. Someone had inscribed it with a series of small dots, several still showing signs of red pigment, incised a series of lines on it, and drilled five holes through it. I wondered why they treated the handle that way and was curious about how it got deposited in the midden, imagining that its owner would have missed it.

I learned how much this one tool might have meant in the context of nineteenth-century Dakota culture when a student working on the project, Sarah Oliver, brought me Royal Hassrick's *The Sioux: Life and Customs of a Warrior Society* (1964). This text provided the key for deciphering the meaning of the inscriptions on the handle.

Hassrick's book is about the nineteenth-century Lakota, a group linguistically and culturally related to the Eastern Dakota. Citing a Lakota woman named Blue Whirlwind as the source for much of his information about women he wrote:

> *In the same way that men kept war records, so did women keep count of their accomplishments. Ambition to excel was real among females. Accomplishments were recorded by means of dots incised along the handles of polished elkhorn scraping tools. The dots on one side were black, on the other red. Each black dot represented a tanned robe; each red dot represented ten hides or one tipi. When a woman had completed one hundred robes or ten tipis, she was privileged to placed an incised circle at the base of the handle of her scraper. (Hassrick 1964: 42)*

Hassrick implies that awls were also important material symbols of women's skills and values. He was told that in the nineteenth century when a girl experienced her first menses

> *. . . she notified her mother, who took her to a separate wigwam or small tipi. Isolated there for four days, the mother would ceremoniously teach her the art of quill embroidery and moccasin-making. As one old person expressed it, "Even though she has learned quilling before, the girl must quill continuously for four days. If she does this she will be good with the awl; if she does not, she will never be industrious." (Hassrick 1964: 41–2)*

Though documentation about Wahpeton women's hideworking tools was not so detailed, I was able to confirm that they were also inscribed to record accomplishments. The practice is briefly mentioned in *Ehanna Woyakapi* a history of the Sisseton-Wahpeton Tribe written by members of that community in South Dakota. In describing elkhorn and wooden handled scrapers, the authors report that "it was a custom to make marks on the handle to show the number of hides and tipis completed" (Black Thunder et al. 1975: 106).

Very soon after learning all of this I abandoned the task analysis and wrote the narrative below, based on the archaeology at Little Rapid's, documentary and oral accounts, my relationships with Mazomani's family, information from the Dakota–English dictionary, and my general impressions from having worked for four summers at the same place that the Wahpeton people had their planting village 150 years earlier. This narrative is not meant to stand alone as an interpretation of life at Little Rapids. Rather, it will be the centerpiece of a book containing descriptions, photographs, and interpretations of site materials, reproductions of Seth Eastman's sketches and paintings (Eastman 1853), and a series of essays. The essays will elaborate and annotate elements in the awl narrative, providing the basis for my inferences or discuss other aspects of Dakota life represented at Little Rapids. Other essays will expand on this discussion of feminist archaeology.

The point of presenting the narrative here is to provide a concrete example of a new way of writing archaeology. It conveys a very different sense of the Little Rapids community and the nineteenth-century historical context than is possible employing more conventional ways of writing.

What This Awl Means

A time of loss one summer day at Little Rapids

The women and children from Inyan cetake atowan (Little Rapids) had been working at the sugar camps since the Moon of Sore Eyes (March), while at the same time, most of the men had been far from the village trapping muskrat. The members of the 12 households that formed the community were glad to be reunited in their bark lodges in the Moon for Planting (May) despite the hard work they now anticipated as they began to replenish their stores of food and other supplies used over the winter months.

One day some of the people brought their finished furs and sugar over to the lodge of the trader Faribault, who lived among them a few months each year with his Dakota wife Pelagee, to exchange for glass beads, silver ornaments, tin kettles, and the iron knives, axes, hatchets, and awls they used for most of their summer tasks. They could tell Faribault was uneasy as he told them the news he'd just heard: that one of the "praying-men" named Riggs planned to visit them soon.

Faribault admired Mazomani (Iron Walker), one of the most prominent men of the community. He knew he was an important leader of the Medicine Dance among the Wahpeton and he knew that Mazomani had already announced a Dance to be held just at the time Riggs was to arrive. Faribault also knew that the missionaries were contemptuous of the Medicine Lodge and found the practices associated with it both imposing and absurd. In hopes of preventing an inevitable conflict between Riggs and Mazomani if the Dance were held as scheduled, he suggested a delay in the Medicine Dance which the elders, after some discussion and deliberation, agree to.

Riggs didn't stay long at Little Rapids. Speaking Dakota as well as he could despite his failure to understand Dakota ways, he asked to speak to the "chief men". Mazomani and several others came forward curious to see what he wanted. They were surprised at how little he knew when he asked to establish a mission there. First, Riggs offered to teach the men how to plow as if they would ever consider such an idea, or if the women would willingly give up their cornfields. They found his ideas about proper men's and women's work amusing and his suggestion of injuring the earth by cutting it with a plow incomprehensible. Then Riggs unknowingly insulted them further by suggesting that he could replace Mazomani as the spiritual leader of the community. They told Riggs to leave, and after only half a day, he and his party left to continue up the Minnesota River looking for another station for their mission, never really understanding why they refused his offers. The next day, Mazomani announced that the Medicine Dance would be held during the Month the Corn was Gathered (August) and the community resumed their summer work without further intrusions by such outsiders.

Ha-za win (Blueberry Woman) and Mazomani were proud of their daughter, Mazo okiye win (One who talks to Iron). One day after visiting Faribault, they brought her a new iron awl tip and some glass beads. Even though she was still young (unmarried), she had already established a reputation among the people at Inyan cetake atonwan for hard work, creativity, and excellence through her skills in quill and bead work.

Her mothers and grandmothers taught her to keep careful record of her accomplishments, so whenever she finished quilling or beading a skin bag or pair of moccasins, she remembered to impress a small dot on the fine antler awl handle Ha-za win had made for her when she first went to dwell alone ("isnati", i.e. at the time of her first menses). When Mazo okiye win completed more laborious work like sewing and decorating buckskin dresses or leggings, she created diamond-shaped clusters of four small dots, one to the north, one south, one east, and one west, a pattern she designed to represent the powers of the four directions which guided her life in so many ways. She liked to expose the handle of this small tool as she carried it in its beaded carrying case so others could see that she was doing her best to ensure the well being of their community.

When she engraved the dots into her awl she carefully marked each with pigment she made by boiling the tops of sumac plants with a small root found in the ground near the village. Red, she knew, was a color associated with women and their life forces. Everyone in her own and other Dakota communities knew the significance of that color: it represented the east where the sun rose giving all knowledge, wisdom, and understanding. It was the appropriate color to symbolize her aspirations toward these highly valued qualities.

One hot day in the Month the Moon Corn is Gathered (August), just after Mazomani had led people in the Medicine Dance near the burial place of her ancestors, Mazo Okiye win gathered together all of the work she'd completed since they had returned to Inyan cetake atonwan after the spring hunt and sugar season. Now, after several months back at their planting village, the women were getting ready to harvest the corn, much of which they would dry and store in the large bark barrels kept underground in storage areas near their lodges for winter use when fresh vegetables were not available. They had already finished making new clothes, bags, moccasins, and tools in anticipation of the fall deer hunt.

Mazo okiye win eagerly anticipated the quilling contest and feast which had been announced by a woman of a neighbouring household to honour a family member who'd just been initiated into the Medicine Lodge. She knew she'd produced more beaded and quilled articles than most of the young women her age and she looked forward to bringing recognition to her parents and grandparents.

The lodge where the contest was held grew hot during the day as the women spread out their articles for others to admire. They stayed inside for shade to avoid the intense heat and sun, but as an impending thunderstorm grew closer, the lodge grew stifling. One of the elders asked Mazo okiye win to bring more water for the women in the lodge. She ran down the slope to the spring near the slough, glad to be out of the heat of the lodge and close to the cool water. She thought of taking a quick swim but the thunder grew closer and soon it started to rain, lightly at first, and then, as it did so often on those hot summer days, the rain fell in great sheets across the village.

She started uphill carrying her "miniapahtapi" (skin bottles for water) carefully and with practiced skill, but near the quilling contest lodge, she slipped on the wet and worn footpath where water had pooled in the driving rain. As she struggled to regain her footing and balance without dropping the water, the leather strap holding her awl in its case broke and the small awl dropped into the grass outside the lodge entrance.

She didn't miss it until the next day because as she entered the lodge with the water, the host of the contest took her hand and escorted her to the center of the crowd. When the host had counted each woman's work, distributing sticks for each piece, Mazo okiye win had accumulated more sticks in front of her work than all but three other women. With them, she was taken to the place of honor in the lodge and as the feast began, these four were given food first to honor them. Later, the results of this contest were recorded with marks representing the women's names and their works on the hides lining the walls of the lodge for all to see. Ha-za win and Mazomani were pleased.

The heavy rainstorm had scattered debris all over the village so the day after the quilling contest and the Medicine Dance, people were called together to clean up their community. They used old hides and baskets to carry loads of fallen branches, wet ash and charcoal from fires, and the remains of the feasts held the previous day to the dump on top of the crest overlooking the slough. Mazo okiye win's awl handle was swept up and carried off with the other garbage from the quilling contest lodge without anyone noticing. It was quickly buried as one basketload after another was emptied into the dump where it rested until it was found 140 years later.

Mazo okiye win and Ha-za win were saddened by the loss of this awl handle. They knew it was nearly worn out and both realized it was more a girl's tool than a woman's. Still, its finely incised dots and engraved lines showed how well Mazo okiye win had learned adult tasks, and she took as much pleasure in displaying it as her mother did watching others admire it. Mazo okiye win intended to keep this awl even though, following Dakota practice, she had already drilled five holes through the handle, symbolically killing it to mark an important transition in her life. She was now a woman ready to establish her own household, no longer a child of her mother's lodge. It was time to put aside her girl-tools.

Both mother and daughter knew that the awl handle was an object of the past, not of the future. But when the handle was lost, it saddened them more deeply than they could explain. One evening as they sorted the last of the harvested corn they laughed together remembering the "prayer-man" Riggs and his ideas about men planting corn. Then for some reason each thought of the antler awl handle and they shared their sadness about its loss. They realized that the feeling of loss they experienced wasn't simply about the small tool. Instead, they discovered each shared a pervasive sense of loss about the past and, even more, they felt troubling premonitions about the future.

Some Other Archaeological Stories about Awls

The discovery of the awl and its meaning allowed me to experiment with a new way of writing archaeology. It gave me a context and vantage point to describe and interpret aspects of Dakota culture and gender in a format I found far more compatible with my archaeological and feminist interests and commitments than any of the usual archaeological modes of writing. Let me illustrate this by showing how I would have described awls from Little Rapids using conventional writing formats in Great Lakes archaeology.

Both Lyle Stone (1974) and Ronald Mason (1986) discovered and described awls and awl handles like those at Little Rapids at historic sites in Michigan and Wisconsin. Had I followed their style, I would have classified and discussed awls along with other, presumably related, artifact types under a heading like "Household Context of Utilization – Maintenance and Repair" (Stone 1974: 155–62). My description of the metal awls' tips might read something like this:

> *A total of 4 metal awls were found during excavations at Little Rapids. The description of awls is based on four attributes: (1) means of attachment of awl to handle, (2) cross-section shape, (3) size as defined by the dimension of length, and (4) material of manufacture. Two levels of taxonomic distinction are based on two of the above attributes: (1) Type which is distinguished by different materials, and (2) Variety which is distinguished by means of attachment.*

TYPES

> *Type 1: Iron*
> *　Variety a: Offset Attachment*
> *　Figure A–3 specimens (see photo); dimensions:*
> *　Length average —; standard deviation —*

and so on until all the metal awls had been described and illustrated. Then, in a section called "Discussion", I might note Stone directly and report that:

> *Although awls have been reported from several other sites . . . this limited evidence does not permit cross-dating. The . . . quantity and . . . spatial distribution of awls indicate that they were commonly used . . . throughout the period of site occupation . . . trade-good lists indicate that awls were an important trade item with the Indians. (Stone 1974: 159)*

Stone does not discuss the bone or antler awl handles shown in a photograph, though like the metal tips they too vary in size, shape and form (Stone 1974: 156).

Mason does allude to awl handles but only obliquely. In one chapter of his Rock Island report he shows photographs of some metal awls, including one hafted in a bone handle. The awl tips are presented in tables entitled: "European Trade Goods and Aboriginal Artifacts Made from Trade Materials" (e.g. Mason 1986: 60–1). He discusses neither the awls nor the handle in the text, although in a paragraph next to the photo he remarks: "It appears that bone and antler tool making survived longer in the native repertoire than pottery making and common flint knapping" (ibid.: 53).

These formats channel our attention as readers in specific ways but without acknowledgement from the authors. Messages pervade the text and authored stories are buried there despite the neutral, value-free, objective-sound language. Unlike my narrative, which I intentionally crafted to reveal things I have found important and interesting about life at Little Rapids, Stone and Mason have conveyed stories about their sites which are not entirely conscious.

For example, a dominant theme in their presentations is that the European-produced metal awl tips are more significant than the Indian-produced handles. This story is built into their classifications, table titles, and general emphasis. It is then reinforced as the authors reiterate the significance of metal awl tips as markers of European influence on Indians and the disintegration of native culture in their discussions. I imagine Dakota (and undoubtedly other Indian) women would have found such stories amusing, irritating, or perhaps just wrong, particularly those who inscribed their bone or antler handles as a means to visually and publicly express their accomplishments.

Different plot elements are contained in Stone's classification scheme which states that awls functioned exclusively in the context of maintenance and repair, specifically within the household or domestic sphere. In the first place, awls here are classified with tools that (merely) maintain or repair other useful and completed objects and are differentiated, presumably, from primary tools essential in the production of new items. An implied ranking places "maintenance and repair" tools below "productive" tools that are needed to make things. Secondly, awls are placed in the context of the domestic sphere. Indeed, we today live in a culture where the domestic/public dichotomy is real, both socially and spatially. Political and economic life is often divided into two differentially valued parts, and the parts are gendered. The domestic sphere is seen as female and less important than the male-dominated public domain. Stone's classification system with its implied public/domestic split distorts the cultural reality of many Indian groups and uncritically imposes it on them through an artifact classification scheme. This leads us away from rather than toward any insights about the meaning or use of awl tips or handles in their original cultural context. Projecting the dichotomy back in time reveals as much or more about our own gender ideology and divisions as it does about groups in the past, a familiar androcentric theme in archaeology.

The awl descriptions communicate other unacknowledged messages. There are no people and no activities in these narratives. There is no sense of people making, trading for, displaying, or working with awls. The awls are without specific context, without associations, without meaning except in so far as they mark time or measure the influence of whites on Indians. Though the writing style is entirely depersonalized and object-centred, it is not without feeling, regardless of the intentions of the authors. The awl descriptions are dull, tedious, boring, hard to grasp. Do readers absorb these same feelings and transfer them to the people who once made or used these tools?

Some Conclusions

I developed the task differentiation framework in response to the feminist criticism of archaeology which documented pervasive androcentrism in conventional portrayals of the past. Through it, I hoped to study aspects of gender archaeologically, so that we might revise prevailing theories which perpetuate and reinforce western ideologies about women and gender arrangements. While the framework does succeed in drawing attention to the significance of gender in its material dimensions, it does not alter the way we present our insights and interpretations, an issue which increasingly captured my attention after working collaboratively with Dakota people.

That experience made me acutely aware of the ramifications of Indian exclusion from archaeology. As I tried to write about Little Rapids using the task differentiation framework, I found Wahpeton people and their history subordinated by the taxonomic device.

The contrast between the awl narrative and more conventional ways of writing about this class of artifacts reinforced and clarified my ideas about what it means to do more inclusive feminist archaeology. Including Dakota people in the project certainly deepened my knowledge and appreciation of their culture and their recent history. I also came to understand their resentment toward archaeologists and our rendering of Indian Culture.

In the awl narrative I attempted to present aspects of Wahpeton life as I'd come to understand them – particularly aspects of women's lives as materially expressed and enacted. It provided a way to write accessibly and emphatically about Wahpeton people during a particularly turbulent period of their history, hopefully capturing some essences or images of how people under very different conditions from our own may have thought about and confronted certain fundamental changes.

As with most enthnographies (see Rosaldo 1987) the dominant forms of writing archaeology produce problematic representations. Androcentric archaeology imposes culturally specific and often demeaning stereotypes of women onto women living in other times and places, reinforcing discrimination on the basis of gender. In a similar way, archaeological presentations of Indian histories and cultures reinforces their continued oppression. An inclusive feminist archaeology will emphasize gender as a centrally important category of difference and diversity. Ultimately, this approach will challenge all phases of archaeological practice from research design, funding, and fieldwork to publication.

Acknowledgements

My thinking and writing have been enormously enriched by discussions with graduate students and colleagues. The Wedge conference was an extraordinary and illuminating experience. I am grateful to Meg Conkey and Joan Gero for organizing it. I was encouraged and helped by the lively discussion which followed my presentation to the University of Minnesota "History and Society Workshop". In particular, Susan Cahn's insightful comments about feminist dimensions of the narrative helped crystallize my thinking.

I have had stimulating and ongoing discussions about the Little Rapids project and about the awl narrative with Randy Withrow, Diane Stolen, Sharon Doherty, and Beth Scott who each read and commented on early versions of this paper. They have been a great source of energy and inspiration.

Black feminist scholars like Barbara Smith and bell hooks have had a strong influence on the development of more inclusive feminist approaches and studies in recent years.

My thinking about the socio-politics of academic writing and representations of "others" was galvanized by Renato Rosaldo when he presented his powerful paper, "Where Objectivity Lies: The Rhetoric of Anthropology" at the University of Minnesota in the Spring of 1987.

Finally, I wish to thank Susan Geiger for her skillful editing, her insights, her prodding and her confidence.

References

Black Thunder, Elijah et al. (1975). *Ehanna Woyakapi, History and Culture of the Sisseton-Wahpeton Sioux Tribe of South Dakota*. Sisseton: Sisseton-Wahpeton Sioux Tribe.

Conkey, Margaret and Janet D. Spector (1984). "Archaeology and the Study of Gender." *Advances in Archaeological Method and Theory*, vol. 7, M. Schiffer, ed. New York: Academic Press, 1–38.

Eastman, Charles (1971). *Indian Boyhood*. New York: Dover Publications. Originally published 1902.

Eastman, Mary (1853). *The American Aboriginal Portofolio*, illustrated by Seth Eastman. Philadelphia: Lippincott, Grambo.

Gero, Joan (1985). "Socio-Politics and the Woman-at-Home Ideology." *American Antiquity* 50(2): 342–50.

Hassrick, Royal (1964). *The Sioux Life and Customs of a Warrior Society*. Norman: University of Oklahoma Press.

Martin, Calvin, ed. (1987). *The American Indian and the Problems of History*. New York: Oxford University Press.

Mason, Ronald (1986). *Rock Island: Historical Indian Archaeology in the Northern Lake Michigan Basin*. Kent: Kent State University Press.

McNickle, D'arcy (1972). "American Indians Who Never Were." In *American Indian Reader*, Jeannette Henry, ed. San Francisco: The Indian Historian Press.

Moore, Henrietta (1988). *Feminism and Anthropology*. Minneapolis: University of Minnesota Press.

Minnich, Elizabeth (1982). "A Devastating Conceptual Error: How Can We *Not* be Feminist Scholars?" *Change Magazine*, April: 7–9.

Pond, Samuel W. (1986). *The Dakotas or Sioux as They Were in 1834*. St. Paul: Minnesota Historical Society Press. Originally published 1908.

Prescott, Philander (1852). "Contributions to the History, Customs, and Opinions of the Dacota Tribe." In Schoolcraft 1851–4: 168–99.

Riggs, Stephen Return (1893). *Dakota Grammar, Texts, and Ethnography*. Washington Government Printing Office.

Rosaldo, Renato (1986). "Where Objectivity Lies: The Rhetoric of Anthropology." Paper presented at the University of Minnesota.

Schoolcraft, Henry R. (1851–4). *Information Respecting the History, Condition and Prospects of the Indian Tribes of the United States*, Part II. Philadelphia: Lippincott, Grambo.

Spector, Janet D. (1983). "Male/Female Task Differentiation Among the Hidatsa: Toward the Development of an Archaeological Approach to the Study of Gender." In *The Hidden Half: Studies of Plains Indian Women*, Patricia Albers and Beatrice Medicine, eds. Washington: University Press of America, 77–99.

(1985). "Ethnoarchaeology and Little Rapids: A New Approach to 19th Century Eastern Dakota Sites." In *Archaeology, Ecology and Ethnohistory of the Prairie-Forest Border Zone of Minnesota and Manitoba*, Janet Spector and Elden Johnson, eds. Lincoln, NB: J&L Reprints in Anthropology 31, 167–203.

Spector, Janet D. and Mary K. Whelan (1989). "Incorporating Gender into Archaeology Courses." In *Gender and Anthropology: Critical Reviews for Research and Teaching*, Sandra Morgen, ed. Washington: American Anthropological Association, 65–94.

Stone, Lyle M. (1974). *Fort Michilimackinac 1715-1781: An Archaeological Perspective on the Revolutionary Frontier*. East Lansing: Michigan State University Anthropological Series 2, in cooperation with Mackinac Island State Park Commission.

Trigger, Bruce (1980). Archaeology and the Image of the American Indian. *American Antiquity* 45: 662–76.

19

Dorothy Hughes Popenoe:
Eve in an Archaeological Garden

Rosemary A. Joyce

Young Wife, Young Archaeologist

Down in Honduras, Dorothy Popenoe, young wife of a botanist, obtained important information about the forerunners of Middle-America's early civilizations. Choosing to dig at the Beach of the Dead, in a sodden, cracking shelf of land, overhanging the swift current of the Ulua River, Mrs. Popenoe tied a rope round her waist and set to work. Twice, without warning, the treacherous shelf cracked and dissolved

Figure 19.1 [orig. figure 1]   Dorothy Popenoe examines an exposed skeleton and burial goods in her excavation 5 at Playa de los Muertos, on the Ulua River, Honduras
(Courtesy Peabody Museum of Archaeology and Ethnology, Photo #N11543).

beneath her feet. But the safety rope held, and she survived her adventure [figure 19.1].

From that exploit, the young archaeologist brought away nothing very spectacular to capture a public's fancy. The objects she salvaged are chiefly pottery of plain brown color. The pieces lay buried in the Beach of the Dead with the bones of an ancient people, whose manner of living was simpler, and, it seems, earlier than the glories of Mayan, Aztec and other Middle American civilizations. Following her first struggle with the river, Mrs. Popenoe returned again when the capricious Ulua permitted. Then, December 30, 1932, she died of a sudden illness.

... "the plain colored pottery that she dug from fifteen graves ... [is] sufficiently numerous and prevalent to represent a distinct group of people with a culture of their own," according to Dr. George Vaillant, of the American Museum of Natural History, who places the clay wares as "affiliated to other pre-Mayan culture groups in Central America, though probably not the product of the same tribe or people." *(El Palacio 1935: 124)*

How can we tell the story of a woman's life? Carolyn Heilbrun (1988) has explored the dilemma that this task poses. Women's lives are always refracted through the "marriage plot," their independent action ending when they marry, or else their failure to marry viewed as the central enigma to be unraveled. Any enactment of the "quest plot," the search for expression and achievement, is shattered into the pieces of a puzzle, re-arranged along the chronological narrative of marriage / not-marriage.

How much more problematic does it seem, then, to tell the story of a woman's life as a scientist, an explorer and archaeologist? Such a life be must recovered by sifting the broken fragments that remain for the clues they give about the decisions made, theories adopted and abandoned, understanding arrived at and embodied, finally, in written texts. A scientist writes her life in her papers, and they give her voice. What could be more tragic than the loss of that voice, the slippage from the quest plot to the marriage plot?

My first encounter with Dorothy Hughes Popenoe was a folktale, part of the lore of Honduran archaeology, an allegory with mythic overtones. Much of what I was told was false, and its central image may be questionable. This work is my attempt to recover the myriad threads of her life.[1]

---

[1] The present paper is a version from a computer-based hypertext document I have been developing. Hypertext, which links information in nonlinear fashion and allows for multiple ways of reading, allows an experience that cannot be translated to the page. I use the hypertextual conventions of the printed text (footnotes, indented quotes, and varied typefaces) to give some impression of the quality of hypertexts, but nonetheless this is a single fixed reading. To recapture some of the nonlinear effects, readers should consider following Dorothy Popenoe's own words (italicized throughout), or the quotations from primary texts (set apart from my own commentary by typeface). Letters from other people are indented.

The source hypertext was developed using Storyspace™, a writing environment developed for the Macintosh computer published by Eastgate Software in Cambridge, Massachusetts.

A Chorus of Voices

To tell her story, a murmuring of voices must be admitted, the nuances of their speech considered. For Dorothy Popenoe, there is only her own writing to speak. And this writing has been layered over by other, more authoritative tones: George C. Vaillant, promulgating the true significance of her work at Playa de los Muertos (the only voice in the chorus heard in *A History of American Archaeology*); A.M. Tozzer, guiding Dorothy's decisions in research, and placing his own interpretation on her life; Doris Stone, retelling her work at Playa, Cerro Palenque, and Tenampua, writing out Dorothy Popenoe's own conclusions based on her pursuit of stratigraphic control; and my own encounters with her photographs, objects, unpublished reports, and ignored interpretations of her own work.[2]

First Voice

The first voice must surely be that of History, the chronicle of a life stitched together from contradictory sources. What stands out here is the pace of this life, the uncompromising commitment to research which makes the presence of five children an almost irreconcilable contradiction.

CHRONOLOGY
1899   Born June 19 or June 16
1914   Left school at start of World War I
1918   Began work at Kew Gardens
1923   Invited to join staff of US National Herbarium, July
        Married Wilson Popenoe, November
1924   Birth of son (Peter)
1925   Move to Tela, Honduras with Wilson, December
1926   Birth of daughter (Nancy)
1927   Exploration of Tenampua
        Exploration of Cerro Palenque
        First writing: typescript on bells in Tozzer library

---

[2] My own engagement with Popenoe began when, as a novice in Honduras, I first was told a slightly inaccurate version of her death, describing her as childless at the time. She preceded me at my dissertation site:

> Cerro Palenque first entered the archaeological record in Doris Stone's brief commentaries, based in part on the unpublished work of Dorothy Popenoe. Popenoe referred to her work at Cerro Palenque in 1927 in her discussion of Playa de los Muertos. Unpublished photographs by Popenoe in the Peabody Museum pinpoint the areas where she worked . . . Popenoe's photographs show massive cut stone balustrades, steps, and U-shaped drain stones, features still in place at the hilltop site today. The building associated with these features is part of a group which shows signs of major excavations, perhaps to be attributed to Popenoe. (Joyce 1991:35–36)

It was only in researching the Peabody's Honduran collections that I began to realize how much of her legacy had been lost.

1928   Initial work at Playa de los Muertos, November 5
        Publication in Spanish of report on Tenampua
1929   Renewed work at Playa de los Muertos, February
        Birth of son (Hugh)
1930   Move to Guatemala with Wilson
        Birth of daughter (Marion)
1931   First English publication, with Wilson, in *Unifruitco Magazine*
1932   Birth of daughter (Pauline)
        Return to Tela with Wilson, December
        Operation and death, December 30
1934   Publication of study of Playa de los Muertos
1936   English publication of study of Tenampua by Smithsonian Institution

Second Voice

The second voice must be her own, writing for scientific guidance to A.M. Tozzer, to Harvard's Peabody Museum. Her own vision of her task was brilliantly clear. By seeking stratified deposits – years before the authoritative history states that this became accepted practice in Central America – she would place the abundant material remains of the Ulua Valley in their proper order.

> Dear Dr. Tozzer,
>   I have just returned from making your Ulua River Expedition to Playa de los Muertos. As soon as the report is complete I will mail it to you and seek some way to send you all the artifacts and skeletal material . . .
>   I am daring to hope that you will consider the work satisfactory. My greatest desire is to win your approval and confirm the confidence you so generously placed in me. This was the thought that overshadowed all others throughout the trip. And now I must await your frank criticism of the report before knowing if I have succeeded . . .
>   Hoping, more earnestly than I can say, that you will consider your expedition to have been worth while; with warm personal regards to yourself and Mrs. Tozzer. (Dorothy Popenoe 1929)
>
> Dear Dr. Tozzer,
>   You may have heard by now that the Popenoes have been transferred back to Tela. This gives me a good opportunity to resume my studies of the Ulua Valley. I am now writing up my report on the expeditions of 1930 and 1931. It should be ready for you in a few weeks . . .
>   As always I shall be more than grateful for any advice or guidance you can give me. I am paying particular attention to stratification and types of deposits. Are there any other points I might be able to help clarify? (Dorothy Popenoe 1932)

Third Voice

George Vaillant, placing a value on her work:

> In 1896 George Byron Gordon . . . distinguished several types of decoration, which he was unable to reduce to chronological sequence. The freakish changes of course made by the Ulua River and its tributaries during the flood seasons redistributed the refuse lenses, so that Gordon found none fit for stratigraphical dissection.[3] . . .
>
> The preceding report by Dorothy H. Popenoe . . . lays a firm basis for an orderly historical and ethnographical arrangement of Uloa Valley archaeology. It is a tragedy for all her co-workers in the Central American field that Mrs. Popenoe could not have been spared to complete a work with so promising an inception. Nonetheless her finds have great value, since they reduce to specific problems some of the outstanding general questions relating to Central American ceramics.
>
> The outstanding results of Mrs. Popenoe's excavations are the separation of the monochrome from the polychrome wares . . . Mrs. Popenoe's work at Playa de los Muertos should take its place among the definitive descriptions of culture groups upon which rest the foundations of Central American archaeology. (Vaillant 1934:87, 96–97)

Faint Voices

And now Dorothy Popenoe is lost, a murmur comes from her successors, each taking as guide Vaillant's work:

> Gordon excavated . . . on the Ulua River, and indicated a difference in depth of deposit between the monochrome and polychrome wares . . . Late, Dorothy Popenoe (1934) isolated at Playa de los Muertos a series of burials which were quickly recognized as a phase of the Mesoamerican Formative or Preclassic (Vaillant 1934). Further excavation at the site by Strong, Kidder, and Paul confirmed the stratigraphic position of the Playa de los Muertos phase. (Glass 1966:162).

> No study of the north coast of Honduras . . . can be complete without at least a brief examination of Playa de los Muertos culture.
>
> The earliest report . . . is that by Gordon who conducted the Peabody Museum expedition in 1896–1897. It was Mrs. Dorothy Popenoe, however, whose excavations . . . and subsequent report led to the naming of this type of ware. Dr. George Vaillant has pointed out the presence in the Playa de los Muertos culture of many of the traits prevalent in the Q culture.
>
> Strong, Kidder and Paul have enlarged the scope of Playa de los Muertos ware . . .
>
> They have called attention to the relationship between the Playa de los Muertos culture and that of the early Guatemalan highlands . . .

[3] In fact, Gordon's notes indicate that he dug in a primitive attempt at stratigraphy, with levels of 1–2 feet recorded. The materials he found were clearly stratified, not mixed as seems to be implied in this passage. They confirm the sequence Popenoe hoped to demonstrate, although absolute depths of similar materials vary markedly.

If we accept the excavations of Strong, Kidder and Paul at face value, then we are forced to admit that objects of Playa de los Muertos culture are indeed the most ancient recorded from the Sula-Ulua. According to Mrs. Popenoe the only hint at stratification was the absence of jadeite in the upper stratum . . . Mrs Popenoe stresses the lack of uniformity encountered among the burials, and goes so far as to say "that whatever code of burial rules the people possessed, it must have been a lax one." This comment suggests that here in the Sula-Ulua were divers groups living simultaneously . . .

With regard to the age of the Playa de los Muertos culture, the writer . . . believes the presence of this ware does not necessarily suggest that each piece is of great age . . . the writer accept[s] the possibility that people made Playa de los Muertos articles . . . until quite late during the Indian occupation.[4] (Stone 1941: 56–57)

Yarumela and Los Naranjos contrast in basic ceramic inventory at this time period. This regionalization of Period IV Honduran ceramic complexes extends also to Copan and to the Playa de los Muertos culture of the Ulua Valley, although all of these sites share an emphasis on monochrome pottery and decoration by plastic techniques, including incision, zoned burnishing, applique, and modelling. Only the rare burial ceramics seem comparable across the area . . . Playa de los Muertos lacks the elaborate incised decoration noted in early Middle Formative burials elsewhere in Honduras, and instead shares the Mesoamerica-wide adoption of the "double-line-break" motif on bowl rims. (Joyce 1991a:23–24)

Ventriloquism

Only through the lens of George Vaillant's interpretation is Dorothy Popenoe's work inscribed in *A History of American Archaeology*, entwined in the early stage of classification, establishing chronology and defining cultures. Popenoe herself transgresses the categories of this history. Like significant figures from before World War I, she had no formal affiliation with an institution and worked as a lone explorer. But her reports, published and unpublished, are concerned with more than mere chronology. Her lack of formal training in archaeology led her to develop her own structures of meaning, and these fit poorly into the main strands that authoritatively account for the development of Americanist archaeology.

According to Willey and Sabloff (1974:83), the great developments of the period to 1914 were "a steadily growing professionalization of the discipline in an academic alliance with anthropology as a whole." People like Dorothy Popenoe, access to the emerging centers of research denied them, could only work on the margins. Popenoe turned to A.M. Tozzer of the Peabody Museum for guidance and legitimation.

During the period of classification and culture history (1914–1960), Willey and Sabloff recognize several important methodological developments and common

---

[4] Radiocarbon dates for Playa de los Muertos range from ca. 240BC +/– 150 to 430 BC +/– 180 (Kennedy 1981: 110–111).

goals. The "stratigraphic revolution" resulted in the recognition of a means to place deposits in sequence. George Vaillant, Dorothy Popenoe's alter-ego, appears again and again in this account of the unified mission of archaeology:

> Outside of the Southwest, G.C. Vaillant, who had been a student assistant of Kidder's at Pecos, published his first detailed stratigraphic work on the Valley of Mexico in 1930 . . . Kidder appears to have been one of the few, or perhaps the only, American stratigrapher of the 1920s and 1930s who favored the natural as opposed to the metrical method . . . The reasons for this difference between the American stratigraphic digging methods and the more frequent use of the natural or physical soil zone unit of digging in the Old World are, like the reasons for the delay in the acceptance of the method as a whole in the Americas, uncertain and open to speculation . . . Vaillant argues that the physical complexities of the Zacatenco site, in which refuse and semi-destroyed architectural features were found over a hill slope, made physical strata digging impossible or inadvisable . . . (1974:96-98)

> Both Vaillant and Bennett tended to look upon the pottery complex or the "pottery period" as a whole. That is, certain forms and features characterized a period, in contrast to another period. (1974:109)

> In fact, even as early as the late 1920s, G.C. Vaillant was beginning to question Spinden's chronological ordering . . . Vaillant had actually begun such a synthesis in 1927 in an unpublished Ph.D. dissertation . . . in 1941, he gave his ideas detailed expression . . .
> Spinden's "Archaic Hypothesis" . . . had both chronological and developmental implications . . . In other words, this "Archaic" was a kind of American Neolithic. Having its origins in the Valley of Mexico, it had spread outward to other parts of the hemisphere from this center . . . Vaillant, among others, took issue with Spinden. (1974: 120, 124–125)[5]

Dorothy Popenoe

Dorothy Hughes Popenoe was born on June 19, 1899 and died on December 30, 1932. At the center of the life written for her is an allegory. Twisting through the allegory is another reading of her life. Carolyn Heilbrun, in *Writing a Woman's Life* (1988), suggests that each woman's life has four narratives: the one she may envision before she lives it; the one she may write as fiction; the one she may write as "autobiography"; and the one that may be written for her as "biography." This is my reading of Dorothy Popenoe's life, intent on seeing an alternative to the tragic allegory in which she has been cast.

---

[5] A footnote on Vaillant's arguments against the Valley of Mexico origin of the "Archaic" cites his interpretation of Popenoe's excavations at Playa de los Muertos in Honduras, the only echo of her voice in this history.

The Marriage Plot

In July 1923, Dorothy K. Hughes, an attractive, intelligent young British woman, was hired by the Bureau of Plant Industry. Born at Ashford, Middlesex, England, in June 1899, Dorothy had studied at the University of London and worked for several years on African grasses in the herbarium at Kew. She had become a capable botanist and botanical illustrator . . .

It was love at first sight. A few days later she called him and asked if he had any work for her.[6] Wilson thought to himself, "Yes, I have a lifetime of work for you." He soon proposed to Dorothy and they were married in November 1923. (Rosengarten 1991:91–92)

In 1925 Wilson Popenoe resigned from the USDA and accepted a job with the United Fruit Company in Honduras. "His wife, Dorothy, *was very much in favor of this move.*"[7] (*Rosengarten 1991:97*)

Eve

When she first came to Honduras, Dorothy had a pink and white complexion and a youthful appearance. By 1932, however, having given birth to five children in just a few years while continuing to work on archaeology in Honduras and the reconstruction of a seventeenth-century house in Antigua, Guatemala, she seemed tired. In December of that year, a very tragic event took place in Lancetilla. Dorothy Popenoe ate an unripe, uncooked akee fruit which is said to have poisoned her. (Rosengarten 1991: 108–109)

A Sermon

If this were only a little sermon I should choose for its text a single word. That word would be gallantry, and why this word was chosen will be evident to the reader of this short life history, for it tells of the most gallant soul I have ever known. I chose the word to indicate dynamic, not static, qualities and for want of a better. Steadfast she was, but one might be steadfast and lack the verve, the vision, and the personal valor of Dorothy Popenoe.

Dorothy Hughes Popenoe was born 19 June, 1899, at Ashford, Middlesex, England. She attended the Welsh Girls' School at Ashford until the beginning of the Great War. Then she went into "land work" until she suffered an injury in Anglesea which made necessary an operation and which forced her to remain inactive until 1918. During this year she entered the Royal Botanical Gardens at Kew as student-assistant to Dr. Otto Stapf. Here at Kew she remained five years, but studied during all her spare hours at the University of London. Dorothy had a brilliant, acquisitive mind, and she soon became an authority on several genera of African grasses and described a number of new species in the Kew Bulletin.

---

[6] Whispers of Dorothy's voice?
[7] More whispers?

In July, 1923, by invitation of Mrs. Agnes Chase of the United States National Herbarium, she came to Washington and entered the Office of Foreign Plant Introduction, of which her husband-to-be's old friend Dr. David Fairchild was the distinguished head. Here she carried on taxonomic studies of the cultivated bamboos, and so in Washington she met Dr. Wilson Popenoe, himself a distinguished botanical explorer. They were married on 17th November, 1923 . . .

It is hard for a woman to go to live in the American tropics, especially in the hot wet coastal zone of the more backward Central American states. Life in India, Ceylon, or Malaya presents a very different aspect. In the East there is in many places a considerable European society, and the amenities of life have developed naturally with the long occupation of the land by cultivated folk. To be sure there were congenial Americans at Tela who soon became warm friends, but Dorothy was much more than usually fearful of stagnation of mind and indolence of body.

In 1927, with only Jorge Benitez, her Ecuadorian assistant and friend, she travelled for days on muleback and finally reached and described and mapped the prehistoric mountain-top fortress city of Tenampua, abandoned centuries ago and a site which few explorers have ever seen . . .

At odd moments for a long time Dorothy had been reading avidly on Maya art and archaeology, and from 1928 to 1932 she spent weeks at a time, when the waters were low, excavating a rich pre-Columbian [sic] cemetery at La Playa de los Muertos on the Ulua River. She unearthed several splendid collections of pottery and many skeletons, and prepared a scholarly report . . . She never hesitated to camp alone at this wild and lonely spot among the most notoriously unreliable people in Central America . . .

From time to time five children came, but these events never held up Dorothy's explorations for long . . .

On 23rd December, 1932, she wrote me: *"We have been transferred back again to Tela and I have written Professor Tozzer that I am ready again to struggle with the problems of the Ulua Valley pottery." . . .*

Three days after her last letter to me she died suddenly at Tela, after an emergency operation. So passed another young Valiant-for-Truth, and who can doubt but all the angel's trumpets sounded on the other side? (Thomas Barbour 1933:vii–x)

Death Retold

Dear Doctor Barbour:

Thank you for your letter of January 5th. I knew how terribly you would feel about Dorothy Popenoe's death. It is unutterably sad. On December 30th she suddenly felt very badly and telephoned the Tela hospital. The doctor came for her in a car and on examination deemed an immediate operation necessary . . . The operation was performed at once and the surgeon was entirely satisfied with her condition. He stepped out of the hospital to telegraph as much to Dr. Popenoe, and when he returned to the hospital, Dorothy had died . . . It now appears possible that eating overripe akees, the fruit of Blighia sapida, may have contributed to her sudden illness.

The last time I saw her we spent the day together at her house in Antigua, which you know. After an absence in Tela she was like a freed bird in her joy at being in the place she loved . . . What a companion she was, with her youthful gaiety and her mature and cultivated mind. There were times when she looked like a little girl with her smallness, her pink and white complexion and her bright happy expression. Behind this she possessed the mind of a born scholar, accurate, penetrating and untiring. With her keen intellect, went a feeling for beauty and romance and a sound common sense. I have known no woman so gifted and none so modest . . .

Dorothy was my nearest neighbor, and often when I dropped in to see her she was in bed resting before or after the birth of one of the babies . . . Her husband often came in with an old painting or a frame for their collection, which he had just bought. If it was a portrait, every clue would be followed up to identify the subject – costumes, coat of arms, etc. – all were carefully studied . . .

Dorothy radiated cheerfulness and strength even when far from well herself. For her strength was that of the Spirit and she was completely selfless. Her death touches all who knew her deeply. This gay and fascinating girl in her early thirties has been taken from her devoted husband and her large family of children, and her life, full of accomplishment and promise, is over. (Mary Alexander Whitehouse, in Barbour 1933:xi)

Allegory

It now appears that eating overripe akees, the fruit of *Blighia sapida*, may have contributed to her sudden illness. (Mary Alexander Whitehouse, in Barbour 1933:xi)

Dorothy Popenoe ate an unripe, uncooked akee fruit which is said to have poisoned her. (Rosengarten 1991:109)

The significance of akee in Dorothy Popenoe's death seems more as symbol, less as fact; unconfirmed in all sources and varying in its poisonous stage, unripe or overripe. It is one of the accepted stories for women: warned by her husband not to eat the fruit of one particular tree in his garden, yet she does: Eve in an archaeological garden.

Second Voice Returns

What is the intellectual course of Dorothy Popenoe's work and thoughts? The motives for her first trip to Tenampua are lost and only speculation can provide some idea of the forces that drove this woman to ride, accompanied only by a Spanish-speaking colleague, leaving her husband and children behind, far from their coastal garden home.

Lancetilla/Eden.

The Tela Railroad Company, the Honduran guise of the United Fruit Company, established an experimental botanical station at Lancetilla in 1925 under the direction of Wilson Popenoe. The Popenoes published a study of the archaeological material encountered here (W. and D. Popenoe 1931). At times they seem to treat it as products of the contact period; at others, they apply developmental frameworks implying earlier dates. Lancetilla is presented as a unified culture, not an archaeological component in stratigraphic context, a striking contrast with Dorothy Popenoe's later work:

> The greater part of the collection from Lancetilla is made up of stonework. Pottery is generally of coarse sandy clay, poorly baked . . . The knowledge of chipping stone was followed by another discovery, that of the effect produced by grinding and polishing the chipped articles . . .
> All of the objects so far described seem more suitable for the use of men than for that of women. But the one illustrated at the bottom of Figure 3 was most likely employed by the latter. It is a bark-beater, and provides a clue as to the type of clothing worn by these people. (W. and D. Popenoe 1931:6–8)

A tension was maintained in this early work between classification, always developmental, and interpretation in human terms.

Playa de los Muertos/The Beach of the Dead.

It is at this juncture that Dorothy Popenoe's contact with the Peabody Museum began. In the wide reading she had done, she encountered G.B. Gordon's work (1898). Here he set the problem of monochrome and polychrome ceramics in its place, and it was this problem Popenoe set out to solve.

> Thirty-five years ago, when the Ulua Valley was still clothed in a tangle of dense jungle, an incident occurred which served to arouse the suspicion that beneath its tropical forests and within its stratified banks there lay hidden the story of a vanished race . . .
> In February 1928, while I was engaged in an investigation of some ruins on a hill near Pimienta, one of my workmen mentioned Playa de los Muertos . . . I had long wanted to visit this site where Byron Gordon had worked, but had hitherto been uncertain as to its exact location. Upon ascertaining that my informant knew the place well, I secured him as a guide, and with two others of my men, rode across the country from Pimienta . . .
> Perhaps one of the most striking problems is the riddle of the different types of pottery. At certain points in the river – for example, Playa de los Muertos, described in this report – all the pottery found in both upper and lower strata is of the simple monochrome type (figure 19.2), while at Rancheria, about eight kilometers upstream on the same side, a rich dump of polychrome ware yielded fragments as beautiful as some of the finest Central American examples . . . It seems inconceivable that these two distinct types of ware could have been manufactured by the same people, and equally strange, that tribes differing widely in cultural traits could have been found living synchronously in such close proximity. (Popenoe 1934:61-62, 79–80)

With Tozzer's encouragement, she extended her stratigraphic studies to other sites, seeking to clarify the relationship of monochrome and polychrome pottery complexes in the valley:

> In 1930 we wished to direct our attention to the problem of the Ulua Polychrome pottery . . . The uncovering of the burial ground at Playa de los Muertos in 1929 and the finding of much entire plain pottery together with the complete absence of polychrome

Figure 19.2 [orig. figure 2]   Photograph by Dorothy Popenoe of objects from burials at Playa de los Muertos, presented against a background of modern Maya textiles
(Courtesy Peabody Museum of Archaeology and Ethnology, Photo #N11516).

fragments led us to suspect that the latter might lie in a different type of deposit . . . The horizontal or "onion-peel" method of digging disclosed in a number of cases that the pieces of a single vessel would be scattered over a large area. (Popenoe 1930)

In her earliest works at Lancetilla, Popenoe classified material remains as passive reflections of cultures. In her study of Tenampua she demonstrated an emerging concern with process. Tenampua, she argued, was a hilltop fortress, like others known archaeologically and described ethnographically. Its strategic location, water sources, and walls were her evidence, and direct historic analogy her confirmation. Her unpublished work at Cerro Palenque must have been a comparative investigation of another presumed hilltop redoubt. Rapidly thereafter, her emphasis shifted, and she sought to demonstrate stratigraphic relationships. Her final manuscript on Playa de los Muertos describes a series of burials exposed in a fresh river cut. She examined environmental data to explain the sedimentation and recutting of these sites, an early essay in site-formation processes. She left unfinished her report on the work she hoped would win her A. M. Tozzer's approval:

On going through her notes and files, I failed to find much regarding the polychrome pottery work. She had taken it up a few weeks before her death, on completing the little book on Antigua, and I know that she was about ready to write up the whole subject.

But I am afraid she had put very little in writing at the time her work came to an end.
(Wilson Popenoe 1933b)

Erasure

How did Dorothy Popenoe's death come to mean more than the work she wrote?
I return here to Heilbrun's (1988) observations about the limited nature of stories
available for women's lives. How can the quest plot be combined with the marriage
plot? Not since Eve has this combination been easily accepted. Dying a young
mother and wife, with most of her work unfinished, Dorothy Popenoe's life was
subject to evaluation by others in control of her essential meaning.

Her Mentor's Voice

Although she had no formal affiliation with the Peabody Museum, A.M. Tozzer
was the scholar to whom she turned for guidance and approval. He acted as the
filter for her ideas both during her life and after her death.

To Dorothy:

It has been a long time since I have heard from you, and along with your letter comes
a fine collection of polychromes . . . As I have already told you, this polychrome with its
background is most important. Your report will furnish the background and fit it into the
complex where it belongs in relation to the unpainted wares which you have already
sent us. (Tozzer 1932a)

To the archaeological community:

Dorothy Hughes Popenoe was born on June 16, 1899 at Ashford, Middlesex, England.
As a student assistant at the Royal Botanical Gardens at Kent and at the University of
London, she acquired that knowledge of botany which led to a position in 1923 at the
United States National Herbarium. Here she met and married Dr. Wilson Popenoe, the
distinguished botanist. In 1925 they moved to Tela, Honduras, to organize a plant introduction station and undertake agronomic research for the United Fruit Company. In
1927 after great hardships she described and mapped the fortress city of Tenampua.
This report was published by the Government of Honduras. From this time onward to
her death she was intensely interested in the Maya ruins. She devoured the old and the
modern authorities and made many most arduous trips which yielded important results.
Her special field was the Playa de los Muertos on the Ulua River. Most of her work was
undertaken under her own initiative and with no outside aid. From time to time the
Peabody Museum gladly gave her small grants for her expenses. The present paper,
printed exactly as she left it, is the account of a series of burials of unpainted pottery on
the Ulua. She was about to search for a burial yielding polychrome pottery, at the time
of her death on December 30, 1932 . . . Archaeology has lost one of its most inspired
students and her friends one whose life was marvellous and full of beauty. (Tozzer
1934b:86)

To Wilson:

I am looking forward to Mrs. Wilson writing up in detail this collection from the Playa de los Muertos. She has with her investigations a good background for fitting in the other material. As I wrote her, I wish some time that a grave with polychrome pottery could be found and investigated as this would place this type of ceramics into the context. (Tozzer 1932b)

Tom and I are very anxious to publish a paper by her on the Ulloa Valley. I have in my hands her finished report on the excavations at Playa de lost Muertos, which could be printed almost as is. If, in the near future, you could send me the material on which she was working, the reports for the seasons 1930 and 1931, I think we could get together an excellent paper. (Tozzer 1933)

With your permission, I am going to publish Dorothy's paper on the Ulua. I am writing a short note on her life and Dr. Vaillant is going to write on the place of Ulua ceramics in the Maya pottery complex. (Tozzer 1934a)

The Final Voice

I cannot tell you how much I appreciated your letter about Dorothy. Both she and I always felt extremely grateful to you and Mrs. Tozzer for the deep interest you took in her. As I think you know, you were her inspiration and her mentor, and she always looked forward to the day, – now never to arrive, – when she might do more serious work under your sympathetic guidance. (Wilson Popenoe 1933a)

References

Barbour, Thomas 1933 "Introduction." *In Santiago de los Caballeros de Guatemala*, by Dorothy H. Popenoe, vii–xii. Cambridge, MA: Harvard University Press.

El Palacio 1935 "New Pottery Found in Honduras." *El Palacio* 38(21-22-23): 124.

Glass, John B. 1966 "Archaeological Survey of Western Honduras." In *Handbook of Middle American Indians*, vol. 4, edited by G. Eckholm and Gordon Willey, 157–79. Austin: University of Texas Press.

Gordon, George Byron 1898 *Researches in the Uloa Valley, Honduras*. Peabody Museum of Ethnology and Archaeology, Harvard University Memoirs 1(4).

Heilbrun, Carolyn 1988 *Writing a Woman's Life*. New York: Norton.

Joyce, Rosemary A. 1991 *Cerro Palenque: Power and Identity on the Southern Mesoamerican Periphery*. Austin: University of Texas Press.

Kennedy, Nedenia. 1981 "The Formative Period Ceramic Sequence from Playa de los Muertos, Honduras." Ph.D. dissertation, Department of Anthropology, University of Illinois.

Popenoe, Dorothy 1929 Letter to A. M. Tozzer, February 21. Harvard University, Peabody Museum of Archaeology and Ethnology, accession file 29–15.

1930 Two Expeditions in Search of Painted Pottery. Unpublished Report March 30. Harvard University, Peabody Museum of Archaeology and Ethnology, accession file 30–46.

1932 Letter to A.M. Tozzer, December 8. Harvard University, Peabody Museum of Archaeology and Ethnology, accession file 33–18.

1934 "Some Excavations at Playa de los Muertos, Ulua River, Honduras." *Maya Research* 1: 62–86.

Popenoe, Wilson 1933a Letter to A. M. Tozzer, January 20. Harvard University, Peabody Museum of Archaeology and Ethnology, accession file 33–18.

1933b Letter to A. M. Tozzer, July 2. Harvard University, Peabody Museum of Archaeology and Ethnology, accession file 31–43.

Popenoe, Wilson and Dorothy Popenoe 1931 "The Human Background of Lancetilla." *Unifruitco Magazine*, August: 6–10.

Rosengarten, Frederic Jr. 1991 *Wilson Popenoe: Agricultural Explorer, Educator, and Friend of Latin America*. Lawai, Kauai, Hawaii: National Tropical Botanical Garden.

Stone, Doris Z. 1941 *Archaeology of the North Coast of Honduras*. Cambridge, MA: Memoirs of the Peabody Museum of Archaeology and Ethnology, IX(1).

Tozzer, A. M. 1932a Letter to Dorothy Popenoe, December 22. Harvard University, Peabody Museum of Archaeology and Ethnology, accession file 33–18.

1932b Letter to Wilson Popenoe, January 22. Harvard University, Peabody Museum of Archaeology and Ethnology, accession file 31–43.

1933 Letter to Wilson Popenoe, January 10. Harvard University, Peabody Museum of Archaeology and Ethnology, accession file 33–18.

1934a Letter to Wilson Popenoe, March 23. Harvard University, Peabody Museum of Archaeology and Ethnology, accession file 31–43.

1934b "Obituary of Dorothy H. Popenoe." *Maya Research* 1:86.

Vaillant, George C. 1934 "The Archaeological Setting of the Playa de los Muertos Culture." *Maya Research* 1: 87–100.

Willey, Gordon R. and Jeremy A. Sabloff 1974 *A History of American Archaeology*. London: Thames and Hudson.

Part VII

The Past as Power

Representations and Antirepresentations

The past is and always has been constructed as part of power relations in the present. Perhaps most archaeologists, of whatever theoretical hue, would agree with some version of this thesis. What have changed, and what are continuously debated, are the ways in which we conceptualize power and knowledge, how we relate knowledge of the past to power relations in the present (Gathercole and Lowenthal 1989). All archaeologists share the view that the past can and should be used to the "benefit" of contemporary society. But they differ in their visions of the ideal society and of how archaeology is to contribute to its realization. For culture historical archaeologists, knowledge about the past can educate, civilize, teach about progress, and instill in people a sense of a common humanity. For processual archaeologists, the past can be used to demonstrate cultural diversity within an overall universality of the human condition. It can demonstrate the methods of science and help to plan a better future. For postprocessual archaeologists, knowledge of the past can be used to demonstrate the contingency of human action and the historical nature of our taken-for-granteds. These insights can serve as ways to confront different forms of oppression in the present.

The explicit theorizing of power has called into question the confidence with which we wield our authority derived from being guardians of the material past. Traditional archaeologists had few doubts that they should speak, in a paternalistic way, for all people. Their role was educative and enlightening. This "top down and center out" view was retained in later archaeologies, but it was gradually confronted by the democratization process – that is by the diversity of groups who increasingly sought to present their own versions of the past. Power had to be shared. While it could be used positively it could also, as in the Nazi case, be used negatively. Those in power through their control of the past became increasingly required to justify that their version of how to use the past was the right one, or at least the right one for all groups of people. A major change was that, in archaeology as in society as a whole, confidence in science itself came to be questioned. The certainty that science would reduce bias by being external to social interests was undermined by examples of the misuse of science. Self-reflexivity gradually led to the view that a "down up and margin in" dialogue should be created. Even the way we write needed to be transformed so that the terms of the debate did not exclude alternative perspectives.

The history of Anglo-American archaeology can thus be understood in terms of the tensions between strategies of control of the past and visions of the ideal society. Regardless of theoretical approach, archaeologists have shared a concern to make the past more widely available and accessible to the public with the view that this democratization would benefit society. And indeed, the differences between culture historical, processual, and postprocessual programs are grounded in the perceived failures of the previous approaches to deal adequately with the democratization of the past. But coupled with this is a reluctance to give over authority and share responsibility for interpreting the past. This reluctance can be seen, for example, in the sharp reactions of the profession to indigenous perspectives on the past (Part VIII). The recent postprocessual debates have firmly positioned archaeology within its cultural context. They suggest that the tensions between power and knowledge cannot be resolved in any final sense since the past resists control by any one single interest group. The past cannot be fully possessed; meaning eludes attempts to pin it down for now and always. The process of negotiating the meaning of the past is thus part of the social reproduction of society. We need to understand the historical conditions of our own existence.

Paternalism and Elitism

Prior to the development of a scientific archaeology in the nineteenth century, archaeology was largely in the hands of the educated upper classes and professionals (clergy and military etc.), who formed the main local and national antiquary societies and Boards of Directors of museums (Daniel 1981). It was an elite pastime, and authoritative statements about the past were closely tied to social position and privilege. As the state took an increasing interest in curating and presenting the past, in the later nineteenth and early twentieth centuries, by providing a legal framework and public funds, it became necessary for statements about the past not to be based on privilege but to be open to public scrutiny. Archaeology had thus to be accountable, its statements based on agreed and open procedures. This accountability was uniquely supplied by science and the scientific method, which allowed for the neutral, unbiased gathering of knowledge for its own sake. This concern with accountability in archaeology went hand in hand with a wider set of public concerns about democratization – the extension of the franchise, the extension of workers' rights, public health reform and so on (Clark 1934).

The social concerns of many of the founding figures of scientific archaeology in this period were paternalistic. The archaeological past was to have an educative and cultural role, especially in the context of museums. In 1905 Franz Boas wrote, "Just as our school system requires, beside primary and grammar schools, high schools and universities, so a large museum should fulfill the function of a primary objective school for the general public . . ." and ". . . if the underlying idea of the exhibit can be brought out with sufficient clearness, some great truths may be impressed upon them [the public] . . ." (cited in Jacknis 1985, p. 86). A message about the past was provided from the educated to the less educated in a culturing process that would benefit society as a whole. In Britain and America archaeological excavation was often conducted as part of public-works programs. The democratization of the past was from the top down, or from the centre out. From a critical perspective this process naturalized the interests of the dominant groups and contrived to create a more "civilized" and docile work force.

The paternalistic view often had enormous vision and scope – an imperial or colonial enterprise was at stake. In America the *National Geographic* magazine promoted progress, democracy and expansionism as part of American imperialism (Gero and Root, **chapter 20**; Lutz and Collins 1993). This viewpoint was closely linked to the embrace of a neutral, objective, scientific perspective. Indeed this very objectivity "proved" the ideological claims being made. Equally important, the methodology of science provided a common thread that connected human cultural diversity together. Perhaps the clearest individual expression of a global humanitarian vision is seen in the writing of Grahame Clark. In his books on a "World Prehistory" (e.g. 1961) a common humanity was asserted within the framework of an archaeological science. Archaeology crossed the borders of the modern world and showed that the cultural relationships in the past linked everyone together. In particular, common themes could be emphasized such as the Origins of Culture, Agriculture, and Civilization. The search for "Origins" created a common order that did not respect the boundaries of the modern political world. There was, according to this vision, something for everybody in the first hand axe.

But despite its humanitarian ring, Clark's call for a One World archaeology was again "top down and center out." There was little concern with alternative views about what a common humanity might consist of. A set of essential truths is supposed to be attainable through archaeological enquiry. The main political contexts for this viewpoint, as we have seen, are Western imperialism, colonialism and capitalism (see Trigger, **chapter 23**). And yet there is also another important and very specific context for Clark's views of a common world heritage crossing and undermining national borders – and that is the use of the past in relation to nationalism throughout the nineteenth and twentieth centuries in Europe. The rise of archaeological societies and museums in Europe is intimately connected to the rise of nation states. The past became an important medium for the assertion of a common national identity (Silberman 1988). Indeed, the whole democratization process can be seen as promoting a popular nationalism – a popular appreciation for the treasures of the national heritage.

The clearest and most dangerous outcome of the dual processes of democratization and nationalism can be seen in the use of the past in Nazi Germany, as described by Arnold (**chapter 21**). The abuse of the past in the Third Reich reinforced the empiricism and skepticism of most archaeologists in Europe. Although the aim of culture historical archaeologists had been to produce a scientific archaeology, the procedures used prior to the 1960s emphasized detailed knowledge, not straying far from the data. Theoretical excursions were seen as dangerous, both scientifically and politically. As a result, in practice, the past remained locked up in esoteric knowledge. Detailed knowledge of culture-historical sequences was a prerequisite for an archaeological career. Understanding of the past was linked to a relatively high level of education and cultural knowledge. Archaeology largely remained in the hands of an educated elite. It remained top down and center out.

Science and Objectivity

The main social thrust of the processual program was to eliminate this lurking and recalcitrant elitism and paternalism and replace it with an unbiased, objective account of the past. Processual archaeology decried the way in which statements about the past were based on the intuition of "authorities" in the discipline (Binford 1962). Indeed the whole aim of the development of a positivist, law-and-order approach was to ensure that statements about the past could be based on regular, open, repeatable procedures rather than on the murky musings of armchair theoriticans. Once a scientific hypothesis had been proposed, anyone could test it. A true democratization was thus sought. Statements about the past were to be based on science rather than privilege.

The agenda was, of course, the same as that set out by scientific archaeologists from the late nineteenth century onwards. But it differed in two respects. First, it introduced a method which opened up the past to hypothesis testing and reconstruction. While the positivism espoused retained an emphasis on testing against observable data, the earlier empircism was tempered by an emphasis on theory building. As a result, a wider range of theories, taken from a cross-cultural range of sources, came to be applied to the data. Knowledge about cultures became less specific and inward-looking. The past did become more open. Secondly, this new openness was allied to an enormous expansion in the numbers of people involved in archaeology through the growth of university systems and rescue or cultural-resource management archaeology. At one level these changes simply brought more and a wider range of people into the discipline. But at a more fundamental level they necessitated the standardization and formalization of archaeological procedures. Public accountability again came to the fore. Archaeologists not only became scientists; they also became professionals with a clear role to play in the community, and using methods open to scrutiny by all. The definition of "an archaeologist" became more clearly regulated (e.g. the Society of Professional Archaeologists in the United States and the Institute of Field Archaeologists in Britain), and membership in the profession more clearly demarcated. Membership was based on knowledge and skill rather than on status.

Much of the earlier emphasis on searching for common themes of humanity remained. An evolutionary emphasis gave added support to the search for Origins (of agriculture, or ranking, of the state) and for a global perspective. Certainly there was a prime concern with variability and diversity – the different behavioral adaptations to environments. But this diversity was subsumed within the assumption of and search for cross-cultural regularities. Other cultures were treated as specimens for laboratory analysis. The aim was to subsume diversity within general scientific statements of universal validity. There was almost no concern with alternative indigenous views. Even in the ethno-archaeology, what "they" had to say was of little interest. The adaptationist views and materialist assumptions meant that the observer tried to be "outside" culture (Binford 1989). Behavior could be related to cross-cultural regularities regardless of what people thought they were doing.

So archaeology remained "top down and center out." The scientific assumptions and methodologies were defined at the center as being universal – there was only one way of doing archaeological science and that was as defined by Western white male academics. David Clarke's (1973) "loss of innocence" had still not occurred, in that there was little reflection on the basis for *a priori* statements about the nature of archaeological science. Instead of paternalism, we find the technocrat intent on providing useful information and a public service. For example, the identification of cross-cultural regularities valid for all times and places was thought to be useful in the planning of future societal development (Schiffer 1976; Watson, Redman and Leblanc 1971).

We have seen that the twin prongs of the New Archaeological assault on culture historical archaeology were simply extensions of two already present trends – a scientific methodology and a professional status. The two in fact depended on each other. A professional field archaeology depended on the use of repeatable and accountable, objective procedures – procedures overtly above vested interest. However, the hypothetico-deductive method embraced by many archaeologists in theoretical and research contexts often proved difficult to apply, particularly in the professional context of cultural resource management. Here contradictions began to emerge between the goals of a neutral scientific archaeology seeking to acquire knowledge, and those of business interests seeking to maximize profits. The practicalities of running contract programs as businesses meant that only certain aspects of science could be implemented. The most obvious casualty was problem-oriented research and the hypothesis-testing procedure. The constraints of time and money meant that archaeologists had to focus on the specifics of each contract and pay less attention to regional patterns and processes. In addition, publication usually consisted of manuscript reports, the "grey literature," of limited circulation. When it comes to cultural-resource management, processual archaeology does not seem so democratic after all.

Pluralism and Inclusion

The basic critique that led to the development of postprocessual archaeology is remarkably similar to that which led to the emergence of traditional and processual archaeology, namely that archaeological interpretation is too narrow, too privileged, not sufficiently responsive to a wide audience. The "objective" methods of processual archaeology are seen not as ensuring public access, but rather as misrepresenting the subjectivity involved in all scientific endeavors. They thus frustrate real public engagement with the past. They present a partial perspective as neutral and universal and thus inhibit the possibilities of critique and debate from radically different positions. The approach is again democratizing and widening.

A starting point for this new commitment to pluralism is often the critique of the dominant ideology. For example, Gero and Root (**chapter 20**) explore the ways in which popular images of archaeology helped reinforce the dominant political ideology of the United States of America. The text and the pictures in *National Geographic* used a variety of techniques to support nationalism and patriotism – as well as racism, materialism, and sexism. A commoditized view is expressed in the emphasis on artifacts evaluated in universal terms. Such critical analyses often take an explicitly Marxist or critical-theory perspective. For example, the Shanks and Tilley (1987) analysis of museums is primarily an ideology critique, and is at least partly based on the Frankfurt school of critical theory. A broad construal of critical theory is presented by Leone, Potter and Shackel (1987) in their account of the historic-heritage project at Annapolis, Maryland. They look at the way in which public presentations of the past may help to prevent people from being aware of their true interests. The past becomes part of an ideology which makes coercion acceptable, natural or rational.

These studies assume that we can uncover what a message (any type of archaeological "text") is "really" saying – for example, that the message may serve to naturalize or misrepresent what is "really" going on. Thus Leone, Potter and Shackel (1987, p. 284) argue that critical theory helps people to achieve enlightenment so that they can see what their "true" interests are. What is "really' or "truly" going on is usually some form of exploitation of people's time, labor or material resources. But there are elements of paternalism which remain here – can the analyst see what is "really' going on any better than those being duped by the system. There is still a tendency to try to speak for others. There is still a commitment to positivism, a belief that what is "really" going on may be uncovered through the proper use of the scientific method. Leone, Potter and Shackel (1987, p. 285), for example, claim that critical theory and positivism can work side by side to produce a less biased and more reliable and accurate account of the past. Positivism together with a materialist or dailectical Marxism can thus lead to an objective statement about what "really" happened.

One characteristic of capitalism is that it seeks to segment knowledge and deny its social matrix. Leone and Potter (1992) have explored this issue in the context of historical preservation. Their question is how the significance of archaeological sites is assessed. The existing standard, and the one codified by National Register Criterion D, is that a site can be registered if it has yielded, or is likely to yield, information important in prehistory or history. Leone and Potter show that this rather vague criterion actually privileges professional archaeological concerns at the expense of legitimate nonscientific interests. They then point out that archaeological information is important, but so are highways, electric lines, and low-income housing. Archaeology cannot somehow stand "above" the social. The crucial question is how these different interests can be brought together so that effective action can result. The suggestion offered by Leone and Potter centers on the notion of dialogue in an "ideal speech situation." Essentially, this is a context in which it is possible for everyone to participate in forging a consensus (see Part VIII for another application of this idea). Archaeology thus needs to acknowledge its embeddedness in larger social and political frameworks and this may mean that purely archaeological interests will not always win out in the end.

Such viewpoints are valuable in that they begin to open up dominant ideologies to critique. Yet it can also be argued that they themselves are not sufficiently self-reflective. They do not question the basis of the critical theorist's own claims to "truth" or "reality." They take their own Enlightenment position for granted. A more radical position is that there is no way of saying with certainty what "really" or "truly" happened in the past. This extreme relativist position has been introduced most recently in archaeology by a small group of poststructuralist writers (e.g. Bapty 1990; Yates 1990). Poststructuralism argues that a meaning of a word depends on its relations with other words in an unstable and fluid process. It is critical of any sort of essentialism, as might be implied by the use of terms such as culture, behavior, meaning, and it is critical of any notion that we can reconstruct what "really" happened in the past – both because there were many interpretations in the past of what was happening, and because our present understanding of the past is arbitrary and provisional. The way we reconstruct the past can thus always be deconstructed to show that it is based on arbitrary assumptions and to show that its supposed coherence is internally contradictory.

The poststructuralist emphasis, in contrast to critical theory, tends to focus more on language and representation rather than on the material conditions which make certain types of representation of the past possible. An example of this trend is Shanks and Tilley's (1987) critique of museums and representations. Although their work is presented as an ideology critique it concentrates on narrative and rhetoric. It refers to writers in critical theory, and there is again an emphasis on commodification of the past within capitalism, but there is also a poststructuralist emphasis on the play of differences within a system of signs. The objects in museums are only signs of the past – they refer to an absent signified (past meanings). We experience the signs but their meaning is constructed in the present. It is a delusion to think that their meaning is the meaning of the past. That meaning (what they meant in the past) is absent. Rather, a meaning is constructed in the present by, for example, creating the artifact as aesthetic, or by constructing a situation or context which appears to give meaning to the artifact. But this is all delusion – a play of signifiers in the present. And yet the fascination of objects is their materiality: they appear to us as the "real thing." We are doubly duped – by the object as sign of an absence, and by the sign masquerading as a "real" material object connecting us to the past. The past seems separate from us and "really there," but in fact it is only a product of the present.

But where does all this deconstruction leave us? Isn't this just another discourse with another set of rules, concepts, and terms, the mastery of which is used to accumulate power and authority in the academy? The answer is yes, of course. This discourse, like all academic discourses, does lend itself to hierarchies and power. This point has been well made by feminists who have pointed out that post-processualism is simply the latest in a series of male-dominated discourses with little to say to women in the present or about women in the past (Engelstad 1991; Smith 1994). And the fact that this same tension between poststructuralism and feminism can be seen across the social sciences (Waugh 1992). This "deconstruction of deconstruction" is accurate as far as it goes, but it doesn't acknowledge an important aspect of this kind of discourse which sets itself apart from all other discourses. Critical discourse helps create the conditions for the possibility of the participation of alternative voices, voices such as feminists, indigenous people, and nationalist perspectives. The challenge yet to be faced by archaeology is how to create structures and organizations that will allow for the construction of a more inclusive and democratic profession.

Value-Committed Archaeologies

It is almost ten years since Shanks and Tilley's (1987) call for the reconstruction of archaeology in terms of value commitment. At that time they regarded as archaeology an active mediation between past and present grounded in three interrelated areas – understanding, critique, and commitment. The first of these, *understanding*, refers to a consideration of how material culture works in the social construction of reality. The second, *critique*, is an acknowledgment of the indeterminacy of archaeological knowledge and an exploration of the uses of the archaeological project in the present. The third, *value commitment*, describes the abandonment of the standard notion of objectivity in favor of the view that knowledge production is constrained by the local contexts and conditions.

A number of projects have now addressed the issue of what a value-committed archaeology might look like and these have met with varying degrees of success. Leone and Potter (Leone, Potter and Shackel 1987), for example, have experimented with several ways to empower the public at historic Annapolis (see Part VIII). The site tours and guides are intended to teach visitors and tourists how to question and challenge their guides and others who present the past. In a pamphlet specially created for public distribution Nancy Jo Chabot (in Leone and Potter, **chapter 22**) tells us why historical photographs should not be regarded as merely pictures of the past since their meaning is in part determined by their contemporary uses. Two photos of the same building are not the same simply because they have the same subject; there are often important differences in terms of perspective, or viewpoint differences in the circumstances of production. The past is thus reproduced in the present. In other words, the aim is to equip the general public with the tools needed to identify the ideological basis of different reconstructions of the past. This notion of empowerment means that the past is not to be used only by dominant groups, such as archaeologists, but rather is to be used by all groups in relation to their interests.

As we have seen, empowerment is a central focus of feminist archaeologies. This is typically accomplished by raising the consciousness of women and men archaeologists by demonstrating the existence of gender bias and exploring the ways in which it has an impact on professional careers (see Part VI). Here feminists are drawing upon the common experiences of women within the profession and appealing to notions of democracy and fairness. The recent publication of a special archaeological paper of the American Anthropological Association on equity issues for women in archaeology (Nelson, Nelson, and Wylie 1994) and the formation of professional task forces and workgroups is testimony to the seriousness with which the profession now views these issues. However, it is one thing to publish a collection of papers and quite another to tenure more women. The profession has been rather slow to respond in this area despite the critiques offered by Gero (1983, 1985), Kramer and Stark (1988) and others.

Empowerment is also associated with the encouragement of nationalist and indigenous archaeologies. Perhaps the best example of this is the One World archaeology of the World Archaeology Congress. At first glance, this One World might be seen as reminiscent of Clark's world archaeology and the cross-cultural emphasis so characteristic of processual archaeology. But this is a different "One World" in which "they" are speaking on all matters, including archaeological theory (Ucko 1995). Indigenous and non-Western groups are being encouraged to participate from their own perspectives rather than being spoken for through paternalism or universal science. This kind of empowerment is not easily accomplished and, indeed, is highly controversial both within and outside the profession, as the bitter debate concerning the Southampton World Archaeological Congress (WAC) conference in 1986 (Hodder 1986) and as the controversies surround the Native American Graves Protection and Repatriation Act (NAGPRA) and its implementation demonstrate (see Part VIII).

A difficulty which remains, however, is that empowerment is taught in the terms of the dominant discourse. Disadvantaged groups are often expected to engage with archaeologists in a universal scientific language which determines the very terms used in the debate and limits the directions criticism can take (see Part VIII). This extends as well to international archaeology. Olsen (1991) has drawn attention to the fact that any discussion of power in the production of archaeological knowledge must include a consideration of the context of the discussion. He suggests that archaeological discourse is presently dominated by the West in ways which might be termed "scientific colonialism." Why is it, he asks, that a paper on Southwestern archaeology published in *American Antiquity* is regarded as international while a conference attended by Norwegian and Swedish scholars is not, and, more to the point, why is it that the latter archaeologists concur with this categorization?

Another difficulty is that empowerment does not guarantee agreement or accord. The result is, as often as not, a cacophony of voices all claiming interests in the past, in the present. We have already seen why this happens. The past is routinely used to legitimize particular interests in the present and these interests may be at odds with one another. Does this mean that radical relativism must prevail, and that anything goes? Not at all. We feel that this criticism is misguided and suspect that it is motivated by the desire to retain disciplinary authority at all costs. It ignores the fact that we do have the ability to distinguish between different pasts and in fact we do it routinely in much the same way that we are able to distinguish between different interests in the present. Neither, as Wylie (1989) has pointed out, are data infinitely plastic; they effectively constrain our interpretations in very specific ways.

It can be argued that all archaeological approaches use some mixture of the following four strategies, whether consciously or not (Hesse 1995). The first is some commitment to the objectivity of the data. We have seen that even the most radical writers are concerned to deal with detail in the data (Shanks 1993; Tilley 1991; Yates 1993). The objectivity of the data is seen as "guarded" or "bracketed." It is not absolute, but there is a concern to demonstrate that the interpretive claims that are made are grounded in at least one reading of the data, construed in quantifiable terms. The second strategy is coherence. To be persuasive, the different types and levels of theory used must be compatible. This may be one of the reasons that most studies use a limited range of theories. The third strategy involves extending coherence into the social realm. Theories must make sense not only internally, but also externally in a particular historical context. A fourth strategy involves experience and autobiography. From a variety of different perspectives, authority is created through claims to have "encountered" the Other either through fieldwork, laboratory analysis of even just visiting a site. What counts is not only how this experience is publicly validated, but also how it affects the author in the light of his or her social and political identity.

Conclusion

We have seen that the control and representation of the past is thus a central arena of contest and negotiation in the social reproduction of society. The past cannot be set off, divorced from the present. It is always here, the past is present. This has as many implications for how we constitute ourselves as social beings as it does for the practice of archaeology as an academic discipline. We are continually reflecting on our experience, which is always "past experience" even if only a few moments ago. We do not so much "exist" in a static present as "become" in a continual process, in the continual flow of time. We have identified strategies of control and utopian visions of society and suggested that culture-historical, processual, and postprocessual can be understood in terms of different strategic responses to achieve these ideal societies. All three exhibit a concern for the democratization of the past, opening it up to greater participation by others, however defined. At the same time, this opening up has increasingly forced archaeologists to problematize their own authority as privileged guardians of and commentators on the past.

It could be argued that democratization, at least as it is applied in the opening up of specialized fields of knowledge, is not desirable since it has the potential to lead to a dispersal of meaning and will only result in further confusion and misinterpretations. Our own view is that power has a tendency to represent the world as unitary, monolithic, and stable, and, for this reason, must always be questioned; it is only by championing diversity that we can ensure further debate and critique of our taken-for-granteds. As cultural debate continues to be enlivened by the emergence of multiple voices, we expect the process to lead to revision of the terms in which it is expressed. For example, the emphasis on power can itself be seen as one-dimensional. The past is socially constructed, and the ways we have described that social construction here are themselves socially constructed. A critique of the emphasis on power and ideology has already emerged in archaeology (e.g. Tarlow 1992). Another critique of power emerges from various indigenous perspectives (Layton 1989). The relationship between the past and the present will itself be constructed in varied historical ways.

However, just as this diversity is beginning to be expressed it is being counteracted by the process of globalization, what might be called the spread of informational capitalism. This has both positive and negative aspects. On the positive side, new developments in computer technologies and networking have led to interactive displays, geographical information systems, multi-media, the world-wide web, and virtual reality. These allow for multiple experiences, hands-on museums, multiple interpretations, indigenous participation in exhibit planning and presentation. Many of the new theoretical developments in our understanding of the relationship between the past and the present are informed by, and made possible by, these new technologies. But at the same time, issues of access and control remain. Perhaps these new technologies will only increase the sophistication with which special interests manipulate the past to support their images of the present. Our historical experience with different forms of capitalism should lead us to be skeptical of claims by multicorporations that the information highway will automatically yield a more inclusive, democratic world. Our reflexivity needs to extend from the social and cultural to the material and technological. Archaeology thus has a very special role to play in society, a role which has come to the fore through the rise of postprocessual approaches and postmodernism more generally. That role is to investigate how the past and present mutually construct each other in the historical interplay of knowledge and power, in an "archaeology of knowledge" (Foucault 1972).

References

Bapty, I. 1990. Nietzsche, Derrida and Foucault: re-excavating the meaning of archaeology. In Bapty, I. and Yates, T. (eds) *Archaeology after Structuralism*. London, pp. 240–77.
Binford, L. 1962. Archaeology an anthropology. *American Antiquity* 28, 217–25.
Binford, L. 1989. *Debating Archaeology*. New York.
Clark, J.G.D. 1934. Archaeology and the state. *Antiquity* 8, 414–28.
Clark, J.G.D. 1961. *World Prehistory: An Outline*. Cambridge.
Clarke, D.L. 1973. Archaeology: the loss of innocence. *Antiquity* 47, 6–18.
Daniel, G. 1981. *A Short History of Archaeology*. London.
Engelstad, E. 1991. Images of power and contradiction: feminist theory and post-processual archaeology. *Antiquity* 65, 502–14.

Foucault, M. 1972. *The Archaeology of Knowledge and the Discourse on Language*. London.

Gathercole, P. and Lowenthal, D. (eds) 1989. *The Politics of the Past*. London.

Gero, J.M. 1983. Gender bias in archaeology: a cross-cultural perspective. In Gero, J.M., Lacey, D.M. and Blakey, M.L. (eds) *The Socio-Politics of Archaeology*. Department of Anthropology, University of Massachusetts, Research Report No. 23. Amherst, pp. 51–7.

Gero, J. 1985. Socio-politics of archaeology and the woman-at-home ideology. *American Antiquity* 50, 342–50.

Hesse, M. 1995. Past realities. In Hodder, I. and Shanks, M. et al. (eds) *Interpreting Archaeology*. London, pp. 45–7.

Hodder, I. 1986. Politics and ideology in the World Archaeological Congress 1986. *Archaeological Review from Cambridge* 5, 113–19.

Jacknis, I. 1985. Franz Boas and exhibits: on the limitations of the museum method in anthropology. In Stocking, G.W.Jr. (ed.) *Objects and Others: Essays on Museums and Material Culture*. Madison, pp. 75–111.

Kramer, C. and Stark, B. 1988. The status of women in archaeology. *Anthropology Newsletter* 29, 1, 11–12.

Layton, R. 1989. *Conflict in the Archaeology of Living Traditions*. London.

Leone, M. and Potter, P. Jr. 1992. Legitimation and the classification of archaeological sites. *American Antiquity* 57, 137–45.

Leone, M., Potter, P. and Shackel, P. 1987. Toward a critical archaeology. *Current Anthropology* 28, 283–302.

Lutz, C. A. and Collins, J. L. 1993. *Reading National Geographic*. Chicago.

Nelson, M., Nelson, S. and Wylie, A. 1994. (eds) *Equity Issues for women in Archaeology*. Archaeological Papers of the American Anthropological Association No. 5. Washington D. C.

Olsen, B. J. 1991. Metropolises and satellites in archaeology: on power and asymmetry in global archaeological discourse. In Preucel, R.W. (ed.) *Processual and Postprocessual Archaeologies: Multiple Ways of Knowing the Past*. Center for Archaeological Investigations, Occasional Paper No. 10, pp. 211–24.

Schiffer, M.B. 1976. *Behavioral Archaeology*. New York.

Shanks, M. and Tilley, C. 1987. *Reconstructing Archaeology*. Cambridge.

Silbermann, N.A. 1988 *Between Past and Present: Archaeology, Ideology and Nationalism in the Modern Near East*. New York.

Smith, L. 1994. Heritage management as postprocessual archaeology. *Antiquity* 8, 300–9.

Tarlow, S. 1992. Each slow dusk a drawing down of blinds. *Archaeological Review from Cambridge* 11, 125–40.

Tilley, C. 1991. *Material Culture and Text: The Art of Ambiguity*. London.

Ucko, P. 1995. *World Archaeological Theory*. London.

Watson, P. J., Redman, C. and Leblanc, S. 1971. *Explanation in Archaeology*. New York.

Waugh, P. 1992. *Modernism, Postmodernism, Feminism: Gender and Autonomy Theory*. London.

Wylie, A. 1989. Matters of fact and matters of interest. In Shennan, S.J. (ed.) *Archaeological Approaches to Cultural Identity*. London, pp. 94–109.

Yates, T. 1990. Archaeology through the looking-glass. In Bapty, I. and Yates, T. (eds) *Archaeology after Structuralism*. London, pp. 154–202.

Yates, T. 1993. Frameworks for an archaeology of the body. In Tilley, C. (ed.) *Interpretive Archaeology*. Oxford, pp. 31–72.

20

Public Presentations and Private Concerns: Archaeology in the Pages of *National Geographic*

Joan Gero and Dolores Root

This study attempts to understand how archaeology participates in the formation of the dominant political ideology of America. We start with the premise that the way in which any group of people charts its past, and what is valued from that past, are social practices, embedded in a larger logic and broader set of actions (Gero in press). The prehistoric past, like other aspects of knowledge, is mediated and constrained by a contemporary social context which provides an ideology for interpretation. At the same time, interpretations of the past play an active function, a *political* function, in legitimating the present context, naturalizing the past so that it appears to lead logically to present social practices and values (Conkey & Spector 1984, Leone 1984). In this chapter, we inspect how archaeology is presented in the pages of *National Geographic Magazine* and how, in this particular context, archaeology is touted, exploited, and capitalized upon to reinforce the dominant ideology that produced it. Thus, we hope to demonstrate the closeness of fit between archaeology as a particular means of organizing and presenting the past and the North American industrialized, capitalist state whose past it so effectively tells.

National Geographic Magazine, which in 1988 celebrated its hundredth year of publication, has enjoyed a particularly long history and wide circulation record in comparison with other popular American magazines. In fact, it is hardly an exaggeration to say that the sum total of what many Americans know about archaeology comes directly from its pages, or at least that it has often served as an introduction to and stimulus for learning more about the subject. Evidently the version of archaeology it presents is extremely effective in fixing images and transmitting messages about the past into American homes. Moreover, the origins, intellectual ancestry, and social lineage of the *National Geographic Magazine* are all peculiarly American, advancing the democratic principles on which the USA was founded and embodying the contradictions inherent in a capitalist class society. How then do images and accounts of archaeology in the magazine perpetuate the ideological interests and perspectives of American expansionism and capitalism?

The History of *National Geographic Magazine*

Before we delve into the familiar yellow-covered, glossy-paged magazine, some history is essential. The founding of the National Geographic Society in 1888 coincided with a transformed world view. There was a growing American faith in the production and distribution of goods as a primary means of improving the human condition. At the turn of the century, when *National Geographic Magazine* was modernized and assumed its present publication form, America's quest for new frontiers, new markets, and a knowledge of the world expanded in the larger context of a developing capitalist world order. Education, science, and research were promoted as the paths to American progress and to the growth of American power and influence (see Arnove 1980, Cawleti 1968, Harris 1978, Oleson & Voss 1979). The recognition that American progress depended on trained experts, together with an abundance of surplus capital, led to the formation of universities as we know them today and to national organizations of specialists and philanthropic foundations that sponsored scientific research. By the late 19th and early 20th centuries, once-isolated regional learned societies had become centred in an expanding network of national organizations dedicated to the advancement of specialized knowledge. These new organizations were seen as 'fundamental instruments of material and cultural progress' (Oleson & Voss 1979, p. ix). The formation of the National Geographic Society, dedicated to the advancement and dissemination of specialized geographic knowledge, was part of this movement.

National Geographic *and the democratic ideal*

The National Geographic Society's origins were exclusive and intellectual, growing out of a meeting between a group of genteel avocational scholars and a few celebrated geographers and explorers in January 1888, in the prestigious Cosmos Club in Washington, DC. Gardiner Greene Hubbard, a well-known lawyer and financial underwriter of the newly invented telephone, became the Society's first president; on his death in 1897, Alexander Graham Bell, a distinguished inventor, a founding father of the Society, and Hubbard's son-in-law, assumed the presidency of the Society, along with its then floundering publication. Bell's first step was to hand-pick and personally subsidize a new publications editor, choosing a recent Amherst College graduate and son of a close friend, Gilbert Hovey Grosvenor, who proceeded in 1900 to marry Bell's daughter Elsie May. In 1903, the Hubbard and Bell families presented the society with a permanent facility, Hubbard Memorial Hall, laying the foundations for a tight family venture that rapidly became a popular national institution.

In 1899, in a climate of increasing professionalism and specialization of knowledge, the educational distance between elite scholars and general readers was thought to be unbridgeable; the idea of making geography or any other scholarly pursuit accessible to a general audience was revolutionary in this context. One of Gilbert Hovey Grosvenor's first battles was to convince the Board of Managers that the best way to fulfil the mission of the Society's founding fathers – and the key to the magazine's solvency – was to take geography into the homes of the American people. He reasoned:

Why not transform the Society's magazine from one of cold geographic fact, expressed in hiero-glyphic terms which the layman could not understand, into a vehicle for carrying the living, breathing, human interest truth about this great world of ours? Would not that be the greatest agency of all for the diffusion of geographic knowledge? It was my job to change that bright vision into fact. But how to do it? Where to start? . . . Finally I was convinced I had the answer: each [article] was [to be] an accurate, eyewitness, firsthand account. Each contained simple, straightforward writing – writing that sought to make pictures in the reader's mind. (Grosvenor 1957, pp. 23–4)

Along with non-technical language, pictorial illustrations became the hallmark of the *National Geographic* making faraway places and people real and immediate while also humanizing them. The success of the first series of exotic photographs (1903), featuring Filipino women naked from the waist up, quickly confirmed Grosvenor's conviction of the power of pictures to make geography come alive and initiated a long-standing interest on the part of American male readers in the geography of foreign women.

As Grosvenor gained greater control over the magazine, becoming in 1907 its chief executive and a trustee of the Society, he increasingly asserted his populist vision of a magazine for large masses of people: 'We [felt we] should give our members what they wanted, not what some specialist thought they should have' (Grosvenor 1957, p. 34). A wide variety of natural phenomena, including plants and animals, prehistory and exotic peoples, became subjects of *National Geographic* articles and extended the life of the old rubric of 'natural history' into a time when scholars were parcelling it up among their various specialities (Pauly 1979, p. 527).

In the spirit of popularization and entrepreneurship, Grosvenor's second battle involved opening up membership of the National Geographic Society to anyone and everyone regardless of education, occupation, or social status, and using membership subscriptions to sponsor expeditions and underwrite publication costs. No distinctions were to be made between scholars and laymen, nor were there to be special fellows who alone would discuss and decide technical matters: "Class distinctions of this kind, which are very well in a monarchial country where aristocratic distinctions are recognized . . . [are] somewhat out of place in a republic like the United States" (Bell 1912, pp. 274–5).

At the same time, while assuring the membership that a professional elite did not dominate the Society, Grosvenor made membership appear special and exclusive. Membership was only to be by sponsorship, and if someone did not personally know a member, the Society would provide a list of people living close by who might become sponsors (Grosvenor 1957). In advising Grosvenor on this procedure, Alexander Graham Bell noted in 1904:

I think therefore the applicant should not be asked to enclose a check in payment of his dues as this suggests OF COURSE he will be elected a member if he sends his money. Such an impres-

sion should be avoided as tending to lower the dignity of the Society. (cited in Pauly 1979, p. 529)

Yet the membership has no voice in policy-making nor in the selection of research projects, which are partly funded through annual membership dues.

As recounted by Grosvenor (1936, 1957), it took several difficult years for his ideas of popularizing geography and subscription by membership to win the full support of the Board. By 1910, however, *National Geographic*'s mission of increasing membership subscriptions had become a frequent theme of editorial statements in the magazine that proudly asserted the financial independence of the democratic institution:

> *The society has no endowment, nothing coming to it but the membership fees. No millionaire has since come forward to help us out, yet the society today has a great endowment raised by its own efforts . . . We have never had to take off our hats to any multi-millionaire for having endowed the society with a million dollars; we have done it ourselves. (Bell 1912, p. 273)*

The reiterated myth of a membership of common people building their own society and responsible for their own fates has undoubtedly contributed to the outstanding success of the National Geographic Society; we trace its growth from 900 members in 1899 to more than 750 000 in 1920, to over a million in 1930, to two million by 1950, with membership topping 10 500 000 in 1981.

From the time of its populist reorganization, then, the National Geographic Society embodied a set of contradictions. On the one hand, we note its obviously elitist and intellectual foundations within a network of interrelated, intermarrying American blue-blood families who are closely aligned with the political and financial interests of the American capitalist establishment. On the other hand, we see in *National Geographic Magazine* the consistent promulgation of an ideology replicating the most sacred ideals of American democracy: participation by the common man on an equal footing in all endeavours, and the image of the rugged individual making it on his own. This was clearly stated in 1938: *National Geographic Magazine* 'helps to open up the highways and by-ways of the world . . . [and] the janitor, plumber and loneliest lighthouse keeper share with kings and scientists the fun of sending an expedition to Peru or an explorer to the South Pole' (Ross 1938, p. 24). Here, congruent with widely shared American values, the ideology of democracy has been used to mask the reality of elite control within the Society. This marked parallelism suggests that the magazine's popularity may depend in part on its ability to replicate American ideology so ingenuously, selling back to its readers what they already believe.

National Geographic *and American expansionism*

The growth of *National Geographic Magazine* also parallels the growth of American global influence. The turn of the century marks the beginning of economic and political expansionism beyond American continental borders, a strategy promoted in humanistic terms by the magazine. The National Geographic Society recognized that it 'could assist the nation in dealing effectively with its new global responsibilities through research in political and economic geography' (Pauly 1979, p. 521), and undertook to advertise the benefits of colonialism in a format that could be broadly embraced and widely understood. After building up military strength in the late 19th century, the United States moved to forge a confederation of North and South America in the so-called Pan American Union. The Spanish–American War of 1898 yielded new US possessions: the Philippines, Cuba, and Puerto Rico; Latin American countries and customs suddenly became of great interest and concern to Americans (Abramson 1987, p. 57).

National Geographic Magazine monitored territorial acquisitions and reported on geographical areas where changes of power seemed imminent. But it was the coverage of the First World War that really consolidated its readership around a national policy concern: each issue of the early war years summarized the preceding month's military highlights and plotted the combatants' positions; every article in 1917 and 1918 related directly to the war effort. Moreover, the National Geographic Society's maps were placed at the service of the military and when the draw law was passed, the Society offered the use of its stencil machines to help mail out the ten million notices, and its employees volunteered to run the machines. Copies of *National Geographic Magazine* were sent free to all army bases, camps, YMCAs, and to American soldiers fighting in Europe (Abramson 1987, p. 118).

When the war began in 1914, the National Geographic Society had 285 000 members; by the armistice in November 1918, membership had reached 650 000 (Abramson 1987, p. 119). Thereafter, the acquisition of territory, cheap labour, and political influence was inextricably linked to the acquisition of knowledge for American readers, all packaged together in winning smiles and hearty handshakes as *National Geographic* editors travelled the world, acting as self-proclaimed US good will ambassadors.

In aligning the interests of the Society with those of the nation, the editors associated themselves (and continue to do so) with the political and military leaders of the nation. Like large corporations and philanthropic foundations with their interlocking directorates, the Society has always invited policy-makers, captains of industry, statesmen, heads of government bureaus, and high-ranking military officials to serve as directors, extending its influence considerably beyond the realm of geographic research into the sphere of national and international

---

[1] The Board of Trustees for the National Geographic Society in 1960, for example, included the Director of the National Park Service, the Deputy Administrator of the National Aeronautics and Space Administration, the Director Emeritus of the National Bureau of Standards, the Vice Chief of Staff of the U.S. Air Force, the former Director of the U.S. Coast and Geodetic Survey, and the Secretary of the Smithsonian Institution, as well as the Chairman of the Board of Riggs National Bank, the Honorary Board Chairman of Chesapeake & Potomac Telephone Co., and the Vice President (retired) of the American Telephone and Telegraph Co. This roster of military, economic, and scholarly interests is typical of decades of National Geographic Society Boards of Trustees.

policy.[1] For many years, most contributors to *National Geographic Magazine* enjoyed official positions with various departments of the government and included United States presidents and vice-presidents, congressmen, justices of the Supreme Court, and members of the cabinet (Mott 1957, p. 625). It is the President of the United States who bestows the Society's Hubbard Medal for exceptional achievements in geography, although the head of state is obviously not involved in less politically relevant lines of scholarship.

Not only is the Society linked to national policy through its board of directors, but it has served the government in various ways. Its maps and photographs have provided 'a veritable goldmine' of information to the government and to intelligence sections of the armed services (1943, Vol. 83: 277[2]), and articles such as 'Maps for victory: National Geographic Society's charts used in war on land, sea and in the air' (1942, Vol. 81: 667) are typical wartime entries. Many articles assume a strong editorial tone, directly asserting US foreign policy in the framework of geographic concerns, as suggested by such titles as: 'Wards of the United States: notes on what our country is doing for Santo Domingo, Nicaragua, and Haiti' (1916, Vol. 30: 143); 'Germany's dream of world domination' (1918, Vol. 33: 559); 'The Hawaiian Islands: America's strongest outpost for defense – the volcanic and floral wonderland of the world' (1924, Vol. 45: 115); 'New map reveals the progress and wonders of our country' (1933, Vol. 63: 650); 'Your Society aids war effort' (1943, Vol. 83: 277); 'Pacific wards of Uncle Sam' (1948, Vol. 94: 80); and, 'Iraq – where oil and water mix' (1958, Vol. 114: 443).

National Geographic expressly perceives its role as an extension of American diplomacy. During the First World War, Grosvenor wrote, 'The months that lie ahead are pregnant with opportunities for national service and for achievements in the increase and diffusion of geographic knowledge . . . With the sustaining support of each individual member, the Society cannot fail to prove equal to and worthy of these opportunities' (1918, p. 375). In a letter to a friend in 1918 (1957, p. 5), he explicitly stated, 'I intend to use *National Geographic Magazine* to the best of my ability to promote a better understanding between Great Britain and the United States.'

National Geographic, then, is all-American, as American as Mom, apple-pie, and industrial capitalism. Its themes are expansion and discovery, homage to boundless American ability, ambition, and resourcefulness, showing that Americans can go anywhere and do anything, and that strategic resources for some is knowledge for all. Here is geography at the service of society, promoting America, democracy, and internationalism through exploration, expansion, and imperialism:

> *The clerk in the store or the mechanic in a mill may not consciously engage in any enterprise [of discovery], but when he learns that the government of which he is a part has . . . opened a town on the shores of the North Pacific . . . and has driven a railroad nearly 40 miles inland toward the Arctic Circle on its way to the coal fields of the Matanuska and gold fields of the*

---

[2] Throughout this chapter, all references to volumes without authors are citations from particular issues of *National Geographic Magazine*.

Tanana, he has a feeling that he, too, is participating in the making of this new world. (Secretary of the Interior Franklin Lane in National Geographic Magazine, 1915, Vol. 28: 590)

National Geographic readers are swept along in the expansionist, imperialist enterprise, given gorgeous pictures and thrilling undertakings in the name of American goodwill, accepting the ideology of a collective good derived from a course of national imperialism. Yet official editorial policy maintained (and maintains) a contradictory neutrality. Clearly formulated the same year as Lane's expansionist pronouncement, it was encapsulated in 'Seven [editorial] principles' (Vol. 28: 318–20):

1 The first principle is absolute accuracy;
2 An abundance of beautiful, instructive and artistic illustrations;
3 Everything printed in the Magazine must have permanent value;
4 All personalities and notes of a trivial character are avoided;
5 Nothing of a partisan or controversial character is printed;
6 Only what is of a kindly nature is printed about any country or people, everything unpleasant or unduly critical being avoided;
7 The contents of each number is planned with a view of being timely.

These same principles were reaffirmed almost verbatim in the magazine in 1936 and again in 1957, during the second half of Gilbert Hovey Grosvenor's 54 years as editor and director, and then again by his son Melville Bell Grosvenor in 1967, ten years after assuming the editorship, and yet again by his grandson, Gilbert M. Grosvenor, the Society's current president, in 1974 and in 1978. The bloodline continuity of leadership underscores the remarkable consistency of editorial policy and publication programme maintained by the magazine throughout its existence. As the principles are repeated, they reiterate a journalistic honour code, insisting on the impartiality of the magazine. It is the disavowed propaganda which we now examine in seeing how archaeology is treated in its pages.

Analysis of Archaeology in *National Geographic Magazine*

The archaeological content of *National Geographic Magazine* reveals various ways that archaeology is used to build and promote a nationalist ideology. The information presented here is based on a survey of the distribution of all the magazine's archaeological articles from 1900 to 1985, and on a more intensive systematic sample of archaeology articles that appeared every third year of publication, supplemented by additional volumes when historically needed. In total, more than 50 per cent of the volumes published between 1900 and 1985 were researched. We discuss our findings under three broad categories that delineate ways in which we believe the magazine used archaeological research to further its goals.

The thrill of archaeology

J.O. LaGorce, G.H. Grosvenor's first paid employee and a long-time *National Geographic* editor, recognized the power of glamourized knowledge: 'Behind the term geography is exploration. Behind that is adventure and just over the hill is romance' (Hellman 1943, p. 29). Behind archaeology in the magazine is an intensification of drama that portrays archaeology as a process of exploration and discovery, emphasizing resource extraction and a search for treasure. Archaeology validates the exploration of exotic landscapes in the name of scientific enterprise, using tales of archaeological discovery to heighten knowledge into super-drama, entertaining a popular fascination with the remote and the spectacular while progressive inroads are made to extract the resources of foreign lands. Archaeological sites are overtly cast as reservoirs of enormous riches, as seen in article titles spanning decades of publication:

1912   'Forgotten ruins of Indo-China: the most profusely and richly carved group of buildings in the world' (Vol. 10: 392)
1930   'A new alphabet of the ancients is unearthed: an inconspicuous mound in northern Syria yields archaeological treasures of far reaching significance' (Vol. 58: 477)
1942   'Finding jewels of jade in a Mexican swamp' (Vol. 82: 635)
1955   'Fresh treasures from Egypt's ancient sands' (Vol. 108: 611)
1965   'Drowned galleons yield Spanish gold' (Vol. 127: 1)
1978   'Regal treasures from a Macedonian tomb' (Vol. 154: 55)

The hint of treasure is always gleaming behind the edge of the archaeologists' shovel or trowel, as *National Geographic* systematically blurs the distinction between 'treasures of scientific value' and items that would bring huge prices on the international art and antiquities market.

There is one significant caveat to acquiring archaeological treasure: in contrast with other geoscientific endeavours, archaeology offers rewards of data, artefactual and associated, only to the investigator who arrives *first* at the site. Subsequent scholars who come to study find little but architectural foundations, backdirt piles, and debitage. The difference between actually opening the tomb/raising the galleon/finding the jewels or jade *versus* getting to the site even shortly after the excavations are closed underscores archaeology as the particular kind of all-or-nothing enterprise that demands Americans be quick and aggressive, daring and venturesome. First-person accounts emphasize the drama of personal risk:

1924   'Discovering the oldest statues in the world! A daring explorer swims thru subterranean river of the Pyrenes and finds rock carvings made 20,000 years ago' (Vol. 46: 123)
1933   'Air adventures in Peru: cruising among Andean peaks, pilots and cameraman discover wondrous works of an ancient people' (Vol. 63: 81)
1942   'Discovering Alaska's oldest Arctic town: a scientist finds ivory eyed skeletons of

a mysterious people and joins modern Eskimoes in dangerous spring whale hunt'
(Vol. 82: 319)

1953   'Hunting prehistory in Panama jungles' (Vol. 104: 271)

The implicit involvement of the magazine in promoting these ventures, and the
almost universal domination of American archaeologists at these scenes, dramatically illustrate that these riches are Americans' for the taking, and shows
Americans as 'right for the job'.

The appeal of exploration and treasure seeking in the magazine depends heavily
on high-quality, close-up photographs that heighten the impact of discovery and
convey the immediacy of being at the scene. Photographs, too, abbreviate and
intensify action, obviating the textual narration for 'readers' who want a fast and
dramatic skim of the material. Although most archaeologists recognize that data
collection requires patient planning and the often tedious conducting of fieldwork,
the archaeologists pictured in *National Geographic Magazine* exhibit extraordinary
hyperactivity. Photographs depict archaeologists crawling, clambering, climbing,
scaling, burrowing, swimming, diving, slinging sledgehammers, driving dog
teams, and more, all in the direct line of duty. A particularly splashy piece in 1963,
'Relics from the rapids' (Vol. 124: 412–35), illustrates the recovery of historic artefacts from a voyageur canoe dump site; the archaeologists are shown splashing and
tumbling in the rapids, holding artefacts above their heads and bobbing through
chutes and standing waves, an absurdly improbable dramatization of doing
archaeology.

But this ruggedness ties archaeologists to other explorers and exemplifies the
bold, competitive spirit that made the United States a world power. Moreover, the
explorer-archaeologist in *National Geographic Magazine* equates spatial frontiers
with scientific frontiers, as Secretary of the Interior Franklin K. Lane suggested
(1915, p. 595): The 'absorbing determination [of the American people] to "go forth
and find" ' is directly linked to learning 'what this land is, what it will yield to
research, and *how it may best be used*' [emphasis ours]. Archaeology argues that to
gain new knowledge you have to get to new places, and to get there first you have
to be tough.

To dramatize the lengths to which archaeologists will go to acquire knowledge,
archaeological photographs in *National Geographic* regularly feature context or
overview shots that situate sites in the most remote and challenging locations,
surrounded and isolated by jungle or desert, or in the middle of vast spaces without
roads or airstrips. Aerial views of Angkor Wat show it standing inviolate in its
remote jungle setting (Vol. 161: 554–5); Pueblo Bonito is dwarfed by mesas and
butes stretching in unbroken vastness in all directions (Vol. 162: 555); Mayan caves
are photographed from across the river, suggesting one more barrier to their exploration (Vol. 160: 223). Knowledge, again, consists of covering (or uncovering) new
ground; greater remoteness means greater knowledge.

National Geographic's coverage of archaeology never dwells on explanations of
prehistory or technical aspects of excavation. Rather, the editorial emphasis is on
the quest: the quest in which one must be first, and for which one must traverse

great distances in order to acquire artefacts, and, above all, the unique artefact. The most frequent photographic image in its articles on archaeology displays the *unique artefact*, torn from its original production and use context and cleared from its recent archaeological matrix. These hand-held or free-standing treasures abound from the earliest to the most recent volumes of the magazine, almost invariably representing whole artefacts (fragments, sherds, flakes, or parts are seldom illustrated). The beauty and costliness of items, the intensity of labour involved in their production, are highlighted; especially common are pieces of jewellery (necklaces, brooches, rings, pins, pendants), elaborately decorated vessels, pots or amphorae, pieces of technological paraphernalia (watches, measuring instruments, tools used in production) – the finest, the first, the biggest, the best. These are the possessions of elite consumers and specialist producers; other classes of material culture from which the archaeologist could construct a typology or derive a seriated sequence are virtually never included. Image after image makes it clear that unique artefacts are the hunted treasure, exaggerating but also distorting the archaeological tendency towards an entirely material representation of the past. Long after the professionals have declared scientific explanation to the the goal of archaeology, *National Geographic Magazine* still promotes an object-centered view of the past.

Humanizing and homogenizing the past

National Geographic also manipulates prehistory and archaeology by investing prehistoric individuals with feelings, personalities, and thoughts, offering 'portraits' of past ways of life, emphasizing first-person narratives of the archaeologist, and juxtaposing photographs of archaeological research with modern natives. Early archaeologists often patronizingly describe the foreign places in which they worked; W. M. Flinders Petrie (1903, p. 359) characterizes Egypt for its 'lawlessness . . . bribery and the suppression of truth'; Hiram Bingham (1915, 1916) notes the prehistoric simplicity of present-day Peruvian primitives. Now increasingly written by staff reporters, articles endeavour to capture professional personalities, scholarly passions, or strong emotions at the time of discovery. In a 1978 article on Minoan and Mycenean civilizations, Dr Heinrich Schliemann and Sir Arthur Evans come alive as 'two brilliant, eccentric and rich men [who] almost single handedly revealed the Bronze Age origins of European civilization to a stunned world' (Vol. 153:148). Readers are invited to experience the past directly through *National Geographic's* reporting, as when Mary Leakey projects her emotions upon discovering preserved Pliocene footprints:

> At one point, and you need not be an expert tracker to discover this, the traveller stops, pauses, turns to the left to glance at some possible threat or irregularity, then continues to the north. This motion, so intensely human, transcends time. Three million seven hundred thousand years ago, our remote ancestor – just as you or I – experienced a moment of doubt. (1985, Vol. 168:592)

Frequently, the past is made more accessible through the lens of contemporary American concepts, categories, and social relations, homogenizing all pasts to look like ours, and marking all prehistoric events along a timeline of the rise of Western civilization. The ruins of Tiahuanacu in Bolivia are compared to Stonehenge and other European dolmens (1927, Vol. 51: 218); the timescale of strata from Russell Cave in Alabama is correlated to great events in Western civilization, including the landing of the Pilgrims in 1620, the birth of Christ, the construction of Egypt's pyramids, etc. (1956, Vol. 110: 542–58). A 1936 article on Mexican archaeology is entitled 'In the empire of the Aztecs: Mexico City is rich in relics by a people who practiced human sacrifice, yet loved flowers, education and art, (Vol. 71: 725), as though sacrifice and flowers were incongruous in any terms but our own. Everyday life at Russell Cave, Alabama, is depicted in the following terms:

> *Naked children dash hither and yon about the mouth of the cave, playing the boisterous games of youth. As sunset nears, the men return to divide their kill . . . Soon each family gathers around its fire to eat, laugh, and boast of the day's experiences . . . Only the glow of dying embers testifies that humans are here asleep. Generation after generation life goes on . . . (1958, Vol. 113: 430)*

Skeletons are given flesh and evaluated accordingly, as in an article on Herculaneum, where the caption beneath an artist's reconstruction reads, 'Beauty more than skin deep . . . in life she was about 35 years old . . . with a lovely face of rare proportion, perfect teeth and a dainty nose' (1984, Vol. 165: 588–9). Again and again, present-day American values are extended into the past, onto the peoples of the past, appropriated by us to represent us in an earlier state.

The photographs of modern natives also humanize archaeological landscapes, again connecting the past with the present. In the 91 archaeology articles canvassed in our survey, close to one half of the photographs show modern natives of the country in which the site is located. Natives are often pictured associated with excavations, as workmen or labourers, or used for scale or to point out artefacts or site features. Early photographs of workmen usually cast them as children: 'The men's vitality is remarkable, after a hard day's work excavating they will run home singing and dancing' (1930, Vol. 57: 111), and as exotics: 'A neat hand with a dagger is often a neat hand with a pick. The workmen in the Near East cannot always be selected according to European standards of reliability' (ibid.). Since large-scale archaeological projects seem to be *National Geographic*'s preference, photographs characteristically feature hundreds of workmen, necessitating some assurance to readers that scientific methods are still in use. Beneath the photograph of an archaeologists perched on a high tower is the caption: 'Though the 250 native workers, soldiers and prisoners displayed habitual good humor, constant diligence was needed to prevent careless handling of precious ancient objects unearthed' (1933, Vol. 64:126).

Readers are also bombarded with photographic images of 'the Other', the *non-*American, often manipulated to maximize contrast with American lives and values. Frequently, natives with no apparent connection to the archaeological

Figure 20.1 [orig. figure 2.1]   Maya man, used almost as a scale against a sculpted figure from his
glorious past
(Carnegie Institution – National Geographic Magazine, *January 1925, p. 86).*

project are posed either standing or striding in front of ruins, human scales for
more than the size of archaeological features – scale, too, for differences in the
human condition (figure 20.1). We are told explicitly that these modern natives
represent the living, breathing descendents of a glorious past, but the photographs
reveal a present-day material impoverishment far below our level of modern
American technology. 'Though kingdoms rise and fall, these Kurdish ferrymen
carry on' (1930, Vol. 57: 103). Again and again, the equation is made between what
is unearthed and a native material culture, between the indigenous technology and
what was practised millennia before, between a modern phsyiognomy and physical characteristics depicted in antiquity. A contrastive photograph juxtaposes
dancing figures on a painted prehistoric vessel against modern Cretans: 'Across
the gulf of countless generations, the Minoan love of dance still find expression in
Crete where villagers at Lasithi (right) need little excuse to take to their feet' (1978,
Vol. 153: 146).

   The emphasis is always on the changelessness of backward peoples, even in the
face of modernization coming from the West; picture the photograph with this
caption: 'Bedouins, camels, goats, sheep, a happy desert family camp beside a well
at Al Jauf . . . A pipeline, gift of Americans who drilled here for oil, leads to a diesel
pump. Black goat-hair tents of nomads date back to Biblical times' (1948, Vol. 93:
492). Rich Clarkson (1986), director of photography for the magazine, tells of hiring
a camel train and directing its route in front of Egyptian pyramids for one
published cover. The message from *National Geographic* is clear: over time, 'they'

Figure 20.2 [orig. figure 2.2]   Europeans in suits and hats at the Theseum, Athens
(*Keystone Press* – National Geographic Magazine, *September 1916, p. 272).*

have progressed so little (or have even retrogressed), while 'we' have come so far, superseding and by implication surpassing the ancient civilizations which they represent. Are not these innocents *with* their ruins quite *'in ruins'* themselves?

One significant exception to the patterned pairing of ruins and natives can be observed. In pictures of classical Greek and Roman sites, or clearly Eurocentric sites, raggedy Greek or Italian children or backward-looking natives are notably absent. Instead, a highly evolved European type is consistently paired with his architectural origins, standing in suit and top hat at the Temple of Jupiter in Baalbeck (1912, Vol. 23) or in front of the Theseum in Athens (1916, Vol. 30). These images stress the evolutionary progress of Europeans by contrast with the evolutionary arrest of Others (figure 20.2). Decade after decade, classical sites of Greece record changing American fashions as tourists are posed with their 'origins' (1963, Vol. 124; 1980, vol. 157), while non-European sites exhibit the exotic native in timeless garb. This same distinction is reflected in the treatments accorded to jewellery recovered from the African site of Jenne Jeno, modelled by an indigenous African woman, and the jewellery from Herculaneum adorning the neck, arm, and finger of a modern high-fashion blonde model. Supposedly primitive natives are matched with the remains from African countries; whites are paired with remains of our own self-declared heritage. In all these comparisons, archaeology becomes a convenient vehicle for examining the exotic 'Other' in relation to ourselves, and for promoting self-congratulatory American well-being. Moreover, by reiterating the primitiveness of peoples from backward lands, and by posing Americans beside the cultural remains they claim as their heritage, the right of Americans to excavate everywhere, to dig anyone's past, is proclaimed and validated.

Selective slants in National Geographic *archaeology*

Archaeological reporting and imagery in *National Geographic Magazine* are also slanted by systematic geographic, topical, and chronological emphases. Selections are ostensibly guided by Grosvenor's seven sacrosanct editorial principles: topics are to be accurately reported, photogenic, impersonal, of permanent value, non-partisan, non-critical, timely. In fact, the magazine's ideological and nationalistic bent overrides these concerns, distorting archaeological inquiries in various ways.

Throughout the magazine's history, whole continents and subcontinents – Australia, India, China, Southeast Asia and Africa – receive little attention. Except for Leakeys' contributions, our sample contains only two archaeological articles on Africa exclusive of Egypt[3] (one treats the Roman site of Carthage). South American archaeology is largely restricted to Hiram Bingham's work at Macchu Picchu; Central American archaeology is almost entirely devoted to the Maya. Preponderant coverage is given to archaeological investigations in the Middle East (23 per cent) and Europe (15 per cent). Within these geographic areas, Middle Eastern archaeology in *National Geographic* focuses on biblical history and other antecedents of Western civilization, while European prehistory emphasizes classical Greek and Roman sites. The magazine gives disproportionate attention to the cultural development of Western civilization and to the origins of the Judaeo-Christian tradition.

In highlighting these aspects of the archaeological record, it is not surprising that the magazine concentrates on the archaeology of state-level societies. To be sure, early seafaring, temple-building, and biblical states leave behind dramatically photogenic monuments, tombs, and artefactual evidence. But such images make the past appear to be like the present and lead the public to believe that the state has always existed and is the norm as well as the most successful form of social organization. This misrepresentation of the past conveniently gives a time-depth to the American state, underwriting a logic that portrays this system of governance as innately human and intrinsic to the human condition.

The archaeology presented is also dominated by the actions and images of males,

---

[3] Egypt is considered as part of the Middle East.

reiterating the sexual bias that makes exploration and discovery unambiguously man's work in a man's world. Out of the 74 articles in which the gender of the archaeologist could be identified, only two articles feature female archaeologists, with another five recognizing females as co-partners with males. The naked eye of the camera shows the occasional female participant in archaeology in postures of near repose, seated in the laboratory or sometimes in an excavation unit, often merely observing what is being pointed out to her (Gero 1983, 1985) and never engaged in the frenzied physical action characteristic of males doing 'proper' archaeology. Photographs of male and female co-investigators poring over data show the females recording dictated notes or being shown the niceties of artefacts indicated by the males; yet the captions ('Two doctors look for disease in ancient bones from Crete') clarify that both individuals are in charge of the research (Vols 148: 769 & 159: 219). Inevitably, it is the rugged adult male with his virile vitality who best exemplifies the ethic of aggressive American expansionism that is part and parcel of the *National Geographic* image of the archaeological endeavour.

Images of natives in *National Geographic Magazine* serve to humanize and interpret the past well into the present. After 1950, however, they are overshadowed by images of technological prowess in archaeology, emphasizing a new reliance on scientific technology for uncovering the secrets of the human past. Technological innovations appear soon after their earliest applications in archaeological research: radiocarbon dating is reported in 1950; deep-sea diving advances are frequently presented and continually updated after the early 1960s; computer applications to archaeological reconstructions are featured in 1970. In the international arena, *National Geographic* asserts America's technological superiority, which enables, and even guarantees, accurate interpretation of the archaeological record. The primacy given to scientific technology confirms that those nations possessing sophisticated technology must be at the forefront of geographic and archaeological research. Moreover, images of technological prowess underscore these nations' right to extract and to interpret the archaeological resources of the world, thereby legitimizing American expansionism and the accompanying asymmetrical social relations.

Conclusion

For close to one hundred years, *National Geographic* has played an active role in promulgating a nationalist ideology, presenting a view of the past that promotes technological progress as cultural superiority, expansionism as scientific inquiry for the benefit of humankind, and democratic state systems as inevitable and normative outgrowths of the great civilizations of the ancient Western world. Beginning with Gilbert Hovey Grosvenor in 1915, the editors have claimed an unbiased, objective reporting of the facts; in 1978 Gilbert Melville Grosvenor reasserted that the magazine 'will continue to travel the world unencumbered by ideology . . . as the world goes its way, we will record it, accurately and clearly' (Vol. 153: 1). But the articles identified here reverberate with messages that naturalize the material and social conditions of an expanding capitalist society: the past is represented in objects, particularly exquisite objects associated with prehistoric elites; the lavish material conditions enjoyed by Americans are contrasted with those of other times and other peoples; and prehistory is concentrated into those parts of the globe that illuminate the cultural antecedents of Western industrial society.

Photography is *National Geographic*'s principal medium of communication, crucial to its interpretation of archaeology. It is not used, as in archaeological scholarship, to record strata, assemblages, fragments of artefacts, or architectural detail. Instead, it brings into the American living room the exotic 'Other' together with the romance of the undiscovered past, making American expansionism and imperialism picturesque. *National Geographic* graphically illustrates archaeology-as-exploration, turning the discovery of rare resources into high drama and humanistic exchange. Implicitly building on the assertion that photography is precise and accurate, the magazine's photographs guilefully assert the inherent superiority of Euro-American males and the morality of cultural progress. Lessons of power, of national and racial hierarchies, and of the social relations of domination are frozen in the hardware and logic of the photograph (after Haraway 1984–5).

In popularizing archaeology for an American audience, *National Geographic* distorts archaeological practice by stressing exploration in remote places and the physical demands of field archaeology, overemphasizing the discovery of 'lost' civilizations, opulent artefacts, and bizarre social practices. Its analysis and interpretation of the archaeological record are generally limited to depictions and descriptions of the spectacular remains of prehistory, frequently embellished with characterizations that promote the American mythos. Filtered through a contemporary vision and rationale, *National Geographic*'s telling of the past replicates and extends back in time the values and structures of our dominant ideology: Eurocentrism, nationalism, racism, materialism, sexism, and emphasis on state-level society.

It was the opening premise of this chapter that our constructions of the past are mediated by present social contexts and serve a political function in legitimating our social and material conditions of existence. We have argued that *National Geographic*'s popularization of archaeology advances a nationalist ideology and legitimizes American expansionism abroad. But how much of this promulgation of American ideology stems from *National Geographic*'s popularization of archaeology? And, conversely, how much does the American ideology promulgated by the magazine overlap with the agenda of archaeological scholarship?

North American archaeology and *National Geographic* share a common heritage: both grew out of industrial capitalism and prospered with American imperialism. Archaeology as practised in North America (and Western Europe) is fundamentally a Western science (Hall 1984); its approach to understanding the past is part and parcel of the objectified and commoditized view of the world inherent in the capitalist mode of production. The artefact-laden past portrayed in *National Geographic Magazine* only slightly exaggerates the role of archaeology in Western industrialized society, where units of production and labour and time are measured against a value standardized the whole world over. The material record, the central focus for most archaeological investigations, is often held to represent a distillation of individual, material solutions to problems, such that the past is universally measured in terms of rational utility. The embeddedness of persons and objects in a social world is disjoined by a Western ideology that maintains a natural discontinuity between social and material spheres (Comaroff 1985). It is these commoditized views of the world, integral to scientific archaeology, that are sold to the public by *National Geographic Magazine*.

The past we construct, then, is more than passively conditioned by our political and economic system; it is a direct product of, and an effective vehicle for, that system's ideological messages. As a product of Western logic controlled by Western practice, archaeology reduces the cultural distance between past and present by reifying a commoditized view of the world and the values that support that view. Archaeology as an enterprise legitimizes the hegemony of Western culture and Western imperialism and imposes a congruent view onto the past, one that is ably promoted by successful media such as *National Geographic*.

Acknowledgements

We wish to thank James Faris for lending enthusiasm to the undertaking. The content and images of many *National Geographic* archaeology articles were creatively and systematically researched by Kimberly Grimes, Richard Handler made important contributions to this chapter after a careful, critical reading of an earlier draft, and Stephen Loring's powers of perception produced important insights. In the end, however, we acknowledge full responsibility for the final form our argument has taken.

References

Abramson, H.S. 1987. *National Geographic: behind America's lens on the world*. New York: Crown.
Arnove, R. (ed.) 1980. *Philanthropy and cultural imperialism*. Boston: G.K. Hall.
Bell, A.G. 1912. History of the magazine. *National Geographic Magazine* 23, 273–4.
Bingham, H. 1915. The story of Macchu Picchu: the Peruvian expeditions of the National Geographic Society and Yale University. *National Geographic Magazine* 27, 172–217.
Bingham, H. 1916. Further explorations in the land of the Incas by the National Geographic Society. *National Geographic Magazine* 29, 431–73.
Cawleti, J.G. 1968. America on display: the World's Fairs of 1876, 1893 and 1933. In *The age of industrialism in America: essays in social science and cultural values*, F.C. Jaher (ed.), 317–63. New York: Free Press.
Clarkson, R. 1986. 'Mediocrity and the Golden Age'. The Niels Lauritzen Lecture, presented at the University of South Carolina, Columbia, 22 September.
Comaroff, J. 1985. *Body of power, spirit of resistance*. Chicago: University of Chicago Press.
Conkey, M.W. & J. Spector 1984. Archaeology and the study of gender. In *Advances in archaeological method and theory, Vol. 7*, M.B. Schiffer (ed.), 1–38. New York: Academic Press.
Gero, J.M. 1983. Gender bias in archaeology: a cross-cultural perspective. In *The socio-politics*

of archaeology, J.M. Gero, D.M. Lacey & M.L. Blakey (eds), 51–7. *Amherst: University of Massachusetts, Department of Anthropology Research Report No. 23.*

Gero, J.M. 1985. *Socio-politics of archaeology and the woman-at-home ideology. American Antiquity* 50, 342–50.

Gero, J.M. In press. Producing prehistory, controlling the past: the case of the New England Beehives. In *Critical traditions in archaeology*, V. Pinksy & A. Wylie (eds). Cambridge University Press.

Grosvenor, G. 1936. The National Geographic Society and its magazine. *National Geographic Magazine* 69, 123–64.

Grosvenor, G. 1957. *National Geographic Society and its magazine: a history.* Washington, DC: National Geographic Society.

Hall, M. 1984. The burden of tribalism: the social context of southern African Iron Age studies. *American Antiquity* 49, 455–67.

Haraway, D. 1984–5. Teddy bear patriarchy: taxidermy in the Garden of Eden, New York City, 1908-1936. *Social Text* 11, 20–64.

Harris, N. 1978. Museums, merchandising and popular taste: the struggle for influence. In *Material culture and the study of American life*, I.M.G. Quimby (ed.), 140–74. New York: Norton.

Hellman, G. 1943. Geography unshackled – part I. *New Yorker Magazine*, 25 September, 26–34.

Lane, F.K. 1915. The nation's pride. *National Geographic Magazine* 28, 589–606.

Leone, M.L. 1984. Interpreting ideology in historical archaeology: using the rules of perspective in the William Paca Garden in Annapolis, Maryland. In *Ideology, power, and prehistory*, D. Miller & C. Tilley (eds), 25–35. Cambridge: Cambridge University Press.

Mott, F.L. 1957. *A history of American magazines, volume IV: 1885-1905.* Cambridge, Mass.: Harvard University Press.

Oleson, A. & J. Voss 1979. Introduction. In *The organization of knowledge in modern America, 1860–1920*, A. Oleson & J. Voss (eds), vii-xxi. Baltimore: Johns Hopkins University Press.

Pauly, P. 1979. 'The world and all that is in it': The National Geographic Society, 1888–1918. *American Quarterly* 31, 517–32.

Petrie, W.M. Flinders 1903. Excavations at Abydos. *National Geographic Magazine* 14, 358–9.

Ross, I. 1938. Geography, Inc. *Scribner's Magazine* 103, 23–7 and ff.

21

The Past as Propaganda: Totalitarian Archaeology in Nazi Germany

Bettina Arnold

After almost six decades, there is no comprehensive account by a German-speaking prehistorian of the effects of prehistoric scholarship on the National Socialist regime, or the rôle played by archaeology in legitimating it. This paper addresses the following questions: What were the foundations of German prehistoric research under the National Socialists (NS)? What rôle did prehistory play in the process of political legitimation from 1933 to 1945? What did the NS system offer to prehistorians in exchange for their part in this legitimation process? What was the official Party policy regarding prehistoric archaeology? What was the response of the discipline to this Faustian bargain? What were the effects of state control on excavation and research? How is German prehistoric archaeology affected by this legacy today?

The Foundations of the 'Preeminently National Discipline'

To understand events in German prehistoric archaeology under the National Socialists, it is necessary to look at the discipline well before Hiltler's rise to power in 1933 and the beginning of the *Umbruch* period of radical change. Archaeology in Central Europe at the eve of the First World War was marked by a return of the ethnohistoric approach to theory: in German-speaking regions there was a new name for the discipline to go with its new orientation. The term *Vorgeschichte* (prehistory) was rejected as a survival of anthropological thinking: *Urgeschichte* (early history) was preferred as better emphasizing the continuity of prehistory with documentary history (Sklenar 1983: 132). The writings of the 19th-century French racial philosopher Gobineau provided a doctrine of the inequality of different races (Daniel & Renfrew 1988: 104–6). Journals and publications dealing with the subject of race and genetic engineering increasingly appeared in Germany in the early 20th century, among them *Volk und Rasse*, which was founded in 1926, and *Fortschritte der Erbpathologie und Rassenhygiene*, founded in 1929. Neither publication survived the Second World War.

The groundwork for an ethnocentric German prehistory was laid by Gustaf

Figure 21.1 [orig. figure 1]   Gustaf Kossinna (Mannus 1931: 337).

Kossinna (1858–1932), a linguist who was a late convert to prehistory, (figure 21.1). Kossinna proposed cultural diffusion as a process whereby influences, ideas and models were passed on by more advanced peoples to the less advanced with which they came into contact. This concept, wedded to Kossinna's *Kulturkreis* theory, the identification of geographical regions with specific ethnic groups on the basis of material culture, lent theoretical support to the expansionist policies of Nazi Germany. 'Distribution maps of archaeological types became a convincing argument for expansionist aims: wherever a single find of a type designated as Germanic was found, the land was declared ancient German territory. . .' (Sklenar 1983: 151) (figure 21.2).

Alfred Rosenberg, the Party's ideologist, codified this ethnocentric and xenophobic perspective: 'An individual to whom the tradition of his people (*Volkstum*) and the honor of his people (*Volksehre*) is not a supreme value, has forfeited the right to be protected by that people' (*Germanenerbe 1938:105*). Applied to prehistoric archaeology, this perspective resulted in the neglect or distortion of data which did not directly apply to Germanic peoples: during the 1930s scholars whose main interests were provincial Roman archaeology were labeled *Römlinge* by the extremists and considered anti-German (Jacob-Friesen 1950: 4). The Römisch Germanische Kommission in Mainz, founded in 1907 by Schuchhardt and his circle (Eggers 1986: 220), was the object of defamatory attacks, first by Kossinna and later

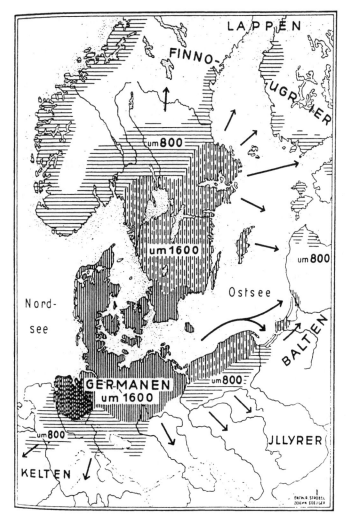

Figure 21.2 [orig. figure 2]   A distribution map of "Germanic" territory during the Bronze Age
(Reinerth 1945: figure 2).

by Rosenberg and his organization, primarily because it concentrated on the excavation and study of provincial Roman Germany (Bollmus 1970: Eggers 1986: 234).

The connection between prehistory and politics was of long standing, not a new product of the National Socialist regime. The fledgling discipline evolved from the pan-European geographic divisions and rise of nationalism that followed the First World War (Sklenar 1983: 131). Politicians began to take an interest in prehistoric archaeology, which seemed well suited to nationalist visions. Hindenburg's interest in Kossinna's work is well documented (*Mannus-Bibliothek* 1928: Frontispiece). Kaiser Wilhelm II was a frequent visitor to Schuchhardt's excavations at the Römerschanze near Potsdam: after one visit, he sent Schuchhardt a telegram: 'Continue excavations and ascertain whether [Römerschanze] still Volksburg or already Fürstensitz' (Eggers 1986: 224). Between 1905 and 1914 the Kaiser also helped finance a number of archaeological excavations undertaken by the Duchess of Mecklenburg, in what is now the Yugoslav Republic of Slovenia, and at Hallstatt in Austria. The skull of a well-preserved skeleton from Hallstatt was sent to the Kaiser by the Duchess as a gift (Wells 1981: 1, 16).

Prehistory as Political Legitimation

Prehistory played an important role in rehabilitating German self-respect after the humiliation of defeat in 1918, the perceived insult of Versailles, and the imposed Weimar regime. The dedication of the 1921 edition of Gustav Kossinna's seminal *German prehistory: a preeminently national discipline* reads: 'To the German people, as a building block in the reconstruction of the externally as well as internally disintegrated fatherland' (1921: Dedication).

Kossinna acquired great influence after the death of Rudolf Virchow (1821–1902), who was the most prominent German prehistorian of the late 19th century. Virchow was one of the first proponents of the ethnohistoric approach to prehistory, although he is perhaps remembered more for his misinterpretation of the first Neanderthal skeletal remains in 1856 (Eggers 1986: 202–5). In 1909 Kossinna founded the German Society for Prehistory in Berlin, later more aptly named the Society for German Prehistory (*Gesellschaft für Deutsche Vorgeschichte*). This was much more than a semantic alteration; as Alfred Götze wrote (1933:68):

> The name of an organization is its business card . . . In order to understand correctly what the Society for German Prehistory means one must remember what it was originally called . . . [It means] a prehistory of Germanness, independent of its present-day political or ethnic boundaries, reaching back to its roots and following these wherever the ancestors of the Germans originated in antiquity – and that was on occasion all of Europe.

Kossinna's influence increased interest in archaeology as a political tool; as the path which German National Socialism was to follow became more clearly defined, archaeological data were used to endorse it. Gradual changes manifested themselves in new journal titles and cover illustrations. The publication series *Mannus-Bibliothek*, for example, changed its title from the latinate original to the germanic *Mannus-Bücherei* (it was named *Mannus-Bibliothek* again after the war). *Mannus Zeitschrift für Vorgeschichte* became *Zeitschrift für Deutsche Vorgeschichte* in 1934; by 1975 it was *Deutsche Zeitschrift für Vor-und Frühgeschichte*. The editorial staff of these and other journals turned over rapidly between 1933 and 1935, as dissenting archaeologists were replaced by 'right-thinking' party liners. The Berlin-based *Prähistorische Zeitschrift* was one of the few journals relatively unaffected in form and content by the political transformations of the 1930's.

Many prehistoric archaeologists were drawn to the National Socialists because they felt themselves second-class citizens in the academic arena with regard to the classical and Near Eastern archaeologists; they were generally bitter about their lack of state funding and public recognition. The Party benefited from a dual inferiority complex on the part of its constituency of prehistorians, feeling both the general sense of injustice provoked by the Treaty of Versailles and a particular perception of prehistory as a neglected academic discipline. On the creation of the new Polish state in 1919, Kossinna published an article, 'The German *Ostmark*, home territory of the *Germanen*' (1919), which used archaeological evidence to support Germany's claim to the area. He sent the article to Versailles in an attempt to apply his ethnic interpretation of archaeological evidence directly to the politics of the day. He never received a reply (Eggers 1986: 236). Kossinna's identification of 'Germanic' material culture in Polish territory led to a debate with Josef Kostrzewski, one of his former students, who was rather predictably convinced that the ethnic group described by Kossinna was in fact Slavic. As Veit points out, Kostrzewski's criticism was directed not at Kossinna's *method*, but at his results (1989: 40).

This defensively ethnocentric attitude manifested itself in the intentional exaggeration of the importance of Germanic cultural influences in Western civilization (Sklenar 1983: 145). Hitler contributed his own views on this subject in a dinnertable monologue, referring to the Greeks as Germans who had survived a northern natural catastrophe and evolved a highly developed culture in southern contexts (Picker 1976: 93). This common piece of wishful thinking was supported by some otherwise reputable archaeologists. The Research Report of the Reichsbund for German Prehistory, July to December 1941, for example, reported the nine-week expedition of the archaeologist Hans Reinerth and a few colleagues to Greece where they claimed to have discovered major new evidence of Indogermanic migration to Greece during the Neolithic (*Mannus Zeitschrift für Deutsche Vorgeschichte* 1942 33: 599).

The Faustian Bargain: State Support under the NS Regime

The nature of prehistoric archaeology itself in its European context is crucial to understanding its rôle in Nazi Germany. Peter Goessler stated unequivocally, 'prehistory is an historic discipline, not a natural science . . . and it serves historic goals even if its sources are generally quite different ones' (1950: 7). The same point is made by Eggers: 'There is only one history, and prehistory is part of it in its entirety. These two types of scholarship differ only in their different sources: on the one hand written texts, on the other material culture' (1986: 16).

Prehistoric archaeology in Nazi Germany differed from history as a discipline in one important respect. It was not a recognized and well-funded academic subject before the rise of National Socialism. The first chair in prehistory was established in Marburg in 1928 (Sklenar 1983: 160). The subject was taught by lecturers whose university status was unquestionably lower than that of classical and Near Eastern archaeologists or art historians. Alfred Götze (1933: 69–72) blamed this phenomenon on the

> *obsession, unfortunately embedded in the blood of every German, to value the foreign more highly than the indigenous, an evil characteristic which affects archaeology as well as other disciplines . . . It also manifests itself however in the unequal treatment by the authorities and other controlling official organizations. One need only compare the financial support which is allocated to the German archaeological projects inside and outside Germany. . . Without bureaucratic support worth mentioning, without the financial means at the disposal of other disciplines, German prehistory has grown from hand to mouth, attacked and ridiculed to boot by its older sister disciplines. These are hard words, but I know whereof I speak, for I witnessed these developments in my student days.*

And Hans Reinerth explained in the introduction to his *Federseemoor* volume (1936a: 5):

> We have found the courage once more to admit to the deeds of our ancestors. Their honor is our honor! The millennia separate us no longer. The eternal stream of blood binds us across the ages to those Nordic farmer's sons, who had to fight for southern German soil twice in the course of four millennia.

Eggers, writing four decades after the war, believes this inferiority complex was more perceived than real; it was exploited by scholars like Kossinna who projected their personal professional disappointments on to the discipline (1986: 231). I think the truth lies somewhere in between; the interest shown in some excavations by high government officials and members of the nobility before 1933, which Eggers cites to support his case, did not compensate for the general lack of funds, the inadequate museum space and the paucity of academic positions. Reinerth's description of 'ideologically correct' prehistorians as engaged in a 'battle against the barbaric lie of the uncultured character of our Germanic forbears' (*Mannus Zeitschrift für Deutsche Vorgeschichte* 1940: Dedication to Alfred Götze) was an exaggeration which contained a grain of truth (Sklenar 1983: 160; Veit 1989: 37).

Prehistoric archaeologists seemed, in 1933, to have everything to gain by an association with the rising Nazi party. Between 1933 and 1945, eight new chairs were created in German prehistory, and funding became available for prehistoric excavations across Germany and Eastern Europe on an unprecedented scale (Reinerth 1936b: 66; Sklenar 1983: 160). New institutes sprang up – the Institute for Prehistory in Bonn in 1938 (*Nachrichtenblatt für Deutsche Vorzeit* 1938) and the Institut for Pre- and Early History in Cologne in 1939 (von Stokar 1939: 269ff). Museums for protohistory were established, such as the one in Freiburg (*Nachrichtenblatt für Deutsche Vorzeit* 1938). Prehistoric collections were brought out of storage and given exhibition space, in many cases for the first time. Institutes for Rune Research were founded at the Universities of Göttingen and Giessen (*Nachrichtenblatt für Deutsche Vorzeit* 1939: 73). The Römisch Germanisches Zentral Museum in Mainz became the Zentral Museum für Deutsche Vor- und Frühgeschichte in 1939 (Behrens 1939: 266–9). (Today it has its pre-war title once more).

Open-air museums like the reconstructed Neolithic and Bronze Age lake settle-ment at Unteruhldingen on Lake Constanz popularized prehistory. An archaeological film series, produced and directed by the prehistorian Lothar Zotz, included titles like 'Threatened by the steam plow', 'Germany's Bronze Age', 'The flames of prehistory' and 'On the trail of the eastern Germans' (Zotz 1933: 50). Popular journals, such as *Die Kunde* and *Germanenerbe* – a publication of the Ahnenerbe organization under the offical direction of Reichsführer SS Heinrich Himmler – proliferated.

These journals contained abundant visual material. One advertisement shows the reconstruction of a Neolithic drum from a pile of meaningless sherds. The text exhorts readers to 'keep your eyes open, for every *Volksgenosse* [fellow German] can contribute to this important national project! Do not assume that a ceramic vessel is useless because it falls apart during excavation. Carefully preserve even the smallest fragment!' An underlined sentence emphasizes the principal message: '*Every single find is important because it represents a document of our ancestors!* (*Nachrichtenblatt für Deutsche Vorzeit* 1939: figure 48).

Members of amateur organizations were actively recruited by appeal to patrio-tism. The membership flyer for the official national Confederation for German Prehistory (*Reichsbund für Deutsche Vorgeschichte*), under the direction of Hans Reinerth of the Amt Rosenberg, proclaimed: 'Responsibility with respect to our indigenous prehistory must again fill every German with pride!' The organization stated its goals as 'the interpretation and dissemination of unfalsified knowledge regarding the history and cultural achievements of our northern Germanic ances-tors on German and foreign soil' (*Mannus Zeitschrift für Deutsche Vorgeschichte* 1938: flyleaf).

The Offical Policy Regarding Prehistoric Archaeology

What was the official Party policy towards prehistoric archaeology? Different bureaucratic divisions within the NS organization produced their own policies, at times in conflict with one another. The power struggle between the Amt Rosen-berg and Himmler's Ahnenerbe organization from 1933 to 1937 (Bollmus 1970) exemplifies this internal confusion.

The Ahnenerbe organization was founded in 1935 at the Research and Teaching Society 'Ancestral Heritage', (*Forschungs- und Lehrgemeinschaft Ahnenerbe (Ahnenerbe- Stiftung)*); after 1936 it included the Society for the Advancement and Preservation of German Cultural Monuments (*Die Gesellschaft zur Förderung und Pflege Deutscher Kulturdenkmäler*). The Ahnenerbe organization, a personal project of Himmler's, was funded by interested German individuals and firms to research, excavate and restore real and imagined Germanic cultural relics (Koehl 1983; Kater 1974). The rôles played both by the Ahnenerbe and by the Amt Rosenberg in archaeological research, the conflict between Rosenberg and Himmler with regard to a central state-controlled archaeological organization, are discussed in detail by Bollmus (1970: 153–235). The absence of a unified central party policy with regard to prehistoric research is typical of the bureaucratic chaos which characterized the command system of the National Socialists. To some extent prehistorians benefited from this internecine strife. It effectively sabotaged plans for an umbrella organization, the Confederation for German Prehistory (*Reichsbund für Deutsche Vorgeschichte*), intended to coordinate and control all prehistoric research in German territory under the direction of Rosenberg's operative Hans Reinerth.

At the top of the command pyramid the response was equally contradictory. Party ideologues Alfred Rosenberg and Reichsführer Heinrich Himmler were ridiculed by Hitler and his inner circle as 'crack pot otherworld apostles' who formulated 'homemade Germanic myths' (Picker 1976: 44). According to Hitler's architect and armaments minister Albert Speer, Rosenberg's best-selling 700-page *Myth of the Twentieth Century* – which, among other contortions, 'proved' the existence of Atlantis and that Christ was not a Jew – was 'considered by the public to be the standard text for party ideology, but Hitler in his teatime conversations bluntly called it "stuff nobody can understand" written by "a narrow-minded Baltic German who thinks in horribly complicated terms". He expressed wonderment that such a book could ever have attained such sales' (1970: 96). Hitler attacked Himmler as well (Speer 1970: 94–5), saying

> *Why do we call the whole world's attention to the fact that we have no past? It's bad enough that the Romans were erecting great buildings when our forefathers were still living in mud huts: now Himmler is starting to dig up these villages of mud huts and enthusing over every potsherd and stone axe he finds. All we prove by that is that we were still throwing stone hatchets and crouching around open fires when Greece and Rome had already reached the highest stage of culture. We really should do our best to keep quiet about this past. Instead Himmler makes a great fuss about it all. The present-day Romans must be having a laugh at these revelations.*

Beyond its convenience for propaganda purposes and as justification of the expansion into countries like Czechoslovakia and Poland, the archaeological activities of the Amt Rosenberg and Himmler's Ahnenerbe were just so much window dressing for the upper echelons of the Party. There was no real respect for the past or its remains; while Party prehistorians like Reinerth distorted the facts, the SS destroyed archaeological sites like Biskupin in Poland (Sklenar 1983: 62).

'Official' involvement in archaeology consisted of visits by Himmler and corps SS officers to SS-funded and staffed excavations, like the one on the Erdenburg in the Rhineland (Buttler & Schleif 1939), or press shots of Hitler and Goebbels viewing a reconstructed 'Germanic' Late Bronze Age burial in its tree trunk coffin, part of the 1934 '*Deutsches Volk-Deutsche Arbeit*' exhibition in Berlin (Petersen 1934). Party appropriation of prehistoric data was evident in the use of Indo-European and Germanic design symbols in NS uniforms and regalia. The double lightning bolt, symbol of Himmler's SS organization, was adapted from a Germanic rune (Kohlmann 1942: 99–108). The swastika is an Indo-European sun symbol which appears in ceramic designs as early as the Neolithic in western Europe and continues well into early medieval times (figure 21.3: *Die Kunde* 1936: Title page; *Germanenerbe* 1938: Title page).

Figure 21.3 [orig. figure 3]   Title page of the journal Die Kunde (1936).

The Response of the Discipline to NS Control

German prehistorians of the 1930s can be regarded as falling into three basic categories: the party-liners; the acquiescent and passive majority; and the critical opposition.

The party-liners

The party-liners either achieved academic legitimacy under the Nazis, or were already established scholars promoted within the Party, who furthered their careers by conducting 'politically correct' research. The lunatic fringe of this category were derisively called *Germanomanen* (Jacob-Friesen 1934: 131) or Germanomaniacs by the mainstream. Herman Wirth, co-founder of the Ahnenerbe organization, attempted to prove that northern Europe was the cradle of Western civilization and was taken in by the 'Ura-Linda-Chronicle', an obvious forgery (Jacob-Friesen 1934: 130–5). Herman Wille, another of these extremists, interpreted the megaliths of Scandinavia as Germanic temples, identified as the inspiration for Greek and Roman temples as well as early medieval churches (Jacob-Friesen 1950: 2–3). Wilhelm Teudt's interpretation of the Externsteine near Detmold as a Germanic temple (figure 21.4) was supported by a large number of amateur

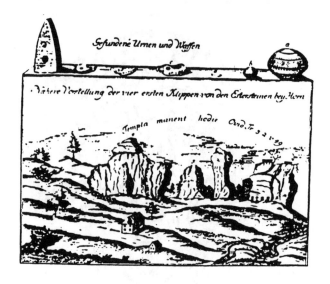

Figure 21.4 [orig. figure 4]   Etching of the Externsteine near Horn, Kreis Lippe from 1748
(Teudt 1934: figure 17).

prehistorians, and his encyclopaedic *Germanische Heiligtümer* (1934) identified, among other things, a complex system of solar observatories throughout areas of Germanic settlement.

The interpretation of the Externsteine generated heated and often vindictive debate, demonstrating the extent to which fringe research was rejected by the mainstream (Focke 1943). As Koehl points out, 'the second- and third-rate minds of the "scientists" which the Ahnenerbe, for example, sponsored tended to make SS "research" the laughingstock of the universities Himmler wished to penetrate' (1983: 115). The phenomenon of *Germanenkitsch* was parodied in *Germanenerbe* in a regular humour column (figure 21.5), partly to disassociate the Ahnenerbe prehistorians from the 'fringe' (*Germanenerbe* 1936: 87; 265).

Some researchers established before 1933 became high-ranking party officials, among them Hans Reinerth and the Austrian Oswald Menghin. These individuals consciously participated in what was at best a distortion of scholarship, and at worst a contribution to the legitimation of a genocidal authoritarian regime. They were certainly aware of what they were doing, and they must have been equally aware that much of the work they were producing under the auspices of Nazi ideology had absolutely no basis in archaeological fact.

As a result of his party career and his antisemitic writings (Menghin 1934), Oswald Menghin was summarily removed from his post as Austrian Minister of Education and Culture in 1945, spent some time in an American internment camp and ended up in South America, where he continued to excavate and publish, primarily in Spanish (*Der Schlern: Festgabe für Oswald Menghin* 1958: 73–6). His

Spanish publications, interestingly enough, begin around 1942, well before the disastrous end of the war.

Hans Reinerth was Rosenberg's *Reichsbeauftragter für deutsche Vorgeschichte* (a plenipotentiary position) from 1934 to the end of the war; he remained active on the archaeological scene in Baden-Württemberg, and his works continue to be published and sold, including the volume *Pfahlbauten am Bodensee* (1986); although most of its conclusions and interpretations are outdated. Recently officials in the town of Bad Buchau, where Reinerth excavated the Wasserburg Buchau in the 1920s, suppressed a pamphlet prepared by young archaeologists presently working in the area because it described Reinerth's party activities (*Pfahlbauten* 1984(3): 6–7).

Figure 21.5 [orig. figure 5]   Example of 'Germanenkitsch' advertisement from the journal *Germanenerbe* (1936).

The racist tone of Reinerth's writing is well illustrated by the three-volume tome entitled *The Prehistory of the German Tribes* (1945). Key passages deal with the genetic superiority of the Germanic peoples and their natural right to those territories to the east of Germany or anywhere else inhabited presently or at any time in the past by German peoples. Reinerth's unprofessional harassment of colleagues who disagreed with his views is described in detail by Bollmus (1970: 153–235).

The Mitläufer

The majority of German archaeologists were *Mitläufer* or passive fellow-travellers, to translate an untranslatable German term. These were the unnamed thousands who taught what they were told to teach in schools and universities, and accepted state funding with little question or comment. J.G.D. Clark's discussion in *Archaeology and Society* clearly states the dilemma of German prehistorians: 'Will it not happen that under dictatorial conditions activities paid for by the state will be used for state purposes?' (1939: 202).

Although the *Mitläufer* clearly constituted the critical mass in the attempted *Gleichschaltung* (political and ideological coordination of all intellectual pursuits) of the discipline by the Party, their inactive rôle makes their contribution difficult to assess. Yet it is precisely their inaction which explains how the discipline could practise 12 years of self-delusion so effectively. The acquiescent silence of the *Mitläufer* was crucial, their passivity representing a *de facto* sanctioning of NS policies and attitudes – a phenomenon that extended to all other areas of public life.

The opposition

A third category is constituted by the critical opposition and the victims of the regime. These archaeologists were both highly visible and relatively few in number, so their rôle can be studied more easily. Victims of the regime were persecuted on the basis of race or political views, and occasionally both. Gerhard Bersu, who had trained a generation of post-war archaeologists in the field techniques of settlement archaeology, was prematurely retired by the National Socialists from the directorship of the Römisch Germanische Kommission in 1935. His refusal to condone or conduct research tailored to NS ideological requirements, in addition to his rejection of the Kossinna school and its nationalist, racist doctrine of hyper-diffusionism, led to the abrupt interruption of his career as a prehistorian until the end of the war (Krämer 1965). The official reason given for the witch-hunt led by Reinerth under the auspices of the Amt Rosenberg was Bersu's Jewish heritage (Bollmus 1970: 163; Sklenar 1983: 160). By 1950 Bersu was back in Germany, again directing the Römisch Germanische Kommission.

Hans Kühn and Peter Goessler were also forced to leave, together with Jewish prehistorians like Paul Jacobsthal, who finished his *magnum opus* on Celtic art in English at Cambridge. Hugo Obermaier resided in Spain and Switzerland, having turned down a chair at the University in Berlin 'because the National Socialists had already taken possession of the field' (*IPEK* 1956: 104). Franz Weidenreich, who had to give up his chair at the University in Frankfurt, went to Chicago as Director of the Geological Institute in China from 1935 to 1941, and as Professor at the Museum of Natural History in New York after 1941 (*IPEK* 1956: 104). Gero von Merhart was another victim of the Reinerth witch-hunt. Despite the efforts made by his student Werner Buttler, a member of Himmler's private corps, to fend off the defamatory attacks, von Merhart was prematurely retired in 1940. In a letter to Buttler, who was in the front lines during this period of harrassment, von Merhart is both bitter and resigned (Bollmus 1970: 210):

> *All I can say, Buttler, is that I am being treated in an unbearable manner. My way of life has been destroyed, I have been defamed in a way which can never be made good, since my resilience has been dealt a fatal blow. . . No one will ever be able to convince me that I have not been carelessly and irresponsibly accused, condemned without a trial, and finished as an honest and dutiful citizen of the state . . .*

A critical faction, consisting of archaeologists like K.H. Jacob-Friesen, Ernst Wahle and Carl Schuchhardt, were cautious in their opposition yet managed to hold on to their postions. Jacob-Friesen openly criticized the lunatic fringe, especially Herman Wirth and his support of the Ura-Linda-Chronicle. In a 1934 article he claimed to speak for the professional mainstream in warning against the excesses of nationalistic and racist manipulation of archaeological data (1934).

Jacob-Friesen saw himself as a patriotic German prehistorian for whom the complete distortion of archaeological data by party doctrine was a defamatory attack on German scholarship and the international reputation of German scholars. Dogma requires complete, unquestioning faith in its precepts, and 'faith', according to Jacob-Friesen, 'generally begins where knowledge ends' (1950: 1). As early as 1928 his article 'Fundamental questions of prehistoric research', criticized research along the lines of Gobineau's doctrine of racial superiority, remarking: 'Racial philosophy in our time has mutated into racial fanaticism and has even been extended into politics' (1950: 2). As he himself noted, by 1933 this was an unpopular opinion, and he was asked, in the tradition of the medieval inquisition, to retract these statements publicly. He refused; in response W. Hülle, Reinerth's second-in-command, issued a statement warning against such heresies. 'That was how scholarship was conducted in the Third Reich!' Jacob-Friesen concluded bitterly in his 1950 *apologia* (1950: 2).

In 1941 Ernst Wahle published a critical analysis of Kossinna's theories, 'On the ethnic interpretation of prehistoric cultural provinces', which, as Eggers points out, took a considerable amount of courage (1986: 237). Unfortunately most of these gestures remained isolated incidents, and real debate on topics like Kossinna's research did not begin until after the war. Men like Wahle, Jacob-Friesen and Wilhelm Unverzagt, the editor of the relatively independent *Prähistorische Zeitschrift*, represented the voice of reason in German archaeology which attempted to maintain standards of scholarly objectivity, with little effect, as Jacob-Friesen himself admits (1950: 4). Without support in the Party machine, organized resistance was impossible, and most criticism either ignored or censured.

It is dificult to assess the effectiveness of these individuals, or the reasons for their survival. Internal conflicts and the absence of a general policy with regard to dissenting scholars were certainly part of the reason. Arousing the personal enmity of a man like Reinerth could be enough to destroy a career. Although the situation in Germany was less life-threatening than in the Soviet Union under Josef Stalin, where hundreds of prehistorians and archaeologists were killed (Childe 1935; Clark 1939: 196–7), it was a difficult time for researchers committed to an international, rather than a National Socialist, perspective.

Effects on Excavations and Research

Some research designs and interpretations of SS excavations were explicitly geared toward the Party's goal of investigating Germanic remains in all modern geographic regions, especially in eastern Europe where it was politic to prove previous Germanic habitation on the basis of material culture (e.g. Kunkel 1935). In general, however, excavation reports paid lip-service to the party in introduction and conclusion, while the rest was 'business as usual' (Clark 1939: 202). Sound work was done during this period in spite of political pressure. The vocabulary carefully conformed to the policies of the funding source, but the methodology was relatively unaffected. Given enough time, of course, this would have changed, as new terms and concepts made a significant transformation in the orientation of the discipline inevitable. In 1935, the entire prehistoric and early historic chronology was officially renamed: the Bronze and Pre-Roman Iron Ages became the 'Early Germanic Period' (figure 21.6), the Roman Iron Age the 'Climax Germanic Period', the Migration Period the 'Late Germanic' Period and everything from the Carolingians to the 13th century the 'German Middle Ages' (Peterson 1935: 147). A site continuously occupied from prehistoric times through to the present was to be excavated by Rosenberg's organisation until Roman remains were uncovered, at which point the Römisch Germanische Kommission would deal with this 'non-German' material. The prehistoric strata underneath would again be excavated by the Amt Rosenberg (Bollmus 1970: 166). This patently ridiculous and impractical arrangement, engineered by Reinerth and Rosenberg, was never adopted. It was one reason many previously committed archaeologists, disenchanted with the Amt Rosenberg and its plenipotentiary, began to turn more and more, after 1937, to Himmler's Ahnenerbe for official support.

Several well-known sites began as Ahnenerbe projects at this time: the Viking trading post of Haithabu in Schleswig-Holstein, excavated by Herbert Jankuhn under SS supervision beginning in 1938 (Jankuhn 1935; 1938; 1939; 1940), the Neolithic settlement of Köln-Lindenthal excavated by Werner Buttler (Buttler & Haberey 1936), and the Hohmichele tumulus at the Early Iron Age Heuneburg, excavated by Gustav Riek (1962).

Many smaller excavations, conducted with SS funding (Doppelfeld 1939), served a very specific purpose apart from their dubious scholarly value. They were intended to unite Germans – interested amateurs, locals, soldiers in the SS and the

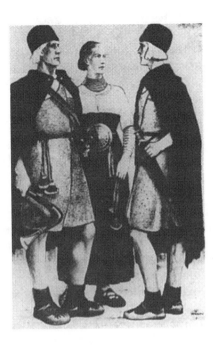

Figure 21.6 [orig. figure 5] Bronze Age "Germans"
(Reinerth 1945: plate 5a).

SA – in the retrieval, preservation and interpretation of prehistoric remains. Langsdorff and Schleif state specifically in a 1937 article that the primary beneficiary of such research was to be Germany's young people, not scholarship as such (1937: 82). Much of this rhetoric was reserved for official statements. Since it was necessary to use the proper code words to ensure continued support, their use does not prove that the writer accepted the general principles implied. Langsdorff and Schleif, in fact, appear as unsung heroes in Bollmus' account of their part in maintaining standards of archaeological research within the Ahnenerbe organization. Borderline research like the Externsteine excavations was discouraged by the Ahnenerbe after 1936, largely due to the influence of these two individuals (1970: 180–1). Götze warned against pseudo-archaeology of this sort as early as 1933, although he was careful to explain that it was exaggerated claims of Germanic achievements he deplored, not the principle of Germanic superiority itself (1933: 70).

Field schools for young archaeologists combined political indoctrination with the Party emphasis on the outdoors and on healthy communion with one's peers. The director of a field school held in 1935 for 65 participants, one fifth of whom were women, stated: 'Naturally the intellectual and material culture of the Germanic world was the focus of the relevant presentations' (Geschwendt 1935: 74).

Aftermath and Legacy

The paralysis felt by many scholars from 1933 to 1945 continued to affect research in the decades after the war. The *anomie* and intellectual dislocation of this period are described by Wilhelm Unverzagt in his essay (1959: 163):

> *After Germany's collapse it initially seemed virtually impossible to begin rebuilding the discipline with any hope of success. The new wielders of political power viewed prehistory with deep mistrust, an attitude which seemed understandable in view of the abuse of the results of prehistoric research on the part of National Socialist leaders with regard to questions of education and politics.*

Veit (1989) interprets the predominantly pragmatic orientation of prehistoric research in West Germany today as a direct result of intellectual shellshock, 'a reaction against the inflated claims of Nazi studies in prehistory', especially the ethnic interpretation of the Kossinna school (1989: 48). As Veit also points out, 'the reasons for the misuse of his [Kossinna's] ideas, which were, after all, based on the nature of archaeological knowledge, remained largely unexplained' (1989: 39).

The surviving older generation were faced with a terribly reduced student population after 1945. The journals between 1939 and 1945 contain hundreds of obituaries, written mainly by senior scholars, occasionally in the front lines themselves, who watched a whole generation of young archaeologists die. It has taken several decades to replace the losses of war, emigration and extermination. Most of the scholars who were graduate students during this 12-year period had to grapple with a double burden: a humiliating defeat and the disorienting experience of being methodologically 'deprogrammed'. There was neither time nor desire to examine the reasons for the 'German prostitution of archaeology' (Piggott 1983: Foreword).

The essence of propaganda, as Himmler and Rosenberg were well aware, is the ability to manipulate language and symbols. A race, nation or individual can be defamed by terms with negative implications – 'barbarian', 'under-developed', 'primitive'. Rosenberg was adept at twisting archaeological and anthropological data to impugn Jews, the Catholic church and Communists alike. Terms like 'hebraic parasites', 'ruling priest class' and 'red subhumanity' are liberally sprinkled throughout his *magnum opus* with invocations of the classics, the natural sciences, Goethe and any other authority which could be pressed into service (Rosenberg 1930).

Archaeology lends itself particularly well to intentional misinterpretation. Almost-truths and half-facts have been used in archaeological contexts other than Nazi Germany to support racist doctrines and colonial military expansion, or to establish political legitimacy for shaky regimes (Clark 1939: 197*ff.*; Silberman 1982; 1988; Garlake 1984; Silverberg 1986; McConnell 1989; etc.). One particularly dangerous aspect of archaeological writing is its tendency toward professional jargon which tends to obscure rather than reveal meaning. The multidisciplinary nature of prehistoric research, in and of itself an admirable thing, lends itself too early to abuse under the guise of science or other falsely appropriated authority.

Prehistory is particularly vulnerable to manipulation because it so often depends on a minimum of data and a maximum of interpretation (Klejn 1971: 8).

It is difficult to read Rosenberg's *Myth of the 20th Century* today and remember that his theories – however preposterous and absurd they now sound – constituted part of the platform for the Nazi doctrine of racial purity that culminated in the extermination of over six million human beings. Germany's archaeological community played a part in legitimating notions of Germanic racial and cultural superiority; yet prehistoric archaeology is the only social science discipline in Germany which has still to publish a self-critical study of its rôle in the events of the 1930's. Historians and Germanists have published several such studies. The historian Karl Ferdinand Werner says of this phenomenon of denial among historians (1967: 103):

> One didn't want to hear about one's past, of which one was now ashamed (how could one have believed in this Hitler person!), and expressed this basically praiseworthy attitude by simply denying this past. Since the great majority of Germans was interested in such suppression, very little opposition could arise. After the fact they all became, if not resistance fighters at least sympathetic to the resistance; indeed, they are perhaps resisting even now, when it is no longer dangerous to do so, to make up for the missed opportunity.

It is easy to condemn the men and women who were part of the events which transformed the German archaeological community between 1933 and 1945, more difficult really to understand the choices they made or avoided in the context of the time. Many researchers who began as advocates of Reinerth's policies in the Amt Rosenberg and Himmler's Ahnenerbe organization later became disenchanted. Others, who saw the system as a way to develop and support prehistory as a discipline, were willing to accept the costs of the Faustian bargain it offered.

The benefits were real. Many of them still exist today – in government programmes, museums and institutes, amateur organizations, and a widespread popular support of and interest in prehistory. Academic scholarship outside Germany also benefited; not all of Kossinna's theories or those of his advocates can be dismissed out of hand (Eggers 1986: 200), and quite a lot of the work done from 1933 until the end of the war was ground-breaking research. Scholars like V. Gordon Childe adapted Kossinna's theories to their own work. Ideas such as the identification of ethnic groups in the archaeological record and the concept of independent invention on the part of indigenous European cultures unaffected by Eastern influence are some examples (Klejn 1974: 8). Settlement archaeology benefited from excavations like those at Köln-Lindenthal and Haithabu (C. Evans 1989).

More recently a number of studies dealing with certain aspects of the use and abuse of archaeology under the National Socialists in Germany have been published by non-German researchers (Schnapp 1977; Baker 1988; McCann 1988; 1989; C. Evans 1989). The only German prehistorian who has approached the topic to date has done so indirectly through the study of Kossinna's theories and their political and cultural significance (Veit 1984; 1989). Yet organizations like the ones recently formed by graduate students in prehistory at the Universities of Berlin

(West) and Kiel (*Offener Brief* 1989) seem to indicate that a new wind is blowing in the corridors of German academe. The theme of a symposium held recently in Berlin by the organizations '*AUTONOME SEMINAR*' (Berlin) and '*Arbeitsgemein-schaft Archäologie und Faschismus*' (Kiel) was '*Ur-und Frühgeschichtsforschung und Nationalsozialismus*'. The topics under discussion indicate a critical awareness not just of the forces that transformed prehistoric research from 1933 to 1945, but of the enduring legacy of that period in the academic community today.

Unfortunately, conservative elements in German prehistoric archaeology which turn a blind eye to the abuses of the 1930s labour under the influence of a continuing 'unconscious ethnocentric fixation' (Veit 1989: 50). Dieter Korell (1989: 178), for example, attempts to resuscitate Kossinna's concept of prehistory as a 'pre-eminently national discipline':

> *Gustaf Kossinna spoke programmatically of a 'pre-eminently national discipline'... The term 'national' has nothing whatsoever to do with the current discussion and labeling of 'nationalism'... German prehistory is a national discipline. The life and suffering of a living people are represented by the discipline, and in the final analysis can only be understood in its entire significance by Germans and their close ethnic kin.*

This trend can be seen in the context of a lengthy term in power for the current conservative government and is a subtext of the *Historikerstreit* which has made revisionist history the topic of much recent debate (R.J. Evans 1989). I mention it here because it emphasizes the importance of an in-depth critical study of prehistoric archaeology under the National Socialists.

As C. Evans says: 'It is precisely because so much archaeological evidence is ambiguous, and therefore open to re-interpretation, that there is a need to understand the rôle and historic constitution of archaeology's disciplinary consensus over time' (1989: 447). History (and by association, prehistory) informs communal self-image. An awareness of origins is necessary to construct and maintain self-esteem and self-understanding. History legitimizes individuals and their actions within society. In this context the distortion of prehistoric research for political purposes has grave implications for the integrity of the structual framework of a society as a whole. This is the most important legacy of the German example. We cannot afford to ignore the responsibility the relationship between archaeology and politics places upon interpreters of the past.

Acknowledgements

A preliminary version of this paper was presented at the Joint Archaeological Congress in Baltimore (MD) in January 1989. I would like to thank John Mulvaney for first encouraging me to pursue the topic of prehistory and politics. I also would like to thank Stephen L. Dyson, Neil A. Silberman and Brian McConnell for their useful suggestions. Special thanks go to Herbert A. Arnold and Matthew L. Murray for their comments on earlier drafts of this paper. Thanks also go to Thomas H. Hruby for bearing with me, and to Gloria P. Greis for acting as general *factotum*. Any omissions or inaccuracies are entirely my own.

References

Baker, F. 1988. History that hurts: excavation 1933–1945, *Archaeological Review from Cambridge* 7(1): 93–109.

Behrens, G. 1939. Das Zentralmuseum für Deutsche Vor-und Frühgeschichte in Mainz, *Nachrichtenblatt für Deutsche Vorzeit* 15 (9/10): 266–9.

Bollmus, R. 1970. *Das amt Rosenberg und seine Gegner: zum Machtkampf im Nationalsozialistischen Herrschaftssystem*. Stuttgart: Deutsche Verlagsanstalt. Studien zur Zeitgeschichte, Institut für Zeitgeschichte.

Buttler, W. & W. Haberey. 1936. *Die bandkeramische Ansiedlung bei Köln-Lindenthal*. Berlin: Walter de Gruyter.

Buttler, W. & H. Schleif. 1939. Die Erdenburg bei Bensberg (Rheinisch-bergischer Kreis), Eine Ausgrabung des Reichsführers SS, *Prähistorische Zeitschrift* 28–29: 184–232.

Childe, V.G. 1935. Prehistory in the USSR, *Proceedings of the Prehistoric Society* 1: 151*ff*.

Clark, J.G.D. 1939. *Archaeology and society*. London: Methuen.

Daniel, G. & C. Renfrew. 1988. *The idea of prehistory*. Edinburgh: Edinburgh University Press.

Doppelfeld, O. 1939. Das germanische Dorf auf dem Bärhorst bei Nauen, *Prähistorische Zeitschrift* 28–29 (1937–38): 284–9.

Eggers, H.J. 1986. *Einführung in die Vorgeschichte*. 3rd edition. Munich: Serie Piper.

Evans, C. 1989. Bersu's Woodbury 1938 & 1939, *Antiquity* 63: 436–50.

Evans, R.J. 1989. *In Hitler's shadow: West German historians and the attempt to escape from the Nazi past*. New York: Pantheon Books.

Focke, F. 1943. *Beiträge zur Geschichte der Externsteine*. Stuttgart/Berlin: W. Kohlhammer.

Garlake, P. 1984. Ken Mufuka and Great Zimbabwe, *Antiquity* 58: 121–3.

Germanenerbe. 1936. Monatsheft für Deutsche Vorgeschichte.

1938. Monatsheft für Deutsche Vorgeschichte.

Geschwendt, F. 1935. Schulungslager für Vorgeschichte, *Nachrichtenblatt für Deutsche Vorzeit* 11(4): 73–4.

Goessler, P. 1950. Geschichte in der Vorgeschichte, *Prähistorische Zeitschrift* 34: 5–17.

Götze, A. 1933. Ziele und Wege: Eröffnungsrede zur 12. Tagung der Gesellschaft für Deutsche Vorgeschichte 1.10.32, *Mannus Zeitschrift für Vorgeschichte* 25(1): 66–72.

Hawkes, J. 1968. The proper study of mankind, *Antiquity* 42: 258*ff*.

Hohenschwert, F. 1985. Archäologische Forschung und Bodendenkmalpflege im ehemaligen Land Lippe, *Führer zu archäologischen Denkmälern in Deutschland, Der Kreis Lippe*, 10: 34–46. Stuttgart: Konrad Theiss Verlag.

IPEK 1943–1948. 1956. 7: 104–5.

Jacob-Friesen, K.H. 1934. Herman Wirth's Ura-Linda-Chronik und die deutschen Vorgeschichtsforscher, *Nachrichtenblatt für Deutsche Vorzeit* 10(6): 130–5.

—1950. Wissenschaft und Weltanschauung in der Urgeschichtsforschung, *Die Kunde* N.F. 1 & 2: 1–5.

Jankuhn, H. 1935. Die Ergebnisse der Grabung in Haithabu 1935, *Nachrichtenblatt für Deutsche Vorgeschichte* 11(11): 242–4.

—1938. Haithabu, der erste Ostseehafen des Deutschen Reiches, *Germanien*: 309–19.

—1939. Die Ergebnisse der Grabungen in Haithabu 1938, *Nachrichtenblatt für Deutsche Vorgeschichte* 15(1): 27–30.

—1940. Die SS-Grabung von Haithabu 1939, *Nachrichtenblatt für Deutsche Vorzeit* 16(4&5): 103–4.

Kater, M. 1974. *Das Ahnenerbe der SS 1935–1945: ein Beitrag zur Kulturpolitik des Dritten*

Reiches. Stuttgart: Deutsche Verlagsanstalt. Studien zur Zeitgeschichte, Institut für Zeit-geschichte.

Klejn, Leo S. 1971. Marxism, the systemic approach, and archaeology, in C. Renfrew (ed.), *The explanation of culture change: models in prehistory:* 691–710. London: Duckworth.

—1974. Kossinna im Abstand von vierzig Jahren, *Jahresschrift für mitteldeutsche Vorgeschichte* 58: 7–55.

Koehl, R.L. 1983. *The Black Corps: the structure and power struggles of the Nazi SS.* Madison: University of Wisconsin Press.

Kohlmann, M. 1942. Kossinna's Blitzzeichen, *Mannus Zeitschrift für Deutsche Vorgeschichte* 34(1–2): 99–108.

Korell, D. 1989. Zum Wesen der Vor- und Frühgeschichte, Mannus Deutsche Zeitschrift für Vor und Frühgeschichte 55(3): 169–84.

Kossinna, G. 1919. *Die deutsche Ostmark: ein Heimatboden der Germanen.* Berlin.

—1921. Die deutsche Vorgeschichte: eine hervorragend nationale Wissenschaft, *Mannus-Bibliothek* 9.

Krämer, W. 1965. Gerhard Bersu zum Gedächtnis, *Deutsches Archäologisches Institut Römisch-Germanische Kommission Berichte* 45: 1–2.

Die Kunde. 1936. Title page.

Kunkel, D. 1935. Ausgrabungen Wollin 1935, *Nachrichtenblatt für Deutsche Vorgeschichte* 11(12): 257–63.

Langsdorff, F. & H. Schleif. 1937. Ausgrabungen auf dem Schlossberg von Alt-Christburg, Kr. Mohrungen, *Nachrichtenblatt für Deutsche Vorgeschichte* 13(4): 80–2.

Mannus-Bibliothek, 1928: Frontispiece.

Mannus Zeitschrift für Deutsche Vorgeschichte, 1938.

—1940.

—1942.

McCann, W.J. 1988. The National Socialist perversion of archaeology, *World Archaeology Bulletin* 2: 51–4.

—1989. 'Volk and Germanentum': the presentation of the past in Nazi Germany, in P. Gathercole and D. Lowenthal (ed.), *The politics of the past:* 74–88. London: Unwin Hyman. One World Archaeology 12.

McConnell, B. 1989. Mediterranean archaeology and modern nationalism. Unpublished paper presented at the First Joint Archaeological Congress in Baltimore, January 1989.

Menghin, O. 1934. *Geist und Blut.* Vienna.

Nachrichtenblatt für Deutsche Vorzeit. 1938. 1939.

Offener Brief An Alle Ur-und Frühgeschichts-Studentinnen In Der Bundesrepublik. 1989. Kurzbericht über ein Seminarwochenende in Berlin, Thema: Ur- und Frühgeschichtsforschung und Nationalsozialismus.

Petersen, E. 1934. Die Deutsche Vorgeschichte auf der Ausstellung 'Deutsches Volk – Deutsche Arbeit', *Nachrichtenblatt für Deutsche Vorgschichte* 10: 56ff.

—1935. Vorschläge zur Einführung neuer Zeitstufenbenennungen in der deutschen Frühgeschichte. *Nachrichtenblatt für Vorgeschichte* 11(8): 145–8.

Pfahlbauten. 1984. Archäologische Ausgrabungen in Reute-Schorrenried Bad Buchau-Federsee – Südschwäbische Nachrichten Sonderdruck.

Picker, H. 1976. *Hitler's Tischgespräche im Führer Hauptquartier.* Stuttgart: Seewald Verlag.

Piggott, S. 1983. Foreword, in Sklenar (1983).

Reinerth, H. 1936a. *Das Federseemoor als Siedlungsland des Vorzeitmenschen.* Leipzig.

—1936b. Das politische Bild Alteuropas: Aus der Arbeit der nationalsozialistischen Vorgeschichtsforschung, *Germanenerbe* 1936: 66–75.

—1940. Festschrift für Alfred Götze, *Mannus Zeitschrift für Deutsche Vorgeschichte* 32: Dedication.

—1945. *Vorgeschichte der deutschen Stämme: Germanische Tat und Kultur auf deutschem Boden.* Berlin.

—1986. *Pfahlbauten am Bodensee.* Überlingen.

Riek, G. 1962. *Der Hohmichele.* Berlin: De Gruyter.

Rosenberg, A. 1930. *Der Mythus des 20. Jahrhunderts.* Munich.

—1934. Aufbau der deutschen Vorgeschichte, *Nachrichtenblatt für Deutsche Vorgeschichte* 10(3): 4*ff.*

Der Schlern, 1958. Festgabe für Oswald Menghin 32: 73–80.

Schnapp, A. 1977. Archéologie et nazisme, *Quaderni Storia* 3(5): 1–26.

Silberman, N.A. 1982. *Digging for God and country.* New York: Knopf.

—1988. *Between the past and the present: archaeology, ideology, and nationalism in the modern Near East.* New York: Holt, Rinehart & Winston.

Silverberg, R. 1986. *The moundbuilders.* Athens (OH): Ohio University Press.

Sklenar, K. 1983. *Archaeology in central Europe: the first 500 years.* New York: St. Martin's Press.

Speer, A. 1970. *Inside the Third Reich.* New York (NY): Macmillan.

Von Stokar, W. 1939. Das Insitut für Vor- und Frühgeschichte an der Universität Köln, *Nachrichtenblatt für Deutsche Vorzeit* 15(9/10): 269*ff.*

Teudt, W. 1934. *Germanische Heiligtümer: Beiträge zur Aufdeckung der Vorgeschichte, ausgehend von den Externsteinen, den Lippequellen und der Teutoburg.* Lippe.

Unverzagt, W. 1959. Die Vor- und Frühgeschichtsforschung am 10. Jahrestag der Deutschen Demokratischen Republik, *Ausgrabungen und Funde* 4(4): 163–5.

Veit, U. 1984. Gustaf Kossinna und V.G. Childe: Ansätze zu einer theoretischen Grundlegung der Vorgeschichte, *Saeculum* 35 (3-4): 326–64.

—1989. Ethnic concepts in German prehistory: a case study on the relationship between cultural identity and archaeological objectivity, in S. Shennan (ed.), *Archaeological approaches to cultural identity*: 35–56. Unwin Hyman: London. One World Archaeology 10.

Wahle, E. 1941. Zur ethnischen Deutung frühgeschichtlicher Kulturprovinzen, *Grenzen der frühgeschichtlichen Erkenntnis I.* Heidelberg.

Wells, P.S. 1981. *The emergence of an Iron Age economy: the Mecklenburg grave groups from Hallstatt and Sticna, Mecklenburg Collection, Part III.* Cambridge: Peabody Museum Press. American School of Prehistoric Research Bulletin 33.

Werner, K.F. 1967. *Das NS-Geschichtsbild und die deutsche Geschichtswissenschaft.* Stuttgart: Kohlhammer.

Zotz, L. 1933. Die Deutsche Vorgeschichte im Film, *Nachrichtenblatt für Deutsche Vorgeschichte* 9(4): 50–2.

ARCHAEOLOGICAL ANNAPOLIS

A GUIDE TO SEEING
AND UNDERSTANDING
THREE CENTURIES
OF CHANGE

(A)

(B)

(C)

(D)

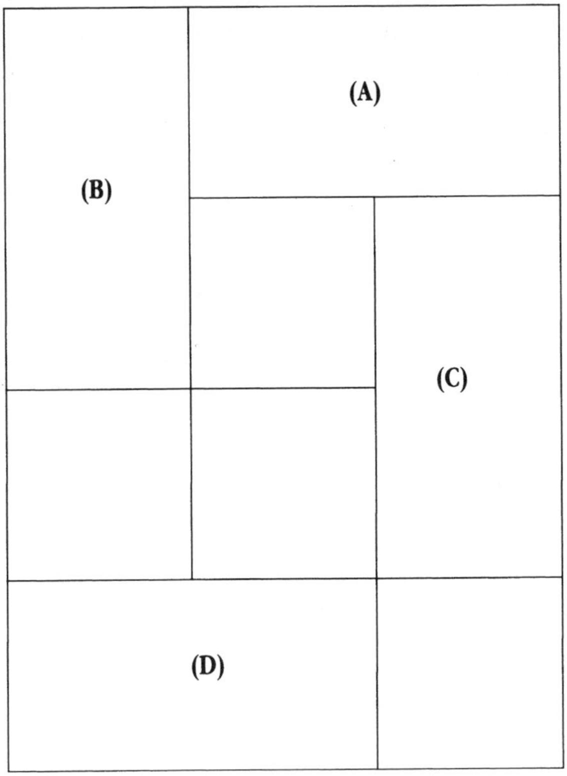

While the Maryland State House (started in 1772 and the third on this site) may look unchanging or timeless, it has been altered constantly either to suit popular tastes or to meet historical needs. As the dome was originally designed, its horizontal emphasis (**A**) did not visually dominate the buildings around it. By 1786 the large dome had been added (**B**, *a view from 1886*). The vertical emphasis of the 1780s remains today (**C**) and now, as then, the State House dome dominates the Annapolis skyline (**D**).

You are about to take a walk that will give you a glimpse into the last three centuries of history in a bustling port city. You will see remnants and artifacts, from above and below ground that will help you to understand the many changes that have taken place. Annapolis is a splendid example of how a city's past is being unearthed both literally and through the use of historical documents. Much of it is intact and easily viewed.

Through the centuries, this history has come to have many meanings. Like the pottery or timbers uncovered at an archaeological "dig," historical interpretations, too, are artifacts of the past. Each individual forms his or her own version of what might have taken place. Few professionals still believe that the past is neutral or can be discovered impartially, even though they try to be as accurate as they can. Through the insights of professionals and amateurs, each of us uses the various versions of the past to help us to see ourselves and our society more clearly. So, this is a guide based on the archaeology of the city and on the archaeology of how the city has used its past.

As you explore these sites, we hope you will ask questions, challenge historical theories, and form your own theories about the past. Your interpretations will be based on what you see, on the present mingled with the past. History changes, and so do historical interpretations. This guide encourages you to take responsibility for mentally digging into the layers of history to understand how they are formed.

Mark P. Leone

Parker B. Potter, Jr.

If you turn to the fold-out, walking-tour map at the back, you will see eight numbers. Each number is keyed to a two-page section in this guide beginning with pages 4-5. On your walking tour, as you come to a place numbered on the map, turn to the appropriate section, read the short essay, and look at the historic photographs on the facing page. Our purpose is to present a different way to look at history in Annapolis. We hope this guide will also help you to appreciate the historical significance of other parts of the city and of other cities as well. On pages 20-23 you will find brief notes about some more historic buildings in Annapolis.

In the essays, we have tried to go beyond merely presenting facts. We want to share with visitors the intense excitement that comes from a very important understanding: Not everybody has always seen the past in the same way. Each era actively creates the past through the perspective of the present. This guide tells how archaeologists associated with the project, "Archaeology in Annapolis," have chosen to look at the remains of the past.

Often, when you visit a museum or even a living history exhibit, you see a view of the past as it is supposed to have been. But archaeologists, historians, architects, and museum experts know that such exhibits do not always bring the visitor up-to-date on what has happened in their own fields in the last 25 years or so.

With "Archaeology in Annapolis," you will discover history that may have been "dug up" only last week. For several summers, professionals and volunteers have been painstakingly excavating at several of the sites included in this publication. They have also been giving guided tours of some of the sites to share with visitors the ways that archaeologists think about the past. Anthropologists and archaeologists from The University of Maryland work cooperatively with Historic Annapolis, Inc., on the excavations. This guide extends the process of sharing our work. Grants from the Maryland Humanities Council and the National Endowment for the Humanities support the project.

The Annapolis Historic District is a Registered National Historic Landmark. Many of the sites in this guide have connections with each other and with other locations in the city. The city's unique history—and the story of each building and site in it—play a part in the ever-evolving historical interpretation. Generations of people have added patches and stitches to this rich historical fabric, which has been passed down to us. As you take part in this walking tour, you, too, play a role in interpreting the past in terms of the present.

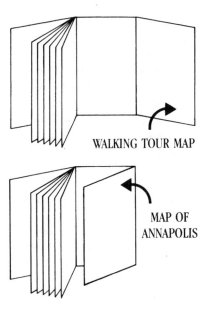

WALKING TOUR MAP

MAP OF
ANNAPOLIS

Historians use photographs to document the past. A photo may be seen as a fact, as evidence that an event occurred or that a building looked a certain way at a given time. Yet the powerful document of the photograph is a product of a split-second. Each image, directed by the individual behind the camera, reflects the photographer's motives for wanting to record that scene.

Photographs are not merely pictures of the past. The *use* of historic photographs is based on the contemporary context. By "cropping" or otherwise highlighting certain portions of an old photo, we choose from the past what is relevant today. Two photos of the same building are not similar because their subject is the same; they differ in perspective, in viewpoint, in the circumstances of the moment of creation.

In Annapolis, Maryland's capital city, the popularity of photography coincided with the growing interest in written history. In the 1860s Annapolis was a popular subject with Civil War photographers. By the 1880s, Elihu Riley had begun writing popular histories of Annapolis and Henry Schaefer, also an Annapolitan, had begun photographing the town: people, landscape scenes, buildings, the Naval Academy. Today, much of Schaefer's work forms a historic record, something he probably never intended it to do. In the 1920s and 1930s, George Forbes collected more than 2,000 historic photographs of Annapolis. He then took pictures of these older photographs, printing them in uniform size and contrast (though the originals probably varied greatly). In the 1930s, the Company for the Restoration of Colonial Annapolis praised Forbes' collection as evidence of what the past looked like.

In reshooting the original photographs, Forbes changed their appearance. In this guide, we have changed them even more by cropping them to focus your attention on the physical features pointed out in the text.

That is another way of saying that each of us brings to the study of history our own special perspective. The original photographer saw the scene one way; Forbes reshaped that vision in his darkroom; we have made a new use of details of those photographs. You become an important part of this process as well, for in agreeing with or in challenging an interpretation, you are part of a consensus that ties together the loose threads of the past that make up history.

Nancy J. Chabot

A *1890-91*

B *after 1908*

C *1886-1901*

D *c. 1960*

Photos **A, B,** and **D** show an 18th-century streetscape—a rare scene in modern cities. Francis Street is on the right; Main Street on the left. In general, over the past 300 years, the street pattern and topography have not been altered much here or in the rest of the Historic District of Annapolis. A view like this can be especially useful if we learn how to read the many pasts visible in it. Of course, we cannot always walk around in a historic environment and pick up the lessons of the past. The buildings do not speak for themselves. Current uses and appearances of buildings control how much we can see; alterations and facades can hide history from us.

But here, despite all the changes that have taken place, you can see some features of an 18th-century city, such as streetwidth and direction, and the height of the buildings. Such streetscapes no longer exist in New York, Philadelphia, or Boston, which unlike Annapolis, grew in size by going deeper and beyond their 18th-century limits, destroying their earlier appearances.

How has this street scene changed? The State House *(center of* **A***)* frequently has been visibly altered or restored. Originally it had a smaller porch and no cellar. Its roofing has changed from copper to shingles to slate. The hilltop, graded to its present form in the late 18th century, once was the site for the city market. Later on the site was crowded with adjoining buildings, removed in 1902 when the northwest annex was built and when the trees and statues of the present park were added. Only recently, a second retaining wall and staircases were built around the House.

Even though the scale is unchanged, the view has been subject to various tastes. Some of the individuals making the changes valued the past and others chose to ignore it. The blend of the new and the old styles gives us the varied streetscape you see here. At times, the "latest fashion" in architecture meant borrowing from earlier eras. In the 1930s, and in the 1950s as well, "new" meant in the form of older models; Annapolis built public buildings in the neo-Georgian style or with false colonial fronts that often covered Victorian and Federal architecture. At other times, architects tried for a new, different look that made no pretense at restoring a previous style; this was particularly true in the 1870s and 1880s, and again in the 1950s and 1960s. Notice the Victorian chimneys on the State House (**C**) and the commercial buildings dressed up in Victorian taste *(right side of* **A***)*. Since 1969, the city has attempted to maintain its original periods of architecture by city ordinance.

In the small building at the base of the "V" in Main and Francis Streets *(center of* **A, B,** *and* **D***)*, you can see some of the continual alterations: modern-day Georgian windows with many panes, paneled woodwork, and the removal of electric signs and wires. A modern purpose sometimes determines the part of the past put on view. While in Annapolis the past remains in abundance to be read and seen, it has not always meant the same thing to each age. The reasons history is important to us are not the same reasons chosen by some past era nor will they necessarily be the ones chosen by a future one.

A *1882-91*

B *1889-90*

C *1961*

577

In 1695, Governor Francis Nicholson created the Baroque town plan of Annapolis — two large circles with radiating "spokes" and a grid pattern of streets *(see the Annapolis map on the reverse of the walking-tour map at the back)*. He used streets, topography, and buildings to create views of important places intended to send social, cultural, and political messages. His street plan is largely unchanged today and the views still speak to our age, guiding our eyes to important structures *and* to the water surrounding the town.

The two main focal points in Annapolis are St. Anne's Episcopal Church (**A**) and the Maryland State House, each in a circle, on a hill, and at the junction of several major city streets. The colonists in Maryland linked these two buildings by adjoining circles and gave them equal visibility to show that the church and the state were closely connected. With American Independence in 1776, the connection disappeared. While public funds supported the construction of both St. Anne's and the State House before Independence, afterwards, only the State House continued to receive public money. The church was supported privately and more modestly. After Independence, the State House's shallow dome was replaced with the large one that still dominates the Annapolis skyline. This newer dome for two centuries has symbolized the separation of church and state. Its classical design also signaled the connection between the newly created American form of government and the Greek ideal. It is hard to find a spot in Annapolis from which the dome is not visible. Notice how it appears in the background of many of the photographs in this guide.

Many places in Annapolis, for instance the State House, the Wm. Paca House, and the Naval Academy Chapel (1905), were sited to look out over Spa Creek, the Chesapeake Bay, or the Severn River. Many Annapolitans saw their town as significantly connected with the water surrounding it. The town's Golden Age in the 1760s in part grew from its transatlantic maritime activity. But during the 1800s the town had a marked decline in such trade and the port dwindled to only local importance. During this era, many of the town's views of the water became blocked off by other buildings (**B**). In 1845 the U. S. Naval Academy was established along the Severn, separating the town from a part of its shoreline. Later in the century several businesses — including a fish market, a lumber yard, warehouses, and crab-packing houses — were built at the foot of Main Street *(left center of **B**)*, hiding the view of Creek and Bay. Ways of making money on the waterfront changed between the 18th and 19th centuries. Transatlantic commerce called for an open harbor. But as Annapolis came to handle only small, bay-going vessels, the harbor became constricted and the shoreline built up.

Within the last 30 years things have changed again. Now that Annapolis prides itself on being an important yachting center and is celebrating its maritime resources, the city has restored the view of the water from Main Street — a view which was blocked until the early 1960s (**C**). To be a successful yachting town, Annapolis has built an open, prominent harbor; scenic views of the water boost the maritime ambiance.

A *1950*

B *1983*

C *1888-95*

D *1888-95*

The Annapolis waterfront (**A**) has undergone many transformations during the city's history. Today yachts and historic exhibits share the harbor. At the waterfront we see celebrations of those aspects of the past that most nearly resemble the present — or what we would like the future to be.

For 100 years, published histories of Annapolis have stressed the city's national role in the years before, during, and just after the American Revolution. While not nearly as large as Boston, New York, or Philadelphia, Annapolis was an important pre-Revolutionary port. Its waterfront was an entrance to the city and to the colony for commodities and people from England, Scotland, Ireland, the West Indies, Africa, and American ports.

Shortly after the Revolution, Annapolis lost much of its business to Baltimore's larger harbor. Waterfront property in Annapolis decreased in value, a point well illustrated by archaeology sponsored by the Maryland Humanities Council at the Victualling Warehouse site (**B**) at the dock. Here, two warehouses used by the American side during the Revolution burned in 1790. One was never rebuilt. Excavations in its foundations show that its burned-out shell stood for several years before the land was reused.

Through much of the 19th and 20th centuries, lumber mills (**C**) and crab-packing houses replaced the small, 18th-century warehouses used for transatlantic shipping; the harbor decreased to the size of today's city slip. Fewer visitors entered by way of the city dock; West Street became the primary entrance. City dwellers in the 19th century reused property from the century before but paid little attention to earlier uses or meanings.

Redevelopment occurred again in the 1960s as Annapolis began to transform itself from a harbor for working boats (**D**) into a well known yachting center. In this redevelopment, 18th- and 19th-century buildings were restored. The harbor again became what it had not been for 150 years: nationally prominent and an important entrance to the city. Currently, nine Historic Annapolis, Inc., restorations and two historical museums for waterfront visitors (the Victualling Warehouse Museum and the Tobacco Prise House) focus on the 18th century, the period in which the harbor was the city's entrance and major source of wealth. In the mid-1970s, when these buildings were restored, the American Bicentennial was in full swing and it was easier to raise funds for Revolutionary period projects than for those of other eras. And a future era may choose to tell the story of all those Afro-Americans who began their history here.

Nineteenth century Bay watermen are absent from the town's presentation of history but were an integral part of Annapolis. To interpret this aspect of waterfront development, Historic Annapolis, Inc., has initiated the soon-to-be-built Maritime Inn/Museum complex on the Eastport side of Spa Creek; it will feature a reconstructed 19th-century shipyard where the wooden boats of the Chesapeake Bay will be built in the traditional way. This project, based on current historical — and environmental — interest in the Bay, demonstrates that history is in many ways a product of the time in which it is created.

These narrow streets (**A**) give a sense of residential life in Annapolis; workers and tradesmen lived here 300 years ago. Now blue-collar workers and professionals make their homes in a mix of restored and unrestored 19th-century buildings and a few structures from the 18th century.

From the beginning, houses on these streets were mostly built of wood. Inventories list warehouses, stables, a boat house, milk house, and dependencies. In 1713, Shiplap House (**B**) at 18 Pinkney Street was owned by a sawyer and innkeeper. Nearby there was a pumpmaker and block-maker for ships' equipment. A cabinetmaker, a brassfounder, barber, wigmaker, blacksmith, and wheelwright lived and worked on or near Pinkney Street (**C**), making it a kind of manufacturing alley. Attached to the houses were workyards, wells, privies, sheds, and stables. The alley was surfaced with cobblestones.

On Fleet, Cornhill, and Pinkney Streets, lots and houses were used both as shops and businesses. In 18th-century Annapolis, ownership of land could be divided from ownership of the buildings on it, a practice that permitted a merchant or artisan with limited means to buy or construct a *building only* on rented land; leases were usually for a 99-year period. Lots or houses were rented out to craftsmen and shopkeepers, thus producing a considerable profit for the owners. By the Revolution, only a small percentage of the inherited land in Annapolis was owned by laborers like those in the Cornhill, Fleet, and Pinkney Streets' area. In fact, because such a small number of families owned such a high percentage of the land, many inhabitants had to become wage earners to support their families.

Notice how close the buildings are: This 19th-century buildup in what was formerly open workyards and gardens came about as the city's population grew and lots were filled in. Nonetheless, the scale, the look of the buildings, and the closeness to the rest of the city represent how the environment would have appeared in the 18th century.

The residence at 43 Pinkney Street (**D**) is typical of an 18th-century artisan's house—small, with two rooms on each floor and a kitchen in the cellar. For years, it was masked by modern siding and roofing. In 1975 its original construction features were uncovered and archaeologists discovered its cellar kitchen, which verified the building's dimensions as those of a modest 18th-century habitation.

Had Annapolis become a reconstructed outdoor museum like Williamsburg, this area would not likely have retained its working-class, residential look. Had Annapolis become a big city in the last century, this area would have become apartment houses, tenements, office buildings, and parking lots. Cornhill, Fleet, and Pinkney Streets were saved by a combination of 20th-century circumstances: 1) World War II and rent controls made the properties unprofitable; 2) the city adopted a housing code; 3) the federal government for a brief interlude financed rehabilitation; and 4) Historic Annapolis, Inc., has for 25 years worked to establish a value for this area. The organization purchased easements to help owners rehabilitate and it used its Revolving Fund to buy properties to demonstrate the benefits of rehabbing.

A *date unknown*

C *1983*

B *1983*

583

In Annapolis, history has an important function. You can see its changing uses and meanings piled up against each other in places like Calvert House (**A**), where different generations, all aware that the past was important, made different uses of it — and still do. Calvert House, with numerous changes and alterations superimposed one upon the other, has stood on this site for more than 250 years.

The House is a good illustration of architectural and archaeological stratigraphy, or layering. One use succeeded another; buildings have been used and reused. The pattern of stratigraphy at Calvert House is a common one in the city and has played a part in preserving it.

The recently finished Historic Inn is a modern hotel that fills a large lot first occupied about 1690. The earliest remains on this land are among the oldest archaeological artifacts found in Annapolis. Excavated in 1982 and 1983, the pieces of plates, cups, and bottles can be dated (1690s) by their shape.

In 1984, an early 1700s building made of timber posts set in the ground was excavated in the front yard (**B**). The second building to stand here, built in the 1720s, was Governor Calvert's brick house. Its first floor now forms the first floor of the front of the hotel. Most of the 1720s' building was drastically renovated in the 19th century. But the walls of the 1720s building were preserved within a later Victorian building and remain as part of the hotel.

Also preserved from the 1720s is the brick foundation of the heating system (**C**) of what was likely a greenhouse. The heating system, called a hypocaust, conducted hot air through brick channels underneath the structure, probably used to grow tropical plants that would not survive Maryland's cold winters. This is one of the earliest such heating systems known in the American colonies; it dates from the era when two governors of Maryland (relatives of Lord Baltimore, the Lord Proprietor of the province) occupied the house.

In the 1760s the heating system, no longer used, was partly torn up and filled in with refuse. Normally such trash rots. But an addition to the 1720 house was built over it, thus keeping dry and preserving thousands of such items as bones, pins, buttons, hair, bits of paper, lace, cloth, seeds, and fish scales. This refuse cast off by rather rich people (as you would expect the Calverts to be) is a revealing and rare find for archaeologists.

In the top floors of this house — built by the Claude family who have been politically prominent in Annapolis since the late 18th century — you can see what remains of the fashionable Victorian residence.

A layered relationship like this would be special in almost any American city, but it is especially unusual to see all the elements in one modern building. Such a preserving relationship — deliberate as well as accidental — is a long-standing tradition in Annapolis. Even the Continental Congress took note of the city's antiquity. And in the 1890's, the first historic house opened to tourists. Modern preservation began over 30 years ago. During some decades, for example the 1950s, there was little success in keeping intact the remains of earlier eras. But in the last two decades, businesspeople, preservationists, and city officials have begun to make new use of the past.

A *before 1893*　　　　　　　　　**B** *1858*

C *before 1893*

D *after 1908*

As you look down Bladen Street, you see a harmonious view of Georgian Revival buildings: the Governor's residence, the State Office Buildings (built from the 1930s to the '70s), and even the heating plant (to the right beyond the parking lot).

To create this homogeneous architecture, many changes had to be made. When the Governor's mansion was built in 1868 (**A**), it was a conventional Victorian structure built to replace a 1740 Governor's mansion (**B**) which was demolished to make room for the Naval Academy. This Victorian building was changed dramatically during the 1930s in an attempt to make it look like a five-part colonial mansion.

Most of Bladen Street used to be a residential area (**C**) and was laid out as one in 1695. Since the 1930s, the construction of state office buildings has enabled Annapolis to continue to be used as the capital. The city — particularly its business community — was determined to keep the capital here rather than having it moved to Baltimore.

The present Georgian Revival structures in Annapolis demonstrate the compromise that was reached. Georgian buildings were rarely as large as the present state offices, but modern needs required — and modern construction methods made possible — these large and efficient buildings to be built. These, along with other governmental offices in Baltimore fulfill the needs of a modern state government. Architecture expresses the compromise between efficiency and scale thought to be appropriate. Cities and neighborhoods can and do change their functions, and architecture and urban design reflect those changes. The strategy of replacing one func-

tion with another but softening the change by using an older style of architecture is especially noticeable on Bladen Street.

As Annapolis advanced into modern times, the main entryway into the town switched from crowded West Street to Roscoe Rowe Boulevard, which did not even exist until 1950. Motor access to Annapolis was easily accommodated on the vacant land that led to the new Route 50.

West Street (**D**) remains a commercial, and secondarily, a residential place. Rowe Boulevard created a ceremonial way into the city, leading to the foot of the State House and emphasizing the increased importance of state government. Whether or not deliberate, this change continues the historic use of vistas to indicate important parts of the city. This practice was standard in European cities, including the rebuilding of Rome in the 1400s and the redesigning of London after the 1666 fire, which Governor Nicholson knew about. Urban designers have been managing the views to the capitol for nearly 300 years. They have used architecture, landscape, and street scapes to indicate what they consider to be important and what should remain unnoticed. Here, the style of architecture minimizes the changes and is designed to enhance your impression of the government.

We cannot know by direct experience what life was like centuries ago. But through viewing historical buildings and the various changes architects have made to them, we increase our appreciation of the uses that people have made of the past. These ever-evolving compromises between the present and the past help to make history more alive.

A *1900-05 postcard*

B *1900-05 postcard*

C *c. 1902 postcard*

The Chase-Lloyd House (**A**) was built between 1769 and 1774 by Samuel Chase, a Maryland lawyer who signed the Declaration of Independence, and by Col. Edward Lloyd, IV, a wealthy Eastern Shore planter. (Chase sold the unfinished house to Lloyd when he couldn't afford to complete it.) These associations with well-known historical figures are only one reason why the house is of interest. The Chase-Lloyd House is also important because it became in the 1890s the first of the great Georgian mansions in Annapolis to be opened to the public.

Today the first floor of Chase-Lloyd is a museum and the top two floors are an Episcopal home for elderly women. The museum emphasizes the architecture of this house designed by William Buckland, with its ornamental plaster ceiling, and the Palladian window on the second floor landing. (The window was considered significant and was termed "a three-part window" long before guidebook writers knew to call it "Palladian.")

The Chase-Lloyd museum could have emphasized furnishings. It could have focused on 18th-century lifestyles. Or it could have been a shrine to Samuel Chase, a signer of the Declaration of Independence. But instead it emphasizes architecture. This is the nature of all historical writing and presentation. Decisions are made about what to highlight and what to leave out. In this way history is largely a product of the circumstances in which it is written.

The opening of Chase-Lloyd in the 1890s was one of the earliest and most obvious ways that Annapolis began to present itself as a historic place. At around that same time, the city saw its first preservation move-ment; many guidebooks and histories, large and small, were written; and some historic celebrations took place. Buildings, institutions, and cities are not historic just because they are old; people must make a conscious decision to consider old things historically significant. Annapolis developed a sense of itself as being historic 30 years after Mt. Vernon was saved and many years before Williamsburg was rebuilt.

The 1920s and 1930s were another period of historical activity in Annapolis. Two lengthy historical guidebooks were published, the Company for the Restoration of Colonial Annapolis (which wanted to make a Williamsburg of Annapolis) was formed, and the Hammond-Harwood House (**B**) (directly across the street from Chase-Lloyd) was opened. Today Hammond-Harwood, a Georgian mansion, is a museum of 18th-century decorative arts, furniture, paintings, silver, and other objects.

In 1976, Historic Annapolis, Inc., opened the Wm. Paca House (**C**), the third of the great Annapolis mansions to become a museum (*it is Tour Site 8 on the map*). The museum depicts the lifestyles of the wealthy colonial leaders in Annapolis. Paca House displays few objects owned by William Paca because many of his possessions were lost in a fire at his Wye Island estate late in the 1800s. Thus, a 19th-century fire has greatly influenced the 20th-century presentation of an 18th-century mansion.

Each of Annapolis's three important museum houses is different. Each museum has a point of view, shaped by the circumstances under which it was made historic.

A *c. 1860*

B *1948-49*

C *early 1950s*

D *c. 1970*

The Wm. Paca House has been considered a historic place for 140 years, and during the past 80 has been presented as historic in two very different ways.

The house was built between 1763 and 1765 by 23-year-old William Paca, an Annapolis lawyer who signed the Declaration of Independence a decade later. He sold the house in 1780. An 1860s' view of the house (**A**) shows a vegetable garden for the Naval Academy.

By the mid-19th century it had become a popular lodging place for Naval officers. Throughout the century people were aware of the historic quality of the house and garden behind it. In 1907 the house was incorporated into a 200-room hotel called Carvel Hall *(**B**, back view; **C**, front view)*. The name came from the title of the 1899 novel, *Richard Carvel of Carvel Hall,* the most popular of the dozen or so romantic historical novels set in Annapolis during its Golden Age in the 1760s. By calling the hotel Carvel Hall, its owners tried to link it with the favorite historical perception Annapolis held of itself at the turn of the 20th century: a romantic colonial capital. Paca was not forgotten however; the hotel had a portrait of him and a chair he supposedly used. Yet in 1907, the fictional Richard Carvel was a more important "historical" figure than William Paca — at least for the purpose of filling hotel rooms.

Carvel Hall stood for almost 60 years. By the time the hotel, now obsolete, went out of business and was demolished in 1965, it, too, had a history — and sentimental memories for some visitors. The hotel hosted Naval Academy functions and was an important gathering place for members of the state legislature. Many Annapolitans worked at Carvel Hall and many others dined and celebrated weddings and anniversaries there.

In the mid-60s, a high-rise building was proposed to take its place. Local popular sentiment was very much against the demolition of the old building, which by that time was an important landmark both as the Wm. Paca House and as Carvel Hall Hotel. Opposed to the development of oversized buildings in the Historic District, Historic Annapolis, Inc., purchased William Paca's house, which was still intact, and the State of Maryland purchased the land that had been Paca's garden. Photo **D** shows the garden being restored.

With the restoration of the house and garden, the romantic view based on literary associations was replaced by a view based on archaeological and historical accuracy. Archaeologists excavated all of the foundations, paths, and drains around the house, as well as the garden walls, its terraces, the pond, the pavilion, and even the remains of plants. Careful restoration has been a practice since the 1930s in this country, but this was the first archaeology in Annapolis to aid in establishing historical identity.

The Wm. Paca House, as does any historic place, shows aspects of the past, but at the same time cannot help but show how the present understands the past. At one time, the "history" of the house centered more on artistically portraying fictionalized people in a real colonial house. But our own age has chosen to interpret the history of this house and its era through displaying genuine period objects and through applying scientific accuracy.

Back of 10 Francis Street

1. 10 FRANCIS STREET

This stylish 19th-century facade conceals a much earlier building, one of the oldest in Annapolis, with interior architecture and a rear facade that date from the early 1700s, if not the late 1600s. For many years historians believed that it housed the "Kentish Inn" early in its existence and in 1773 it was the "Sign of the Indian King." *(See page 4, photo A, third building from right.)*

2. VICTUALLING WAREHOUSE
(77 Main Street)

Known as "The Warehouse of the Victualling Office," the building (which had been confiscated by the state from its colonial owner, a loyalist) served as a supply center for goods awaiting shipment to the Maryland Navy and the Continental Army during the Revolution. Rebuilt shortly afterwards and more recently restored, it houses an exhibit depicting maritime aspects of 18th-century Annapolis. *(See page 6, photograph B, base of Main Street.)*

3. MARKET HOUSE

Annapolis originally had an open, semi-weekly market where householders brought in produce from surrounding farms and seafood from the Chesapeake Bay. Later a market house was built and several times relocated. One was at the head of the dock in 1728. Another, built there in 1784 on land deeded to the city by seven Annapolitans, was replaced in 1858 by the present one, which has been restored as a result of Historic Annapolis's intervention. The 1784 deed of gift requires that, unless the Market House function continues, the land will revert to their heirs of its original owners.

4. FACTOR'S ROW
(26-28 Market Space)

The four buildings that stood here in the early 1770s served merchants (or "factors") as counting houses and storage space for goods imported from Great Britain and the West Indies. Gutted by fire in 1883, they were rebuilt in the style of that period, incorporating what remained of their late colonial walls.

5. MIDDLETON TAVERN
(Market Space)
Built about 1740, this tavern was bought in 1750 by Samuel Horatio Middleton, who had operated it for some years as an "inn for seafaring men." He also ran sailing ferries to the Eastern Shore that were patronized by Washington, Jefferson, and other notables. Later the inn was one of the foremost hostelries in Annapolis — the place where the Jockey Club, the Free Masons, the Tuesday Club, and convocations of the colonial clergy met. In the 1780s it housed members of the Continental Congress, then meeting in Annapolis. The interior, used as a merchant's store in the 1790s, was gutted by fire in the 1960s. The exterior facade was rehabbed with a federal grant. *(See page 8, photo D, building on far left.)*

6. TOBACCO PRISE HOUSE
(4 Pinkney Street)
Here you can see evidence of the tobacco trade that sustained the colonial economy — and is still the chief crop of the counties of southern Maryland. The building is typical of a small pre-Revolutionary warehouse often used to store tobacco. In the yard alongside is a replica of a colonial "prise" (or "prize"), a device like a huge potato masher, for compressing tobacco into a "hogshead," a container like a barrel but four times as large, used to ship tobacco abroad.

7. SHIPLAP HOUSE
(18 Pinkney Street)
Built as early as 1713, if not earlier, this house has been put to many uses.

Originally a tavern owned by a sawyer, it later housed a shipbuilder, a cabinetmaker, and — in the 1880s — the artist, Frank B. Mayer. He painted "The Planting of the Colony of Maryland" and "The Burning of the Peggy Stewart," which hang in the State House. Mayer was the first person we know of who appealed to Annapolitans to preserve their colonial buildings. In Mayer's period it was acceptable to alter the style of the original architecture to fit the functions of the time. In 1958, Historic Annapolis, Inc., followed the preservation principles of its period and returned Shiplap House architecture to its original style. *(See page 10, photos B and C.)*

8. 45 FLEET STREET
Built about 1720, this gambrel-roofed house is one of the best surviving examples of a modest residence of early Annapolis. Note the Flemish bond chimneys and the galleted stone foundation.

45 Fleet Street

9. 37-39 CORNHILL STREET

In 1740, John Brewer built these two houses as one structure housing a residence and a tavern. His niece, Rachel, married Charles Willson Peale, a saddler in Annapolis who later became the famous portrait painter. When the Continental Congress met in Annapolis in 1783-84, Jefferson housed his groom here and also purchased gloves, salt, and cotton stockings from Brewer. Conversion to a two-family house and the diverging tastes of property owners led to such changes on the facade as the two doors and porch railings.

10. OLD CANNON
(in front of the State House)

The pitted iron cannon was among those brought from England in 1634. The first governor, Leonard Calvert (a brother of Lord Baltimore, to whom King Charles I had granted the province of Maryland) mounted the guns on the fort he built to protect St. Mary's from possible marauders — Indians, Spaniards, Frenchmen, or pirates. In time the cannons were toppled into the water. Two hundred years later, 10 were recovered. This relic of our past was brought to Annapolis and reminds us of Maryland's beginning in 1634.

11. OLD TREASURY
(State Circle)

This sturdily built cruciform building was erected about 1735 as an office for issuing Maryland's first paper money, which was so well funded that it was ultimately redeemed at face value. In later years the building served other functions and came to be known as the Old Treasury.

Old Cannon

14. JAMES BRICE HOUSE
(42 East Street)
Towering over its neighbors, the Brice House chimneys rise 90 feet above street level. The house was built in the years 1767-75 by a wealthy merchant who was a mayor of Annapolis; a vestryman of St. Anne's parish; and, for a short time, governor of Maryland. It is an outstanding example of a late colonial mansion and is noted for its intricate interior woodwork, which is among the finest surviving from pre-Revolutionary days.

12. JOHN BRICE II HOUSE
(195 Prince George Street)
This early 18th-century house was purchased in 1737 by John Brice II, a lawyer and merchant, who had his office in a wing that is no longer standing. It is of a very early architectural style, a version of the 1700-1730s gambrel-roof house with double-end chimneys.

13. GASSAWAY-FELDMEYER HOUSE
(194 Prince George Street)
Built between 1867 and 1870, this elegant Italianate-style residence, with museum rooms awaiting restoration, serves as the headquarters of Historic Annapolis, Inc.

Entrance to Gassaway-Feldmeyer House

The essays in this guide were written by Dr. Mark P. Leone and Parker B. Potter with considerable help from St. Clair Wright, Dr. Arthur Pierce Middleton, Ann Webster Smith, Dr. Jean Russo, Dr. Lorena Walsh, Donna Shoemaker, and Nancy Chabot. Students and staff of The University of Maryland Field School in Urban Archaeology, including Barbara Little, Nigel Holman, Patricia Lockeman, Naomi Leach, Theresa Churchill, David Sachs, Charles Stearns, Vincent Chick, and Juliet Burch, provided comments on a draft of this guide. Jacquelyn Winter and Carmen Keister did the typing. Lisa Royse gathered and collated much of this material, and provided essential logistical support for the project.

The photos of 10 Francis Street *(page 20)*, 45 Fleet Street *(page 21)*, and John Brice II House *(page 23)* appear courtesy of the Historic American Buildings Survey. Photo A on the cover is courtesy of the Special Collections Division, Milton S. Eisenhower Library, The Johns Hopkins University. Photo B, page 8 is by Philip Arnoult. All other photographs come from M. E. Warren who either took them or collected them. Mr. Warren also made the prints used in producing this guide. His assistance aided considerably in the completion of the guide.

Kell & Chadick, Inc., of Silver Spring, Maryland, designed the guide; Hodges Typographers of Silver Spring composed it; and The Woods Group of Baltimore did the printing and binding. Charles Aldrich, director of university publications at The University of Maryland, supervised its production.

This guide is a product of "Archaeology in Annapolis," a collaborative project of Historic Annapolis, Inc., and the Department of Anthropology of The University of Maryland College Park. The project is co-directed by Drs. Richard J. Dent, Mark P. Leone, and Anne E. Yentsch. Dr. Yentsch was in charge of the excavation at the Calvert House site. Connie Crosby was in charge of the excavation at the Victualling Warehouse site. The Wm. Paca House was excavated by Stanley South; the Wm. Paca Garden was excavated by Bruce B. Powell, Kenneth G. and Ronald G. Orr, Contract Archaeology, Inc., and Dr. Yentsch. Barbara Liggett excavated 43 Pinkney Street, as well as the Victualling Warehouse.

This publication was produced with funds from the Maryland Humanities Council and the National Endowment for the Humanities.

Support for "Archaeology in Annapolis" comes from the Maryland Commission on the Capitol City; the Maryland Heritage Committee; Historic Annapolis, Inc.; The University of Maryland; Paul Pearson's Historic Inns of Annapolis; the Mayor and City Council of Annapolis; Mr. Charles Schelberg of the Farmer's National Bank; The Colonial Dames of America, Chapter I; Preservation Maryland; Annapolis Institute; and George M. (Reese) King Construction Company. Assistance for "Archaeology in Annapolis" has been provided by the State of Maryland, the Maryland Historical Trust, the Hammond-Harwood House Association, and the Smithsonian Institution.

The authors used records from the Historic Annapolis, Inc., Preservation Data Bank and the Maryland Hall of Records. The interpretations of Annapolis's history are the authors'.

Banneker-Douglas Museum of Afro-American Life and History
84 Franklin Street
Annapolis, MD 21401
(301) 269-3955; 269-2609
(Baltimore-Annapolis)
(202) 565-0450 *(D.C. area)*
Closed Mon.
Tues.-Fri. 10-3 p.m.
Sat.-Sun. 12-4 p.m.

Chase-Lloyd House
22 Maryland Avenue
Annapolis, MD 21401
(301) 263-2723
Open 2-4 p.m. daily
except Wed. & Sun.

Hammond-Harwood House
19 Maryland Avenue
Annapolis, MD 21401
(301) 269-1714
Open Mon.-Sat. 10-5 p.m.
Sun. 2-5 p.m.

Historic Annapolis, Inc., Tours
Annapolis, MD 21401
(301) 267-8149
March-Oct., 10 a.m., 1:30 p.m., and
3:00 p.m. daily
Nov.-Feb., 1:30 p.m., Mon.-Fri.
(These tours start at the Old Treasury Building.)
Contact also for arranged tours and Historic Annapolis special events.

Londontowne Publik House & Garden
Londontowne Road *(off Rt. 253)*
Edgewater, MD 21037
(301) 956-4900
Tues.-Sat. 10-4 p.m.
Sun. 12-4 p.m.

Maryland State House
State Circle
Annapolis, MD 21401
(301) 269-3400
Open daily 9-5 p.m.
except Christmas

Old Treasury Building
State Circle
Annapolis, MD 21401
(301) 267-8149
Mon.-Fri. 9-4:30 p.m., Sept.-May
Mon.-Sun. 9-4:30 p.m., June-Aug.

St. Anne's Church
Church Circle
Annapolis, MD 21401

Tobacco Prise House
4 Pinkney Street
Annapolis, MD 21401
Open 11 a.m.-4:30 p.m., weekends,
mid-April through October

U. S. Naval Academy
Ricketts Hall
Annapolis, MD 21402
Open daily 9-4 p.m.

Victualling Warehouse
(Maritime Museum)
77 Main Street
Annapolis, MD 21401
(301) 268-5576
Open daily 11-4:30 p.m.

Wm. Paca House
186 Prince George Street
Annapolis, MD 21401
(301) 263-5553
Tues.-Sat. 10-4 p.m.
Sun. 12-4 p.m.

Wm. Paca Garden
1 Martin Street
Annapolis, MD 21401
(301) 267-6656
Mon.-Sat. 10-4 p.m.
Sun 12-4 p.m.

Archaeological Annapolis

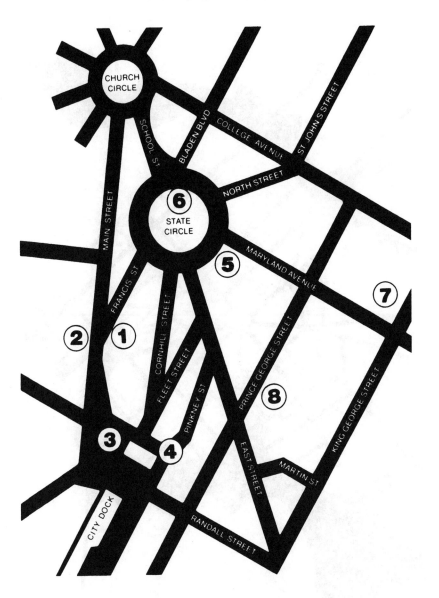

ABOUT THIS MAP: Each of the eight tour sites noted here is keyed to a two-page section in this guide, beginning with Tour Site 1, pages 4-5. As you come to each numbered site, turn to the appropriate section in the guide for help in seeing and understanding a portion of Annapolis's rich heritage.

Part VIII

Responses of "the Other"

Constructing Identities

One of the signal contributions of anthropology to the postmodern debates is the self-reflexive theorizing of identity. How do people recognize similarity; how do they mark difference? This, of course, has been a traditional topic of interest since the founding of anthropology as a discipline in the nineteenth century. Postmodern anthropologies have extended this question to how anthropology creates its subject as an object of analysis: that is, how "the Other" is created. There is a newfound awareness of the colonial origins of traditional anthropology and a growing recognition of the power relations embedded within the discipline (Marcus and Fischer 1986). Increasingly, there is a focus on how the practice of anthropology has constituted society through its preoccupation with the exotic, the foreign, the primitive. This process is bound up in the construction of time as a category to set off indigenous people from the West (Fabian 1983), and in the production and consumption of material culture (Clifford 1985; Miller 1987).

This section is devoted to the archaeology of and by "Other" groups. But we use the term "the Other" not simply to refer to non-Western, or less developed, or indigenous peoples. The archaeologies of these peoples have been long studied. The notion of "the Other" means something more than this. It refers to the idea that those in dominant Western countries have tended to construct the past and culture of non-Western countries as inverse images of themselves. In the way that the Greeks and Romans constructed largely fictive images of the "Barbarians" around their fringes, so the West has constructed its own imaginary world. A good example of this tendency is the way the West has constructed "the Orient," as stagnant, despotic, steeped in religion. In archaeology, Childe's (1925) construction of the ancient Near East, as autocratic, weighed down with religion and slow to change, fits exactly the image described by Said (1978). For Said, this image of the Orient has less to do with the societies we call Oriental, than with an idealized inversion of the Western view of itself as dynamic, democratic, and rational. Indeed, it was precisely these qualities which Childe identified as distinctively European. As for so many "Others," when we are studying the Orient we are as much studying ourselves.

Not surprisingly, this construction of the "Other" has served our political and economic interests as the dominant culture. The term "primitive" is no longer acceptable precisely because it assumed some correspondence between a distant past and an unchanging present on the margins of developed countries. "The Other" was a residue of the past, stopped in time. Fabian (1983) has shown not only how this temporal dimension underlay Western attitudes to less developed societies in general, but also how such conceptions affected anthropological enquiry. Timeless, "Other" groups were also often denied a spatial referent, often displaced and separated from homelands to which they might make claim. McGuire (1992) argues a related point regarding North American Indian peoples, who were often all lumped together in a single homogenous group. This denied them an identity except in relation to Whites. Spaceless, their specific local identities were denied. Defining Native American people as alien allowed them to be placed outside the rights of White society. In these ways, the historical and dynamic West was contrasted with an ahistorical, static "Other."

This same point can be made in a number of different contexts. For example, some feminists argue that the category "female" has been constructed as an inverse of the male (Part VI). However "significant" this "Other" might be it remains defined in negative terms, in absence. Thus the female lacks male genitalia and, in the Freudian view, is in envy. More generally, the female is described as submissive, dependent, attractive etc. so that males can constuct themselves as dominant and protective. Likewise a Marxist analysis would point to differences between elite and worker classes. The elites are dominant, controlling, masters while the workers are passive, submissive, slaves. So again we have a category that is defined by absence. In order to understand the full impact of archaeology on the construction of "the Other," it is important to explore how and why archaeology developed in the West.

Distancing past and present

We saw in Part VII that the development of archaeology in the West is intimately connected to the rise of a scientific, distanced, objective view of the past. This notion of archaeology emerges out of a very particular nineteenth-century context. There are many aspects of this context which remain to be explored and a full history of Western archaeology as discourse has yet to be written (but see Patterson 1995). In Part VII we concentrated on the rise of scientific archaeology in relation to the wresting of power from traditional authority. But why should the past have played such an important role in the emergence of new economic and social strategies? Certainly ideas of progress could be championed by contrast with a primitive past. The role of archaeology in the rise of nationalism has also been long recognized (see Trigger, **chapter 23**); but there are also other factors. For example, Trigger mentions Romanticism.

The role of Romanticism in the rise of archaeology is extremely important but has been largely ignored, mainly because archaeologists have preferred to emphasize their scientific pedigree in geology and the natural sciences in keeping with the growing prestige of science. Nineteenth-century Romantic thought was concerned with ideals of a better past or future, with, for example, millenarianism and Utopias (Brisbane 1840; Carlyle 1844). Archaeology contributed to the building of these ideals. For example, it was central to the search for a Celtic Spirit which was thought to pervade both national (French, Irish etc.) and European identities (Merriman 1987). As Colin Campbell (1987) has shown, the Romantic ethic was linked to the rise of consumerism – Romanticism was integral to the creation of desire for a better material world. Archaeology also contributed to this consumerism by providing the example of objects which could be valued and fetishized, and often in an idealized, exotic, Romantic context.

Another important aspect of Romanticism was the development of what might be termed "sensibility." A sense of humanity and of care for the disadvantaged became a distinctive characteristic of nineteenth-century thought. Tarlow (1996) has shown that the massive increase of stone gravestones in the eighteenth and early nineteenth centuries can be explained in terms of changing attitudes to death – in particular an emerging sensitivity to death, a point also made by Deetz (1977) for New England. In parallel way, people also became sensible toward the past. The scientific working over of the remains of the past became a way of dealing with the past in a sensitive and humanitarian way. But in objectifying the past within a scientific archaeology, the past was separated from life – it was made dead. This is the beginning of the process which Lowenthal (1985) refers to when he says that the past became a "foreign country." In Foucault's (1979) terms we might argue that the scientific objectifying of the past within archaeology alienated people from their past, and in doing so it created us as individuals, separated from our past. So, while deriving from a sensibility to the past, the end result was that the past became sanitized and scientifically cleansed. Although personal collections of heirlooms and momentos have remained a central part of many people's lives (Merriman 1991), the profession of archaeology "disciplined" this personal experience within a depersonalized, objectified past. As we saw in Part VII, the rise of scientific archaeology is intimately linked to the rise of state control of archaeology and "public" monuments.

It could be argued that the notion of a lived (as opposed to a dead) past is itself a retreat to Romanticism. But this is too simple. Habermas (1984, 1987) provides another way of looking at this difference in terms of two kinds of rationality. *Instrumental rationality* refers to the acquisition of knowledge necessary to adapt to and manipulate the environment. This is the kind of rationality we are all familiar with in scientific discourse. It results in a past that is objective, dead, and distanced. *Communicative rationality* is based on the social experience of consensus building. Through it we seek to achieve a shared understanding. Significantly, it has its own form of discourse similar to that of town meetings and public debates. This results in a subjective, lived, and connected past. The key point is that these forms of rationality are not mirror images of each other, they are not equivalent. Rather, communicative rationality is the more general by virtue of its being shared by all the world's peoples. So the notion of a lived past is an appeal to our submerged communicative rationality, and indeed this may be why we can all respond to it, why the Romanticist view is so attractive. The lived past reminds us that the past is not simply a Western product, and that even though we tend to see it all in terms of instrumental rationality there are other ways to view it. And the reason why this claim is so powerful is that it comes from the concrete experiences of marginalized groups, people who do not currently have full access to the resources and political structures of the West.

This opposition between a dead Western and a lived indigenous past is, of course, artificial and conceals much variation. In Part VII we showed that the past in developed countries is used actively in many types of social strategy. The archaeological past is used in strategies of power and so evidently it is not dead. While this may be true, it is instructive to note the variation in the depth of the lived past, differences for example between the attitudes involved in digging up a recent Christian burial and in the excavation of a Beaker (late Neolithic) burial in England. Excavating recent remains involves a whole set of religious, emotional, and legal issues which do not pertain in the Beaker case. The historic past is alive for us in a way that the prehistoric is not. Those societies which lacked writing are seen by Western scholars as having no history, as if the only type of history worth having is that which is written (Wolf 1982). As Mamani Condori (**chapter 24**) writes "we were condemned to inhabit prehistory." But Beaker people and indigenous Bolivians had histories as much as did those in contemporary Christian burials. And yet it is only the latter that are seen as alive, linked to us. Prehistoric individuals are thus doubly dead – without life and without history.

Certainly the past is used in Western contexts as part of power strategies, but the way it is used within the discipline is via science and the "objective gaze". Therefore, regardless of whether the results of archaeology are manipulated for contemporary ends, the very doing of archaeology (as traditionally defined) creates the past as a distanced, remote object of study. New interpretive and phenomenological approaches to the past, coupled with new ways of writing narratives about the past, attempt to break down this view of archaeology. There is certainly a potential affinity between interpretive approaches and indigenous concerns to retain a "lived" past (see Parts V and VI). However, as we shall see below, the languages in which these two approaches are expressed may not be fully compatible. Because these experiments and explorations are only now underway, it may be premature to render final judgment.

Conflict and Resistance

The contrast between a "dead" and a "living" past underlies many of the responses of indigenous peoples to archaeology. Almost by definition, archaeology separates people from their past. It involves inserting a surgical knife into monuments which are constituents of many indigenous peoples identities, parts of themselves. So any use of archaeology (at least as that term is conventionally understood) is alienating in the sense that it involves viewing the past as an objective representation, a record. But many indigenous people reject the Western opposition of past and present. For many, the past and present mutually constitute each other in daily life, time is not linear and progressive but rather cyclical and immanent (see contributions in Layton 1989a, b). Anawak (**chapter 25**) shows how his own name Illuitock connects him to the past and the future by creating a matrix of relationships with all the people who have ever held this name and all those who will hold it in the future.

An example of an indigenous response to this objectifying archaeology is provided by Rosalind Langford on behalf of the Tasmanian Aboriginal Community. Even her way of writing contrasts with the distanced scientific mode. She writes:

> "The issue is control. You seek to say that as scientists you have a right to obtain and study information of our culture. You seek to say that because you are Australians you have a right to study and explore our heritage because it is a heritage to be shared by all Australians, white and black. From our point of view we say you have come as invaders, you have tried to destroy our culture, you have built your fortunes upon the lands and bodies of our people and now, having said sorry, want a share in picking out the bones of what you regard as a dead past. We say that it is our past, our culture and heritage, and forms part of our present life. As such it is ours to control and it is ours to share on our terms. That is the central issue in this debate".
> (Langford 1983, p. 2)

Here she explicitly contrasts a dead past of archaeological science with a lived past of contemporary aboriginal people. This example also illustrates the point made above about the attempt by dominant groups to make native groups "placeless" within a wider identity. This then is the effect of invoking a transcendental past to be shared in by all, since the term "all" always refers to those in power.

Mamani Condori (**chapter 24**) provides a South American perspective on the conflict between a past made dead and past lived every day. As he says, Bolivian Indians "were 'integrated' on the condition that we renounced our cultural heritage, which was supposed to be relegated to the museums, alienated and converted into a mere souvenir of a dead past." He reminds us that for many native peoples, archaeological sites are not inert or dead. Ancestors still live and walk about in them. In fact, colonial invaders quickly recognized this and re-categorized them in terms of Christian beliefs, claiming that such places were for "devil worship." More recently, the sacred character of Aymara sites has been confronted by a positivist scientific attitude which treated them as objects of knowledge. As a result a "dead and silent past" was produced with no connection to the contemporary living people. Oral tradition and myths, the indigenous ways of knowing about the past, became marginalized discourses. "We were condemned . . . to know our own past only in a clandestine way in the darkness of the night."

One strategy that some native peoples are adopting in response to this objectification is the formation of pan-native groups and taskforces. These organizations are quite varied, ranging from ad hoc alliances to address a common need, such as the confederation of five Northeast tribes (Abenaki, Penobscot, Passamaquoddy,

Micmac, and Maliseet) to deal with reburial issues, to more formal organizations seeking to redress a variety of human-rights issues, such as the Native American Rights Fund (NARF) and National Congress of American Indians (NCAI). These pan-native groups often serve as lobbying groups; NARF and NCAI, for example, have played major roles in the establishment of the new National Museum of the American Indian and the passage of the Native American Graves Protection and Repatriation Act (NAGPRA). However, even within the native community issues of representation remain and the extent to which these groups can be said to actually speak for individual tribes is not clear.

For some native peoples, anthropology and archaeology have contributed to political tensions within local communities. The dissemination of secret traditional knowledge without permission can be literally life-threatening. In extreme cases of conflict such as the killings associated with the tearing down of the Ayodya mosque in India, archaeology plays a difficult and dangerous role if it seeks to claim an absolute objectivity. More normally, in disputes of this nature, the archaeology can be shown to be interpretable in different ways. Even in legal cases dealing with development, land rights and cultural-resource management in Western contexts, archaeologists sometimes find themselves speaking for both the prosecution and the defence. Indeed, the solution to the problem of conflicting and indigenous perspectives of the past seems to be dialogue.

Dialogue and Communication

One context that clearly demonstrates the importance of communication and dialogue in effecting change is the reburial and repatriation debates in North America and Australia. Only ten years ago, there was a broad sense within the academic community that to acknowledge the interests of indigenous people would compromise the integrity of science. The scientific position was that the return of skeletal remains would shut down archaeological research on mortuary practices, demography, genetic relationships, health and disease, and diet. It was argued that the curation of existing collections was necessary to permit future reanalyses using new technologies. Many archaeologists held that science was properly objective, neutral and for the benefit of all, while the religious claims of indigenous people were sectarian, subjective and for the benefit of the few. As more and more archaeologists came into contact with native peoples, abstract issues became grounded in social contexts and personalities. This caused some archaeologists to rethink their professional interests. Zimmerman (1989), for example, recounts how he was "made radical by his own," and how the insensitivity of his archaeological colleagues almost caused him to leave the profession.

The story of the passage of the Native American Graves Protection and Repatriation Act (NAGPRA) is complex, convoluted, and inextricably tied to the American Indian Religious Freedom Act (AIRFA) and the new National Museum of the American Indian in Washington DC. It is a historic piece of legislation that recognizes for the first time the rights of native people to religious freedom, rights that have long been guaranteed to US citizens under the Constitution. NAGPRA has four basic provisions: (1) it requires federal agencies and private museums which receive federal funds to inventory their collections of native American human remains and associated funerary remains; (2) it states that tribes have control over human remains and cultural items found on tribal or federal land; (3) its prohibits trafficking in human remains and cultural items; and (4) it requires museums to create summaries of unassociated funerary objects, sacred objects, and objects of cultural patrimony. These inventories and summaries are to be sent to all federally recognized tribes according to a specified timetable. The repatriation process begins when a tribe can prove cultural affiliation or can show that the museum obtained the remains without the consent of the legal owner.

Prior to the passage of NAGPRA the predictions from the academic community were dire, that museums would be emptied out, and anthropologists would be robbed of their objects of study. The Society for American Archaeology, for example, initially opposed the bill on scientific grounds, only to reverse its decision six months later when it became clear that public opinion was sympathetic to native Americans. Since the passage of the bill the majority of museums have in good faith made efforts to comply with the new legislation and have mailed out their inventories and summaries. Somewhat to the surprise of the museums, tribes have not made wholesale claims for either skeletal remains or cultural materials and are proceeding cautiously. One reason for this is the practical problem of processing this material and initiating claims; some tribes received over 600 mailings. But another more important reason is that the tribes must determine the appropriate individuals to conduct funerary rites and handle sacred materials, and this is not always a straightforward matter. Regardless of these problems, many tribes are using this process as an opportunity to renew interest in cultural traditions and language programs. Rather than the loss of scientific information, the legislation is generating a wealth of new information for both native peoples and museums. As traditional leaders visit museums and personally examine collections, they often share information about the proper handling of specific objects. On the reservations, new organizations composed of elders and traditional leaders are being created which may serve multiple purposes (Leigh Jenkins, personal communication).

This emphasis on dialogue has direct parallels with the debates in ethnography (e.g. Clifford and Marcus 1986) concerning the incorporation of "Other" voices within ethnographic texts. And yet it might be claimed that the situation in archaeology is radically different in that "they" – the subjects of study – are no longer alive and cannot "speak back." As we have seen, this view of the past as dead is a particular Western conception. It is a product of our own commodification of the past, whereas in Other traditions the past is alive in the present. In Vizenor's view (**chapter 26**) the past can speak in the present – by being represented in "bone courts." More generally, the past is always owned by someone, it always has some meaning in the present, and there is always someone to take its voice. Dead people cannot speak. But this does not mean that there are not multiple voices who would wish to speak for them. Increasingly, these voices are finding ways of being heard, in a dialogue with "scientific experts".

A Dialogue on Whose Terms?

How is dialogue to be structured? One solution is to attempt to create the conditions for an ideal speech situation. As defined by Habermas (1970), an ideal speech situation refers to contexts where every participant has roughly equal chances to participate in consensus making. This context is never totally achieved in practice, but it is useful to develop as an ideal model for discourse and dialogue. Habermas describes four different speech acts and related validity claims that are necessary for an ideal speech situation. Communicative speech acts are those acts associated with initiating and furthering discourse. They are related to questions of comprehensibility. Is the speaker clear and understandable? Representative speech acts are those that are associated with expressing attitudes, feelings, and intentions. They are linked to questions of sincerity and trustworthiness. Regulative speech acts are associated with commanding and opposing, controlling the flow of speech. They are related to questions of legitimacy. Finally, constative speech acts are associated with providing interpretations, offering explanations and raising critique. They are associated with questions of believability. All of these speech acts are used in the course of ordinary speech, but when conflicts arise substantiation must be worked out through further discourse.

   Leone and Preucel (1992) have examined the repatriation debate in terms of discourse analysis. They show that the media have contributed to the politicization of the context by portraying scientific and native concerns as being 'at war'. An article published in *Nation* (10 October 1988) is entitled "Indians Gaining on the U.S. in Battle over Ancestral Bones." Even an article in the news and comment section of *Science* (245: 1184–6) is entitled "Smithsonian, Indian Leaders Call a Truce". The active metaphor here is clearly one of battle confrontation, conflict between longtime adversaries. They then propose a more nuanced understanding of the debate by drawing on Habermas's (1984, 1987) notion of system and lifeworld. A systems perspective is the basis of the capitalist foundations of American society and is expressed through the segmentation of time, the specialization of labor, and the commodification of objects. This is contrasted with a lifeworld perspective which is the product of generations of oral traditions and myths which give meaning and guidance to everyday life. The repatriation debate can thus be viewed as a context where the systems perspective is "colonizing" the lifeworld. This suggests that the central problem is how to redefine the relationship between system and lifeworld so that lifeworld structures can actively participate in the larger system and yet remain strong enough to resist the system.

   But Habermas's notion of an ideal speech situation can itself be challenged. Critics have pointed out that it severely underestimates the roles of ideology, false consciousness and power differentials in dialogue. It fails to address the cultural context within which dialogue takes place. An example of how dialogue is often unbalanced is that it often takes place in the language of, and on the terms of, the dominant partner. "We" in the Anglo-American context often take it for granted that we write in English. Others have to decide in what language to write. Olsen (1991), writing from Norway, points out that in order for his words to have an impact on wider theoretical debate outside his country, he must use the English language. Perhaps this would be acceptable if language was a collection of neutral signifiers. But it is not. Language is not transparent. It forms and constrains how we see the world. For example, we have already seen that the term "prehistory" as it is defined in English as "before writing," implies that people before or without writing had no history. Anawak (**chapter 25**) asserts that the Inuit do have a past, even without written history. We have also seen (Part V) that the word "meaning" in English cannot be translated easily into either French or Malagasy. The whole debate about meaning in this volume is thus based on an assumed category in language. As further examples, Mamani Condori (**chapter 24**) discusses Aymara ideas of *pacha*. This concept may be close to concepts used in space–time geography (e.g. Giddens 1984) but there does not seem to be any obvious equivalent word in English. Similarly the Aymara idea of *nagra*, that "the future is behind our backs," seems counter-intuitive to an English speaker.

Another example is our Western legal system. We take it for granted that our justice system permits the fair hearing of individual cases. But does it? What is it like for indigenous people to take the stand and testify about sacred knowledge, about religious beliefs that are meant to be shared only with the initiated? This point is well made by Weldon Johnson, Assistant Director of the Colorado River Indian Tribal Museum,

> I don't think we should waste a lot of time talking about going to court, because I would like you to really know what it is like to go to court and stand up and speak on cultural resources and religion. It's very rough because you have to pick your words. You have to pick what you can and cannot say, and you have to do a lot of – those lawyers really drill you sometimes, on what you know and don't know. The Mojave for instance. They were told by their creator in the beginning not to have a written language. There are other forms of communications, such as petroglyphs, pictographs, and intaglios, that took this form of communication because they couldn't have a written language form. And I found myself doing something sacrilegious by writing about religion. In that sense, in the Mojave view, that is wrong. It is wrong to do that. So we're doing these sacrilegious things to try to protect our religious ways. That's the very hard part about going to court. You're doing one thing good for your tribe on one hand, yet on the other hand it's bad. (in Quick 1986, p. 146)

Here Johnson is literally caught in between system and lifeworld. He must adopt Western legal procedures to defend his case in court, yet this very act may represent a betrayal of his tribal community.

Dialogue would thus seem to be possible only if both sides accept some of the terms of the debate. Language provides only one set of terms – and perhaps the least important. What happens if scientific methodology and even archaeology as a systematic body of knowledge are rejected? Does dialogue then break down? In

Australia, Langford (1983) questions whether training Aboriginal people in a "white value science" is desirable. For Langford, there are too many injustices which have been committed in the name of science for Western science to be trusted. McGuire (1992, p. 829) notes that some native North Americans do not recognize the value of archaeology and scholarship. In these cases, there seems to be little room for negotiation or compromise. One solution may be that indigenous groups develop their own ways of doing archaeology and conceiving science. Mamani Condori suggests that an Indian-controlled archaeology making use of indigenous concepts of time and space may assist in winning back indigenous history from colonial domination. Radically different ways of conceiving archaeology within Other traditions are also beginning to be discussed (e.g. Barnes 1990, for Japan). This has parallels to the attempt by both feminist authors (Part VI) and poststructuralists (Part V) to explore different ways of writing about the past which confront distanced, objectified accounts.

But do such strategies actually further dialogue? Is it possible to negotiate even the terms of the debate? Is everything up for grabs? The signs are mixed. Traditional stories as well as radical new structures are often not taken seriously by the archaeological community or the legal establishment. Anawak's account might be criticized as being overly personal and particularistic. He doesn't talk about the past in a way that might be called scientific. Vizenor's idea of a "bone court" is secular, theoretical, postmodern. But it is a different way of thinking, radical and shocking. It is of interest that in his solution – the provision of "bone courts" – the past is brought alive. Bones are seen as having inalienable human rights. They are not dead but are seen as mediators of narratives. The objective measuring and recording, dead objective archaeology, is replaced with a living past. An initial response to the difference is to laugh and make fun. Indeed, in a footnote Vizenor says that when presented at a scholarly seminar, "the idea invited some humour." Certainly we have found when teaching this paper in graduate seminars that the immediate response is often to assume that he is not serious. But making fun of something is not only derogatory, it also helps us to deal with something unexpected, "coming out of left field." Students do normally come to see the value of the Vizenor proposal after debate and discussion. As Vizenor himself points out, the idea is not so strange. Other abstract entities like natural resources, states and universities have lawyers who speak for them, in a way parallel to speaking for bones.

Conclusion

The concept of "the Other" refers not only to difference and diversity but also to the idea of identity – in the sense that difference is constructed referentially. The "Other" is simply the opposite of "Self." Thus the "Other" can be seen as an example of the wider point made by poststructuralists that meanings of signs are always deferred, always over the next hill (Part V). Thus the meaning of female, primitive, or black is defined in reference to male, developed, or white. But the response of indigenous groups takes us beyond a theoretical debate about the meanings of words. Indigenous groups find themselves in "real" subordinate positions. They are not an abstract, dehumanized "Other." They refuse to be defined as negatives. They are people with a rich history and have a positive and independent role on their own terms. Dialogue, therefore, must include the attempt to understand these different terms through a process of negotiation and adjustment.

Some contemporary archaeological debate aims to explore the possibilities of discovering a past which is radically "different" from the present. Writers such as Barrett (1988) and Hill (1992) follow Foucault in identifying rupture, radical breaks in our "taken-for-granteds." Everything we take to be essential and universal is thought potentially to have been different in the past. But there is a danger here, a danger that we are just engaging with the past as the play of difference – the past as sign. However much we might try to embed the past in historical context, the effect is simply to produce more difference, more "Others" which are little more than fragmented and imperfect reflections of ourselves. The voice of indigenous people forcefully reminds us of the inadequacies and inhumanity of this view. The rights of indigenous groups to their past should not be alienated in the imposition of the contemporary "language game" that is interpretive archaeology. For indigenous peoples their past may not be different or "Other", but rather an integral part of themselves.

One way that archaeology can begin to construct radically different and integrated views of the past is to encourage the participation of indigenous people. And indeed the number of indigenous people trained in the profession is increasing. But this too has its difficulties and limitations. Academic archaeology is currently the controlling discourse, and the danger is that indigenous people within academia may begin to devalue or criticize their own traditions, lose respect for their elders and traditional leaders. A very real problem is that the values of mainstream archaeology can come into direct conflict with those of tribal traditions. As an example of this we need only look as far as the sharp differences between scientific and indigenous views of the origins of native people in the Americas. Traditional leaders of some tribes state that their stories and myths tell them that their people have always been there after having emerged from the underworld, while archaeological accounts identify post-Pleistocene migrations from Siberia. It is necessary to understand in what senses both of these accounts are correct. This is not the simple project of correlating emergence with migration, or seeing one as a transformation of the other, but rather, understanding the different historical contexts giving rise to these different narratives. As Naranjo (1995, p. 249) writes, we live not in an universe, but a multi-verse where "there are many levels of simultaneous existence and these understandings predate time."

There is now a growing body of evidence to show that the collaboration of archaeologists and indigenous peoples can work for the benefit of both. Archaeology has played an important role in Alutiiq cultural identity on Kodiak Island (Knecht 1994). The collaboration between professionals and Alutiiq people on a series of projects, including the Exxon Valdez oil spill, has created a context for Alutiiq to gain control of the preservation and interpretation of their own history and stimulated some Alutiiq people to consider careers in museum studies, anthropology and archaeology. Archaeologists and Hopi elders are working together in the Hopi Cultural Preservation Office to address issues such as archaeology, ethnology, the recovery of stolen sacred artifacts, farming, and the preservation of the Hopi language (Ferguson et al. 1995a, b). The office is presently developing ways for Hopi villages, clans, and religious societies to participate in program activities without compromising the nature of sacred esoteric knowledge. The Annapolis Project has worked closely with the African-American community and in the process learned that issues of freedom both before and during emancipation were of greater concern to the community than slavery (Leone et al. 1995). Examples from other countries can be found in Layton (1989a, b). As McGuire (1992, p. 829) notes, these kinds of collaborative projects forcefully demonstrate that addressing the concerns of other interest groups "does not automatically, or necessarily, destroy research or scholarship."

This pluralism opens up the possibility of other kinds of archaeology, archaeology by and for indigenous peoples. The professional response has been to resist this pluralism on the grounds that it encourages relativism. After all, so the argument goes, how are we to distinguish between those reconstructions of Olmec society that discuss local development from its formative-period roots, those which cite mythological stories of emergence from the jaws of the underworld, and those which cite African colonization? But the existence of multiple interpretations does not necessarily mean that all are equally valid or tenable. There may be guidelines for arguing that some are better than others for specific purposes and in particular contexts. If archaeology is to engage with the lived world, rather than being a science of the dead, we need to explore the historical contexts of these different interpretations. We need to understand why some African Americans interpret the Egyptian civilization as their ancestors, why some native Americans believe in the possibility of pre-Columbian European civilizations in the New World, and why modern Druids wish to claim Stonehenge as an ancestral site.

References

Barnes, G. 1990. The "idea of prehistory" in Japan. *Antiquity* 64, 929–40.

Barrett, J. 1988. Fields of discourse: reconstituting a social archaeology. *Critique of Anthropology* 7, 5–16.

Brisbane, A. 1840. *The Social Destiny of Man: Or Association and Reorginization of Industry.* Philadelphia.

Campbell, C. 1987. *The Romantic Ethic and the Spirit of Modern Consumerism.* Oxford.

Carlyle, T. 1844. *Past and Present.* New York.

Childe, V.G. 1925. *The Dawn of European Civilisation.* London.

Clifford, J. 1985. Objects and selves – an afterword. In Stocking, G. W., Jr. (ed.) *Objects and Others: Essays on Museums and Material Culture.* History of Anthropology Vol. 3, Madison, pp. 236–46.

Clifford, J. and Marcus, G. 1986. *Writing Culture: The Poetics and Politics of Ethnography.* Berkeley.

Deetz, J. 1977. *In Small Things Forgotten.* New York.

Fabian, J. 1983. *Time and the Other: How Anthropology Makes its Object.* New York.

Ferguson, T.J., Dongoske, K., Yeatts, M. and Jenkins, L. 1995a. Hopi oral history and archaeology, Part I: The consultation process. *Society for American Archaeology Bulletin* 13(2), 12–15.

Ferguson, T.J., Dongoske, K., Yeatts, M. and Jenkins, L. 1995b. Hopi oral history and archaeology, Part II: Implementation. *Society for American Archaeology Bulletin* 13(3), 10–13.

Foucault, M. 1979. *Discipline and Punish: The Birth of the Prison.* London.

Giddens, A. 1984. *The Constitution of Society: Outline of the Theory of Structuration.* Berkeley.

Habermas, J. 1970. Toward a theory of communicative competence. *Inquiry* 13, 360–76.

Habermas, J. 1984. *The Theory of Communicative Action, Vol. 1: Reason and the Rationalization of Society.* Boston.

Habermas, J. 1987. *The Theory of Communicative Action, Vol. 2: Lifeworld and System: A Critique of Functionalist Reason.* Boston.

Hill, J.D. 1992. Can we recognise a different European past? *Journal of European Archaeology* 1, 57–75.

Knecht, R. 1994. Archaeology and Aleutiiq identity on Kodiak Island. *Society for American Archaeology Bulletin* 12(5), 8–10.

Langford, R.F. 1983. Our heritage – your playground. *Australian Archaeology* 16, 1–6.

Layton, R. 1989a. (ed.) *Conflict in the Archaeology of Living Traditions.* London.

Layton, R. 1989b. (ed.) *Who Needs the Past? Indigenous Values and Archaeology.* London.

Leone, M.P. 1995. A historical archaeology of capitalism. *American Anthropologist* 97, 251–68.

Leone, P., Mullins, P.R., Creveling, M.C., Hurst, L., Jackson-Nash, B., Jones, L.D., Kaiser, H.J., Logan, G.C. and Warner, M.S. 1995. Can an African American Historical Archaeology be an alternative voice? In Hodder, I., Shanks, M., Alexandri, V., Buchli, Carman, J., Last, J. and Lucas, G. (eds) *Interpreting Archaeology: Finding Meaning in the Past.* London, pp. 110–240.

Leone, M.P. and Preucel, R.W. 1992. Archaeology in a democratic society: a critical theory approach. In Wandsnider, L. (ed.) *Quandaries and Quests: Visions of Archaeology's Future.* Southern Illinois University, Centre for Archaeological Investigations, Occasional Paper No. 20. Carbondale, pp. 115–35.

Lowenthal, D. 1985. *The Past is a Foreign Country.* Cambridge.

McGuire, R. 1992. Archaeology and the first Americans. *American Anthropologist* 94, 816–36.

Marcus, G.E. and Fischer, M.M. 1986. *Anthropology as Cultural Critique: An Experimental Moment in the Human Sciences.* Chicago.

Merriman, N. 1987. An investigation into the archaeological evidence for "Celtic spirit." In Hodder, I. (ed.) *Archaeology of Contextual Meanings.* Cambridge, pp. 111–16.

Merriman, N. 1991. *Beyond the Glass Case: The Past, the Heritage and the Public in Britain.* Leicester.

Miller, D. 1987. *Material Culture and Mass Consumption.* Oxford

Naranjo, T. 1995. Thoughts on migration by Santa Clara Pueblo. *Journal of Anthropological Archaeology* 14, 247–50.

Olsen, B. 1991. Metropolises and satellites in archaeology: on power and asymmetry in global archaeological discourse. In Preucel, R. (ed.) *Processual and Postprocessual Archaeologies: Multiple Ways of Knowing the Past.* Southern Illinois University, Center for Archaeological Investigations, Occasional Paper No. 10. Carbondale, pp. 211–24.

Patterson, T.C. 1995. *Toward a Social History of Archaeology in the United States.* Orlando.

Quick, P. McW. 1986. (ed.) *Proceedings: Conference on Reburial Issues*. Society for American Archaeology and Society for Professional Archaeologists, Washington D.C.

Said, E. 1978. *Orientalism.* London

Tarlow, S. 1996. Each slow dusk a drawing down of blinds. *Archaeological Review from Cambridge* 11, 125–40.

Wolf, E.R. 1982. *Europe and the People without History.* Berkeley.

Zimmerman, L. 1989. Made radical by my own: an archaeologist learns to accept reburial. In Layton, R. (ed.) *Conflict in the Archaeology of Living Traditions.* London, pp. 60–7.

23

Alternative Archaeologies: Nationalist, Colonialist, Imperialist

Bruce G. Trigger

This article evolved from the editing by Ian Glover and myself of two numbers of *World Archaeology* (vol. 13, no. 2; vol. 13, no. 3) that explored 'Regional traditions in archaeological research'. It has long been recognized that there is considerable variation from one country or part of the world to another in the kinds of problems that archaeologists think it worth investigating and in what they are predisposed to regard as acceptable interpretations of evidence. It is widely believed that this variation represents the infancy of the discipline and that in due course what D. L. Clarke (1979:154) called the 'unformulated precepts of limited academic traditions' will be winnowed and consolidated to produce a 'single coherent empirical discipline of archaeology'. It may be questioned whether, in the long run, such 'coherence' would be in the best interests of archaeology or whether variability is a better guarantee of scholarly vitality and adaptability. The problem addressed in this article is rather whether it is remotely possible to achieve such unity. While the accumulation of hard evidence and the development of new techniques for interpreting these data inevitably constrain wild speculation among professionally-responsible archaeologists, it does not appear that national variations in archaeology are disappearing or even significantly diminishing as Clarke's view would imply. Moreover, our examination of variations in national traditions indicated that they were far from random, as would be the case if they were simply the result of historical accidents. Similar orientations were found in diverse parts of the world that were not especially closely connected in terms of archaeological practice or academic interaction (Trigger & Glover 1981). This suggested that something more fundamental than local idiosyncrasies and historical accident was at work and that examining this variation more closely might reveal important factors that influenced the nature of archaeological research.

As a result of these observations, I began to consider what factors might shape similarities and differences in the general orientation of archaeology from one country to another. This article presents the conclusions that have been reached so far. I do not claim to be able to explain all the variations of this sort or even to do summary justice to many complex issues that are involved. Doing so would involve considering factors such as differences in the funds and technical resources available to archaeologists in different countries and in the dynamism, charisma, and capacity for innovation among those archaeologists whose research sets the standard for work in various parts of the world. Yet my investigation leads me to believe that there is a close relationship between the nature of archaeological research and the social milieu in which it is practised. More specifically, I would suggest that the nature of archaeological research is shaped to a significant degree by the roles that particular nation states play, economically, politically, and culturally, as interdependent parts of the modern world-system (Wallerstein 1974: 3–11). I do not rule out the possibility that different kinds of archaeology (Palaeolithic, prehistoric, ancient, medieval, industrial) may have different social orientations within the same country, but investigating these differences is beyond the scope of this article. The emphasis is placed primarily on prehistoric and ancient archaeology, which are the two types of most general interest to anthropologists.

It is generally recognised that the development of scientific archaeology corresponds with a specific stage of social development. A systematic antiquarian study of material artefacts as a supplement to written records has been traced back to the Song Dynasty (A.D. 960–1279) in China (Chang 1981: 158–61), to the Italian renaissance in Europe (Daniel 1950: 17–18), and apparently as an independent phenomenon to the Tokugawa period (A.D. 1603–1868) in Japan (Ikawa-Smith 1982: 297–8). A less systematic and perhaps less specifically historical interest in the material remains of the past has been noted for Classical Greek and Roman civilisations and for the later phases of the still earlier Egyptian and Mesopotamian ones (Rouse 1972: 29–30). Yet the notion that the material remains of the past could be a source of information about human history independently of written records had to await the replacement of cyclical and degenerationist views of human development by the widespread intellectual acceptance of an evolutionary perspective (Daniel 1950: 38–56). This occurred within the context of accelerating technological change that characterised the Industrial Revolution in Europe (Toulmin & Goodfield 1966). It was also accompanied by the development of modern nationalism, in which a sense of the solidarity of states became focused less on kings or princes and more on its citizens as a collective group (Wallerstein 1974: 145). At least in western Europe, the leading role in the development of prehistoric archaeology was played by the middle classes, which benefited the most, economically and politically, from the social changes that were being brought about by the Industrial Revolution. It is perhaps significant that, as early as the sixteenth century in northern and western Europe, local antiquarian studies had been a phenomenon of the gentry and middle classes, even if in some areas, such as Scandinavia, they enjoyed royal patronage, by virtue of which they were also to some degree subject to royal control (Daniel 1950: 17–19; Klindt–Jensen 1975: 14–31). In various forms and combinations, nationalism, social evolutionism and the interests of the middle class have proved to be significant variables in the development of various traditions of archaeological research.

Today archaeologists are employed in most countries or regions of the world. Since 1945, there has been a considerable expansion of archaeological research even in third-world countries where economists might consider it a rather wasteful luxury. The spread of archaeology as a locally-based activity throughout the world appears to correlate with the emergence of nation states within the modern world-system. Yet we are not witnessing parallel developments. Scientific archaeology originated early in the nineteenth century in Scandinavia and diffused from there to Scotland and Switzerland and eventually throughout Europe as a whole (Morlot 1861). Prehistoric archaeology developed in America within the context of an awareness of what was happening in Europe, while Europeans initiated archaeological research in many other parts of the world within colonial or semi-colonial settings; often carrying out the first archaeological investigations and training (as in India) the first generations of local archaeologists. The rapid spread throughout the world of technical innovations in archaeological research, such as radio-carbon dating or flotation, demonstrates the continuing interconnectedness of archaeological investigation on a planetary scale, while the leading role of certain countries in training archaeologists and supplying them to others further reinforces such ties (Murray & White 1981). It is simply not true that local traditions of research reflect the isolation of archaeologists from each other, either in the past or at present.

A final introductory observation is that, while archaeologists generally are caricatured as embodiments of the myopic, the unworldly and the inconsequential, the findings of archaeology have always been sources of public controversy. Many of these controversies have centered around conflicting claims of national priority and superiority. Indeed, Scandinavian antiquarians, such as Ole Wurm and Johan Bure, engaged in such disputes long before the development of scientific archaeology (Klindt-Jensen 1975: 15–16). Other disputes have been about matters of more worldwide interest. Archaeological evidence has played, and continues to play, a major role in the struggle between evolutionists and creationists, which in turn has a host of additional ideological implications (Grayson 1983). It is also looked to for support by those who believe in or deny the literal truth of the Bible or the Book of Mormon. The widespread belief among supporters of Erich von Däniken that professional archaeologists are wilfully concealing evidence of the existence of extraterrestrial benefactors is an extreme example of the bizarre passions that interpretations of archaeological evidence currently arouse. Further evidence of the significance of archaeology is provided by the fact that many totalitarian governments have thought it worthwhile to control the interpretation of archaeological data. A striking example occurred in Japan during the 1930's and early 1940's, when restrictions were placed on prehistoric and protohistoric research that might touch on sacred traditions concerning the origin and early history of the royal family (Ikawa-Smith 1982: 302–4). In some other countries, public beliefs and expectations have been scarcely less constraining. Such examples clearly demonstrate that archaeology operates within a social econtext. It is reasonable to conclude that if archaeology is highly relevant to society, society has played an important role in shaping archaeology.

I will now attempt to distinguish three different social contexts, each of which produces a distinctive type of archaeology. I will label these contexts and the archaeology associated with them nationalist, colonialist, and imperialist or world-oriented. These formulations capture only certain broad features of very complex situations. As ideal types, they also fail to express the varying intensity with which the characteristics of each type are realised in specific cases.

Nationalist Archaeology

Most archaeological traditions are probably nationalistic in orientation. The development of European prehistoric archaeology was greatly encouraged by the post-Napoleonic upsurge of nationalism and romanticism. Some of this archaeological activity was directed towards strengthening patriotic sentiments and in these cases it often received substantial government patronage. For example, Napoleon III ordered the excavation of the fortresses at Mont Auxois and Mont Réa, which illustrated Celtic life in France at the time of the Roman conquest (Daniel 1950: 110). In eastern Europe, representatives of suppressed nationalities, such as the Czechs, turned to archaeology as a means of glorifying their national past and encouraging resistance to Habsburg, Russian and Turkish domination (Sklenar 1981; 1983). After the 1880's, as class conflicts became more pronounced in western Europe, archaeology and history also were used to glorify the national past in an effort to encourage a spirit of unity and cooperation within industrialised states. In so far as it was concerned with Europe, prehistoric archaeology was regarded as a historical discipline.

Denmark provides a precocious example of the development of prehistoric archaeology in Europe. Danish national pride had suffered badly during the Napoleonic period and was to receive further blows from the Germans in the course of the nineteenth century. It is not surprising that the Danes (at first largely upper-middle class functionaries but later, as they grew more powerful, the lower-middle class [Kristiansen 1981]) turned to history and archaeology to find consolation in thoughts of their past national greatness. In particular, they took pride in the fact that Denmark, unlike its southern neighbours, had not been conquered by the Romans. They were also powerfully attracted to the Viking period. Scandinavian archaeologists attempted to reconstruct what life had been like in the past and to that degree their research projected a nationalistic interest in folklore into prehistoric times. Throughout southern Scandinavia, it was assumed that ethnic continuity extended back into the prehistoric period, so that Iron Age, and possibly Bronze Age and Neolithic archaeology as well, were studying the ancestors of the modern Scandinavian peoples. Moberg (1981) has noted the continuing fascination with the Viking period and the disproportionate time and resources that are still devoted to its study.

In modern Israel, archaeology plays an important role in affirming the links between an intrusive population and its own ancient past and by doing so asserts the right of that population to the land. In particular, Masada, the site of the last Zealot resistance to the Romans in A.D. 73, has become a monument possessing great symbolic value for the Israeli people. Its excavation was one of the most massive archaeological projects undertaken by Isreali archaeologists. For the most part Israeli archaeologists are trained in historical and biblical research and devote much time to studying history, philology, and art history. Palaeolithic archaeology is much less important and the impact of anthropological archaeology has generally been limited to encouraging the use of technical aids in the analysis of data (Bar-Yosef & Mazar 1982).

In some countries, where the emphasis of archaeology is on the historical period, the situation is more ambiguous. In particular, Egypt and Iran tend to emphasise the glories of pre-Islamic times in periods when nationalistic and relatively secular politics prevail, but de-emphasise them in favour of the Islamic period when political movements favour a pan-Islamic or (in the case of Egypt) a pan-Arab orientation (J. A. Wilson 1964). During the latter periods, attitudes towards the pre-Islamic period can vary from lack of interest to hostility. In recent years, such shifts have been dramatically displayed with respect to the monuments of Achaemenid Persia.

In Mexico, since the Revolution of 1910, it has been official policy to encourage archaeologists to increase knowledge and public awareness of the pre-Hispanic civilisations of that country. This is done to promote national unity by glorifying Mexico's past and honouring the achievements of the native people who constitute a large part of the population. It is also intended to assert Mexico's cultural distinctiveness to the rest of the world. An important part of this policy is the development of major archaeological sites as open air museums for the entertainment and instruction of Mexicans and tourists alike (Lorenzo 1981; Bernal 1980: 160–89). To some degree, however, this policy of integrating Indian peasants into Mexican life by dignifying their past seems to have become a substitute for the far-reaching economic and social reforms that were promised by the revolution.

Despite China's size and potential political importance, its archaeology has been of the nationalistic variety. It remains so today even though the discipline's very right to exist was attacked during the cultural revolution. During that period, the view that the study of the past was itself reactionary led to the disruption of archaeological excavations and publications and to attacks on some archaeological sites. Today archaeology is extensively encouraged as a means of cultivating national dignity and confidence, though at least lip service is paid to a socialist ideology by interpreting the past in terms of a Marxist perspective and by lauding its cultural achievements as testimonials to the skills of workers-artisans in ancient times. Significantly, the interpretation of the archaeological record remains in accord with the northern-centred views of traditional Chinese historiography and centrist politics (Chang 1981; Watson 1981). The importance of southern China as an area of independent cultural development has been recognised only in recent years by some Western archaeologists and by Vietnamese archaeologists who reject the view that northern China was the only significant centre of cultural development in each Asia. The latter see in the archaeological record of southeast Asia evidence of a 'deep and solid basis' for Vietnamese culture which, despite heavy pressure, 'refused to be submerged by Chinese culture while many other cultures . . . were subjugated and annihilated' (Van Trong 1979: 6).

Although Germany had imperialist ambitions, its archaeology also never transcended the limits of a nationalistic tradition. In the nineteenth and early twentieth

centuries, patriotic German archaeologists sought to project far back into prehistoric times the ethnic continuity that historians emphasised had characterised
their homeland throughout the historic period. Gustaf Kossinna (1911; 1912)
sought to demonstrate archaeologically that Germany was the homeland of the
Indoeuropean peoples and the centre of cultural creativity in prehistoric times.
While the other Indoeuropean-speaking peoples had moved off and interbred with
allegedly inferior races, the Germans alone had preserved their racial purity and
hence their full powers of creativity (Klejn 1974). While such views were a powerful
stimulus to nationalism and were enthusiastically endorsed by prominent Nazi
leaders, they failed because of their parochial nature to attract major support
among archaeologists elsewhere.

The primary function of nationalistic archaeology, like nationalistic history of
which it is normally regarded as an extension, is to bolster the pride and morale
of nations or ethnic groups. It is probably strongest amongst peoples who feel politically threatened, insecure or deprived of their collective rights by more powerful
nations or in countries where appeals for national unity are being made to counteract serious divisions along class lines. Nationalistic archaeology tends to
emphasise the more recent past rather that the Palaeolithic period and, in particular, to draw attention to the political and cultural achievements of ancient
civilisations or other forms of complex societies. There is also, as Daniel Wilson
(1876, 1: 247) noted long ago, a tendency to glorify the 'primitive vigour' and
creativeness of peoples assumed to be national ancestors.

Colonialist Archaeology

By colonialist archaeology I mean that which developed either in countries whose
native population was wholly replaced or overwhelmed by European settlement
or in ones where Europeans remained politically and economically dominant for
a considerable period of time. In these countries, archaeology was practised by a
colonising population that had no historical ties with the peoples whose past they
were studying. While the colonisers had every reason to glorify their own past,
they had no reason to extol the past of the peoples they were subjugating and
supplanting. Indeed, they sought by emphasising the primitiveness and lack of
accomplishments of these peoples to justify their own poor treatment of them.
While history and the specialised social sciences, such as economics and political
science, studied the accomplishments and behaviour of white people in Europe
and around the world, the study of colonised peoples, past and present, became
the domain of anthropology. Modern native peoples were seen as comparable only
to the earliest and most primitive phases of European development and as differentiated from Europeans by possessing no record of change and development and
hence no history.

The oldest and most complex example of colonialist archaeology was that which
developed in the United States. Long before the beginnings of significant antiquarian research in the late eighteenth century, native people were regarded as

being inherently unprogressive and incapable of adopting a civilised pattern of life (Vaughan 1982). Hence, from the start, archaeologists assumed that their work would reveal little evidence of change or development in prehistoric times. Past and present were not seen as qualitatively distinct and much effort was expended using local ethnographic knowledge to interpret the archaeological finds for a particular region (Meltzer 1983: 38–40). When cultures that were strikingly different from those known in historical times and seemingly much more elaborate were discovered in the Ohio and Mississippi Valleys beginning in the late eighteenth century, it was fashionable to assign these to a lost race of Moundbuilders who were distinct from the North American Indians and had been either destroyed by the latter or driven out of North America by them (Silverberg 1968). Archaeology thus identified the Indians not only as being unprogressive but also as having wilfully destroyed a civilisation; which made their own destruction seem all the more justifiable. Where cultural change was obvious in the archaeological record, it was assumed to reflect not internal development but one static tribe replacing another as a result of warfare or the aimless wanderings of peoples on a large and thinly populated continent. In the absence of satisfactory chronological data, it was widely accepted that elaborate artefacts had been made by the Indians only after they had obtained the metal tools and inspriation necessary for doing so from white intruders. Finally, while some archaeologists sought to discover a North American equivalent for the Palaeolithic period, convincing evidence was not forthcoming until the 1920's; in part as the result of a general reluctance to believe that native people had been established in North America that long (Meltzer 1983).

After 1910, American archaeology became chronologically-orientated and it also became obvious that internal changes had taken place within native cultures. Yet, until the 1960's, these chages generally were attributed to cultural diffusion. Moreover, all the major innovations that loomed large in the archaeological record, such as pottery, agriculture, and burial mounds, were habitually traced to a point of origin outside of North America, either in Mesoamerica or in eastern Siberia. This suggested that, while North American Indians were flexible enough to adopt innovations coming to them from abroad, they were not capable of innovating on their own. Throughout what has been called the culture-historical period (1910–1960), major changes continued to be attributed to diffusion and migration (Willey & Sabloff 1980: 109–21; Trigger 1981).

Archaeology began later and, until recently, was practised on a much smaller scale in Canada, Australia, and New Zealand than it was in the United States. Canadian anthropologists argued that because of the limited funds that were available for research, it was more important to record the vanishing customs of living Indian peoples than to excavate their prehistoric remains, which it was wrongly thought would survive in the ground for centuries (Jenness 1932: 71). Yet the history of archaeology in these countries has much in common with that of American archaeology. In Australia, the image of the 'unchanging Aborigine' (fostered by social anthropologists, by the evolutionist belief that hunter-gatherers possessed the simplest of human life-styles, and by an apparent lack of evidence for a high antiquity of human occupation) discouraged the archaeological study of changes in cultural patterns and ecological adaptations. W. B. Spencer interpreted all differences in the form and function of Australian tools as synchronic reponses to raw materials and local conditions and it was thought that a harsh environment rendered the stratigraphic interpretation of deeply buried materials hazardous. The building of chronologies and a more dynamic view of Australian prehistory had to await the 1960's (Mulvaney 1981; Murray & White 1981).

Prior to 1950, such archaeological work as was done in New Zealand tended to be focused on whether or not the prehistoric 'Moa-hunters' were related to the historic Maori. It was generally assumed that everything else that needed to be known about the Maori could be learned from ethnology and oral traditions. Although oral traditions conveyed an awareness of historical events, New Zealand archaeologists did not develop an accompanying sense of change in material culture that would have stimulated the archaeological investigation of Maori (i.e., post-Moa-hunter) prehistory. Culture change was attributed almost entirely to migration (Gathercole 1981).

During the colonial period, archaeologists and ethnologists regarded the so-called tribal cultures of sub-Saharan Africa as a living but largely static museum of the past (Clark 1969: 181). They also tended to underestimate the technological, cultural and political achievements of African peoples past and present and to attribute such accomplishments as were recognised to diffusion from the north. The role that was assigned to prehistoric Hamitic peoples in transmitting to sub-Saharan Africa a smattering of more advanced traits that were assumed to be ultimately of Near Eastern origin bore a striking resemblance to the civilising missions that European colonists were claiming for themselves (MacGaffey 1966). There was also a tendancy for European archaeologists to devote a larger share of attention to Palaeolithic archaeology than to studying the Iron Age. While there 'were few incentives to study cultures that were considered to be "native" or "recent" ' (Fagan 1981: 49), Palaeolithic ones were valued because they seemed to be ancestral to European societies no less than to African ones. Later phases of African history were generally regarded as ones of stagnation that were of little general interest (Posnansky 1982).

The most spectacular example of the colonialist mentality operative in African archaeology is provided by the controversies surrounding the Zimbabwe ruins. Early white investigators of these monuments, beginning in 1868, saw them as proof of ancient white settlement in southern Africa, by Sabaeans or Phoenicians. Cecil Rhodes appreciated the propaganda value of such speculations. When, in 1904, the archaeologist D. Randall-MacIver dated these ruins to the second millennium A.D., he so angered local whites that it was almost twenty-five years before serious and archaeological research was again carried out there. Although Gertrude Caton-Thompson confirmed Randall-MacIver's work and the Bantu origins of Zimbabwe in 1930, amateur archaeologists kept alive the notion that Zimbabwe was the work of foreign invaders, merchants, or metal workers. For white settlers, such claims served to deprecate African talents and past accomplishments and to justify their own control of the country. Extraordinarily, in 1971, P.

S. Garlake was forced to resign as a Rhodesian Inspector of Monuments because he was unwilling to interpret Zimbabwe to the satisfaction of the white settler government of the day (Fagan 1981: 45–6; Posnansky 1982: 347).

In post-colonial Africa there has been a considerable re-orientation of archaeology. As Posnansky (1982: 355) points out, African archaeologists are not necessarily interested in the same problems as are foreign scholars. They tend to be concerned more with recent prehistory than Palaeolithic archaeology and with problems that relate to their national history. These include the origin of states, the early development of trade, the evolution of historically-attested social and economical institutions, and relations among ethnic groups that live within the boundaries of modern African states. There is also an interest in the excavation of famous sites and monuments that relate to the national past. At the same time, anthropology is not well regarded and archaeological research is being increasingly aligned with history, just as ethnological studies are being redefined as sociology (Ki-Zerbo 1981). In our terms, the archaeology of post-colonial Africa is being transformed from a colonialist into a nationalist type.

Colonialist archaeology, wherever practised, served to denigrate native societies and peoples by trying to demonstrate that they had been static in prehistoric times and lacked the initiative to develop on their own. Such archaeology was closely aligned with ethnology, which in the opinion of the general public also documented the primitive condition of modern native cultures. This primitiveness was seen as justifying European colonists assuming control over such people or supplanting them. In Africa and elsewhere where native peoples have regained control of their own lands, archaeology is now severing its connexions with anthropology and is being transformed into a branch of history. The situation for archaeology in countries where native peoples have been largely or wholly supplanted by European colonists is considerably more complex and involves new ways of either symbolically coopting or continuing to ignore native people in changing social conditions.

Imperialist Archaeology

Imperialist or world-orientated archaeology is associated with a small number of states that enjoy or have exerted political dominance over large areas of the world. As one aspect of this hegemony, such nations exert powerful cultural, as well as political and economic, influence over their neighbours. The archaeologists in two of the three cases we will be examining engage in much research in other countries, and play a major role in training students who find employment abroad (this is also true of some nonhegemonous countries). Through their writings, archaeologists in these countries also exert a disproportionate influence on research throughout the world.

The first imperialist archaeology developed in the United Kingdom. Scientific archaeology was introduced there from Scandinavia in the 1850's, at a time when the British middle class were fascinated by technological progress. Britain had become the 'workshop of the world' and industrialisation promoted by individual enterprise had greatly strengthened the middle class both economically and politically. By offering evidence that such progress was the continuation of what had been going on more slowly throughout human history, prehistoric archaeology bolstered the confidence of the British middle class and strengthened their pride in the leading role that Britain was playing in this process (Trigger 1981: 141–2). With the development of Palaeolithic archaeology, beginning in 1859, archaeology became more than ever the science of progress in prehistoric times. It is no accident that British archaeologists and geologists played the leading role in winning scientific recognition for this new field (Grayson 1983). The populariser John Lubbock, whose book *Pre-historic times,* went through seven editions between 1865 and 1913, assured his readers that progress was inevitable and benefited every facet of human life. He asserted that, as a result of technological progress, future generations of humanity would be wiser, healthier, happier and more moral than are present ones (1913: 594). Yet in order to counteract anti-evolutionary arguments, he adopted a position that was similar to, and reinforced, that of colonialist archaeology. He believed that technologically less evolved peoples were also intellectually and emotionally less advanced than were civilised ones, to the extent that the most primitive groups could never catch up with more advanced ones and because of this were doomed to extinction as a result of the spread of civilisation. The study of prehistory was seen as proving that, among European peoples, culture had evolved rapidly, while elsewhere it had either developed more slowly or remained static. Through this version of cultural evolution, prehistoric archaeology was linked to a doctrine of European pre-eminence. Lubbock's formulation, which was not conceived in a narrowly chauvinistic fashion, but rather sought to explain the expanding world-system that was dominated by western Europe with Britain at its head, had appeal far beyond Britain itself and served to integrate much archaeological interpretation. Above all, it was echoed in the unilinear evolutionary views of Gabriel de Mortillet in France and provided a broader perspective and greater intellectual respectability for colonialist archaeology, espeacially in the United States.

By the 1880's, growing economic competition abroad, the proliferation of slums and discontent among the lower classes, and the incipient challenge of working-class political movements caused many middle-class intellectuals in Britain and elsewhere in Europe to have grave doubts about the inevitability of technological progress or its beneficial effects (Trevelyan 1949, 4: 119). British archaeologists grew increasingly uncertain about the creativity even of Europeans, doubted that there was a fixed order to history and explained cultural variation to an ever greater degree in terms of biological differences. All this encouraged increasing belief in diffusion as a mechanism of change.

Towards the end of the nineteenth century, British archaeologists accepted the view of the Swedish archaeologist Oscar Montelius that the prehistoric development of Europe had been stimulated by the diffusion of culture from the Near East. Their reactions to this view were deeply influenced by the understanding of more recent British history, when successive waves of invaders and settlers were portrayed as having brought fresh ideas to Britain which in the long run accounted for British pre-eminence in world affairs. They did not, as Kossinna had done for Germany, attribute national greatness to their ethnic and cultural purity (Rouse 1972: 72). The achievements of ancient Near Eastern civilisations were appropriated for western Europe by claiming that western Europeans rather than the people who lived in the Near East today were their true spiritual heirs. British archaeologists also stressed that Britain was located where several streams of cultural influence from the Near East had converged; hence Britain, and especially England, had been able to develop more rapidly than its neighbours (Myres 1911; Childe 1925). Thus, despite growing pessimism about human creativity, they continued to stress the capacity of Europeans, and especially of the British, to use innovations creatively. One is tempted to see these developments as evidence of a shift towards a more nationalistic archaeology and this in turn as a reflection of the growing insecurity of the British middle class.

The second archaeology with a world mission was created by government decree in the Soviet Union beginning in 1929. Prior to that time, many Russian archaeologists had continued the nationalistic approach of the Czarist period. While stressing the spectacular achievements of the inhabitants of Russia in prehistoric times, they hoped that because they studied material culture their work would satisfy the new political order. In 1929, existing theories and methods were subjected to severe criticism and pronounced to be unacceptable. Archaeologists were called upon to explain change not simplistically in terms of technological development, as the disciples of Montelius had done, but within the context of social organisation. They were required not only to describe archaeological remains but also to reconstruct the society that had produced them. This involved defining its mode of production and determining as much as possible about its technology, social organisation, and ideological conceptions. Changes were to be seen as coming about as a result of the development of contradictions within societies between different social classes and ultimately between the forces and relations of production (Miller 1956: 79).

Yet Marxist archaeologists had to labour under some severe ideological constraints. A belief in psychic unity was reasserted and with it a unilinear scheme of socio-economic formations or stages of development that was loosely derived from Friedrich Engels's *The origin of the family, private property and the state*. No criticism of this scheme was possible. Under the influence of Nicholai Marr, a linguist turned prehistorian, all discussion of diffusion and migration was suppressed in favour of the belief that each ethnic group had evolved spontaneously in its historical homeland from earliest times to the present. Finally, too much concern with typology and chronological detail was likely to be viewed as evidence of lingering anti-Soviet attitudes (Bulkin *et al.* 1982: 274–6).

Soviet archaeology presented a world scheme which, while not denying creative powers to any ethnic group, implied that the Soviet Union represented the direction in which all other societies were evolving, thus giving it pre-eminence in a world-historical sense. Despite the limitations under which it laboured, early Soviet archaeology was innovative in many ways. By directing the attention of archaeologists to studying how ordinary people had lived in prehistoric times, it pioneered the careful excavation of settlements, campsites and workshops. Archaeologists were also encouraged to try to explain cultural change internally in terms of the development of social systems, rather than to attribute it to diffusion and migration. In addition, an interest in the processes of labour encouraged the development of use–wear analysis.

In the period prior to and following the second world war, the external threat of the Soviet Union produced a strong emphasis in archaeology on tracing the origins of the various national groups that made up the Soviet federal state and in particular on lauding the prehistoric achievements of the Slavic peoples. This attempt to counteract German archaeologically-based propaganda had much in common with the nationalistic archaeologies of central Europe (Miller 1956: 107–56; Klijn 1977: 13–14). In the post-Stalin era, Soviet archaeology has reacquired a more distinctively Marxist orientation but Soviet archaeologists have rejected the excesses of the 1930's. Unilinear views of cultural evolution have been muted, diffusion and migration are accepted as historical realities and there in increasing emphasis on the formal analyses of archaeological data and on ecology. Soviet archaeologists see these developments as making archaeological findings even more useful for a Marxist analysis of history (Bulkin *et al*. 1982).

Soviet archaeology counts as a world archaeology not only because it has influenced archaeological practice in countries allied to the Soviet Union but also because it offeres a view of the significance of archaeological data that, both directly and through the works of western archaeologists such as A. M. Tallgren and V. Gordon Childe, has influenced archaeological research far beyond the Soviet sphere of political control.

American archaeology remained colonialist in orientation until the advent of the New Archaeology in the early 1960's. By stressing internal change and adaptation, the New Archaeology climinated the previous tendency of American archaeology to stigmatise native peoples by failing to recognise their creativity. Yet the New Archaeology took no more serious account of native peoples than earlier versions of American archaeology had done. The goal of the New Archaeology was not to understand prehistory but to use archaeological data to establish universal generalisations about human behaviour that would be of practical value in modern society (Martin & Plog 1973: 364–8). That it studied data produced by native peoples was a matter of only incidental concern. The New Archaeology's emphasis on generalisations in part reflects the low prestige accorded to historical studies by American social scientists. It may also reflect a general tendency in American society to prefer knowledge that has specifically utilitarian applications (Gardin 1980: 178).

In a more general sense, however, the New Archaeology can be seen as the archaeological expression of post-War American imperialism. Its emphasis on nomothetic generalisations implies not simply that the study of native American prehistory as an end in itself is trivial but also that this is true of the investigation of any national tradition. By denying the validity of studying the prehistory of specific parts of the world, the New Archaeology asserts the unimportance of national traditions themselves and of anything that stands in the way of American economic activity and political influence. Of the three imperialist archaeologies we have examined, the American is the only one that is also explicitly anti-national. Lest this seem too strong a claim, one may point to the aggressive American promotion after the second world war of abstract expressionist art as the dominant international style, apparently with financial support from the American government as well as from private foundations. As a result of this activity, many national or regional artistic traditions were suppressed or trivialised (Fuller 1980: 114–15; Lord 1974: 198–214).

The impact of the New Archaeology throughout the western world and in particular in Britain has been very considerable. In recent British symposia, it has become fashionable to invite leading American exponents of the New Archaeology to pass judgement on the proceedings; which usually involves their pointing out to what degree British archaeologists, depsite their good intentions, have failed to live up to the exacting standards of the new 'international archaeology' (Renfrew & Shennan 1982; Hodder 1982). Yet, in Britain and the rest of Europe, the New Archaeology has not succeeded in dissolving the sense of an important relationship between past and present and hence of a historical perspective as a significant part of archaeology.

Within American archaeology, interesting developments have taken place in the 1970's. The New Archaeology was primarily a technical innovation concerned with what archaeologists should do and how they should do it. Its view of humanity in relationship to a broader context was provided at first by neo-evolutionsim; an anthropological paradigm that expressed an optimistic view of technological progress, well suited for a period of economic prosperity and unchallenged political power. During the 1970's, however, this view gave way to a pessimistic and even tragic version of cultural evolution that sees population growth and other factors constraining cultural change to take place along lines that most people do not regard as desirable. The development of food production and urbanism, which previous generations of archaeologists interpreted as desirable products of humanity's ability to solve problems and make life easier and more fulfilling, is now widely viewed as a response to forces that are beyond human control and which throughout history have compelled the majority of people to work harder, suffer increasing exploitation and degrade their environment. In place of the belief that most important changes took place in a slow and gradual fashion, catastrophic reversals are now seen as common occurrences. Humanity is imagined to be the victim of forces that lie beyond its understanding or control. There is more than a hint in this eschatological materialism that the future is likely to be far worse than the present and that humanity is moving from a primitive Eden, filled with hunter-gatherers, to an atomic hell (Trigger 1981: 149–51).

This cataclysmic evolutionism is all too clearly a reflection of the growing insecurity of middle-class Americans, who have been troubled since the late 1960's by deepening economic crises and the increasing ineffectiveness of American foreign policy. More specifically it has been influenced by the key expressions of this anxiety: fear of catastrophic environmental pollution, fear of unchecked population growth and fear of the depletion of non-renewable resources. It is significant, however, that American archaeologists, and the American public, do not treat these problems as national ones that they can debate and solve politically. Rather they situate them within a universal context. Hence cataclysmic archaeology has become part of the imperialistic formulation of American anthropology, with a willing audience amongst the insecure middle classes of other western nations. This surely reflects the strength of America's conception of its international mission, even in the midst of a serious internal crisis.

Conclusion

The classification I have proposed is not without its problems. Israeli archaeology might be classified as being of the colonialist type, were it not that Israelis claim substantial historical roots in the land they are occupying. Mexican archaeology might also be thought of as an example of colonialist archaeology, as archaeology clearly is in many other Latin American countries. Yet this view does not accurately take account of the complex political and social realities of modern Mexico. German archaeology of the Kossinna school had some of the characteristics of an imperialistic archaeology and these features would undoubtedly have come more pronounced had National Socialism been militarily successful. Yet this archaeology was nationally too specific and its treatment of the evidence too obviously biased to command respect abroad. It is also clear that nationalistic themes have been strong at certain points in both British and Soviet archaeology. These characteristics tend to blur the distinction between different types of archaeology and serve to remind us that we are dealing with ideal types. On the other hand, the rapid transition of American archaeology from a colonialist to an imperialist type or of African archaeology from a colonialist to a nationalist one do not pose problems. Instead, they show the utility of these concepts.

There are also clearly unanswered problems. Why has a country as nationalistic and proud of its past and possessing such important sites as the Republic of Ireland shown relatively little interest in its prehistoric archaeology (Clark 1957: 256–7)? Why does archaeology in India, in spite of its impressive development, continue to appear so foreign to India and so attached to its European origins (Chakrabarti 1982)? In both cases, religion may provide part of the answer. The present model requires many kinds of elaboration and clarification. Nevertheless the regularities that have been noted provide evidence that archaeology does not function independently of the societies in which it is practised. The questions that are asked and the answers that appear reasonable reflect the position that societies occupy within the modern world-system and change as the positions of countries alter within that system. It does not appear likely that the present diversity of views represents merely the immaturity of archaeology or that in the future an objective and value-free archaeology is likely to develop. Instead the past will continue to be studied because it is seen to have value for the present; the nature of that value being highly variable.

This does not mean that archaeologists should abandon the search for objectivity. The findings of archaeology can only have lasting social value if they approximate as closely as possible to an objective understanding of human behaviour. But such understanding requires not only paying scrupulous attention to archaeological and other relevant sources of information but also a deeper awareness of why archaeologists ask the questions and seek the kinds of knowledge that they do. This in turn necessitates investigating the behaviour of archeologists not simply as individuals but as researchers working within the context of social and political groups. Understanding of this sort at the level of the world system is both a point of departure and the ultimate sythesis of such research.

Note

A preliminary version of this article was read in May 1983 to the Canberra Archaeological Society; the Department of History, University of Melbourne; the Anthropological and Archaeological Societies of Western Australia (Perth); and the Anthropological Society of New South Wales (Sydney), while the author was visiting Australia as a guest of the Australian Academy of the Humanities. For helpful comments I wish to thank Sandra Bowdler, Gregory Dening, Jack Golson, Sylvia Hallam, Isabel McBryde, D. J. Mulvaney, Nigel Oram, Jim Specht, Sharon Sullivan, and others. The article has also benefited from discussions with Olav Sverre Johansen, University of Tromsø. At the time of writing, the author was recipient of a Leave Fellowship of the Social Sciences and Humanities Research Council of Canada and on sabbatical leave from McGill University.

References

Bar-Yosef, O. & A. Mazar 1982 Israeli archaeology, *Wld Archaeol.* 13, 310–25.

Bernal, I. 1980. *A history of Mexican archaeology.* London: Thames & Hudson.

Bulkin, V. A., L. S. Klejn & G. S. Lebedev 1982. Attainments and problems of Soviet archaeology. *Wld Archaeol.* 13, 272–95.

Chakrabarti, D. K. 1982. The development of archaeology on the Indian subcontinent. *Wld Archaeol.* 13, 326–44.

Chang, K. C. 1981. Archaeology and Chinese historiography. *Wld Archaeol.* 13, 156–69.

Childe, V. G. 1925. *The dawn of European civilisation.* London: Kegan Paul.

Clark, G. 1957. *Archaeology and society* (3rd edn). London: Methuen.

——1969. *World prehistory: a new outline.* Cambridge: Univ. Press.

Clarke, D. L. 1979. *Analytical archaeologist.* London: Academic Press.

Daniel, G. 1950. *A hundred years of archaeology.* London: Duckworth.

Fagan, B. M. 1981. Two hundred and four years of African archaeology. In *Antiquity and man* (eds) J. D. Evans, B. Cunliffe & C. Renfrew. London: Thames & Hudson.

Fuller, P. 1980. *Beyond the crisis in art.* London: Writers & Readers.

Gardin, J. -C. 1980. *Archaeological constructs.* Cambridge: Univ. Press.

Gathercole, P. 1981. New Zealand prehistory before 1950. In *Towards a history of archaeology* (ed.) G. Daniel. London: Thames & Hudson.

Grayson, D. K. 1983. *The establishment of human antiquity.* New York: Academic Press.

Hodder, I. (ed.) 1982. *Symbolic and structural archaeology.* Cambridge: Univ. Press.

Ikawa-Smith, F. 1982. Co-traditions in Japanese archaeology. *Wld Archaeol.* 13, 296–309.

Jenness, D. 1932. Fifty years of archaeology in Canada, *Anniversary volume, 1882–1932*. Toronto: Royal Society of Canada.

Ki-Zerbo, J. (ed.) 1981. *General history of Africa, I, Methodology and African prehistory*. Berkeley: Univ. of California Press.

Klejn, L. S. 1974. Kossinna in Abstand von vierzig Jahren. *JSchr. mitteldeutsche Vorgesch.* 58, 7–55.

——1977. A panorama of theoretical archaeology, *Curr. Anthrop.* 18, 1–42.

Klindt-Jensen, O. 1975. *A history of Scandinavian archaeology*. London: Thames & Hudson.

Kossinna, G. 1911. *Die Herkunft der Germanen: zur Methode der Siedlungsarchäologie*. Wärzburg: Kabitzsch.

——1912. *Die deutsche Vorgeschichte: eine hervorragend nationale Wissenschaft*. Wärzburg: Kabitzsch.

Kristiansen, K. 1981. A social history of Danish archaeology (1805–1975). In *Towards a history of archaeology* (ed.) G. Daniel. London: Thames & Hudson.

Lord, B. 1974. *The history of painting in Canada*. Toronto: NC Press.

Lorenzo, J. L. 1981. Archaeology south of the Rio Grande. *Wld Archaeol.* 13, 190–208.

Lubbock, J. 1913. *Pre-historic times* (7th edn). New York: Holt.

MacGaffey, W. 1966. Concepts of race in the historiography of north east Africa. *J. Afr. Hist.* 7, 1–17.

Martin, P. S. & F. Plog 1973. *The archaeology of Arizona*. Garden City, NY: Natural History Press.

Meltzer, D. J. 1983. The antiquity of man and the development of American archaeology. In *Advances in archaeological method and theory* (ed.) M. B. Schiffer, New York: Academic Press.

Miller, M. 1956. *Archaeology in the U.S.S.R* London: Atlantic Press.

Moberg, C.-A. 1981. From artefacts to timetables to maps (to mankind?): regional traditions in Scandinavian archaeology. *Wld Archaeol.* 13, 209–21.

Morlot, A. 1861. General views on archaeology. Washington: *Annual Report of the Smithsonian Institution for 1860*, 284–343.

Mulvaney, D. J. 1981. Gum leaves on the Golden Bough: Australia's Palaeolithic survivals discovered. In *Antiquity and man* (eds) J. D. Evans, B. Cunliffe & C. Renfrew. London: Thames & Hudson.

Murray, T. & J. P. White. 1981. Cambridge in the bush? archaeology in Australia and New Guinea. *Wld Archaeol.* 13, 255–63.

Myres, J. L. 1911. *The dawn of history*. London: Williams & Norgate.

Posnansky, M. 1982. African archaeology comes of age. *Wld Archaeol.* 13, 345–58.

Renfrew, C. & S. Shennan (eds) 1982. *Ranking, resource and exchange*. Cambridge: Univ. Press.

Rouse, I. 1972. *Introduction to archaeology*. New York: McGraw-Hill.

Silverberg, R. 1968. *Moundbuilders of ancient America*. Greenwich: New York Graphic Society.

Sklenar, K. 1981. The history of archaeology in Czechoslovakia. In *Towards a history of archaeology* (ed.) G. Daniel, London: Thames & Hudson.

——1983. *Archaeology in Central Europe: the first 500 years*. Leicester: Univ. Press.

Toulmin, S. E. & J. Goodfield 1966. *The discovery of time*. New York: Harper & Row.

Trevelyan, G. M. 1949. *Illustrated English social history* (4 vols). London: Longmans.

Trigger, B. G. 1981. Anglo-American archaeology. *Wld Archaeol.* 13, 138–55.

——& I. Glover 1981. Editorial. *Wld Archaeol.* 13, 133–7.

Van Trong 1979. New knowledge on Dong-s'on culture from archaeological discoveries these twenty years ago. In *Recent discoveries and new views on some archaeological problems in Vietnam*. Hanoi: Institute of Archaeology.

Vaughan, A. T. 1982. From white man to red skin: changing Anglo-American perceptions of the American Indian. *Am. Hist. Rev.* 87, 917–35.

Wallerstein, I. 1974. *The modern world-system, I.* New York: Academic Press.

Watson, W. 1981. The progress of archaeology in China. In *Antiquity and man* (eds) J. D. Evans, B. Cunliffe & C. Renfrew. London: Thames & Hudson.

Willey, G. R. & J. A. Sabloff 1980. *A history of American archaeology* (2nd edn). San Francisco: Freeman.

Wilson, D. 1876. *Prehistoric man* (3rd edn) (2 vols). London: Macmillan.

Wilson, J. A. 1964. *Signs and wonders upon Pharaoh.* Chicago: Univ. Press.

24

History and Prehistory in Bolivia: What About the Indians?

Carlos Mamani Condori
(translated by Olivia Harris)

Introduction

It might be assumed that Bolivia is a nation with a homogeneous national culture, solidly based on a common historical heritage, in which there are no serious national or ethnic contradictions. However, in Bolivia some 70 per cent of the population is Indian, a term which embraces many different linguistic and cultural groups, of which the largest are the Quechua, the Aymara, and the Guarani. All the Indians have suffered colonial oppression since the arrival of the Europeans, but in spite of this, Bolivia is presented by our oppressors as a free nation, whose citizens are 'free and equal', and in which civil liberties exist.

Until the Agrarian Reform of 1953, the Indian was not even considered a person, and did not have even the most basic civil rights. Since the so-called 'National Revolution' of 1952 there has been some attempt to neutralize Indian opposition by extending us some of these rights. We were 'integrated' on condition that we renounced our cultural heritage, which was supposed to be relegated to the museums, alienated and converted into a mere souvenir of a dead past.

This chapter is written from the perspective of the colonized Indians. We are struggling to free ourselves, to become ourselves. There must be many errors, which we hope you will forgive: only in the last 30 years have our people had real access to literacy and everything else that could be called science or 'universal knowledge'.

Bolivian Archaeology, Legitimator of Colonialism

In an article in *América Indígena* Rivera criticizes the many failings of Bolivian archaeology, including lack of professional training, inadequate analysis, and ideological manipulation which ignores the Indian descendants of the people who built the monuments studied by the archaeologists (Rivera 1980, pp. 217–24). Nothing has changed since that article was published, except for the recent establishment of a degree in Archaeology at La Paz University.

The systematic study of archaeology in Bolivia goes back only to 1952. Before that it was the domain of a few antiquarians and interested foreigners who attempted a first systematization of their researches and observations. It was the triumphant National Revolutionary Movement (MNR) which in the person of one of its young militants first took seriously the task of archaeological research. In this sense the 1952 revolution was the most serious attempt by our white colonizers to form a nation; archaeology had an important role in this project, since it had the job of providing the new nation with pre-Spanish cultural roots. The object of their concern was to integrate pre-Spanish archaeological remains into the 'Bolivian' cultural heritage, and at the same time to integrate the Indian population into the stream of civilization (another of the main nationalist projects).

Carlos Ponce, the ideologue of Bolivian archaeology, makes a statement that reveals clearly the aims of the Bolivian nationalists:

> It must be obvious to everbody that the Indian peasants of Bolivia, Perú and México are related to the high civilizations of pre-Spanish times. Although centuries have passed since the Spanish conquest many traces of the former culture remain. In spite of the intensive production of non-indigenous cultural forms, there is a solid cultural nucleus of pre-Columbian origins and a continuity of traditions. The archaeologist in countries of indigenous ancestry must then decipher the profound roots of the people and *the very foundations of the nation* [my emphasis]. In sum, the archaeologist can by no means hide away and engage with his discipline as though it were cold and detached. *(Ponce 1977, p. 4)*

In spite of this pronouncement Ponce is in fact obsessed with creating through archaeology the source of national identity in the sense of white-dominated republican Bolivia, and he does not hesitate to use archaeological data in a maner directly opposed to such statements of principle.

The case of Tiwanaku is the most obvious example. This major site was the centre of one of the Andean 'cultural horizons' between the 6th and 10th centuries. Since it is located in Bolivia near Lake Titicaca, Ponce treats it as the source of Bolivian national identity. He therefore refuses to acknowledge that Tiwanaku was influenced by cultural inputs from the Pacific coast (i.e. what is today Peru) in its early phases, and only admits links between Tiwanaku and the coast in the late expansive phases when Tiwanaku was the centre of an empire (phases 4 and 5 in his periodization). Ponce's distortion goes to extremes; he even claims that 'Bolivia as a nation is witness to the past' (Ponce 1977), whereas Bolivia is a country which actively *oppresses* the Indian majority of its population.

This nationalist archaeology, in spite of its continuous protests against imperalism and external influence, is firmly rooted in a Western ideological framework and as such carries a strong colonialist ideological load. Take the case of the two Portugals (father and son) who belong to the Ponce school. They claim to have 'discovered' archaeological remains, which the Aymaras have known for centuries. In the wake of such achievements Portugal writes of Tiwanaku as follows:

> Tiwanaku evokes the fields and roads which must have led to settlements situated in the altiplano – the immense space which is the theatre for the extraordinary spectacle

of its ruins. It has a special appearance for the traveller or visitor as the outline of a great deserted city, the memory of times long past which call to mind the greatness of other cities of the ancient world: the fortress of Nineveh, the undeniable walls of Babylon overcome by Cyrus, king of the world; the famous palaces of Persepolis, and the fabulous temples of Baalbec and Jerusalem. *(Portugal 1975, pp. 195–6)*

This quotation reveals the deep insecurity of the mestizos who constantly seek points of comparison with the great centres of European and Asian culture in order to identify our past with other empires which perhaps had little in common with ours in terms of social and political organization.

The Portugals are intoxicated by this colonialist spirit; they take no notice of the original culture context of our archaeological sites, and simply rename places whose names a long oral tradition has preserved, as it this was enough to credit them with their discovery. Thus the ruins of *Qalasayaña* (Aymara: lit, upright or standing stone) were changed to *Q'allamarka*, meaning 'origin of the city'. This name fitted their interpretation better, that these ruins were the beginning of Tiwanaku. *Intin Qala* near the sacred Lake Titicaca was also renamed. The name means 'stone which contains sun'; the Portugals called the ruins 'Inka seat' because their shape was like a chair or seat. One after another, 'gallows' and 'baths' of the Inkas appeared in their fever for names, which do nothing to clarify the organization of ancient Andean society and economy.

All the nationalist denunciations of outside domination, all their stress on internal development, have only led to the development of a sort of Monroe Doctrine: they take possession of what is not theirs in order to lay the foundations of their 'nation' in the past which does not belong to them and whose legitimate descendants they continue to oppress.

This appropriation of the eloquent material remains of our past is nothing new; it has been occurring in different ways since the early days of Spanish rule. Tiwanaku was used as a quarry first to build houses for the Spanish in the town of the same name; then its huge worked stones were transported to La Paz in order to build the Presidential Palace, and finally they were used for the railway bridges on the La Paz-Guaqui line. Plundering takes a different form these days; monoliths are carted off on the demands of their 'discoverers' to decorate squares and private houses in the city, for example the Plaza del Stadium and Posnansky's house. The expropriation is not only symbolic but also material: they have built earthworks round the ruins so that today we can no longer get in to Tiwanaku. The Aymara people have to pay an entrance fee to visit the ruins as tourists where they listen to invented accounts of the meaning of our history. The archaeologists completely ignore the fact that for our culture the site is sacred. It is a *wak'a*, a place where our ancestors lived and through which they communicate with us in various ways.[1]

---

[1] *Wak'a* is a concept of the sacred which embraces the works of humans as well as the deities. Thus Mount Illimani which dominates the city of La Paz is a *wak'a mallku*, which in Aymara means high god. Below Illimani in rank come other intermediate deities in more accessible, even everyday, locations

Archaeology, Prehistory and History

If our independent historical development had continued, the discipline of archaeology would today be studied with seriousness and scientific rigour. Not only
would there be fewer gaps in our knowledge, but since we understand the social
and cultural practices which are still alive in our society we would be able to interpret better the central features of the social, economic, and religious-political
organization of antiquity.

The traumatic fact of colonial invasion changed our contact with the sacred sites
of our ancestors. It was claimed that they were places of 'devil worship'; thus
leaving us with only a mythological understanding both of our past and the material remains of the past.

The archaeological ruins left by ancient cultures are not inert or dead objects: they
have a reality which actively influences our lives both individually and collectively.
They are the link with a dignified and autonomous past in which we had our own
government and were the subjects of our own history. In short, they are the source
of our identity. This is why many of these sites are held to be links with the past. In
many areas the Indians believe that the *gentiles* – that is, our pre-Christian ancestors
– still live and walk about in the ruins.[2] We are thus able to live with our ancestors
and share our world with them. By day we live in a foreign time system, and by night
we are reunited in secret with our own past, our own identity.

These ruins and the myths that they generate, are considered sacred (*wak'a*) but
we believe that they are not the same as all the beings called *wak'a*. For example the
sacred mountains (*achachilas*) are also thought to be *wak'a*, but are linked directly
to religious practice, whereas the ruins are treated in a way more similar to how
Western society honours outstanding citizens. Ruins are as it were historical *wak'a*
related to social circumstances. An example of this can be seen in my own community in Pacajes Province. There is a ruin called Inka Uyu – a pen in which according
to tradition Inka herds were kept. Today the community invokes its help when we
have economic difficulties, or conflict either with neighbouring *ayllus*[3], or with the
State. We make regular offerings, particularly of sweets, fat, and *q'uwa* (an aromatic
plant burnt as incense); and in times of crisis we hold a llama service (*wilani*). Ruins
also play a part in rituals connected with the argricultural cycle. For example, in
the newly revived festival of Inti Raymi at the winter solstice (21 June) in Tiwanaku
we perform propitiatory rites, including llama sacrifices, in order to affirm our faith
in the re-establishment of Tawantinsuyu.[4]

---

which are called *katxasiri* and may be individual as well as collective. Finally there are the *illas* materialized in an object which may be kept in the house or carried around. 'Historical' *wak'as* on the other
hand are not deities nor created by deities, but are the work of human hands.

[2] A point confirmed to me recently in an interview with two Bolivian archaeologists – Roberto Santos
and Juan Faldin – from the National Institute of Archaeology (INAR).

[3] *Ayllus* are the basic units of Andean society; in the Aymara region they are in principle endogamous
and territorially based.

[4] Tawantinsuyu is the Quechua name for the Inka state, meaning literally the 'four divisions'.

Those who have studied the 16th-century anti-Christian millenarian movement of Taki Onqoy suggest that such rites were an escape from Spanish-dominated space and time (e.g. Curatola 1977). This is incorrect, since our colonial oppressors did not effectively wrest from us our control over space. Time on the other hand is another matter: we need to regain control of our own historical time and end the foreign domination of our history. I do not believe that this counts as 'escapism'. As for ritual time, the writings of Eliade can help us to understand the issue. He states: 'All liturgical time consists in making alive in the present a sacred event which took place in a mythical past at "the beginning"' (Eliade 1959). His next sentence on the other hand does not fit our experience so well. He writes: 'To participate in a religious festival implies leaving normal durational time' (1959). It seems to me that the Aymaras do not need to leave normal durational time, since Bolivian colonial domination is so ineffective that it can be seen as a sort of enclave with partial control only in the cities.

The city is the centre of colonial power par excellence. Nonetheless in the case of La Paz it is in practice dominated by Aymara shamans or priests (*yatiris*, in Aymara literally 'he who knows'). These *yatiris* challenge the power of the official Catholic church from the calvary chapels where they perform their rites. Even the upper classes go to consult them when they have personal or family problems, revealing in this way their fragile sense of identity, and equally their fragile dominion over the country as a whole.

In these ways Indian society constantly reaffirms its links with the past through myth and ritual on both a daily and a calendrical basis. One could argue that in the *ayllus* and in the Indian neighbourhoods of the cities we live in a different time, one in which the 'sacred' and the 'profane' are united. This experience of time is interrupted only by the superficial contact we have to make with our oppressors.

For all these reasons it will be clear that the relationship we have with the material evidence of our past goes beyond a simple 'positivist' attitude which would treat them as mere objects of knowledge. Rather, they are for us sources of moral strength and a reaffirmation of our cultural autonomy. This is why the archaeological *wak'as* are surrounded by a mythical aura and are the object of individual and collective rituals. This proves that the attempt of the colonists to turn our culture into 'devil worship' has failed, and we are still able to approach them with respect, when we seek guidance or healing. The rites and offerings to the *wak'as* are acts of reaffirmation.

Let us compare this attitude with the one adopted by Bolivian archaeology. The statements by Ponce make clear its aims and position. According to him, the mission of archaeology is:

> to provide ancestral roots for the national culture. In the case of a people which is testimony of the past, therefore, archaeology uncovers the alienation in national consciousness *and regains legitimate possession of pre-Spanish antecedents. [my emphasis]* (Ponce 1977, p. 6)

The use of the term 'antecedents' reveals clearly that for Ponce History only begins with the European colonial invasion.

Historians are no different in their conception of the history of native peoples. When Adolfo de Morales [5] was admitted to the Bolivian Academy of History in June 1986, one of the other academicians (who is a history lecturer in La Paz University) announced firmly in his speech of reply:

> Here and now we must once again emphasise that Bolivian history began 451 years ago with the arrival of Diego de Almagro and his advance guard to the banks of Lake Titicaca and from there across the altiplano. What happened before is prehistory, or at best protohistory. *(Siles 1986)*

The message of both archaeology and history in Bolivia is clear: the evidence of our past, the age-old historical development of our societies and the Indians are for them only prehistory, a dead and silent past.

Prehistory is a Western concept according to which those societies which have not developed writing – or an equivalent system of graphic representation – *have no history*. This fits perfectly into the framework of evolutionist thought typical of Western culture. All we can say by way of reply is that writing was only one among many of the great inventions which regulated both relations between human beings, and with the natural and supernatural worlds. While it has the advantage of leaving traces for posterity, writing is not the only, or even necessarily the best, form of knowledge and transmission of a society's historical experience.

On the other hand, we know that in Tawantinsuyu there were specialist historians, as there are today in our Indian communities. Even a chronicler openly hostile to our forms of social organization was forced to register the indigenous means of recording history:

> In addition there used to be, and still are, particular historians in these nations whose craft is inherited from father to son. We must also mention the great diligence of Pachacuti Inca who called together all the old historians from each of the provinces subjugated by him and of many others in this country. He kept them in Cusco a long time questioning them about ancient times, the origins and the notable things in the whole country. And when he had properly ascertained all the most important elements of their antiquities and history, he had everything painted in order on great wooden boards, and arranged a large room in the Temples of the Sun where they placed these boards decorated with gold. They were like our libraries; he established learned people who knew how to interpret them and tell their meaning. Nobody could enter the place where these boards were except the historians themselves or the Inca unless by express permission of the King. *(de Gamboa 1942, p. 54)*

---

[5] Adolf de Morales is known mainly for his genealogical researches in the Archivo General de las Indias in Seville, where he concentrates on demonstrating the noble ancestry of members of the Bolivian ruling elite. As a result of his 'researches' it has been 'proved' that almost all of them are direct descendants of El Cid!

This specialist, independent development of a historiographical tradition, universalized as 'official history' under direct State control, stagnated and went backwards as a result of the colonial invasion. In a way, we were condemned to inhabit prehistory, and to know our own past only in a clandestine way in the darkness of the night, that is, by oral tradition, which is transmitted from one generation to the next, and especially by myth, which has become the vehicle for our history and archaeology. These academic disciplines as practised by our oppressors treat us as part of prehistory, and undoubtedly they see in myth one more example of our 'backwardness'. We cannot, however, afford to abandon myth since it is a form of knowledge of our past, and a deposit of our own modes of thought and historical interpretation. Myths form the main basis of our historiography and philosophy of history.

The Myth of the World Ages: Liberty and Order in Our Autonomous History

History, not only in the (Andean) Indian version, but also as a universal human concept and heritage, can be understood as a process of transforming and ordering the internal relations of society and the relations between society and nature which nourishes it.

In the mythical account of the world ages (*pacha*) independent Indian society passed through four distinct ages.[6] The first, the time of darkness (*ch'amakpacha*) was the origin of human life. That long night of birth has left no record; it develops without internal differentation in total darkness (*ch'amaka, tuta*). This age was succeeded by the *sunsupacha*, the age of silliness or the nebulous age of childhood. Human beings were not distinguished from animals and other creatures of nature, and animals intervened actively in social life. We are still living out the consequences of many of these interventions today. In the *sunsupacha* a distinction between society and nature also begins to emerge.[7] It is the time of confrontation between humans and animals, revealed in many myths which show how society and nature re-establish a new balance.

An example of this is the myth of the 'Son of Jukumari', a type of bear which inhabits the tropical frontiers of the Andean world. The bear gathers wild pepper (*ulupika*) to exchange with humans and has a son by a girl whom he seduces. The boy when he grows up is extraordinarily strong, and kills people with a flick of his finger. He is able to defend himself against the attempts of the local people to get rid of him, but in the end he is killed in the forest. All versions of this myth end

---

[6] The concept *pacha* has multiple resonances in Andean languages. These will be discussed below (see the final section of this chapter).

[7] *Sunsu* is a Spanish word – *sonso* – which as been incorporated into Aymara. It may have replaced the Aymara term *q'inaya*, which means a cloud of fog, and is used to refer to children in that they lack the faculty of reason. If this is the case, it would support my argument that the early mythical ages reflect the stages of human growth.

with the question: 'What would have happened if the Jukumari's son were still alive?'

The first two ages are obviously mythical. They are followed by two more which represent civilization and include more directly historical elements. The third age or *pacha* is that of the *chullpa*, the population living before the expansion of the Inka state which practised burials known by the name *chullpa*. These people practised agriculture and had domesticated animals; they left behind burials and remains of pottery and metalwork, and also numerous food plants which are thought to be the predecessors of those grown today. Thus the *q'apharuma* is the previous form of the potato, *ajara* of quinua grain, and *illamankhu* of *kañawa* grain.

They were succeeded by the culminating moment of the *inkapacha*, a time when humans, personified in the Inka himself, ordered both society and space. For example, one myth tells how Mount Illimani grew too tall and was threatening to unbalance the earth; the Inka decided to put a stop to its growth so he made it fall down and sent the highest peak to the western part of the cordillera, where today it has become the volcano of Sajama. The Inka age is also remembered as an age of plenty, of agricultural production and social order. Nobody died of hunger, there was enough of everything and the earth's wealth was at the disposition of humanity. When anybody committed a wrongdoing the Inka as a punishment made them pull up *wichhu* grass, and under it silver appeared. People also say that the huge buildings of the Inka period were created as a result of his power over nature: he gave orders and the stones moved into place of their own accord.

This independent historical development, representing a progressive ordering and differentiation of human society, was violently brought to an end when foreign forces burst onto our civilization and invaded Tawantinsuyu. The Inka was killed by the Spanish and order was broken and eroded. This event is also recounted in myths: the Inka used his control over natural forces to order the sea to enclose the Spanish. The Spanish were saved by the treachery of an Indian; this enabled them to take the Inka king prisoner, and to justify their rule because he was unable to read the letter brought to him from the King of Spain by the soldiers. Before he died the Inka ordered that all the wealth should be hidden, and put all his cities, fortresses, and sacred places under a spell. As a result they are all underground and frozen in time. The spell will last until Indian society frees itself from its oppressors.

Jichhapacha: the Present Colonized Age

While historiography was rigorous, scientific, under the Inkas, the rupture that resulted from colonization condemned our forebears to orality and illegality. Myth, an 'underground' means of transmitting and reflecting on history, was used to keep alive our memory. In Andean thought, there is a concept – *pacha* – which unites the two dimensions of space and time; *pacha* was unified so long as our society controlled both dimensions. Colonization meant for us the loss of control over time, that is over history, but not over space; one of the ways we think of our fight against the rupture of colonialism is through mythical thought, for example our aim is to reunite time and space in the unity of *pacha*.

Although our lands suffered one incursion after another under the colonial order, we still basically control them and thus our own space. History on the other hand was stopped in its tracks: Tawantinsuyu was cut off in 1532 and history will only recover its coherent course by going back in time to when that rupture occurred, truncating our historical development. This in turn can only be achieved within the forms and spaces in which our collective life is lived, the *ayllus*. *Ayllus* are the social units on which Andean society is based; although quite fragmented today they remain the vital centre of our cultural and social life, of our relationship with nature and with our forebears.

What has occurred in the course of the long period of colonialism? Have we just become part of nature, part of the land? Have we just vegetated? The answer is no; in a clandestine way *pacha* and the historical development of our autonomous time are maintained. From the moment of the colonial rupture, Tupac Amaru I and all the Incas of Willkapampa took up the struggle to recover continuity of time, and preserve the unity of *pacha*.[8] Since then, intermittently anticolonial movements flower on the surface, like flashes in which we momentarily regain control over our history and our identity as historical subjects. This process continues through movements like that of Tupac Amaru II, the Katari brothers, Zárate Willca and Santos Marka T'ula, violently bursting into the world of civilization in an attempt to overturn and thus restore the course of history.[9] In the most recent bursting forth (1952–3) we managed to destroy the feudal estates and restore our identity as historical subjects, but in that case only as individual subjects. Meanwhile Bolivian historiography merely treats us as a background – part of the landscape – except during times of war when we become useful as cannon fodder, for example the Chaco War (1932–5).

Chukir Qamir Wirnita: Savagery and Freedom versus Civilization and Colonial Subjugation

Let us follow the lead of myth in order to examine the ways in which the Indians confront the colonial order. The myth of Chukir Qamir Wirnita tells of an event that supposedly occurred in colonial times, but it is also reproduced again and again in contemporary history. The myth is well known in my community, which

---

[8] The Andean forces of resistance to the Spanish withdrew under Manco Inka to the forests of Willka-pampa (written Vilcabamba in Spanish) after their unsuccessful seige of Cusco (1536). The Inka state in Willkapampa maintained its resistance to the Spanish until 1572, when Tupac Amaru, the nephew of Inka Atawallpa, was captured and beheaded.

[9] Tupac Amaru II and the Katari brothers were leaders of the great Indian uprising of the late 18th century. Zárate Willka led the Aymara forces against those of the Bolivian republic in the so-called 'Federal War' of 1899 (see Condarco 1984); Santos Marka T'ula led a massive resistance movement against the attack on Indian land rights in the first decades of the 20th century (see THOA 1984).

is located along the frontier between the high Andes and the tropical forest to the east.

Chukir Qamir Wirnita was the daughter of the most noted citizen of a Spanish town, which like all colonial towns was an enclave within a large territory beyond its control. Although many suitors came to court her, she accepted the suit of one called Katari, which in Aymara means snake. The personage appeared as a human being (as in the age of *sunsupacha*) – a fair-skinned Spaniard with elegant clothes and covered in jewels. He only came at night, and by day after visiting her would slither back as a snake to sleep in his cave (*chinkana*). The girl's parents realized that she was being wooed by a stranger and tried to find out who he was. By a trick they discovered that he was a snake living deep in the most dense part of the forest. (As is well known, for Christians the snake is the personification of the devil.)

However, the affair between Katari and the Spanish maiden had already gone far, and she was pregnant. Her children were also born as snakes, and her parents decided to burn these offspring of the devil and exorcise their daughter. But when they tried to do so they were cast under a spell. The area which had been controlled by the Spanish was invaded by snakes who brought darkness to the light of day. Ever since the town has remained under this spell. When an Indian goes there without bad intentions Wirnita herself looks after him, but people who go there in search of gold or to try and undo the spell lose all their wealth. The bewitched town is guarded by snakes and the Spanish and whites try to set off the church bells by firing their rifles in order to break the spell and return to civilization.

Other versions of this myth say that the snake children of Wirnita still live in particular church towers, for example, in Sicasica, Peñas and San Francisco in La Paz. All these places are of central importance to Aymara colonial history.[10] In the case of La Paz there is a belief, or a hope, that one of these days the whole city will be bewitched by the *kataris*, that is, that civilization will be invaded and taken over by darkness and 'savagery'.

This myth is constantly re-created. For example, between August and October 1979 people said that a new Wirnita had appeared in the town of Viacha and she had given birth to her children in the public hospital in La Paz. The news was even broadcast on the radios, although they added that since it was only a 'superstition' no one need worry about it. Nonetheless, many people went in search of her and many claim to have seen her. People said that the city of La Paz would soon be bewitched by the *kataris*. The fact is that in November of the same year, the whole country was convulsed by a series of peasant mobilizations of which the most radical centre was among the Aymaras of the altiplano. Road blocks were established and lasted over two weeks, repeating in a way the seige of La Paz by Tupac Katari in 1781. No agricultural produce could reach the city and people were terrified by the prospect of an Indian invasion. These events are another indication of the historical power of myth. The ideological climate of anticolonial resistance

---

[10] Sicasica was the birthplace of Zárate Willka; Peñas was the centre of his resistance to the republican armies; and San Francisco was the first 'Indian church' built after the city of La Paz was founded. It remains a neighbourhood particularly dominated by the Indian population.

and the hope of victory over our oppressors contributed to this historic mobilization of the Aymara peasantry, and was an important ingredient in this apparently spontaneous action.

Cyclical Vision of History

It seems clear that a cyclical vision of history is typically found in societies affected by profound crisis. This it seems is why Toynbee (1946) offered a cyclical philosphy of history at a time when the West was plunged in crisis and looking for some divine plan to save it from the Depression of the interwar period. It also explains Carr's (1961) refutation of Toynbee at a time when Europe was emerging from the mire (see also *Who needs the past?*, also in the One World Archaeology series).

Since 1532, Tawantinsuyu has been in crisis. It seems likely that our concepts of history have not always been cyclical, and that Indian culture developed this vision under colonial domination as a defence mechanism and as a means of recovering its historical destiny. In any event, it is clear that colonial oppression has been a major factor in shaping our own ideology.

While our process of development started from darkness (the first age of *ch'a-makpacha*), the arrival of the colonial power forced on us a foreign light which turned our own light to darkness. For this reason, as can be seen in the myth of Chukir Qamir Wirnita, the victory of darkness over light is also the victory of our own freedom over a light which for us has meant oppression and disorder.

Our freedom movements are therefore orientated around the theme of return, and of the positive value of 'savagery' as a means of liberation from colonial oppression. The leaders of Indian movements give up their civilized Christian names and adopt names which to Western eyes conjure up the spectacle of the devil. Often they become snakes in order to uproot a 'civilization' which is pernicious and chaotic. For example, of the leaders of the great uprising against the colonial order in the late 18th century, those of the Chayanta region already bore the surname Katari; Julian Apaza, leader of the uprising round La Paz took the name Tupac Katari, and José Gabriel Condorcanqui, the leader in the Cusco region, was called Tupac Amaru (*amaru* also meaning snake in Quechua). At such times, often the use of Western clothes is forbidden by Indian insurgents (see for example Lewin (1957) in the 18th century, and Condarco (1977) for the Aymaras at the end of the 19th century).

But return is not simply going backwards; it means the recovery of our independent history. Since colonial times the wheel of our own history has not moved on; time has stagnated, damaging and imprisoning us. We wish to move on in pursuit of our own vision, a vision which is both in the past – before 1532 – but also in the future. For this reason it is essential to return to the past. This does not mean to push the wheel of history backwards, but that we ourselves set it turning once again.

This idea of history, rooted in the experience of anticolonial resistance, can be clearly illustrated by means of two concepts, one which we have used throughout this chapter – *pacha* – and a second, *nayra*, meaning both the eye and the past.

Pacha as time/space

Let us start with the most concrete uses, such as the seasons: *Jallupacha* means the season of rains (Aymara: *jallu*, rain); *juyphipacha* is season of frost, *awtipacha* dry season, and *lapakpacha* the season of scarcity. These seasons are linked to agricultural tasks and to different spatial locations (sowing, harvest, making *ch'uñu*, journeys to other climatic zones), and they follow on from each other through the annual cycle. *Pacha* refers to a specific time: *ukapacha* means that time, that period. *Ukapachay ukhamanx*: at that time things were like this.

Longer time periods, and historical stages which refer to less specific time-spans, are also expressed by the concepts of *pacha* as we have already seen in discussing the mythology of world-ages. According to Szeminski (1985) these ages each last a millenium; for Chukiwanka (1983) they are spans of 500 years. Each span has a spatial referent or *suyu*. In Chukiwanka's reckoning we are today living in the fifth world-age, which is the age of disorder and chaos. It will soon be ended, and will be replaced by a cyclical return to the independent temporal order of Indian society.

Pacha can also designate a spatial orientation. The sky can be called *pacha*: when it is cloudy we say *pacha q'inayataway*, and as a joke we call very tall people *pacha k'umphu*, which means 'holder-up of the sky'. Probably through the impact of Christian ideas the cosmic division of space acquired a value distinction; thus *alaxpacha* is heaven, the upper space, and also the most venerated; *akapacha* is the world we inhabit, and *manqhapacha* is hell or the underworld.[11]

Another well-known context in which the concept *pacha* is used is the living space of *pachamama*. White Bolivians translate this concept as 'the earth mother', but according to Aymara tradition it is related more to the principles of fertility, nourishment, and protection, and is a cosmic category distinguished from the physical earth (known in Aymara as *uraqi*). *Pachamama* has a relation of correspondence and reciprocity with Indian society, offering food as the fruit of labour, which for us is a source of pride not a curse. The agricultural cycle is marked out by ritual offerings and libations to *pachamama*. The sowing is a propitiatory rite, a feast both for humans and for draught animals, which are decorated with vicuña skins, flowers, and flags. *Qhachwa* and *anata* are ritual dances performed to ensure a good harvest and offered to *pachamama* at specific moments in the agricultural calendar. In August too there are rituals in order to renew the reciprocal relationship with *pachamama*. This celebratory and festive spirit has been turned into 'devil worship' by Christianity, so that today the month of August is said to be the 'devil's month', a time when the earth's mouth is open and hungry for sacrifices.

Then there is *akapacha* which means both the present time and the space inhabited by humans, the 'here and now'. It can be called 'our space-time' (*jiwaspacha*),

---

[11] See also Bouysse-Cassagne & Harris (1987) for a further discussion of the concept *pacha*, and Platt (1983).

which also means 'we ourselves'. Thus the term *jiwaspacha* expresses the unity between humans and the space around them, in a harmonious relationship which was broken by the chaos of colonial time.

Nayra

In its basic restricted sense this word means the eye, the organ of sight, but it also means the past. The past is as it were in front of our eyes. By contrast the word *qhipa* which means literally the back, is used to refer to time after, i.e. the future. We thus reach a concept of time in which the future is behind our backs and the past before our eyes, both in time and space. The present brings together this conjunction between past and future, and between space and time.

A phrase which vividly expresses this is *qhiparu nayaru uñtas sartañani*. Literally it means 'let us go backwards looking in front of our eyes', but translated meaningfully it is 'let us go into the future looking into the past'. The authorities of the ayllu, when they hand over office to their successors, end their speech of advice to the new authorities (*iwxa*) with this phrase. To look into the past, to know our history, to know how our people have lived and struggled throughout the centuries, is an indispensable condition in order to know how to orient future action. *Pacha* and *nayra* thus incorporate notions of both past, present, and future. The two words together (*nayrapacha*) mean the past, former time, but former time is not past in the sense of dead and gone, lacking any renovating function. *Pacha* and *nayra* imply that this world can be reversed, that the past can also be the future.

If we were to talk of an Aymara philosophy of history, it would not be a vision of forward progress as a simple succession of stages which develop by the process of moving from one to the next. The past is not inert or dead, and it does not remain in some previous place. It is precisely by means of the past that the hope of a free future can be nourished, in which the past can be regenerated.

It is this idea which makes us believe that an Indian archaeology, under our control and systematized according to our concepts of time and space, could perhaps form part of our enterprise of winning back our own history and freeing it from the centuries of colonial subjugation. Archaeology has been up until now a means of domination and the colonial dispossession of our identity. If it were to be taken back by the Indians themselves it could provide us with new tools to understand our historical development, and so strengthen our present demands and our projects for the future.

References

Bouysse-Cassagne, T. & O. Harris 1987. *Pacha. En torno al pensamiento aymara'* in *El pensamiento andino en al Quallasuyu: tres reflexiones*. La Paz: HISBOL.

Carr, E. H. 1961. *What is history?* London: Macmillan.

Chukiwanka, K. 1983. *Marawata. Calendario Indio*. La Paz.

Condarco, R. 1977. *Origines de la nacion boliviana: interpretacion, historico sociologica de la fundacion de la republica*. La Paz: Urquizo.

Condarco, R. 1984. *Zárate el 'temible Willka'*. La Paz: Urquizo.

Curatola, M. 1977. El movimiento del Muro Onkoy. *Allpanchis*. 10, Cusco.

Eliade, M. 1959. *The sacred and the profane*. New York: Harcourt Brace.

Gamboa, S. de. 1972. *Historia de los Incas* [1942]. Buenos Aires: Emecé.

Lewin, B. 1957. *La rebelión de Tupac Amaru*. Buenos Aires: Hachette.

Platt, T. 1983. Religion andina y conciencia proletaria. *Qhuyaruna y ayllu en el Norte de Potosi*. HISLA II. Lima.

Ponce, C. 1977. El INAR: *su organizatión y proyecciones*. La Paz: Instituto Nacional de Arqueologia.

Rivera, S. 1980. La antropologiía y arqueologia boliviana: límites y perspectivas. *América Indígena* XL (2). México.

Siles, J. 1986. Respuesta a Adolfo de Morales. *Presencia Literaria*. 15 June, La Paz.

Szeminski, J. 1984. *La utopía tupamarista*. Lima: Universite Católica del Perú.

THOA, 1984. *El indio Santos Marka T'ula, Cacique Principal de los Ayllus de Qallapa y Apoderado Gerneral de las Comunidades Originarias de la República*. La Paz: Universite Mayor de San Andrés (Taller de Historia Oral).

Toynbee, A. 1946. *The study of history* (first 6 vols abridged by D. C. Somervell). Oxford: Oxford University Press.

25

Inuit Perceptions of the Past

Jack Anawak

My people the Inuit (Arctic Eskimo) have a continuing high regard for the past, and throughout our life we are taught by example and observation that it is through the knowledge gained over time that our people have managed to survive.

From the earliest possible time an Inuit child is given an Inuktitut name by which he or she will be known. This name is bestowed and 'twins' him or her with someone else much older, who may be living or deceased, and who is of importance to the child's family or group and was also known by that name. This name may have come to the child's parents or close relative in a dream or a penetrating thought. In any event the child is thenceforth dealt with by all as bearing that name. All members of the family and extended group then respond to the child according to the relationship they had with the previous bearers of that name.

Hence, Illuitok, a respected, elderly woman from the community of Pelly Bay near the Arctic Circle has a son who, later in his life, when she is old and ill, names his own son Illuitok. This child is now the old lady's namesake. The passing on of his mother's name to the man's son signifies the importance of this system in preserving the past on an intimate daily level. It also carries with it the necessity of repeating an oral history, and causes our people to relate to the figures who throughout time have held his name.

Great reverence is shown by those who most closely relate to a bearer of a name. In this case the man who gave his son his mother's name at birth relates to the baby by addressing it as 'my mother'. As the baby grows up and becomes aware of the name he carries, he will in turn address his parent as 'my child'. Others who were related to old Illuitok will also address this small male child in the exact manner and with the same degree of intimacy as they would have displayed to the old lady, with no distinction by gender. Thus, we as Inuit are taught that all things stem from and continue to be tied to the past, and that it must continue to be respected and preserved.

In the harsh environment such as our home in the Canadian Arctic, it is necessary to hand down from generation the knowledge and skills to ensure survival. Learning these skills is not optional. The recent arrival of the 'White men', or *Kabloona* as we call them, has brought with it the introduction of clothing, vehicles, implements and adornments. Many are now being utilized, but they prove to be of limited use compared with time-honoured ways of creating shelter and providing transport on the land. We continue to rely on caribou and sealskin clothing for hunting, and erect snowhouses, called igloos, in which to sleep. Our tools, although often made from metal, still reflect the designs that have proved most suitable since our people first came to be a part of our land.

From birth, through stories and legends about survival, endurance and respect for nature and all mankind, children are taught. Toys and playthings are fashioned for them, including tools and traditional dress so that they may learn early about the roles they will assume. Girls are provided with packing parkas, called *amoutis*, and carry their dolls on their back as they will carry their children in the future, and they are taught the traditional styles and methods for sewing and designing clothing. Boys are dealt with from an early age as budding hunters, and are introduced to traditional games, group play and exercises to learn agility, improvisation and endurance.

Children quickly come to understand in my culture that time-honoured skills and attitudes can never be relegated solely to the past; that they ensure a way of life and survival in the present and for the future.

A great amount of time is spent by the child in listening to the elders as they recount tales of their past, and in hearing through individual songs, called *Ai-yai-yahs*, the experiences of the singers who are the owners of each specific song. These songs usually speak of events that occurred in the singer's past, and detail their reaction to them.

The school system in the Eastern Arctic reflects this same emphasis and the budget of the Government's Department of Education places importance upon this respect for the past, ensuring that Cultural Inclusion funds are provided to enable elderly people to function as Land Instructors to acquaint students with survival skills, legends, hunting techniques and terminology, traditional food and skin-clothing preparation, production of implements and shared on-the-land living experiences.

The ties to the past have essentially been passed verbally through legends, anecdotes and song. Information is now being set down on paper for dissemination and for preservation by the Inuit Cultural Institute. One of their main activities has been to standardize the Inuit syllabic writing system, which until recently had been taught differently by Roman Catholic and Protestant missionaries and government educators. Another goal has been to develop a Roman orthography. Audio-visual techniques have recently been employed to tape elders' stories, which are then played over the local community radio. A project for creating a tape library and making film and musical recordings, for the enjoyment of old and young alike, is now under way.

In winter, while the majority of women and children now remain in the settlements which have sprung up over the past 25 years, the hunters actively hunt on the land, practising the same hunting methods as their fathers in pursuing game. In spring, summer and autumn families relocate from the settlements to live on the land. Although canvas has replaced skin tent, the anchoring is still achieved by placing large stones around the tent. Stone fishing traps called weirs, are rebuilt annually in which fish are trapped and speared. Fish and caribou meat are hung to dry or stored in stone caches using the same method our ancestors used. When families vacate these camping areas the sites often resemble, at a glance, those archaeological sites which have been found to be hundreds of years old.

The necessity of facing what is considered to be such a harsh environment makes it imperative to learn that the traditional methods for coping must always be practised. This means not only acquiring the skills associated with procuring food and shelter, but actively practising the traditional skills and attitudes and coping mechanisms that allow for adaptation and survival as a distinct people. These skills are only attained through incorporating the past into the present.

I am Illuitok. As my namesake was taught, there will be many bearers of this name in the future, as there was in the past. I am part of something that time has not erased. As an Inuk I have learned first-hand that the knowledge handed down by my people on survival in our land is not to be disregarded, and failure to practise and uphold this wisdom can only result in tragedy or disharmony to an individual or a group. We, as Inuit, have a strong sense of self – of who we are, and why we are as we are. Although our north is changing, and at times we select those things that are of use to us that stem from other cultures, we maintain to ourselves that which is passed on to us and will be passed on by us.

The past as I refer to it is measured in three distinct ways. I have a *recent* past, and I refer here to the years in which I pursued a more outwardly traditional style of life – that of being a small child of less than 10 years of age, living a nomadic life with members of my family group before the creation of permanent settlements. We lived in igloos and travelled by dog-team before contact with White men. These are the years in which the skills were taught to me through legends, stories and observation, and by example.

Most Inuit adults make the same delineation with regard to a recent past, and describe it as being associated with the years in their life which were before settlement living and the impact of settlement living, permanent housing, school system–wage economy and the presence of a non-Inuit government bureaucracy in our land. We are aware of the tales and stories associated with the earliest contact with non-Inuit – in the form of traders, missionaries, geographers and whalers – that occurred from the period AD 1700 to 1900, and our older people speak of their parents meeting the early visitors and sharing our food and shelter with them. Remains of the early whalers' look-outs, stone winter houses and shipwrecks dot our landscape. Beyond that period there is no precise measuring stick when it comes to time. The past stretches back over the years, and stories and legends are handed down which do not contain within them any specific references in the manner of other societies which had developed and utilized a writing system which set down their history on paper and measured time in terms of other happenings. Although the timespan that we refer to is general, the information handed down is very specific and detailed.

Through our legends we Inuit speak of our close ties with the spiritual world, and of our reverence for and understanding of wildlife. Stories handed down through time depict our interrelationship with the animal world, and tell of animals and humans exchanging roles, acquiring supernatural powers, and teaching and providing for one another. Our artwork also reflects these relationships, and we have rituals that show our respect for and acceptance of this oneness and this harmony, which are displayed in our world-famous Inuit soapstone carvings and silk-screen prints.

As a people we are aware that others have come before us to our land. Elders pass on stories of a people who were known to us as the Tunnit, described as being much taller and possessing great strength, and who preceded the Inuit.

Because we lived a nomadic life until 25 years ago, there is evidence of our campsites, graves, fox traps, storage caches, stone weirs, stone kayak rests and semi-subterranean houses throughout the north. As there was no written system before the coming of the missionaries, there have only been recent initiatives to document these sites. However, as stated earlier, great emphasis is placed on transmitting oral history, and most adults can readily identify he old structures and many of the tools and implements found around them.

Most of the sites, while known, have been of limited historical interest to the Inuit, as they have simply accepted their existence as a part of their life. At times they utilize portions of them while out camping on the land. However, this attitude may be changing as outside pressures intrude which have resulted in a new awareness of these sites as the key to preserving the past. As the population grows in the Canadian North and my people become increasingly concerned about the threat to the environment and way of life that oil, gas and mining exploration coupled with an increasing outside population poses, there are initiatives being taken by the Inuit through our organizations to press for additional legislation to protect various sites.

As we are now conducting Land Claims negotiations with the Government of Canada, we are developing key agreements, including an archaeological sub-agreement which awaits ratification. Various Land Use and Occupancy Studies have been carried out by Inuit organizations to bolster our Land Claim negotiating positions. Funding has been received to conduct Unmarked Graves projects, utilizing a military grid system for mapping. These studies are carried out by elders in each of our settlements, who also interview other old people about their knowledge of the locations and information surrounding these sites.

As Canada's North becomes a growing tourist destination, there is also an awareness that these sites can be utilized to acquaint and educate visitors regarding the Inuit way of life, and many settlements are exploring ways to cater to this market, while also serving to increase their own awareness and that of their children by developing historical sites and trails, signage and information brochures. This new interest in these old sites sometimes gives way to concern as the Inuit survey the large quantity of artefacts that have been removed over the years by non-Inuit, and which are presently housed in private collections, universities and museums throughout the world. Our people want to find wasy to house and preserve these artefacts within our homeland.

Whereas there was minimal response to archaeological teams conducting digs many years ago, recently a feeling of concern has arisen if Inuit organizations or elected Municipal Hamlet Councils are not consulted and see themselves to be directly involved or benefiting from such activity. This heightened awareness on the part of our people to protect, preserve and retain control of our past is now supported by Northwest Territories legislation which prohibits excavation or investigation of any site unless a permit has been obtained. No land-use operation can now be conducted within 30 metres of a known or suspected archaeological site or burial area unless authorized by an inspector, and if any such site is unearthed such land-use activity must be suspended and the location and unearthed materials, structures or artefacts must be reported.

It is necessary for the archaeologists and the Inuit to share their understanding and knowledge of the past. At times archaeological teams have spent a minimal time in communities in discussion with Inuit and our organizations, developing a common approach to sites or enlisting their assistance in identifying artefacts. More time and attention will have to be paid to the strong concerns we have regarding the removal of artefacts to distant museum locations, where we question whether we shall ever get an opportunity to view them again and utilize them to educate our own children.

There is also a continuing need to train more of our people to be involved in the investigation and interpretation of these sites. Few Inuit have gained a secondary education, and almost none have gone to university. However, the pressures upon us and the times we live in demand quicker and more innovative training methods than the standard secondary school and university route to obtain a grasp of archaeological principles and procedures if we are to work hand-in-hand with people in this profession.

Although archaeologists working in our homeland have been able to identify a wide variety of artefacts through seasoned practice, it remains to be seen how much more could have been known or how much more refined their studies could have been if they had enlisted our elders to work side-by-side with them to challenge and share each other's perceptions. Both of us can only gain from this process, and I hope that, in the future, innovative programmes will be developed within the archaeological community to meet the needs of the Inuit and other aboriginal peoples of the world in preserving, interpreting and protecting yesterday for tommorrow.

As we view with such concern the newcomers to our land, some of us feel that we cannot wait for additional legislation and increased Northwest Territories Government funding and programmes to begin to protect some of the sites. People such as myself and my family have gone ahead and spent time at the sites to monitor, mark and protect them from being disturbed. Last summer we set up our tent camp as close as we thought necessary to a Thule site, thought to be several hundred years old, on the banks of the Meliadine River. Throughout the next two and half months we cleaned and maintained the area, while showing visitors through it along designated walking paths so as to prevent damage and disruption to it.

We realize that it will take many more of us actively doing our part to preserve areas such as this if we are to move sufficiently quickly in the next few years to locate and protect them while they are still relatively intact. Already I can see how valuable an experience caring for this site has been to me and to my children. As we spend time there, we look at our way of life.

Often visitors come by in the form of families or local groups, and somtimes tourists from southern Canada and the USA. We spend time touring the tent rings, meat caches, kayak stands, graves and semi-subterranean winter houses. From time to time we are joined by a friendly sik-sik and birds, who watch our progress as we walk through the site. I am aware, as they may be, that their ancestors probably watched mine in the same manner and in this same place hundreds of years ago. Here, at this site, nothing has changed through time. I – Illuitok – and the land and the animals are all still here. This is my past, and this has become a special place. Even though I am young, I too am the past as much as I am the future.

The formal education I received has made me aware that my country – Canada – and other cultures, for the most part through their long written history, have developed reference points and time-frames through which they view their history. My people have developed and passed on the wisdom and stories of the generations without the assistance of a written history spanning hundreds of years.

Our unique way of passing on this knowledge which allows our young to know who they are, and to see how they belong to time immemorial, has allowed us to survive.

26

Bone Courts: the Rights and Narrative Representation of Tribal Bones

Gerald Vizenor

Ishi, the last survivor of his tribe, died seventy years ago in a museum at the University of California. Alfred Kroeber was in New York at the time and wrote to the curator of the museum, "If there is any talk about the interests of science, say for me that science can go to hell."

"We propose to stand by our friends," the distinguished anthropologist continued. "Besides, I cannot believe that any scientific value is materially involved. We have hundreds of Indian skeletons that nobody ever comes to study. The prime interest in this case would be of a morbid romantic nature."[1]

Kroeber protected the remains of his tribal friend, and, in his letter to the curator, anticipated by two generations the debate over the disinterment of aboriginal bones and the reburial of tribal remains. Three hundred thousand tribal bodies have been taken from their graves to museums and laboratories, asserted a tribal advocate. "If this would happen in any other segment of society there would be outrage.'. . . Whether they were buried last year or thousands of years ago, they have the right to the sanctity of the grave."[2]

This is a contentious discourse on the prima facie rights of human remains, sovereign tribal bones, to be their own narrators, and a modest proposal to establish a Bone Court. This new forum would have federal judicial power to hear and decide disputes over burial sites, research on bones, reburial, and to protect the rights of tribal bones to be represented in court.

The rights of bones are neither absolute nor abolished at death; bone rights are abstract, secular, and understood here in narrative and constitutional legal

---

[1] Kroeber, Theodora, *Ishi in Two Worlds* (Berkeley: University of California Press, 1961), 234. Ishi was cremated and his remains "placed in a niche at Mount Olivet Cemetery. Pope and Waterman decided and I agreed," wrote the museum curator to Alfred Kroeber, "that a small black Pueblo jar would be far more appropriate than one of the bronze or onyx urns." The inscription reads: *Ishi, the last Yana Indian, 1916*. "The funeral was private and no flowers were brought."

[2] *The New York Times*, "MX Cable Gives Air Force and Sioux a Bond," Thursday, November 15, 1984. Jan Hammil, a Mescalero Apache from New Mexico, directs American Indians Against Desecration. She said, "What we're interested in is respect for the dead because for us it's just another step in life."

theories. The rights of bones to be represented in federal court is substantive; these rights are based on the premise that human rights continue at death.

Most human remains were buried with ceremonial heed, an implied communal continuation of human rights; death, cremation, subaerial exposure, earth burial, and other interments, are proper courses, not the termination of human rights. The rights we hold over our bodies and organs at death are the same rights we must hold over our bones and ashes.[3] Brain death, or heart death, is not a constitutional divestment; death is not the absolute termination of human rights. In the Bone Court the last rites are never the last words.

This proposal to hear bones is not an ontological argument to discover the soul or to measure the duration of human consciousness; however, concern over the evolution of the soul, and the spiritual return of souls, is pertinent in a wider discourse on tribal remains. "Conscious persons consist of body and soul," wrote Richard Swinburne in *The Evolution of the Soul*, but "humans cannot discover what else is needed to get souls to function again, unless they can discover the ultimate force behind nature itself."[4] Here, the proposal for bone rights is a postmodern language game with theories on narration and legal philosophies to direct the discourse. Narrative theories augment the proposition that bones have the right to be represented and heard in court; moreover, tribal bones would become their own narrators and confront their oppressors in a language game, in a legal forum – the proper person, mode, and perspective in narrative mediation.

The Narrative Rights of Bones

Franz Karl Stanzel, in his theoretical research on narrative structures, defines three fictional narrative mediations: the narrator belongs to the world in the story; the narrator conveys information; the narrator gives the reader or listener an external view. These three categories – person, mode, and perspective – are based on the idea of a mediator; in this discourse, tribal bones are mediators and narrators. Stanzel explains that "whenever something is reported, there is a mediator." He terms this phenomenon "mediacy," or the "generic characteristic which distinguishes narration from other forms of literary art."[5] Narrative theories are language games; here, bones are the "mediacy" with representation in court. Tribal bones as narrators could be considered the *real* authors of their time and place on the earth; the representation of their voices in a court would overturn the neo-colonial perspectives, written and invented tribal cultures.

Roland Barthes, in *Image – Music – Text*, wrote that "writing is that neutral, composite, oblique space where our subject slips away, the negative where all

---

[3] Bendann, Effie, *Death Customs: The Analytical Study of Burial Rites* (New York: Alfred A. Knopf, 1930), 45–46, 268–283. See also *The Archaeology of Death*, edited by Robert Chapman, Ian Kinnes, and Klavs Randsborg (Cambridge: Cambridge University Press, 1981).

[4] Swinburne, Richard, *The Evolution of the Soul* (Oxford: Clarendon Press, 1986), 176, 311.

[5] Stanzel, Franz Karl, *A Theory of Narrative* (Cambridge: Cambridge University Press, 1984), xi, 4.

identity is lost. . . . As soon as fact is *narrated* no longer with a view to acting directly on reality but intrasitively, that is to say, finally outside of any function other than that of the very practice of the symbol itself . . . the voice loses its origin, the author enters into his own death, writing begins. . . . Narrative is first and foremost a prodigious variety of genres, themselves distributed amongst different substances – as though any material would fit to receive man's stories."[6] Tribal narratives are located in stones, trees, birds, water, bears, and tribal bones. In modern research the narrative perspective on tribal remains has been neocolonial; tribal bones held in linguistic servitude, measured and compared in autistic social science monologues. Tribal bones are liberated in this proposal, represented in court as narrators and mediators; manumission in postmodern language games. Social and moral contention does not arise in tribal remains, but in research demands, academic power, material possession, criminal and accidental exhumation. Archaeologists and anthropologists have assumed an absolute right to burial sites, an improper right to research tribal remains and narratives. Tribal bones must oppose science and narrative apocopation; bones have a right to be represented and to have their interests heard and recorded in a federal Bone Court.

This modest proposal to hear the rights of tribal bones in a new federal court is based on the constitutional premise that congress has the power to establish courts with plenary jurisdiction; and, that federal judicial power is proper in cases that arise under constitutional definitions, such a human and civil rights, treaties, and tribal sovereignties. Human remains, tribal bones, have rights, human rights, protected by a creative and pragmatic interpretation of the Bill of Rights which forbids the taking of life, liberty, or property, without due process of law. Tribal bones are sovereign, a moral measure of properties, and an agonistic contnuation of narrative rights in language – a postmodern language game. Tribal remains bear the same rights to be represented in court as those human and civil rights provided in constitutional interpretations; moreover, bones are in human communion with the earth, a natural disposition, and cannot be taken for public use – such as archaeological research and museum servitude – without legal consideration and compensation.

The rights of tribal remains would abolish ownership claims on bones, those policies and provisions that sustain research, discoveries, and hidden treasures; bones are not properties in the same categories as precious stones and metals, or abandoned sea treasure.[7]

---

[6] Barthes, Roland, "Introduction to the Structural Analysis of Narratives," and "The Death of the Author," In *Image – Music – Text* (New York: Hill and Wang, 1977), 79, 142.

[7] *Twentieth Judicial District Court*, Parish of West Feliciana, State of Louisiana, Suit Number 5,552, March 18, 1985. Human remains, however, are viewed in terms of property rights or in some cases as religious issues. In the Louisiana decision the court pointed out that a "*treasure* is a thing hidden or buried in the earth, on which no one can prove his property, and which is discovered by chance." This provision "requiring discovery *by chance* admits to no misunderstanding. Its intent is to deny ownership to one who goes on the property of another with reasonable knowledge that he will discover something of value on that property. The court decided that ownership of "discovered" artifacts should be awarded

This proposal to estblish bone rights in a new court does not rest on primitivism, naive religionism, or semantic binaries, engendered in the recent spiritual and institutional bone wars, but is based on secular, theoretical propositions, and legal philosophies. "The reliance on contradiction is the most familiar trait of dialectic," argues Robert Cumming, "whether it be sophistic or Socratic,"[8] but the dialectic seems better suited to the criticism of social science methodologies and mono- logues than to an interpretation of the rights of human remains.

Ronald Dworkin asserts that even legal pragmatists argue that "judges must sometimes act *as if* people had legal rights, because acting that way will serve society better in the long run. The argument for this as-if strategy is straightfor- ward enough: civilization is impossible unless the decisions of some well-defined person or group are accepted by everyone as setting public standards that will be enforced. . . ."[9] The pragmatists, it seems, would salute the proposition to establish a new court and to provide bones the right to be represented; bone rights would resolve the grievances and servitude of tribal remains. Legal pragmatists would liberate bones, and the courts, in this legal language game, would "act *as if*" tribal bones had rights to their own narratives.

The Color of Tribal Bones

Social scientists are loath to associate archaeologists with necrophilism, even in semiotic ironies; however, the disinctions between some methodologies and the peculiar practices of collecting aboriginal bones, are blurred causeries in modern tribal consciousness. There is, to be sure, a color and culture variance in the collec- tion of tribal bones; white bones are reburied, tribal bones are studied in racist institutions. The bone robber barons, as some archaeologists would be appre- hended, are academic neocolonialists and racial technocrats who now seem to posture as liberal humanists; the institutional emblems distended in world views that deliver models and the hyper-realities of the "absolute fake."[10] These bone barons protect their "rights" to advance science and careers on the backs of tribal bones. The tribal dead become the academic chattel, the aboriginal bone slaves to advance archaeological technicism and the political power of institutional science. The methodologists, and liberal apologists, assume that tribal bones have no rights,

---

to the Tunica-Biloxi Tribe. "Its principal concern is that of title to the burial grouds which was not put at issue in these proceedings."

[8] Cumming, Robert Denoon, *Starting Point: An Introduction to the Dialectic of Existence* (Chicago: The University of Chicago, 1979), 186.

[9] Dworkin, Ronald, *Law's Empire* (Cambridge: Harvard University Press, 1986), 152–153.

[10] Eco, Umberto, *Travels in Hyperreality* (San Diego: Harcaourt Brace Jovanovich, 1986), 3–58. Eco writes that Americans live in a "more to come" consumer culture. "This is the reason for this journey into hyperreality, in search of instances where the American imagination demands the real thing and, to attain it, must fabricate the absolute fake. . . ." Tribal cultures, in this sense, have been invented as "absolute fakes" in social science models, cinema, and popular media.

that bones are the properties of an advanced civilization – science appropriates aboriginal bones as research chattel.

Thomas Rock, the fictional character in *The Doctor and the Devils*, a film scenario by Dylan Thomas, lectured to his students in an amphitheater, "Let no scruples stand in the way of the progress of medical science!" Rock was an anatomist, a remote trope to science in this discourse, but his dramatic monologue is borrowed as a moral lesson. "I stand before you gentlemen," lectured Rock, "a *material* man to whom the heart, for instance, is an elaborate physical organ and not the 'seat of love', a man to whom the 'soul', because it has not shape, does not exist. . . . Our aim for ever must be the pursuit of the knowledge of Man in his entirety. To study the flesh, the skin, the bones, the organs, the nerves of Man, is to equip our minds with a knowledge that will enable us to search *beyond* the body."[11] The real doctor behind this scenario purchased murder victims and bodies stolen from graves to continue his research.

Fifteen years ago a "bulldozer blade uncovered an unmarked cemetery" and overturned the basic assumptions and practices of archaeologists. "As the road-work continued bits of tombstone and the bodies twenty-seven people were uncovered," wrote Vine Deloria, Jr.[12] "One of the bodies had next to it several hundred glass beads. . . . This body was tentatively identified as the remains of an Indian girl. The remains of the twenty-six other bodies were reverently taken to the Glenwood Cemetery and reburied. The remains believed to be Indian had another destination." The state archaeologist "demanded that the bones be sent to him under the provisions of an Iowa law. . . ." Running Moccasins, a tribal woman, protested and "demanded that the bones be given proper burial. She discovered that the bones had been taken to Iowa City, where they were destined for space in a museum."

Duane Anderson, in his article "Reburial: Is It Reasonable?" wrote that the "incident brought to light the inadequacies of the Iowa legal code for dealing with such situations, and left archaeologists without a procedure for conducting investigations of aboriginal remains."[13] These bones bound to a museum resulted in state legislation to recover human remains, to establish a cemetery for aboriginal remains, and to measure responsibilities of state archaeologists.[14]

These reburial issues demonstrate the real need for a Bone Court; a new forum where the rights of human remains, and aboriginal bone narratives, would be represented. The Bone Court would establish a proper record of rights and

---

[11] Thomas, Dylan, *The Doctor and the Devils* (London: J.M. Dent, 1953), 10. Donald Taylor (he commissioned Dylan Thomas to write the film scenario) wrote that the *real* doctor who practiced in the last century had an "abiding passion" for ethnography and lectured to "invited audiences, using for demonstration purposes a group of North American Indians who were appearing in a circus" in the United Kingdom.

[12] Deloria, Vine, Jr., *God is Red* (New York: Grosset & Dunlap, 1973), 32, 33, 66.

[13] Anderson, Duane, "Reburial: Is It Reasonable?" *Archaeology*, Volume 38, September/October 1985, 48.

[14] Anderson, 49.

narratives, and the measured interests of the various parties – state politicians, archaeologists, the public, tribal rights organizations – would be balanced with the rights of the bones.[15] The Bone Court decisions would occasion legal philosophies over research and reburial; the discourse would be based on the rights of tribal bones. These decisions would establish legal histories and anticipate research and contention over human remains. Reburial narratives are muddled in local politics when the prima facie rights of bones are determined in state or local governments. Bones have a right to be represented and heard in court; these rights, not the assumed rights of science, or the interests of politicians, must be the principle concern in court. Science and academic power would survive; bones without representation would continue to be chattel, servitude to science.

In Iowa the issues were research and reburial, but bone rights and narratives were not represented in legislation. "Both scientists and Indians have encountered some difficulties with the new legislation," wrote Duane Anderson. "For archaeologists and physical anthropologists, two problems stand out. First, the intent of the law is to provide for investigation of only those cemetery areas threatened with destruction. . . . Their second difficulty with the law is its reburial requirements; no scientist likes to bury comparative research material."[16]

The rights of tribal bones to be represented in court are not based on religion or interpretations of the American Indian Religious Freedom Act. The right of bones are abstract, secular, and procedural; religion would be a consideration in certain reburial issues argued in Bone Court, but the rights of bones to be represented in court are not absolute – neither religious nor doctrinal. The rights of bones in this proposal would not violate the constitutional amendment restricting the "establishment of religion."[17]

---

[15] Logan Slagle pointed out that in some cases a skeleton would invite a "competency hearing" to determine "standing" and how many actual bones were present to be represented. Slagle is assistant professor of Native American Studies, University of California, Berkeley.

[16] Anderson, 49.

[17] Sewell, Ellen M.W., "The Indian Religious Freedom Act," *Arizona Law Review*, Volume 25, 1983, 429–472. Sewell wrote that the "American Indian Religious Freedom Act intends extensive protections of Indian traditional practices, whether or not those practices would necessarily be protected by the free exercise clause, as judicially interpreted, and the the Act's protections are not prohibited by the establishment clause."

"The American Indian Religious Freedom Act, passed with almost no opposition," Sewell continued, "was signed into law by President Jimmy Carter in August 1978. The Law is unusually general and cryptic. It states that it is the 'policy of the United States to protect and preserve for American Indians their inherent right of freedom to believe, express, and exercise the traditional religions. . . . The statute specifically protects three aspects of religious practice: 'access to sites, use and possession of sacred objects, and the freedom to worship through ceremonies and traditional rites.'"

For more general discussion see "Civil Rights, Indian Rights," by Robert Michaelsen, *Society*, Volume 21, Number 4, May/June 1984; reprinted in *The American Indian: Past and Present*, by Roger Nichols (New York: Alfred A. Knopf, 1986), third edition.

Standing in the Bone Court

Human remains have rights and those rights should be honored as legal standing; bones, the continuation of human rights, would be saluted with the same legal standing in court as corporate bodies, ships at sea, church, state, and municipalities. These inanimate associations possess legal rights that oceans, red pine, owls, rainbow trout, are denied. The asseveration of insensate corporate bodies should include the natural and constitutional rights of bones in court.

Christopher Stone, in his legal thesis, *Should Trees Have Standing? Toward Legal Rights for National Objects,* proposed that "we recognize legal rights of forests, oceans, rivers, and other so-called 'natural objects' in the environment – indeed, of the natural environment as a whole." "As strange as such a notion may sound, it is neither fanciful nor without considerable operational significance,"[18] he continued. "It is not inevitable, nor is it wise, that natural objects should have no rights to seek redress in their own behalf. It is no answer to say that streams and forests cannot have standing because streams and forests cannot speak. Corporations, cannot speak either, nor can states, estates, infants, incompetents, municipalities or universities. Lawyers speak for them, as they customarily do for the ordinary citizen who has legal problems."[19]

The Legal Veil of Ignorance

"Justice is the first virtue of social institutions," John Rawls asserted in a *Theory of Justice,* "as truth is of systems of thought. A theory however elegant and economical must be rejected if it is untrue; likewise laws and institutions no matter how efficient and well-arranged must be reformed or abolished if they are unjust."[20]

Roger Finzel, counsel for American Indians Against Desecration, pointed out that tribal organizations have demanded the "reburial of the three hundred thousand to six hundred thousand remains of ancestors in museums," laboratories, and those bones held at universities.[21] These, and other recorded reburial issues, demand professional reformation and the abolition of research on remains that denies the rights of tribal bones.

The Bone Court, however, would not abolish the academic attention to tribal remains; rather, archaeologists, osteologists, anthropologists, and others, would answer to the rights of tribal bones; the rights and interests of bones would be represented and narrated in court.

---

[18] Stone, Christopher, *Should Trees Have Legal Standing?* (New York: Avon Books, 1975) 25, 26. (Southern California Law Review, 1972).

[19] Stone, 40, 41.

[20] Rawls, John, *A Theory of Justice,* (Cambridge: Harvard University Press, 1971) 3.

[21] Finzel, Roger, "Indian Burial Site Issues," unpublished outline presented at *Indian Law Training Conference,* University of California, Berkeley, July 1985.

Rawls argues, "Each person possesses an inviolability founded on justice that even the welfare of society as a whole cannot override." Here, in this discourse, bones hold the continuance of human rights, and, to include the argument above, human remains possess "an inviolability founded on justice" that cannot be reversed. "For this reason justice denies that the loss of freedom for some is made right by a greater good shared by others. It does not allow that the sacrifices imposed on a few are outweighed by the larger sum of advantages enjoyed by many."[22] Clearly, the power of academic institutions and the freedom demanded by archaeologists and anthropologists to conduct their research has been the loss of tribal rights, and the rights of human remains. The proposed Bone Court would not abolish research on tribal bones, but the rights of human remains would be represented; the injustices, not freedom, would be denied. Tribal bones would cease to be the neocolonial research chattel of the social sciences.

Concurrence, and association, is significant in research; the representation of human remains is inviolable and justice is possible in a new court where the narratives of tribal bones are heard and recorded; these rights and legal procedures would enrich social science research and unburden the language games. Rawls asserted that the "circumstances of justice may be described as the normal conditions under which human cooperation is both possible and necessary."[23] The Bone Court would provide a practical forum for cooperation between tribal bones, their narratives, and the demands of science.

The rights of tribal bones, however, will not be discovered in conservative semantic theories that establish legal criteria. The legal realist movement, for example, "insisted on the propostion that legal rules cannot guide courts to definite results in particular cases and demanded that legal scholarship recognize the social forces influencing legal change."[24] These forces, in the proposition for the rights of bones, include the critical issue of "standing," and, as Justice William O. Douglas reasoned, would allow "environmental issues to be litigated before federal agencies or federal courts in the name of the inanimate object. . . ."[25]

The theoretical proposition that bones have legal rights, and the proposal to establish a federal forum to hear bone narratives, is based on the concept that law is interpretive, and that justice "is a matter of the right outcome of the political system. . . ."[26] Ronald Dworkin argues, "Fairness is a matter of the right structure for that system, the structure that distributes influence over political decisions in the right way. Procedural due process is a matter of the right procedures for enforcing rules and regulations the system has produced."[27] Political positions, public policies, limited legislation, new social values, and religious consciousness,

---

[22] Rawls, 4.

[23] Rawls, 126.

[24] *Harvard Law Review*, "'Round and 'Round the Bramble Bush: From Legal Realism to Critical Legal Scholarship," Volume 95, May 1982, 1669–1690.

[25] Justice William O. Douglas, quoted in *Should Trees Have Standing?* by Christopher Stone.

[26] Dworkin, *Law's Empire*, 404.

[27] Dworkin, *Law's Empire*, 404, 405.

have issued from the controversies over the exhumation of tribal remains and the demands for reburial. [28] Some rules and regulations have been published on these issues; now, what must follow is the due process of bones, the procedural rights to be represented, the right to *voice* a narrative in a new federal court.

Dworkin, in *Taking Rights Seriously*, reasoned that "Constitutional law can make no genuine advance until it isolates the problem of rights against the state and makes that problem part of its own agenda. That argues for a fusion of constitutional law and moral theory, a connection that, incredibly, has yet to take place. It is perfectly understandable that lawyers dread contamination with moral philosophy, and particularly with those philosophers who talk about rights, because the spooky overtones of that concept threaten the graveyard of reason."[29]

Indeed, the idea of bone rights and narrative representation threatens the "graveyard of reason" in archaeology, anthropology, and other social science monologues.

Bones Narratives and Language Games

"Arguments of principle are arguments intended to establish an individual right; arguments of policy are arguments intended to establish a collective goal," argued Ronald Dworkin.

"Principles are propositions that describe rights; policies are propositions that describe goals."[30] The proposition that bones should be represented in court is a right, a principle of justice based on human rights; however, tribal bones are dominated by academic policies and must oppose the goals of institutions. Tribal bones must counter institutional power to be represented and heard in their own narratives in a legal language game.

The power of science, and social science methodologies, is intractable because that power, reduced to goals, is located in institutions; academic power has prevailed in structural opposition and metonymic binaries – tribal narratives, popular memories, and political resistance, have been reduced to models and dialectics. Alan Sheridan, in *Michel Foucault: The Will to Truth*, construes that "power and knowledge are two sides of the same process. Knowledge cannot be neutral, pure. All knowledge is political not because it may have political conse-

---

[28] *New York Times*, "Smithsonian in Dispute Over Indian Skeletons," February 14, 1986. "Officials of the Smithsonian Institution"s Museum of Natural History" said "they would turn over to recognized tribal units," the article reported. "But the museum officiaals estimated. . . that this description would apply to fewer than 10 percent of the Smithsonian's collection of 14,000 Indian skeletons, since most of the remains are of undermined prehistoric origin. The Indian organizations want all the remains returned to Indians for reburial, citing religious reasons."

[29] Dworkin, Ronald, *Taking Rights Seriously* (Cambridge: Harvard University Press, 1977), 149. Walter Berns, "Equally Endowed with Rights." in *Justice and Equality Here and Now*, edited by Frank Lucash (Ithaca: Cornell University Press, 1986), asserts that "Dworkin recognizes that there can be no constitutional law independent of philosophy but he maintains that until recently there has been no philisophy – or, at least, no *good* philosophy – to which constitutional law can be attached."

[30] Dworkin, *Taking Rights Seriously*, 90.

quences or be politically useful, but because knowledge has its conditions of possibility in power relations."[31]

Cultural *anthropologies* and *archaeologies*, for example, are not discourse but monologues with science and power; moreover, social science languages subdue tribal rights and imagination. These *anthropologies* and *archaeologies* are neocolonial tropes to power – causal methodologies, reductive expiries, but not an agonistic discourse on *anthropos* or humans and their *real* narrative remains. Those who reduced tribal cultures to models, and invented the tribes in dioramas, imposed dominant material world views in their research on ceremonies and tribal remains. Now, the tribal survivors are summoned to the universities and museums, roused to be proud, cited to abide by the monologues, the dubious splendors of neocolonial tropes on tribal cultures, invented narratives, and aboriginal remains.

Roy Wagner argues that "anthropology exists through the idea of culture," which is a monologue with science. "The study of culture *is* culture . . . The study of culture is in fact *our* [dominant material] culture; it operates through our forms, creates in our terms, borrows our words and concepts for its meanings, and re-creates us through our efforts." The dominant culture "is a vast accumulation of material and spiritual achievements and resources stemming from the conquest of nature and necessary to the continuance of this effort."[32]

George Marcus and Michael Fischer, in *Anthropology as Cultural Critique*, explain that what "has propelled many modern anthropologists into the field and motivated resultant ethnographic accounts is a desire to enlighten their readers about other ways of life, but often with the aim of disturbing their cultural self-satisfaction." In their descriptions of other cultures, "ethnographers have simultaneously had a marginal or hidden agenda of critique of their own culture, namely, the bourgeois, middle-class life of mass liberal societies, which industrial capitalism has produced."[33]

Paul Feyerabend, on the other hand, argues that when some anthropologists "collected and systematized" tribal cultures, the scientific emphasis was on the "psychological meaning, the social functions, the existential temper of a culture," while the "ontological implications" were disregarded. Feyerabend contends that, to the anthropologists who transformed tribal cultures, the "oracles, rain dances, the treatment of mind and body, *express* the needs of the members of a society, they *function* as a social glue, they *reveal* basic structures of the relations between man and man and man and nature but without an accompanying *knowledge* of distant events, rain, mind, body. Such interpretations were hardly ever the result of critical thought – most of the time they were simply a consequence of popular antimetaphysical tendencies combined with a firm belief in the excellence. . . of science."[34]

[31] Sheridan, Alan, *Michel Foucault: The Will to Truth* (London: Tavistock Publications, 1980), 220.

[32] Wagner, Roy, *The Invention of Culture* (Chicago: The University of Chicago Press, 1981).

[33] Marcus, George, and Michael M.J. Fischer, *Anthropology as Cultural Critique: An Experimental Moment in the Human Sciences* (Chicago: The University of Chicago Press, 1986), 111.

[34] Feyerabend, Paul, *Science in a Free Society* (London: Verso Editions, 1978), 77.

James Clifford and George Marcus, in the introduction to *Writing Culture: The Poetics and Politics of Ethnography*, warrant that ethnographic truth are "inherently *partial* – and resisted at strategic points by those who fear the collapse of clear standards of verification. But once accepted and built into ethnographic art, a rigorous sense of partiality can be a source of representational tact. . . . Ethnographic work has indeed been enmeshed in a world of enduring and changing power inequalities, and it continues to be implicated. It enacts power relations. But its function within these relations is complex, often ambivalent, potentially counter-hegemonic."[35]

Manfred Stanley, in *The Technological Conscience*, a study of "linguistic technicism – the misuse of scientific and technological vocabularies with regard to human activities," argues that technicism is a special case of "cultural imperialism."[36] He explains that his "course is not revolution against science. The enemy, rather, is our universal complicity in the degradation of linguistic discipline." Stanley outlines a "modern scientific world view" as materialistic and nihilistic; he asserts that "knowledge based upon sensuous relations of human beings to perceived object world is downgraded in favour of knowledge conceived in terms of conceptual operations performed upon the world."[37]

Tribal bones and those who assert their relations with tribal remains, must oppose those social science "conceptual operations" on tribal cultures and narratives. The rights of bones, legal practices, and narratives, are argumentative; science has no absolute rights to objects, methods, narratives. Tribal bones have earned the right to their own popular memories, to their own narrative properties; bones have earned the rights to be represented and heard in court.

Rights, arguments, narratives, are discourses not isolated monologues. The rights of bones to be represented are not semantic, positivist, or religious, but a secular, theoretical, and agonistic interpretation of legal propositions.[38] To overbear tribal narratives, to oppose discourse on bone rights, and to reduce arguments to a religious or radical performance, as the social sciences have done, could "demonize science and technology to a point of some great religious convulsion of primitivist simplification."[39]

Clifford Geertz, in "Blurred Genres: The Refiguration of Social Thought," concludes that the "relation between thought and action in social life can no more be conceived of in terms of wisdom than it can in terms of expertise. How is it to be conceived, how the games, dramas, or texts which we do not just invent or

[35] Clifford, James, and George Marcus, editors, *Writing Culture: The Poetics and Politics of Ethnography* (Berkeley: University of California Press, 1986), 7, 9. (A School of American Research Advanced Seminar, Santa Fe, New Mexico, April 1984).
[36] Stanley, Manfred, *The Technological Conscience: Survival and Dignity in an Age of Expertise* (Chicago: The University of Chicago Press, 1978), xii, 14.
[37] Stanley, 23, 142.
[38] Dworkin, *Law's Empire*, 33–37.
[39] Stanley, 16.

witness but live, have the consequence they do remains very far from clear. It will take the wariest of wary reasonings, on all sides of all divides, to get it clear."[40]

First, however, we must establish the sides, the forums, the narrative persons, modes, and perspectives in this cultural discourse and these postmodern language games. The Bone Court is the best place to begin, where tribal bones are the narrators; where tribal bones have the legal right to be represented. There are no better operative tropes in these cultural language games than the narrative rights of tribal bones; the genres, but not tribal bones, are blurred.

Notes

I proposed the Bone Court, and the rights of bones to be represented, last year at the School of American Research in Santa Fe, New Mexico. The response from other resident scholars, archaeologists and anthropologists, was tolerent; the idea invited some humor as critical abatement, but a discourse never matured at the seminars.

---

[40] Geertz, Clifford, "Blurred Genres: The Refiguration of Social Thought," *The American Scholar*, Volume 49, Spring 1980, 179.

Part IX

Dialogue

Theoretical Archaeological Discourse

a: Let me try to sum things up. It seems to me that the main conclusion we can draw from all this is that archaeological theories are gradually coverging. The sharp 1980s dichotomies between processual and postprocessual are breaking down. There is widespread agreement that both materials and meanings are important, that both individual agency and social and economic structures need to be taken into account, that material culture is both adaptive and active, that both historical and evolutionary perspectives are useful. There is even some convergence on positivism and relativism. A qualified objectivity is argued by Hodder (1992), some form of empirical constraint is accepted by Shanks and Tilley (1987), Wylie (1989) discusses "tacking" between theory and data, and Renfrew (1989) accepts that the data are theory laden while retaining positivism. The differences between these positions all seem relatively minor.

b: Are you saying that we are getting close to a global theory that integrates all aspects of archaeological inquiry and which allows us to write a grand narrative about the development of human societies over the long term?

a: Well, perhaps not quite as grand as that – there will always be unknowns and uncertainties and there will always be exceptions and local variation, but yes, I think we are progressing toward a unified and coherent account. We can see this, for example, in Sherratt's recent discussion of return to "grand narrative" (Sherratt 1995).

b: But there is *so much* diversity surely? In terms of theory, on the one hand you have people arguing for the relevance of biological models of culture change. Some such people deny the relevance of social agency. On the other hand, you have social theorists who deny the relevance of the natural sciences for understanding the uniquely human attributes of intentionality and meaning. Of course, everyone accepts that scientific techniques are essential for recovering pattern and information, but it is not widely accepted that the processes of biology or physics can be extended to human culture. Many believe in the difference between the single and the double hermeneutic. So there is much diversity in theoretical approaches.

a: But the variation you are talking about can be accommodated by the concept of a multiscalar approach. Agency theorists are concerned with the day-to-day lived experience of people in their social practices. In the social sciences generally there are approaches such as phenomenology and symbolic interactionism which focus on this small scale. Other approaches such as Marxism, structuralism and neo-Darwinianism paint a picture with a broader brush – they are more concerned with the constraints within which individual action works. It is quite acceptable to have one set of theories dealing with the small scale and another set dealing with larger-scale constraints and consequences.

b: What about the differences between, since you have brought them up, Marxism, structuralism and neo-Darwinian theories? They all seem to work at the same, larger scale.

a: I'm not sure that is true. Neo-Darwinian theories provide reasons for the continuance and transformation of cultural traits which go beyond the social issues identified in Marxism. The contradictions between classes or between forces and relations of production can be seen as proximate causes for social change – but what survives and is selected for over the longer term needs to be linked to "fitness" in a wider sense.

b: But what about *mentalité* and the *longue durée* identified by the Annalistes or long-term structures of structuralism? In such cases one is arguing that structures are retained over the long term. Thus the division of the world into four colour-coded quarters in Mesoamerica (Flannery and Marcus 1976), or the existence of a Central Cattle Complex in southern Africa (Huffman 1984) are argued as long-term structures. Structuralists argue that such a code is transmitted because it is embedded in the mind or in culture or society – it is the arbitrary way the world is organized in that region. It just is. This has nothing to do with enhancing the culture's adaptive fitness.

a: It is interesting you should include the Mesoamerican example. Flannery and Marcus (1976) themselves say that structure is the mechanism through which people adapt to their environment. At one level one can look at the code, its operation in a particular context. At another level one can explore how the code was selected because it allowed the continued reproduction of the group in its local environment.

b: But your two ways of looking at code don't work. Take the example of pottery fabric. Selectionists such as O'Brien and Holland (1992) argue that the different types of paste contribute to the cooking qualities of the ceramic vessel. Put crudely, better pots allow for more efficient cooking which leads to increased reproductive fitness. On first glance this may seem reasonable, but if you think about it the selectionists presume that cultures are isolated from one another for long periods of time and that they tend to monopolize certain inventions. Remember Kohl's (**chapter 6**) arguments about transferable technologies? Cultures exist and indeed reproduce themselves through a continual process of action and interaction.

Now don't get me wrong, I'm not arguing that natural selection doesn't operate on humans. I only find it of limited value in understanding the vast majority of variability in the archaeological record. In a sense, we are back to the old opposition between the natural sciences and the humanities, between a dehumanizing and a humanizing vision. You cannot ignore these differences. They are fundamental.

a: But you do not have to see the world in terms of those tired oppositions, those age-old philosophical debates. There is no reason at all why the paste used in cooking vessels should not contribute both to food consumption and thus to survival and adapation and to the social negotiation of meanings. Indeed it would be an interesting research question to explore the relationships between these different factors rather than oppose them. If we embrace a global theory we can start to break down the dichotomies in archaeology. This will open up new areas of research as the interactions between different types and scales of factors are explored.

b: I'm still not convinced, although I can see the advantages of your last point. Let me take another tack. The evidence of past trajectories through time in different regions is looking extremely variable. The idea of writing a grand narrative for the origins of agriculture, for example, is increasingly difficult to imagine. Local sequences seem very diverse the more that the trend for regional studies is followed. Agriculture appears to have been adopted in very different ways in the different parts of Europe and the Near East for example. And if we look at a more global scale there is enormous diversity – consider the very early evidence for water management and taro gardening at Kuk Swamp and Kosipi in Papua New Guinea compared with the better known trajectories in the Near East. The diversity is enormous. How can you write a grand narrative out of that or say that similar things were happening within one global theory?

a: It is true that archaeologists have not had much success in isolating common causal factors for the origins of agriculture and the rise of the state.

b: Yes. If you look at the evolutionary theories discussed in Part IV you will see a gradual movement away from deterministic models. Recent work, by Yoffee (1993) for example, seems to be moving away from clear categories and toward more generalized process. This is true in all areas. Take the Annales school discussed in the same Part. There research has turned toward the contingent and the specific. Or take the shift from structuralism to poststructuralism, or from Marxism to neo-Marxism or structural-Marxism. The debate about gender has taken a similar line – away from categories of men and women based on biological differences and toward the complex process of identity construction in which gender plays a central role. In all these cases there is a clear trend – from grand narratives, overall structures, global theories to the breaking down of universals, the incorporation of diversity, contingency, uncertainty. This all seems to be part of the larger shift to a less certain postmodern world.

a: Yes, I agree there does seem to be that trend, although I am worried about it. It seems to undermine any idea of a scientific discipline of archaeology.

b: You cannot ignore what is happening and stick your head in the positivist sand – it *is* sand, and it is moving. It is difficult now to imagine people writing about the "Rise of civilization," the "Rise of the West," the "Dawn of European prehistory," or even "Before civilization" or the "Domestication of Europe." Even "Origins" research has come under attack (Conkey with Williams 1991). The ideas of the "Origins of Inequality," the "Origins of Humanity," the "Origins of Agriculture" or "Origins of the State" seem anachronistic. We seem more concerned now with local diversity and multiple beginnings. Things seemed to happen differently in different places. As Foucault argued, nothing seems essential any more. We are wary of totalizing accounts. We seem attracted by contingency and complexity.

a: But I think a new breed of theory is emerging which accepts this complexity and indeterminacy. In a way, I think this is part of the attraction of the neo-Darwinian theories. Here there is no idea of grand developmental theory. Things happen locally for a variety of reasons although constrained by what is already there – there are historical constraints on variation. Within these constraints variation can be considered chaotic or random but what survives has minimally to allow biological fitness or enhance group survival.

b: I don't buy that. Neo-Darwinian theories are still grand schemes. Indeed the criticism of them is precisely that they present a totalizing account which assumes that biology and reproductive success are at the center of human endeavor. What happens if I say that there is no evidence that what human beings do *is* regularly adaptive? What happens if I argue that most cultural traits are adaptively neutral or even maladaptive? What if I argue that cultural selection is much more important than natural selection, even in the long term? Although neo-Darwinian models allow for a degree of indeterminacy, such theories still remain essentialist and totalizing.

a: What about chaos theory and the non-linear modeling of complex adaptive systems? These theories emphasize rupture and discontinuity (Gumerman and Gell-Mann 1994, Renfrew and Cooke 1979; van der Leeuw 1989). They show how small perturbations can lead to large-scale effects. They emphasize emergent behaviour in the inter-relationships between variables which themselves are continuously changing. They focus on self-organization and "phase transitions".

Surely here we have a global theory which is in tune with the desire for and the evidence of local contingency and complexity.

b: I buy that even less. Non-linear modeling is just a more sophisticated form of simulation and it has the same problems. Human relationships are forced into mathematical formulations. The overall aim is to discover structure, albeit very complex structure, within systems. It may aim to be more realistic and less deterministic, but it is hardly going to get us toward an understanding of how different people experienced their worlds (McGuire 1994).

a: Ok, but let me take another tack which, I think, will certainly undermine your position. Surely a coherence is emerging regarding the methods archaeologists use in going about their work. All archaeologists, whatever they think they are doing and whatever they call what they are doing, employ hermeneutic procedures. I think we can all agree that how we look at the past changes through time. I think we can all agree too that, although there may be differences of opinion regarding what happens in the present and what happened in the past, material traces are and were left which are organized and structured.

Archaeological interpretation involves a to-and-fro movement between hypotheses and the data. Rather than "testing" hypotheses "against" entirely objective and independent data, most people seem to accept a softer view – that theories and data are accommodated to each other. Theories are "fitted" rather than "tested." Although we may talk loosely and colloquially about "testing," what we are realling doing is working between or around theory and data in order to make it all "fit" in a coherent way. If this is what you mean by hermeneutics, I think that there is a convergence on this view although some might call it modified positivism, or even realism (Bhaskar 1975; Wyle 1982). Renfrew (1989) talks of going back and forth between theory and data, Wylie (1989) describes a process of tacking, and Hodder (1992) describes a spiral. The image, metaphor, or name do not matter. There is a convergence.

b: I am afraid you have taken a rather self-serving definition of hermeneutics. You must at least modify your view by saying that no one thing happened in the past. A muliplicity of things happened depending on the perspective of the participant. In addition, your account – that theories can be evaluated on the basis of an appeal to neutral evidence – neglects the social context of the production of interpretations. This is why many writers have linked hermeneutics to a critical position (for example, see Shanks and Tilley 1987; Hodder 1992). The assessment of the plausibility of an account depends on numerous factors beyond the disinterested evaluation of "fit" – such as the authority of the author, the place and form of publication, the rhetorical tropes used in the writing. Writing is always for a purpose, and assessment of the coherence of interpretations is always interested. Thus, even if we could all agree (which I doubt) that archaeology is a hermeneutic enterprise, the result is a diverse and dichotomous past, a past engaged in the conflict of life in the present.

a: So you are rejecting the possibility of Grand Theory on both theoretical and practical grounds?

b: Yes, but not in the way you seem to think. The main point I want to make is that this theory/data dichotomy that you rely upon cannot be sustained, because of the interrelationship between knowlege and human interests (Habermas 1971). There can be no coherent and plausible integrative Grand Theory which is not partisan or linked to a specific perspective. Theory cannot be abstracted from the contexts of its own production. There is no disinterested theoretical labor. As a result, a plurality of theoretical interpretations is to be expected, many of them contradictory, as long as there are different interest groups within societies. And, for purely political reasons, diversity is preferable to unity since it is harder for those in power to manipulate.

a: Wait a minute . . .

c: I've had enough of this! You archaeologists are always getting stuck in endless debates such as this one – one of you emphasizing convergence toward a global theory, the other emphasizing diversity and contingency. But don't you see both of you are arguing from essential first principles. Both of you say there is something fundamental – either that the world is coherent and structured and can be known in and of itself, or that the world is diverse and can only be known provisionally. But both of these discourses are Western discourses. Whether it is positivism, or hermeneutics, these are discourses specific to a particular history, a particular point in time. Both are essentialist. I don't accept either of them.

b: I am shocked by your intervention! I thought I was speaking on your behalf. I am arguing that there are no essential truths, that everything is contingent and provisional. I do not think there is an overall trend toward greater complexity – only that there are specific historical sequences which, in the case of capitalism, have led to global dependence.

c: But earlier you yourself said that there are fundamental differences between a dehumanizing systems view and a humanizing agency view.

b: Yes, I guess it is true that I did make that claim. But I do this for political reasons, in that I argue for the rights of indigenous peoples to assert their own relationships with the past and to react against the dominant culture. Your past can be used to form an identity separate from a global homogenized humanity. Why do you disagree with me?

c: Because I'm suspicious of your political claim. I see all this emphasis on diversity and contingency as part of a postmodern trend in the West. It's part of the new dominant ideology. It doesn't grow out of our experiences of being dominated. Your interest in diversity and multivocality has led to products such as the "One

World Archaeology" series sponsored by the World Archaeological Congress. But whose "One World" is this? It's a "One World" defined in your terms and your interests; it's you who set the agenda. But we aren't just part of some postmodern pastiche. We have real needs and concerns. Our past is real to us. It plays a real part in our lives. It's the *Ndee bi atee*.

a: Aha! Then what your really need is a scientific and positivist approach such as I have been arguing. Why do you challenge my position? Surely, if you want to make land claims using archaeological evidence of cultural continuity you need to be able to say what really happened in the past. You need to be able to debate the objective evidence in a court of law. You need science in order to assert your rights. The beauty of science is that no matter who you are, if your claim is just, it can be evaluated objectively.

c: I'm afraid too much injustice has been perpetrated in the name of your Western science for us to have much confidence in it. The neutrality you assert always seems to work in your favor. You use assumptions that are alien to us. Do you remember the Mashpee case, the native people from Cape Cod who were denied legal status as a tribe because they weren't deemed "Indian enough" (Campesi 1991)? Why do you and your courts have the power to say who is or isn't a native person? You desecrate our ancestral shrines and appropriate our cultural heritage – all in the name of a neutral science. How many of you have ever bothered to communicate the results of one of your studies to us? Don't you see? The deck is stacked against us, you set the agenda on your terms.

b: But look, we care about native peoples and are trying to be appropriately self-reflexive and self-critical about this. We have included a number of feminist authors throughout the book. We have also devoted an entire section to the indigenous voice because we wish to highlight its "difference" and "integrity", not subsume it under some artificial academic discourse.

c: Why do you think that it's ok to group all our experiences together and then ghetto-ize them in a section of this book? – and by the way, even in that section, I note that the agenda is set by one of you, a male, Bruce Trigger. As a *Ndee* person, I feel what you have done is patronizing to women and indigenous people everywhere. Even here in this discussion we have come in as the third voice, again we are marginalized: the First, the Second, and then the Third World. There is no generic indigenous voice. You seem to have an idealized, romanticized view of a generalized "Other." Stop trying to speak for me!

＊　　　＊　　　＊

d: Perhaps I might come in here. I noticed the long silence that followed the last exchange. There seemed to be a breakdown of communication. I am worried that there is a real danger that by taking up adversarial positions we can only end in silence, as you have just done. Lived experience is not about opposed Cartesian categories, it is about give and take, compromise and negotiation. The trouble with theoretical debate, indeed the trouble with this whole book, is that theoretical debate involves abstractions removed from the contexts of lived experience.

b: You mean we have to develop a theory of practice. That is what I have been saying all along.

d: No, I do not mean that. A theory of practice is still a totalizing narrative, built on dichotomies and produced within a particular set of academic relations. No, I mean more, that when we actually *do* archaeology we *live* a particular set of experiences which are inclusive and integrated. Interpretation and theoretical discussion might pick these experiences apart, but they seem much less good at putting them together again and understanding them in their entirety. So an adversarial debate does not take us closer to understanding. What is needed is an inclusive discussion. We need to see that different perspectives are valid. Different ideas add to, rather that oppose each other. We need to learn how to listen.

c: I can't stand this warm integrative stuff. How can you have an inclusive, non-adversarial discourse when there are people in this world fighting and dying over interpretations of the past? Look at the tragedy between the Serbs and Muslims in Bosnia-Herzgovena and the difficulty the United Nations faced trying to achieve a peaceful resolution. How do you think that history will be written? What linkages will be forged with past cultures to legitimize the new power structures that arise there (Chapman 1994)?

b: I do not like it either (*a*: nor I). But theoretical debate *is* necessary in order to stop complacency about taken-for-granted assumptions. The theories and assumptions used in interpreting the past need to be open to critique. And I certainly will not accept that archaeology is just what archaeologists do. That is a recipe for an uncritical *laissez-faire* discipline, unconcerned with the implications of what is done and said.

d: Ok, but can you all accept that the only way forward is as a communicative discourse? In other words we need to open up the past to multiple voices. We all have personal relationship with the past – indeed with many pasts. We all have gender, ethnic, religious and other identities which are forged with the past. From different perspectives we will want to mobilize that past in different ways. It is too easy to use the past in order to support entrenched views. Hiding behind our essentialist positions and our taken-for-granteds simply leads to incomprehension and silence. There has been too little discussion across the full range of archaeological theories and practices. Even the types of comparisons explored in this book have rarely been tried. What is needed is the notion that all interpretations are simply stages in a communicative process, however dichotomous and violent.

Archaeology is not a thing but a process – a process of debate informed by material evidence.

e: Archaeology is not a thing, but a process. Yes, we all seem to like the sound of that, from our very different perspectives. We all seem to be aware of the dangers of global homogenization, the spread of informational capitalism. We all live in an increasingly global culture where an increasingly narrow range of experiences is portrayed by the media as progressive, sophisticated, and modern. There is a danger that we all will become "the same," but this "sameness" will always be defined in the interests of the dominant. As indigenous cultures are increasingly colonized and subsumed by our Western economy, we might come to live in an increasingly homogeneous world where the range of differences is lost. Our taken-for-granteds will seem universal and our debates will become increasingly sterile.

We are already destroying the diversity of plants and animals in the rain forests that might one day hold the key to our own resilience. Our ability to fight disease depends on retaining that diversity of species. In much the same way, our ability to point out the arbitrary nature of "universal truths" depends on retaining a diversity of human experience. Societies can be destroyed and histories rewritten. But what is in the ground, the trace of past societies, is covered over, hidden from view. It has the potential always to surprise us – to cause us to rethink our assumptions and biases. Beneath the ground is a diversity that can be used to construct different presents.

Pious words perhaps, especially since it is clear that humans have the curious ability always to reinterpret what they find to suit their own interests. And yet the unexpectedness of the past, however quickly it is absorbed within totalizing narratives, provides a moment of doubt, and that is an opening for critique. The opening can be pried apart in order to explore the difference of the past, and thus to confront the present. It is in the communication of these different readings and doings that archaeology plays out its role in society. It is in communication and debate that the discipline takes its multifaceted and chameleon form. Archaeology is not a thing but a process – a process of doing and communicating.

f: Let me get this straight. You seem to be saying that an essential part of archaeology is digging things up so that they can play a role, however uncertain and unpredictable, in confronting our Western society. But not all of us agree that society is in as bad a shape as you seem to believe. Some of us feel that archaeology has no business taking a political stance and instead should focus on the importance of conservation and preservation and advancing knowledge for knowlege's sake. We have a responsibility to protect and conserve archaeological sites for the future generations. We also have a responsibility to learn as much as possible from the past for the benefit of the present and future.

e: But can't you see that what you have just articulated amounts to a political stance. If the past is protected, preserved, frozen, it can play no role in the present except to reinforce and support what we already know and believe. So we are not really debating whether the uses of archaeology are political, but rather which are the best political uses of archaeology.

It may be useful to rethink what archaeology is. Archaeology is not a thing but a process of engagement. Increasingly the past is being taken out of its glass case and held up to the light. Museums and heritage centers are opening up the past to diverse experiences and interpretations. This is a political act which reflects a commitment to diversity and multiplicity as opposed to singularity and totality. It is certainly in the interests of some to argue that archaeology is a thing, like the monuments it protects. But even the monuments change as we look at them.

f: But what about those situations where archaeological sites are directly impacted by the construction of shopping malls, housing developments, and road-ways? Don't we have an ethical responsibility to excavate, or better yet, preserve these sites? What *are* the proper roles for cultural-resource management and the heritage industry? (Kerber 1994, Walsh 1992)

e: What you are really asking me is how to balance our responsibilities as professional archaeologists and our responsibilities as citizens. But you are actually creating an artifical dichotomy of the kind which is encouraged by our capitalist society. Why can't you be a citizen archaeologist?

We need to begin by acknowledging that cultural–resource management and the heritage industry are examples of archaeology in the service of special interest groups. Some of these are oil and gas companies, towns and municipalites, and even commonwealths and nations, to name just a few. But there are always other interests which are hidden or glossed over. The question we always have to ask is whose interests are being served and why in the production of archaeological knowledge.

If you agree with me that democratic principles are desirable then I think you will also agree that we need to pay close attention to who participates in cultural–resource management and the heritage industry, how representative they are of the range of public interests, and how the process of selection works. Now you may protest that there are very few businesses which operate under these constraints, but this is precisely the point. How we do business needs to be trans-formed before we can claim that we live in a democratic society.

Personally, and I know that I differ with some of my more radical colleagues on this point, I feel this can be accomplished through a program of raising public awareness of the uses of the past in the present and by creating more representa-tive structures for the funding, analysis, and communication of the past. In this way we may bring about the conditions for the possibility of a democratic archaeology.

f: I'm surprised to hear you say that. I thought that all critical theorists were intent on deconstructing our society through the analysis of colonial New England museums or the pages of *National Geographic*.

e: Well not exactly. What many of us are trying to do is to show how our belief systems are historically constructed. The truths we believe in today are not natural or absolute in any sense, but are the result of continual reinterpretation and nego-tiation. This is part of the process of social reproduction and we ourselves are not immune to it. Hopefully, this kind of research will make us all a little more self-conscious in debate and in work, a little more tolerant of others, and a little less quick to act in judgment. If it inspires some to comfront the forms of oppression sanctioned by our government, so much the better.

c: But the truths of my people endure. Despite all the intrusions by the Bureau of Indian Affairs, the forced education programs, the requirements to settle down and farm, the meddling of inquisitive anthropologists and tourists, we are still here.

References

Bhaskar, R. 1975. *A Realist Theory of Science*. Leeds.

Campesi, J. 1991. *The Mashpee Indians: Tribe on Trial*. Syracuse.

Chapman, J. 1994. Destruction of a common heritage: the archaeology of war in Croatia, Bosnia and Herzegovina. *Antiquity* 68, 120–6

Conkey, M. with Williams, S. 1991. Original narratives: the political economy of gender in archaeology. In DiLeonardo, M. (ed.) *Gender at the Crossroads of Knowledge*. Berkeley, pp. 102–39.

Flannery, K. and Marcus, J. 1976. Formative Oaxaca and the Zapotec cosmos. *American Scientist* 64, 374–83.

Flannery, K. and Marcus, J. 1993. Cognitive archaeology. *Cambridge Archaeological Journal* 3, 260–70.

Gumerman, G.J. and Gell-Mann, M. (ed.) 1994. *Understanding Complexity in the Prehistoric Southwest*. Santa Fe Institute Studies in the Sciences of Complexity, Proc. Vol. XVI, Reading.

Habermas, J. 1971. *Knowledge and Human Interests*. Boston.

Hodder, I. 1992. *Theory and Practice in Archaeology*. London.

Huffman, T. 1984. Expressive space in the Zimbabwe culture. *Man* 19, 593–612.

Kerber, J.E. (ed.) 1994. *Cultural Resource Management: Archaeological Research, Preservation Planning, and Public Education in Northeastern United States*. Westport.

McGuire, R. 1994. Why complexity is too simple. Paper presented at the Chacmool Conference, Calgary.

O"Brien, M.J. and Holland, T.D. 1992. The role of adaptation in archaeological explanation. *American Antiquity* 57, 36–59.

Renfrew, A.C. 1989. Comment on archaeology into the 1990s. *Norwegian Archaeological Review* 22, 33–41.

Renfrew, A.C. and Cooke, K.L. 1979. *Transformations: Mathematical Approaches to Culture Change*. New York.

Shanks, M. and Tilley, C. 1987. *Reconstructing Archaeology*. Cambridge.

Sherratt, A. 1995. Reviving the grand narrative: Archaeology and long-term change. *Journal of European Archaeology* 3, 1–32.

Van der Leeuw, S.E. 1989. Modelling innovations and change. In Van der Leeuw, S.E. and Torrence, R. (eds) *What's New? A Closer Look at the Process of Innovation*. London, pp. 258–80.

Walsh, K. 1992. *The Representations of the Past: Museums and Heritage in the Post-modern World*. London.

Wylie, M. A. 1982. Epistemological issues raised by a structuralist archaeology. In Hodder, I. (ed.) *Symbolic and Structural Archaeology*. Cambridge, pp. 39–46.

Wylie, A. 1989. Archaeological cables and tacking: the implications of practice for Bernstein's "options beyond objectivism and realism." *Philosophy of Social Science* 19, 1–18.

Yoffee, N. 1993. Too many chiefs? (or, safe texts for the '90s). In Yoffee, N. and Sherratt, A. (eds) *Archaeological Theory: Who Sets the Agenda?* Cambridge, pp. 60–78.